W9-BCZ-369

PEKING AND MOSCOW

PEKING
AND MOSCOW

Klaus Mehnert

Translated from the German by
LEILA VENNEWITZ

G. P. PUTNAM'S SONS
NEW YORK

CONTENTS

MAP

The Soviet Union and China

PREFACE

WHEN THE AUTHOR, after World War II, surveyed those areas in the field of international politics with which he was familiar, it seemed to him that two questions emerged, of vital importance for the next few decades. The first was that of developments within the Soviet Union which, hard on the heels of the leading world power, was rapidly rising to second place; the author's views and experiences on this subject are contained in his book *Der Sowjetmensch*.* The second crucial question, as Mao Tse-tung's eventual victory over Chiang Kai-shek became increasingly apparent, concerned China's relationship with the Soviet Union. For the rest of the world, much depends on whether the Communist bloc, with its one billion inhabitants, represents a solid, indivisible monolith, or a complex structure fraught with internal dissension and contradiction. The present book is devoted to an examination of this question.

Since the triumph of Communism in China the author has studied the relations between the two Red neighbors and has asked hundreds of qualified observers all over the world for their views. Since Stalin's death he has spent twenty months on six journeys on Asian soil and visited all the Asian countries with the exception of North Korea and North Vietnam, including the Chinese and Mongolian People's Republics. Altogether he has lived some ten years in the USSR and China—five years in each. However, the meager distribution of visas on the part of the Red Chinese government has made it virtually impossible to come by firsthand knowledge of the realities of present-day China; since 1958 the entry of Western observers has been permitted in exceptional cases only. The reader's indulgence is therefore requested in cases where the author has not

* Published in Great Britain under the title *The Anatomy of Soviet Man* and in the United States as *Soviet Man and His World*.

xi

always painted his pictures in the fresh colors of personal experience, as he was able to in his previous book. However, he has made every effort to obtain all available statements from reliable witnesses, and he has made as complete use as possible of the relevant Western literature—which has enormously increased in recent years—in English, Russian, and German.

For nearly a century Western Sinologists were so overcome by the splendor of Confucian civilization and culture that they tended to pay but fleeting attention to other aspects of China. This in turn gave rise to the image, fed still further by the often superficial reports supplied by Western observers, of a supposedly unchanging China which had preserved itself for two thousand years from all foreign influence and which was hence immune to Communism. But the downfall of the imperial house in 1911 was followed within a few decades by that which had been considered impossible: the Communist seizure of power. The demand for a new interpretation of Chinese history and the Chinese national character became imperative, and today it is in full swing.

In the age of Khrushchev we know more about the Soviet Union than ever before. By contrast, the difficulty in obtaining reliable material on Communist China is comparable to that facing a student of the Soviet Union during Stalin's time. The export of Chinese newspapers is, with few exceptions, prohibited; in Hongkong the newspapers smuggled at enormous risk out of Red China are sold at prices reminiscent of the heyday of opium-trafficking. Nevertheless, it would be a full-time job to keep up with the information reaching us from Red China, including Chinese radio stations. News items whose authenticity is in doubt have been deliberately omitted from this book, and the borderline between facts and suppositions has always been clearly defined.

The differences and contradictions in the relationship between Peking and Moscow require that a firm foundation, some stable factor be found, which will determine the relationship between the two giants in the Red 'camp' now and in the foreseeable future. One factor of this kind may be looked for in the character of the two peoples themselves. The fresh insight derived from a comparison of these peoples will lead to a better understanding of each of the partners. Just as a color is apt to look different when another color is put next to it, so Russia and China, when observed side by side, appear in a somewhat different light.

Rather than present the material historically, the author has chosen to arrange it according to subject, his aim being, in comparing the Chinese and the Russians as well as in depicting the themes around which the dialogue between Peking and Moscow revolves, to give a clear picture of the crucial issues and their interrelation. Once these are grasped, a basis exists on which to follow the course of relations between the two powers.

*

A word concerning the transliteration of Chinese and Russian words. The standard Wade system has been used for the former, except in cases where names of people and places are in such common use today that they have virtually become part of the English language, and to use anything but the familiar form would seem an affectation. Russian words and names have been transcribed according to a consistent method; although the Russian language has no accents, these appear in the Index to indicate emphasis.

In line with present practice, constantly recurring expressions such as Communist Party, Central Committee, and Kuomintang, have been abbreviated to CP, CC, and KMT.

The footnotes at the end of the book corresponding to the numbers in the text give sources and references only. Although this information is not essential to an understanding of the text, the interested reader should be able to check the author's statements. The author hopes the Sinologists will forgive him for encroaching upon their territory; he is very conscious of his deep indebtedness to their painstaking research. Many of these experts appear in the bibliography as the authors of definitive works.

Among those not named are numerous members of the diplomatic services of the United States, Great Britain, and the West German Federal Republic, as well as of the research staff of the United States Consulate-General in Hongkong. To all of these the author is grateful for the time and expert knowledge placed at his disposal. His gratitude is also expressed to the Ford Foundation for a research and travel grant of several months accorded him in 1959, and to Harvard University and the Universities of California and Hawaii, as well as the (Chinese) Union Research Institute in Hongkong, for kind permission to make full use of their library facilities over a period of many months. In particular he is indebted to his closest associates,

Ruth Henning, Karl Eugen Waedekin, Hans Schneider, and Joachim Glaubitz, all of whom, working with him for many years, greatly contributed to this book, and especially to Leila Vennewitz for her translation.

KLAUS MEHNERT

Stuttgart and Aachen
15 July 1963

TRANSLATOR'S ACKNOWLEDGMENT

I am very grateful to the following for their assistance and advice in certain aspects of the work of translating this book: Miss Tung-king Ng, librarian at the Asian Studies Library, University of British Columbia; Dr. Stanley Z. Pech, Associate Professor in the Department of Slavonic Studies, University of British Columbia; and, most of all, my husband, William Vennewitz.

LEILA VENNEWITZ

Vancouver, Canada

Part I

PEOPLES

INTRODUCTION

WHEN WE TRY TO UNDERSTAND the problems of a marriage we do not limit ourselves to a description of external events—the dates the couple met, became engaged, or got married, the occasions on which they quarreled and made up again, the family celebrations and the visits of relatives. Instead we try to understand each marriage partner as an individual, the background and environment of his or her upbringing, the characteristics and habits, the temperament and degree of intelligence, the political, moral, and religious outlook—in short, the character of each. This is all the more vital when the two partners have undertaken not merely a marriage bond but the joint achievement of some definite end. In that case we have to examine the contribution made by each of the partners toward the achievement of such goals.

Looked at from this point of view, what contribution have the Chinese on the one hand and the Russians on the other made to the association in which we find them today? The first part of our study will be devoted to this question. Since Communism lays claim to the lives of human beings at all levels, the scope of our observations must be a wide one.

The question of whether one can speak of 'the' Chinese, 'the' Russians, 'the' Soviet people, 'the' Americans, has been the subject of thorough and often heated discussion. The late Felix M. Keesing, the New Zealand anthropologist, summarized his findings in two theses:[1] first, in the case of each nation it is possible to prove the existence of a certain national character which distinguishes it from other nations; second, this national character is a variable, not a constant, quantity. In other words: the Chinese differ from the Russians. And the Chinese of today are different from the Chinese of the Confucian era; the Soviet Russian is no longer the muzhik of the days of the Tsars. Therefore, although national minorities, often

3

with sharply distinguishing characteristics, have long existed both in China and in Russia, we may speak of 'the Chinese' and 'the Russians', for in both cases a politically powerful and culturally outstanding race—in China the Han (i.e., the real Chinese), in Russia the Great Russians—constituted the vital element which characterized the population as a whole.

At this point one thing must be made clear. That China forms part of Asia, both ethnically and culturally, is taken for granted by everyone; but that Russia is part of Europe has not always been an accepted fact. Even in Napoleon's times it used to be said: 'Scratch a Russian and you'll find a Tatar'; and in our own day we hear of 'Asiatic Bolshevism'—its victory over the Russians being attributed to their Asiatic 'blood'.

Ignorance and prejudice have been partly responsible for this error. The Polish-Lithuanian empire stood for centuries between Central and Eastern Europe, and it was only with Peter the Great's advance to the Baltic and the downfall of Poland that Russia became an immediate neighbor of the Occident. But even stronger was the influence of a spiritual barrier: the schism in the Church between West and East. This split had originated with the proselytizing activities of two divergent centers; it had then been completed by the schism of 1054, advanced northward when Moscow assumed the role of fallen Byzantium, and had been accentuated and hardened by mutual reproaches of apostasy. With the progressive secularization of daily life, religious barriers faded; but the difference in the level of civilization between West and East put Russia at a disadvantage when that country finally came face to face with Europe as a result of Peter the Great's actions. To the Westerner, especially when he came as an invader, Russia appeared incomprehensible, wild and barbaric.

The term 'Asiatic' applied to Russia is nothing but a new formula for this feeling of incomprehensibility. I have always found that it is used by people who have no personal knowledge of either Russia or Asia. It may be necessary to have lived there in order to know where the borderline between Europe and Asia lies. Anyone entering a Russian church from the streets of Peking or Harbin and remaining merely for the duration of the service will feel the difference between Asia and Europe as unmistakably as if he had gone into a Catholic church in one of these cities.

*

Although we may still be in the dark as to some aspects of the original home and history of the Slavs, no one disputes that linguistically and ethnically they form part of the Indo-European family of nations. In the case of the Eastern Slavs, this relationship has been modified and deepened, not dissolved, by their close ties with Byzantium. It was through them that the Russians shared in the Hellenistic-Christian culture of this Second Rome, and as a 'Third Rome' carried on the tradition of Byzantium after its conquest by the Turks. But the invasions of Asiatic steppe-dwellers, and even the two hundred years of foreign rule by the Tatars, left fewer traces than, say, the Osmanli in the southeast or the Arabs in the south and southwest of Europe.

Even less marked was the influence of the Asiatic peoples and cultures which later became part of the far-flung empire of the Tsars. The millions of Russians who settled in these Asiatic regions remained Russians, however little aversion they had to mixed marriages. Russia's entry into European history does not constitute the entry of Asia into Europe; on the contrary, the Russians carried the boundaries of Europe as far as the Pacific and into the steppes of Central Asia. Russia's closeness to Europe needs no description here. Its intellectual life since the eighteenth century is unthinkable without Leibniz or Voltaire, without Byron or the Swedish-Baltic influences. And who is not aware of the influence on Western Europe of Pushkin and Gogol, Dostoyevsky and Tolstoy! Of course, we also find evidence of Asia and its peoples in Russian literature, and there are Oriental themes to be found in music, painting, and architecture, in folk culture and handicrafts. But these are all the ornaments of folklore, at most a symptom of contact with the Orient, not of a dominating Oriental influence. We doubt if anyone would be inclined to see in Kipling's books about India proof of the dominating influence of the East on England.

Asiatic influence on Russian philosophy is no greater than on German philosophy, which, with Schopenhauer, turned so willingly to the heritage of India, and Russian natural science knew only the Western model. Even the Slavophiles of the nineteenth century struggled less against Europe than against those things in Europe which seemed to them to be decadent. They believed they could create something better, and the periodical which outlined their program was called *The European*. The 'Eurasians', however, who at the turn of the century tried to evolve a Eurasian *mystique* for the

Russian people as a basis for the Messianic spirit, were never more than a sect.

Is it necessary to add that Communism came to Russia as the legitimate offspring of Western intellectual and social history, that Lenin dreamed of making Berlin, not Moscow, the capital of the world revolution? Since he was successful in seizing power in Russia and only in Russia, and since the further development of the ideology fell to him and to a lesser extent his successors, Bolshevism and Soviet Communism as we know them today have absorbed much that is Russian. But Asiatic? Stalin's totalitarianism has such a terrifying number of parallels in totalitarianism under Hitler that only someone who is prepared to include Hitler and Himmler among the Asiatics could call Stalinism Asiatic. Moreover, the immense influence in the Soviet Union of typically Western methods and scientific thinking has led to the industrialized and (compared with old Russia) highly intellectualized Soviet Russian being in many ways far more European than was his peasant great-grandfather.

As long as Stalin was in power, it would have been premature to make even a partially valid pronouncement on the Soviet Russian; with the aid of totalitarian terrorism and under conditions of extreme hardship it is possible to force human nature into an almost unrecognizable state. And even with Stalin's death, Stalinism did not end immediately; a certain length of time was necessary before the enormous pressures under which the people had lived began to relax. Only then was a more or less reliable analysis of the Soviet Russian possible, and this was at once undertaken in various quarters and using various methods, but with, on the whole, similar results. Soviet man, it was found, was nothing but the Russian of the industrial age.

*

China is still living under a harsh dictatorship of a 'Stalinist' type, so that in China the visitor can see many things which are only temporary, whilst others, though camouflaged or pushed into the background, nevertheless continue to exist. But the people themselves live and act under totally abnormal conditions, and for this reason the time is not yet ripe for an accurate presentation of the 'Soviet Chinese' based on the behavior of the Chinese under the Communist regime. It may be possible in fifteen or twenty years' time, but we cannot wait that long. Hence we must base our answer to the question of the future attitude of the Chinese to Communism and to

Moscow not so much on the last twelve or fifteen years as on the last twenty-four centuries.

This method, the only possible one, entails a further difficulty. The interpretation of Chinese history is still very much in dispute among the experts. Moreover, the research of Sinologists is based chiefly on the official history, the 'scholarly' history, so to speak, of China; the sociologists, however, came to China a hundred years too late. And if in the case of other races we know far more about the classes of society which left written chronicles of their ideas and deeds than about the inarticulate masses, this is particularly true when applied to the Chinese and Russians, the majority of whom, until the penetration by the West, were illiterate. Thus it would be wrong to extend our image of the leading intellectual classes indiscriminately to the population as a whole, and such words as 'typical' and 'characteristic' should only be used with care. On the other hand, the extraordinary wealth of this classical tradition compels us to choose the truly representative.

In two and a half millennia the Chinese have pondered a great deal, and of this they have written down an incredible amount. There can scarcely be a single idea capable of being thought which has remained unformulated and unexplored. Although China's spiritual evolution took place at a fairly constant pace and was seldom disturbed by external influences, it has its dialectic and its swing of the pendulum between extremes of ideas—between idealism and materialism, for example, or between such theses as 'Man is good' and 'Man is evil', or between 'The State is there for the people' and its antithesis, 'Man is there for the State'. If Lenin's thirty-nine volumes could supply Stalin and Trotsky, Khrushchev and Mao, with intellectual ammunition for their disputes, then indeed we might say that it is possible to prove almost anything in the world with the aid of the millions of volumes which go to make up the intellectual history of China. It is not surprising, therefore, that interpretations vary.

A comparative study can certainly not evaluate everything the Chinese have ever thought or felt or done in the course of their history. The reader must not expect an encyclopedia of the Chinese (or Russian) people. The confusing complexity begins to sort itself out when we extract from the superabundance of types of behavior, thought forms, and ideas, those which eventually prevailed and proved lasting. And even among these we can only look at a few.

*

The task of Part 1 of this book is, in short, to provide a basis for the study of the following questions:

To what conclusions are we led by a comparison of the Chinese and the Russians as to the present and future relationship of the two nations?

What are the powers of resistance—or the susceptibility—of the Chinese and Russian peoples to Communism, yesterday, today, and tomorrow?

And above all: is it correct to say that Chinese or Russian Communism is the logical crowning of their history, or is it more accurate to regard it as being in complete contradiction to all that is Chinese or Russian? The thesis of Communism as the continuation, the culmination, of the history of these two peoples is propagated not only by Communist leaders, by Stalin, Khrushchev, and Mao, but also—although of course with different arguments and different prognoses—by some Western observers, for example Amaury de Riencourt when he writes: 'The triumph of Marxism in China implies to a very great extent a return to the past,' or 'Marxism . . . restored China's traditional way of thinking.' Riencourt, who is anything but a Communist, has described Chinese Communism as 'psychologically predetermined'.[2] A similarly one-sided view is expressed by an Indian observer: 'To substitute the gospel according to Mao for the gospel according to Confucius, conforms to this [i.e., traditional Chinese] pattern.'[3]

A second thesis, that Communism is the complete antithesis of the true nature of China and Russia, is maintained by the Chinese and Russian opponents of Communism (Chiang Kai-shek, for instance, and the leaders of the Russian émigrés) and many foreigners who, as businessmen and missionaries, became personally acquainted with the China and Russia of the past, and who are convinced that the people whom they came to know and respect as human beings are enduring the Communist regime solely because they are compelled to do so by the most brutal terrorism, and are yearning for the day when China will re-emerge 'as a free united nation' and they can take part in the 'triumph of freedom over slavery throughout the world'.[4]

Reality, as we shall see, corresponds to neither of these two theses; it is more complicated and thus more interesting, and still leaves the door open to all kinds of possibilities.

CHAPTER I

THE MAN

IN THE TWELVE-FLOOR APARTMENT BUILDING in which we spent the greater part of our years in Shanghai, we were not the only Europeans. A few floors below us lived a highly excitable Russian family. At times things would get rather hectic—the father shouting that he would kill (or leave) his family that very day, the children sobbing, the wife going into paroxysms of weeping. Anyone who was interested could look on, as all the apartments ón each floor opened onto the kitchen veranda running along the back of the building. Whenever these scenes took place, the Chinese servants of the European families, as well as a number of other Chinese living in the building, gathered eagerly to watch the spectacle, which they enjoyed as if it were some strange theatrical performance.

It is in fact difficult to imagine a more violent contrast of temperaments. On the one hand the 'expansive nature' of the Russian, broad enough to embrace every human emotion, inclined to sudden changes of mood from one extreme to the other and to utterances often both uninhibited and explosive; on the other, the face of the Far East, so mysterious to the Occidental, a face which in its unchanging expression is a far cry from being a 'mirror of the soul'. It is not proper to reveal what is going on in the family—one would lose 'face'. 'The tree lives by its bark, man by his face', says a Chinese proverb.

Here we already come up against a trait which is as essential to the Chinese individual as it is to the social and political patterns by which he has lived for thousands of years. Indeed, any attempt to interpret the psychology of the individual without a socio-psychological foundation would be doomed, and in the end we would be left with an even greater feeling of remoteness and bewilderment, and totally at a loss to what attitude to adopt toward him. When Aristotle defined man as a *zoon politikon*, a 'social animal', he had no idea that in a highly developed culture there already existed a classic example of

9

this concept unlike anything in the Hellenistic world. If the Occidental has always been inclined to give priority to the individual over society, to freedom over bondage, and to pursue individualism to the point of egoism, hedonism, and solipsism, and liberalism to the point of anarchy, the very opposite is true of the Chinese. The Chinese is conditioned by his surroundings, 'situation centered', to use the formula of a Chinese sociologist,[1] to an extent almost beyond our Western comprehension, a fact we must accept if we are to understand him.

The Chinese never for an instant separates himself from his surroundings. This applies not only to his actions but also to his thoughts and feelings. He remains always within the network of personal relationships, and these bind him just as much to his contemporaries as to those who preceded him and those who will come after him. He looks outward, not inward; it is not to his conscience that he looks for the norm in his conduct, but to the possible effect of his actions on his environment. A Chinese scholar has the following to say on corruption, a subject to which we shall return later on:

Social response in China is rarely an independent single action but rather an additional entry in a long balance sheet which registers the personal relations between two individuals or two families. Conditioned by already established personal relations, a given response can easily have an effect, or at least an appearance, of nepotism or favoritism.[2]

As a device toward the understanding of different peoples, American anthropologists have made use of the distinction between 'shame' and 'guilt'. According to this, shame is the disgrace we are conscious of in the eyes of others, and guilt is what we feel inwardly. In other words: 'Shame requires an audience who knows about the misdeed, whereas guilt operates in the psyche without an audience.'[3] Or: a sense of shame resulting from wrongdoing disturbs a person not so much because he has done wrong as because this wrongdoing was observed by others.

The sociologist Ruth Benedict has found in Japan expressions such as these: one cultivates self-respect because of society; if there were no society one would not need to respect oneself; shame is the root of virtue. In a brilliant book on Japan she draws the following conclusions:

Where shame is the major sanction, a man does not experience relief when he makes his fault public even to a confessor. So long as his bad behavior does not 'get out into the world' he need not be troubled and

confession appears to him merely a way of courting trouble. Shame
cultures therefore do not provide for confessions, even to the Gods.[4]

China, like Japan—which was for a long time under the spiritual
influence of China—represents a 'shame culture' as distinct from the
'guilt culture' which is a product of Christianity. One Chinese has in
fact explained the relatively small success of Christian missions in
China by the fact that missionaries, especially in their Protestant
variations, relate everything to personal conscience, and in China,
where more importance is attached to shame than guilt, conscience is
not greatly developed.[5] In the same way, many sociologists believe
the formation of a guilt culture through Christianity to be one of the
reasons behind the spiritual and hence the civilizing dynamism of the
Occident, whereas in China (and in Asia generally) they see in the
priority of shame over guilt a definite factor contributing to the desire
for conformity, to be inconspicuous, and inhibiting any wish to stand
out as a reformer, let alone a revolutionary.[6]

*

We must now consider the effect on the individual of being conditioned by his environment. How strong this trait has remained even
after the upheavals of the last few decades is shown by the results of a
survey of one hundred and eighty Chinese living in the United States,
which was carried out after the Second World War by American
psychologists and sociologists. The Chinese, it was discovered, dislike making decisions by themselves; they prefer to act after consulting their families or friends, faithful to the old saying: 'In the home
one must depend on parents, outside the home one must depend on
friends.' They choose to use the services of a middleman (and not
only in marriage negotiations) in order, if for no other reason, not to
expose themselves to a refusal. Even business decisions are felt to be
of a personal nature, creating as they do bonds and hence obligations
between the parties. Although a sense of general responsibility,
such as civic duties toward an anonymous state, scarcely exists, that
of concrete responsibility, toward the family or anyone else to whom
one may be bound in one way or another, is very strong indeed.[7]

The immense importance and the lasting quality of personal relationships in China are something I discovered for myself at the end of
the Second World War. In the months following the Japanese surrender, when German nationals in China were virtually without

protection or rights, it was possible to divide them into two categories: those who had reliable Chinese friends and so did not have much to worry about, and those who had only themselves to depend on and had no idea from one day to the next what was going to happen to them.

Only a few years ago I had the following experience: In the summer of 1960 I took on a Chinese assistant in Hongkong to help me look through newspapers and pamphlets from Communist China. His help was particularly valuable to me because he had recently escaped from Red China, which made it much easier for him to cope with the Red Chinese jargon than it would have been for a refugee of long standing. But this young man, who at the risk of life and limb had fled from Communist China, avoided committing himself against the regime he hated; instead he tried to rationalize his attitude, both to himself and to others, as a sort of 'third position'.

Certainly not in every case, but generally speaking, another observer may be right when he says that in the West people ask, when they are faced with a conflict: 'What do the two sides want, and which one is right?' but that in China the question is: 'Who is most likely to win, and what must I do to be on good terms with him?'[8] It was a Chinese who came to this conclusion: 'When a Chinese acts in an opportunist fashion in order to meet the demands of a situation, he does not have to square his opportunism with his conscience.'[9]

*

Chinese opportunism expresses itself with an ingenuity and naturalness that are rather disarming, especially as it is at the same time both rational and wise. The European, with his inhibitions and his preoccupation with principles, is at a loss to find the right word for it; 'matter-of-factness' is perhaps the closest. Why get upset about things we can do nothing about anyway! As long as the storm rages over the countryside, the bamboo bends; when calm returns, it rises up again.

One afternoon in Peking during the summer of 1957 I went to an exhibition of works by Dürer on loan from East Berlin. Among the crowd of visitors I noticed a young Chinese woman. She was quite smartly dressed, and this, combined with her poise, made her stand out from the other rather drab-looking people. She was standing alone in front of a picture and chuckling to herself. Curiosity made me glance at the object of her amusement: it was a sketch which

Dürer had made for one of his larger works, consisting of nothing but ordinary pillows in varying shapes and shadings. It was doubtless a strange picture to Chinese eyes, for sketching is unknown in China. I must have seen this sketch before without finding it amusing, but now I had to laugh too. So we became acquainted, and for a while I led the young lady from picture to picture, telling her about Dürer and Germany.

We agreed to go for a walk the next day through the Forbidden City. When she arrived, she had a parcel in her hand, and I offered to carry it for her. We wandered through the courtyards and palaces of the old Imperial City. Her name was Lan Er, and she came from a family of former court officials that had lost everything as a result of the Communist revolution. Moreover, since she was regarded as politically unreliable on account of her background, she had not been able to find a decent job. Meanwhile I had noticed that her dress was made of cheap material and was shabby in places. But no word of complaint escaped her, and she told me quite cheerfully that she spent her free time looking at beautiful things and doing some painting of her own; in fact, she had brought some of her pictures in the parcel to show me later.

Suddenly I realized, and I felt myself go hot all over, that I no longer had the parcel with me. I remembered I had put it down somewhere so as to leave my hands free for my camera. I asked Lan Er to wait and ran to the spot—the parcel was gone. I hurried from one place to another, to the administration office of the Forbidden City, to the guards at the North Gate, at the South Gate—no one knew anything about it. Overcome with guilt and bathed in perspiration, I finally got back to Lan Er. She was sitting on a bench, and, just as if nothing had happened, drew my attention to the exquisite view she was feasting her eyes on: a pond with lotus blossoms, some old trees, red walls, roof tiles glazed a golden yellow, and over all the fabulous blue sky of North China. But I had no eyes for such things and loudly reproached myself for my inexcusable carelessness. Then Lan Er said, without raising her voice: 'Don't upset yourself. It is nothing. It's only when you get upset that the loss becomes unpleasant.' Embarrassed and ashamed I fell silent; we went on with our walk without another word about the parcel. Incidentally, the following day Lan Er went to the municipal Lost and Found; there was her parcel. It was quite true—I had been upset for nothing.

In 1959 a Chinese of thoroughly anti-Communistic leanings said to me in all seriousness, with a gesture of reassurance: 'It will pass. After all, even the rule of the Manchus lasted less than three hundred years.' The Russian expression *nichevo* has its counterpart in Chinese; in fact there are three variations of it: *mei kuan hsi, mei fa tzu,* and *mei pan fa,* all meaning: 'never mind, it can't be helped'. In neither country do the Communists like this attitude; in China they are trying to displace *mei pan fa* by their *yu pan fa* ('yes, it *can* be helped!')

Anyone who has lived even for a short time in China is aware of the versatility and adaptability of its people, qualities which enable them to cope with sudden surprises as well as with external pressures which may have been going on for years. It always seemed to me that they positively enjoyed being confronted with the unexpected. For example, our Chinese servants were never happier than when twelve guests turned up for dinner instead of the expected four. They outdid themselves in imagination and inspiration and bustled about, hurrying to the shops across the street, borrowing from the cook of the family downstairs, changing the menu, and stretching whatever food was on hand with the aid of camouflaging sauces.

*

During the war years, the Japanese, who were occupying large parts of China, were continually thinking up new regulations designed to restrict the population's freedom of movement. But it often seemed that the annoyance of the Chinese was outweighed by the challenge of getting round each new regulation with even greater ingenuity. The rationing of rice, for example, the staple food, was organized by the occupation authorities in the following manner: on the days when rice was distributed, each person entitled to a ration had his hand stamped with indelible ink when he received his portion. Only those with no stamp on their hands got their bowls filled. Actually it was not a bad way of doing away with the need for ration cards, but it was totally unsuitable for China, for of course there were clever Chinese who knew how to remove the ink with a chemical solution. Wherever there was a line-up in front of a rice shop, there would be the 'chemists', squatting on their little stools right out in the street. For a fee the stamp would be washed off. In this way one could go back into the line-up, and it was good fun as well.

In an effort to hold up a mirror to his people and to render them comprehensible to Western readers, the witty Chinese author Lin Yutang says frankly: 'There is nothing on earth that can make a

Chinese angry; sin, greed and corruption only make us laugh, and high and fine ideals only make us laugh all the more.' He speaks of 'our tendency to turn everything and anything into a joke, our inability to take anything seriously, not even when it concerns the salvation of our country'.[10]

This is even true, according to Lin Yutang, of funerals. A certain number of people are brought in from the street, dressed in magnificent funeral robes and made to walk behind the coffin to increase the size of the procession. They don't even have their faces washed, for that, Lin Yutang says, would be taking the whole thing much too seriously. And when one knows that the daughter-in-law at the burial of her mother-in-law (seldom an object of affection) is told to sob loudly at a given signal and to stop sobbing with equal suddenness at another, how can anybody believe in her grief? But, Lin Yutang goes on, what else is there for the Chinese to do, considering the exaggerated formalism of his whole life, but look on the lighter side of things!

This may be merely the view of a man who is a moralist and furthermore tries to win his readers' attention by extreme statements. There is, of course, in the Chinese a streak of fanaticism, but it too is situation centered and to be found mainly in the form of mass hysteria, for example in the bloodthirsty *hsia! hsia!* (kill! kill!) of the Taiping rebels, or in the abandon with which Chinese participate in wild demonstrations.

Anyone who has witnessed Chinese funeral ceremonies has seen for himself to what extent feelings of grief are drowned out by bustle and movement and by the noises (originally intended to scare away devils) produced by firecrackers. In the same way the process of death itself is accepted without particular emotion or sympathy. Never in Russia but more than once in China have I seen people chatting and laughing as they walked by a dying person.

*

This unfeeling attitude, which enables Chinese of all walks of life to look on unmoved at the sufferings of their fellowmen, was, naturally enough, the chief cause of indignation among Christian missionaries. It was they who took up the fight against footbinding among Chinese women, and against the slave-system which still existed in private houses well into our century. During the Second World War, when starvation and disease were rife, it was mainly the few Christian organizations which supplied food, shelter, and medical aid, and which each morning collected from the streets the bodies of those who had died during the night. There is little of the spirit of the Good Samaritan to be found in China: the desire to avoid the trouble and vexation which might arise from looking after strangers is usually much stronger than the willingness to help one's neighbor.

There is more to this, however, than mere personal convenience. If someone is suffering—be he ill or poor or otherwise a victim of misfortune—then there is something the matter with him; it is better to have nothing to do with him so as not to come within the spell of this disorder. The idea of dedicating oneself to the service of the suffering was strange to the Chinese. Would that not be tantamount to meddling in something which is the business only of the clan and the family? 'If another man sells his daughter into prostitution,' writes a Chinese sociologist, 'that is their affair.'[11]

Ethical rules and taboos apply mainly to behavior toward the family and its members, also toward members of the same sect, but hardly ever to one's 'neighbor'. Reformers like Mo-tzu, who preached love toward all men (rather than only toward relatives and friends), were not in the long run successful. Mencius, the great restorer of Confucianism, went so far as to assert that a general love for humanity would have an unfavorable effect on filial piety and public justice: to acknowledge neither king nor father was 'to be in the state of a beast'.[12] Lao-tzu's teaching, the main theme of which was 'non-action', was, of course, still less designed to promote humanitarian feelings. It was said of Yang Chu, a kindred spirit of Lao-tzu's: 'Though he might benefit the whole world by merely plucking out one of his hairs, he would refuse to do it.'[13]

The progress of Buddhism in China from the third to the ninth century seems to show that, on many levels of society, a need for human warmth existed which was not filled by the teachings of the philosophers. But Buddhism too was transformed and given a pronounced Chinese character, and in that process sacrificed those very characteristics of universal love which make it so attractive to many Westerners who have tired of the Occidental way of life. One must also remember that the doctrine of *karma* does not exactly encourage compassion: the sufferer is expiating his own deeds of an earlier life. Only in the worship of Kuan-yin might one perhaps find a somewhat modified attitude toward suffering, a need for divine compassion.

Nor are there in the classical literature of China more than a very few examples of compassion, and nothing which could be compared to the socio-Utopian literature of Europe. The great novel, *All Men Are Brothers*,[14] written about the year 1500, although it describes the deeds and misdeeds of a robber band with dramatic realism, always remains completely matter-of-fact, and only in a negative sense could it be called a social criticism: it is the injustice of the officials which is responsible for the evil deeds of the robbers. The moral: a good robber is better than a bad official.

It is a peculiar gift of the Chinese to rise above unpleasant things and reject anything which might disturb his inner equilibrium. Kavalam Panikkar, India's last ambassador to the government of Chiang Kai-shek and its first to that of Mao Tse-tung, was certainly more sympathetically inclined toward China—even Red China— than to the West, about which he is so critical in his books; yet he once said: 'The Chinese are not revolted by cruelty as we are. They would as soon slit a man's throat as they would a frog's.'[15]

*

To an Indian, who has grown up in the tradition of sharing the suffering of all creatures, such observations must be particularly shocking. But in this underdevelopment—and often total absence— of human feeling on the part of the Chinese, this inadequacy of their emotional range, the psychologist sees only the negative side of that typical matter-of-factness which so readily enables the Chinese to cope with life and to meet adversity with calm composure. Extremes of feeling or behavior do not appeal to these people. They prefer the middle way, the compromise, the universally acceptable expedient. There is a saying in China: 'When you are given an inch, do not take a foot.' It is—or was before the Communists—considered unseemly to hound an enemy to his last breath, and the phrase 'unconditional surrender' was unknown to the traditional Chinese. Here lies, in the belief of a Chinese sociologist, one explanation for the stagnation which took place centuries ago in Chinese evolution; for 'conflict brings in its wake not only human tragedy but human progress as well'.[16]

When directed inwardly, however, as a force not only shaping but penetrating human nature, this attitude is bound to have an anti-impulsive, anti-emotional effect. The imperturbability with which a Chinese can accept his own misfortunes as well as those of others is more than a mask, assumed as the result of generations of caution

and training, to hide otherwise uncontrollable passions. He does not
demand of life an opportunity to develop his personality, a demand
taken for granted by the Western man. As a result, when this opportunity is denied him, he does not suffer, or at least he suffers less. He
finds no difficulty in conforming to his environment.

My years in China have left me with an unforgettable impression of
the Chinese capacity for happiness even when his days are spent in
unimaginable poverty. With the most perfect naturalness he has
mastered the art of the simple life, the ability to enjoy the little
pleasures of existence, and to forget his troubles and anxieties. The
picturesque festivals, carried on with such enthusiasm and noise, the
gay family picnics in temple courtyards, the chattering funeral proces-
sions, the intimate, childlike worship of the kitchen-god—since time
immemorial this and much else has been part of the very nature, one
is tempted to say of the very charm, of the Chinese people. No one
who has lived for a time in China can fail to have experienced these
things, and whenever 'old China hands' meet anywhere in the world
and exchange reminiscences, these are the memories that return.

Chinese know not only how to live happily, but also how to die
serenely, 'with philosophical tranquillity and a look of transfigure-
ment on their faces', as Lily Abegg, with her intimate knowledge of
China and its people, once put it.[17] Even in death the Chinese is
sustained by the knowledge that he is a link in the chain of his clan
which began in the mists of antiquity and reaches out into the distant
future. He has a vision of the little mound of earth in the family field
under which he will rest, surrounded by his sons and grandsons who
will go on tilling the fields, and often long before his death he has
chosen his own coffin, taking a businesslike interest in its quality and
price.

*

The same attitude of calm composure strikes the foreign visitor
watching the Chinese at his daily tasks. It would not occur to a
Chinese to regard his daily work as a divine curse, as a punishment
for the Fall, or as the stigma of his expulsion from the Garden of
Eden. Even when the work is hard, and he has to go on, for low
wages, until he is exhausted, it never becomes for him a problem of
divine justice or a measure of moral achievement. Not without justification have the Chinese been called the most industrious people on
earth. The long working hours have always astonished—or shocked

—their neighbors and foreign visitors. From dawn to dark they are to be seen at work, in the fields, the workshops, and the factories. Their zeal never seems to flag, nor the care they take over their work, whether they are planting rice shoots by hand, one by one, or picking caterpillars off cabbages. The intellectual is no different: in 1889 among the candidates for the provincial examinations in Foochow there were nine who were over eighty and two over ninety, and in Anhwei thirty-five over eighty and eighteen over ninety. According to the governor's report, they submitted to an ordeal lasting nine days and wrote essays which were absolutely accurate and showed no sign of senility.[18]

This industry, however, has nothing in common with that obsession with work so characteristic of Occidentals, who see in everything a 'challenge' and who desire to do each job 'for its own sake'. In post-war Germany this obsession has acquired neurotic dimensions. In America parents speak with pride of their children who earn ten or twenty cents by doing housework, or show an early talent for business by delivering newspapers. The Oriental observer remarks, unimpressed: 'The idea of earning money from one's parents is considered laughable by Chinese.'[19]

The historical explanation of the Chinese capacity for hard work is probably to be found in the age-old battle with nature and in the vicissitudes of China's history. This capacity, aided by a sense of family obligation, is lasting proof of the innate Chinese vitality. It can be a source of resentment to others, as for example to the Indonesians, among whom hundreds of thousands of Chinese families are conspicuous by virtue of their unflagging activity, or to Russian students who despair at the sight of their tireless Chinese classmates constantly increasing the norms.

Before the Communists introduced a note of fanaticism into this industry, it was by no means incompatible with the joy of living. It was, so to speak, a cheerful approach to hard work; in China people did not live in order to work, but they worked in order to live, and they were quite prepared to enjoy the fruits of their labors in comfort when the goal had been reached. This art of enjoying life extends from the material and sensual world—we have only to think of the exquisite Chinese cuisine—to the highest spheres of aesthetic refinement, not only in art but in the forms and patterns of daily life, in a cult of beauty going beyond almost anything known to any other people.

As regards the somewhat off-beat field of specialized pleasures, in particular the use of narcotics, an astute Chinese has hit on a new example of the Chinese unwillingness to emerge actively from his environment: he points out that the Chinese prefers the sleep-inducing opium while the American taste is for the stimulating marijuana.[20]

*

Even the basic urges of love and sex take different guises in China. Rather than trust to Western observers, who all too easily succumb to the temptations of the spicy and the sensational, we shall rely here on a Chinese who has inside knowledge of this aspect of Chinese reality and is thus more competent to convey Chinese feelings about it than even the most sensitive Western novelist:

> For centuries they [the Chinese] have considered parental arrangement in betrothal and marriage to be part of the order of nature. For centuries Chinese lovers have shied away from all public showing of affection, and they have exhibited, neither in public nor in private, the familiar signs of love so common in the West. In fact, when a man said that he loved a girl the statement usually carried the implication that something irregular was afoot. If a woman told anyone that she loved some man it would be tantamount to her downfall.
> These Chinese manners are the natural expression of a way of life in which individual feelings must be subordinated to the requirements of the group, while sex and all activities associated with it must be restricted to the compartments of life where it is socially appropriate. . . . To a Chinese in love his love occupies a place among other considerations, especially his obligations to his parents.[21]

In cases where the marriage partnership was monogamous, habit usually developed into affection in a manner essentially no different from that of our own lifelong marriages; but side by side with the marriage partnership there were other spheres of sex. Ancient China had a highly developed culture of prostitution, and her courtesans were expert in every type of pleasure, including perversions. The cruel custom of footbinding has been explained in modern times by the suggestion that the ensuing alteration in the woman's gait served to enhance her attractiveness to the Chinese male.[22]

But free-ranging pleasure is one thing, and duty toward the family another. It was just because within the framework of the Chinese family system more importance was attached to continuity and outward solidarity than to the happiness of the individual, that it was possible to separate the erotic from the sexual; we can see this even in classical literature. In the eighteenth-century novel *Dream of the Red Chamber*, Pao-yü and Black Jade exemplify the ideal pair of lovers, yet they are never united. It is in no way detrimental to their love that Pao-yü should have relations with numerous women, including servants, and even with an actor.[23]

The theory has been put forward that the comparatively small number of sex crimes—indeed, of all crimes of violence—in China is due to the fact that the Chinese, sustained as they are by the solidarity of the clan, feel less need than other races to prove themselves by deeds of violence. Westerners, on the other hand, who revel in the type of crime to be found in Mickey Spillane's novels, are, it is said, haunted by a feeling of inner insecurity and suspicion of their fellowmen.[24]

In a recently published work on the sexual history of China[25] it has been shown that, since pre-Confucian times, one theme has occupied a position of prime importance in the erotic literature of China (and India as well, incidentally),[26] and that is the practice of withholding the seminal fluid during coition in cases where conception is not intended. It was apparently believed that the semen thus retained would be rerouted to the brain and result in the prolongation of the life of the male. Is it too far-fetched to see in this pseudo-medical justification of the most extreme form of restraint a symptom of the Chinese aversion to self-communication?

*

If we have so far tried to grasp the psyche of the Chinese principally in his relation to his natural environment, we must now take a look at the powerful historical factor in the formation of his character: his language, both spoken and written. This factor chiefly affects the educated upper classes, but through them and beyond them—although to what extent it is hard to say—the broad masses of the people as well.

China has never revealed itself readily to the foreigner; the difficulty of its language has become proverbial. But even those who know the language well, or who try to overcome the barrier by means of translations, do not find the way open to China's innermost self. The Chinese himself is of not much help to us, for analysis, at least self-analysis, is not in his nature: for thousands of years he has regarded himself simply as a human being, not as a member of a race comparable with others. Occidentals have indeed tried to understand the

Chinese, but for a long time they made use of the totally inadequate means of general impressions—inadequate because they approached the Chinese from a prejudiced point of view and measured them with the yardstick of the 'normal' European, or, to be more exact, the 'normal'—or rather 'ideal'—Christian. *The* book about the Chinese which could be used here as the basis for a psychological portrait of his character, whether from the individual or social point of view, does not yet exist.

On closer inspection, however, we find that it is this very language of China, differing radically as it does from all other languages and forms of writing familiar to us, which enables us to draw some interesting conclusions. During the five years I spent in China I devoted a good deal of time to the Chinese language—too little to master it but enough to get some idea of its peculiarities. The greatest difficulty for me—as for everyone else trying to learn it—was the fact that, with its tens of thousands of characters, Chinese holds the world record for the largest number of symbols and simultaneously for the smallest number of sounds.

Today the Chinese language still employs the characters in use thousands of years ago. Instead of representing sounds, as in the case of our own (and the Russian) alphabet, these characters signify whole words or ideas. A Chinese wanting to read newspapers and books has to know at least several thousand characters. (It is too early to evaluate the effects of Communist reform.) Each character corresponds in sound to a single syllable—*kung*, *tang*, *mao*, etc. As a result, all basic words, apart from the numerous combinations formed by several characters, are monosyllabic. As there are far more characters (words) than syllables, most syllables have more than one meaning; some can have ten, fifty, even eighty or more different meanings and hence must be written in as many different ways. The syllable *li* can, according to the context, signify custom, mile, carp, or plum. In order to increase the possibility of differentiation, a system of tones evolved, the same syllable having different meanings to be identified by different tones.

This is enough to show the extraordinary importance of Chinese characters. Moreover, they represent the chief means by which Chinese culture, one might even say the Chinese empire, is held together. Wherever Chinese influence extends, the characters are always the same, while the spoken languages and dialects vary widely. A man from Peking cannot converse with a man from Canton who only speaks Cantonese. However, they have no difficulty in corresponding, just as an American who speaks no Italian knows exactly what is meant when an Italian writes $2 \times 2 = 4$.

*

In contrast, therefore, to the sound-writing which is so natural to us, Chinese writing originated as word-writing, although eventually it also acquired some of the characteristics of phonetic writing. For us, letters are tools of secondary importance. We can concentrate on the substance of what is written, just as when we are eating we concentrate on the food and do not waste time thinking about knives and forks. To the Chinese, however, many characters instantly evoke the picture of the object in question. Whether he thinks about it or not, his eye absorbs it, it reverberates in his mind and conjures up further associations. This applies even to abstract ideas: the character for 'think', for example, consists of strokes which contain the sign for 'heart' (which, incidentally, throws some light on the Chinese mentality). In his mind's eye the educated Chinese sees the character for a word not only when he reads it but also when he hears it.

This fact can also be of importance in propaganda. When Communism was introduced into China about 1920, the word *kung* (common) was taken, and the expression *kung chan* (to produce in common, i.e., communism) was formed. However, there is another *kung*, spoken in a different tone and written with a totally different character, and this *kung* recalls to the educated Chinese a Golden Age, an image dating from ancient times. With this the word *kung she* was formed: commune.[27] In China the people's communes only emerged in 1958. If Mao Tse-tung had introduced the word 'communism' in Chinese in 1958, he might possibly have preferred to use the *kung* meaning Golden Age, with its rich, glowing overtones of tradition, instead of the colorless *kung* meaning simply 'common'.

From earliest times, however, Chinese have delighted in puns. The founder of the Communist Party in China, Ch'en Tu-hsiu, for example, used to make Communism palatable to his bourgeois audiences by resorting to the following reassuring formula: hitherto capital had been *ssu yu* (private); henceforth it was to be *kung yu* (public). So one had only to replace the character for *ssu* by that for *kung* and, abracadabra, Capitalism became Communism.[28]

For thousands of years countless generations played their part in the formation of the characters, until from pictures of, let us say, a tree, or two hands, grew characters or parts of characters bearing little resemblance to their original forms. This process has been neither uniform nor definitive. In fact quite recently, under the Communists, drastic modifications have been undertaken in order to simplify some characters. (This has nothing to do with the simultaneous but independent decision to use the Roman alphabet as well.)

Numerals occupied a special place in the vocabulary. The mystique of numbers has almost entirely vanished from European consciousness, and only rudimentary traces of it are still to be found in fairy tales and superstitions; in everyday speech, numbers have retained their serial function only. In China, on the other hand, numerology has flourished (cf. page 221).

With us, the joining of words into sentences is governed by the rules of grammar, the wealth of whose forms is so familiar to every Western schoolboy. If he had to learn Chinese he could at least sigh with relief at the discovery that Chinese has practically no morphology. The same word can be a noun, an adjective, a verb, or an adverb, and in none of these functions does it decline. The only clue to its function is its position in the sentence, supported by a few particles. The rules for this position, however, are not absolute, and they may be broken for stylistic, i.e., subjective, reasons. The abundance of rules and the strictness of syntax in Indo-European languages make such liberties well-nigh impossible and compel us to a much more precise formulation than is possible in Chinese.

So we see that language makes different demands on the mental powers of Chinese and Westerners. The Chinese requires thousands of hours (almost his whole life if he is an intellectual or professional) just to become—and remain—proficient in reading and writing. On the one hand this learning process develops to an astonishing degree his memory, his visual powers of absorption for even minute details, and his aesthetic sense; but on the other hand it does not encourage the faculty for logical, analytical thought which has become such a firm tradition in the West since Greek and Roman times. And how indeed should it be exercised, when a sentence is created merely by stringing together a series of undeclined words!

The Sinologist Wolfram Eberhard has described this as follows: 'While thinkers in the subordinating languages [e.g., Russian] arrive at a "vertical" logic (cause and effect), the Chinese language results in a "horizontal" logic, a logic functioning by means of parallelisms.'[29]

C. G. Jung, who in co-operation with the Sinologue Richard

Wilhelm attempted to arrive at an understanding of Chinese thought, calls it 'synchronistic', and he defends this kind of thinking by saying that 'there are psychological phenomena which are parallel and positively cannot be causally made to relate to each other but which must be left to stand in some other context of events'.[30]

Lily Abegg, who spent most of her life in the Orient, emphasizes that Chinese writing 'influences thought in an antigrammatical, that is to say, an antilogical and antidiscursive sense', whilst Occidental languages led to discursive thought proceeding consecutively from one idea to the next. She points out that Chinese characters have a life of their own, and compares a Chinese engaged in writing with a domino player who chooses from among the dominoes (i.e., characters) at his disposal, those most suited to his purpose. It often happens that a character is chosen, not because it gives the clearest rendering of the sense, but because it appeals to the writer on the strength of its aesthetic or symbolic value. 'In this case the decision is made more from emotional and artistic reasons, for it is the use of this character and no other that evokes a particular mood.' She comes to the conclusion that:

The relationship between writing and thinking in China has been reciprocal. The Chinese psyche evolved the system of writing and out of its own need it has continued to cling to it. Once created, it possessed a life of its own, quite apart from the language and in distinction to alphabet-writing. Like a steel scaffolding or a corset, it has served to strengthen and maintain the conservatism of a Chinese culture already by nature conservative.[31]

Indeed, an understanding of the reciprocity between language and thought must be regarded as basic to the modern science of linguistics. Races and cultures have evolved their own immutable forms of linguistic expression, and these in turn exert a formative influence on men: they are 'very much at the mercy of the particular language which has become the medium of expression of their society'.[32]

*

I myself have a vivid memory of the Chinese aversion to logic and systematism from the days when I was editing a magazine in Shanghai. The manuscripts of Chinese contributors, at least of those who had not had a Western education, consisted simply of a number of facts or thoughts strung together without logical or causal connection, with not even a conclusion drawn from the sum total. A manuscript concerning, say, modern film-making or some recently published books resembled a catalogue. No attempt was made to arrange the films or books according to subject, significance, or political views of the writer, or any other point of view, or to draw any conclusion or lay down any consistent thesis. Mao Tse-tung once described this Chinese peculiarity as an arrangement of 'items in A, B, C, D . . . as if setting up a Chinese drug-store'.[33]

A further personal experience may serve to show the difference between European and Chinese ways of thinking even in the very young. 'Abstract or Concrete?' was the name given by the children with whom I grew up in Moscow before the First World War to the familiar game where one thinks of an object which the others have to guess. Invariably the guesser tried to find out with the very first question whether the object to be guessed was abstract or concrete, after which a systematic attempt was made to solve the riddle. The players who were the most logical and methodical in their questions were considered the best. The distinction between concrete and abstract comes as naturally to the Westerner as the desire at all times —even in games—to be logical and systematic.

Years later, when I taught Chinese children this guessing game, we could not begin with the same question. It did not even interest them: in fact, it was hardly intelligible to them, apart from those who went to Western schools. The questions these Chinese youngsters put were completely random: they jumped about all over the place without any obvious reason, got 'warmer', went off again, and then suddenly hit the nail on the head.

In talking to an adult Chinese one finds exactly the same thing, even in rational discussion. Unless he has been Western-trained, he does not express his opinion by logical steps but advances it in little thrusts, first from one side, then from the other. His thinking is an 'encircling or embracing' process, to quote Lily Abegg again. She compares Chinese thinking with arrows which begin by flying around in all directions and only converge on a certain target (the goal or result of the thought) when they sense its nearness.[34] In this process the Chinese is capable of a degree of concentration which the Occidental, without the Ariadne thread of logical connection, could never attain.

In Hawaii and Shanghai I used to watch my Chinese students writing essays; they sat motionless for a long time beside their Western classmates. These were already busy writing and erasing, but the Chinese would wait till they had completed the composition in their heads and then proceed to write it down at great speed and without further reflection. This method extends from the most ordinary daily task to the highest level of intellectual activity. A Chinese cook takes hours to discuss the meal, buy the ingredients, and otherwise make his preparations, while the cooking itself takes only a few minutes. And the Chinese artist knows nothing of the sketch or study, of overpainting, or of any other form of correcting the emerging picture. He does it all, so to speak, in his head first, and only then is it transferred with swift strokes of the brush to the blank sheet of paper. Every stroke must be 'just right', for nothing may be altered afterwards. Such feats of concentration are in their turn the fruit of systematic and patient training. An Anglo-Saxon psychologist has remarked that the method of learning in China—that is, the constant repetition of set sentences—is based on the assumption that in this way the lesson eventually becomes part of the student himself. He calls this 'a process of gradual integration of external models and personal experiences through repetition'.[35] In Part II we shall deal with the significance of this method with regard to 'brainwashing'.

Finally, one must mention the revealing fact that the use of analogies for the comprehension of the laws of nature resulting from the magical view of the world (a view no longer to be found among Europeans) has continued to exist in China until recent times, although, of course, not under the Communists. Chinese medicine, for instance, was founded on analogies of the following kind (wind, acidity, and anger affect the liver adversely, and so on):

east— wind— wood—acid— liver— muscles—anger
west—dryness—metal—sharp—lungs—hair— anxiety[36]

Accordingly it was not uncommon for a sick person to consult a chronicler rather than a doctor.[37] It is only to us that such things seem like a nonsensical game; for the Chinese they proceed from the close relationship of all things in the cosmos, from the reciprocity between the largest and the smallest, the macro- and the microcosm, between natural events and human actions. Chinese thinking is 'complementary' (H. Wilhelm[38]), 'totalistic' (L. Abegg[39]), 'universalistic' (de Groot[40]). 'A single principle is sufficient to understand everything' (Confucius[41]).

*

If at this point, where our observations turn from patterns of thought to content of thought, we look back once again, we are immediately struck by the contrast between the Chinese and the Russians on the emotional as well as the rational plane. As long as they were permitted to be themselves, the Russians were conditioned more by emotion than by the mind or the will, and were inclined to dream rather than to act, to suffer rather than to resist, to an amiable laziness rather than to systematic effort. When their consciousness was awakened, it was often the best among them who suffered from their inability to emerge from their deep and passionate discussions onto the road of determined action, and they felt they were 'superfluous'. And even after his victory Lenin let fly with the rebuke: 'Russians are lazybones, softies,' . . . 'It's a bowl of mush we have, and not a dictatorship.'[42]

This emotional and impulsive temperament of the Russians exemplifies, among all the people of Europe, the strongest contrast to the rational wisdom of the Chinese, at least of the educated Chinese, to his self-control arising out of his continual state of harmony with his environment. More passionately, more fervently than the West, Russia has proclaimed the message of the priority of the soul over the body, the spiritual over the material, of eternal salvation over worldly profit, and, even in our mass age, its great writers have presented the introvert in his most radical form. At the same time it has provided a vast reserve of wide-eyed, self-immolating idealism, indeed of the utmost fanaticism, for the cultivation of doctrines of salvation and Utopias of a very different kind and origin.

Yet how could such Messianic fanaticism have flourished in the Middle Kingdom, in the land of the longest tradition, of the most static race known to human history, among a people who have always lived in the past and the present rather than the future, who have evolved the spirit of scepticism and relativity, the wisdom of compromise and the ethos of moderation!

It has often been said that Christian dualism, face to face inexorably with the Absolute, has given rise to a new dynamism and has impelled the European spirit to embark on ever new voyages of search and discovery and active reshaping of the world. Max Weber taught us to understand even the robust nature of 'big business' as an offshoot of secularized Puritanism. It was the dialectic principle which led European thought, blossoming to its first full perfection in Ancient Greece, later to take its decisive turn toward the idea of constant and inevitable progress. That the first country to be conquered by this idea in its extreme form of Marxism should have been Russia, a country that had experienced neither the strict discipline of the Roman spirit nor the awakening of the Renaissance and of humanism, and that had been affected by the age of reason on the highest social level only, is in my opinion but a further proof of the power of the common European heritage. It is a mistake to believe that this ideology (as distinct from many of the practices of its disciples) had to be forced on the Russians. During the early thirties I found scarcely any indication of a basic rejection of its principles; on the contrary, I often came across a lively interest in it and a desire to learn more about it. Today in the Soviet Union the belief that the dialectic process leads inevitably from Capitalism via Socialism to Communism is no longer limited to active Communists.

In China, as we have seen, these fundamental conditions were lacking: not only the dialectic principle itself, but causal thought in general, the reasoning of strict logic, the reciprocity of analysis and synthesis, of knowledge and its practical application, are all imports from the West and must be systematically acquired if China is to catch up with the West—including the Soviet Union. Meanwhile, those familiar with the industry, the endurance, and the patience of the Chinese know better than to pronounce such a thing as 'impossible'; why, by another token, should not China succeed in a task which scarcely a hundred years ago the Japanese people achieved in a few decades?

CHAPTER II

THE HERITAGE

View of the World

IN ITS THEORY AND PRACTICE, in its historical roots as well as in all its developing power today, Communism can only be grasped when seen in the context of its close ties with the industrial revolution. In the early days of the Russian revolution, the Communists' attitude toward the machine was nothing short of worship, and from Red China comes similar evidence of faith in salvation through technical progress. We need only recall the cult of the 'people's furnaces' which in 1958, at the time of the Great Leap Forward, millions of Chinese were forced to pursue.

The revolutionary nature of the most recent stage in Russian and Chinese history becomes all the more apparent when we examine the spiritual heritage of these people. Up to the time of their first encounter with the West, the center of gravity of their spiritual and intellectual life was to be found in areas which had nothing to do with science and technology.

It is true that the Soviets began very early to correct their history so as to prove that every important discovery and invention was first made in Russia. The whipping up of Soviet patriotism in the Second World War gave new impetus to these efforts, and there are still many learned scholars in the USSR today who are engaged in tracing Russia's 'native natural science' as far back as possible in order to prove its independent origin. But their success was limited. Even the semi-official review of natural science in Russia prior to 1917,[1] published since 1957 by the Academy of Sciences in Moscow, reveals no independent beginnings of modern natural science and technology in the 181 pages devoted to the era preceding Peter the Great; such beginnings were limited to translations of Central and Western European works. Nor is the truth of these facts affected by the device of including in Soviet history the Central Asian regions conquered by the Tsars in the nineteenth century. These areas, having previously been under Islam-Arab influence, provided the Soviets with an excuse to claim for themselves the Arab sciences which were already highly developed by the Middle Ages.

Until the first half of the eighteenth century the Russian contribution had been scant. It began with M. V. Lomonosov who, after studying in Germany from 1736 to 1741, produced with the eruptive power of genius a spate of works dealing with the arts and sciences, and even poetry.

The rise of mathematics, for which the Russian people had a special gift, is mainly attributable to the activity of Leonhard Euler, a Swiss who lived almost continuously from 1727 to 1783 in St. Petersburg. Euler, of whom the great Laplace said, 'Everything we know we learned from him', made mathematics the backbone of the Academy of Sciences, which had been opened just before his arrival in Russia. This school has produced Russian mathematicians of international stature since the mid-nineteenth century. They were given special support from the state, so that mathematics could actually be called the Russian 'governmental science'.[2]

Today the whole world knows what followed. Although, for reasons which their history explains, the Russians stepped over the threshold from ancient to modern science later than the peoples of Western and Central Europe, once this step had been taken it was not long before they were on an equal footing with their Western colleagues. Not only did they take over the West's stimulating ideas, but they developed them creatively. 'For thirty years Ilya Muromets [one of ancient Russia's most popular heroes] sat on the same spot without moving. But when he was thirty he began to plant his feet firmly on the ground, and he felt within himself a mighty force.'[3]

*

China entered upon this evolutionary stage still later. There are, of course, those who say that our ideas concerning the unity of matter and energy were known in the days of Neo-Confucianism and even in the teachings of Lao-tzu, and that China was thus ahead of the West by some hundreds of years.[4] But this is not to be taken seriously; one might as well declare that the early natural philosophers and mystics of European history were atomic physicists.

The Chinese are no more lacking in technical intelligence than the

Russians. In many fields this intelligence led them thousands of years ago to perform feats which would have been unthinkable in the Europe of that time and which the Greeks, had they known about them, would almost certainly have included among the Wonders of the World. Many of their irrigation systems and dams which were built two thousand years ago are functioning today as well as they did then. To Marco Polo, coming from a part of Europe that was particularly advanced for those days, the China of the thirteenth century seemed a highly developed wonderland. The printing press, as well as gunpowder and the compass, were known to China long before Europe; the first of these inventions certainly came to Europe from China, and probably the others did too. These are but a few outstanding examples. Joseph Needham's monumental work, the first systematic presentation of Chinese natural science and technology, will comprise seven volumes.[5]

But between Marco Polo's days and our own, nothing much has been added. Generally speaking, things remained as they were until well into the nineteenth century, and we may assume they would have continued to do so had it not been for the stimulus from the West. For thousands of years the Chinese lived beside the Pacific without bothering to find out how far it extended or what shores bounded it on the other side, while the Europeans had hardly reached it before they had crossed it; and gunpowder was used by the Chinese chiefly for filling firecrackers. Not that they were particularly peaceloving— far from it, for their history resounds with battle cries. But their attitude to the forces of nature was of a less serious kind, and they totally lacked that overwhelming, systematic curiosity which existed in Europe since the end of the Middle Ages—whether for the good of humanity is not a matter for discussion here. For thousands of years the intelligent Chinese had watched the steam from boiling water, but not one of them hit upon the idea of making use of this natural energy; if he had we would know, for their chronicles preserved everything that seemed even remotely interesting. Their inventive spirit was given wings by the practical needs of the hour; their curiosity ended at the point where these needs were satisfied.

It cannot be denied that there have been rudiments of scientific thinking in China during the past two and a half thousand years. The so-called dialectic school of Chinese philosophy in the fourth century B.C. seemed to open up a trend in this direction, and in the following century the adherents of Mo-tzu, known as the Neo-Mohists, tried to tread new paths as logicians. Their writings contain such phrases as: 'To estimate the heaviness and lightness of bodies is called weighing. This weighing does not consist of finding out the right or wrong of things. It consists in balancing them correctly.'[6]

On closer inspection, however, we see that even this conclusion, which seems to constitute an objective, morally neutral statement, one which to us appears to conform to our understanding of natural science, was to be interpreted in the traditional sense, i.e., that it concerned the weighing of motives and thus in turn human behavior. The passion for exact weighing, measuring, counting, and experimenting, without which modern natural science could not exist, is typically Occidental.

The man who went furthest in the direction of an 'applied' science was Hsün-tzu, who in the third century B.C. wrote a poem which was quite revolutionary:

> You glorify Nature and meditate on her;
> Why not domesticate and regulate her?
> You follow Nature and sing her praise;
> Why not control her course and use it?[7]

And two hundred years later Wang Ch'ung, in his *Critical Essays*, attacked the prevailing superstitions of the day in a manner reminiscent of modern times.[8] But such things never progressed beyond the initial stage. The conservative spirit of the Chinese promptly turned against these innovators and prevented them from further development.

There is more to this than mere superstition, however tenacious it may seem to be. Not more than twenty years ago I had the following experience in China—and, what is more, in China's most Westernized city. The German Medical Academy, built at considerable expense for the benefit of the Chinese (the previous one having been destroyed in the Sino-Japanese war), very nearly turned out to be a magnificent failure as an investment. After a few days the students fled from it in panic—they said it was haunted. Many years previously, in the days when Shanghai was still only a small settlement, there had been a number of graves on this site, which at that time was outside the city walls. As the city grew, a gambling den arose here, and this, it was now explained, so infuriated the spirits of those who had been buried there that they continued to haunt the place. Taoist priests spent days in the building exorcising the spirits before students would return. And this was not all: a rather odd problem arose, for the German Consulate's books contained no column in which the considerable costs of the exorcism could be entered.

Every 'old China hand' has a tale to tell of the difficulties liable to arise in the construction of railways, roads, factories, and warehouses because the spirits and magic powers prevailing in the chosen sites had first to be considered.

All this was, on the level of popular religion only, an expression of a far broader and deeper *Weltanschauung*, of that ancient Chinese conception of the interrelationship of all things in the cosmos— embracing all mankind and its actions—whose harmony was inviolate even to the educated Confucian. When he tried to explore this cosmos, it was only in order to become a part of it, to act in harmony with it, not to rule it, let alone change it. When Mencius said: 'The reason why I hate that holding to one point is the injury it does to the way of right principle. It takes up one point and disregards a hundred others,'[9] even this conservative principle can only be grasped when seen as part of Confucius' cosmic moral code:

It is through the power of right behavior that heaven and earth work together, that the four seasons harmonize, that the sun and moon shine, that the stars trace their courses, that the rivers flow, that all things flourish, that good and evil are differentiated, that joy and anger find their proper expression, that inferior men obey, that superior men are enlightened, that all things regardless of change are not brought into confusion. If one departs from it, all perishes.[10]

Confucius proceeds from the all-embracing, all-governing principle of Tao, which includes heaven and earth, the world of the gods and the world of men. By contrast to the popular Taoist belief in devils and magic, he develops this principle further into a moral, social, and political doctrine rooted in the cosmos. In countless variations the philosophers of China have repeated the principle that heaven and earth and the ten thousand things are one.

From earliest times the Chinese have aimed at achieving harmony, and this word *ho* appears in the names of people, places, palaces, temples, and streets.[11] One often comes across the following quotation from the classics: 'Let the states of equilibrium and harmony exist in perfection, and a happy order will prevail throughout heaven and earth and all things will be nourished and flourish.'[12]

*

It is not the task of this book to introduce the reader to the magnificent edifice of China's classical philosophy, which takes its place side by side with the highest achievements of the West; there is no lack of reliable literature available today, most of it readily understandable and focussed on the essentials. What we are concerned with here is the extent to which this philosophy has shaped the thinking and behavior, the spiritual, social and political evolution, of the Chinese people, at least of the upper classes. Considering the all-powerful influence of Confucius and his disciples (and later his successors), this effect was bound to be unequivocally conservative, anti-revolutionary, and even anti-reformatory. If man has to fear that his wrong actions may upset not only the order of his human environment but also the balance of nature, he will act with greater circumspection and caution, if not with more trepidation, than if the only obstacles in his path are punishment at the hands of the law or his neighbors' disapproval—even if he does not, with Lao-tzu, subscribe to the ideal of non-action (*wu wei*). It is here that we find the real reason for the static element in Chinese culture and history which places China at the opposite end of the scale from the dynamism of the West.

Another factor is that this philosophy—again with Confucianism in the lead—is concerned expressly with problems of daily life; in other words, it is pragmatic. Its interest in metaphysics and in epistomology is slight, and 'unfortunately there has been but little development of logic in Chinese philosophy'.[13] In essence, then, this philosophy is almost synonymous with ethics. The index to the English edition of Fung Yu-lan's work on the history of Chinese philosophy prefers to dispense with the word 'ethics' as Chinese philosophy is in any event largely concerned with ethics.[14]

According to this view, thought must serve the purposes of behavior and in particular behavior in human society; this was where, after generations of political chaos, Confucius felt his historical mission to lie. More than two thousand years before Karl Marx (and a good hundred years before Plato), Confucius demanded that philosophers reshape the world; thought and knowledge as ends in themselves are rejected. 'Though a man may be able to recite the three hundred odes, yet if, when entrusted with a governmental charge, he knows not how to act, ... notwithstanding the extent of his learning, of what practical use is it?'[15]

Thought should restrict itself to what is in practice attainable. 'To know the unknowable, to attain the unattainable, ... those are things

I would never attempt.'[16] This saying has also been attributed to Confucius. We are reminded of the lines in Goethe's *Faust*: 'A man who ruminates/Is like an ox whom evil spirits/Lead round and round on barren heath,/While just beyond lies verdant pasture.' But that unquenchable urge toward what seems unattainable, that desire for knowledge for its own sake, 'pure' research without aim or objective —those are the things to which science and technology owe their proudest triumphs.

Yet to call Confucius' teaching utilitarian would be to misunderstand the Master completely. That which benefits, not the individual, but society, is right. Confucian ethics are social ethics. This sentence from *The Book of Rites* could be taken as its motto: 'Right behavior wards off rising disorder as a dike wards off the rising waters.'[17]

One must, then, do right regardless of whether it is beneficial or injurious to oneself. One might say that, just as the Greeks fused the ideas of 'beautiful' and 'good' to form the one higher concept of *kalokagathia*, so for Confucius the right and the useful (in its highest sense) were to a certain extent identical. That Confucius did not, of course, expect everyone to have this attitude is proved by his saying: 'The mind of the superior man is conversant with righteousness; the mind of the mean man is conversant with gain.'[18]

In fact, Confucius was imbued with the conviction that men could be taught to become better men, certainly better fellowmen and thus presumably happier men. In this he has sometimes been justifiably compared to Socrates, born ten years after Confucius' death. Five hundred years before Christ, Confucius taught the basic rule of 'What you do not want done to yourself, do not do to others.'[19] It is characteristic of his moderate estimation of mankind that he gave his exhortation a negative form in contrast to the positive one pronounced by Christ.

And yet a fundamental mood of optimism is to be found running throughout Chinese philospohy. Apart from the sceptic Hsün-tzu and the so-called legalistic ideology of the third century B.C., one finds that man is regarded as being by nature good, or at least capable of being taught to be good. Mencius, the great Confucian, was foremost in contributing to the victory of this concept. If a man sees a child about to fall into a well, he says, he will feel horror and pity. This will occur quite spontaneously, and not because he wants to find favor with the child's parents or be praised by his neighbors.[20]

This natural disposition toward good must, as Mencius taught and as many Chinese believe, be supplemented by teaching men to be good. This teaching must lead to an enlightened egoism which will make men realize that to do right is in accordance with human nature and thus contributes to his happiness. To paraphrase Mencius: If you want a child to learn the dialect of Ts'e, send him to Ts'e. If you wish to develop your virtues, keep the company of virtuous men.[21]

For Mencius, even desires are not in themselves bad if they are understood and guided properly. The thinker Hu Shih, who died on Taiwan in 1962, defines 'the perfection of the individual through intellectual training' as the true goal of mankind.[22] In contrast to Socrates, this training consists of the acquisition and mastery of certain formulas, rules, and practices by means of protracted learning or contemplation; but the belief in the possibility of acquiring virtue by learning is common to both and distinguishes them radically from the Christian image of man.

In spite of its philosophical basis, the Chinese moral code is lacking in the principle of absolute commitment. Confucius himself described his own maxims as being relative: 'I have no course for which I am predetermined, and no course against which I am predetermined.'[23] It is true that the weight of his authority together with a tradition of two and a half thousand years have endowed his teachings with a semblance of absoluteness; in their origin, however, they are directed toward the practical demands of life in human society, and they are based on understanding and good will rather than on divine revelation. Instead of invoking the gods as the bestowers and guardians of moral law, Confucianism transformed them into impersonal cosmic forces and ethical principles.

When the Occidental—and in the end that meant the Christian— observer was confronted with this world of ideas, he was bound to ask, no matter how much he respected its spiritual intensity: could one speak here of what had long been familiar to him as the most powerful force in his whole existence: was this religion?

And Beyond?

THE ARGUMENT AS TO WHETHER or not the Chinese have a religion is as old as the appearance of the first Europeans in China. The sharp division between the masses and the educated upper classes makes a uniform answer impossible, so let us look first at the upper class. If one takes this class as a whole and considers only its basic elements, we arrive at the following picture for the last two and a half thousand years.

The original concept, common throughout China, of a supreme deity (*shang ti*) gradually dissolves into an anonymous force—that of *tao*, for example; out of the rivalry of the various gods grows the interplay of natural principles such as the male and female (*yin* and *yang*). Although Confucius still often speaks of 'heaven' (*t'ien*), this word, which had previously been but another name for the deity itself, is for him merely a kind of impersonal force in the universe.

Did they exist at all, the gods? Confucius declared that he knew nothing about them and reinforced this agnosticism with the words: 'When you know a thing, to hold that you know it; and when you do not know a thing, to allow that you do not know it: this is knowledge.'[24] He advised keeping a careful distance: 'While respecting spiritual beings, to keep aloof from them, may be called wisdom.'[25] His practical, if sceptical, advice was to behave as if they existed, and *The Book of Rites* demands that one should continue to offer the traditional sacrifices,[26] just as one is polite to one's fellowmen, not because it is 'to one's advantage' but because it is proper to do so.

Mo-tzu, the enlightened humanist, replied scornfully to this: 'To hold that there are no spirits and learn sacrificial ceremonials, is like learning the ceremonials of hospitality when there is no guest, or making fish nets, when there are no fish.'[27] But for Confucius the sacrifices, the rites and ceremonies, which played so large a role in ancient China, had a predominantly ethical significance; the fact that they brought man into harmony with the laws of the universe meant that they disciplined him and trained him in the way of moral conduct. It is this aim of educating the people that explains the supreme importance attached to the ceremonial system, especially to *The Book of Rites*, ever since the time of Confucius.[28]

The meaning given by Confucius to ancestor-worship was also beyond all else an ethical one. It forms the basis for moral training by encouraging and giving outward form to filial piety and by raising clan and family ties to an ethical level. He taught that, if a people respected burial customs and remembered its ancestors in sacrificial ceremonies, its morals would incline toward perfection.[29] And today Hu Shih explains that Confucius

sought to establish a new moral sanction without the benefit of the Gods. The constant consideration of never disgracing one's sacred inheritance from the parents was regarded as sufficient moral sanction for human action. . . . His parents thus take the place of God or the Gods.[30]

Thus God and the gods have become dim shadowy forms, and in their social function too they are now almost superfluous. To the Chinese intellectual they never meant anything; he has no feeling whatsoever for the existential power of religion. The passionate search for a path to God and the world beyond, for redemption and salvation, a search which has never ceased to occupy the finest minds of Russia, in fact of the entire West, is—always allowing for exceptions—unknown to him. The powerful polarization existing between God and the world is to the Christian a positive experience, and from the Volga to the Atlantic it has been *the* subject not only of religious history but of all spiritual and intellectual history as well. In China, however, there has been scarcely a trace of it since Confucius. Nothing shows this more clearly than the word *chiao*, which means 'teaching' (especially religious teaching) as well as 'education' or 'training', thus embracing religion, training, and culture as a unit. Chan Wing-tsit, an authority on the intellectual history of his people, and during the thirties one of my colleagues at the University of Hawaii, has the following to say:

In Indian, Persian, and Western literature, great expressions about God have been full and abundant. In Chinese literature, however, such expressions are isolated and few. . . . There have been comparatively few religious leaders in Chinese history. Not a single member throughout Confucianism's long history of twenty-five hundred years may be labeled a religious leader. There were great priests in both Buddhism and Taoism, to be sure, but most of them existed before the twelfth century, and since that time there have been fewer and fewer prominent religionists. In recent Chinese history one cannot find a Ramakrishna or even a Kagawa.[31]

In comparison to Europe it might be said that in China enlightenment and rationalism won important victories in the fifth century B.C., with the result that China's educated upper classes were never again able to accept a religion of revelation. To the extent that the intellectual Chinese believes at all in gods, he only does so in an extremely vague and, as it were, diluted metaphorical sense. He speaks of heaven, of the absolute, of natural law, and of course of the principle of order embracing all human life, *tao*. The only 'immortality' he knows is that of living on in his children and grandchildren, as a link in the chain of the generations, or, more vaguely still, as a part of the cosmos seen as a unity and hence eternal. Even in his language the soul has no place, and the concept of the soul's indestructibility has been 'fundamentally . . . discarded. The question was settled once and for all in the sixth century.'[32]

The passion of ecstasy, the mystical desire for union with the divine, are unknown to the Chinese; and since he knows no 'hereafter' he feels no need to prepare himself for it in this world. Even when he retreated into solitude, as often happened, his aim was either to enjoy life—not in a coarse materialistic sense but with the refined hedonism of the epicure—or to turn his back on some particular ruler or dynasty.[33]

The Chinese has no need of asceticism because he has no conception of sin, let alone original sin. Lin Yutang remarks with an ironical shake of the head: 'You can't make a man a Christian unless you first make him believe that he is a sinner.'[34] That which for the Christian is an offence against divine law is for the Chinese a violation of good behavior (and thus of course at the same time a disturbance of the social order and of the balance of all things). For the Confucian, evil is basically a social phenomenon. 'All immorality arises from want' we read in an apocryphal Confucian dialogue from the Han period.[35]

Nevertheless, the idea did exist that good deeds were rewarded, if not in one's own life then at any rate in the life of one's descendants. But there was no heaven for the devout nor was there a hell for the punishment of the wicked. The satanic element is entirely absent from Chinese religious feeling, hence man is not called upon to prove himself in combat with Satan. Buddhism was the first to introduce hell, and then not merely one but eighteen all at once.[36] However, this has had little effect on the optimistic outlook of the Chinese.

*

This ethical principle is also a marked characteristic of popular religion, so far as we know it. It is noticeable that, in the most widespread sects, moral precepts of a practical nature prevail: filial piety, respect for old age, gratitude, willingness to serve, and loyalty; patience, freedom from envy, tolerance; moderation in drinking and gambling; active co-operation in such community projects as treeplanting, road-building, and education of the ignorant.[37] However, we know too little about popular religion in China to be able to judge its spiritual strength, its power of resistance to atheism and materialism. According to a Chinese philosopher and expert on religious matters, its study has been shockingly neglected, and he complains that since the turn of the century not a single book has been published dealing with Chinese folk religion.[38]

Earlier works[39] present a picture of an almost staggering diversity of involved superstitions and occult practices connected with agriculture and family life, such as spells to promote a good harvest or drive out illness, combined with a mixture of Taoist, Buddhist, and Confucian ideas in their vulgar form. Everything foreign was assimilated and adapted by China. The Chinese showed his strong family feeling by extending the Indian idea of *karma* (man is rewarded or punished for his deeds in his next reincarnation) to the family (the good and bad deeds of the individual affect his descendants), thus introducing a kind of 'family-*karma*'. Again, he showed his sense of history by merging Yama, the Buddhist Lord of Hell, and an imperial official into one figure.[40]

This popular religion has no clearly defined limits and no solid structure, other than the Taoist church of the first century A.D., which disintegrated at the beginning of the Tang period (about 600). Imperial religious practices were mainly of a ceremonial nature and had little in common with popular religion. The Chinese peasant did not profess to be either a Buddhist or a Taoist; instead he worshipped gods, spirits, and temples of every imaginable kind and derivation, and sought help against demons and the forces of nature wherever he could. Occasions of various kinds might cause him to enlist the services of Taoist priests and Buddhist monks all in the same week, not forgetting, of course, to pay his respects to his own ancestors. The magicians and shamans who operated among the people made use of the concepts of classical philosophy in order to acquire some sort of legitimacy in the eyes of the ruling educated class, but these concepts were ruthlessly vulgarized. Between the superstitions of so-called Taoism and the *Tao Te Ching*, of which Lao-tzu is said to be the author, there exists an even more tenuous connection than between popularized 'Buddhism' and the original teachings of Buddha. One should make a distinction between the philosophy of Lao-tzu and that type of popular religion called Taoism.

The pre-Confucian belief in the interrelationship of all things, and thus also between the human and the nonhuman, offered far-reaching possibilities to the shamans. This parallelism was pushed by them to absurd limits and built up into a contrived system of relationships devoid of any basis in reality, such as that between the 'five planets' and the 'five senses of man'. The number of occult forces which had to be considered, of images derived from characters and analogies (cf. page 27), was countless: a man suffering from a disease, the written character for which contained the symbol for rat, must eat a cat, because cats eat rats; and under no circumstances must one sharpen a knife at a well because the combined symbols for knife and well constitute the character for beheading.[41]

Geomancy, the science of the earth's secrets, provided a living for whole armies of priests. Every early account of travel in China mentions it; in fact, nowhere else in the world was it of such significance. Geomancers knew all there was to know about the spirit world of the mountains, rivers, trees, graves, indeed of almost every square foot of ground, and in every building enterprise, large or small, they delivered their opinion—for a fee. Their colleagues the chronomancers were hired in all ventures of any importance at all to calculate the correct day and hour.

In view of the distinctly worldly nature of these concepts and practices, one might well speak of a practical materialism. The deities and spirits most worshipped by the masses were those who had best proved their efficacy by the granting of offspring, wealth, and health; and the particular art of prolonging life was served by various highly specialized systems of magic rites. Prayers often resembled business transactions: if you, God, give me this or that, I will do this or that for you. The various deities were, so to speak, responsible for rain or health according to their offices, and they were harshly treated if they failed to live up to expectations. Not without reason have Chinese gods been compared to high-ranking officials;[42] and their priests and monks, regardless of the diversity of their spiritual derivation, practised a highly secular magic aimed toward well-being in this life. They were little more than ritualistic functionaries and had nothing of the divine authority with which we associate the mediator of the Divine. True religious yearning found no satisfaction here; it turned away—in the last few decades more than ever—from the priests and the monasteries toward religious societies, some of which were secret.

The ruling class was surprised by such events because it had failed to satisfy the needs of the masses for religious security and protection from the forces of nature, and had withdrawn to a dignified distance. It looked on the pre-Confucian beliefs as disorderly, in a way even objectionable. The educated Confucians made no attempt to wipe out the practice of magic; although they despised it, they tolerated certain aspects of it—as long, that is, as its adherents did not intrude upon government affairs and administration (or occupy high government positions!). The gulf which was thus formed was never to be bridged. One may assume with certainty that it contributed in no small measure to the downfall of the old upper classes and in the end facilitated the influence of Communism among the masses.

One must not underestimate the psychological effect of the lack of any church order such as moulded Christian Europe: its religious services and sacraments in which all could participate; the orderly annual succession of feast-days, a definite creed, and a divine Founder without which there could be no binding authority. What the Chinese intellectual lacks most of all, however, is the basic principle underlying all this: the belief in the exclusive truth of one particular religion—that is to say, one's own. The Chinese people are really the classic example of a mixture of faiths, of syncretism.

*

Buddhism found its readiest response in China at a time when Confucianism was going through a phase of spiritual fatigue and when the downfall of the Han dynasty, which was in existence at the time these changes were taking place, had resulted in a widespread feeling of insecurity. The form in which Buddhism took root in China no longer had much in common with the teachings of Buddha; it had become a Chinese folk religion. The Chinese masses welcomed it on account of its doctrine of incarnation. According to this doctrine, the righteous could look forward to a future of happiness as a compensation for their suffering, whereas punishment awaited their masters and tormentors. For a long time Buddhism was the most powerful spiritual force in China. It reached its highest level in the sixth century, but in the middle of the ninth century it suffered persecutions under Emperor Wu Tsung from which it never fully recovered, probably because at the same time the spiritual sources of Buddhism in India were drying up.

The old upper class had begun to take control again. In its intensive battle with Buddhism (and the popular religion of Taoism) traditional philosophy grew strong: Confucianism was reborn. Although this rebirth took place some thousand years ago, we still call it Neo-Confucianism. This Neo-Confucianism lasted for hundreds of years, and until 1905 it continued to form the basis of the official government examination subjects. In the nineteenth century it was reborn yet again as a result of contact with the West, which gave rise to a new spiritual movement, a second Neo-Confucianism, as it were.

Neo-Confucianism was no more a mere revival of the old, just as the Renaissance in Europe was not simply a repetition of antiquity; rather, it contained the elements of Buddhism and Taoism in new forms. As soon as Buddhism appeared on the Chinese horizon, it underwent a change simply by the translation of ideas. For 'perfection' Chinese translators used the character for 'round'; they translated 'essence' as 'pupil of the eye', 'one's true nature' as 'original face and eyes'; the Sanskrit word *śīla* (morality) as 'filial submission and obedience'; and for 'nirvana' they used their old 'non-action'.[43]

As an instance of what can happen to Buddhism at the hands of the Chinese, here is an amusing little tale from the Second World War. There was a noticeable food shortage in Shanghai. The sea route was almost entirely eliminated as a result of the destruction of the Japanese merchant navy, and from the interior, which guerrillas of all kinds had made unsafe, very few goods were reaching the city, in which—counting the Japanese garrison—some six million people were living. The patience and self-control with which the population endured all the shortages were as astonishing as the inventiveness which continually found ways and means of making these shortages tolerable. One day my Chinese friends laughingly told me the story of a new '*ch'an*'.

The Japanese military authorities had set up stocks of sugar in a warehouse down by the docks, and these stocks were heavily guarded. What the Japanese did not know was that suddenly, all around the harbor district, in backyards, on roofs and on verandas, beehives appeared, and the denizens of these beehives industriously carried back the sugar from the warehouse, over the heads of the sentries and into the hives of their owners. The actual point of this story, however, is to be found in the expression *ch'an*, which my friends used to describe the trick: it is simply the Chinese word for a Buddhist concept derived from India which originally meant 'religious intuition'. (In Japanese the character is *zen*, as in Zen Buddhism, so much discussed in the West today.) Among the Chinese the word gradually took on a highly secular meaning of 'intuition', somewhat as we might say: 'It suddenly dawned on me,' or 'I had a flash of inspiration.' The masters of this particular type of Buddhism are well known for their artful tricks in which evil always gets the worst of it.[44] This explains how the beehive-trick played on the Japanese was jestingly described by a word that once had a sacred and profound meaning.

But this 'translation' of Buddhism from the abstract into the concrete constitutes only one aspect of the process. Indian Buddhism —insofar as it did not live on in specifically Chinese forms, particularly in Zen—had, it is true, been dissolved in the ocean of the Chinese spirit; in other words, it had largely surrendered its identity. But the ocean had also been changed by this process. Neo-Confucianism had to a very great extent absorbed elements of ideology, speculation, and even metaphysics; now it possessed a cosmology, since it had taken the traditional Chinese principles of *yin* and *yang* and incorporated them as moving forces into the structure of the Indian concept of eternal creation and decay of the worlds. Moreover, the idea of dedication, so typical of later Buddhism—that is to say, a dedication not only to one's fellowmen but to all living creatures— gave rise in China to the beginnings of a social understanding, of a social way of thinking which was not at all characteristic of the Chinese.

We need not go into the question of Islam here, as generally speaking it found its way among the non-Chinese peoples only. The acceptance of Christianity in China, however, merits our attention, as far as this throws any light on the Chinese mentality.

*

After centuries of constant endeavor, Christian missions in China have had very limited success. Why? Because the nature of Christianity prevented it from paying the price that Buddhism paid: namely, becoming largely Chinese in character. There was no lack of effort in this direction. The Jesuit missionaries of the seventeenth and eighteenth centuries, headed by the first great Sinologist Matteo Ricci, not only adapted themselves outwardly to their Chinese surroundings in speech, dress, and way of life, but even accepted the Chinese word *shang ti* for 'God', and tolerated ancestor-worship and reverence for Confucius. It might be said that they anticipated Mao Tse-tung's formula of 'a uniting of the universal truths of Marxism with the national characteristics of China', if one replaces the word 'Marxism' with 'Christianity'. They appealed quite consciously not to the masses but to the intellectual élite, and their instinct told them that this élite was not to be won over by flying in the face of the basic Chinese traditions. However, the Dominicans and Franciscans opposed this Jesuit attitude. Tired of the quarreling between the orders and becoming increasingly suspicious of their motives, the Throne withdrew its favor in the eighteenth century and finally became actively hostile.

The methods by which leading Chinese Protestants tried to make use of the fresh chance offered in China after the collapse of the Japanese occupation and before Mao Tse-tung's assumption of power are very revealing. In 1946 F. C. M. Wei, a Chinese Christian, gave a series of lectures, also published in book form, at Union Theological Seminary, in New York.[45] His advice was that churches be erected, not in the city, but 'on a hill top surrounded by beautiful shade trees' and in 'the architectural style of local ancestral temples, ... a clubhouse as well as a church. There ought to be a family atmosphere in it. It is a place to which people would love to go and go naturally. There they meet God and there they meet their friends. ... Adjacent would be a cemetery where the leading Christians are buried. ... In this way we build up a Christian shrine to which we hope the Chinese sentiments at present centered around the clan may be gradually transferred, because the spiritual ancestors of the Christians are commemorated there.'

Under no circumstances should young clergymen be sent, for Chinese respect old age. One must acknowledge the baptism of all Christian faiths, and no one, no matter to which branch of Christianity he belongs, should be excluded from Holy Communion. The Chinese inclination to compromise is shown here. The contents of the Creed were also given a Chinese interpretation:

'He [God] has sought to reveal Himself ... in the person of Jesus of Nazareth, ... by living as the obedient Son of God who knows intimately His Father's heart and mind. He lived and died in filial obedience and He conquered death as the Son of the living God. ... As head of the great family embracing the whole of mankind, God exercises His will as the supreme authority. ... From their Confucian culture they [the Chinese] will find it easy to understand the Fatherhood of God and the brotherhood of man. ... They know what it means to submit to the Father's will and make it their own. When they are told that there is a Will in the universe and that there is a Purpose in history, they will readily grasp its meaning. While they believe in the inner light within the human heart, it is not strange to them that the mysteries of life are revealed to them in the lives of great historical personages who are the spiritual geniuses of the race. ... All that is necessary is for Christianity to bring in the new idea of man's personal relationship with God, for personal relationship as the basis of life is the familiar Chinese way of thinking. ... The standard of the good and of the true is higher than man. It is the cosmic harmony according to Confucianism. Put the Christian God in the place of *ch'eng*, which we have proposed to translate as Cosmic Harmony, and the framework of the Confucian moral and religious philosophy may keep its old form but its spirit will be changed; it will have a new life. . . . We may expect the theological development of Christianity in China to be along the historical and moral rather than the speculative line. But after all, Christianity is fundamentally historical and moral, not speculative. . . . Sin for the Chinese is not so much an existential fact as a failure of the will. It is moral in nature rather than metaphysical. . . .'

Dr. Wei's American audiences were given no opportunity to put his recommendations of 1946 into practice. Nevertheless they are still valid: they indicate the extent to which, in Chinese eyes, a foreign ideology must adapt itself to Chinese ways of thinking if it is to achieve lasting success in that country.

*

Here we must say something about the renowned tolerance of the Chinese. This is often contrasted with the intolerance practised in Europe (including Russia, from the schism of the Church in 1666 to Stalin's 'purges') and the persecution and branding of dissenters as heretics. One has only to recall the generosity of outstanding emperors of the Mongol and Manchu dynasties, the religious discussions among Christians, Mohammedans, Hindus, and Buddhists at the court of Kublai Khan, and the respected positions held by Jesuits as close advisers to the Dragon Throne. But the Mongols and the Manchus were foreign conquerors; and even before their time the history of China offers examples of extreme intolerance.

In a work written during the anti-European Boxer rebellion and still showing the effects of the agitation of that time, J. J. M. de Groot has compiled a long list of religious persecutions and religious wars in China.[46] He begins with Confucius himself, who in the *Analects* said: 'The study of strange doctrines is injurious indeed!'[47] De Groot points out that Mencius condemned the philosopher Mo-tzu, who preached love of one's fellowmen, as a heretic; and he reminds us of the law established by the Ming emperors against heretics, a law which was taken over by their successors and was valid until well into the nineteenth century. This provided for death by strangling, or for one hundred blows (which many did not survive) followed by exile. The destruction of many thousands of Buddhist monasteries under the T'ang emperors in the ninth century, and civil wars with a religious background (from the 'Yellow Turbans' of the second century to the Taipings of the nineteenth) form part of this picture.

When we examine this more closely, however, we see that the causes of this suppression were mainly political. The ruling class in China restricted its tolerance to such manifestations as did not jeopardize the basic structure of their personal and public life. The accusations which they leveled against their opponents are, therefore, not philosophical in nature but of a social and political kind. They accused the Buddhists, for example, of betraying family tradition and ancestor-worship by their practice of celibacy, of withdrawing in their monasteries from productive work and military service, of depriving the country of the agricultural use of their very considerable lands and properties, and of not paying taxes.

We see, then, that it is not intolerance as such, which exists in Russia as well as in China, that is of interest, but the direction taken by its attacks. In the West it was largely concerned with faith and dogma; in China with state and society. Even the Chinese sense of mission is secular; it is expressed in the term 'Middle Kingdom' which they gave to their country, thus claiming to be a force bringing order and civilization to mankind and having a mission, so to speak, of an administrative rather than religious nature. But even this mission does not seem to have found much response beyond the circles of military and political leadership. The Chinese simply does not like to emerge from his private sphere and commit himself to 'ideas' or 'movements'.

However, the absence of reformatory zeal, so characteristic of China's internal history—or, when it does appear, its rapid exhaustion —is not merely a matter of temperament. Reformatory zeal can only exist where there is a clear, well-nigh passionate belief in a distinction between right and wrong, good and evil. To expect him to make such a distinction seems to the Chinese highly unreasonable; his thinking lies along lines not of mutually exclusive opposites but of polar extremes which, like night and day, merge into one another, and this in itself is not conducive to drastic progressive action. For him, even spirit and matter—the two extremes which have governed the history of the West for two thousand years—are not mutually exclusive; for him they belong not to two different worlds but to one and the same cosmos, and they are linked together by a variety of transitional stages. So how can he decide definitely in favor of one rather than the other?

Among the deeds of the Emperor Shih Huang Ti, known to subsequent historians as the wickedest of all the Chinese emperors, the most wicked was the 'Burning of the [Confucian] Books' in the year 213 B.C. For the Chinese intellectual, who after more than two thousand years still recalls this event with horror, the unprotesting acceptance today of the extreme intolerance of the Communist doctrine is sheer torture, as is also the consequent insistence on 'confessions' and denunciation. With what relief, then, did he grasp in 1957 at the dream of the Hundred Flowers that bloom side by side, of the Hundred Schools of Thought that were to compete with one another! His despair when these flowery dreams suddenly faded is something I saw for myself in China in the summer of 1957.

The precious possession of tolerance was won by the West only after centuries of bitter religious wars. Chinese history has nothing comparable to offer: in that country, apart from the brief flashes of revolutionary movements, religion was never the governing force. The gods—insofar as they were still believed in—had their clearly defined authority and as such were called upon as the occasion arose. Beyond this they had no power; they were not a force whose laws and taboos determined man's whole existence, his earthly fortunes and eternal salvation. In life as in death, the educated Chinese can manage very well without them. This is expressed in the much-quoted saying from the eleventh century: 'In life I shall serve unresistingly, and when death comes, I shall be at peace.'[48]

Among the common people, Buddhist priests are often called in for prayers for the dead—just to be on the safe side, but this does not constitute an avowal of Buddhism. The idea of the migration of souls can hardly be any consolation for a people who prize life not only as such but life in the family community, for it is an idea which holds out the promise of a reincarnation unconnected with present existence or one's companions in this life.

One thing is certain, and that is that even among the people the old beliefs and religious practices had already been seriously undermined long before the Communist seizure of power. I shall return to this in Chapter IV. Their feeble powers of resistance against new influences, including the most recent, should not surprise us. The imperishable achievements of the Chinese spirit lie in other fields than the religious: the religious pattern was and is still much less in evidence in China than the economic and particularly the aesthetic.

*

Few Europeans have any conception of the venerable age, the
wealth and artistic maturity, of Chinese literature. It will be sufficient
for us to give one historical detail: when during the Manchu dynasty
an anthology was compiled of the poems of the Tang period (a
thousand years earlier!) which were considered worthy of literary
immortality, these numbered forty-eight thousand poems by two
thousand three hundred poets.

On the other hand, many an art-lover is familiar with the genius
of Chinese painting. It has become part of mankind's cultural heritage
and is represented today in every illustrated work offering any selection, big or small, of 'World Art'. Calligraphy must also be considered as belonging to this category, as in China it involves the use
of the brush. Nowhere else in the world has calligraphy achieved
such significance. Even an uneducated man is capable of appreciating
the beauty of the characters whose meaning he may not understand,
and he can tell you the names of the great calligraphists of the past
and present. Hundreds of generations succeeded one another in
dedicated efforts to paint these characters with increasing beauty and
elegance, with the result that Chinese writing at its best is of breath-
taking beauty.[49]

The products of Chinese arts and crafts have long been sought
after by collectors all over the world: bronzes, porcelain, artistically
embroidered robes. There is also a never-ending charm in the rhyth-
mic vitality of Chinese architecture, particularly in the art of land-
scape-gardening, which has been brought to the highest pitch of
refinement. To comment further on the renown of Chinese art would
be to overstep the boundaries of political observation; for our purposes the only important thing is the element to be found throughout
all these exquisite creations: the delight in beauty, pure and simple
and sufficient unto itself. It is the highest and noblest expression of
that preoccupation with earthly existence, that affirmation of life,
which we have come to know as the all-pervading characteristic of the
Chinese and which qualifies him even less as a champion of rigid
ideologies than as a resistance-fighter.

*

In its spiritual heritage, old Russia is, of all the peoples of Europe,
the antithesis of classical China. The Russian people have been conditioned, permeated, and moulded by Christianity more forcefully

and more exclusively than any other, except perhaps the Spanish. For almost a thousand years—in 988 it became the state religion—Christianity has been the most powerful spiritual force in Russia, for the peasants until well into the twentieth century, for the upper classes as a whole until the time of Peter the Great, and even later for the overwhelming majority of them.

Intellectual life in Russia was until the sixteenth century entirely, and until the eighteenth century almost entirely identical with the life of the Church and was carried on by men of the Church. It was not until the eighteenth century that the influence of the secular West became noticeable. But the great writers—Gogol, Dostoyevsky, Leskov, Tolstoy—to whom not only Russia but the whole world was beginning to listen, remained searchers after God. The formation of a separate intellectual stratum of partially atheistic leanings did not take place until the last two or three generations. The fact that some of its leaders—Chernyshevsky, Dobrolyubov, and the professional revolutionary Stalin, to cite but a few—owed their earliest education to theological seminaries is one of the ironies of history.

Because in Russia Christianity did not follow in the wake of foreign conquerors, it met with less opposition there as a spiritual force than it did elsewhere. Besides, not only were the Slavs' own religious ideas too weak and too vague, as witness the mass baptisms which took place toward the end of the tenth century, but they lacked the support of an organized priesthood. Within a few generations, patterns of thought and speech were moulded in the Christian image. During the rule of the Tatars (from the beginning of the thirteenth to the end of the fifteenth century) the Church was not hampered by the tolerant foreign masters, with the result that it gained in prestige, also in its role as political spokesman of the people. This situation persisted until the influx of atheistic ideas from the West in the eighteenth and nineteenth centuries. Apart from a few conflicts of a political nature, the Tsars' despotic claims to supremacy, far from damaging the Church, actually enhanced its power, for only the Church was capable of endowing Tsarist rule with divine authority.

Nor was the Church harmed by its trend toward outward display and ritualism, a trend which was first perceptible in the fifteenth century and which found full expression in the victory of the stern religious organizer, Abbot Joseph of Volokolamsk, over the contemplative hermit Nil Sorsky at the Council of 1503, the effects of which were to last for centuries. Even the most terrible atrocities of the power-crazed Tsars did not prevent the Russians from calling their country Holy Russia.

For the devout, of course, this Church, ruled by the state and parading about in gold vestments, was not much more than the vessel which they filled with their own religious feelings. The grimy village priest could hardly be an object of respect. Since the schism of the Old Believers in 1666, millions lived outside the official Orthodox Church, which to them was no longer the authentic mediator for the salvation they longed for so ardently.

These searching millions produced no new religious organization or theology of their own; it was only with the influx of Western influences that a certain interest was aroused in the rationalization of the Christian message. They swarmed about some great individuals, hermits and saints, who were the real religious leaders of Russia, about men like Nil Sorsky, like Tikhon of Zadonsk, who with the quiet light of his mystical piety cast a radiance over the turbulent eighteenth century, convulsed as it was by the advent of rationalism, just as Serafim of Sarov did in the Napoleonic era with his works of mercy. Their ascetic lives made a greater impression on the common people, who for centuries had endured poverty and oppression, than the ostentatious splendor of the monasteries and bishops. It was here that the masses saw men who did not bother about transitory temporal power; here they saw poverty voluntarily assumed, cures, and other miracles; here they sought spiritual guidance and intercession. The weary and heavy-laden set up camp around their huts, often hidden in the forests, and spread the news of the consolation they received near and far.

The hermits remained an integral part of Russian life until the downfall of old Russia. In *The Brothers Karamazov*, Dostoyevsky immortalized them in his figure of saintly old Zosima. In 1924, when in my student days I was on a walking tour through Finland, I came across one of the last of these men on Valaam Island in Lake Ladoga. When the frontiers were redrawn this island had fallen to Finland (meanwhile it has become part of Soviet Russia); that was why the monastery founded nearly a thousand years earlier was able to continue undisturbed, while on the other side of the nearby frontier not far away the Bolshevik *bezbozhniki* (atheists) were turning churches into barns and cinemas. In the hut of the holy hermit I came upon two fishermen, who at the risk of their lives had come across from the Soviet shore. The conversation, which was held in an ancient form of

Russian that I found hard to follow, was not about the miseries of everyday life, about starvation and oppression, but about the divine meaning of pain and suffering. When darkness had fallen the two men returned to the other shore.

*

In figures such as these we still see flashes of that absoluteness, that refusal to compromise, of the Christian faith which in our modern times has largely disappeared from the life of the practising Christian but which in Russia remained alive for a long time. Thus in ten centuries of Russian thought the supreme, the most passionate interest has been devoted not to the improvement of earthly existence or the best possible organization of human society: Russian thought has been—and still is—of an intensely speculative nature; it ponders ultimate and sublime things, roams infinite spaces (one of the reasons why the Russian loves and extols his own country is its vast size), and only reluctantly finds its way to the shaping of concrete reality.

The reverse side of the holy man's (and the philosopher's) sense of spiritual superiority toward the doings of the 'world' has always been a certain sense of insecurity, of helplessness even, in the face of the requirements of daily life and of the demands of authority for total obedience. He seldom has more to offer in opposition than the negative heroism of suffering, which in turn ranks nowhere so high as in Russia. Before the advent of Western influences it was rare to hear a critical voice such as that of the priest Fyodor Karpov who, in the mid-sixteenth century, countered the eulogy of his superior in praise of 'the patience of the ruled' by condemning 'the slavery of patience'; patience, he maintained, might be a virtue for monks but it could not form the basis of the state as it aided and abetted corrupt practices.[50]

Suffering itself appears as a distinctive virtue. The very words for suffering, endurance, patience, 'long-suffering' (dolgoterpenie), had for the Russians a sacred ring. Nothing could be more typical of this than the choice of their first saints, Boris and Gleb. These two sons of the Grand Duke Vladimir, under whom Russia became Christian, were murdered by their elder brother for purely political reasons. During their lives they were not renowned for their holiness; the simple fact that, according to legend, they submitted without resistance to the crime which was perpetrated on them sufficed to make them, following upon their death, the object of a fast-spreading

veneration as *strastoterptsy* (sufferers of violence), and to have them
declared saints within five years of their death.[51]

Prince Andrey Bogolyubsky, the stern tyrant who in the twelfth
century ruled one of the Russian principalities and reduced the noble
city of Kiev and its churches to ashes, was nevertheless made a saint
—for the sole reason that he himself later fell victim to a crime of
violence. Again, the half-mad Tsar Paul I, whose murder by his
confidants brought his reign of terror to an end in 1801, owed his
undeserved reputation among the people to this violent death. And
Ivan the Terrible, in an extraordinary perversion of this notion,
wrote to Prince Kurbsky, who had fled from his tyranny: 'If you are
just and pious, why should you not accept suffering from me, the
harsh ruler, and receive the [martyr's] crown of life?'[52]

So the concept that suffering was the special mission of the Russian people finally evolved. Thus in 1812, after the burning of Moscow forced the French conqueror to retreat, Tsar Alexander I was
able to say to his subjects that God Himself had chosen the ancient
and noble capital of the empire to save all Europe through its
suffering. Dostoyevsky too meant it in a purely spiritual sense when
he cried: 'All men must become Russian! First, and above all things,
become Russian!'

One must not, however, fall prey, like so many of those in authority, to an illusion: although the Christian's willingness to suffer
may manifest itself in non-resistance to force, it is still an outward
rather than an inward submission. It becomes active resistance the
moment this force, supposing itself absolute, violates spiritual freedom and attempts to set itself above faith and conscience. In no case
have the totalitarian forces of the twentieth century escaped this
experience. Divine commands and interdictions, where acknowledged,
are absolute; at this point compromise and tolerance cease. Absolute
truth excludes all other: hence the relentless cruelty of religious wars.

On Russian soil the first great religious schism, the Raskol, in
the seventeenth century, arose from causes which do not compare in
importance with those which led to the Reformation in Central and
Western Europe. Both factions were conservative: however, what the
Old Believers considered old and worth retaining was everything that
had developed during the preceding few centuries, whereas the
Patriarch Nikon, as leader of the reformers, wanted to return from
the largely corrupted Russian texts to those of the late-Byzantine
period. In the final analysis, all that the common people were

concerned with was whether they should cross themselves with two fingers or three. For the sake of this difference, countless people flung themselves voluntarily into the flames. Since that time, schisms have been a characteristic feature of Russian intellectual life.[53]

Passionate sectarian movements have dramatically demonstrated the inclination of the Russian nature for extreme and radical upheavals. At times—the most impressive example being Dostoyevsky —these movements took on the proportions of Messianic missionary faith embracing the whole human race. In all of them there existed the anticipation of an everlasting kingdom, a kingdom toward which, so they believed, the whole history of mankind was moving.

*

Thus the ground was psychologically prepared for the new doctrine of world salvation, albeit only of this world. Idealistic devotion to Utopian ideas, the sacrifice of the present in favor of a better future, were as familiar to the Russian as the demand—so puzzling to Westerners—for 'partisanship' (*partiynost*). Indeed, as I found often enough in talking even to non-Communist Russians, they were inclined to regard tolerance and willingness for discussion as weakness, or even as a denial of truth.

But the Christian essence of the Russian people contributed a still further element to Lenin's revolution, an element to which it, like the French revolution, owes a considerable part of its innate strength and vital impetus: the concept of brotherly love.

The European of the twentieth century, especially when his personal ties with the Church have been loosened or severed, is seldom fully aware of the vital part Christianity has played in moulding our society. Whether by direct tradition—in recent times as 'Christian socialism'—or secularized in the form of humanitarianism, the Christian image still continues to be effective in our day. What we call 'social consciousness' today—and who would dare to ignore this concept?—was once called (although we cannot say it actually was) Christian brotherly love. It wrought decisive changes in the social structure of the various peoples; it weakened the natural groupings of society and realigned them in the higher spiritual community of religion—and by no means least of all in old Russia, where the traditional Christian greeting, familiarized in the words 'little brother', remained in use until supplanted by the Bolshevik's *tovarishch* (comrade) or *grazhdanin* (citizen).

In the sphere of ethics, too, religion has been the cornerstone and sole determining factor in old Russia. Examples of this are: the oldest book of moral instruction, the *Izbornik* of 1076; the aristocratic moral code in the *Instruction* of Vladimir Monomakh, Grand Duke of Kiev from 1113 to 1125; the teaching of decorum and propriety of Joseph of Volokolamsk early in the sixteenth century; and at the outset of our own century Leo Tolstoy's call for a drastic revival of Christian morality, which made a deep impression on our fathers' generation. In fact it is the example of Tolstoy and the influence he still exerts in Russia which clearly indicate that we are dealing here less with doctrine and systems than with mental attitudes. It is a standing reproach in Russia that the 'apostate' West, in abandoning pure doctrine, also forsook piety of heart and the brotherliness of the early communities; in the Eastern Church, especially in the Russian, this brotherliness has remained a living reality. Anyone who has spent Holy Week among Russians and who has taken part in their Eastern midnight service, heard the joyful 'Christ is risen!', seen the brotherly kiss exchanged on all sides and experienced the feeling of salvation and joy on Easter Sunday, will carry with him an unforgettable memory.

*

Let us now at the close of this second chapter try to sum up our comparative observations from the point of view of the theme of this book. To what extent have the spiritual heritage and the historically rooted cultures of both races provided a favourable soil for Communism? To what extent are they likely to make it endure? Or will they contribute to its transformation into a less explosive force, one capable of true co-existence (not a tactically limited co-existence) with the free world? Will they perhaps in the end even lead to its downfall? Three conclusions present themselves.

First, old Russia owes almost all its cultural impulses to the one among all the great religions of the world which is most concerned with the Hereafter; it was this that gave metaphysical depth to the innate restlessness of the Russian, endowing him with a dynamic impulse toward the Absolute; it was this that shaped the type of man capable of religious devotion and boundless self-sacrifice, without which Communism's secular doctrine of salvation cannot exist either.

These psychological conditions could not be produced by the classical culture of China, with its marked preoccupation with this world, with its emphasis on harmony and beauty as the highest of all values. For this reason it will not be easy for Mao and his followers to maintain the revolutionary impetus of the early days and to renew it from generation to generation. For the first time in Chinese history, Communism subordinates the existence of every individual to an absolute goal. Until now, the Chinese were completely indifferent to the fate of others; those who were not Chinese were barbarians. Dostoyevsky's words, 'We are all responsible for one another' would have been unthinkable from the lips of a Chinese. Now he is called upon not only to accept the Communist doctrine of salvation himself and to act upon it, but, at the expense of his own sacrifices, to spread it throughout the world. Countless millions of Chinese have taken part in demonstrations in support of Lumumba, Algerians, and Cubans.

But did these people really mean anything to them? Or was this merely one more instance of the age-old talent and inclination of the Chinese to bend before the storm like the bamboo, to bow without complaint to the inevitable and to withdraw into himself—without surrendering himself? Drought, typhoon, and flood, conquerors from abroad and tyrants at home—these are the facts of life, these are the things which one must somehow survive. Is not 'action through non-action' really the best form of resistance under the conditions of a Communist dictatorship?

Second, however, the very nature of the Christian tradition in Russia was bound to be the chief obstacle in the way of Communism's final victory. Between the materialistic view, which sees every event as a process either of natural law or of economics, and the belief in an almighty creator and preserver of the world, there can be no reconciliation. Even during the last few years I found people in the Soviet Union who said quite openly to me, a foreigner, that they regarded Stalin as the Antichrist. It speaks for itself that, in World War II, after many years of bitter anti-religious strife, Stalin found himself forced to conclude a truce with the Orthodox Church, a truce which, considering the circumstances at the time, was by and large not unfavorable to the Church. This truce extended even beyond the end of the war—a clear defeat for Communism and one not to be taken lightly. Complaints are heard to this day in the Soviet press about the continued existence of strong religious sentiments in the population, even among young people.[54]

In China, however, there has never been a religious force with anything like comparable powers of resistance. Philosophical convictions, even of so ancient a tradition as the Confucian, are no substitute; they exist in outstanding individuals, but not in the masses. As for popular religion, this was declining long before the advent of Communism; in any case, in its variety and typically Chinese polytheism, it would be incapable of offering any prolonged resistance to the totalitarian *ersatz* religion.

In short, of the two forces at work in world Communism— Materialism and Messianism—the Chinese respond to materialism, but not to one of an intolerant Messianic type, while the Russians respond to Messianism, although not necessarily to one which seeks salvation on the materialistic-utilitarian level.

Third, although Communism was remote to the Russians, it was no more remote than a distant relative; for it, too, was an offshoot of the European religious and social history of which they were a part. To the Chinese, however, Communism was as remote as Buddhism (or Christianity) had once been; that is why it was worth while glancing at the way in which Buddhism was adapted to the Chinese mentality. Although this transformation process began practically at the very moment the first messengers of Buddhism set foot on Chinese soil, nevertheless it lasted almost a thousand years. It is not, therefore, of much significance that, fourteen years after its conquest in China, Communism has so little to show in the way of sensational signs of Chinese adaptation. Buddhism, on the other hand, transformed China, and this without the aid of an Indian 'Kremlin' or a totalitarian government in the background. Anyone wishing to draw conclusions from the history of Buddhism in China to apply to the acceptance and further evolution of Communism will have to take both these aspects into account.

What, then, will happen in the Middle Kingdom, when one day dictatorship loosens its grip and its power declines? The Communists are doing their best to weaken the family, the strongest of all the pillars of the old China. Is it possible for a system to endure without tyranny if it recognizes neither God nor ancestors, and if, in their place, it puts world revolution as the yardstick of human behavior? Will the end be disintegration and anarchy? Or will tradition, built up through thousands of years of orderly community life, continue to be effective in Communist China?

In old Russia there was no such civic tradition, and it was necessary for the state to have divine authority in the eyes of the people. Dostoyevsky's message to his people was: Between you and chaos there stands only faith in God. And many years later a devout Russian *émigré* raised a warning voice: 'When the Russian loses his faith in God and the immortality of the soul, he will find anything excusable, for the values of civilization as such mean nothing to him.'[55] That does not necessarily mean chaos; the stabilizing force emanating from the new Soviet élite may be enough to prevent this. But one may say this much: Stalin replaced divine authority with tyranny and the worship of the machine. Krushchev sought to win the support of the Russian people by an attempt to rekindle belief in the mystical 'transition to Communism'. Whether the Russians will in the long run be content with that depends not least on the state of their belief in God.

CHAPTER III

THE SOCIETY

China's Own Road

IN ANY DISCUSSION OF RED CHINA, the standard question recurs: how was it possible for Communism to triumph in a country in which the family is so strong? That family and clan possess an overriding importance in China has long been one of the basic facts about Asia of which the educated Occidental was aware. Indeed, nowhere else in the world is—or at any rate was—the 'family man' such a dominant figure, such a distinct type, as in China.

The same Chinese who could unfeelingly pass by the misery, suffering, and death of his fellowmen manifested an almost unsurpassed capacity for devotion and self-sacrifice within the circle of his clan. Can we imagine more forceful, more terrifying, examples of this than, say, the story of the sons who cut pieces of flesh out of their arms to make a stronger broth for their sick father—incidents which not only appear in moralizing fairy tales but which are reported in ancient chronicles as having really happened?[1] The duty of self-sacrifice was therefore affirmed in its most extreme form, but at the same time it was restricted to a human environment that was not freely chosen but preordained: the family and the clan.

Filial piety required the uttermost sacrifices, such as in other traditions may be demanded only by the deity. In the following astonishing parallel to the story of Isaac's or Iphigenia's sacrifice, the characteristics which it has in common are as interesting as those which distinguish it: a man by the name of Kuo persuades his wife to kill their three-year-old child because they are too poor to feed both the child and his sick mother. Just as they are about to bury the child—alive—they come upon a heap of gold deep down in the earth: the gods, moved by Kuo's filial devotion, have made it possible for him to look after his mother without sacrificing his child.

This tale is one of the 'Twenty-four Examples of Filial Piety' from the time of the Mongol dynasty which for centuries have provided material for plays and professional storytellers. But even the realities of the twentieth century may offer some surprises to the foreign visitor. In Shanghai during the forties we had for some years a house-boy who lived with his mother in our apartment; there were no signs of any other relatives. When the old lady died, he asked for a few days' leave. On his return he brought with him a wife and two children. We thought he had married a widow and were about to congratulate him on the wedding, when he informed us he had been married to this woman for six years, but, as his mother could not get along with her, she had lived till now in the village.

The Chinese family system was run on strict hierarchical lines and was governed by two dominating principles: the older generation always took precedence over the younger (likewise the older members of each generation had priority over the younger); and the man had priority over the woman. Hence the younger relative owed obedience to the older one (even when they did not live under the same roof), and the woman owed obedience to the man. This system survived more than two thousand years of Chinese history without any noticeable opposition until the penetration of Western ideas. Those who could not endure it did not rebel but voluntarily departed this life, as has often been reported of young women. But this system also surrounded the life of the individual with human warmth and affection, and gave it the outward and inward security which today, in our highly civilized world, shut in by the 'walls of loneliness', he often so painfully lacks.

Countless Chinese novels paint a vivid picture for us of the way in which the real life of a human being is lived within the family and how it is sustained in joy and sorrow by the family. The harshness of the system mainly affected the woman: wedded to a man not of her choosing, often literally bought by his family, living in his family's house as a stranger, separated from her own clan (which was not even allowed to take part in the wedding ceremonies), a servant of her parents-in-law, above all expected to bear sons, virtually without recourse to divorce but at the same time not assured of respect as the sole wife, since the husband, if she gave him no son (and even, if he was a rich man, simply for prestige reasons), was free to take concubines. To be sure, she could, if she outlived her husband, in her old age become the highly respected head of the family, ruling over sons and grandsons (there was, for example, no lack of masterful female figures on the imperial throne); but her fate was all the more cruel when she was widowed young, without having borne sons. Prospects of a second marriage scarcely existed, for it was now her duty to look after the parents of her deceased husband. According to one Chinese sociologist: 'The unity of the big family was insured at the expense of the wife.'[2]

With more certainty than their sisters, the growing sons could look forward to a future in which one day they would be in authority; but when death was late in claiming the parents, this could take half a lifetime, and meanwhile there could be no question of freedom or self-determination.

We must begin by dispelling a widespread misconception. Recent research has clearly shown that the very big family (*chia*), uniting several dozen people under one roof, was far from being the rule. This concept was only possible abroad because the family of that size formed part of the life of the ruling class, and it is representatives of that class who play the leading roles in many Chinese novels, especially in those which have become well known in the West, and which constituted the favorite, if not the only, contact of the Western observer with China. The large family represented the personal retinue of the successful man rather than a firm institution; for among a people with the strong family feeling of the Chinese, a man's prestige was enhanced by the presence of great numbers of relatives and servants in his house. Large households of this kind, therefore, usually lasted only as long as the founder held the reins as the patriarch, seldom for more than three or at most four generations. Disintegration was hastened by the laws of inheritance which, instead of the law of primogeniture, provided for equal division of the property among *all* the sons of the testator.

By far the majority of families, particularly in the country, differed little in size and way of life from those of other peoples at a similar stage of development. Usually they formed a production unit, in farming as well as in handicrafts and trade, and were small, consisting of parents and children, with the grandparents often living with them. Their size has been calculated, after painstaking statistical research, at from four to seven persons, depending on the regions studied.[3]

*

If, then, certain exaggerated elements have been eliminated from our image of the Chinese family, we must now stress the overwhelming importance (compared to the West) of the larger family unit: the clan (*tsu*). For Occidentals the clan is today no more than a historical or literary conception, but in China it was till yesterday a living reality. The members of a clan were descended on their fathers' side from the same ancestors; they therefore bore the same family name and usually lived together in the same area, often in the same village. The importance of the clan was greater in the country than in the town, and in South China than in the North.[4]

There were one-clan villages, multi-clan villages, and also villages where the population was all mixed up together and hence without any solid clan-organization. The size of the clans ranged from a few hundred heads to many thousands. Their strength and importance depended on whether their members attained rank and dignity, thus bringing honor and worldly goods to the clan. A rise of this kind was usually followed after a few generations by impoverishment, sometimes decay. There have been many clans, however, which have managed to retain their solidarity, if not their respected position, for hundreds of years. A sociologist who was doing some research in a village in South China shortly before the victory of the Communists reports that in the ancestral hall of one clan twenty-four generations were venerated; the original ancestor had come from the North Chinese province of Hopei in the year 1091.[5] All the members of a clan had a right to assistance from the clan, regardless of their economic or social position. The clan was headed, however, by the richest and most respected of the various families belonging to it; these also held the leading position in the clan council, which looked after the duties of the clan.

These duties were of both a spiritual and a practical nature. Chief among the spiritual duties was the worship of ancestors, the joint celebration of feast-days, the keeping of genealogical books (the clans tried to trace their origins back to the most impressive ancestor they could find: in one case they even resorted to a hero from a novel for this purpose!). Among the material responsibilities were the maintenance of schools, the support of the aged and ill, the education of gifted members of the clan who were sent at the clan's expense to sit for the state examinations, the upkeep of the irrigation systems, dams, bridges and other types of construction from which the clan members—although not only they—benefited. Furthermore, the clan kept a watch on morals and manners, and punished the wrongdoers in their ranks—in extreme cases even with death. P'eng Teh-huai,

later one of the leading Communist generals and for some years (till
1959) Minister of Defence, as a young man narrowly escaped a death
sentence by his clan, as they accused him of insufficient respect for
his stepmother.[6] For good sons and honorable widows, the clan
erected memorial arches. It settled quarrels among its members, and
often even set up a kind of clan-militia. The material basis for their
numerous expenses was the land which belonged to the clan as such
(as distinct, that is, from the private property of the individual clan
members) and which in most cases consisted of endowments to the
clan by rich members.

In this way the family and the clan embraced a man's life from birth
to death and even beyond, and were the measure and the core of his
existence. As a child he came to know not only the grandparents who
were living in the house, but how to distinguish accurately among the
whole circle of relatives. For each degree of relationship there was a
special term. In order to name correctly all his relatives who were
descended on his father's side from his great-great-grandfather down
to his own great-great-grandsons, he needed seventy-six different
terms; for his mother's relatives, seventy; for his wife's, sixteen. The
married woman had additional terms for her relatives. Where we
merely say uncle or aunt, the Chinese differentiates: his father's older
brother, the wife of his father's older brother, his father's younger
brother, the wife of his father's younger brother, his father's sister,
the husband of his father's sister, the son of his grandfather's older
brother, the wife of his grandfather's older brother, and dozens more
subsidiary groups of uncles and aunts on the father's side alone, down
to the son of the granddaughter of his great-grandfather's sister—
altogether 262 degrees of relationship![7] A slight relief was offered by
the fact that brothers bore the same generation-name as a component
part of their name: Chiang Kai-shek's sons, for example, are called
Chiang Ching-kuo and Chiang Wei-kuo.

And so the young Chinese grew up in a clan community, aware
that he was part of a group which would look after his needs. Even
the dead ancestors were still present in the house—in the ancestral
hall, the best-kept room in the house which could thus also serve as a
parlor. As late as 1960, when I was on a walking tour on Taiwan, I
was hospitably invited into the ancestral hall of a farmhouse and
given tea there.

The earliest literary works bear witness to the importance of the
family and the clan. In *The Book of Songs* (thought to be from the

eighth and seventh centuries B.C.) we find a song of praise to the ancestors, another to brotherly love, a family drinking-song, and among the many love-songs a surprising number relating to marriage —forty-seven according to the compilation of an English Sinologist.[8] Confucius made the family the focal point of his moral code, and the State protected its authority with the threat of drastic punishment. The legislation of the T'ang emperors, part of which remained in force until the twentieth century, provided for particularly severe penalties for acts of violence against relatives, for destruction of ancestral shrines, even for offences against filial piety or harmony within the clan. Similar crimes against persons who were not relatives were far less severely punished. That is hardly surprising, since the clan system assumed a considerable part of the duties of the State, not the least of which were those relating to social security; it became the bulwark of the social structure for a society whose stability survived for thousands of years.

*

It is, of course, true that the constant emphasis on respect for old age and for the traditions of the past resulted in the inner stagnation of the country. This is also the best explanation for the nepotism which is so typical of China: everyone felt obliged to look after the interests of his own relatives at all times in the first instance. When he had the chance to do this, he gained 'face', and this, as we have already seen, was more than riches. 'Riches are dirt, face is the true gold' says a proverb.

The same basic principle of superior and inferior rank to be found within the rigid circle of the clan was a governing principle through-out social relations as a whole. Here, too, in China 'face'—or, to use a term fashionable in our times, 'status'—was more than riches: it was the essential condition to all life in the community. Not the least of the ways in which the man of good position demonstrated this was by taking liberties which were not open to the little man: for example, when he drove his car through the city streets a great deal faster than the speed limit allowed and the policeman, after discovering that he was a respected personage, let him drive on without giving him a ticket, he, the driver, gained considerable 'face'. Equality in the eyes of the law existed mainly on paper, because the application of the law depended on the situation, an evil which Lin Yutang condemned when he said that not until there was a government by law instead of a government by 'face' would Chinese live in a true republic.[9]

The complaint is a natural one, for closely related to the cult of 'face' was the cultivation of personal connections. These were not always of a family nature, although very often they were. What was expected and obtained by the inferior from his superior, by one relative from another, was personal advancement, preference, and protection. In Chinese this system is known as *pao*, one of those words which it is almost impossible to translate. The way in which *pao* was taken for granted could scarcely be better demonstrated than by this little story from the ninth century A.D.:

When Prime Minister Tsui Ch'üan was urged by his wife to buy some land for purposes of financial security, he refused, saying he already had thirty magnificent properties—by which he meant thirty men who, during the years when he had been commissioner in charge of the state examinations, had passed the highest examinations, and who therefore owed him a debt of gratitude. This same Tsui Ch'üan went down in history as a model of incorruptibility.[10]

That the average man, especially the official of intermediate rank, was bound to be corrupted by this system, as soon as it went beyond certain limits, has been repeatedly proved by the history of China right up to the downfall of Chiang Kai-shek's regime, which was attributable to corruption. Will the Communist regime turn out in the long run to be capable of resistance? Powerful rulers such as the Han Emperor Wu (140–87 B.C.), under whom the empire achieved its greatest expansion, and reformers like Chancellor Wang An-shih (1021–80), tried to replace this web of protection with an enlightened absolutism, and egalitarian mass movements did their best to uproot it by revolutionary force. Thus in the revolt of the 'Yellow Turbans' (in the second century A.D., a reaction against the general confusion of the declining Han period) a system of communal labor and meals was set up, and—an especially interesting fact—of public confession of misdeeds. The leaders of the Taiping Rebellion, which after the violent upheavals of the Opium War plunged the country into fifteen years of civil war (1851–66) demanded that all landed property be divided up among the peasants and that all movable goods be under common ownership. However, not only were these reformative and revolutionary attempts unsuccessful, but, being associated with exceptional situations, they are only partially representative. The history of other peoples, including the Russian, has similar examples to offer in times of crisis.

*

Eventually the forces of conservatism proved superior, both in political and spiritual strength. They relied on the unique authority of Confucius, who had preached a distinctly aristocratic social system, although he believed that the aristocracy of blood should be replaced by that of education. He himself, as we have seen, adjudged only the noble in spirit to be capable of doing right for its own sake and without regard to profit. And the Confucian Hsün-tzu wrote in the third century B.C.:

> To divide the people, to cause them to have the classes of poor and rich, of noble and inferior, so that everyone would be under someone's control—this is the fundamental thing in caring for the whole country. . . . The prince and minister, the father and son, the older and younger brother, husband and wife—here we have a beginning and end, an end and a beginning; this social structure exhibits the same principles as Heaven and Earth; it is of equal permanence with the universe—this is called the great foundation. . . . For the purpose of rescuing people from trouble and eliminating calamity there is no method as good as that of making social distinctions plain.[11]

In his book Hsün-tzu also offered an economic argument which has a modern ring to it: inequality is unavoidable since there are not yet enough goods to go round. Even for Marx and his successors the creation of a superfluity of goods is essential for the transition to Communism.

A sharp differentiation in rank, a distinct and conscious division of authority, applied not only to social relationships but to daily life and work. Every foreigner who settled in China soon learned that the household which ran the most smoothly was the one in which the duties of the various servants were most clearly defined.

Even in the twentieth century the intellectuals knew how to defend their place in society with the utmost tenacity. On my first visit to China, in 1929, I was commissioned by an international student organization to visit a series of universities in order to explain the Western system of student self-help, and to recommend its adoption. With my reports of student-operated cafeterias and laundries, etc. I first met with astonishment, then icy rejection: they had not come to the university to dirty their hands with manual labor; what they expected according to ancient Chinese tradition was stipends and other privileges. Nor did they lack sayings which they could quote from the classics: 'Superior men should labor with their minds and smaller men labor with their strength. . . . The government men

devote themselves to governing and the smaller men devote themselves to labor. . . . Those who govern others are supported by them.'[12]

*

However, in the pyramid of occupations to which we will now turn it
was neither the peasants nor the artisans who found themselves at the
bottom, but—the merchants. At times they were even put in the same
category as slaves and prostitutes, actors, jugglers and musicians,
barbers and mercenaries, all of whom were regarded as being outside
society as such, and all of whom were excluded from sitting for civil
service examinations. This may surprise many who have seen for
themselves the remarkable business ability of the Chinese. But the
Confucian state of scholar-officials had a moral code according to
which the merchants, who neither were learned nor—like the
peasants and artisans—produced goods, who in other words operated
not at the 'root' level but at the 'branch' level of the economy, were
not very highly regarded. And Lao-tzu's exhortation to moderation
could hardly tend to enhance public respect for them: 'When one is
moderate in one's desires, there is no want,' or, 'Too much accumu-
lation must lead to great spoilage.'[13]

Neither did legislation or the administration of justice favor the
merchant profession. What they protected was not so much the
property system as the moral system.[14] Moreover, the practical application of the law by the judge depended on the circumstances and the
persons involved. Hence there was no strict framework of laws with
which the merchant could reckon in his calculations.

In such circumstances no free and continuous development of the
merchant class was possible. Whenever they succeeded in raising
themselves, they were quickly slapped down again. During the Han
and T'ang dynasties, for example, there were times when merchants
were forbidden to wear silk or ride on horseback. During the Ming
and Manchu periods their situation improved, although they were
excluded from certain branches of business such as the salt trade and
mining, these being government monopolies. In these fields they
could at best operate as lessors, but not as contractors. Even where
they could carry on their business legally they were subject to
arbitrary bureaucratic action. By far the greater majority of them
remained at the level of the shopkeeper, or even of the itinerant
streethawker, that picturesque figure of old China with his cries and
sounds varying according to his wares—the drum of the paper-

collector, or the tinkling little metal clappers of the refreshment-vendor.

But even the rich merchant was not nearly as important as his colleague in the pre-industrial West or in the Islamic world. Not until the nineteenth century did the picture radically change—too late to allow for the growth of a strong, economically independent, self-confident middle class such as became the most powerful counter-weight to royal bureaucracy in the West. Hence the merchants' drive for the development of an autonomous city community was lacking; the Chinese city never progressed beyond the role of an adminis-trative and economic center for the surrounding countryside.

The artisan, himself the creator of objects of value, was ranked higher, owing to the value placed on beautiful articles of every kind. By and large his position was hardly different from that of his Euro-pean fellow craftsmen of pre-industrial times. Family businesses, with apprentices and journeymen, were the rule here too; and, as used to be the case in Europe, and sometimes still is, workshops of the same trade gathered together in the same street. There were also guilds whose main purpose was to control price and quality and represent the interests of their members to the public. We find no mention of the existence of large businesses from which an early type of capitalism might have evolved.

*

The Confucian order of precedence placed the peasant even higher than the artisan. The esteem in which agriculture was held in China since earliest times is evident in the venerable figure of the mythical ruler Shen Nung (*heavenly farmer*). According to ancient tradition, he is said to have invented ploughing tools, taught the people farm-ing, and studied plants and herbs for their curative powers. The high rank of the peasant in the social scale was attributable to two things which were lost to the European peasant to a large extent and to the Russian peasant almost entirely: personal liberty, and freedom to do as he pleased with the soil. In China there has been virtually no peasant serfdom for over two thousand years, and the proportion of financially dependent peasants, either tenant-farmers or those who hired themselves out to work for landowners, was comparatively small. Even in the thirties of this century, when the situation had sharply deteriorated as compared to earlier times, the Chinese peasant class consisted, according to the reliable research of J. L.

Buck, of fifty-four per cent property-owners only, seventeen per cent tenant-farmers only, and the remaining twenty-nine per cent of peasants who farmed their own as well as leased land.[15] On the other hand, the larger estates were modest compared to European, and particularly Russian holdings. There was no clearly defined border-line between them and ordinary farmland, even down to the smallest holdings. In fact, large properties were usually leased in allotments, which precluded any large-scale agricultural enterprises.

In contrast to Russia, therefore, until well into the nineteenth cen-tury there were no circumstances favoring a class struggle at the agricultural level—with rich landowners on one side and poor serfs on the other—just as for the past two thousand years there had been no feudalism in China, although the Communists maintain that such existed right up to our own century. After all, the clan itself embraced both rich and poor, thus contributing to the alleviation of social differences. The Confucian tradition, too, had a tranquillizing effect, teaching men to make the best of a situation. Furthermore, as we shall see, anyone could raise himself into the upper class. Another factor contrasting with the situation in Europe even in the eighteenth century was the mobility of the land. From time immemorial, land in China had been regarded—not only on paper—as private property which could be sold without any restriction. The detailed study of a village in the South China province of Kwangtung after the end of World War II revealed, for instance, that among the more than thirty rich families only one had belonged in this category for the past four generations, and the remainder for only one or two genera-tions.[16] Even clan property, of which there was a great deal in South China, did not constitute a restriction on the liberty of the peasant. The clan members could—but they were not obliged to—lease it from the clan in addition to the land which each member already owned. There was also no collective property owned jointly by the whole village and involving legal ties to the land, such as there was in most of Russia. Here, too, then, the rudiments of socialist communal patterns were lacking.

And yet China's history shows a long series of peasant uprisings and disturbances, often lasting many years. The causes lie not so much in political or social oppression as in economic deterioration. In earlier centuries this was chiefly due to continuous wars and the burden of taxes which became heavier in proportion to the amount of fighting among those in power; later, after the end of the eighteenth century, it was due to the ever-increasing population with which the opening up of new land could no longer keep pace. G. B. Cressey has made the following calculations which clearly indicate the trend: there were 5·24 *mou* of arable land per head of land-population in 1666, 4·07 *mou* in 1766, but only 2·49 *mou* in 1872[17] (one *mou*, which varies in size according to district, corresponds at the present time to about a sixth of an acre). Yet agricultural productivity scarcely increased as the peasants continued to use the methods of their forefathers.

An additional burden for the peasant household was the very considerable and economically unproductive outlay for ceremonies and ostentatious display prescribed by custom, especially for such occasions as weddings and funerals. Many a farmer of moderate means spent his total gross income for a whole year on his son's wedding.[18] He had no reserves with which to face drought or floods or the devastations of war. For many there was no alternative but to take to the road and die of starvation.

*

We have roamed through the structure of Chinese society, moving from the bottom toward the top, and we come now to the highest class. Its identification with Chinese culture is as strong as its close ties with government, so that it would seem impossible to separate state and society in old China. This constitutes such a unique phenomenon that no truly satisfactory Western word has been found for it. A literal translation of its Chinese name, *shen shih*, is of not much help, as *shen* means belt or wearer of a belt (of honor), as was the custom with officials and holders of an academic degree, and *shih* means scholar.[19] To speak of officials or of scholars only will not do, since these terms overlapped considerably. On the other hand, the double term 'scholar-official' is too clumsy, and the expression 'literocrat', suggested by C. G. Wang, although pertinent, too artificial. The word 'mandarin' (a garbled Portuguese expression from Southeast Asia) means, as does 'official' with us, merely a man holding office, but not the far greater number of candidates for office who also went to make up the *shen shih*.

To the English who went to China, the name which to them seemed best suited to express the idea in mind was the one they gave to their own upper class, the 'gentry', that is to say, the class composed of the landed aristocracy and the upper middle-class families which had become property-owners. And it is this term which has been adopted by most English-speaking historians and Sinologists although it hardly corresponded to Chinese reality, as the aristocracy of birth had long ceased to exist in China (apart from the imperial princes and their families) and landed property was of secondary importance for the position of the *shen shih*, who based their claim to a place in the administrative hierarchy on their education and state examinations. What this 'gentry' was, we hope to show in the following pages.

As an institution, the gentry was the instrument of the absolutist and centralized state as it was founded following the overthrow of the old feudal system in the third century B.C. The vast expanse of the empire and the multifarious dialects, if not languages, were enough to require an army of officials capable of understanding the language of the capital and of reading orders from headquarters. Who else could be considered for this task but the guardians of ancient writings and traditions, the graduates from the schools of the 'philosophers', headed by and soon consisting exclusively of Confucians, who had always demanded that the rulers be advised by men of wisdom and noble character? Thus the mastery of all the principal areas of Chinese culture, and above all of Confucianism, to be demonstrated in state examinations, became the real proof of qualification of the official.

This system of examination and selection was developed with great consistency, although with certain interruptions and detours, until in the first part of the Sung dynasty (960 to 1067) it more or less found its final form, and one which, apart from a few minor changes, it retained until examinations were abolished in 1905. Every detail was thought out: a gradation of examinations from the provincial to the capital level; guarantees against cheating and outside help; objective valuation through identification of the papers by numbers instead of names; continual testing of an official on active service by means of annual achievement reports based as far as possible on objective criteria, such as the population's increase or decrease in the district concerned, or the number of criminals apprehended. One or two examinations were not sufficient; the life of the Chinese upper class has been called a 'life of examinations'.[20]

Examination standards were very high; in some provincial examinations during the Manchu period, ninety-eight per cent of the candidates failed—one of these was Hung Hsiu-chüan, later leader of the Taiping Rebellion. A carefully restricted staff of top officials, some of whom were chosen personally[21] by the emperor, had the privilege of proposing those candidates considered most suitable for advancement to the highest ranks, and they were then obliged to guarantee the quality and good behavior of their candidates. These guarantees were in turn supervised down to the last detail: among other things it was stipulated exactly what punishments were to be imposed on the guarantor (ranging all the way from small fines to forced labor and exile) should the man whom he had guaranteed commit an offence.

In this way an impressive system of unity arose, and one of its most striking elements was the underlying desire to open the doors of government employment to every kind of talent, regardless of the social level at which it originated, and at the same time to find a solution to one of the principal tasks in the art of government: to reconcile the two conflicting yet mutually essential principles— stability of the whole and mobility of the individual. The achievements of this political system, particularly in the field of hydraulic engineering, would have been impossible without a qualified, centrally directed hierarchy of officials.

Reality, of course, was not quite so democratic. Apart from the members of a few despised occupations, anyone was free to apply for admission to the examinations, but the knowledge required for them demanded years of study, something which only a minority could afford. This was where the clan could come to the rescue with stipends: it was always worth while to have an active representative of the clan in the regional or, better still, the central administration. But here too the outsiders could not compete with the wealth at the disposal of well-established clans, not to mention the possibilities such clans had of furthering the chances of their own people by having relatives in the examination and selection commissions. In the long run there was no remedy for *pao*; with mounting success the ruling class managed to shut itself off from below. During the latter half of the Sung period, some forty per cent of the gentry were descended from gentry families,[22] and in the nineteenth century the proportion had risen to some sixty-five per cent;[23] in other words it was only a minority that had risen from below, and of this minority not a few had evaded the lower examinations and bought their way in—a new symptom of decay. On the other hand, there were many cases in which gentry families sank back into the masses.

*

For early times there are no absolute figures available for the size of the gentry. For the first half of the nineteenth century a fairly recent estimate puts the total number of its members at over a million, that is to say, of men who had advanced at least beyond the first rung of the examination ladder, even if they paid to do so. Of these, however, only 35,000 actually held positions as officials or officers. The remainder were candidates, but these too carried out a great many semi-official functions: planning and construction of roads, bridges, and dams; arbitration, emergency aid in natural disasters, establishment of grain houses, compiling local histories. This is the only explanation for the fact that it was possible to administer this immense empire with a tiny staff of full-time officials: of those 35,000, only some 20,000 were civilian officials, the rest were military.[24]

A great many of the gentry, although just how many it is hard to assess, lived in the country and occupied themselves with the administration of the family property, in which the surplus from their official revenue was invested. However, the economic importance of their land must not be overestimated, for a broad examination of the Manchu period shows that during this time the direct income from official revenues and income due to the gentry status in general represented the principal source of income of the upper classes, while revenue from landed property amounted to only one third of the total.[25]

The economic and social activities of the gentry were not limited to agriculture. As trade began to flourish on a large scale during the Sung period, a lively co-operation developed—to the detriment of the State (favorites had their taxes reduced) and of the consumers, who were forced to pay the prices fixed by the government.

Generally speaking, the strength of the upper classes lay not so much in the exercise of administrative and political functions or in material possessions as in their inner solidarity. They lived on the Confucian heritage which, in spite of many reversals, always renewed itself, and the state examinations were enough to ensure that each successive generation could take possession of it unchanged. The examination subjects remained the same—philosophy, ethics, and history; individual attempts to give a more specialized and practical form to education were unsuccessful.[26]

Nevertheless, this education was unable to avoid the danger of increasing formalism; after all, even Europe's humanistic education succumbed to it at times. But it was this very rejection of positivism, this persistent clinging to the humanities, that nourished its formative power. Confucius had taught that things straighten themselves out when leadership is put into the hands of the right men. Ever since then, apart from certain exceptional periods, the governing principle in China was that it was better to rule by men than by laws. However, these men could only be taught by men who had themselves been taught in the same spirit.

Their monopoly of the mastery of writing—so uniquely difficult—and of the education which this skill alone made possible and without which any rise in the social scale was impossible, assured the gentry of the respect and admiring awe of the populace, elevating them visibly above the common people by special clothes and insignia that varied according to rank, as well as other privileges such as exemption from labor service and humiliating punishments. In periods of social fermentation, their privileged position was sometimes inundated by the flood of revolutionary hatred, but as soon as this ebbed away the old edifice was seen to be still standing.

Being irreplaceable, the gentry survived imperial absolutism, which often crushed its opposition by means of harsh and bloody violence. If they were fond of quoting the Confucian saying, 'All within the four seas will be . . . brothers',[27] what they meant—as is clearly shown by the context—was not the oneness of humanity but the solidarity of their own class.

This solidarity existed at an early stage: when the concubine of one of the princes of the Han period laughed at an official, all his colleagues at court went on strike until the lady was executed.[28] What a difference from the loyal *kanpu* (cadre) of the Communist functionary corps, with which superficial observers are tempted to compare the old Chinese upper class and from which by reason of its education, if nothing else, it is worlds apart!

In spite of all the dramatic vicissitudes of its history, this élite has survived two thousand years and, next to the family system, has proved to be the second pillar supporting classical China. Conservative and loyal to its Confucian heritage, as an institution it remained firmly united to the State. The usual danger—present in Russia too—of a potentially explosive tension between power and intellect was thus largely neutralized and the creation of an anti-government or anarchistic intelligentsia was prevented. The continued existence of intellectuals who were active as writers, scholars, and artists was

guaranteed by the very positions held in government service by their
relatives and fellow-thinkers; why should they undermine these
foundations? Besides, the fact that the government controlled permission to sit for the central and regional state examinations enabled
it to manipulate the extent and composition of the upper class, to
keep out or restrain undesirable elements, and to inject new blood.
On the whole such a strict and highly differentiated hierarchy was
bound to contribute materially to the stability of the bureaucracy, but
at the same time also to its increasing stagnation.

*

It was possible to get along with such a small body of officials
because in the rural areas administrative duties were delegated to
unofficial representatives—not only to the 'candidates' already
familiar to us, but to a number of other organisms. Until recently
attempts have been made to prove that these latter constituted a
highly developed self-government, but now Hsiao Kung-ch'üan[29] has
demonstrated that they must be looked upon as instruments of the
government. Their functionaries were appointed by the district ad-
ministrations and could be recalled at any time.

The *pao chia* (ten households = one *pai*, ten *pai* = one *chia*, ten *chia*
= one *pao*) was a kind of block-warden system. With the aid of current lists it kept the administration informed at all times of the numbers and movements of the population, thus carrying out one of the
duties of a registry office. The *pao chia* system had been in existence
ever since the Sung period and was particularly encouraged by the
Manchu emperors. The Kuomintang took it over, and even the
Japanese made use of it during the Second World War in the territories occupied by them. It was in this latter guise that I encountered
it. When we went to live in overcrowded Shanghai in 1941, the only
apartment we could get was the most expensive one in a tall apartment house in the French Concession. Since the rank of a servant
depended on the rent of the apartment in his care, our houseboy
automatically became *chia chang*, i.e., head of the hundred or so
Chinese families living in the apartment house. It was a purely formal
office which, apart from the keeping of lists, caused him very little
trouble, but it cost me (not him!) a good deal of money as he had to
distribute gifts on all manner of occasions, and the size of these gifts
determined my 'face' (and his).

The collecting of land taxes and, since the Sung period, of the fees paid for exemption from compulsory labor service, was entrusted to the *li chia* system: every hundred and ten households comprised a *li* and paid their taxes jointly to the district administration, and, of the hundred and ten household heads, ten were responsible for the collection of taxes in eleven households each.

The functionaries of a third institution, the *hsiang yüeh*, had on the first and fifteenth day of every month publicly to read out the main governmental laws, down to the smallest village, and to keep watch over the loyalty of the people.

In China, therefore, we have a bureaucratic monarchy which administered the empire with a handful of scholar-officials but with the inclusion of a large number of other, unofficial functionaries and a few semi-official controlling bodies. This was a long way from being a totalitarian state, but it was even further removed from a democracy, since, as we have seen, there were no truly self-governing bodies. Neither could the cities with their guilds and corporations (which were purely trade associations and not political organisms) exercise any democratic or even predemocratic function.

*

There was no such thing as an actual military career: military office was a government office like any other, and not a particularly desirable one. By comparison with Europe the representatives of the military were not very highly regarded. This was at any rate the case during the last five hundred years of Chinese history, for the two foreign dynasties of the Mongols and the Manchus brought unusually long periods of peace to the empire. As a result, soldiers—who since the Sung period had been mercenaries—were regarded as somewhat superfluous and enjoyed very little respect, as can be seen from one of the best-known Chinese proverbs: 'Good iron is not used to make nails, nor good men to make soldiers.' People did not think much of men who left their families and ran the risk of being buried far from home, for had not the Master taught: 'While his parents are alive, the son may not go abroad to a distance?'[30]

This attitude had an unfavorable effect on the military leaders, although, like their civilian counterparts, they were recruited by examination and thus likewise belonged to the gentry.[31] In importance and popular regard they fell far behind civilian officials, and nothing could have been less martial than their manner and appearance. Even the conquering races soon lost their warlike customs: a hundred years after the conquest of China the Manchurian garrisons were useless from a military point of view.[32] Moreover, the size of the country entailed a divided command. When the test came in the nineteenth century, the Chinese army proved to be hopelessly incapable and outmoded.

The authority of the gentry in civilian positions, on the other hand, was enhanced by the fact that they were also in charge of judicial proceedings. Their dependence on written law was far less than that of European judges.[33] It is true that a harshly legalistic period occurs in Chinese history too—during the absolutist central government of the Ch'in, who under their 'First Emperor' subjugated all China in the year 221 B.C. These 'legalists' wanted to leave nothing to the independent intelligence of their subjects, to regulate every aspect of life by law, and to enforce the strict maintenance of these laws by Draconian penalties. But the early fall of the dynasty in 207 B.C. put an end to the reign of this ideology as well.

Disputes as to whether laws were a good thing and, if so, to what extent, remained a favorite subject for philosophers for hundreds of years, but here too the Confucian spirit showed itself to be the stronger. Confucius' view was diametrically opposed to the ideas of the legalists; he believed in as little state control and as few laws as possible.

> If the people be led by laws, and uniformity sought to be given them by punishments, they will try to avoid the punishment, but have no sense of shame. If they be led by virtue, and uniformity sought to be given them by the rules of propriety, they will have a sense of shame, and moreover will become good.[34]

Here again the Master was following ancient Chinese wisdom. From time immemorial, right conduct, sanctified by custom (*li*), outranked law (*fa*), and as early as the sixth century B.C. we find the following passage:

> The ancient kings . . . did not (write down) their systems of punishment, fearing to awaken a litigious spirit among the people. But since all crimes cannot be prevented, they set up the barrier of righteousness . . . , bound the people by administrative ordinances . . . , treated them according to just usage . . . , guarded them with good faith . . . , and surrounded them with benevolence. . . . I have heard it said that a State has most laws when it is about to perish.[35]

In these circumstances the creation of a legal literature was impossible. As regards the application of the law in jurisdiction, we must not forget that a large number of offences against morals or property were punished within the family or clan. The following two quotations are typical of the attitude toward justice itself: the first dates from the Ming period and the second from the Manchu:

The imperial court must be severe in formulating laws and the officers must be forgiving in executing these laws.

The law is a uniform standard, but situations take on a thousand variations. To use the law with reference to the situation involved is to avoid disturbing the harmony of the natural order.[36]

The conflict between legalists and Confucians, however, is not limited to the doctrine of law: it permeates the entire concept of the State up to and including the rights and duties of the emperor. The Ch'in princes thought and acted like Oriental despots. One of them had some of his subjects punished for sacrificing a bull in honor of his recovery from an illness, for, he said, between subject and ruler there is no room for affection, only absolute obedience.[37] Similar stories are told of Shang Yang, perhaps the most important minister and lawgiver of this regime. Anyone who criticized his laws was executed; anyone who praised them was punished no less severely, because he had presumed to give an opinion.

*

Confucius and his successors, on the other hand, also placed the ruler under the law of the moral code and required that his authority be founded on personal example:

He who exercises government by means of his virtue may be compared to the north polar star, which keeps its place and all the stars turn toward it.

Chi K'ang once asked the Master about the nature of government and requested his advice about the number of thieves in the state:

Confucius replied, 'To govern means to rectify. If you lead on the people with correctness, who will dare not to be correct? . . . If you, sir, were not covetous, although you should reward them to do it, they would not steal.'[38]

And Mencius, the consistent Confucian, was not afraid to say openly: 'The people are the most important element in a nation; the spirits of the land and grain are the next; the sovereign is the lightest.'[39]

Thus the two doctrines of government stood in irreconcilable opposition to each other on almost every point. For the legalist, man was an immoral egoist, while Confucius believed that man was capable of improvement. According to the legalists, men existed for the State and its rulers; according to Confucius, man and society were the main consideration. The legalists wanted to enforce obedience through punishment and reward; Confucius preferred to lead men to the natural order of a moral code through education and example. The legalists applied the laws with equally harsh severity in every case; the Confucians favored a flexible legal system. The legalists needed officials who blindly carried out the will of the ruler; Confucius wanted to place the administration of the State in the hands of morally superior men who, although they served the ruler loyally, were in the final analysis responsible to heaven. What Confucius seems actually to have wanted was rule by men of noble character, independent of birth or inheritance, but he could not say this in so many words, since the rulers were after all hereditary.[40] Thus, far from being a democratic order it was an aristocratic order in the true sense of the word that was being sought here.

The Master said, 'The people may be made to follow a path of action, but they may not be made to understand it. . . . He who is not in any particular office has nothing to do with plans for the administration of its duties.'[41]

But how did the emperors (or their counselors) really behave? This question touches on our theme too. Since the Chinese monarchy never had a constitution, the authority of the monarchy depended almost entirely on the men invested with it. Obviously we cannot expect to find consistency here. Perhaps we could say that many emperors held that Confucianism was the correct view for those who were governed (including the gentry) but that they themselves should keep to the principles of the legalists.[42]

However, there is no lack of evidence of a highly developed imperial sense of responsibility which fully measured up to Confucian requirements. One of the most magnificent documents of this kind is the report which the great Manchu Emperor K'ang Hsi (1661–1722) drew up on the occasion of his seventieth birthday:

I am seventy years old and have occupied the throne for fifty years. The world is more or less at peace, and within the four seas order reigns. It is true that I have not been able to bring about an improvement in morals, nor have I been able to see to it that all families have a livelihood or that the people have a sufficiency; but I have been tirelessly active and constantly attentive, and have not permitted myself the smallest neglect, day or night. The last ten years have passed in the exertion of mind and strength. Have they not all been filled with the words effort and labor? . . . The officials serve as long as they are able to serve, and retire when they are able to retire. When they are old, they give up their government positions and return to their homes, cherish their children and play with their grand-children, and they can devote themselves to their hobbies. But the monarch must exert himself his whole life long.[43]

Another example gives us a better understanding of the meta-physical background of this high ethos. The emperor is in his person the mediator between heaven and earth. His highest duty, therefore, is to bring order into the relationships with the cosmos and to per-form the required rites; in the Peking period of the monarchy, these rites were chiefly carried out in the famous Temple of Heaven and Temple of Agriculture in the southern quarter of the city. Thus the emperor acknowledged himself to be personally responsible for natural disasters, as witness the following prayer of the Emperor Tao Kuang in the year 1832:

Oh, alas! imperial Heaven, were not the world afflicted by extraordinary changes, I would not dare to present extraordinary services. But this year the drought is most unusual. Summer is past, and no rain has fallen. . . . I, the minister of Heaven, am placed over mankind, and am responsible for keeping the world in order and tranquillizing the people. Although it is now impossible for me to sleep or eat with composure, although I am scorched with grief and tremble with anxiety, still, after all, no genial and copious showers have been obtained. . . . Prostrate I beg imperial Heaven . . . to pardon my ignorance and stupidity, and to grant me self-renovation; for myriads of innocent people are involved by me, the One man. My sins are so numerous it is difficult to escape from them. Summer is past and autumn arrived; to wait longer will really be impossible. Knocking head, I pray imperial Heaven to hasten and confer gracious deliverance—a speedy and divinely beneficial rain, to save the people's lives. . . .[44]

In the earliest collection of historical documents, the *Shu Ching* (Book of Records), we read the words of a prince of the eighth century B.C. to his army, which he was leading against the last of the Hsia rulers:

Hearken to my words! It is not my humble self which dares to proclaim a revolt; because the Lord of Hsia has been guilty of many things, *Heaven decrees* [author's italics] that he be destroyed.[45]

And in the first century B.C. we find that 'excessive rain is a sign of the emperor's injustice, prolonged drought indicates that he is making serious mistakes, intense heat accuses him of negligence, extreme cold of lack of consideration, and strong winds . . . show that he is

being apathetic.'[46] Natural phenomena of this kind, therefore, fore-
cast the repudiation of the rulers, of the fall of the dynasty which had
forfeited its mandate from heaven. This relationship has been
defined by Max Weber with great clarity as follows:

> Thus, the Chinese monarch remained primarily a pontifex; he was the
> old rainmaker of magical religion translated into ethics. Since the ethically
> rationalized 'Heaven' guarded eternal order, the charisma of the monarch
> depended on his virtues. Like all genuinely charismatic rulers he was a
> monarch by divine right, and not in the comfortable manner of modern
> sovereigns who, by the grace of God, claim to be responsible to Him only
> for their blunders. The latter are de facto irresponsible, but the Chinese
> emperor ruled in the old genuine sense of charismatic authority. He had to
> prove himself as the 'Son of Heaven' and as the lord approved by Heaven
> insofar as the people fared well under him. If he failed, he simply lacked
> charisma. Thus, if the rivers broke the dikes, or if rain did not fall despite
> the sacrifices made, it was evidence—such was expressly taught—that the
> emperor did not have the charismatic qualities demanded by Heaven.[47]

In practice, the logical step of depriving the ruler and his family of
office when he was obviously repudiated by heaven was taken early
and often; indeed, there was no better justification for men who were
determined to seize power for themselves. In theory, Hsün-tzu stated
as early as the third century B.C.: The government is there for the
people, not for the ruler; a bad ruler can be deposed.[48]

However, let there be no mistake: even then we cannot speak of a
true revolution, with a complete change of the ruling and social
systems. The aim was merely the replacement of the existing dynasty
by another, either by some entirely new one or, if the former one had
been foreign, by the preceding Chinese one. At the time of the
Mongols there were dreams of restoring the Sung dynasty, in the
Manchu period of restoring the Mings. Even when the monarchy
came to an end, the old idea of the mandate from heaven flared up
once more, for the words of the abdication speech of the last Manchu
emperor are more than an attempt merely to preserve face in the
inevitable defeat:

> The thoughts of the people, of the whole empire, incline today more and
> more toward the republic. . . . Wherever the heart of the people inclines,
> it is there that one may learn heavenly destiny. How could I, for the sake
> of the honor of one family, oppose that which the whole people loves and
> hates?[49]

The idea, not merely of deposing a dynasty but of abolishing the
monarchy as such, first came to China with the republican theories of

Europe, and most of all of America. Today 'revolution' in Chinese is still *ko ming* (=to change the mandate). Even Sun Yat-sen started off with the slogan: 'Down with the Manchus, long live the Ming dynasty!' He did not become a republican until much later. According to tradition he—indeed, even Mao—should have founded a new dynasty. This concept is still so ingrained in the people that even in 1957 peasants in North China referred in their conversation with me to Mao as *T'ien-tzu* (*son of heaven*). Possibly the weather disasters and crop failures of recent years gave rise to the question among many Chinese as to whether Mao were not about to forfeit the mandate from heaven.

So we see from the practice and theory of the Chinese doctrine of government the fallacy of automatically applying the familiar concept of an absolute monarch, let alone an Oriental despot, to the 'son of heaven'. It is true that he was bound by no constitution; it is also true that his religious function of mediator raised him high above all other men. But this did not render him inviolate or exempt from the criticism of his subjects; on the contrary, criticism was required of every faithful servant of the state:

> The Master said: 'What is called a great minister, is one who serves his prince according to what is right, and when he finds he cannot do so, he retires.'
> Tsze-lu asked how a ruler should be served. The Master said, 'Do not impose on him, and, moreover, withstand him to his face.'
> The Master said: 'If a ruler's words . . . are not good, and no one opposes them, may there not be expected . . . the ruin of his country?'[50]

Mencius was even stricter in his formulation:

> To repress the prince's perversion may be called reverence to him. . . . For one whose place is near the throne not to remonstrate is to hold his office idly for the sake of gain.[51]

The cautionary and exhortatory role of the high-ranking officials was actually given institutional form in classical China in the so-called censorial system, which on the one hand served the emperor as an additional method of control of his officials and on the other was developed by the officials themselves as a basis for remonstrating against the emperor. Criticism of this kind was, of course, not without danger: after the great remonstration of 1519, for example, thirty-three of the mandarins who had remonstrated against the emperor were imprisoned, a hundred and seven were forced to remain for several days in a kowtow position in front of the palace gates, and a hundred and forty-six were sentenced to flogging from which eleven died.[52] This institution, whose origins go back to the most distant past, remained in force until the end of the monarchy, when it was taken over by Sun Yat-sen and Chiang Kai-shek as one of the Five Powers and incorporated into the structure of the Republic.

After all this one might wonder that the monarchy could have so easily and almost without resistance been uprooted by Sun Yat-sen and his revolutionaries. But in the thousands of years of history which it spanned, had it ever been really deeply rooted in the consciousness and emotions of the people? Of course, the peasant needed his 'son of heaven' who—even if he was of foreign race—was the mediator between the cosmos and mankind and thus responsible for the weather. But in that very capacity the emperor was too far above him for any human contact, any emotional tie, to develop. In the flesh he was virtually never visible to the peasant—the vastness of the empire saw to that. It is no wonder, then, that an expert on Chinese rural life maintained: 'The peasants' vocabulary contained the word official but not the term government.'[53] 'Heaven is high and the emperor is distant' is not only a well-known Russian saying but also a Chinese one;[54] and several sources testify to the Chinese peasant song which contains the following words:

> I plough my ground and eat,
> I dig my well and drink;
> For king or emperor
> What use have I?[55]

To serve the emperor: that was the duty of the officials. From them was expected loyalty even to an already declining dynasty—and even, although to a lesser degree, at the fall of foreign dynasties.[56] Emperors came and went, dynasties rose and fell, but fields, family, and clan remained. In their self-sufficient life the peasants felt no need whatever to wax enthusiastic about distant emperors or other heroes. 'Their own emotional needs were already cared for and relatively stable', is the opinion of a Chinese sociologist.[57]

*

Side by side with the clans, the secret societies constituted a second home for many Chinese. For thousands of years these have played a role which is difficult to grasp but which was undoubtedly to a very large extent anti-government and anti-authority, and often revolutionary. We would know a lot more about China if our knowledge of these societies were not so fragmentary. The fact that it is so, is of course inherent in their nature. The development of the secret societies goes back to the very beginnings of Chinese history, and they are far too diverse to bring under one common denominator. Their roots were often a mixture of religious, superstitious, and sectarian ideas (originating from Taoist, Buddhist, and later Christian motives); others were political, especially during the rule of foreign dynasties. Many were economic in character, when large sections of the population had no recourse against authority other than to participate in a conspiracy; and others again, as self-help organizations, restricted themselves to certain individual occupations. Some secret societies were not at all secret to begin with; some changed their name in the course of their existence, others their character: in its earliest beginnings the 'White Lotus' was Buddhist, later it became political and revolutionary, aimed at the Mongolian and later at the Manchurian foreign domination. Others degenerated into piracy and banditry, and some were even used by the government for its own purposes—the 'Boxers', for instance, at the turn of the century, whose fighting spirit was channeled by the government against the 'foreign devils'. To what extent these movements took root in the broad masses and thus undermined the foundations of the classical systems of State and society before the penetration of the West and prepared the soil for the revolution, has not, as far as I know, been studied in detail by the West, nor by Chinese or Russian Communists.

One must, therefore, in considering the relationship of the Chinese to freedom, distinguish between two things: in his clan and in his secret society he was not free; there he was bound up in a network of relationships, subject to countless rules and limitations of his freedom of movement and choice. But in his relationship to the State he enjoyed a great deal of freedom; he could travel unhindered about the whole empire and needed no documents of identification. He was free to exercise whatever trade he chose, and there was no compulsory military service. The law seldom intervened in his life: the State relied —in normal times, at any rate—on the clan providing for the orderly behavior of the individual. Not even in the days of the First Emperor in the third century B.C., and certainly never since that time, have the Chinese people known a government as severe and totalitarian as that of the Communist State.

*

If any feeling of positive identity with the State was entirely absent, there was also very little nationalist feeling in traditional China. Inwardly, the clan claimed the loyalty of the individual; outwardly, China did not indulge in constant quarrels with other powers of similar strength. After the conquerors had been absorbed, it could quietly go on developing as the 'Middle Kingdom', which, with its superior power and culture, looked down upon other races as barbarians. Its feeling of cultural superiority—which finally reached the stage of belief in a Chinese cultural monopoly—was so strong that for centuries the people endured the rule of foreign dynasties without losing their sense of inner security. It was not until the nineteenth century that, as a result of the challenge of the West, the Chinese became nationalistic in our sense of the word. Until that time we should speak of a cultural rather than of a political nationalism.

So this people achieved unity principally through a common cultural heritage, and not least—bridging all variations in dialect and all outside influences of the times—through a common system of writing. Regardless of his place of origin, the literate Chinese of yesterday could read the two-thousand-year-old texts of Confucius as easily as the morning newspaper. This superb continuity is taken so much for granted by the Chinese that, unlike Europeans, they have developed no historical sense and attach no particular importance to the preservation of material examples of their cultural heritage. While in the West—and in Russia—historic buildings are constantly being restored, the Imperial City in Peking was looked after better under the Japanese occupation authorities, and under Mao, than during the years of the Monarchy.

This sense of continuity is not limited to the intellectual upper class; it is very much alive in the people, encouraged by a great number of professional storytellers and by the theater, whose material is in many cases taken from history and which is much patronized by the masses. However, this feeling of continuity is not linear in the sense of a progressive development, but cyclic: in the course of some twenty dynasties the Chinese have again and again gone through the same cycle of growth and decay. This idea of the rhythm of history was presented to them at the very beginning of the popular novel, *The Three Kingdoms* (from the fourteenth century), which starts off with the words: 'If the kingdom has long been divided, it must be united again; if it has long been united, it must be divided again.' And it continued to predominate until the penetration by the West.

There was no desire to create anything absolutely new. In 1869 an English observer wrote as follows:

> The idea of establishing a new order of things, which shall be an improvement on the old, never enters the mind of anyone. . . . Such a change the people neither expect nor desire. All they look for is the removal of certain grievances arising from maladministration, the rectification of corrupted manners, the reformation of abuses, and the complete restoration of the primeval order. Beyond this point their hopes and aspirations never go.[58]

Chinese historical thought received its first linear—as opposed to cyclical—direction with the penetration of the West, and the Communists are now emphasizing this trend. However, no one can yet say how successful they have been. To understand the rigid inflexibility of the Chinese we must see it as originating from that consciousness of intellectual and moral superiority which is revealed by the two names the Chinese use for their country: *T'ien-hsia* (under heaven) and *Chung-kuo* (middle kingdom). The idea of associating their national feeling with, or limiting it to, race is so foreign to them that they have not even defined themselves with a name of their own. They call themselves, after the great Han dynasty, the People of Han, or, more often, simply the People of the Middle Kingdom. They have never used the European term China which (according to a disputed theory) applies the name of the founder of the united country, the warlike Ch'in, to the people as a whole, nor the Russian term of *Kitay* (Cathay), after the non-Chinese race of the Khitans who attacked China from the north in the tenth century.

*

However, this lack of ethnic barriers has, in conjunction with their cultural superiority, endowed the Chinese people with an unusual power of assimilation. Anyone, without regard to his origin, became 'Chinese' who was prepared to take his place in the Chinese civilization. This in turn explains the success of the Chinese expansion movement, unparalleled both in its extent and its duration, a movement which, since it is still under way today, we must outline if only in a few sentences.

This expansion has, as we know, led the Chinese as far afield as the Himalayas (and beyond), and deep into the islands of Indonesia. It was actively supported by outstanding rulers; as early as the third century B.C. the First Emperor sent half a million people to China's 'tropical Siberia', i.e., what are today the provinces of Kwangsi and Kwangtung, and he directed the establishment of a military frontier with settlements of armed peasants. But the expansion was more than the expression of government power politics: it was joined by powerful spontaneous movements. Great waves of Chinese continued to pour down into the southern part of the country, often beyond its present borders, and in our century toward the north too, especially Manchuria, which until the end of the Manchu period was closed to immigrants as being the native country of the ruling dynasty, and in which the Chinese population then soared within a few decades from a few thousand to forty million. An important internal migration took place in a westerly direction during the last war with Japan, when hundreds of thousands fled from the enemy-occupied coastal areas to the interior. Here we must note as being typically Chinese the way in which for generations the immigrants preserved their ties with their native province, even with their native village.[59]

Von Eickstedt provides the following convincing picture of the whole process: in the favorite settlement areas, particularly the Yellow River and the Yangtze, new 'pressure chambers' were constantly being formed. As soon as one area of settlement was filled, it burst, and the tide of humanity flowed into the next.[60]

Among the legalists we already find an indication of this population pressure: in Han Fei's writings we read that in ancient times there were few people and hence few problems; but now (in the third century B.C.) there was a large and rapidly growing population.

For this reason commodities are scarce and people many, so that although they work hard they still get only a poor living. Therefore, the people contend with each other. Even though rewards were doubled and punishments multiplied, it would be impossible to get rid of disorder.[61]

Nevertheless, quantitatively speaking, the population movement at that time does not seem to have assumed dangerous proportions, for the population figure, which for more than a thousand years probably stood at some fifty to sixty million, was still under a hundred million at the beginning of the Manchu period. Then, however, the situation became serious, for in the long period of peace which ensued the population began to grow rapidly, and at the time of the impact with the West, in the mid-nineteenth century, it stood at four hundred million.[62]

*

When we look back and try once more to picture the social and political structure of China before the penetration of the West, we are struck by the clearly drawn line of demarcation (so different from anything we know in Europe) between private and public life. The 'State' intervened in the existence of its citizens to a far lesser extent than we in the West have for centuries taken for granted. It had delegated a considerable part of its functions to the clan associations; others were carried out by organisms which, although they did not strictly speaking constitute self-government, were familiar and closely akin to the citizens since their members were drawn from their own circles. Even the gentry, the main support of this State, was not a closed body of officials, responsible only to the State and owing their existence only to the State. In the actual daily life of the gentry, government restrictions and responsibilities were secondary to private ones. The gentry was much more thoroughly integrated in the whole orbit of concrete personal existence than in the anonymous 'State', whose only visible representative was the distant emperor; for it was this existence which was governed and upheld by the most personal, the most private, of all social forms—the family and the clan.

Russia is European Here Too

AGAINST THIS BACKGROUND, the Russia of Tsarist times moves still closer to the rest of Europe, all the more so as recent experience has taught us that Russia's technological backwardness as compared to the West was to be overcome more quickly than expected. While in China the clan, legitimized by the State and a powerful moral factor in the people's life, was able to maintain itself until the clash came with the West, in Russia, as far back as the beginning of recorded history, we find it existing as a real power virtually only among the nobility; internal migrations, which took place very early on and far exceeded anything known to the West, may have contributed considerably to the clan's decay. What remained did not differ essentially from the normal European family before the latter began to shrink to the small family of our day. It is true that the Russian's delight in social gatherings often brought the more distant relatives together at family celebrations, and this is still, although to a lesser degree, the case today; but this was not sufficient to make the clan an organized social force.

Within the family, strict patriarchal discipline, as it existed in the upper classes at least, was soon relaxed by the adoption of Western ideals of education. The educational policy of Catherine II, founder of the famous Smolny Institute for Young Ladies of the Nobility in 1764, may be regarded as the first stage on the road to the emancipation of Russian women. In contrast to this, the peasant and middle classes clung obstinately to the old order, and the conflicts to which this gave rise proved a rich source of subject matter to the literature of the nineteenth century—to epics and dramas, to tragedy, satire, and grotesque humor. We recall the family tyrant, who controls his children's property as well as their choice of career and marriage partner, leaving them with the alternatives of humiliating submission or open revolt; the young, or even the not-so-young, woman who wants to break away, or who actually does break away, from marriage to a man she does not like—a whole gallery of portraits relating to women's problems, with such figures as Yekaterina in Alexander Ostrovsky's most frequently performed play, *Born of the Storm* (1860) and Tolstoy's *Anna Karenina* (1877–79). All this, however, the social reality as well as its literary sublimation, is European, in spite of the time-differential in East-West development and the particular characteristics of the Russian temperament.

*

All the more pronounced was the integration of the Russian with his class, his social environment; on the lowest level this amounted for hundreds of years to a total integration. As distinct from China, the mass of the peasants was relegated to this lowest level, and the longer this continued the more marked it became. In what they were forced to produce in taxes and labor they formed the broad base of the Muscovite State. The creation of a new service nobility (since Ivan IV and later by Peter the Great and his successors, in particular Catherine II) would have been impossible without the economic maintenance of this service nobility by land and 'souls', i.e., without the peasants who worked for it. The difference which originally existed on the great estates between free peasants and serfs gradually disappeared because the estate owner possessed jurisdiction over both and, since the introduction of the 'souls tax' (head tax replacing the previous land tax in 1722), had to collect taxes from both, as he was personally responsible for the whole amount. In the 1760's the proportion of serfs in the total population was as high as forty-five per cent, and in less than two decades it rose to fifty-six per cent.

This Russian form of serfdom was far harsher than that of Central and Western Europe, and it came very close to slavery; there were no legal restrictions on the exploitation of the human work-force. To quote a reformer from the time of Peter the Great, the accepted view was: 'Let not the peasant grow a fleece, but shear him bald like a sheep.'[63] The sale of serfs (and their families) had been possible practically without restriction since the eighteenth century, and naturally professional talent commanded the best prices. For example, Prince Potyomkin bought the entire private orchestra of Count Razumovsky for 40,000 roubles. Anyone who needed money advertised living possessions unashamedly in the newspapers; it was not until 1822 that such advertisements were finally declared illegal—although not the transactions themselves. A picture of conditions as they still existed in the nineteenth century is to be found in Gogol's immortal novel, *Dead Souls*, which appeared in 1841.

The peasants broke out in bloody revolts which sometimes lasted for years; that of Stenka Razin in the seventeenth century and of Yemelyan Pugachov in the eighteenth are the best known. They sought the road to freedom in mass flights, mainly into the southern and southeastern steppe regions but also to the forests of the north and east, and this contributed considerably to the expansion of the Russian empire. Legislation and administration did their utmost to cut off even this escape route and to chain the peasants, both in fact and in law, to the soil. According to the laws of 1648–49, the 'owners' had the right to fetch back runaway peasants no matter how many years had elapsed.

All peasants, however, even those who were not serfs, were firmly bound to the soil almost all over Russia by the peasant system of land-ownership, the *obshchina*. This system, so enthusiastically extolled by the Slavophiles of the nineteenth century, dates only from the sixteenth century as far as its most striking feature—the periodic redistribution of common land—is concerned. Under this system the individual peasants did not own certain plots, and they therefore could not sell them, but they had the right to the use of the land, all of which was common property and (except for house and garden) was distributed among the individual families of the village, usually according to their size. The village community (*mir*) as a whole was responsible for the peasants' payment of taxes as well as—after the

agrarian reform of 1861—of their debts arising out of the purchase of
land from the manorial property, and even for the supplying of the
village's contingent of recruits; in addition it took over the police
duties formerly carried out by the lord of the manor. Thus the Russian village community was, like the Chinese institutions we have
discussed, more an instrument of the state than a self-governing
body.

The bourgeoisie was too small to exert much influence. We need
not waste time here on the politically inactive artisan class; more
important were the merchants. Like their Western counterparts, they
did not let the low value placed on worldly goods by church doctrine
affect their enterprising spirit. (Yermolay-Erasm and Vassian
Patrikeyev, both in the sixteenth century, declared outright that
riches were a product of robbery.[64]) The far-reaching extent of their
undertakings is astonishing. The best-known examples are the
Stroganovs, who under Ivan IV built up an economic empire on both
sides of the Urals. The great annual fairs, too, in particular that of
Nizhny Novgorod (since 1550), spread their influence far into the
hinterland. On the other hand, the city republic of Novgorod lost its
significance when it lost its political independence (1478), and after
that none of the Russian cities was able to achieve an autonomy comparable to that of urban communities in the West. The decline of the
bourgeoisie's initiative and sense of responsibility and the rise of an
all-powerful aristocracy were visible when Peter, and later Catherine
II, failed in their attempts to foster economic progress by granting
limited autonomy to the cities. Not until the following century was
the time ripe for a fresh start; self-government, renewed in 1864 on
the district and provincial level (*zemstvo*), gained a new lease of life
and also played a role in the internal disputes of the ensuing decades.
Nevertheless the *zemstvos* remained subject to the control of the
provincial governors and were deprived of a right of amalgamation
for purposes of joint representation.

*

The phenomenon of the Chinese gentry is inconceivable either in
Russia or the West. The formation of the typically Russian 'intelligentsia' could not take place until the encounter with Western
culture had advanced on a wide front; but the scarcely less typical
figure of the *chinovnik*, i.e., the lower or middle-class official, immortalized by Gogol in *The Inspector-General*—dull, primitive, coarse,

uneducated, but endowed with a peasant's cunning, the very anti-thesis of the Chinese mandarin—belongs to more modern times. Tsar Alexis and his son Peter the Great were the first to set up a corps of paid professional officials, in which the sons of the nobility—those, that is, who did not choose a military career—were obliged to serve, and which by way of its higher ranks enabled the middle classes to enter the nobility.

After Ivan IV had crushed the boyar high nobility and deprived it of power, the government as well as the army of old Russia had relied on the newly developed service nobility, which the Tsars endowed with official estates. The despotism of the later Tsars played havoc with these too; history reveals countless names of favorites—often men of humble origin—who were raised to the nobility by Peter and the Tsarinas Anna, Elizabeth, and Catherine II. One thing was unknown to the Russian upper class: the horror of physical exertion. Here they differed from the Chinese, many of whom liked to let their fingernails grow to an immense length as proof of their remoteness from any kind of manual labor.

The Russian service nobility remained far behind the Chinese gentry in intellectual and professional solidarity, and for this reason could not oppose the ruler in the manner of the Chinese censorial tradition. In addition, however, we must take into account—since Russia, unlike China, was never granted long periods of peace—the continuing preponderance of the military element over the civilian; the system of military discipline strengthened the authority of the Tsar himself as well. The transition from the feudal liegeman-relationship of the Middle Ages to the modern service-relationship of the officer to his monarch and supreme war commander took place in Russia in much the same way as in the armies of Louis XIV and the Hohenzollerns. The officers' corps remained pledged to personal loyalty to the Tsars throughout all upheavals. When individuals raised their hands as regicides (Peter III, Paul I), they could appear as saviors of the State (and the dynasty) from a crazed despot. The conspiracy of 1825, which was of a different kind, involved only a small segment of the officers' corps. On the other hand, thousands of officers remained loyal to the ruling house long after the family of the Tsar came to its violent end; they fought for years as 'White Russians' against the Bolsheviks, and as emigrants continued to proclaim their devotion to the surviving Romanovs.

Under such circumstances, corporative representation of the nobles (which until the seventeenth century still carried some weight in the form of a 'national assembly', *Zemsky Sobor*), much less opposition, could not flourish; in fact, they were doomed altogether once absolutism had assumed its classical form, starting with Peter. This situation—with variations depending on the particular ruler at the time—persisted until the first revolution of 1905. The Tsar alone chose, appointed, and dismissed the ministers as he pleased, and they were responsible only to him. After the Byzantine pattern he called himself an autocrat (*samoderzhavets*), and his subjects—including the nobility—his 'servants' (*kholopy*). Peter the Great personally thrashed Prince Menshikov, who, after himself, was the most powerful man in the country. According to Western standards, Peter identified himself with the state, but for the masses, and for his devout predecessors on the throne, the power of the Tsar came from God.

This sacred quality was bestowed on the Grand Dukes by chronicles going back to the twelfth century. It became a permanent tradition when in 1503 Ivan III concluded his alliance with the defenders of Church property against the monastic critics of such worldliness; in return, the autocracy received the acknowledgment and support of the Church. Once again it was Joseph of Volokolamsk who raised his voice the loudest. He taught outright that the Tsar was God's representative on earth and hence called upon to guide the Church; he 'resembled all men in his nature, but in his power he resembled God almighty'. By virtue of this authority Ivan IV cried out to his enemies: 'He who rises up against the power of the State, rises up against God,' as the State 'receives its orders from God' and also its duty is 'to bring salvation through fear'. And the deeply devout Tsar Alexis said to one of his subjects who had not carried out an order: 'Whom do you not obey? Christ Himself!'

Peter the Great later altered the alliance between throne and altar in such a way that he replaced the patriarch by the authority of the Holy Synod, in which the Chief Procurator, who was appointed by him (i.e., not by the Church), had the decisive voice, and government officials administered Church property. Thus the Church came under government control and was made dependent on the State for its material existence. What is more important for us, however, is that the Church, in proclaiming to the devout that obedience to the Tsar was a divine duty and manifesting this continually in ceremony and prayer, contributed in large measure, if not decisively, toward making the concept of the 'Little Father' a living reality to the people, and so to rooting it much more firmly and intimately among the masses than was ever possible with the far-off 'son of heaven'.

Russia had only two dynasties, as opposed to the seven (including female succession) in English history and the eight (not counting outsiders) in Germany. And when, after the first Tsarist house of Rurikides had died out, a new one was enthroned with Michael Romanov, reference was made in the national assembly to the fact that the new house was related to the old one. Notwithstanding Tsars who were despotic, weak, or not yet even of age, the dynastic sense of the people clung to the hereditary ruling house; and even usurpers like the False Dmitri (who died in 1606) and the rebel Pugachov (died 1775) who represented himself as the 'returned Tsar Peter' (III), surrounded themselves with the semblance of dynastic legitimacy. The strength of these emotional ties came once more to the fore with the last of the Romanovs: during the war he blessed the departing regiments himself, and from the first weeks which followed the outbreak of war in 1914, when I was a boy in Moscow, the antiphonal singing of the marching columns still rings in my ears:

> Little soldier! Little brother! Who is your father?
> Our father is the Tsar, our great *Gosudar* (ruler).

Here, then, we have something, in the upper classes *as well as* in the masses, which in China has scarcely ever existed: a positive and, in its intensely personal character, extremely effective patriotic feeling for State and nation. Historical events contributed considerably to this patriotism by forcing the Russians to maintain themselves in bitter and fluctuating battles, first against the nomads of the steppes, whose influence was much stronger on Russian evolution than on the Chinese, and later against Turks, Swedes, Poles, and Germans. The fact that these enemies were all of other faiths gave a particular flavor to Russian patriotism; it often happened that religious men were its upholders and monasteries its refuge, such as the Abbot Sergius and his Trinity Monastery in the days of the Tatars.

Patriotism may also be regarded as a product of the reaction to foreign advisers. The second Romanov, Alexis, found himself obliged to concentrate all foreigners outside the walls of Moscow in the 'German suburb'; and after the Patriarch Nikon had begun the revision of Church books according to the Greek texts, the Old Believer Archpriest Avvakum cried out to the Tsar: 'Spit on the Greeks! You are a Russian, after all, not a Greek. Speak your mother-tongue.' Later Romanovs were reproached for their German descent and their German wives; rumors of alleged secret alliances between the last Tsarina (who had been a princess of Hesse) and the German enemy contributed to the fall of the dynasty.

However, what distinguishes Russian patriotism even more from the Chinese variety and was not to be found in such a highly developed form anywhere among the peoples of Europe was that, beyond the mere warding off of foreign power and influence, it possessed a concrete element which the simple man was able to grasp: the concept, already familiar to us, of a Third Rome. At a time when in the West the Holy Roman Empire had faded to a more or less constitutional concept, and as a result of the Reformation the schism in faith was already on the threshold, the monk Filofey wrote from the Pskov Monastery to Tsar Vassily (1505–33) as follows:

> Two Romes have fallen, but the third is still standing, and there will be no fourth. . . . The sole apostolic Church . . . fled to the Third Rome, that is to say, to the New Great Russia . . . and the great pious Russian Tsar alone guides it and preserves it.[65]

According to this line of thought, the fall of Constantinople to the Turks in 1453 was merely the just punishment for the 'Betrayal of Florence', that is to say, for the alliance with the Roman Church accepted by the Greeks at the Council in Florence in 1439 as a desperate measure to obtain aid against the Turks. The role of protector which thus fell to Ivan III was given dynastic emphasis by his marriage with Zoë (Sofia), the niece of the last of the Byzantine emperors, who met his death in the defence of his capital city.

From these traditions, therefore, the Russian people drew a good portion of their national strength: first in maintaining themselves even under foreign domination, then in long defensive struggles against superior enemies, and later as a driving, dynamic, often aggressive force such as could never result from the cyclical historical thinking of the Chinese. In spite of all the savagery of the struggle for power and all the harshness of oppression, this dynamic force created a community extending from the Tsar to the serf, and as a result the Russian people were far better equipped for their encounter with the West than were the Chinese. Even the periodically recurring peasant revolts did not jeopardize it, for as a rule the peasants did not regard the Tsar as their enemy but rather as one from whom they were inclined to hope for protection from their oppressors; even later on, after the liberation of 1861, their anger did not turn against him but against the landowning class which—so they believed—had fraudulently substituted for their true freedom, given them by the Tsar, a 'forged' freedom. Later uprisings were launched with the aid of 'golden Tsar letters' which in this case really were forged.

Apart from movements of national resistance by non-Russian subjects, the only actual repudiation of the State was that of the Old Believers and the countless sects, but in these cases too it was almost always because—and to the extent that—the State identified itself with the Orthodox Church which they regarded as heretical, and because they were persecuted by the Church, at times with almost unbelievable severity. Admittedly some sects, in their radical rejection of the 'world', refused to do military service or pay taxes; in their own way they were, by the repudiation of all authority, a typical example of that anarchistic undercurrent which could so easily break out with unpredictable violence in the political and social history of Russia, and which on the intellectual level permitted the emergence of the principal representatives of nihilism on Russian soil. The attempt has been made to link it with the limitless expanse of the land itself, and indeed this unrest, this ungovernable urge for freedom, is most strongly in evidence in the home of the old Cossack and frontier tradition—in the steppes of the south and southeast. It was from there that rebels such as Razin and Pugachov came, and it was there that the bitterest foes of the Reds originated in the civil war.

*

If we try once again to sum up the results of our comparative observations, we clearly see that the preconditions for the Communist seizure and retention of power differ even more radically in the social and political structure of China and Russia than on the intellectual plane. In both countries a tradition of freedom is lacking; and in both the individual has become accustomed over the years—thousands of years, even—to find his place in the ranks of a society not of his choosing; but, in its extent and nature, this process differed considerably in the Tsarist empire and classical China. Not only had the Chinese peasant as an individual remained a free man; even the clan, which so largely circumscribed his life, never held him in almost total servitude, as did the serfdom imposed on the Russian peasant and the tyrannical political power of centuries. Furthermore, the ties of the Chinese peasant were of a completely personal nature and so were not felt to be compulsory to the same extent as the Russian obligations which degraded those subjected to them to the status of slaves.

When we look at the solidly constructed, self-supporting framework of China's social system, we can sum up with Riencourt:

> This [Confucian] civilization could have gone on uninterruptedly for hundreds, thousands, even tens of thousands of years on its momentum like a dead planet revolving mechanically and smoothly until an unexpected comet comes along and explodes it.[66]

But the comet was on its way; it came from the West.

CHAPTER IV

THE PENETRATION OF THE WEST

The Historical Course

THE PENETRATION OF THE WEST into the Chinese world and the reaction of the latter are among the most absorbing processes of modern history. A self-contained culture with strongly defined characteristics, its own particular social patterns, and an autarchic economy, is suddenly invaded by a completely different world and sees itself obliged to undergo a life-and-death struggle with it—all within a few decades. The fact that Russia, the other great Communist power of today, also had to contend with an invasion of the West, lends a particular interest to the study of this historical process.

In China contact with the West took place in two stages. The first —before and during the age of discoveries—need not concern us here; geographically, intellectually, and economically speaking, it hardly touched China at all. The Chinese people and its body politic were strong and self-assured; they felt far superior to the handful of European traders and missionaries and paid but little attention to them.

The second phase of the Western invasion, and the only one of interest to us here, began as long ago as the seventeenth century with the Russian thrust to the Amur, but this affected China on the distant northern periphery only and was, moreover, halted by the Manchu emperors in the Treaty of Nerchinsk (1689); it did not gain full force until the Opium War of 1839. To the British traders, as to the other Europeans, only two tiny trading posts on the South China coast (in Macao and near Canton) were open at that time; in their search for a suitable article of exchange for China's most sought-after products, such as silk and tea, they hit on opium, which was cheaply produced in their expanding Indian colonial empire and could be sold for high prices in China. At the beginning of the nineteenth century opium was the chief import article in China; tens of thousands of cases of this drug found their way into the country every year. Opium not only damaged the health and morals of millions of Chinese, but ate up the reserves of silver in the country, as tea and silk no longer sufficed to pay for the import of opium.

In 1839 the Commissioner of the Chinese Government in Canton, Lin Tse-hsü, prohibited the importation of the drug and ordered thousands of cases of opium destroyed. The resulting Opium War ended with China's ignominious defeat. In the Treaty of Nanking in 1842 (followed by similar treaties with other Western powers), five ports, among which the most important were Canton and Shanghai, were opened up to foreign trade, and great quantities of opium continued to flow unchecked into the country.

The West developed the positions won in the Opium War with almost explosive energy and speed. In the five treaty ports 'little Europes' sprang up with their own foreign jurisdiction; the transformation of Shanghai from a poverty-stricken river village into a queen of the sea was particularly remarkable. Yet although Peking found all this undesirable, it did not at first consider it reason enough to take drastic steps. Not until the 1850's and the Taiping Rebellion did the events take a new turn.

*

The southern provinces, the hinterland behind Macao and Canton, were the first to feel the effects of trade with Europe in their social and economic structure. Here, furthermore, the second wave of Christian missions had had more time to penetrate than elsewhere in China. Economic distress and an ideology of equality arising out of a misinterpreted Christianity led first to minor, then to increasingly bigger disturbances. Hung Hsiu-chüan, who came from that part of South China and who had failed the state examinations, became the leader of one of the largest and bloodiest rebellions in human history. It shook the empire to its very foundations in the years 1850 to 1864.[1] The last stage of this rebellion coincided with a second war against the West (1857–60), in which France and England extended the positions they had won in the Opium War (they later joined in putting down the rebellion). The year 1860 saw the nadir of imperial might: a severe defeat near Nanking by the Taiping rebels, and the flight of the emperor from Peking before the advancing English and French, who in revenge for the maltreatment of emissaries destroyed the

Summer Palace at Peking. In the treaties of Tientsin (1858) and Peking (1860), eleven further ports were opened up to foreigners, the Yangtze River was yielded as a route of commerce, the establishment of embassies in the Imperial City of Peking was granted, and missionary activity in the country was permitted.

If Western research during the last few decades has firmly established that, with the entry of Russia into the modern world, the encounter of Russia's intellectual élite with the ideas and economic patterns of the West was a crucial factor in this process, this conclusion applies all the more to China, since China's intellectual élite was much more unequivocally and for a much longer time—more than two thousand years—truly representative of the country.

But what could the answer be to this challenge, this threat? The Western invasion was far too violent to be simply ignored. There were, of course, still men who uncompromisingly defended the old traditions, men like Hsü T'ung (1819–1900), who said: 'Better to see the nation die than its way of life change';[2] or the scholar Wo-Jen, who in his letter to the emperor in 1867 said that men's attitude was more important than technology; one could not bring about the rise of a nation by means of mathematics; furthermore, the West had not even introduced anything new, but instead had merely developed early Chinese beginnings in the field of natural science which the Chinese had intentionally neglected as being unimportant.[3]

The majority of leading men, however, under the strong influence of the technical-military superiority of the West, inclined toward the opinion that, while it was necessary to learn these skills of the West, for the rest the traditional China, the Confucian substance, must be retained. In his work 'Exhortation to Study', Chang Chih-tung (1837–1909), for many years governor-general of the southern provinces of the empire, coined a phrase which was to become typical of this attitude:

Chinese learning for the fundamental principles, Western learning for practical application.[4]

A generation earlier, in the midst of the Taiping Rebellion, the respected official and scholar Feng Kuei-fen (1809–74) had proclaimed:

We have only one thing to learn from the barbarians and that is—strong ships and effective guns. . . . At first they [the Chinese] may take the foreigners as their teachers and models; then they may come to the same level and be their equals; finally they may move ahead and surpass them. Herein lies the way to self-strengthening. . . . We should use the instruments of the barbarians, but not adopt the way of the barbarians. We should use them so that we can repel them.[5]

The great leader of these conservative reformers was Tseng Kuo-fan (1811–72), who as a vigorous military commander and farsighted organizer had been largely responsible for crushing the Taiping Rebellion; as a result, he is often described in the history books of Communist China as a traitor to the people.[6] Tseng wanted both arms from the West for use against internal and external enemies, and many other Western inventions for the further development of China, but he was so deeply rooted in his Confucianism that he saw no danger of any kind in the use of these techniques.

As the 1860's drew to a close, the reformers had made amazing progress: internally the biggest and most menacing rebellion had been put down, and externally China had recovered from the wars with the Western expeditionary forces. The treaty of October 1869 which the British ambassador Rutherford Alcock negotiated in Peking with the Chinese Government seemed to open the way to China's entry nto the society of the other nations.

But the foreign-political success of the 'self-strengtheners' was short-lived. The British merchants in China violently opposed the Alcock treaty as it failed to fulfil many of their wishes, and the British Government refused to ratify it. In June 1870 occurred what is known as the massacre of Tientsin. Provoked by the French consul, who in an argument over the excessive zeal of certain missionaries had shot a Chinese, the maddened crowd killed the consul together with his companions and a number of French nuns and priests as well as several baptized Chinese, and set fire to a church and various missionary buildings. Developments in Europe, in particular the outbreak of the Franco-Prussian War, which followed immediately upon the Tientsin massacre, saved China from drastic military reprisals.

Two years later Tseng Kuo-fan died, and with him died the hope that Confucian China could be strengthened by the new technology from the West without altering its substance. It became increasingly evident (and the example of Emperor Meiji's reforms in Japan emphasized this realization) that the dynamic forces of the West were not going to allow themselves to be used as an obedient instrument of a tradition-bound Asiatic government. The West itself was shaken to its very roots by this modern age, which was its own child, yet the West was far better equipped, both intellectually and sociologically, for the transition and had had centuries in which to become accustomed to it. To China the modern age came as something essentially foreign; moreover, Chinese thought had not, as we have seen, known the separation between spirit and matter which is typical of the West. Thus intellectually and spiritually the Chinese were more deeply affected by material changes than were the European nations. The tremendous dynamic force of Western civilization, and its power to alter the very nature of society; its spirit of enterprise and lust for profit; its private initiative and reckless joy in experiment—all this had been sorely underestimated by Tseng. And so one of the most respected Western experts on the spiritual and intellectual evolution of that time comes to the conclusion that the new China which was then being created was not Confucian China 'with Western technical interests pasted on, but the Confucian world transformed by the Western interests, the Classics paling into functional insignificance'.[7]

In China itself there was already talk of the necessity of reform which 'should extend to all things—from trunk to branch, from inside to outside, from great to small—and not merely to Western methods'.[8]

Indeed, there was no time to lose. The age of imperialism was moving ahead, and China seemed to be falling a defenseless prey to the other world powers. Frenchmen, Englishmen, Russians, Germans, and Japanese made known their claims, despatched their soldiers, established their bases, and built their railways. China was divided into 'spheres of interest', and there were already indications of its complete disintegration into a number of foreign colonies. Above all the humiliating defeat in the war against Japan (1895), so much smaller than China and until now despised, served as an alarm signal of the first order.

The Chinese had been beaten, although—like the Japanese—they had taken over ships and guns from the West. But while the island race had, with these instruments of the West, absorbed something of the spirit of the West (especially in administration and education), the Chinese still believed they could limit themselves to the adoption of Western technology and otherwise leave everything else—the whole unwieldy apparatus of a bureaucratic, nepotism-ridden, and corrupt state—as it was. Even the acquisition of Western techniques was a very slow business to start with; in the thirty years from 1864 to 1894 a total of only 13,000 copies of Western technical works were sold in Chinese translation.[9] When the Chinese batteries lay defenseless under Japanese fire, the money for shells having long since found its way into numerous open pockets, Tseng Kuo-fan's world finally collapsed.

*

The philosopher and politician K'ang Yu-wei (1858–1927), one of the most original minds of the last hundred years of Chinese history, now realized that fundamental, drastic reforms were necessary. In order to overcome the resistance of the conservative forces, however, he had to base his proposals on the old Confucian tradition, and he therefore boldly undertook to interpret the teachings of the Master in a completely new way—that is to say, in a way which showed the Master in the light, not of a preserver of the old, but of an apostle of progress. To this end he made great use of a section from *The Book of Rites*, the chapter 'Li Yün', critically annotated by him. A glorious picture of the good old days was painted in such sentences as 'They did not labor for their own advantage. There was an end to all wiles and scheming. That was the age of great unity.'[10]

Moreover in his book *Ta T'ung Shu*, K'ang Yu-wei portrayed a Utopian society corresponding to those which repeatedly appeared in similar literary works of the West: it even included the dissolution of family and property.[11] This book was of no great practical significance at the time as K'ang only gave it to a few of his closest disciples to read; but it demonstrates how far the author was prepared to go in his reinterpretation of Confucius. In his memorandum to the emperor written early in 1898, which of course was much more carefully worded, K'ang argued with those who rejected any change in tradition inherited from the ancestors as follows:

> Institutions are for the purpose of preserving one's territories. Now that the ancestral territory cannot be preserved what good is it to maintain the ancestral institutions? Consequently I beg your Majesty to adopt the purpose of Peter the Great of Russia as our purpose and to take the Meiji Reform of Japan as the model for our reform.[12]

References to the reforms of Tsar Peter and Emperor Meiji occurred constantly in Chinese thought in those years. Even the British ambassador Alcock had recommended imitating the example of 'Russian self-strengthening through Westernization'.[13]

Toward the public at large K'ang had to be even more cautious.

His goal, so he declared, was, by the removal of the crust of countless overpaintings, to penetrate to the true Confucius. The fact that even such a radical reformer was able to justify, in the eyes of his contemporaries and in his own eyes, an actual break with the Confucian tradition only by an appeal to Confucius—even if it was a Confucius which had been reinterpreted by him to the point of unrecognizability—is one more proof of the extraordinary power of tradition in China.

But K'ang, too, was denied success. He managed, it is true, in 1898 to present five reform memoranda to the emperor, the radical nature of which recalled the measures of a Peter the Great. Had they been put into effect, the provincial governors, who were becoming increasingly independent, would have once again been replaced by a close-knit central administration, an adjustment of the educational system from the mere repetition of Confucian formulas to modern demands would have taken place; the outmoded system of examinations would have disappeared; constitutional monarchy would have displaced absolute monarchy, and the way would have been opened up for a rapid economic development. But after exactly one hundred days the dream came to an end: Empress-Dowager T'zu Hsi (1835–1909), who was to go down in history as the 'Old Buddha', had the emperor (her adopted son) arrested, and the reformers—as many as she could get hold of—executed. K'ang Yu-wei fled to Japan. In the years that followed some of his plans for reform were realized after all, the examination system, for example, being finally abolished in 1905;[14] but what K'ang had seen as a grand design became merely a disjointed piecework.

This failure represented the end of the grandiose attempts to merge the old and the new. It had been proved that the conservative, reactionary forces were still very powerful. Many high government officials were unfavorably inclined to any kind of innovation because, in the case of a surrender of the Confucian system, they were afraid the gentry would lose their governmental monopoly (and the perquisites that went with it!). Their hatred was increasingly directed toward the 'foreign devils', whom—often rightly, as we have seen—they blamed for the country's unrest. They clung to the hope that, by means of a revival of Confucianism, they would be able to lead the people back to peace and quiet; they succeeded in persuading the Empress-Dowager, shortly before the fall of the dynasty, to raise Confucianism to the position of state religion, in order to shore up the tottering foundations of the monarchy. Whether a man of the stature of Tseng Kuo-fan would have been able to breathe new life into the Confucian tradition in the twentieth century, we cannot tell, but it seems unlikely. Even Chiang Kai-shek, who patterned himself on Tseng and can be compared to him, if not on the intellectual plane, certainly on the military and political, foundered in the end; the Confucianism which Chiang (who incidentally became a Christian) sought to evoke had been undermined by the developments of the preceding decades and had lost its power of attraction for the younger generation.

*

Meanwhile China's intellectual class, especially the younger element, had turned to the most drastic of all the possible reactions to Western penetration: it had decided to discard the whole Confucian bag of tricks and set off on the march toward modernization. The key word was 'nationalism'. It was a nationalism of a special kind, at first directed less against foreign countries than against its own past, for it was here that the reasons for China's weakness were most obvious.

In these circles China was no longer identified with the word *t'ien hsia* (under heaven), but instead the emphasis was on calling it *kuo* (nation, state). As long as China was unquestionably the kingdom 'under heaven' it represented a cultural unity held together chiefly by Confucian traditions of life and government, a unity without connotations of either race or nation. But when the Confucian prop collapsed China was forced, if it wished to remain united, to become a nation.[15]

Henceforward the question was no longer: what did Confucius teach? but only: what benefits China today? In order to gain these benefits, the country had to be modernized as quickly as possible, and everything which stood in the path of modernization had to be swept away—Confucianism and the Manchu dynasty, and there was even a growing conviction that the monarchy itself would have to go. Admittedly it proved easier to bring about the fall of a dynasty which had in any case exhausted its powers of achievement, and was foreign into the bargain, than to do away with an ancient philosophy and pattern of life. It was the younger academic generation that set itself this latter task, especially those who had been educated at Western-style schools or universities or who had returned from studying abroad, and they used slogans such as 'Down with Confucius and

Sons!'[16] or catch-phrases like 'cannibalistic Confucianism'.[17] In this they received the approval and often financial support of the overseas Chinese, many of whom were wealthy and most of whom thought along modern lines, and whose aid Sun Yat-sen had invoked in the early years of his struggles against the Manchus.

In the years following the turn of the century, and more than ever after the fall of the dynasty, a flood of modern ideas—mainly in the form of Western European liberalism—came streaming in; expressions like progress, pragmatism, individualism, scepticism, suffice to indicate the trend. Christianity, on the other hand, did not turn out to be very successful in the intellectual upper class and particularly among young intellectuals; it was considered old-fashioned—another idea taken over from Western intellectuals. The swing toward the liberal ideas and ideals of the West occurred with such vehemence and single-mindedness that it looked as if it were going to carry all before it. But at that point an external event intervened: World War I. The fratricide of the Western nations on the battlefields of Europe had a powerfully sobering effect; the idealized West suddenly revealed a problematical, not to say repugnant, side. Moreover, the patriotic youth of China felt extremely bitter when it was found that the Western powers had given the Japanese a more or less free hand in China in order to bring them into the war against Germany.

And so the outbreak of Chinese nationalism in the square in front of the Gateway of Heavenly Peace in Peking on May 4, 1919, came about. Anti-foreign and revolutionary-minded students gave vent to their indignation over the Peace Conference then sitting in Paris with slogans such as 'China is the China of the Chinese' and forced the recalling of the Chinese delegation from Paris.[18]

The 'Movement of the Fourth of May' thus born constituted a victory of liberalism, but at the same time it contained, as a consequence of anti-foreign feeling, seeds of a new radicalism. This new radicalism no longer found its inspiration in the West of the British and the French, who advised the Chinese—as if they were schoolboys who had failed their examinations—first to catch up on their democracy, but in German and Russian thought, in the ideas of Marx and Lenin. Typical of this trend are the careers of Professors Ch'en Tu-hsiu (1880–1942) and Li Ta-chao (1888–1927), who started out as liberals and later became the first leaders of Chinese Communism. Before anyone knew what was happening, many other adherents to liberal thought, even to Christianity, had gone over to Communism. Ch'ü Ch'iu-pai, who later became one of the leading Communists, had published his first rebellious article in a magazine supported by the Y.M.C.A. (The Christian teaching of the fundamental equality of all men before God has, we know, often enough been misinterpreted as the basis for social-revolutionary doctrines.)

From now on there were two variations of the modern theme in China: the liberal and the Communistic. As long as Sun Yat-sen, the 'father of the Chinese revolution', was alive, they could live side by side under the one roof of his party, the Kuomintang; in the imprecise imagination of Sun Yat-sen, whose spiritual nourishment was drawn from somewhat shallow roots—Chinese as well as vaguely understood Western ones—and who was far more interested in plots and revolutions than in the building up and safeguarding of political power, there was room for both. But in 1925 he died, and immediately a sharp front was established between the Kuomintang, soon taken over by Chiang Kai-shek, and the Communist Party, which had existed since 1921 but which had collaborated with the Kuomintang. At first the Kuomintang was by far the more powerful. Behind it stood the port cities with all their dynamic force together with the fast-rising bourgeoisie; the young intelligentsia were also on its side to begin with, although they disliked the increasing Confucianizing of the Kuomintang.[19] It also enjoyed the favor of the Western powers (although this did not preclude scattered conflicts with them) and had the aid of German military advisers.

When I saw Chiang Kai-shek for the first time in 1929, he had just completed taking decisive steps toward the political unification of the country, and it looked then as if he would succeed in checking the disintegration of the State, which had been threatening since the Taiping Rebellion, into satrapies of individual military governors. The next time, in 1936, I found him already at the peak of his power: most of the regional overlords had either made peace with him or capitulated, and the Communists were on their 'Long March' from their former bases in South China, which had been encircled by Chiang Kai-shek, to far-off Yenan, situated on the fringe of the Chinese world. China seemed to be engaged in an extraordinarily swift and impressive rise to the status of a great modern power under the Kuomintang government.

*

In the following year this dream, too, had come to an end—and again intervention by a foreign power was responsible. Once again Japan interfered in the life of its neighbor, and this time with disastrous results, both for itself and for China. The Sino-Japanese War, which had been heralded by various incidents in the preceding years but which did not erupt in all its violence until the summer of 1937 and at the end of 1941—with Pearl Harbor—merged into World War II, was the salvation of the hard-pressed Chinese Communists, and brought in its wake the end of the liberal revolution and the victory of the Communist one. By forcing the Chinese armies, and with them a large part of the educated younger generation and its teachers, to retreat into the interior of the country, and by cutting off the coastal regions—which were the most advanced by modern Western standards—from unoccupied China, Japan was responsible in large measure for the weakening of Western liberal influence in China. Besides, since Chiang Kai-shek was deprived of the aid of the liberal coastal provinces, he found himself forced into an increasingly closer alliance with the conservative, reactionary forces in the interior; and this in turn led to a swiftly mounting estrangement of the young intellectuals from the Kuomintang.

This young intelligentsia now found itself in a desperate position. The possibility of a return to the path of Confucianism at this late date no longer existed, for practical reasons alone: Confucian scholarship, once the foundation for every respected career, was no longer in demand; the prospects of employment in the economy of the country, after eight years of destructive war and the total loss of the coastal provinces, were limited; and the now reactionary government of Chiang Kai-shek was disinclined to employ these sceptical, often hostile intellectuals in government positions. The young people regarded China more and more as a police state, albeit one which could not even exhibit the strict discipline and internal order of a police state.

Tired of China's internal squabbles and of economic and intellectual uncertainty, disoriented by the collapse of a three-thousand-year-old civilization, overwhelmed and confused by the irruption of totally new ideas of Christian, humanistic, rationalistic, and finally Marxist origin, eager, after 'a century of inferiority, maltreatment, and humiliation'[20] for a government which would at last keep the 'foreign devils' within bounds; plagued, moreover, with guilt-complexes on account of their years of fighting against their fathers

and their fathers' world—the intellectuals, now rootless and, since
the loss of their natural and traditional ties, desperately looking for
the 'meaning of life', were searching for an emotionally appealing
(and easily understandable) idea which would endow their lives with
a meaning and a goal. They longed for a strong government which
would replace their lost father,[21] they yearned for the support of a
firm dogma. All this the Communist Party offered them. They succumbed to it in ever-increasing numbers; the student Mao Tse-tung
was only one of them, although among the first.

*

In contrast to China, the Russian people had long been associated
with the rest of Europe through Christianity as well as alliances and
at times royal marriages. As far back as the eleventh century
Yaroslav I had the King of Sweden for a father-in-law, and the kings
of Norway, Hungary, and France as sons-in-law. In those years
Novgorod had been an important trading partner of the German
Hansa. Even Mongolian rule did not sever this contact completely.
In the fifteenth century we find Western armorers, doctors, and
builders in Russia; German, Dutch, and English merchants came;
Italian architects built the Kremlin's walls and first cathedral.

The decisive break-through to the West took place with Peter the
Great. When in 1697 the twenty-five-year-old Tsar started off on his
incognito journey to the West, he was scarcely aware of all the
consequences his undertaking would entail. But his impressions were
so strong that on his return he ordered a vigorous, well-nigh brutal
speeding-up of Europeanization; with his own hands he cut off the
boyars' beards; ruthlessly he insisted on Western dress, Western use
of tobacco, court festivities with ladies present, and Western dances.
Hundreds and even thousands of instructors and teachers came to
Russia during the following years from the West, and many young
Russians were sent there to study. The impatient violence with which
Peter flung open the 'window to the West' created a deep gulf
between the masses, who continued to live according to the old
customs, and the upper classes, who were influenced by the West, and
it made the conflict with the West particularly sharp. In Russia, too,
a common attitude at first was: all we need from abroad is ships and
guns; everything else can remain as it is. This view found its ideologist in Ivan Pososhkov (1652–1726)—Russia only needed the
foreigners for a while as instructors, he declared, afterwards it could

manage without them. But while in China this view prevailed for many years, it did not last long in Russia: the power of Western influence was too strong.

The second possibility, that of rejecting the West and rigidly clinging to the old, was to be found in its uncompromising, negative form chiefly among representatives of the Church, and especially, as we know, among the Old Believers, who were hostile to everything that was new. But the West had already moved too close for this trend to succeed; underground it continued to operate into the nineteenth century, and it is still not dead today. In a different guise it had a lasting influence on the thought as well as political actions of Russia, in the form known as Slavophilism, which really should have been called Russophilism since it was concerned with the glorification of what was Russian rather than Slavic in general. Their patriotism stirred by the mighty thrust forward of the West on the road to modernization, the Slavophiles—as they called themselves—sought compensation and a spiritual reassurance by evoking the deeper and hence stronger forces of the Russian soul with which they opposed the allegedly decaying West; Peter, they said, had taken the wrong turning, and Russia must find its way back again. The fathers of Slavophilism were Ivan Kireyevsky (1806–56) who, impressed by a journey he made in 1831 to the West, especially Germany, began by favoring Western orientation but later became a Slavophile, and Alexis Khomyakov (1804–60) who also, and to an even greater extent, believed Russia's mission to lie in the preservation of the true Christian faith. All the principal Slavophiles knew Europe well; for the most part their criticisms corresponded with those of Westerners themselves. One would be justified in calling them Europeans rebelling against Europe—as it was at that time.

The larger circle of Slavophiles also included those who placed their hopes on the peasant whom they idealized: the Narodniki (from *narod* = people; they were active mainly in the 1860's); the conservative wing among the champions of peasant liberation; and finally the Pan-Slavists, who dreamed of a great empire of the Slavs under the leadership of the Russians and regarded the Turkish and Habsburg multiracial states as their deadly enemies. In the Stalinist variations of Bolshevik patriotism, particularly after 1941, there are many echoes of these ideas.

By far the most important for the further development of Russia was the third type of reaction to contact with the West; that of the

'Westerners', the Western-oriented—in Russian *Zapadniki* (from *Zapad* = West). Their vigorous ancestor was Peter the Great, in whose time, however, Westernization bore all the marks of compulsion and artificiality. But since the time of Catherine II Russia absorbed all the intellectual trends of Europe, and these trends often acquired a radical nature on Russian soil which had not been theirs in their country of origin. Just as the West, since it first began to influence Russian thought, has produced an abundance of ideas, so it is impossible to reduce the Russian 'Westerners' to one common denominator. Even among the very first of them we find the most varying influences—Catholic, socialist, democratic, anarchistic. Among the later ones we find representatives of materialism, of pragmatism and positivism, of liberalism and of Marxism. This latter split into two factions: one more moderate, and the radical one which Vladimir Lenin (1870–1924) led to victory.

The decisive factor, however, is that, while in foreign policy the Pan-Slavic trend continued to be the predominant one, in Russia's internal life after the end of the 1860's the 'Westerners' led the way. And although many convinced advocates of the old Russia—such as the adviser of the last two Romanovs, Constantine Pobedonostsev (1827–1907), for years the guiding spirit in domestic policy—opposed the progressive assimilation of Russia to Western development, this assimilation could no longer be halted. But, as we have seen, the 'Westerners' were not united. Not only the Socialists but the Liberals, too, were split into those who wanted Russia to retain the monarchy and those who wanted to reform Russia on the ruins of the monarchy. In the summer of 1914 Lenin was the leader of a little group, a bystander of history, so it seemed, and Russia was on the road, difficult though it might be, to a modern, constitutional monarchy. But in August 'the lights went out all over Europe'. Two and a half years later Russia collapsed—first Tsarist Russia (in the bourgeois-liberal February revolution), then bourgeois-liberal Russia (in Lenin's Bolshevik October revolution).

*

In its conflict with the ideas of the West, Russia, when compared with China, displays a certain similarity which both countries share with other 'developing nations'—for example, the late formation of a middle class—as well as certain differences arising partly out of the characteristics of both peoples and partly from their very different historical destinies. From a sociological point of view, China lacked the intelligentsia which in Russia provided the soil and the support for revolutionary ideas. While the Russian intelligentsia was prevented by censorship and the police from any direct participation in government affairs, and their most active representatives were driven into the political underground, where the typical professional revolutionary of the stamp of Lenin flourished, in China an intelligentsia which was hostile to the government, let alone revolutionary or nihilistic, scarcely existed until the twentieth century. The Chinese literati were, after all, themselves the governing class and in many ways interested in the maintenance of the old order. Even those most critical of it, men like K'ang Yu-wei, tried to accomplish their plans for reform through the emperor and not in opposition to him. Independent criticism, whether in journalistic or literary form—as in Chernyshevsky's famous novel *What's To Be Done?* (1864)—appeared very late in China, actually only with Lu Hsün (1881–1936) and even then not until he published his *A Madman's Diary* in April of 1918.

Psychologically, China lacked the powerful impetus of religion, the Messianic conception of a mission to renew mankind, such as developed in Russia from the idea of the Third Rome. Even where this Messianic spirit did not appear in religious garb, as, for example, in the case of Nikolay Danilevsky, author of *Russia and Europe* (1869), it is still unmistakably apparent.

In addition to this, a third factor is evident in Russia which is obviously of Western origin, so that we have not dealt with it until now: the veneration—which following on Rousseau and the age of romanticism became a sentimental glorification—of the simple, unspoiled, and therefore ideal, 'people'. In Russia this meant the peasants. To the idealists of the middle class, it seemed a worthwhile goal to help them toward a life of human dignity and equal rights, not merely by making education available to them but also by means of political and social reforms. At the same time they believed they saw germ cells of a better future in the peasant way of life, especially in the village community, a future which, they thought, would one day also prevail in the West.

It was only with the Marxists that the peasants were gradually replaced by the proletariat, and the most consistent and successful man in this direction was again Lenin. His claim, therefore, to act simultaneously as liberator and spokesman of the 'masses' fell on well-prepared soil in Russia and endowed him with an authority which not many, even among the non-party intellectuals, dared to dispute. In Chinese history, on the other hand, an idealization of the masses hardly existed before the Communists; being born realists, and Confucianists besides, the Chinese were much too matter-of-fact for that, and by the time they came into contact with the West the idealization of the peasants had already died out. Mao was the first—because, as we shall see, he had no choice—to 'discover' the political importance of the Chinese peasants.

His country's history, moreover, offered a psychological factor which he could use to whip up the emotions of bitterness and hatred indispensable to every revolution: anti-imperialism and anti-colonial feeling. It is obvious that in the prehistory of the Russian revolution this factor did not play a very important part—regardless of its vociferous exploitation by present-day Soviet propaganda—as the Tsarist empire was itself a colonialist power and a leading participant in the creation of the imperialist age of world history. It was not Russians who were oppressed and exploited by foreign rulers, but non-Russian peoples were forcibly swept into the Russian empire in its swift advance, and only the Japanese counter-attack prevented large areas of China from eventually suffering the same fate. (It is true that there were numerous foreign firms in Russia, but the only hostility—if any—expressed toward them consisted of anti-capitalist, not anti-colonialist, feelings.)

In the final analysis the Russian people had more time to digest Western influences, and this was to have an important effect. If one compares the process of modernization with an infectious disease, one might say that Russia's centuries-old and often very close ties with the West 'inoculated' the people so that the course of the conflict with the West was less acute. The body of the Chinese people, however, was totally unprepared for the attack of the Western virus and hence was much more severely affected; it is still in the crisis stage today.

*

If we have so far been looking at the struggles of the two peoples chiefly from the point of view of political and intellectual history, it is now time to take a closer look at that part of the process which has transformed our Western world as well but with which the 'new' nations had—and still have—to cope in a far shorter period: the industrial revolution.

In Russia the initiative lay at first entirely with the State which, in the age of imperialism, needed its own armament industry and so encouraged the growth of heavy industry, and at the same time, for strategic reasons, promoted the construction of a comprehensive railway network. Count Witte, who was at first finance minister in Russia (1893–1903) and then the country's first prime minister, established the Tsarist empire's credit abroad by means of an active trade balance and was responsible for bringing large sums of foreign capital into the country. At the same time, as the growing private economy became increasingly active, partly owing to the influence and direct participation of the banks, the importance of the State in the economy declined. In the eight years preceding 1914 the Russian economy, after its predominantly state-influenced beginnings, approached the form already general in the West—that is to say, chiefly private, while its powerful cartel system and the rise of large industrial enterprises were particularly noticeable. On the eve of World War I, forty-four per cent of all workers in Russia were employed in concerns with more than a thousand workers,[22] a higher percentage than in England, Germany, or even the USA.

The development of the economy was not only interrupted by disturbances from without—in particular the war with Japan and the revolution of 1905–06 which followed—but was also considerably hampered by the plight of the peasantry. As long as the bulk of the people had consisted of serfs who were, practically speaking, without possessions or income, the consumer-goods industry lacked the necessary domestic market; even the abolition of serfdom led only very slowly to an increase in the purchasing power of the village. The growth of the peasant population in the nineteenth century was relatively much faster than the rate at which new land was opened up; in the census of 1897 (the last before the revolution) 97 million of the total of 126 million inhabitants of the Tsarist empire were peasants. Even after the liberation of the peasants in 1861, two principal obstacles stood in the way of increasing agricultural yield through more intensive methods: lack of capital, and lack of private initiative (as a result of the fact that peasants were bound, as already described, to the *mir* system and that collectively owned land was periodically redistributed to all *mir* members).

The exodus from the land which had been going on for decades provided the rapidly expanding industry with a labor force. The available figures are highly inaccurate, but on the eve of the First World War there must have been some three and a half million workers employed in industry. At that time Russia as an industrial producer already held fifth place after the USA, England, France, and Germany (not, of course, in per capita production, which was still very low). In the fifty years from 1860 to 1910 production had increased by over one thousand per cent.[23]

It was characteristic of the Russian (as of the Chinese) working class that strong ties continued to exist between it and the village. Nevertheless, a sense of solidarity was formed within it, more so than in China, which favored the concentration of Russian industry in large enterprises. It was clearly revealed in the first large-scale strikes, for example in St Petersburg in 1896 and in Riga in 1899. However, the failure of the revolution of 1905 led to a sharp decline in the revolutionary spirit of the working class. In the firms which came under the government's factory inspection in European Russia (the very small ones were not included), there were 13,995 strikes in 1905, the year of the revolution, in 93·2 per cent of all firms with 2·8 million strikers participating; in 1911 there were only 466 strikes in 2·8 per cent of firms, with 105,000 strikers.[24] From 1912 on there were again more wage-fights, but these remained within limits that were not alarming. Only the vain exertions of World War I and the bloody defeats of the vast Russian armies—heightened, if not caused, by the backwardness of state and society—led to a new radicalism. In the words of an expert on Russian economic history:

> As far as the general pattern of its industrialization in the second period [1906–1914] was concerned, Russia seemed to duplicate what had happened in Germany in the last decades of the nineteenth century. One might surmise that in the absence of the war Russia would have continued on the road of progressing westernization.[25]

*

The conditions for the establishment of a modern economy in China were far more unfavorable.[26] Classical China had been an autarchy—not only intellectually, but also economically. The country itself produced all the goods considered necessary for life, and it consumed what it produced. Thus there was no foreign trade to speak of, yet it is well known that in the West, especially since the age of discoveries, foreign trade constituted a stimulating force of prime importance, and that it had a profoundly fructifying effect on Russian development. The little that did come and go across the border was of almost no commercial importance; import was looked on as tribute from barbarian neighboring peoples and export as corresponding gifts in return. The State limited its economic initiative to large construction projects (usually carried out by compulsory labor) which served principally for defence, agriculture (irrigation systems), and food distribution (canals for the transportation of grain to the capitals).[27] It is true that from time immemorial the State had a salt and mining monopoly, but its officials acted purely in a supervisory capacity, and the practical operation (manufacture, transportation, and sales) was leased to private individuals for a set fee. There was no question of officials being trained to think along lines of business or capital investment. Among the peasants, of course, such ideas did not exist at all, and among the artisans they were barely developed. Thus the concept of 'economy' as a highly dynamic phenomenon, subject to its own laws, was unknown either to the masses or the educated upper classes. The traditional word for economy, *ching chi*, when literally translated means 'administration of surplus' i.e., it has a purely static connotation.

The impulse to break out of the closed circle, therefore, and enter on a new phase of development, had to come from outside: and this was the enforced opening up of the country to Western trade. What had developed spontaneously in the West was forced on China by the foreign powers through the long series of 'unequal treaties' from 1842 onward: foreign trade on a large scale and 'free cities' in the treaty ports.[28] Not only did the treaty ports serve trade, but after 1895 foreign industries were established in them which supplied effective patterns and training centers for the rising Chinese economic generation. Another factor which compelled economic communication sprang at the same time from the Taiping Rebellion: as it had brought with it a substantial reduction in the country's income from taxes, the government was forced to rely more heavily on import duties, which since the 1850's were being collected for the Chinese government by an efficient Customs administration managed by foreigners.

The beginnings of Chinese industrialization were determined by state initiative even more than in Russia. Here again we have the familiar attempt to oppose the West with its own weapons, its own technology. In 1855 Tseng Kuo-fan built the first small arsenals, in 1861 the arsenal and wharves of Anking; in 1863 he and his colleague Li Hung-chang erected an iron foundry (later an arsenal) in Shanghai. In other words, until that point industries were all state enterprises serving the armament industry. In 1873 on the initiative of Li, the

China Merchants' Steam Navigation Company was formed; in 1877 came the Kaiping Coalmines, in 1881 the first telegraph line, in 1882 the first railway, and in 1889 the Hanyang Ironworks at Wuhan; and in 1890 the first Chinese cotton mills started up in Shanghai.

It was a long and rocky road, with obstacles unknown to the industrialization of any other country. For the social structure of China, as we saw in the preceding chapter, was entirely unsuitable for this task. The main support of economic progress was lacking: a strong, self-assured merchant class; whereas the institutions which had been old China's strength—the clan and gentry—turned out to be a serious handicap to the establishment of a modern economy. This latter demands that every position, but particularly the top positions, be filled from the point of view of achievement. The first duty for the Chinese, on the other hand, was to find a place for his relatives or his friends who were the equivalent of relatives, without regard to actual suitability. Until shortly before Mao's victory it was possible for the personnel of a Chinese firm to be introduced by the manager or owner to a foreign visitor, not as 'my assistant manager' or 'my accountant', but as 'my nephew' or 'my wife's cousin'. And if all over the world the bureaucratic and the business-enterprise temperaments are incompatible, the Chinese gentry were by tradition, education, and professional training (the office supplying the perquisite!) the people least qualified for managerial positions in a modern economy.

Yet these were the very positions they were expected to fill. At the end of 1872 Li Hung-chang devised the formula: 'Official supervision and merchant management'.[29] A division of labor of this kind was good enough for the salt monopoly with its primitive methods of extraction and distribution, but it was hardly suitable for modern industry which by its very nature is dynamic and unbureaucratic. Here the new contractors, under the surveillance of officials, soon became dependent on government patronage and guidance, even where the State did not participate directly—as was often the case—as joint contractor or creditor. The China Merchants' Steam Navigation Company, for example, owed its flourishing existence to the monopoly of rice transportation to the province of the capital city. Other firms enjoyed the favor and patronage of powerful provincial governors (also by means of taxes), but in return were obliged to act according to their wishes. Ideas of state-controlled economy already prevailed in Sun Yat-sen's days[30] and were further developed within the Kuomintang. In Chiang Kai-shek's principal work, *China's Destiny*, they are still clearly perceptible.

The Effects of Western Penetration

WHILE WE HAVE SO FAR TRACED the outward process of China's conflict with the West in broad outline, we must now sum up by asking to what extent China had thereby been changed and prepared for the victory of Communism. In doing this I would like to avoid giving an opinion as to whether and in what way this change has included the spiritual-intellectual structure of the individual Chinese. Only those who were in the country at the time of the change-over, in close contact with the people, are in a position to judge this, and even then, as many cases have shown, there is the danger of one's perspective being narrowed by chance personal experiences.

As we can fall back on decades of journalistic and literary discussions, we can more easily explore changes in the field of culture, world outlook, and moral and religious forces. We have seen how, due to the numerous failures in the first phase of China's resistance, the Confucian heritage was increasingly discredited and finally thrown overboard by the young intelligentsia. Whether this tradition nevertheless possesses the strength to survive a long period of exclusion and suppression underground, is an open question. The devoutly religious person can, whatever the outward circumstances of his life, pray and praise God in his heart; but the Confucian must put his *Weltanschauung*—in the family and every other human relationship—into daily practice, otherwise he ceases to be a Confucian.

Even among the simple people, the traditional patterns of belief have been subjected in the last few decades to the onslaught of modernization. All the things which throughout the centuries had remained as they were with relatively little change and had been accepted as the heritage of the forefathers, began to seem to the Chinese—first in the towns, particularly the Westernized port cities— anachronistic, even somewhat ridiculous. The unselfconscious way in which they used to carry out their religious practices disappeared; doubt began to creep in. I was once made very vividly aware of this when a young Chinese woman, whom we knew, lost her only child, a ten-year-old boy. At first she found some distraction in the various duties which custom prescribed for a bereaved family; for example,

ordering all the paper figures—servants, vehicles, money, and clothing—which were to be burned to smooth the way for the deceased in
the next world. But after a few days she came to us in tears declaring
that she could no longer believe in these practices so that there was
nothing left to console her in her grief. Others have made similar
observations.[31] The temples were visibly falling into ruin, the statues
of the city gods were disappearing, the idols were crumbling—
decades before the victory of Communism.

*

The impact of the Western spirit was bound to have its profoundest
influence on the social structure of the country, for in no other great
culture had man been so intimately related in his thinking and way of
life to his environment, or embedded in such a multiplicity of personal
relationships. And now he was confronted with the new gospel of the
freedom of the individual, its self-assurance still intact and radiating
an aura of victory and superiority. Was it not perhaps freedom which
was responsible for the foreigners' magnificent development of power
and strength, and was it not the lack of freedom, the excess of ties of
all kinds, which was to blame for the hopeless inferiority of the
Chinese people? A violent protest against this system was raised
among the younger generation in particular. It was directed chiefly
against that authority which young people felt to be most restricting:
that of the family and clan. Even this emancipation movement
patterned itself on the West, as is clearly demonstrated by the passionate arguments about Ibsen's Nora which stirred young China at
that time.

Nothing shows the depth of this upheaval more clearly than a
comparison of two great novels, each of which took a large Chinese
family for its setting: Ts'ao Hsüeh-ch'in's *Dream of the Red
Chamber*,[32] written in the eighteenth century, and *The Family*, by Pa
Chin, which appeared in 1933.[33] The former, in spite of the tragedy
and melancholy that pervade it, never once questions the old order;
the latter, however, is a tirade in literary disguise attacking the family
system. It culminates in the death of a young woman who faces her
confinement in a house in which her recently deceased father-in-law
is lying awaiting burial. In order not to disturb the spirit of the deceased by the confinement, she is taken out to the country where there
is neither doctor nor midwife and where after the birth of her child
the woman bleeds to death. Not many decades earlier, superstition

and the unquestioned veneration of the deceased patriarch would have precluded any doubt whatever as to the propriety of such behavior. But in the altered climate of the early 1920's the senseless death of the young wife gives in this novel the final impetus for the younger generation to rise up against the old system.

Freedom: this meant, then, first of all the emancipation of the young and of women. The revolution against the old order began as a revolution against the existing family system. The young people of the towns, especially those of the upper and middle classes, were the first to respond to these ideas. From here, however, the new ideas spread to the rural areas, beginning with those families who had relatives in the towns. Finally, when in 1937 the Japanese began to occupy the coastal regions, the city-dwellers—especially the students —who migrated to the interior carried the family revolution to the villages. The triumphal march of the emancipation movement could no longer be halted. Within a few years girls were going to college and taking up careers, marrying for love, and joining women's battalions; married couples were divorced, and widows remarried.

The speed with which attitudes were transformed can be clearly seen from the history of family law in the new republic. In the first and second drafts (1911 and 1915) the consent of the parents was the only requirement for marriage; from 1916 on the consent of the contracting marriage partners was required as well; in the final text as passed in 1931 only the consent of the marriage partners was required: the parents were no longer mentioned.[34] This family law of the national government also made monogamy the basis for marriage, and it permitted divorce. The foundations of the old family system were destroyed.

*

Other events played their part. The headlong expansion of industry— beginning with the treaty ports—burst the bounds of the family business and led to new patterns of organization. The creation of modern industries and production methods, for which there were no standards in old China, deprived experience (and hence age also) of its value and gave the young people who had been trained in Western schools a distinct advantage. In proportion to the rising tide of young people who were going to school, the marrying age was also raised; but the older the couples were when they got married, the greater was their self-assurance, and the less they were inclined to submit unprotestingly to their parents' wishes as to their marriage.

Veneration of the ancestors, which was about to be left so far behind, declined as well; the activities of the Christian missionaries had had their share in this. Thus families became less and less prepared to spend large sums on sacrifices to the ancestors and other family feasts, yet it was these celebrations which had contributed so immensely to the strengthening of family and clan. The new-rich in the towns, determined to behave as much like Westerners as possible, were the first to sacrifice the old forms of family life. In the country-side, however, increasing poverty deprived many large old families of their land and brought financial distress to clan associations; their temples fell into decay, and many of their members moved away.

Such things had happened before in times of trouble, but this time the crisis in the clan system coincided with the crisis of Confucianism and hence traditional China as a whole. More than two thousand years earlier the school of the totalitarian legalists had evolved an anti-family ideology; they had realized that the Confucian family system, which created countless little 'states within the State', was not compatible with the type of centralized government at which they were aiming. But they and their kind were in power for too short a time to be able really to destroy the family system. Actually Sun Yat-sen strove toward the same end, starting from completely different hypotheses but using similar slogans. Impressed by Western nationalism, and the particularly forceful variety of Japanese nation-alism, he wanted to make State and nation, rather than clan and family, the focal point of all life in China too, and it was to them that all Chinese were to owe their work, allegiance, and loyalty.

The decay of the traditional clan system was not completed from one day to the next. A few examples of powerful family cliques con-tinued to exist for some time, such as the Kung clan, to which Chiang Kai-shek became linked by marriage in 1927; but on the whole this process was a surprisingly fast one. Before the eyes of a shocked world, amid the rejoicing of the young Chinese and the headshaking of the old, the mighty, centuries-old edifice of the Chinese clan fell to pieces. The Communists merely speeded up and intensified a process which had begun long ago.

Compared with these truly revolutionary events, the dislocation in the occupational structure of the country is of secondary importance. We can also deal with it more briefly because China, apart from the downfall of the gentry, shared this experience with Europe, although at a different period of time.

We have briefly made the acquaintance of the newly created capitalist class. In the next chapter, in dealing with the growth of the
Communist Party, we shall speak about the industrial proletariat,
which was slow in developing, weak, and divided among itself.
In the artisan and lower middle classes things changed relatively
little.

To the overwhelming majority of the Chinese peasants the arrival
of the modern age brought more disadvantages than advantages. A
'liberation' on the European model could not be expected, since—as
distinct from their Russian counterparts—they had not become serfs.
But, as we have seen, their economic position deteriorated seriously,
as since the end of the eighteenth century the rapidly increasing village
population had had to get along with a scarcely increasing area of
arable land. An additional factor since the middle of the nineteenth
century was the acceleration in the rate of growth of the large landed
estates: it was no longer only the official families who were investing
their savings in land which they bought up from impoverished peasants, but also those who had acquired new wealth in trade and
industry. By the 1920's in the area around the commercial metro-
polises of Shanghai and Canton, already ninety-five and eighty-five
per cent respectively of the farmers were tenants,[35] and the rents rose
as land became more and more scarce.

Social tension increased. While the landowning gentry—who usually
had family ties with the village, sometimes living there themselves or
returning there in their old age—still had a sense of responsibility
toward the peasants, this was no longer the case with the new-rich in
the port cities. For them, land was merely an object of investment and
speculation. Furthermore, the cottage industries, which brought the
peasants some additional income during the inactive months, especially in the production of textiles, were very hard hit by the flood of
imports from industrial countries, including such newcomers as
Japan and India. Political unrest and destructive civil wars played
their part. Seething discontent and sullen despair took hold of large
areas: there was a rising inclination to resort to acts of violence
against the 'rich'.

*

The gentry had already shown signs of decay. The strictness of the
examination system had been relaxed by the last Manchu rulers
themselves; they had granted an increase to some of the provinces in

their contingent of examinees, in return for which the provinces paid corresponding sums in to the state treasury. This led to a lowering of requirements and thus of the quality of the new gentry generation. Even worse was an abuse which we have already noted and which was now spreading: increasing numbers of wealthy men who wished to get into the upper class were exempted from the lowest examination if they paid a certain fee. It was now possible officially to buy one's way into the gentry; in the second half of the nineteenth century more than a third of it consisted of elements of this type. Admittedly they were much less highly regarded than those qualified by regular examinations, and the passing of the higher examinations remained essential to any further rise in government service. From the point of view of national morale, the possibility of gaining entry to the upper class with the aid of money represented a degeneration which was bound to inflict heavy damage on the reputation of the class as a whole. Its substance diluted, its solidarity weakened, deprived of the authority it had possessed among the masses, the gentry, with its Confucian-humanistic tradition and training, found itself through the impact of the new age faced with problems with which it was unable to cope. Its failures in battle against the foreign devils, against the Taiping Rebellion, against the Japanese, destroyed what was left of its prestige.

*

The heritage of the abdicating gentry passed neither to the middle classes nor to the young intelligentsia, but to the military, which, thanks to the effects of Western penetration, was achieving a position of power hitherto unknown in China. Its form, of course, was no longer the traditional one. The Manchurian 'banner troops' (so called after their campaign banners of different colors), as well as the Chinese 'Green Flag Army' (which consisted of volunteer and drafted soldiers), had failed miserably in their battles against the foreign invaders and the people's army of the Taiping Rebellion. Foreigners laughed at the Chinese 'operetta soldiers' who went into battle carrying umbrellas and fought with the silver bullets of bribery instead of with arms. Tseng Kuo-fan and his friends—among whom the most outstanding was Li Hung-chang, China's leading statesman until his death in 1901—saw themselves forced to create new, élite troops, loyal to them personally, whom they paid out of the tax funds of whatever provinces they were governing at the time, i.e., not from the revenues of central government. The efficacy of this system was proved for the first time in putting down the Taipings and, during the disturbances which followed, what had begun as an emergency measure became the normal method of warfare and military organization.

The government watched the growth of these private armies with all the more anxiety because their leaders were almost all Chinese (that is to say, not Manchus). Where would it lead, if, according to the new slogan, 'the soldiers belong to the generals'! But it had to sanction their existence in order to overcome its domestic and external enemies. The weakness of the imperial armies on the one hand, and the relative (but only relative) strength of the individual provincial armies on the other, crucially altered the balance of power in China from the middle 1850's on. Henceforward the throne could play off the various military commanders against each other, but it could no longer treat them merely as subordinates, or, in the case of a rebellion, remove them from their posts. The result was that respect for the profession of soldier increased considerably, particularly among young people. More and more capable and ambitious young men decided on a military career as the new road to power and glory, especially as before long the first military academies were founded. According to a recent estimate, out of the forty-four governors-general (in charge of more than one province) who were appointed in the years between 1861 and 1890, twenty had risen as military leaders, and of the 117 provincial governors the proportion was more than half.[36]

The energy and desire for reform of the new generation of officers, who were aided by foreign military advisers (particularly German and Japanese), were inspired in no small measure by the example of Japan. Japan proved, first in the war of 1894–95 and then even more effectively by its victory over the great power Russia, that an Asiatic army could develop considerable fighting power. The results were not long in forthcoming. During the Boxer Rebellion (1900–01) the European Expeditionary Force found in its first attempt at a march on Peking that it was no longer dealing with a disorganized rabble. The Force suffered losses, was encircled, and only just managed to make its way back to Tientsin, before it was able—now nearly 20,000 strong—to break through to Peking and relieve the legation quarter.[37]

*

After that China fought no major wars with foreign enemies until 1937. However, the provincial armies which were established during the second half of the nineteenth century continued to determine domestic developments. The most powerful among them was the 'Northern Army', organized by Li Hung-chang in 1888 in the province of the capital city. It later became the instrument of power of General Yüan Shih-k'ai, who gave his services to the empress-dowager during her *coup d'état* of 1898. He was appointed by her to the post of governor-general of that most important of all provinces, and until his dismissal in 1909 he was China's outstanding figure. Recalled and given dictatorial powers after the outbreak of the revolution in 1911, he was no longer able to save the throne, but by inducing the emperor to abdicate he enabled an orderly transition to the new form of government to take place. It is significant that Sun Yat-sen yielded his office of president to Yüan Shih-k'ai after only a few weeks, and thereafter military men—among them three more from the 'Northern Army'—held that office.[38]

But even Yüan Shih-k'ai—who in the last year of his life (1916) was offered the imperial crown by parliament—not to mention his weaker successors, had to reckon with the fact that they could only rely on their 'own' troops. In the meantime the evils of military disintegration had taken a firm hold, and the peculiar system of warlords had become established. These were simultaneously governors (or governors-general) and military commanders. In other words, they had military as well as administrative, political, and financial control, and, in view of the weakness of the central government, they represented the real power within the State. Moreover, the old gentry tradition was still so strong that many of them—although not always with complete conviction—pretended to be classical scholars, or even, like General Wu P'ei-fu, allowed themselves to be regarded as men of letters.

It is no exaggeration to say that the first two decades of the young republic represented the age of the warlords. The old, Confucian-trained governing class had abdicated, and the new one, drawn from the ranks of the middle class and the revolutionary intelligentsia, was not yet strong enough to take up the reins of the nation's destiny. The rule of the warlords was one of the most tragic phases of recent Chinese history. It lasted until Chiang Kai-shek, himself a prominent military man of the school of Yüan Shih-k'ai but at the same time a supporter of new revolutionary ideas, won supremacy over the other warlords in the years 1926 to 1928 (although he was unable to eliminate them entirely: some of them remained in power in their provinces until the victory of Communism, although nominally they came under Chiang's national government).

From this moment on, the way was open for a swift upward surge in the economy, and in fact this began immediately. It now became apparent that a new generation had grown up, a generation of Chinese with 'modern' ideas, most of whom had been educated in the West or in Japan. With the collapse of the gentry system and the disintegration of the old clan tradition, many of the chief obstacles to a 'Western' development were removed or at least considerably lessened. As purely Chinese firms became established in the treaty ports, it became clear that, given the right conditions, the Chinese were perfectly capable of operating a modern economy. The same thing was demonstrated by the commercial success of great numbers of overseas Chinese, in Hongkong, Singapore, San Francisco, and other centers of free commercial competition.

There are even indications that the middle class in process of formation was now awakening to political self-awareness. The revolution of 1911 had had its origin in the resistance offered by businessmen, merchants, and students of the Province of Szechwan to the central government's decision to nationalize the new Hankow–Szechwan railway, which was originally to have been privately financed. One thing is certain: if liberal capitalism in China was still weak, then so was its potential opponent, the working class, both in numbers and striking power.

In the mid-thirties it was perfectly conceivable that the talented and industrious Chinese people, finally (if not entirely) politically united, would turn on to the broad highway of capitalism and democracy and with swift steps catch up with the Occident. But when in 1937 Japan carried war once more into China, it put an end to these hopes.

*

Pre-Bolshevist Russia's chances of normal progress in the Western sense can be argued with greater certainty. One reason why the impact of the West caused less of an upheaval and offered less of a threat to Russia's way of life was that, in spite of the difference in its historical development, it still belonged, ethnically and spiritually, to Europe. And to cope successfully with the impact of the West it had, instead of a few decades, more than two centuries. Unlike China,

Russia was never in the dire situation of having to choose between immediate modernization, without regard to the consequences, and the loss of its national (and cultural) freedom.

'Russian man' had been quite well able to preserve his much-vaunted breadth of personality. The process of his uniformization did not begin till the Soviets, and here technical civilization's own code of laws assisted those in power. Even the intelligentsia had not been fully Westernized. The most radical opponents of the Christian tradition, men like Chernyshevsky, Pisarev, and Dobrolyubov, were not representative of the intelligentsia as a whole; and still less did they succeed in making any lasting impression on the religious attitude of the masses. It is therefore mistaken to speak of decay and disintegration among the people, of a spiritual void into which the new Communist doctrine of salvation could freely flow; that would be much truer of China, after a few decades of coping with the influx of Western ideas. On the other hand it must not be forgotten that, in contrast to the Chinese gentry, the Russian intelligentsia had become fertile soil for revolutionary impulses as a result of its negative attitude toward the State, an attitude which was less a matter of choice than one which had been forced upon it.

Contact with the West had caused the old Russian sense of mission to take a strange turn. The idea of Moscow's special vocation lived on—in different guise. Many of Russia's leading thinkers, including in a sublimated way its greatest philosopher, Vladimir Solovyov (died 1900), carried it on; and in a coarser, secularized version it gave —and still gives—the Communist doctrine of world salvation, which is actually internationalist in outlook, the mark of a peculiarly Russian mission. Thus Russian propaganda is marked, in spite of the cold severity of its ideology, by an emotional strength which Communism has shown nowhere else. It reveals a pride in its own past and a contempt for the worn-out 'decaying' West with its 'shallowness of intellect' and its 'atrophy of the soul', for the 'rotting corpse and its poisonous miasmas'—phrases which are older than *Das Kapital* and which recur, often in precisely the same words, again and again in the speeches of Soviet politicians and marshals.[39]

One reason for Russia's social pattern being less strongly affected by Western influence was that, like the West, it was not based on the all-powerful position of family and clan. The family, since it curtailed individual freedom much less than in China, did not become, as it did there, the favorite target of literary and journalistic criticism. By comparison with the West it was actually in an even healthier state at the time of the Communist victory, since industrialization, with its harmful consequences for the family, came much later to Russia; the Russian family was able to prove its strength in its conflict with the totalitarian state.[40] Changes in the socio-economic structure among the artisans, merchants, technicians, and workers corresponded to the evolution familiar in the West, allowing, of course, for the fact that the process was less far advanced.

An upheaval of enormous dimensions, however, in drama and importance far exceeding anything in the West or in China, took place among the pre-revolutionary Russian peasantry. For here the very problem had to be overcome which China never knew and which in the West was solved by force during the French revolution and later by reforms in other nations: the problem of the liberation of the peasants. This extraordinarily difficult and stratified process, of supreme importance to the modern history of Russia, cannot be dealt with cursorily here. It can be studied in any comprehensive work on Russian history.[41]

The reforms of Alexander II did not bring complete freedom to the Russian peasant, since they permitted the continued existence of the *mir*, the village community. It was only with the reforms of Witte and Stolypin (1903–11) that the *mir* was abolished, together with collective ownership of land. In the years remaining until the revolution of 1917, about a third of the peasant families concerned in European Russia made use of the opportunity to build up their own farms. From these peasants there emerged with surprising speed a class of active, well-to-do peasants known as *kulaks*, who frequently behaved with a certain harshness toward their economically weaker fellow villagers. Hence a class of free peasants did not exist in Russia (apart from a few fringe areas) except during the period between Stolypin and the introduction of collectivization by Stalin, and even then only under the most adverse conditions caused by war and revolution.

In 1917 the peasants' hunger for land and their seething discontent burst out at the first opportunity in an explosion which flared up over the whole vast country the moment the spark had been lit in the capital. The fact that Lenin handed over to the peasants their masters' land as the spoils of the revolution decided his victory—and the defeat of the White armies in the civil war.

*

But the picture remains incomplete if one thinks only of the dramatic and spectacular events, of assassination and rebellions. The defeat of the first revolution in 1906 was followed by the introduction of a constitution and the first *Duma*. In 1914 the way was open to a constitutional monarchy, and in the summer of 1917 at least to a democratic form of government. That things turned out differently was not, as the Communists maintain, the logical result of a pre-ordained 'law of evolution'. It was the result of an upheaval originating outside the country and the work of the passionate (and lucky) power drive of a determined minority. It was this which forced Russia into the Communist orbit at a moment when—exactly according to the theory of Marxism—it should have been about to blossom into liberal capitalism.

Aside from brief crises, neither Russia's national freedom nor its national unity was ever endangered during its exposure to Western ideas. Moreover, there is nothing in Russian history comparable to the Chinese warlords and their political and economic significance—not even during the terrible crisis of the civil war after the Bolshevist seizure of power. Men like Wrangel, Denikin, Yudenich, or Kolchak, who as leaders of the White armies fought against the Bolsheviks, would have tried to create—had they been victorious—not satrapies, but a strong central government.

Communism Was Not Inevitable

AS WE COME TO THE END of our observations on the basic question of whether the two countries were prepared to a greater or lesser extent for Communism, we find a strangely contradictory picture. On the one hand, to classical China this—or any other—ideology emanating from the West remained, due to the nature and traditions of the people, completely strange; while in Russia, in its psychological and sociological structure, one can trace conditions and forces which provide points of contact for this ideology and which it could turn to its own use. Yet, on the other hand, in its struggles with Western ideas, this same China was far more deeply and fatefully convulsed, and hence prepared for drastic changes at all levels, than was ever the case with Tsarist Russia. This applies to that class in China which would have been the obvious one to develop a new political awareness and to complete the transition to a modern, democratic order: the middle class. After the continual upheavals of the preceding decades, it wanted nothing so much as to live at last under a regime of internal order, so that it was prepared, even sooner than the Russian bourgeoisie had been before it, to put up with Communism as the hoped-for bearer of internal peace and order; all the more so since it had lost its spiritual footing, its spiritual and intellectual sense of direction. The penetration by the West, which the Russian people was in the process of assimilating, brought to the Chinese the end of a world—for thousands of years the only world they could imagine.

One thing we can be sure of: even though the Western impact may have created a pre-revolutionary situation, an existential crisis, this did not entail an advance decision in favor of Communism. This is already clear from the development in other countries which have also completed their entry into the industrial age—formerly Japan, now India, for example. In both the great Communist powers of today, the signs on the eve of the Communist victory were more favorable to the other alternative: the liberal-democratic-capitalistic order. In both countries, the intellectually and politically most active groups looked on the Western model as meaning above all the emancipation of the individual from restrictive ties. They had not fought for freedom in order to lay it upon the altar of a new totalitarianism. This applies to the peasant and his dream of owning his own land; if Communism had not conquered in Russia there would be today, according to the wishes of the peasants, not 40,000 kolkhozes but fifteen or twenty million privately owned farms. Similarly in the Chinese village with its ancient tradition of private ownership of land, there would today, without the victory of Communism, exist neither kolkhozes nor people's communes.

Even among the younger groups of the commerce-oriented bourgeoisie of both countries, among the restless and sometimes seemingly sectarian intelligentsia and the industrial working class to which the radical slogans of Marxism appealed—groups which had grown up entirely during the time when the challenge of the West was being met —the Communist way was never regarded as a possible alternative, except among the party cadres. Even among the Russian working class, after years of war, there was only a minority which actually desired the radical solution offered by Lenin. To the Chinese too, the Communist alternative, on the eve of the war which decided their fate, seemed remote and unreal. But the forces working toward the first alternative, that of a liberal-capitalistic, democratic order, were still young, and their shallow roots were unable to withstand a storm.

Moreover, it would only be accurate to speak of a logical development toward Communism if such a development had not been set in motion or influenced either by disturbances from outside or by the appearance of outstanding individuals who were not necessarily the product of this development. Who could seriously maintain that was the case with the Russian development, which began with Peter, was forced off course and radicalized by Nicholas I's policy of suppression and ended after the disaster of World War I with Lenin? More or less the same applies to the development in China, however one may evaluate the personalities we have met on its way and will continue to meet. That the penetration of the modern world into Russia and China brought immense changes with it, was inevitable; that it should lead to Communism, however, was not inevitable.

It is quite conceivable that, after the Manchu dynasty had lost its 'mandate from heaven', a new, native dynasty might have occupied the throne. That instead of this the cycle of the dynasties came to an end, that the circle was broken and a tangent went off toward an as yet unknown target: that is the result of the collision with the West.

Part II

REVOLUTIONARIES

INTRODUCTION

ON THE EVE OF THE COMMUNIST REVOLUTION both Russia and China, though completely different as to history and mentality, had come to doubt the validity of their former way of life; both had been shaken to their very foundations by the impact of the modern age and by heavy losses in wars against technically superior neighbors. But how different the course taken in these countries by the revolution!

In Russia, Lenin was victorious in a few highly dramatic months, above all in those 'ten days that shook the world' (to use the title of the famous eye-witness report by John Reed); in China, Mao Tse-tung achieved power after a relentless struggle extending over vast areas and lasting a quarter of a century. The main feature—the Long March from South to North China via Western China (which took over a year and covered some 7,500 miles)—offered no such scenes of concentrated impressiveness as Lenin's speech from an armored car in front of Petrograd's Finland Station, the assault on the Winter Palace, the murder of the Tsar's family in a cellar in Yekaterinburg, or the sailors' revolt of Kronstadt.

Yet despite their different roads to power, on closer inspection we see that the two revolutions had a surprising number of features in common. One must not forget that the Bolsheviks, who were the first to travel this road, spent many years experimenting and improvising, and that the Chinese were later able to utilize the results for their own purposes.

In the following four chapters we shall see how the Chinese and the Russian Communists behaved toward the principal population groups (the peasants and workers, the middle class, and the intelligentsia, particularly the writers) and how they in turn reacted. For the time being, however, we shall disregard one subject, that of China's 'Great Leap Forward' of 1958, together with its consequences, as this entirely altered the tone of Peking's policy and its

135

relationship to Moscow and hence merits a separate study (in the last part of this book). Peking's and Moscow's replies to the question: should the population increase be encouraged or discouraged? and their policy toward national minorities, will be examined in Chapter X in connection with the problem of the border territories and the 'population pressure'.

Other fields in which the Chinese have not followed the Soviet example down to the last detail come to mind—education and propaganda, attitude toward family and religion, constitution, administration, and military affairs. But these are minor differences and will not be subjected to close scrutiny here.[1] A look at the Party, however, and the way it works in both countries (in the last chapter of this section) will explain many of Peking's and Moscow's characteristic features.

CHAPTER V

PROLETARIANS OR PEASANTS?

As LONG AGO as the revolution of 1905, organizational talents and revolutionary energies made their appearance in the Russian proletariat, and these Lenin endeavored to use for the furtherance of his aims. Following the collapse of this revolution, the radicalism of the working class declined, to flare up once more during the First World War with its heavy losses and defeats. Lenin's seizure of power in the autumn of 1917 had been preceded by bitter revolts of the workers, mainly in Petrograd. Many of them, indeed, sympathized with the relatively moderate Mensheviks, who were concerned more with improving the economic position of the proletariat than with taking over political power. But in the revolution and civil war (1917–21) the Bolsheviks succeeded in winning over large sections, perhaps even the majority, of the Russian working class, at least in the industrial centers. In the content of its membership (but not, as we shall see in Chapter VIII, on its executive level) Lenin's party became a workers' party.

Many workers lost their lives in the battles of the civil war, and a great many fell victim to the subsequent reign of terror when Stalin, opposing every move toward freedom, delivered up the proletariat to the power of the State, and turned the labor unions from representatives of the workers' interests into mere tools of State and Party. But many, despite all their misgivings, did support the Party throughout the zigzag course of its policy. During the thirties in my travels through the Soviet Union, and in conversation with older workers, I frequently came across men of this kind. Today, of course, they are nothing but living relics of the past.

The transformation of practically the entire Soviet population into state employees, among whom the kolkhoz peasants may also, in a wider sense, be included, renders the study of the present social structure of the Party difficult. Nor are Soviet statistics of much help as they are notoriously reticent on sociological matters. From the figures published on the occasion of the Twenty-second Congress of the Communist Party of the Soviet Union (CPSU) in 1961 it appears evident that among the almost five thousand delegates only 10·6 per cent were workers.[1] The proportion of workers in the Party as a whole is bigger, but is certainly well under fifty per cent. The lack of detailed statistics indicates that the facts represent a too glaring contradiction to the myth of the 'proletarian party'.

The trend in China was quite different. At the very beginning, it is true, the Communists succeeded in many cities in winning over the leading elements of the working class, and in 1922 there were a large number of Communist-led strikes, some of which were successful. However, after a strike of the railway union of the Peking–Hankow Line was crushed in February 1923 with much bloodshed by the troops of the local warlord, there was a change of mood in the working class, and it now inclined toward greater caution. This earned it the impatient contempt of the Party, whose leader at that time declared, as Lenin had done twenty years earlier in regard to the Russian workers:

> The Chinese proletariat is immature both quantitatively and qualitatively. Most of the workers are still imbued with patriarchal notions and their family ties and regional patriotism are extremely strong. These former handicraft workers carry over the habits of their previous existence even when they become industrial workers. They do not feel the need for political action and are still full of ancient superstitions.[2]

*

This 'backwardness' of the Chinese working class corresponded to the backwardness of the Chinese economy, and so it did not seem illogical when the general staff of the world revolution in Moscow demanded of its Chinese comrades that they first strive for a bourgeois revolution and schedule the proletarian revolution for a later stage. The decision of the Communist Party of China (CPC), forced on it by Moscow, to co-operate with the Kuomintang (KMT), the nationalist-bourgeois party of Sun Yat-sen, led to a policy of adventure and the eventual annihilation of the CPC organizations in the coastal cities by Chiang Kai-shek.

It was at this time that the bulk of the Chinese proletariat turned away from the CPC; two years later, according to a report by Chou En-lai, only three per cent of its members were workers.[3] Never again was the CPC to become a party with a majority of workers. The latter were not hostile to the victory of the CPC in 1948–49, their dissatisfaction with conditions at that time being too great, but they did not do much to promote it either; they just let it take its course.

We can only surmise the attitude of the workers toward the CPC after Mao's victory: in totalitarian states the masses are silent. However, in the Chinese press—and not only between the lines—there are frequent indications that, in spite of some improvements, especially in the field of social security, there is in a large section of the working class an attitude of sullen discontent. This attitude has been intensified in recent years by the tremendous pressure of the constantly increasing norms, a pressure which is not compensated for by a corresponding improvement in the standard of living.[4] From a report published in a Peking newspaper of August 1957[5] we know that trade union officials resent being required to drive the workers on to greater productivity and branded as politically immature when they intercede on behalf of the workers' interests. In Red China as in the USSR, the trade unions are not organizations for the workers but, as is freely admitted, organs of State and Party.[6] (It is significant that, in the fifteen-page index of the official Party publication on China's most recent history, the words 'trade unions' do not occur at all.[7]) In other questions, too, concerning the handling of labor in industry, Mao has followed the example of the Soviet Union.

The 'thaw' of 1957, although it brought to light numerous abuses, did not result in any lasting change. According to the labor law of March 1958[8] a worker could no more change his place of work without the consent of his superior than he could under that of May 1954.[9] The forcing of the urban population into 'communes', and the parallel 'mobilization' of women for industry or public projects, have increased the dependence of the worker and his family on the State.

Nor was it possible for the Party to hide the results. Although the statisticians do all in their power to present the CPC in a proletarian guise and thus extend the term 'worker' to cover the widest possible range, at the last regular Party Congress, the Eighth (1956), they could only declare fourteen per cent of all Party comrades to be workers,[10] and a year later only 13·7 per cent.[11]

When I compare my impressions of China in 1957 with those of Russia at the beginning of the thirties, in periods, that is, when both countries were starting on their new industrialization, now Communist-directed and demanding the utmost sacrifices from the people,

I come to the conclusion that at that time the CPSU was more highly regarded by the working class than the CPC was in 1957. The Party functionaries of the USSR, who were at least of urban, if not proletarian, origin, were better able to communicate with the worker than were their Chinese counterparts with their peasant and guerrilla traditions. Since then the general standard of living, as well as the prestige of the Party in the Soviet Union, has risen; in China, as a result of crop failures and economic crises, it has declined.

*

While among Marxists there are—at least theoretically—no important differences of opinion concerning the leading role of the working class, the Communist agrarian policy has been subject to quite a few fluctuations. A contributing factor to the unrealistic nature of Marxist agrarian theories is the fact that among all the leading Communists of Europe, including Russia, not a single one has earned his living for any length of time as a peasant. Most of all, the Communist peasant policy has been discredited through its lack of sincerity.

It may rightly be said that it was not dishonest of Lenin merely to promise the workers leadership in the government and then in actual fact to pre-empt this leadership for a small group first of professional revolutionaries and later professional functionaries. Yet in the case of the peasants this dishonesty went even further: their support was enlisted by promising them the land of the landowners, and then, soon after the seizure of power, not only was the land which had just been allotted them taken away, but also the land they had previously owned.

In their utterances concerning the peasants, Marx and Engels were more or less sincere. They regarded the peasants as a kind of petty bourgeoisie and openly stated that their means of production would have to be made common property, that in other words the peasants would have to be collectivized—an expression at that time not yet in common use. Engels expressly warned against pretending to the peasants that the Communists intended to retain the petty peasantry.[12]

Lenin began to show interest in the Russian peasantry in 1905 when it became apparent that this class was ready to take part in revolutionary violence. From then on he spoke frequently of a Russian 'peasant revolution' and the necessity for 'revolutionary-democratic dictatorship of the proletariat and the peasantry'.[13] In the crucial months before the seizure of power, he promised the peasants that the land of the large landowners would be divided up among them, without bothering to discuss the more distant future. He needed the support of the peasants and knew he would not get it if he told them what he planned to do with them later on. (Moreover, there was no stopping the peasants from seizing the land anyway.) The government set up in 1917 by the Bolsheviks was first known as the 'workers' and peasants' government', and Zinovyev, one of the leading Bolsheviks at that time, said in 1924: 'Leninism is Marxism in the epoch of imperialist war and of the world revolution which began directly in a country where the peasantry predominates.'[14]

Naturally Lenin regarded the peasants merely as an auxiliary force, for even as property-owners on the smallest scale they were, as far as he was concerned, still property-owners, and as such were handicapped by a petty-bourgeois mentality; in other words, they were not suited to be the mainstays of a revolution. His attitude, one which is important for the understanding of the subsequent collectivization measures, is expressed in the following passage: '... small production [i.e., of the peasants] *engenders* capitalism and the bourgeoisie continuously, daily, hourly, spontaneously, and on a mass scale.'[15] It was equally natural for Lenin in the long run to desire the collectivization of the peasants, but he considered this advisable only after certain technological advances had been made, in particular the electrification and motorization of the village.

The turn of events after that is well known.[16] The peasants had no love for the Bolsheviks, especially when the latter began to use brutal methods in requisitioning foodstuffs for the Red Army and the urban working class; but on the whole they preferred the 'Reds' to the 'Whites', whose victory would have brought back the landowners. When Lenin proclaimed the so-called New Economic Policy (NEP) in March 1921 and permitted the peasants to sell some of their products privately so as to encourage them to increase their agricultural productivity, they believed they had at last achieved their desires to be masters of their land and its products. Certain agrarian communes and agrarian state enterprises provided an indication of Lenin's long-range goals, but they did not assume any great significance. Then, of course, the peasants, when they saw they were not receiving adequate compensation from the towns due to the very low industrial production, lost any desire to produce beyond their own needs. Accordingly, the growing urban population continued to suffer food shortages.

Stalin now carried the battle to the rural areas. The peasant was to feed the worker and at the same time provide the financial wherewithal for industrialization. Stalin had been working since 1928 toward the collectivization of peasant property, including their cattle, in a new form of organization, the *kolkhoz* (abbreviation of *kollektivnoye khozyaystvo* = collective enterprise). Soon terror and starvation reigned in the rural areas. By the spring of 1930 the situation had become so serious that Stalin temporarily slowed up the process of collectivization, but nevertheless in the following years it was completed. After the peasant had been crushed, at the cost of terrible losses in human lives, cattle, and equipment, Stalin tried to propitiate him: the Kolkhoz Charter of 1935 was designed to give him a feeling of some security and permanence in existing conditions; among other things, he was permitted to have his own small garden plot and a limited quantity of livestock.

In spite of some ups and downs, there has been little change in the peasant policy of the Soviet Union since 1935. The peasant still has his garden, his cow or his pig, his poultry; he is still allowed to offer his own produce for sale at the market; he is still paid according to his work performance in the kolkhoz, and for some years now he has received part of his wages before the harvest in monthly advance payments, so that in the wage system he approaches the industrial worker who, of course, is also paid according to work performance. The fact that prices for his products have been raised, that the town offers him more industrial goods today than ten or twenty years ago, that in Kazakhstan and Siberia enormous new areas have been brought under cultivation, chiefly by state-owned farms, has not changed his position in principle. The two major changes were the abolition of the state-owned machine-tractor stations (MTS) combined with the sale of their equipment to the kolkhozes in 1958 (until then the State had kept the kolkhoz peasants in line with the aid of the MTS), and the subordination of the agricultural administration to the Party late in 1962. A great deal could be said on each of these points; however, we have been concerned here mainly with the principal stages of Soviet policy.

*

In theory the Chinese Marxists had regarded the proletariat as the mainstay of the revolution. But China also possessed a revolutionary-minded peasantry, and among China's Communist leaders there were some who recognized this,[17] and one who from this recognition was to make world history.

Mao Tse-tung himself was from the country, from a village in the province of Hunan. In his autobiography, as told to the American journalist Edgar Snow in the mid-thirties, he describes his father as having been first a moderately well-off, later a rich peasant and grain-dealer.[18] But in 1911 at the age of eighteen Mao moved to the provincial capital of Changsha, and in 1918 to Peking. Like so many of his age at that time, he became a student, an intellectual, a professional revolutionary, and—after the founding of the CPC in 1921, in which he took part—a Party functionary. As far back as March 1926 he wrote that the industrial proletariat of China 'has become the leading force in the revolutionary movement'.[19] At that time there seemed to be nothing to indicate that he was destined to become the most successful peasant leader in modern history.

In 1926 Mao was sent by the Party to his native province of Hunan. He stayed there thirty-two days. On his return he composed his report, which has since become famous. I quote the key sentences:

In a very short time, in China's central, southern and northern provinces, several hundred million peasants will rise like a tornado or tempest, a force so extraordinarily swift and violent that no power, however great, will be able to suppress it. They will break all trammels that now bind them and rush forward along the road to liberation.[20]

Mao's report was a fighting revolutionary document, a summons to the unshackling of peasant violence and to the destruction of the enemy. It contained no constructive ideas about agrarian reform. Mao praised the peasants for taking the grain from the landowners and for slaughtering the pigs, and expressed his satisfaction that 'the peasants' dirty feet should trample on the ivory beds of the daughters and daughters-in-law of the rich'. He wrote:

A revolution is not the same as inviting people to dinner, or writing an essay, or painting a picture, or doing fancy needlework; it cannot be anything so refined, so calm and gentle, or so mild, kind, courteous, restrained and magnanimous. A revolution is an uprising, an act of violence whereby one class overthrows another. A rural revolution is a revolution by which the peasantry overthrows the authority of the feudal landlord class. If the peasants do not use the maximum of their strength, they can never overthrow the authority of the landlords which has been deeply rooted for thousands of years. In the rural areas, there must be a great, fervent revolutionary upsurge, which alone can arouse hundreds and thousands of the people to form a great force. All the actions . . . labeled as 'going too far', are caused by the power of the peasants, generated by a great, fervent, revolutionary upsurge in the countryside. Such actions were quite necessary in the second period of the peasant movement (the period of revolutionary action). In this period, it was necessary to establish the absolute authority of the peasants. It was necessary to stop malicious criticisms against the peasant association. It was necessary to overthrow all the authority of the gentry, to knock them down and even trample them underfoot. All actions labeled as 'going too far' had a revolutionary significance in the second period. To put it bluntly, it was necessary to bring about a brief reign of terror in every rural area; otherwise one could never suppress the activities of the counter-revolutionaries in the countryside or overthrow the authority of the gentry. To right a wrong it is necessary to exceed the proper limits, and the wrong cannot be righted without the proper limits being exceeded.[21]

Much has been written and there have been many arguments about the ideological significance of this report.[22] From the vantage point of the present, the following may be said: Mao composed it at a moment when co-operation between the CPC and the KMT was still at its peak. Hence he formulated his report with regard not to the Communist revolution but—to use his term—to the 'national' or 'democratic revolution': that is to say, the revolutionary process in which the CPC and the KMT were jointly participating. Furthermore, Mao wrote not as a theoretician but as a practical man. This is the explanation for the following sentence—later suppressed:

If we allot ten points to the accomplishments of the democratic revolution, then the achievements of the urban dwellers and the military units rate only three points, while the remaining seven points should go to the peasants in their rural revolution.[23]

With these figures Mao gave a fair definition of the significance of the various population groups in relation to the revolution. Since the thirty per cent which he allotted to all non-peasant revolutionary forces also included the army and the leftist bourgeoisie, as well as the intellectuals, only a small share remained for the proletariat. This corresponded to the facts.

Relations between Mao and the official Party heads in the years following the Hunan report have not been clarified. Mao himself later claimed that in his peasant-revolutionary efforts he found himself diametrically opposed to them.[24] This may be hindsight and subsequent editing.[25] In Moscow at any rate the Hunan report was duly published without unfavorable criticism[26] and thus implicitly approved.

*

From 1927 on, in the trackless, remote Chingkang Mountains (in the eastern part of Hunan province, southeast of Changsha), Mao, first alone, then with Chu Teh, also a peasant's son, created his predominantly peasant Red army and founded a Soviet republic inhabited chiefly by peasants. As Chiang Kai-shek gradually broke up the urban Party organizations, the center of gravity of the CPC shifted to Mao, that is, to the rural areas held by his Red army, first in the Chingkang Mountains and later, when he had to flee from Chiang's armies on the famous Long March (1934–35), to Yenan, in the great curve of the Yellow River, north of Sian. Having to rely during this time almost entirely on the peasants, Mao pursued a policy which matched their desires: he gave them the land of the landowners and 'rich' peasants and wisely refrained from forcing them into collectives.

When, beginning in 1937, China was fully engaged in defending itself against Japan, the Communists interrupted their expropriation policy; they wished to present themselves as active fighters against the foreign invader who put national duty above the attainment of their own aims. Even after 1945 there was no immediate swing back to the intensive class struggle; instead there was a period of transition marked by a number of changes in the Party's general line, which lasted till 1950.

To deduce a radical difference from these dissimilarities in starting-point and power basis and to suggest that Maoism and Leninism are different in principle, would amount to non-historical and non-political thinking. The professional revolutionary Lenin and the professional revolutionary Mao both made use of every revolutionary force then actually at their disposal in their struggle for power. The fact that Mao leaned far more heavily on the peasants than Lenin did was not because he embraced a different ideology but because of the situation he faced after the destruction of the urban CPC. Neither Lenin nor Mao was following the path of orthodox Marxism when, at the head of a tightly organized group of conspirators, they set about leading economically backward countries with a weak proletariat toward a form of economy which Marx had planned for the highly industrialized countries. Both succeeded in seizing power because they knew how to utilize the forces which were ripe for revolution. The discontent, indeed the despair, of the masses was the dynamite with which they blew up the existing edifice of society and state, and they took the dynamite wherever they found it—in the proletariat, insofar as one existed, among the peasants, the war-weary soldiers, the rebellious intellectual youth. It was the dynamite they cared about, not where it came from.

In Mao's place, Lenin would have behaved as Mao did. After all, it was he who had advised stirring up revolutionary tendencies among the peasants and the forming of peasant soviets (peasant councils) in the so-called colonial and semicolonial areas, i.e., in countries such as China in which there was no, or scarcely any, proletariat. These ideas preoccupied him during the summer of 1920, in connection with the Second Congress of the Communist International; the result was the 'Theses on the National and Colonial Questions', accepted by the Congress on July 28. The guiding principles were emphasized in Section 11:

> It is necessary in the backward countries to give special support to the peasant movement against the landlords, against large landownership, and against all manifestations or survivals of feudalism, and to strive to lend the peasant movement the most revolutionary character and establish the closest possible alliance between the West-European Communist proletariat and the revolutionary peasant movement in the East, in the colonies, and in the backward countries generally.[27]

Admittedly there are sentences to be found (1920) in Lenin's writings such as: 'Only the urban and industrial proletariat, led by the Communist Party, can liberate the rural working masses from the yoke of capital and big landlordism.'[28] But ever since 1902 Lenin had laid far more emphasis on the Communist Party than on the proletariat. For him the Communist Party was *eo ipso* the personification of the proletariat, even when its leaders were not drawn from the proletariat. The passage just quoted, therefore, from a practical rather than from a theoretical point of view, means: only the Communist Party can liberate the peasants. And this was Mao's belief too. But Lenin himself was never in Mao's position and had never had to cope with the question of whether it was possible to carry on the struggle for the victory of Communism in the form of a guerrilla war from remote rural areas over a period of many years, which is what Mao did and, furthermore, justified in speeches and reports.[29]

The actual fact, clear enough in itself, that Mao only applied Lenin's guiding principles to backward rural areas, has been overshadowed by the hairsplitting disputes which followed as a result of the internal conflicts of the CPC and of the various competitors and cliques in Moscow, particularly those between Stalin and Trotsky.

The American scholar Benjamin Schwartz, who emphasizes the special character of Maoism, nevertheless comes to the following conclusion in the last pages of his book on Chinese Communism:

> The Chinese Communist Party under the leadership of Mao Tse-tung has not been the party of the industrial proletariat nor has it been the party of the peasantry in the Marxist-Leninist sense. It has rather been an elite corps of politically articulate leaders organized along Leninist lines but drawn on its top levels from various strata of Chinese society. . . . Under the leadership of Mao Tse-tung this elite group had come to realize in the face of Marxist-Leninist dogma that the peasantry could itself provide the mass basis and the motive power for a revolutionary transformation. . . . It would, however, be a grave error to assume that once having achieved power, the aspirations or intentions of the Communist leaders would necessarily be determined by their peasant background or by the interests of the peasantry. On the contrary, we have every reason to believe that these men had thoroughly absorbed the Leninist abhorrence of 'backwardness' as well as the extravagant Marxist-Leninist belief in the potentialities of industrialization even when circumstances forced them to lurk in the hinterlands. . . . The Chinese Communist Party under the leadership of Mao Tse-tung has been, I would suggest, neither 'the vanguard of the proletariat' in the Marxist-Leninist sense, nor a 'peasant party' in the Marxist-Leninist sense, but an elite of professional revolutionaries which has risen to power by basing itself on the dynamic of peasant discontent.[30]

What, then, was Mao's agrarian policy *after* the foundation of the Chinese People's Republic? Many of the factors which had previously demanded consideration now no longer applied. This altered situation was revealed in the agrarian reform law of June 28, 1950; it called for the distribution of the large and medium-sized properties among the peasants and led to the notorious outrages against landlords and well-to-do farmers. No mention was made of collectivization. The only indication that small-scale farming was far from being Mao's ultimate goal was the establishment under Party patronage of 'mutual-aid teams'. But as these constituted very loose associations and did not run counter to the peasant mentality, their number grew steadily after 1950 and apparently without resistance on the part of the peasants.

The next step, aimed at the formation of 'agricultural producers' co-operatives', was taken by means of the Central Committee's resolutions of February 15 and December 16, 1953. These lower-type co-operatives (as they were to be called later) included an average of twenty to thirty farms; the individual farmer who joined the co-operative received for the land and draft-animals which he contributed

a share of the proceeds, and this share was calculated first according to the value of his invested capital and secondly according to
the work he performed for the co-operative. He was assured that he
was free to resign voluntarily at any time. These producers' co-
operatives also did not represent any radical change, and they rapidly
increased in number.[31]

True collectivization began in 1954–55 with the formation of the
'higher type of agricultural producers' co-operatives'. The details
were contained in Mao's speech of July 31, 1955, and a CC resolution
of October 11, 1955. It was the measures connected with these co-
operatives which formed the real revolution in Chinese agriculture, a
socio-political experiment on a gigantic scale.[32]

In 1957 I thoroughly investigated some Chinese co-operatives, and
in each case I spent a number of hours with the chief accountant and
his books, for I wanted to go into the details of work organization,
norms, and wages, of prices and delivery quotas. I could detect no
difference between these organizations and the kolkhozes of the
Soviet Union, whose development I had followed at first hand since
1930 and of which I had visited countless examples. The Chinese to
whom I talked always showed their displeasure when I spoke of their
'kolkhoz', and they would say: 'This is not a kolkhoz but a higher-
type agricultural producers' co-operative.' But when I asked them
then to tell me in what way the enterprise differed from a Soviet
kolkhoz, they were at a loss for an answer. Their annoyance was
unmistakable; obviously they did not care for the idea that all they
had accomplished was an imitation of the Soviet model.

The 529 Chinese kolkhozes of 1955 had increased a year later to
312,000, and in 1957 to more than 700,000, while the 'mutual-aid
teams' disappeared completely after 1956, and the 'lower type' of
co-operatives after 1957. Collectivization was thus achieved in China
much more quickly and without the severe setbacks with which
Stalin had to cope.

It has often been said that Mao Tse-tung owes this relatively smooth
transition to the care with which he proceeded by intermediate stages,
and that in this way his collectivization differed considerably from the
Soviet pattern. This view, however, overlooks the fact that this step-
by-step transition had been undertaken several years earlier in the
Eastern European countries conquered by the Soviets. What is more,
it was carried out uniformly, almost down to the last detail, in each of
those countries, and in a manner identical with the later Chinese

procedure. Thus this was not a case of a 'Chinese method', but rather of the practical application of the lessons which Stalin had learned from his own experience with collectivization. The following table makes this clear:

THE ROAD TO THE KOLKHOZ

		In Russia	In China
1.	Confiscation of large properties and their distribution among the peasants	1917–1920	1927–1937 and 1950—1953
2a.	'New Economic Policy' with certain liberties for the peasants	1921–1928	—
2b.	Transitional stage with early forms of collectivization	—	1953–1955
3.	Formation of the kolkhoz	1928–1935	1955–1957

Stages 1 and 3 were, as we see, more or less identical in both countries; the only difference is in Stage 2, a result of the different situations in which the two peoples found themselves after the revolution. However, a drastically new and independent Chinese agrarian policy was not long in coming: while for nearly thirty years the Russians had made only trifling changes in the kolkhoz, Mao created the people's commune one year after the completion of collectivization. The people's communes, discussed in detail in the last part of this book, are one of the principal components in the Chinese-Soviet conflict.

CHAPTER VI

WITH OR WITHOUT THE BOURGEOISIE?

THE MARXIST IMAGE OF HISTORY is a simple one. All countries go through the same stages of development: feudalism is followed by capitalism, in which the bourgeoisie is supreme; during the industrial evolution of this era the antagonist of the bourgeoisie is born, the proletariat; this proletariat rises up, overthrows the bourgeoisie, and takes its place; there follows a period of dictatorship by the proletariat, and after that the ideal classless society.

For Lenin, therefore, the bourgeoisie was the enemy. And yet the content of the word fluctuated. Like Marx and Engels before him, and Stalin and other Communists after him, Lenin used it mostly as a collective term for everything which was neither 'feudal' nor 'proletarian'. According to occasion and context, however, Lenin also limited the term to the upper layer of the bourgeoisie, differentiating the petty bourgeoisie as being an element that could, at least from time to time, be won over to the side of the proletariat. The intelligentsia, with which we must deal separately, was usually included by Lenin in the bourgeoisie, although it possessed no means of production. Lack of precision of this kind in sociological terms has always existed in Communist thinking.

That the road to proletariat rule entailed the necessity of going through a bourgeois-capitalist phase was also one of Lenin's teachings; as late as 1912 he attacked Sun Yat-sen's supposition that it was possible to omit the stage of capitalism.[1] In the same way Lenin supported the thesis that the bourgeois revolution must precede the proletarian one. He says quite unequivocally: 'A bourgeois revolution is *absolutely* necessary in the interests of the proletariat.'[2]

So it came about that Lenin's first task was to promote the victory of the mortal enemy, the bourgeoisie, in order afterwards to be able to attack it:

The democratic struggle [i.e., the struggle for the bourgeois revolution]

150

is waged by the workers together with a section of the bourgeoisie, especially the petty bourgeoisie. On the other hand, the socialist struggle is waged by the workers against the whole of the bourgeoisie.[3]

And:

. . . from the democratic revolution we shall at once, and precisely in accordance with the measure of our strength, . . . begin to pass to the socialist revolution. We stand for uninterrupted revolution.[4]

Naturally it was not Lenin's intention that the revolutionary forces of the proletariat should submit to the bourgeoisie in the latter's efforts to bring about the bourgeois-democratic revolution. On the contrary, he wanted to make the proletariat and the Communist Party even in this phase as strong and influential as possible so that they could exert a powerful influence on the course of events. For him there was no question, either, of a truce with the bourgeoisie. His attitude to the bourgeoisie was 'dialectic'; on the one hand he opposed it and on the other he regarded it as a temporary ally in the struggle against the hated 'feudalism' of Tsarism.

Lenin therefore demanded the unequivocal participation of the proletariat and the revolutionary peasantry in the bourgeois revolution, but with the aim of radicalizing it in order eventually to reach that 'revolutionary-democratic dictatorship of the proletariat and the peasantry' (1905).[5] For this purpose he wished to isolate the bourgeoisie and to 'paralyse the instability of the peasantry and the petty bourgeoisie'.[6] When he said in this connection: 'the democratic revolution will not immediately overstep the bounds of bourgeois social and economic relationships',[7] this did not mean that he had any intention of stopping at that stage for even a short time; the 'revolutionary-democratic dictatorship' he aimed at was not compatible with a bourgeois-capitalist order.

In Russia the revolution actually took place in two stages: in March 1917 there occurred the bourgeois-democratic revolution (in our sense of the words) in which the Communists played only a small part, and in November the Bolshevik revolution, which the Bolsheviks themselves called proletarian. Without the support of the peasant masses (a large part of whom were in the army) this revolution would not have been possible, but the Bolsheviks, who claimed to be the spokesmen of the proletariat, were unmistakably the leaders. It is true that after the November revolution (called the 'October revolution' after the Russian calendar at that time) there was talk of a coalition government. But after the Bolsheviks won only a quarter of the seats in the constituent assembly Lenin put a speedy end to it in January 1918, with the aid of his Red Guard. For a while he continued to work with the left wing of the Social-Revolutionary Party as it had strong support from the peasants, but in April he parted company with these allies. Henceforward he ruled with his party only. The revolution had 'grown over into' its 'socialist' stage —not 'immediately' but still remarkably fast.

Scarcely had the new power established itself than the 'first step toward the complete passing of the factories, mines, railroads and other means of production and transportation into the possession of the Soviet Workers' and Peasants' Republic' was announced,[8] and six months later this 'passing' was accomplished, without compensation.[9] (Even when, as a result of the chaos that soon ensued, Lenin was forced, in the period of the New Economic Policy, to decide on a less drastic course, he did not repeal the confiscations.) Some few months after the victory of the revolution, therefore, the economic basis of the Russian bourgeoisie was destroyed and the bourgeoisie itself 'liquidated as a class'.

*

In one important point Lenin altered his views concerning the course of history, but this revision did not affect the Russian people. As Lenin's hopes for the revolution in Europe were proven illusory, he directed his interest toward Asia. In a further development of his thesis, 'Imperialism, the Highest Stage of Capitalism', and with the aim of weakening the Western powers by means of revolts in their colonial empires, Lenin set the revolutionaries of Asia the task of destroying foreign imperialism as well as their own feudalism in national-bourgeois revolutions.[10]

This procedure was intended to clear the path to a domestic capitalism in Asia and—due to the weakening of Western capitalism which was anticipated as a result of anticolonial struggles—to socialism in the West.

For this purpose Lenin recommended 'a *temporary alliance* with the bourgeois democracy of the colonies and of the backward countries' (author's italics), but he warned against any *amalgamation* with these forces and declared that 'the Communist International must . . . under all circumstances preserve the independence of the proletarian movement even if in its most rudimentary form'.[11]

Later, when Lenin had buried his long-cherished hope of an imminent proletarian revolution in the West, he was prepared to make an ally of anyone, anywhere in the world, who seemed to be in a position to damage the stability of the West, particularly of England. An ally of this kind, who later turned out to be an enemy, the Turkish nationalist Enver Pasha, once said jokingly that to Lenin anyone who was anti-British was a Bolshevik.[12] And so it came about that in 1922 Moscow recommended to the Communist Party of China not merely an alliance but a far-reaching amalgamation with the preponderantly bourgeois Kuomintang: members of the CPC were simultaneously to become members of the KMT. In November 1922 the Communist International instructed the Communists in countries like China to use every means to prevent their bourgeoisie uniting with Western imperialism, and even went so far as to declare:

> The refusal of the communists in the colonies to take part in the struggle [of the bourgeois nationalists] against imperialist tyranny, on the ground of the ostensible 'defence' of their independent class interests, is opportunism of the worst kind. . . . In the colonial East the slogan that must be emphasized at the present time is that of the anti-imperialist united front [i.e., co-operation with the bourgeois nationalists].[13]

Mao did not deviate from this line of Moscow's when in 1926 in the first essay contained in his *Selected Works* he discussed the possibilities of co-operation with the bourgeoisie, dividing it into the following categories,[14] to which he from then on always adhered:

1. Landlords and comprador-bourgeoisie. (Comprador was the term used in China for Chinese merchants who worked in partnership with foreigners.) Mao called both these groups enemies of the revolution with whom no alliance was possible.
2. National (or middle) bourgeoisie. Their attitude, he said, was contradictory: on the one hand they were against foreign capital, by which they were oppressed, and to that extent in favor of the anti-imperialist revolution; but on the other hand they were against all the forces at home which might threaten their own economic position, and to that extent they were against the proletarian revolution. In time, he said, this class will fall apart, 'some sections turning left and joining the ranks of the revolution and others turning right and joining the ranks of the counter-revolution'.
3. Petty bourgeoisie: owner-peasants, master handicraftsmen, students, primary and middle school teachers, lower government functionaries and office clerks, small lawyers and petty traders. Mao divides these once again into three sub-groups, all of whom, however, as soon as the 'dawn of victory is discernible', will join the revolution. In this regard he was not a bad prophet.

After the destruction of the urban CPC in 1927 by the KMT and during his years as a peasant leader, Mao had no occasion to devote himself further to the subject of the bourgeoisie. But in spite of the bitter lessons of 1927 he 'fully' accepted Moscow's view that China was in the 'stage of the bourgeois-democratic revolution'.[15] Japan's attack on Manchuria in September 1931 encouraged a rapprochement with the KMT. An initial offer of alliance is to be found in an appeal which Mao made during an interval in the Long March, on August 1, 1935. This appeal contained the following words:

> If the Kuomintang armies will stop their attacks on the Soviet districts and if their forces will fight the Japanese invasion, then, regardless of the animosity and differences of opinion on internal problems that have existed between them and the Red Army in the past, the Red Army will not only immediately cease its action against them, but is ready to join hands with them to carry on a joint fight for the salvation of the country.[16]

This appeal was not yet directed to the hated Chiang Kai-shek but, over his head, to his troops. When the Long March was over, Mao renewed his offer in a speech at the end of December 1935. 'What is the basic tactical task of the Party today?' he asked, and replied: 'It is none other than to form a broad national revolutionary united front' against the Japanese, whom he called 'the chief enemy' of the moment. Critics of his attempts to communicate with the KMT were accused by Mao of 'closed-door sectarianism' because they scared off possible allies or, as he put it, because they chased 'fish to the water and birds to the woods', by which he unmistakably also betrayed his final intentions with regard to the bourgeoisie—to devour it.

As a result of this new general line, Mao announced that he would enlarge the government in that part of China under his control, hitherto a 'government of the bloc of the workers, peasants, and urban petty bourgeoisie', by 'members of all other classes who wish to take part in the national revolution' and thus transform his 'workers' and peasants' republic' into a 'people's republic'. He was even prepared, he said, to take into the government 'those who will not oppose European and American imperialism because of their affiliations, but will oppose Japanese imperialism and its lackeys'. At the same time, in order to reassure the bourgeoisie he added:

> The people's republic will not, in the era of the bourgeois-democratic revolution, abolish non-imperialist and non-feudalist private property but will encourage the development of industrial and commercial enterprises of the national bourgeoisie rather than confiscate them. . . . In the stage of

democratic revolution, a limit is set to the struggle between labour and capital. . . . The transition of the bourgeois-democratic revolution is a thing of the future. In the future the democratic revolution will inevitably be transformed into a socialist revolution . . . it will certainly take quite a long time.[17]

Chiang Kai-shek would have preferred first to triumph in the struggle with the Communists with the aid of provincial troops, and by diplomatic and political means prevent the Japanese from penetrating any further into China, while he prepared his élite troops under German advisers for a decisive clash with the Japanese. But the 'Sian incident' created a new situation: in December 1936 Chiang was taken prisoner in the city of Sian by some officers of the provincial troops who had been ordered to fight the Communists but who wanted to fight the Japanese. What happened during the days of Chiang's captivity, and what obligations he assumed in order to be set free, are matters which even today have not been entirely clarified. But the attacks of Chiang's troops against the Communists ceased. Mao for his part declared in May of 1937 that the territory under his control would from now on no longer be a Soviet republic but become part of the Chinese Republic.[18]

*

We need not concern ourselves here with this second alliance between the CPC and the KMT (1937–41), nor with the ensuing period of their relations up to the end of the war with Japan, relations which at best can only be called a temporary armistice fraught with deep suspicion on both sides. What interests us here is Mao's relationship not with the KMT but with the bourgeoisie, which he dealt with in his publication 'On New Democracy' (January 1940).[19] In the pro-Communist and Red Chinese journalistic world it has been hailed as a masterpiece, as a 'new Marxist classic'[20] of 'historical significance'.[21]

Like Lenin until 1917, Mao in 1940 spoke of the Chinese revolution as a bourgeois-democratic revolution. But he divided it into two stages, with the Russian revolution as the watershed. Until the Russian revolution, 'the bourgeois-democratic revolution in China belonged to the old type of the bourgeois-democratic revolutions, was a part of the *bourgeois-democratic world revolution* of the old type. After that the bourgeois-democratic revolution in China already belonged to the new type of bourgeois-democratic revolutions, and in the common revolutionary front it formed a part of the *proletarian-socialist world revolution*.' (Author's italics.) In other words: the nature of the Chinese revolution itself, declared Mao, had not changed, but the nature of the world revolution had; with the victory of Bolshevism, world revolution entered upon a new phase, and that in turn had reacted on the Chinese revolution which would now no longer be led by the bourgeoisie but by the proletariat (meaning the Communists). 'New democracy', then, was the name given by Mao to that (second) stage of China's bourgeois-democratic revolution in which the proletariat was to replace the bourgeoisie as the guiding force.

The reader will recall that, thirty-five years before Mao, Lenin had taught the same doctrine, with this difference: he had not used the term 'new democracy'. Even Mao's separation of the bourgeois-democratic revolution into two stages, divided by the year 1917, was not original; Stalin had made this separation in 1926 with special reference to China and had referred to Lenin without naming his exact source.[22]

The Seventh Party Congress of the Chinese Communists took place at the end of April 1945. In a report lasting several hours, published under the revealing title 'On the Coalition Government', Mao returned to his offer of co-operation with the bourgeoisie. In order to reassure the bourgeoisie, he announced that, in the new democracy, 'the private capitalist economy' would 'freely develop'; for, he declared, 'we have too little capitalism in our country'. He admitted that the development of private economy represented merely a minimum program of the CPC, that is, a temporary phase, while the maximum program of the Party envisaged the abolition of private economy.[23] At the same time he called for a coalition government and asserted that 'for the whole period of the new democracy' neither the dictatorship of a single class nor the monopoly of a single party was planned. Here, too, Mao did not deviate in principle from Lenin's course, for Lenin had spoken of a dictatorship of the workers *and* peasants and only within this framework of a 'hegemony' of the proletariat.[24] Even the formula 'hegemony of the proletariat' had now been adopted by the Chinese.[25]

It was in this report that Mao for the first time discussed the question of the manner in which at this point the course of the Chinese revolution differed from that of the Soviet revolution. Presumably the contacts between Yenan and Moscow, which for a long time had been so meagre, were somewhat strengthened during the last months of the war, and this prompted Mao to make comparisons which he had not thought of making as long as he was living in almost total isolation. However, what he said on this point was historically incorrect: he explained the removal of the coalition government after the Bolshevik revolution by maintaining that the Russian people had supported 'only the Party of the Bolsheviks'.[26] In reality at that time and for a long time to come, the Bolsheviks represented only a minority among the people.

Let us remember: Mao had not departed from Lenin's general line. Lenin, too, had spoken of a dictatorship of more than one class (namely, of that of the workers *and* peasants; admittedly not of the bourgeoisie, although in 1905 he had still demanded collaboration 'with the mass of the petty-bourgeois urban and rural poor',[27] and had expressly approved, as we have seen, the alliance with the bourgeoisie for the Asiatic peoples); Lenin, too, had declared in the years preceding the Bolshevik victory that Russian capitalism must first of all undergo further development. Nevertheless, there is one difference to be found in Mao's observation:

> For a *long period of time* a particular form of government and power organization will continue to exist in China which is absolutely necessary for us and in accordance with theoretical principles, and which at the same time differs from the order of things in Russia. . . . The general theses of our new-democratic program will remain *for decades* unchanged throughout the whole phase of the bourgeois-democratic revolution.[28] (Author's italics.)

As we have seen, Lenin had had shorter periods of time in mind. But that was a difference in principle, and in actual practice Mao also soon ceased talking about 'decades'. In spite of the enormous difference between China as it was before Mao's seizure of power and pre-revolutionary Russia, in that period Mao followed a surprisingly 'Leninist' line. It was not until 1949 that he went beyond it.

*

The confused history of Chinese domestic policy between 1945 and 1949, as well as the unsuccessful American attempts to effect a stabilization of the situation, do not concern us here.[29] In the spring of 1949 the Communists were on the threshold of victory throughout China. The question Mao had to face was how the Party—after twenty years in the remote hinterland—was to rule a gigantic empire

with densely populated cities and extensive industries. He realized
even more clearly than in the years of the war with Japan that for the
time being he must rely on the co-operation of the bourgeoisie. Once
again in the spring of 1949 he proclaimed a long-term co-operation
with the bourgeois parties,[30] and in July of the same year he called
this co-operation a 'democratic dictatorship'.[31]

Like so many other slogans of world Communism, this paradoxical
formula has its origin in Lenin's vocabulary. As we have seen, he
coined it in the spring of 1905 as 'revolutionary-democratic dictatorship of the proletariat and the peasantry'.[32] In 1926 Stalin had suggested it to the Chinese[33] and then the Chinese Communists adopted
it themselves; it already occurs in the resolution of their Sixth Party
Congress,[34] which was held in 1928 (in Moscow, without Mao), as
well as in the constitution of Mao's Soviet Republic, accepted in 1931,
in which 'the democratic dictatorship of the proletariat and peasantry' is described as being the foundation of the state.[35] And now in
1949 Mao again used this phrase.

At this juncture, however, his offer was no longer made to the
KMT, which was in the process of complete disintegration, but to a
series of small parties founded in the last few years by men who did
not agree with the course of the KMT and stood to the left of it without being Communists. The two oldest were: the Chinese Peasants'
and Workers' Democratic Party which was formed in 1928 as a so-
called Third Party, and the China Democratic League, founded in
1941 and suppressed by Chiang Kai-shek in 1947; their leaders fled
at that time to Hongkong and decided to co-operate with the CPC.

In all there were eight parties or party-like groups which, in addition to the CPC, obtained a licence after the Communists' victory.
In the official handbook of the Chinese People's Republic these eight
parties are listed alongside the CPC as if they were partners of equal
standing.[36] They had a double duty: in the first place they were supposed to show the world that Red China was a true democracy, i.e., a
multi-party democracy, and in the second place they were to provide
an organizational framework for politically active people who
remained outside of the CPC. 'Co-existence' with the other parties
was to last as long as there were classes, in other words 'until we have
successfully built up a socialist society'.[37]

Gradually certain groups among the upper classes were assigned to
these eight parties. Thus the Peasants' and Workers' Democratic
Party was—despite its name—to be the reservoir for officials, doctors,

and scientific and technical employees; the National Construction Association, that of industry and business people, i.e., the 'national bourgeoisie' in the narrower sense; the Chih Kung Party, for overseas Chinese; and the Revolutionary Committee of the Kuomintang for former members of the KMT, particularly for officers. The intellectuals were assigned to three parties: the Democratic League, the Association for Promoting Democracy, and the September 3rd Society. The Chinese from Taiwan were included in the Taiwan Democratic Self-Government League. For workers and peasants, of course, the CPC did not allow the existence of a rival party.

Mao tried to resolve the contradiction in the term 'democratic dictatorship' by saying that democracy applied to the people, and dictatorship to the reactionaries,[38] and that it was up to the Party to determine who belonged to the people and who to the reactionaries. This formula of Mao's does not, of course, mean that true democracy ruled within the 'people', which Mao more than once calculated at some ninety per cent of the population.[39] It is openly stated that within the democratic dictatorship the proletariat holds the leading position[40] and that the proletariat is in turn led by the CPC.[41]

The façade of the coalition with the eight parties was maintained for many years. Their leaders were invited to all public events (insofar as they were not purely Communist Party functions) especially when foreigners were present. Many of them hold (or held) ministerial posts; for example, Chang Po-chun, who was simultaneously Chairman of the Peasants' and Workers' Democratic Party and Minister of Communications, and Lo Lung-chi, leader of the Democratic League and Minister of the Timber Industry; we shall hear more of both these men later on. Many occupied positions in other organizations which Mao needed for the 'new democratic' façade of his State; among the chief of these was the Chinese People's Political Consultative Conference founded in 1949 as a combination of all authorized parties and organizations.

In the Soviet Union itself no such experiments took place, apart from the very first weeks of the regime in the winter of 1917–18. In 1936 Stalin explained in detail that it was only possible to have several parties where there were several antagonistic classes: since the interests of the two classes which remained in the Soviet Union—the workers and the peasants—were not antagonistic, a single party, the CPSU, was sufficient to represent the interests of the entire people.[42] In the Eastern European states, however, including the Soviet Zone of

Germany, Moscow has since 1944—that is, even before the Chinese—not only permitted the façade of a number of parties but actually promoted it.

But before long the true nature of the 'coalition' became increasingly apparent. The extent of the disillusionment among the leaders of the eight parties was revealed during the brief weeks of 'frankness' in the early summer of 1957. After Mao had told these leaders that they ought to express their criticism frankly and openly, they demanded that they be freed from their subservient and humiliating position and that a true democracy be established. What they had in mind was a kind of two-party system that was to consist on the one hand of the CPC and on the other of the remaining eight parties, which would then amalgamate. They suggested that the Chinese People's Political Consultative Conference, in which they were represented in large numbers, be turned from a purely advisory and virtually decorative organ into a kind of upper house with the power to veto the resolutions of the Communist-dominated legislature, the National People's Congress.

Their spokesmen pointed out that, although they were often put on display, in actual fact they had no real voice, not even in their own ministries. In particular they objected to the fact that there was practically no separation between the State and the CPC, and that the strict centralism within the CPC rendered all the fine words about democracy illusory.[43] Here they made use of a formula which evoked a number of mental associations in three characters: *tang t'ien hsia.* *Tang* means party; *t'ien hsia*, as we already know, under heaven, or, that which lies under heaven, i.e., the earth and in particular its central point, China, also the empire or imperial dynasty. These three characters, therefore, expressed the following idea, intelligible to every educated Chinese: the CPC is behaving like a dynasty which regards all China as its property.[44] Mao's 'democratic dictatorship' was after all nothing but a dictatorship of the Communists hiding behind the democratic facade, a dictatorship which was substantially no different from that of the USSR.

In practice Mao's theses on coalition no longer had much political significance, but they did have an economic one. The Chinese Communists can regard the abolition of private ownership in trade and industry as a remarkable achievement of their tactical and psychological skill. The 2,800 large enterprises which had belonged to people openly hostile to the Communists (most of whom had fled) were confiscated by the State without compensation; they comprised four fifths of private business in China.[45] And how did the Communists deal with the many businesses owned by members of the 'national bourgeoisie' who had remained in China?

*

How the Chinese Communists had transformed private economy into state economy was brought home to me very clearly when in 1957 I had a talk with a man who belonged to the 'national bourgeoisie' in an industrial town of China. The official travel bureau had asked me what I would like to see there. 'Two schools, a hospital, a machine factory, and a capitalist,' I replied. This list was taken down without so much as a raised eyebrow; the last item was passed on to the local branch of the All-China Federation of Industry and Commerce, and the next day I was told that Mr. Shao, a capitalist and assistant manager of a factory (which had formerly belonged to him), would see me that afternoon at three o'clock in his home; a gentleman from the travel bureau would accompany me.

Mr. Shao lived in what we would call a residential area. His house stood somewhat back from the road in a garden. The gate was opened by a girl of about sixteen, his daughter, as it turned out. Mr. Shao himself received me at the front door. He was forty years old, tall and broad-shouldered, with strong features. He was wearing well-cut trousers and a clean shirt with open collar and short sleeves. We sat down in the study. A massive desk stood by the window. On the walls were a large photograph of Mao Tse-tung, one of Mr. Shao as a student with his classmates, and a few framed documents.

His daughter brought us some tea. In the ensuing conversation, guest and host not unnaturally pursued different goals: I wanted the most precise description possible of the processes by which Mr. Shao's property had been confiscated; and he made every effort to explain to me what had caused him to give up his property. In my account I will treat the two things separately. To begin, then, with the external events.

Mr. Shao's factory had been founded by his father, and when the Communists came to power in 1949 there were three owners: his father, himself, and his brother. Since his father had become ill in 1938, the management had been in the hands of my host; his brother did not take an active role in running the factory.

In 1948 the firm had shown a profit of some 100,000 yuan. (All the figures given to me by Mr. Shao were in yuan, the currency since March 1955, whose official exchange value has been set at forty US cents.) Its book value, he said, was at that time 1·2 million yuan. In the summer of 1954 Mr. Shao, with the consent of his father and brother, applied for the conversion of the firm, which had till then been a purely family business, into a 'joint public-private enterprise'.

For a whole year the firm and the political views of the Shao family were investigated by the authorities. The investigation showed, according to Mr. Shao, that he had treated his workers well and that the firm was in satisfactory financial shape. The authorities set the value of the business at 700,000 yuan. Indeed, said Mr. Shao with no change of expression, the book value of 1·2 million yuan which he had given earlier for 1948 had been somewhat higher than the actual value.

'Nevertheless,' I said, 'you did at that time show a profit of 100,000 yuan, and the State was the only body which could make you an offer.' Mr. Shao did not respond to this. When one has lost something, his expression seemed to say, it is of relatively little importance to know what it was once worth; if it's gone, it's gone. On July 1, 1955, the solemn deed took place. The State was now in actual fact the sole owner of the 'joint public-private enterprise'. Mr. Shao was appointed assistant manager of the factory at a monthly salary of 120 yuan; the manager was a trusted Party man.

For a period of seven years (later extended to ten)[46] the State pays five per cent annually to the Capitalists—which is what they were called during this time. Thus Mr. Shao was still entitled each year to five per cent of 700,000 yuan, i.e., to 35,000 yuan. He said: 'Of this amount we spend about 20,000 yuan on living expenses—that is, our family, which with my brother's and my own children consists of thirteen people. Out of the remaining 15,000 yuan we buy government bonds every year which carry four per cent interest.'

If the family does this for seven years, Mr. Shao explained, it will own some 100,000 yuan in government bonds and receive 4,000 yuan annually in interest. What the whole thing really amounts to, therefore, is that the Shao family has handed over to the State a business which had been worth between 0·7 and 1·2 million yuan in return for an annual payment of 4,000 yuan.

Such was the external course of events. I gleaned the details in fragments along with Mr. Shao's highly emphatic and personal views. Had we two been alone, I would have listened to his views with great interest. But the presence of the observer caused Mr. Shao to protest repeatedly that his decision to have the State appropriate his firm had been voluntary, that is to say, the result of his complete confidence in the CPC. He made use almost word for word of the official phraseology. 'The liberation of China from foreign domination by the Communists,' he said, for example, 'appealed to my patriotic feelings. I realized that they had only the welfare of the people at heart, and I wanted to co-operate with them. It was not easy to persuade my old father. But I finally managed to do so, and so I applied for state-ownership. I have not regretted this step. I have no more problems with the workers; I can never go bankrupt. I do not even have much to do at the plant—there are months when I spend scarcely five days at the factory. I intend to renounce the interest rates still accruing to me before the proper due date so that I can get out of the capitalist class ahead of time.'

I listened to all this in silence. The whole conversation was becoming more and more embarrassing to me, and I reproached myself for not having spared Mr. Shao and myself this hour and a half. In the presence of a third person he was obviously unable to tell me anything that had not been expounded by the Party leaders on this subject for years, let alone mention the very strong pressures to which he had been exposed.

*

The Chinese prefers indirect methods to direct ones if he thinks that with them he can attain the same ends; they cause less trouble. The Communists wanted Mr. Shao's factory *and* his co-operation. So they decided not merely to dispossess and liquidate him and others like him, but, as they put it, to 'buy him out'. Article 10 of the Constitution defines this policy in the following words:

The State makes use of the positive qualities of capitalist industry and commerce which are beneficial to national welfare and the people's livelihood, restricts their negative qualities which are not beneficial to national welfare and the people's livelihood, encourages and guides their transformation into various forms of state-capitalist economy, gradually replacing capitalist ownership with ownership by the whole people.[47]

The relevant Communist work interprets the process as follows: 'The method of step-by-step transformation . . . helped to avoid the unnecessary losses and confusion that might have resulted from abrupt changes.'[48]

The methods by which Peking persuaded the capitalists to sell out were only partially economic: increasing restriction of freedom of movement—in industry by curtailed allotment of raw materials and orders, in trade by goods-rationing; enormous retroactive payments for alleged tax arrears; frequent intervention on the part of workers and employees who in the short period between 1950 and 1954 for the first and last time really had a chance to voice their opinions—but only in private firms.

Far worse were the psychological pressure tactics; the previous owners were exposed to organized humiliations which reached their low point in the 'Five Anti' campaign of 1952. The five crimes of which each person was automatically suspected consisted of bribery of officials, tax evasion, theft of government property, fraudulence in government contracts, and theft of state economic secrets for the purpose of private speculation. Since the existence of the People's Republic, so many laws and regulations had been promulgated against private businessmen that it was not difficult to prove them guilty of any one of these crimes, or even of all five, to compel them to make public confession, and to wear them down spiritually. In nine cities alone in the course of these campaigns, out of 450,000 large, medium, and small businessmen 340,000 were found guilty.[49] The number of death sentences passed and carried out in the odious 'people's courts' was kept secret, as was the number of suicides.

*

Mr. Shao is intelligent, and he is also a Chinese. He had to ask himself whether there was any point in defending his property against the superior power of a State which was obviously determined to take it away from him. Was it not more sensible to anticipate the inevitable and so gain one or the other small advantage? To make the best of a bad job—that is an art which his people have practiced for thousands of years. And this no doubt is how he came to make his application in the summer of 1954. Presumably Mr. Shao did not pull a long face over all this, which would not have helped matters, but said instead: If I have to sacrifice my property, then it's no use crying over spilled milk —I might as well make the best of it! Many Chinese company owners felt the same way, and the rest of them were 'persuaded' by the Party. Thus during 1955 there were the grotesque parades of 're-joicing', drum-beating and cymbal-clashing 'capitalists' expressing their 'enthusiasm' at having handed over their property to the State. By the beginning of 1956 the whole process was complete.

By his attitude Mr. Shao had distinguished himself in the eyes of the Party and among the former private businessmen. As a reward he was made vice-president of the local branch of the Federation of Industry and Commerce and a member of the Standing Committee of the National Construction Association, one of the eight parties. These offices took up much more of his time than work in his former factory, and it was quite clearly his ambition to become a high official. Meanwhile he has presumably long since renounced the interest payments due to him till 1965; in return for this, he could perhaps exchange his provincial post with a corresponding one in Peking—if he did not have the bad luck to be 'unmasked as a people's enemy' and be forced, as in some parlor games, 'to go back to the beginning'.

When I told Mr. Shao as I was saying goodbye that I would be interested in knowing what effects these changes had had on the labor productivity of his factory, he replied laconically: 'The enthusiasm of the workers has greatly increased.' In what way did this enthusiasm show itself, I asked him? 'In a fifty per cent increase in daily production,' he replied.

I inquired as to whether the number of workers and machines might not have increased.

'Yes, the number of workers has risen by sixty per cent, and the government has acquired extra machinery to the value of 100,000 yuan.' His face remained impassive as he said this, looking past me.

Thus China's private business enterprises were acquired by the State. A total of 1·14 million owners 'voluntarily' gave to the State their firms valued officially at 2·42 billion yuan (but actually worth far more) against payment for ten years of 120 million yuan per year,[50] i.e., for a total of 1·2 billion yuan; of this sum almost half returned to the State immediately in the form of government bonds. The handing over was carried out in relatively orderly fashion: the services and experience of the owners, with few exceptions, were retained for the benefit of the State. Not a bad deal for the State, and more or less tolerable for the former owners—or as many of them as had survived the nightmarish period of the 'Five Anti' campaign.

In 1956 Mikoyan declared in Peking that it had not been possible to follow this path in the Soviet Union because of the close links between the Russian bourgeoisie and that of Western Europe, but that in China the 'national bourgeoisie' had first of all been much weaker than its Russian counterpart, and in the second place, having learned by the example of Russia and because of its anti-imperialist attitude, had been willing to co-operate with the working class.[51] Admittedly this is a distortion of history, but for us it is important that the Kremlin gave its blessing to Peking's policy toward the bourgeoisie in this way. In the autumn of 1961 the Kremlin went one step further: the new (third) program of the CPSU recognized the possibility of buying out the capitalists in future revolutions.[52] It is possible to see here an effect of Chinese experience on Moscow's thinking. Lenin, of course, had also fleetingly considered this possibility,[53] while the Eastern European satellite countries—before China!—used methods differing very little from Mao's.

*

One might sum up the observations made in this chapter by saying that different methods have been used in Russia and China, but the results and goals are identical.

In the Soviet Union there have never been bourgeois parties; in China they exist, but their practical significance is so slight that no one, apart from those directly involved, would notice their disappearance. The façade of the 'democratic dictatorship', however, was kept up.

After the Bolshevik victory in the Soviet Union, private ownership of the means of production ceased to exist, although the clarity of the picture is impaired by the interlude of the New Economic Policy. What the Russian Communists would do today they have shown on their experimental station, the Soviet Zone of Germany, and that closely resembles the methods we have met in China: in the Soviet Zone the large and medium-large concerns were expropriated with the excuse that they had belonged to war criminals, and the same thing happened in China with the justification that such concerns had been the property of 'enemies of the people'. The small and medium-small businesses, on the other hand—large in number, relatively small in importance—were handled rather more carefully both in China and in the Soviet Zone, and the transition to state ownership was only carried out one step at a time, with very similar methods of indirect pressure. In China as well as in the Soviet Zone, this process was completed with less friction and far smaller losses, both human and material, than in Russia.

The difference in methods is only partially explained by the fact that in China, as distinct from the Soviet Union, there was no civil war to lay waste the country after the establishment of the Communist regime, and that no serious danger threatened the country from outside. To my mind the main difference is to be found in the fact that from the very beginning Mao, with his ideas of the 'new democracy' and the 'democratic dictatorship', aimed at a more elastic, more 'Chinese', solution to this problem, without, however, deviating one iota from the Communist goal.

CHAPTER VII

THE TROUBLESOME INTELLECTUALS

How to Treat the Intelligentsia

THE PREMISE ON WHICH LENIN based his attitude toward the Russian intelligentsia is to be found in his famous work *What Is To Be Done?*, dating from 1901 and 1902; in the second chapter he deals with the question of whether the masses are capable of finding the right way by themselves. His answer is a negative one because, he says, the workers had at best a trade-union mentality aimed at an improvement of their material position, but they had no socialistic (i.e., a politically determined) awareness. Then he wrote:

The theory of socialism, however, grew out of the philosophic, historical, and economic theories elaborated by educated representatives of the propertied classes, by intellectuals. By their social status, the founders of modern scientific socialism, Marx and Engels, themselves belonged to the bourgeois intelligentsia.[1]

A great deal has been written about the terms 'intellectuals' and 'intelligentsia.'[2] The intellectuals are made up of two groups which are not identical. One consists of the members of the 'professions'—engineers, doctors, lawyers, professors, and teachers. The other consists of that much smaller number of people who do not necessarily earn their daily bread in the intellectual professions but who try to take an intellectual approach to all of life, especially their immediate social and political environment, and search for universally valid answers. In nineteenth-century Russia the term adopted for such people was 'intelligentsia'. While the majority of the intellectuals were building railways and bridges, treating the sick and teaching children, a small minority—the intelligentsia—were studying all the problems between heaven and earth, drawing up plans for a better future for humanity, throwing bombs at political dignitaries, writing novels and poetry.

To begin with Lenin saw no particular problem in the intelligentsia. They inclined—particularly the younger ones among them—in any event toward revolutionary ideas and were not considered 'class enemies'. The intellectuals among the professions, however, were another matter. Sociologically speaking they belonged to the bourgeoisie, even though they formed the wing of the bourgeoisie which—as a rule—did not own the means of production, factories, or banks, and for this reason (in Russia as well as in China) they were more prepared to co-operate with the Communists than was the capitalistic section of the bourgeoisie. But these were nuances which were not considered in Russia during the violent phase of the revolution. In those days (at the end of 1917) Lenin demanded: 'War to the death on the . . . bourgeois intellectuals.'[3]

Lenin's attitude and the consequent hostile behavior of the Bolsheviks caused numerous intellectuals to boycott the new political power, which in turn led many of them to flight or death. Needless to say, this contributed greatly to the chaos in the country. At the end of April 1918, therefore, Lenin declared that 'the epoch of utilizing bourgeois specialists by the proletarian State . . . is knocking at the door'.[4] In the months that followed, Lenin made more and more remarks in this vein; he even appointed a number of Tsarist officers to train the new Red army. In his great novel *Dr. Zhivago*, Boris Pasternak gives a penetrating account of how the intellectuals sought fulfillment in their work—the vocation of physician, for example.

With the NEP era (from 1921 on) tensions between Party and intellectuals became less acute. As the waves of the civil war subsided, the Bolsheviks loosened their grip of terror and offered the intellectuals the possibility of co-operating (although only on condition of submission, or at least of neutrality in the actual political field) at the same time appealing to their patriotic feelings. These prospects of a reconciliation between the intellectuals and the new regime extended beyond Russia to the *émigrés* as well. However, this did not last long.

*

Measures for forced integration of the intellectuals were initiated simultaneously with the campaign for the first Five-Year Plan. In 1928 the infamous Shakhty trial of a group of engineers took place; it virtually branded all intellectuals as 'parasites'. In the same year a thousand Communists, who had proved politically reliable but were found to be wanting in intellectual training, were despatched to universities and scientific institutions; these were joined in the follow-ing year by a further two thousand. In the autumn of 1929 over a hundred people were dismissed from the staff of the Academy of Sciences in Leningrad, followed soon afterwards by close to three hundred in Kiev. Many of these disappeared for ever, among them the well-known historian S. D. Platonov.

To be nonpolitical, to fail to pledge one's support of the Party's general line, had now become dangerous. In 1930 the Association of Scientists and Educators sent an official communication to the dreaded secret police expressing their gratitude for having purged their ranks of unworthy elements; and at about the same time the Congress of Physiologists elected the country's leading Party bosses to be its honorary chairmen.[5] The famous mathematician D. F. Yegorov, who ostentatiously remained faithful to the Orthodox Church, was arrested and died.

This wave of terror against the intellectuals began to recede in the summer of 1931 after a speech of Stalin's in which he warned against the 'routing' of specialists,[6] and tension between Party and intel-lectuals again relaxed. This could not repair all the damage that had been done, but it accounts for the fact that some of the old intel-lectuals, and especially their sons, are still—or again—to be found in the higher, although not in the leading, positions of Soviet economic and cultural life.[7]

A second period of terrorism coincided with the 'purges' of the years 1936 to 1938. Once again numerous renowned men of letters and science fell victim to this terror, among them the world-famous biologist N. A. Vavilov.[8] This wave of persecution was also stopped by a speech of Stalin's at the Eighteenth Party Congress (March 1939).[9] As a result the climate became more friendly, and efforts were even made—not entirely without success—to bring back the intellectual émigrés. During World War II there was a truce. When the war was over this truce came to an end with angry attacks on the political neutrality of the intellectuals; a new phase of denunciations and persecutions began.

The list of those who in one way or another were 'liquidated' in these three campaigns (1930–31, 1936–38, and 1946–49) is a long one and contains many prominent names. Even Stalin's death did not alter the basic demand for partisanship in favor of Communism, but it was applied less strictly than during his lifetime.

Meanwhile a new generation of intellectuals has emerged in the

Soviet Union, with a largely proletarian or peasant background. The great majority of them progressed in the normal way via the universities. In fact, the intellectual élite turned out to be far more 'normal' than the Party leadership cared for! This became quite clear during the attacks of the Party on the intelligentsia which, beginning late in 1962, quickly proved a major problem for the Kremlin. I have dealt elsewhere in detail with the problems arising for the State from the creation of this new intellectual upper class.[10]

*

And in China? As a young man Mao was a typical specimen of the intelligentsia in the Russian sense of the word. However, for a long time he paid but scant attention to the problem of the intellectuals, first because of his preconceived ideas about the 'proletarian' revolution, and then because of his total involvement in the mobilization of the peasants. It was not until toward the end of the thirties that he began to take a serious look at the intellectuals. As the Japanese armies threatened and then occupied the coastal areas and the cities with their universities, an increasing proportion of the professors and students fled to the interior, the great majority to the areas under national government control and a minority to Mao's domain. Up until then the Communist Party functionaries had been mainly in touch with sympathetic peasants, hostile but intimidated landowners, and unassuming members of the petty bourgeoisie of the artisan type. With the arrival of the intellectuals an unfamiliar element appeared in their midst. Mao's assessment of the situation was apparent from a resolution of the Central Committee formulated by him in December 1939. It was reminiscent of Lenin's words of 1918 (cf. page 169) and was later given the title 'Draw in Large Numbers of Intellectuals'. The following passages are to be found in it:

> . . . many cadres in the army are not yet aware of the importance of the intellectuals and are still afraid of intellectuals or even desire to keep them out of the ranks. Many of our schools still dare not freely admit young students in large numbers. Many local Party organisations are still unwilling to admit intellectuals. All this arises from a failure to understand the importance of the intellectuals for the revolutionary cause, to understand the difference between the intellectuals in colonial and semi-colonial countries and those in capitalist countries, to understand the difference between intellectuals in the service of the landlords and the bourgeoisie and in the service of the working class and the peasantry. [At this point in *Selected Works* the following sentence[11] which occurs in the original

resolution has been omitted: 'The failure to grasp these factors has resulted in certain wrong tendencies with regard to the problem of intellectuals.']. . . .

All Party organisations in the war areas as well as all armed forces led by the Party should draw in large numbers of intellectuals to join our army and our schools and to work in our government. We should by various means draw in all intellectuals who are willing to resist Japan and are relatively loyal and able to endure hardships and work hard; we should educate them, . . . At the same time we should effectively encourage the worker and peasant cadres to intensify their study and raise their cultural level. Thus the worker and peasant cadres can become intellectuals, while the intellectuals can acquire the good qualities of the worker and peasant masses.[12]

Mao looked on the intellectuals as forming part of the petty bourgeoisie,[13] which is why he usually spoke only of the 'alliance of the proletariat, peasants, petty bourgeoisie and national bourgeoisie' and seldom[14] named the intellectuals separately. In the Soviet Union the formula since Stalin's time has been: 'Workers, kolkhozniki, and toiling intelligentsia'. The word bourgeois (in revolutionary jargon: *Burzhuy*) had acquired such a negative implication in the early years of the Russian revolution that it was no longer possible to make use of it.

But Mao regarded the *chih shih fen tzu* (= knowledgeable people), i.e., the intellectuals, with mixed feelings, particularly after he had a few years' experience of them and discovered that the peasants were more willing to accept his ideas than they were. In one of his 'rectification' speeches of 1942 he told the intellectuals who turned up their noses at the workers and peasants that it was they—the intellectuals—who were 'unclean'. 'The workers and peasants are after all the cleanest persons, cleaner than both the bourgeois and the petty-bourgeois intellectuals, even though their hands are soiled and their feet smeared with cow dung.'[15]

'*Thought Reform*'

THE PROBLEMS WHICH MAO had in the Yenan period with the relatively few intellectuals multiplied when his rule began to extend over the whole country. He now decided on a course of action which has never existed in Russia in the same form: that of 'thought reform' (*ssu hsiang kai tsao* = transformation of thoughts). This took place in various stages—according to my calculation, nine so far—which to a certain extent overlap, beginning in 1949 under the maxim of 'study' (*hsüeh hsi*). At first this also looked like merely an imitation of the Russian model. While in 1920 at the Third Komsomol Congress Lenin had cried 'Learn!',[16] in China the echo was heard, 'Learn, learn, and learn again!'[17] But whereas Lenin had expected the younger generation to acquire as quickly as possible the knowledge necessary for the technical and economic development of the Soviet Union, i.e., had used the word in the European sense, to Mao, being Chinese the word 'learning' conveyed a somewhat different meaning.

Since the days of Confucius, learning has signified for the Chinese the acquisition not so much of knowledge as of principles, and their practical application in one's own life. What every Chinese, especially every intellectual, had to have drilled into him in thousands of study hours since the establishment of the People's Republic (in summer an hour and a half, in winter an hour before work began)[18] was not mathematics and mechanics but Marx and Mao.

In conversations with intellectuals in China in 1957, I tried to discover how they reacted to this method. Most of them declared that they had begun by finding it interesting; they had been prepared, they said, to meet Communism half-way since it had brought unity, peace, and order to their country after such a long period of upheaval, and they had been anxious to find out more about it. They even took a sporting interest in passing their ideological examinations with good marks. They still had no idea of what was in store for them. At first they felt no reluctance when the reins were tightened in the 'revolutionary universities' which were temporarily set up for them. It was true that in these universities they had to live at close quarters with their fellow trainees and training leaders, and they had their first taste of mutual analysis and criticism, but even this was at first nothing more than an exhilarating new experience.

The Chinese are a reserved people; because of their confined family life with its strict rules, reticence has become second nature to them. Many now found it a relief to open their hearts to their comrades and to have them do the same, the kind of relief which many people find in the confessional or on the psychoanalyst's couch. At that time everything still seemed simple: stimulated by the revolutionary changes they had just experienced, they got together, spoke their minds, discarded the old, and began a new life in a new China surrounded by like-minded comrades who were all, so to speak, in the same boat. The Party leaders must also have imagined that it would be comparatively easy to re-educate the intellectuals, and they allowed many of them to occupy leading positions in public life.

The second stage of thought reform, that of the mass campaigns, began in 1950. Its banner was a double one: on the one side they had to profess anti-Americanism, which had been whipped up during the Korean war with all the tools of propaganda and which demanded of the intellectuals something that was not easy for them to carry out—the unremitting defamation of the United States, which for decades had to most of them represented the Promised Land. On the other hand they had to take part in agrarian reform: the intellectuals were sent in tens of thousands to the rural areas to be present at the expropriation—and often the execution—of the landowners (at a mass meeting called a 'people's court'). The purpose of this was to give them practical training in class warfare, to discipline them to be relentless toward the 'class enemy', and to involve them in responsibility for the Communists' actions. By forcing them in these two campaigns publicly and against their better judgment to expose themselves and identify themselves with the regime, Mao went far beyond anything which the Confucians or Neo-Confucians, or even Lenin or Stalin, had demanded of the intellectuals.

The third phase (from 1951) brought a further intensification. It began with a five-hour speech by Chou En-lai before three thousand professors of North China at the end of September 1951,[19] in which he summoned his audience to engage in 'thought reform'. Libraries were combed for 'reactionary' literature, and the large publishing houses compelled to destroy unacceptable books. A famous publishing house in Shanghai, for example, was allowed to keep only fourteen per cent of its book stock; another had to turn 317 tons of its own books into waste paper.[20] Regulations aimed at 'suppression of counter-revolutionary actions' were applied with unprecedented severity. Thought reform, which was becoming more and more fanatical, had entirely lost the carefree cameraderie of the first stage.

This was the period of the countless 'confessions' which seem to us so incomprehensible. The official term for this procedure is—presumably on purpose—not the same as the traditional Chinese word for confession, which has a religious implication and furthermore means confession in the private and individual sense. The expression chosen by the Communists, *t'an pai* (*t'an* = plain, straight, *pai* = white, commonly: to explain), has the specific meaning of public confession and is to be heard most frequently in the form of an order: '*Ni t'an pai!*' ('You must confess!')[21]

Many of these confessions are available in European languages[22]— and they make painful reading. Side by side with self-accusations they often contain slanderous attacks on the confessor's own teachers. Since they are not written down spontaneously but are the product of weeks, often months, of strictly supervised effort, one must assume that the defamation of the teacher—that is, of the man who to the Chinese is, next to his father, the highest authority—was an inescapable feature of re-education. Among the older teachers it was Hu Shih (d. 1962) who had most often to bear the brunt of this defamation. This man, one of the leaders of the May Fourth [1919] Movement and for many years a prominent university professor, had been the idol of whole generations of learned Chinese. A large number of these confessions was quickly published, and those who had written them were forced to make public acknowledgment of their authorship. A Chinese scholar living in California, after a study of some one hundred confessions published in 1952 and 1953, has concluded that the following self-accusations are the ones which most frequently appear:[23]

Pro-Americanism. A typical example from the confession of a well-known physicist who had received his scientific training in America: 'I did not realise that the American President and the so-called government officials were slaves of the monopolistic capitalists. . . . In a word, when in 1929 I returned to China . . . my whole body had been saturated with the pernicious germs of the bourgeoisie.'

Individualism. One man confessed: 'I was deeply in love with my wife and we never parted in twenty years of married life. . . . The more children I had, the more I loved them. . . . I used to say to my wife, "We live for our children." My whole life was dominated by individualism.'

Anti-Sovietism. 'I detested the "cruelty" of the Soviet Union. . . . Since I now hate American imperialism, I unconsciously have come to know the Soviet Union as worthy of love, respect and admiration.'

Lacking the spirit of class warfare. A secondary school teacher said that his past life had been perverted by a double dose of bourgeois influence, because he was not only brought up in the family of a 'big landlord', but he married the daughter of a landlord, and 'after that my life became even more corrupt'.

*

At this point, then, we come face to face with that particular feature of Chinese Communism which has become known all over the world as 'brainwashing'. It was aimed chiefly—although not exclusively—

at the intellectuals. Officially the Chinese speak, as we have said, of 'thought reform', also of *hsin yang* (to make new), a term much in use during the Neo-Confucian period. However, the popular expression *hsi nao* (wash brain), thanks to its brutal imagery, has been adopted by the world at large. One Chinese, a member of the Politburo, told an Asian friend of mine that he found the term 'brainwashing' an excellent one even if it was not in official use.

What prompted the State to subject the upper classes, especially the intellectuals, to this procedure, is well known: it wished to commit men publicly in favor of Communism and in opposition to Communism's enemies, and, by means of the humiliation which this involved, to break their spirit; at the same time the State used the confessions as propaganda at home and abroad. But what caused the victims to react in the desired manner? Generally speaking—that is, insofar as they were not regarded as completely hostile, like the foreign missionaries—they were not subjected to physical violence. They were continuously exposed to the emotional pressures of their tormentors as well as of their environment, including their colleagues (or fellow prisoners), until they were prepared to make the desired confession, and their decision to take this step was hastened by the fact that 'everybody' was making similar confessions all around them.

Stages one to three of 'thought reform' are brought home to us in all their reality when we listen to the experiences of the men who went through them. The most outstanding study to date is that made by the American psychiatrist, Robert Lifton. After conducting tests with returning American soldiers who had been taken prisoner in the Korean war and exposed to brainwashing, he went to Hongkong in January 1954 where for seventeen months he questioned a number of persons, among them twelve Chinese intellectuals, who had been brainwashed. He had many sessions with each one of these men, in some cases up to forty hours. As a result of his investigations he defined brainwashing as a 'combination of external force or coercion with an appeal to inner enthusiasm through evangelistic exhortation which gave thought reform its emotional scope and power'.[24]

*

Lifton reconstructs in detail the case of the young leftist intellectual Hu.[25] In his youth Hu had been the victim of a tyrannical grandmother, and his hatred of her was carried over to the traditional order of things, i.e., the Chiang Kai-shek regime. In Communism Hu believed to have found not only an ally against the KMT but also a universal solution to all the problems of mankind. Although he did not actually join the CPC, he worked side by side with it, even before the Communist victory, in the Nanking underground movement. After the victory he entered a revolutionary university, full of the best intentions and with the specific object of undergoing thought reform. Because of his Marxist training he was made the leader of the group of ten to which he was assigned. Ten groups of ten formed a class, for which three 'special assistants' were responsible. In all there were about a thousand persons, most of them intellectuals, with him at the 'university'. Hu has the following to say about his early enthusiasm:

The revolutionary university seemed to be a place which brought together young people from all over with a great deal in common. We ate, slept and talked together, all of us eager to make new friends. The ten of us were at first strangers, but we quickly developed a strong bond. . . . I had very warm feelings toward the group and toward the school. I felt I was being treated well in a very free atmosphere. I was happy and thought that I was on my way to a new life.

In order to be able truly to serve the people, who so urgently needed the services of the intellectuals, he felt that he must lose no time in cutting out the poison inside him which he owed to his bourgeois origin. The others felt the same way. From early morning till late at night, discussions were held in the group of ten, sometimes also in the class of a hundred. Prominent Party men came from Peking and made long speeches which were absorbed with rapt attention and later discussed for hours on end. In the friendly atmosphere surrounding them all, no one found it difficult to talk about himself.

The first clouds appeared on the horizon when Hu found himself under increasing pressure to report on his nine group comrades. He said to Lifton: 'My intention was to help the students to their study about Communism, but I soon began to realize that the Communists were more interested in my helping them to study the students.' Hu inwardly resisted these attempts to make use of him as a spy, but he was not entirely able to escape the suggestion of the 'special assistants' that there was a moral justification and obligation for him to supply reports on his comrades, as in this way he would be furthering the advance of backward students.

Toward the end of the course, Hu, like all the others, had to compose a 'thought summary'. Each one had to write down in what way the course had changed him. The essays were then handed round and discussed in the group. At this point the students in the group felt uncomfortable about expressing their thoughts freely; they realized that what they said would be passed on 'to the top'. The old confidence was gone. Suspicion took its place and tensions arose.

The main accusation to which Hu saw himself exposed was that of individualism. He did not deny this, and he suffered because he was incapable of dedicating himself to the great common cause as wholeheartedly as was expected of him. If he could discipline himself completely, they told him, there were prospects of a brilliant Party career. But he felt increasingly ill at ease. 'I felt disappointed . . . infuriated and disgusted.' Hu was still in favor of Communism, but he had the feeling he was becoming ever more deeply entangled in dangerous webs. He did as he was told and confessed to 'crimes' of his youth, contacts with 'reactionary' groups, friendships with 'backward' girls, his background of a 'rural ruling class' family. The more he surrendered, the more he was praised, but the greater also became his disenchantment. He discovered that the same thing was happening to his comrades, at least to those who were no longer boys, but twenty-five years old or more. The infectious enthusiasm was giving way to an equally infectious disillusionment. Hu began to note increasing signs of nervous ailments and insomnia among his comrades. (No wonder, if we consider the extreme reticence of the Chinese, that, although in the first flush of enthusiasm they were eager to talk about themselves, they finally broke down under the ceaseless demands for constant exposure of their most intimate emotional and mental recesses.) Soon after his training period was over, Hu took the first opportunity that offered and left Red China.[26]

*

That which in Hu's case, the case of a sincere sympathizer, had been attempted by psychological, intellectual, and emotional means, was undertaken in the case of people who were regarded as enemies by brute force—by physical torture, starvation, thirst, and torments of every kind. This torture lasted until the victim succumbed and yielded up the desired declarations, but was renewed with fresh violence in order to force him to new despair, to a still further capitulation; and for every new and increasingly painful step he was

promised the reward of happiness in harmony with the world of today and tomorrow—a process which was repeated again and again
until the victim's spirit was utterly broken. As long ago as 1942, in
Yenan, Mao had given a simple prescription for this 'cure' when he
compared the treatment of the ideological deviationist with that of a
sick person:

... we must begin by administering a shock and shouting at the patient,
'You are ill!' so that he is frightened into a sweat, and then we tell him
gently that he needs treatment.[27]

From a Chinese who was for a long time a leader of the CP but
who veered off in 1938 and moved to Hongkong, we know that at the
end of the twenties the Chinese Communists were already experimenting with brainwashing on captured KMT soldiers.[28] They later
applied their knowledge to captured Japanese, and in the Korean war
to American prisoners, but what they considered most important of
all was the re-education of their own people.

The purpose of brainwashing was always to bring about the break
with a man's past and family background, with the liberal, Western-
influenced outlook of his youth, in short: with his own identity (to
use the psychologists' term). To force a man to defame his own
father—this was an essential ingredient of the 'treatment', a complete
contradiction of the teaching of Confucius: 'The father conceals the
misconduct of the son, and the son conceals the misconduct of the
father.'[29] In order to prevent a mere outward conformity by this
method, which for the Chinese with their 'shame culture' (cf. page
10) was not difficult, the Communists dug up a maxim which is
probably older than Confucius and occurs in ancient legends:[30] *shen
tu* (to keep watch alone), i.e.: 'When you are alone, watch over
yourself!' It is significant that such an out-and-out exponent of the
Russian 'guilt culture' as Tolstoy noted this imperative with satisfaction.[31] The object of all these efforts was the creation of a new
personality—without ties to family, friends, or society, a docile tool,
free of all human considerations, in the hands of the Party.

Something of this kind has existed in the Soviet Union. It was from
the Russian Communists that the Chinese drew their methods, applied
by them a million times over, of criticism, self-criticism, unmasking,
confession (often of the most absurd kind), and above all emphasis
on guilt-consciousness and what can only be called wallowing in
guilt feelings, something which to the Chinese was unnatural, but

which in Orthodox Russia has for many centuries been far from uncommon. But in the Soviet Union this method was not applied to whole classes or professions; it was concentrated mainly on the 'Party enemies', who, before they were turned over to outward extermination, were subjected to 'inner destruction', as a prominent Russian, Bucharin, put it at his trial. The world came to know of these methods during the mock trials of the thirties; in addition there were the first-hand reports of former Communists, of which Wolfgang Leonhard's is the most famous,[32] and the fictional descriptions, the best of which is Arthur Koestler's first-rate novel, *Darkness at Noon*, authentic in atmosphere and based on his own observations.[33]

*

In Russia, the idea of thought as potential action is not unknown,[34] but it arose comparatively late there, in the nineteenth century, and never achieved more than a moderate significance. In China, however, it goes back to ancient times and has always been taken for granted. It is the foundation of 'The Great Learning', one of the Four Books of Confucianism. This book contains the following passage, which for thousands of years has been part of the very lifeblood of the Chinese:

Through the differentiation of things one arrives at complete knowledge; from complete knowledge one arrives at sincerity of purpose; from sincerity of purpose one arrives at the direction of the heart; and from the direction of the heart one arrives at the care of one's own person. When one's own personality is cared for, the family is in good order; when the family is in good order, the State is well governed; and when each individual State is well governed, the whole empire enjoys peace.[35]

All action, all happiness, therefore, depended on right knowledge. It might be pointed out here that Mao also gave his work 'On Practice' (1937) the subtitle 'On the Relation Between Knowledge and Practice—Between Knowing and Doing'.

From this doctrine the thinkers of the Sung period reasoned that man must learn much, then one day everything will become clear to him.[36] Everyone who knows China has noticed (cf. page 27) that lessons there consist mainly of ceaseless repetition of what the teacher says, of repeated reading of the same texts. If someone expressed surprise to the teachers at this method, he was likely to receive the same reply as Lily Abegg describes: If anyone repeats a phrase often enough, she was told, its meaning will eventually become clear to him.[37]

This conception underlying the principle of brainwashing reminds me of Franz Kafka's cruel but brilliant story, *In the Penal Colony*, in which, in his own surrealistic style, he describes an execution machine. This machine consists of a glass sheet called a 'Harrow', on which needles were arranged in letters to form a phrase unknown to the condemned man. Through a vibrating motion the needles slowly bore deeper and deeper into the back of the victim, who is strapped face down on a 'Bed' underneath the 'Harrow', until, shortly before he dies, he suddenly recognizes the words spelled out by the needles. Kafka has the enthusiastic demonstrator of this apparatus say to the foreign visitor:

> But how quiet he grows at just about the sixth hour! Enlightenment comes to the most dull-witted. It begins around the eyes. From there it radiates. . . . The man begins to understand the inscription, he purses his mouth as if he were listening. You have seen how difficult it is to decipher the script with one's eyes; but our man deciphers it with his wounds. To be sure, that is a hard task; he needs six hours to accomplish it.[38]

Here again the Russians are European: learning and understanding are for them rational, not automatic processes. Although of course one comes across senseless 'cramming' in the Soviet Union, there is no belief in 'sudden revelation'. I would even think that the 'purgings' in their own ranks amounted to an admission that there were too many 'unenlightened' for them to be taught rationally, and thus the only solution was to remove them bodily. In this respect the Chinese Communists were more optimistic. And they had dire need of their optimism.

The Russian Communists acceded to power in a country which was economically further developed than China was at the time of Mao's victory. It was thus easier for them to be Marxist, i.e., to suppose that change of environment would (except for the incorrigibles) automatically change people, that the main thing, therefore, was to rouse the 'proletarian consciousness' already created by the beginnings of industrialization, hidden though this consciousness might still be. This was the automatic process in which they believed. Stalin did not think much anyway of discussions and theoretical re-education. As early as 1925, when it was still possible to speak fairly freely in the Soviet Union, he had warned: 'One must not carry discussion too far.' Later on he attacked the 'obsession with the system of propaganda by study groups'. He preferred obedience without discussion.

It is true that Stalin wanted to change consciousness more quickly than he was capable of changing environment, but for this purpose he made use less of persuasion than of terrorism, holding himself up more and more as the years went by as a standard for others. A Communist was a man who acknowledged Stalin to be right in everything. All others he removed—by the hundred thousand, by the million. Hence the zeal for re-education had its limits in Russia; but not in China. In the very first weeks after taking over, the Chinese Communists set to work to alter human nature from the inside out. In view of the economic backwardness of their country there was, as they well knew, no proletarian consciousness waiting to be roused. On the contrary, it had to be newly created. Victory had fallen into their hands so suddenly after the long struggle that they set off in seven-league boots to bring about by force a development in the intellectual superstructure for which the material basis did not yet exist.

*

This is shown by the extraordinary vigor with which the Chinese pursued their 'campaigns', as compared to which those that usually take place in the Soviet Union—unpleasant though they may be for the individual—are harmless ('overfulfilment of the plan', 'in honor of the coming Party Congress Day', 'out of enthusiasm over Gagarin's space flight', etc.). In China, these campaigns are carried out in a manner reminiscent of Kafka's surrealism; one has only to think of the demonstrations of thanks and rejoicing on the part of the abused and expropriated capitalists, or the campaign for the extermination of flies, one of whose phases I saw at first hand.

All China was chasing flies; no one was without a fly-swatter beside him on his desk, and in the middle of the conversation one's companion would slap at a fly to fulfil his quota. I shall never forget the train conductor with whom I traveled for a whole day through Manchuria. He paid hardly any attention to his passengers, but crept through the corridors, crouched like a panther, for ever on the lookout for new victims, which he then liquidated with the fly-swatter.

The campaign against the sparrows was in the highest degree revolting. The birds were to be exterminated because they feed among other things on grain. It did not reach its climax till the following year, and an eyewitness reported as follows:

The day of the great sparrow extermination I was in Hangchow. It was Sunday, May 18, 1958. The entire adult population went up on the roof-tops and banged away for hours to produce a tremendous noise. The terrified sparrows stayed in the air till they were overcome by exhaustion, which took about two hours. Then followed the destruction of the birds, in which the children took part in the streets.[39]

In Peking the 'battle orders' for that day demanded that the popu-lation let the sparrows neither eat, drink, nor rest. Everyone was to take part vigorously and bravely in the battle, and hold out to the end in revolutionary zeal: no troops would be drawn off until final victory had been achieved.[40] Later, of course, it was discovered that the birds feed not only on grain but on grain-destroying insects; the excessive increase of pests after the sparrow-murders was to contribute to the crop failures of the years 1959 to 1961. After that, among the four pests to be combated, the sparrows were replaced by bedbugs.

Although, as far as the industrialization of their country was con-cerned, the Russian Communists started out under more auspicious conditions than their Chinese comrades, their expectations were more modest in regard to the likelihood of changing people. In the chapter called 'The Russian Character' in my book, *Soviet Man*, I have described the attempts of the Kremlin to tame certain characteristics of the Russian, for example, his 'expansive Russian soul'. In doing so the Kremlin was acting contrary to the Russian character, but it was, partially at least, in harmony with the development which was taking place. Even without Bolshevism, the West European and the Ameri-can, through industrialization, urbanization, universal education, and other features of our modern times, have become better able to meet the exigencies of the new age than their grandfathers were. The same thing would have happened to the Russian—with or without Bol-shevism. Naturally Moscow wanted to have a population at its disposal which thought only of carrying out Party directives, but the Kremlin leaders proceeded less radically than the Chinese, and slowed down when they saw that this zeal did more harm than good to their cause—as was the case with their attacks against the family. Starting in the early thirties the Bolsheviks concentrated their efforts on such goals of re-education as benefited technical-economic modernization (steadiness, industriousness, punctuality, sense of time), that is to say, on realizable aims.

The Chinese, however, very soon went beyond that and set their sights at the distant goal of total Communism, of the socialization

not only of things but of human beings. This will be clearly evident in
the chapter dealing with the people's communes.

In 1952 the nightmare of brainwashing more or less came to an
end; the Party seemed to be satisfied with the results. The ensuing
period of almost two years could be called the fourth stage in the
policy of the CPC toward the intellectuals, the stage of comparative
peace. The fifth began in the fall of 1954 with a new attack, directed
primarily against the writers; this will be described at the end of this
chapter. The violence of this attack also spread to the other intellectuals. These latter—including the technicians who were so vital to
the State—became so deeply disturbed that finally it was only with
the greatest reluctance that they fulfilled the tasks set them by the
State. This was pushing matters further than had been intended, and
so, early in 1956, efforts were renewed to gain the confidence and
positive co-operation of the intellectual class.

This new stage, the sixth, was to last until June 1957 and to go
down in history as the episode of the Hundred Flowers. It began in
January 1956 with a Party conference on questions concerning the
intellectuals. On this occasion Chou En-lai promised the intellectuals
better living conditions and less time to be spent on political training,
and he laid part of the blame for a certain coolness between intellectuals and Party on the Party cadres.[41] In March 1956 the *People's
Daily* published an article demanding that greater efforts be made
than in the past to bring intellectuals into the CPC.[42] (Until that time
it had been chiefly the non-Communist 'parties' which had been open
to the intellectuals.) Simultaneously enticing offers were made to
some ten thousand Chinese intellectuals living abroad to return to
China.[43]

Sowing of the Hundred Flowers

ON MAY 2, 1956, Mao made a speech. As far as I know it has never
been published, but two weeks later Lu Ting-yi, Director of the
Propaganda Department of the CPC Central Committee, made known
its contents:

> To artists and writers, we say, 'Let flowers of many kinds blossom.'
> To scientists we say, 'Let diverse schools of thought contend.' This is the
> policy of the Chinese Communist Party. It was announced by Chairman
> Mao Tse-tung at the Supreme State Conference.[44]

The first part of this slogan (*pai hua ch'i fang*) originated with Mao himself; he had already used these words in 1951 (in speaking about a reform of Chinese drama),[45] but at that time they did not attract much attention. The second half (*pai chia cheng ming*) has a classical origin and signifies China's great spiritual and intellectual period from the sixth to the third centuries B.C., the period in which not only Confucianism but almost all the great philosophical and religious systems of China developed.

There is no doubt that this reference to China's Golden Age awakened many hopes among the intellectuals. But while in other countries imagination was captured by Mao's picturesque expression as such, the Chinese took note of the many reservations which Lu emphasized. Art and literature were, he said, part of the class struggle —no liberty should be accorded the enemies of the revolution, the only way to deal with them was by the path of dictatorship. 'A clear political line must be drawn between friend and foe.' He added threateningly: 'The work of ferreting out hidden counter-revolutionaries has not yet been completed.' As a weapon against these he called for the kind of criticism 'that kills at a blow'.[46]

In a commentary on Mao's speech, Kuo Mo-jo, President of the Academy of Science, cautioned against misunderstandings. He compared the 'hundred schools' contending with each other to a hundred musicians in an orchestra who could not play as each happened to feel but had to abide by the music:

> We want to 'contend' but we must not do so in confusion. . . . We not only 'contend'; we must contend properly and contend in such a way as to advance socialist construction. If you contend in confusion or beat the instruments any way you want to, then other people will simply cover their ears or even ask you to leave the concert hall.[47]

It is not surprising that most of the intellectuals continued to keep quiet. Relations with the Party remained tense, although there were increasing signs of relaxation. In this one can discern, as in the other countries of the Communist bloc, a consequence of the de-Stalinization process which had begun early in the year, at the Twentieth Party Congress of the CPSU. These signs became especially noticeable in the late summer of 1956—when 'flowers' began to bloom in Poland and Hungary. In the University of Peking lectures were scheduled on the philosophy of Hegel and Bertrand Russell;[48] the number of newspapers and magazines emanating from non-Communist countries soared and overtook those originating from the

Eastern bloc;[49] and the Peking *People's Daily* declared that students should be trained to think for themselves.[50]

On February 27, 1957, Mao made another speech, the famous 'On the Correct Handling of Contradictions Among the People', which, however, was not published until four months later, and then, as was admitted, in revised form.[51] But the main contents of this speech reached the public from articles in the Party press and from the reports of the many people who had heard the lecture. By the end of April it was generally known what Mao had said in this speech.[52]

Despite what had happened the previous autumn in Poland and Hungary, Mao spoke on this occasion in favor of a better under-standing between Party and intellectuals, an understanding he had begun to promote nine months earlier in his Hundred Flowers speech. The differences between them (unless they actually belonged to the enemy camp) and the Party were not of an 'antagonistic' (i.e., irrecon-cilable) kind, and for that reason were not to be settled by brutal methods, but rather by objective discussion and reasoning—'like a gentle breeze and a soft rain'. Mao expressly called for frank criti-cism of Party measures.

Marxists should not be afraid of criticism from any quarter. Quite the contrary, they need to steel and improve themselves and win new positions in the teeth of criticism and the storm and stress of struggle. Fighting against wrong ideas is like being vaccinated—a man develops greater immunity from disease after the vaccine takes effect. Plants raised in hot-houses are not likely to be robust.

A number of well-known intellectuals ventured out onto the thin ice of open criticism: the German-trained Chang Po-chun called for a speedy development of the non-Communist parties and their amal-gamation; Lo Lung-chi, who had received his doctorate from New York's Columbia University and who complained of the undignified treatment of intellectuals, recalled the old saying: 'A scholar would rather accept death than humiliation'; and Professor Fei Hsiao-t'ung, also well known in the West because of his books on China's social structure, expressed the fear that a sudden political frost might destroy the Hundred Flowers.[53]

As these and similar pronouncements went by unchallenged by the Communist propaganda machine, and indeed were printed verbatim in the Party newspapers, the courage of the intellectuals grew. The man responsible for the co-ordination of the CPC with the non-Communist parties even requested from them an 'uninhibited

contending, frank criticism, and criticism without reserve'.[54] More
and more intellectuals dared to utter an honest opinion without being
called to account for it. The actual eruption started in the middle of
May.

I was then in Hongkong, and I could scarcely believe my eyes when
I saw what was being written every day in the Red Chinese newspapers, which at that time were being fairly freely exported: on the
necessity of an amalgamation of a number of non-Communist
organizations in one large party of intellectuals;[55] and on the 'cleft
between Communists and non-Communists'.[56] A professor at the
People's University in Peking, founded in 1950 as a training-center of
Communism, declared in public meetings:

> There is a shortage of pork and the people cannot get it. Some call this a
> higher standard of living, but who are the people who enjoy the higher
> standard? They are the Party members and cadres who used to wear
> worn-out shoes but now ride in luxury cars and wear woollen uniforms. . . .
> The 'I-am-the-state' attitude you [the Party members] hold cannot be
> tolerated. . . . You must not be arrogant and conceited, you must not
> distrust the intellectuals. If you do well, fine; if not, the masses will knock
> you down, will kill the Communists, and overthrow you. And they cannot
> be considered unpatriotic, inasmuch as the Communists no longer serve
> the people. The downfall of the Communist Party will not be the downfall
> of China.[57]

*

This Chinese spring of 1957—as distinct from the Polish 'spring in
October' of the previous year—lasted exactly a month. There is in
existence an entire book of incontestable quotations taken direct
from the Red Chinese press during these extraordinary weeks.[58]

The Party's counter-offensive, ushering in the seventh stage of its
policy toward the intellectuals, began with editorials in the *People's
Daily* on June 8, 9, and 10 which once again called for an attack on the
enemies of the revolution. Within a few days the hue and cry after all
those who had uttered critical comments in the previous weeks was
in full swing. A wave of denunciations, and soon also of confessions
on the part of those attacked, flooded the country.

Early in July 1957, after a trip to Japan, I set foot for the first time
in eleven years on the Chinese mainland, in Shanghai. In the hotel
the first thing I came across was the latest edition of the Chinese
newspaper (still being published at that time) in the Russian language,
Drushba (= Friendship), containing the translation of an editorial

which had appeared a few days earlier in the *People's Daily* and which contained the following passage:

To publish no or little positive views and to refrain from counter-criticizing the erroneous views for a certain period of time—is that wrong? From May 8 to June 7, our paper and all Party papers carried out exactly this policy in accordance with the directive of the CPC Central Committee. The purpose is to let the evil spirits and demons of all kinds 'contend freely' and to let the poisonous weeds gain a luxuriant growth so that the people will be startled at such things and will take action to wipe out these low scamps. That is to say, the Communist Party sees an inevitable class struggle between the bourgeoisie and the proletariat. The bourgeoisie and bourgeois intellectuals are allowed to start this war; for a time our press carries no or little positive views and deals no counter-blows to the frantic attacks of the bourgeois reactionaries and rightists; for a time also the Party organizations in all organs and schools carrying on the rectification campaign deal no counter-blows to such frantic attacks. Thus the masses are enabled to see clearly what criticisms are well-intentioned and what so-called criticisms are ill-intentioned, so that forces may be concentrated and counter-blows are dealt when the time is ripe. Some say: this is a dark scheme. We say: this is an open scheme. For we told the enemy before-hand: demons can be wiped out only when they are let out of the cage and poisonous weeds can be got rid of only when they are allowed to come out of the soil. Do peasants not weed several times a year? The weeds removed can be used as fertilizer.[59]

In the weeks that followed I was constantly meeting Chinese intellectuals. But after the barrage of attacks which they had had to endure on and after June 8, they were apprehensive and reserved—with the exception of the students. One Sunday toward the end of July, on my way back from the Summer Palace to Peking, I passed the university gate. Years ago I had frequently visited the university; now I thought I would like to see what had become of it.

I was stopped by watchmen, but after some discussion they let me through the gate. Then I found myself once again in the great park among the familiar lecture halls and dormitories, and once again enjoyed the architectural style, a happy blend of traditional-Chinese with modern-Western; there was a noble rhythm to the curves of the green-tiled roofs above the gray walls. One could not deny that the buildings looked dilapidated and neglected compared with earlier days, as is the case with so much in the China of today (apart from the buildings kept up for display purposes). I wrote down my impressions of the next few hours shortly afterwards in my hotel. I will give them again here now; only a few details, which I did not find out till later, have been added since.

The university vacation having started on July 1, I expected to walk through an empty park, and I was surprised to see students everywhere. The main road crossing the university grounds was particularly crowded. In the square in the middle of the campus hundreds of students were standing around. What gave this square and the main road a strange appearance were the countless hand-written and handdrawn posters and notices which had been affixed to special billboards and in some cases to the buildings.

I got into conversation with some of the students. 'Don't you have any vacation then?' I asked. 'Oh yes, we do,' one of them said, and pulled a face.

'Well?' I inquired.

'We have to stay behind,' he said, 'we've already been here for weeks.'

'But why?' I asked. The following picture emerged from their answers.

When Mao Tse-tung's appeal for frank criticism of all abuses was publicized at the end of April, at first no one dared to utter a sound. But in mid-May the wave of public criticism began. On May 19 a few posters appeared in the university grounds. They were allowed to remain, and the next day there were hundreds all over the walls.

It must have been a kind of ecstasy which seized the students, an ecstasy of freedom. One wrote in huge letters, 'road of freedom', another 'road of truth', on that very road where all this was happening; and the great wall which they covered all over with placards was called by the students the 'democratic wall'. An intensely active 'Hundred Flowers Society' was founded; its motto was: 'Marxism is obsolete'.

If criticism was at first directed toward bad living conditions (the food, the cramped barrack-like quarters shared by six or eight students) a political note soon began to creep in. 'Why always only Russian physics and chemistry? Is there no research going on in other countries as well?' was written on one placard; or even more force-fully: 'In America the students read Khrushchev's secret speech long ago. We want to read it too!' (The following day extracts from the secret speech of February 25, 1956, were in fact put up on one of the walls.) 'Why does the Party interfere in the affairs of the university? Science can only flourish in the air of freedom.' One of the students, Lin Hsi-ling, although a member of the CPC, made impassioned speeches attacking the new class State in which they were living, as well as the Party cadres, whom she described as being as useless as rotten eggs.

The students reeled off so many slogans from those few weeks during the spring that I could hardly write them down fast enough:

'Marxism is dogmatism.'

'Communist society makes human beings inhuman.'

'The *People's Daily* is a prison wall behind which truth is dying.'

'A student who failed his examinations joined the Party and was given a grant.'

'Free choice of reading matter!'

'Free choice of career!'

After all the muzzling and dogmatizing, these days of freedom were an immense and exhilarating experience, in many ways similar to the upsurge which took place in Poland and Hungary in 1956. Spring in October—that was what they had said in Warsaw, and in the spring of 1957 on the walls of the Peking University hung a poster: 'It is still winter, but spring will come.' Faculty members also took part, and some of this criticism got into the press and had repercussions beyond the university. At a university in Tientsin placards were saying 'Capitalism is more democratic than socialism' and 'We've had enough of the Communist bandits!'

This went on for about three weeks. But on May 27 it was announced that two days earlier Mao had declared: 'Words and actions which depart from socialism are bad.' Men arrived from the city with long ladders and pots of white paint and wrote this sentence on a wall in the main square; with bitter looks the students pointed out the still clearly visible characters.

The first Communist counter-attacks were heard. Students who were in the service of the Party tried to answer the opposition's questions and accusations. The posters were removed and replaced by pious proclamations of loyalty—the very ones I now saw on all the walls. The students were told that the last few weeks had proved that a great many of them were ideologically immature, and therefore they could not be allowed to go on vacation on July 1. Instead they would have to undergo a period of serious self-examination; how long this would last was something that time would show.

'And here we are, right in the middle of it,' said one student. 'Every evening there is a meeting here in the main square at which the individual cases of wrong thinking are gone through. This usually lasts several hours.'

'Does everyone have to take part?' I asked.

'Oh, yes, because anyone who didn't come would be revealing his wickedness.'

'And what do you do during the daytime?' I inquired.

'Then we have to get together in small groups, usually fifteen of us, and go through whatever was discussed the evening before at the meeting. We criticize each other and practice self-criticism.' They said this quietly and unemotionally, but one could see from their faces how the whole thing filled them with disgust.

Meanwhile I had noticed a commotion going on in the middle of the square. A small stage was there, looking somewhat like a scaffold, and I went over to it. A placard with writing in red ink on it had been stuck on a post. At the front edge of the 'scaffold' stood a student, his hair wild, eyes staring, head bent, silent; beside and behind him stood a group of twelve or fifteen students, all shouting at him. This lasted several minutes; the shouts got fiercer and more menacing. The student with the staring eyes was mute. Finally the others knocked him off the stage, and he disappeared into the crowd.

'What was all that about?' I asked.

'The placard on the post had been written by that student during the weeks of criticism. Now they accuse him and say the words on the poster were antisocialist and rightist-oppositionist. But on the poster he did not only speak for himself. It said that many others thought as he did. Now they want him to name his comrades who share his views.'

'That's something he obviously didn't do,' I said.

'But he will,' replied the students. 'He is just about through with his university course. He has got this far with a tremendous amount of effort, and his whole family helped him. If he doesn't name his comrades, all his work will be wasted.'

'How's that?' I asked.

'Very simple. A few days ago [on July 20] a government resolution was passed whereby in future every student has to produce proof of being ideologically reliable before he can get a job.'

'There is one thing I can't understand,' I said to one student when I was alone with him for a little while. 'How could you ever have believed that you could express your opinions without being punished for it? After all, you have been living long enough under this regime.'

'We students are quite simply the victims of deliberate propaganda,' he replied. 'Just think for a minute of that editorial in the

People's Daily [of July 1]! After all, it said there quite clearly that they wanted to lure us into a trap. Many of us today believe that the first posters with critical comments which we saw here in May were put up by *agents provocateurs*. In any case, we noticed that, when the Party took action later on, none was taken against the men who had put up the first posters.'

On August 1 the government published a further resolution which brought the crisis in the relations between State and students into sharp relief. This resolution provided for forced labor for persons acting 'against socialism' or refusing to carry out the manual labor duties assigned to them. The most detestable feature of this resolution was the part in which universities and even parents were instructed to give the names of students who were to be punished in this way. The forced labor was to be carried out in factories and agricultural enterprises specially set up for the purpose. The *People's Daily* was not ashamed to claim in its editorial that these barbaric measures demonstrated once again 'the care which the socialist State bestows on the future life of socially harmful elements'.[60]

Although the resolution did not specifically refer to students, it was generally felt to be aimed at the academic youth of the country; it was an admission of serious defeat of the State *vis-à-vis* the young intellectuals.

*

What I saw on that Sunday evening at the University of Peking was going on simultaneously all over China. In tens of thousands, the people who had taken Mao's call for frank criticism seriously were being dragged before tribunals. In Wuhan three students were publicly executed. Countless confessions of remorse were published. (Chang Po-chun: 'I hate myself'; Lo Lung-chi: 'I am ashamed of myself'; Fei Hsiao-t'ung 'thanked the Party for "clubbing me in order to awaken me in good time"'.)[61] Children publicly accused their 'wicked fathers'.

After postponing its session twice the National People's Congress —the Red Chinese 'Parliament'—met at the end of June for a few weeks. On the very first day it heard from Chou En-lai's lips a number of angry accusations of the intellectuals. I attended several of these sessions of Congress and heard some of the declarations of remorse. The following scene is one I shall never forget.

One speaker had just finished. The next one stepped up to the rostrum on the stage of the great hall, formed by roofing over what had been a courtyard in the western section of the former 'Forbidden City' (on the South Lake). I sat on a bench in the box reserved for the press. When the newcomer began to speak, it seemed to me the Chinese journalists around me showed more interest than they had in the words of his predecessor, as if there were a certain tension in the air.

'Who is that?' I asked one of my neighbors.

'The Secretary General of the Peasants' and Workers' Party,' was the answer. This was a man who had been attacked several times in the past few weeks as belonging to the 'rightist opposition'.

But after a few insignificant phrases the tension relaxed; people who had stood up to see better sat down again. Several minutes passed. Then suddenly the speaker's voice cracked, and his words turned to sobs. The whole room was electrified; in the press section many people jumped up and dashed to the balustrade separating us from the hall. I saw the speaker wipe away his tears with a handker-chief. This went on for a while—a few sentences, then sobs and tears. Every time he dried his eyes he had to take off his glasses. What kind of spiritual tortures had this man undergone that had caused him to humiliate himself so abjectly? The assembly listened in stony silence, yet at the same time spellbound, as if they were watching an execution. But Chou En-lai, who was sitting on the stage with the presidium, ostentatiously carried on an animated conversation. Nothing could have shown more clearly his contempt for the weeping man and the whole drama as it was staged by the Communists.

The rest of the year 1957 was spent in witch hunts of one kind or another, and it was only toward the end of that year that the situation began to calm down. The acute struggle characterizing the seventh stage had come to an end. Some of those who had been singled out for special reprimand turned up again in public life, although shorn of all influence. As a result of pressure from above, the intellectuals carried on a new campaign of submissiveness under the slogan of 'to give one's heart [to the Party]'.

In spite of all this, however, one is bound to wonder whether the editorial in the *People's Daily* of July 1 which greeted me when I landed in Shanghai and which represented the whole episode of the month of criticism as having been a Party trick to unmask its enemies, told the whole truth. Had it really been only for this purpose that Mao had called for criticism, as the students in Peking had told me?

Perhaps, but looking back I am more inclined to think that, until May 1957, Mao had been a prisoner of his own illusions as to the people being united behind the Party, believing that Peking, unlike Budapest, could afford to open the flood gates of criticism, since, apart from a few enemies, all China agreed with him in principle, including the intelligentsia and even more so the younger intellectual generation, the students. When Mao realized between May and the beginning of June that this was by no means the case, it must have been a rude shock. If my reasoning is correct, the editorial of July 1 must be explained by the desire of the Party to conceal its loss of face due to its utter miscalculation by claiming that that was exactly what it had intended all along. What actually did happen, how much truth there was in the rumors of serious differences of opinion between Mao and other Party leaders, we shall probably never know.

One thing is indisputable: the extent and violence of the criticism in those four weeks came as a great surprise to the whole world, even to the critically-inclined among the Chinese themselves. If they had till then believed that each was alone in his criticism, they now knew that countless others thought as they did.

The years of thought reform and brainwashing, it now turned out, appeared to have been in vain. That is the vital lesson of the summer of 1957. From the point of view of the Party, the flowers had turned out to be thistles; the illusion of cordial relations with the intellectuals dissolved. Moreover—and this was of the utmost significance for the policy of the CPC in the eighteen months that followed—all hope was gone of possessing an army of intellectuals, politically reliable and ready to aid in the rapid transformation of underdeveloped China into an industrial nation. This realization may have contributed to the decision to concentrate first of all on the muscle power of five hundred million peasants, and to subject the entire population to a still stricter, barrack-like discipline: in other words, to the decision to establish the people's communes.

*

The eighth stage of the Party's policy toward China's intellectual class can be defined as an armistice in an atmosphere of mutual suspicion. The Party had not yielded any of its positions, and the intellectuals maintained their spiritual aloofness from the state and, like their Russian colleagues, tried to retreat into non-political realms, a kind of spiritual emigration. Like the Soviet Party press, the Chinese Party press complained that the experts in the arts and sciences preferred non-political subjects; the historians in particular were accused of 'emphasizing the past and neglecting the present' (*hou ku po chin*).

Further attempts toward a rapprochement with the intellectuals were made by the Party on various occasions after the late summer of 1960. In some respects the Party's vocabulary in this, the ninth, stage recalled that of 1956–57, with the result that here and there a new Hundred Flowers period in China was spoken of. But the difference is unmistakable: in the earlier period the Party had, at any rate after Mao's speech on contradictions, called for frank and general criticism, but now criticism was expressly limited to academic matters and was required to strengthen the 'democratic dictatorship', 'socialism', and the leadership of the people by the Party. After the experiences of 1957 it is not surprising that this watered-down version of the Hundred Flowers failed to impress the intelligentsia.[62]

When we look at Mao's intellectual policy from 1949 till today, we find that, by a shrewd combination of appeals to patriotism, fear, idealism, mob instinct, and the will to live, men can be made to do and say certain things and not to do and not to say certain other things. But does this alter these men in substance, or even in their convictions? We cannot yet give a final answer to this question, but what we have seen to date appears to confirm that changes in a person last only as long as the 'treatment' and the immediate after-effects. American psychiatrists, alarmed by the behavior of US soldiers in Korean and Chinese prisoner-of-war camps, have made a highly intensive study of this formerly little known phenomenon and have come to the conclusion that in the case of these men brainwashing has not resulted in any lasting alteration of character or personality.[63] As far as the Chinese victims of brainwashing are concerned, Lifton's previously mentioned book contains striking accounts of how these men—some quickly, some more slowly—in the freedom of Hongkong gradually lost their habit of staring into space, their so-called 'thousand mile stare', and returned to normal.

But brainwashing must not be underestimated. It can be very effective for obtaining tactical results as, for instance, when under its pressure American prisoners-of-war accused their own country over the Red Chinese radio of using bacteriological weapons in the Korean war although they knew this was not true. It is possible that certain highly sensitive individuals may suffer lasting damage. However, the summer of 1957 has taught us that it is not so easy to change the nature of a whole nation, the Chinese included, by brainwashing. The men around Mao evidently realized this too; brainwashing as a mass phenomenon is no longer in evidence. Faith in the magic powers of thought reform has obviously given way to a more sober view.

It is, therefore, to say the least an unjustified exaggeration for the historian Riencourt to declare summarily that 'what was left of independent minds' in China had been 'brainwashed'.[64] Lifton is more likely to be correct when he describes the great majority of Chinese intellectuals today as 'adapters' and says of them:

> In a historical sense, the adapter was following a long-established pattern of Chinese intellectuals: accepting the change in dynasty as part of the order of things, placing his talents at the disposal of the new rulers, and seeing in the reign both good and evil, but not enough good to win his absolute enthusiasm nor enough evil to provoke his unqualified opposition.[65]

On the other hand, Lifton overlooks the fact that in previous dynastic changes the special position of the gentry, i.e., of the intellectuals of those times, remained unaffected (apart from periods of crisis and transition); each new dynasty soon forged an alliance with the gentry and acknowledged it to be an intellectual-political élite, while the Communists have created their own, wholly unintellectual élite.

I would agree with Lifton, however, that thought reform was most successful in its early stages, that is, in 1951 and 1952, and that its successes then tapered off; thought reform is indeed 'subject to a law of diminishing conversions. Repeated attempts to reform the same man are more likely to increase his hostility of suffocation than to purge him of his "incorrect" thoughts.'[66] There is a point beyond which a man no longer regards his own lies and deceit as immoral—the point at which he knows that everyone else is lying and deceiving. Lies of this kind cease to have any effect on the person who is lying; they leave him untouched, as it were, and amount to no more than meaningless phrases, and that is why the man who is lying no longer feels compelled to try—as the Party desires him to do—to identify himself with his words.

Many observers had expected the intellectuals to regard Marxism-Leninism as a kind of Confucianism which they would appropriate in the same way as they had appropriated Confucianism in the past. But that is not the case. Earlier in our study we saw with what vehemence the young Chinese intellectuals decided against 'Confucius & Co.' in the early 1900's. The chaos in which they landed once they had cut loose from the Master resulted, it is true, in a certain willingness to turn to a new ideology, all the more so when this new ideology appealed to their patriotism by anti-foreign slogans and a struggle against a foreign enemy—Japan, and filled their need for a comprehensible doctrine that had an answer for everything. This explains the remarkable initial successes of the CPC among the intellectuals. But these intellectuals who after the turn of the century had opposed the elevation of native Confucianism to the status of a state religion[67] were not inclined to accept foreign Marxism-Leninism as a new state religion—not, at any rate, once they realized that as a totalitarian ideology it made incomparably greater demands on the people than Confucianism had ever done, and that, intellectually and spiritually speaking, it violated and degraded them. Here lies the most cogent reason for the fact that Mao's policy toward the intellectuals has so far proved a failure.

*

Mao's annoyance at the intellectuals may be one of the reasons for his stipulation that they (like the cadres) perform manual labor. Since Lenin's days the Soviet Union has also had *Subbotniki* (from *Subbota*, Saturday, i.e., unpaid holiday work): planting trees in a municipal park or some such assignment, in which everyone, including students, professors, and cadres, had to participate. But the purpose of this type of work was to perform certain jobs and was not—except in the very earliest days—primarily of an educational nature. Nor was the despatch of trusted Party members to the rural areas by Stalin, and later by Khrushchev, undertaken to teach them respect for manual labor, but to speed up the transformation of the village with the aid of their authority and more dynamic influence. In his speeches on school reform since 1958 Khrushchev has, it is true, continually demanded that the younger generation should not receive a purely theoretical education but that this education should be supplemented by practical training in manual work, and it is more than likely that he had socio-educational aims in mind. But even he never thought of mobilizing his ministers, generals, Party chiefs, and rocket experts to harvest potatoes.

It is symbolic that the Chinese term for this kind of manual labor is *hsia fang* (= to send down). Those who for purposes of improving their ideological awareness are sent to rural areas or to a factory to perform manual labor consist chiefly of members of the upper class, intellectuals, and high-ranking cadres. It was after the sobering experiences of the weeks of criticism in 1957 that *hsia fang* was undertaken with increased impetus. The index of the translation service of the US Consulate-General in Hongkong of November and December 1957 contains seventy-four newspaper and magazine articles from the Red Chinese press on this subject.[68] In his speech early in May 1958 Liu Shao-ch'i declared that leading functionaries must spend 'a third of their time toiling in the organizations under their control and among the masses'.[69] In 1958 and 1959, 1·3 million young intellectuals were sent for a year to rural areas, and officers were obliged to serve temporarily as private soldiers. Early in 1960 another *hsia fang* campaign began.[70] In fact, it may be regarded as a permanent institution. Early in 1961, 7,800 cadres were mobilized from the ministries for the purpose of carrying out the 'four shares' (eating, living, working, and consulting with the peasants) in the rural areas.[71]

The differing methods of Moscow and Peking may be explained by the personal background of the leaders: for twenty years prior to the seizure of power, Lenin and his followers spent their time as *émigrés* in Europe, in the libraries and cafés of the capital cities of the West. Mao and his comrades-in-arms lived a corresponding length of time in the mountains of Chingkang and the caves of Yenan.

The wise Mencius would not have agreed with Mao. When he heard about the teachings of a certain reformer according to whom the kings ought to follow his example and go out into the fields with the peasants and even cook their own food, Mencius inquired whether the reformer made his own saucepans and ploughshares. No, he was told, then he would not have time to work in the fields, whereupon Mencius declared that a prince who rules his people wisely would also not have time to cook and plough.[72]

Writers in frost and thaw

AFTER THIS EXAMINATION of the behavior of the Communists toward intellectuals as a whole, it is worth while looking more closely at that section of the intelligentsia which, in the Soviet Union as in China, is by nature the easiest to analyze: the writers. What happened to them is typical of the fate of other artists.[73]

Russian literature before the revolution differed strongly from pre-Marxist literature in China. Its Golden Age began with Pushkin (1799–1837) and ended with Chekhov's death (1904). In its last phase Russian classical literature, unified in spite of its diversity, had already split up into numerous schools and trends. As in the rest of Europe, these schools and trends varied from formalism, symbolism, and decadence, to naturalism and the 'stormy petrels' of the revolution, and included a great many prominent names. Many writers were lost to national Russian literature through emigration (although some of them, notably Gorki, Ehrenburg, and Alexei Tolstoi, later returned to the Soviet Union). Those who remained—and this was the majority—began by carrying on with the former styles of writing. On the whole they were left in peace as long as they did not declare themselves too openly in favor of the opposition, like the well-known lyric poet Gumilyov, who was shot by the Bolsheviks in 1921.

Attempts to bring the writers—and the rest of the professional intelligentsia—to heel did not begin until 1928,[74] and here Lenin's words were frequently referred to:

Literary activity . . . must not in any way be an individual affair, independent of the common cause of the proletariat. Down with the Party-less writer! . . . Literary activity must become a *part* [author's italics] of the common proletarian cause, a 'cog' in the one uniform, great social-democratic [in later terms: Bolshevik] mechanism.[75]

Although this quotation from Lenin dating from 1905 referred to those writers who had joined the Party, under Stalin (and, in slightly milder form, under Khrushchev) it was applied to all authors and thinkers. According to the newly defined principle of *partynost* (partisanship) the Soviet author was soon only going to be allowed to write in the style of 'socialist realism'. It was his duty to show life 'not simply as "objective reality" but as reality in its revolutionary development', and 'to transform and educate the toiling people in the spirit of socialism'.[76] In other words, the writer had to cultivate a kind of heroic naturalism but apply it to people who in reality did not exist but who were to provide the reader with a model. The Soviet Writers' Federation (founded in 1934), to which everyone had to belong who wished to appear in print, permitted no deviation from this line.

Towering above all other literary figures was still the aged Gorky, poet laureate of the Soviet Union, whose deep concern over the increasing spiritual terrorism of the Stalin era persisted till his death in 1936 (according to the official version: until he was murdered at the hands of 'Party enemies'). Some writers, like Yessenin, Maya-kovski, and Fadeyev, withdrew from the reality they found intoler-able by resorting to suicide; some, like Samyatin, emigrated; many were 'liquidated', like Babel; others retreated into spiritual emi-gration (Pasternak is the outstanding example), and many collabor-ated without visible scruple, as did Ehrenburg. Encouraged by the Party's assertion that anybody could write who felt so inclined, a turbid wave of pseudo-literary publications flooded the country in which the authors described their heroic deeds in the factories and on the kolkhozes. The major achievements of revolutionary literature were produced in the period before socialist realism became an article of faith: Furmanov's *Chapayev* (1923), Serafimovich's *The Iron Flood* (1924), Gladkov's *Cement* (1925) and *Energy* (1933), Sholokhov's *And Quiet Flows the Don* (1928–29–33) and *Virgin Soil Upturned* (1932). The work to receive the highest praise as it came closest to the goal set by the Party, but which from a literary point of view was the weakest, was Nikolay Ostrovsky's novel *How the Steel was Tempered* (1932).

Once they had been made to conform to the Party line, Soviet writers became increasingly uncreative and stereotyped. During the war they enjoyed slightly more freedom (which they utilized to neglect socialistic themes, emphasizing patriotic and even private ones); but shortly after the war new and rigorous measures were introduced (1946–48) to ensure conformity. Stalin's death was the turning point. Even if the first signs of spring which replaced the icy frost of winter—the 'thaw', to use the title of Ehrenburg's post-Stalinist novel—were constantly endangered by new cold waves, such as the campaign against Pasternak (1958–59), the world rejoiced to see that beneath the frozen ground of the Stalin era the seeds of creativity had remained alive.[77] During the next few years the thaw became a veritable spring—until new frosts set in late in 1962.

This, then, is the picture: at the time of the revolution of 1917 the Russian intellectuals were on the way to becoming more and more similar to their Western counterparts. Above all else, they desired freedom for intellectual activity, for research and study, for teaching and creating. For this reason they resisted—and still resist—the one-sided partisanship demanded of them. Since Stalin's death they have managed to create for themselves a relatively broad scope of intel-lectual freedom of movement and in return have put at the disposal of the government their patriotic co-operation toward the strengthening of the power of the state. From their midst there has emerged with increasing clarity a body of men and women highly reminiscent of the intelligentsia of the nineteenth century, of those intellectuals who regarded themselves as being Russia's conscience and who felt that their duty lay in championing the humble and the downtrodden, unmindful of the mighty of this world.

*

For China the point of departure had been an entirely different one. May 4, 1919, a day whose importance for China's political and intellectual development has already been noted, brought with it an abrupt break with the past, and determined steps were taken to reform the Chinese language as well. Next came the first attempts at a new literature, a literature modeled no longer on the Chinese classics but on the contemporary writing of the West. The result was a socio-critical prose that initially showed great immaturity and clumsiness—scarcely to be wondered at in view of the sudden adoption of foreign styles.

In 1921 Lu Hsün (1881–1936) published *The True Story of Ah Q*[78] (dealing with the downfall of a Chinese who was unable to cope with the surrounding change and chaos) and became the leader of the new generation of writers. He spoke for many others when he stated in the foreword to a collection of his short stories (1923) that he had abandoned the study of medicine and devoted himself to literature since it was more important to transform the spirit of the Chinese than to heal their bodies.[79] Many other young Chinese concerned with reform also believed that they, like their predecessors, the intelligentsia in old Russia, could communicate political ideas to the people through the medium of the novel and the short story. The Chinese writer 'had converted "literary revolution" into "revolutionary literature"'.[80]

Since the early twenties Chinese literature had been conducting a revolt on behalf of the wronged and oppressed, against the old and the bad (which were regarded as synonymous) and above all against the traditional family system, which was attacked by the majority of writers in much the same way as we have seen in Pa Chin's novel *The Family*. The injured pride of an ancient, influential nation which had become a pawn in the hands of the great powers served to sharpen the criticism of a social system which was held responsible for this decline. There was a widespread inclination to see evil not in man himself but in social conditions. No matter how the individual may strive, he is powerless in the face of the pitiless wicked world—this was the theme of the novel, *Rickshaw Boy* (1938) by Lao She (1898), which became well known in the West, as well as of numerous other books of that time. It is not surprising that it was the revolutionary literature of Russia that was so widely read and imitated during this period. Many translations appeared, among them all the Soviet novels mentioned above, and a number of Chinese writers, including Pa Chin, learned Russian and did translations into Chinese.

After 1927 the KMT became more and more conservative and less desirous of reform, and Chiang Kai-shek, in his search for a spiritual foundation to his 'New Life' movement, finally recommended a return to Confucius—from whom the intellectuals had but recently managed to emancipate themselves. Hence the writers moved further and further to the left; in Marx, in the Bolshevik revolution, in Stalin's first Five-Year Plan, they believed they had found their stimulus, their model, and their spiritual home. From 1929 on, Lu Hsün called himself a Communist, although he never joined the Party; his tragi-grotesque tales about the dismal fate of the little people of China were written in a style somewhere between Gogol and Gorky, and he would have been justified in adopting the pseudonym 'the Bitter One' (=*gorky*) for himself. He was even more bitter than Gorky, since he also made use of satire. After his death Lu Hsün was made a saint of the revolution by the Chinese Communists, just as Gorky, who died the same year, had virtually become a Soviet saint; his portrait was retouched until it even looked like Gorky's. Just as Gorky's picture is to be seen in Soviet schools throughout the country, so Lu Hsün's is to be found in Chinese classrooms (often side by side with Gorky's); and just as every visitor to Moscow is taken to Gorky Park, so the Lu Hsün Parks were the first things shown to me in 1957 in Tsingtao and Shanghai. In actual fact, Lu Hsün—and here again he resembled Gorky—was much more of a humanist than a Communist, and more of an artist than a propagandist. 'Good literary works,' he declared, 'have never been composed in accordance with other people's orders.'[81]

In 1931 the authoress Ting Ling (1907) joined the CPC. That same year her husband, also a Communist, was arrested by Chiang's police and executed. She herself also spent a considerable time in prison. At about the same time Mao Tun (1896) who, after Lu Hsün's death, was to become the leading Communist author, joined the CPC. Other writers who dedicated their work to Communism were two whom we have already mentioned (Lao She and Pa Chin) and Hsiao Chün (1908), who won fame by his war novel *Village in August* (1942).

Some writers, however, remained outside the Communist current, although a smaller percentage than in Russia. The most outstanding of these, Chang Ai-ling (known in America as Eileen Chang) whose first literary attempts appeared in Shanghai during the war, emigrated in 1952. Her principal work was a realistic but not propagandistic novel, published in English under the title of *Naked Earth*, about the first years of Communist rule.[82] The novelist and essayist Lin Yutang, the contemporary Chinese author best known to the West through his book *My Country and My People*, had already left China in the thirties. Chinese literature even had its 'decadent writer': in the twenties Yü Ta-fu revealed to China the psychological significance of sex in modern writing.

*

In 1942 the writers in the Communist camp got a taste of what was in store for them when Mao, in his reaction against indications of independence, announced a number of new literary directives in a series of lectures in Yenan. These directives were no different from those in effect in the Soviet Union and amounted to three demands: literature was to serve politics; it must first and foremost work toward the re-education of the people in the Communist sense; it was to receive its directives from the CPC. Here again Mao's love-hatred for the intellectuals which we have already noted became apparent, and most clearly of all in the following paragraph of a speech which, significantly enough, is absent in the text of the speech as it later appeared in his *Selected Works*. The work of writers, said Mao, was very simple, and he went on:

In comparison, the cook's task in preparing a meal is difficult. To create something ready to eat, he must use a combination of wood, rice, oil, salt, sauce, vinegar, and other materials. This is certainly not easy, and to cook a good meal is all the more difficult. If there is too much fire, the food will burn, too much vinegar, and it will be sour. (Laughter.) Cooking food and preparing dishes is truly one of the arts. But what about book knowledge? If you do nothing but read, you have only to recognize three to five thousand characters, learn to thumb through a dictionary, hold some book in your hand, and receive millet from the public. Then you nod your head contentedly and start to read. But books cannot walk, and you can open and close a book at will; this is the easiest thing in the world to do, a great deal easier than it is for the cook to prepare a meal, and much easier than it is for him to slaughter a pig. He has to catch the pig . . . the pig squeals. (Laughter.) A book placed on a desk cannot run, nor can it squeal. (Laughter.) You can dispose of it in any manner you wish. Is there anything easier to do?[83]

Mao had already adopted the Moscow catchword when he said: 'We are for socialist realism.'[84] It was at this time that the first signs of disillusionment became discernible among some writers in Yenan. But the war was still on, and the possibility existed—as it also did in the Soviet Union—of replacing the vacillating loyalty to the Communist Party line by militant patriotism. It was not until after the war that disciplinary measures were taken against the writer Hsiao Chün: as a result of his experiences in Manchuria he had criticized the Soviets, and he was sent to a coal mine to do forced labor.[85]

In July 1949, that is to say, a few weeks before the official founding of the Chinese People's Republic, over eight hundred writers and artists were summoned to Peking. They were enjoined by Mao Tse-tung, Chou En-lai, and others henceforward to practice their art in the spirit of Communism only. But this was still during the honeymoon of the new regime, when it believed that, with few exceptions, all writers in China were firmly behind it, and that those exceptions could very soon be brought into line by thought reform.

In the fall of 1954 the temper and tempo of the struggle for the adherence of the writers showed signs of sharpening. Their criticism had been considered desirable as long as they attacked the enemy— Chiang or the Japanese; but now criticism was no longer in demand: they were supposed to devote themselves solely to hymns of praise for the new regime. This heightening of the battle (which coincided with the fourth stage of Mao's policy toward the intellectuals) began with a violent dispute over the novel *Dream of the Red Chamber*, which the Party ideologists, unlike the literary historians of the old schools, insisted on regarding primarily as a work of social criticism. Another attack was directed against Hu Feng, an old friend of Lu Hsün's. Hu Feng was a Marxist essayist, inclined toward independent thinking, who, after years of close co-operation with the Communists, began to resist their spiritual tyranny. Early in the summer of 1955 the *People's Daily* published 169 personal letters which Hu Feng had written over the years to friends and colleagues and which the recipients had been forced to hand over. These letters contained numerous bitter comments on the Party and its bosses. Hu Feng was put into prison for alleged espionage.[86] At the same time the thaw in the Soviet Union was already approaching its first peak.

The next victim was Ting Ling. An impulsive woman, who was rumored to have had intimate relations with a number of leading Communists, including the military commander P'eng Teh-huai, she was among those who in 1942 in Yenan had found the narrow Communist dogmatism irksome; but she had then reverted to the general line, and in 1949 she published a perfect Communist propaganda novel, *Sun Over the Sangkan River*, containing remarkably frank descriptions of the brutal agrarian reform. For this novel she was awarded a Stalin prize in 1951. But she could not get used to this tedious conformity. From the summer of 1955 on, she became the target of angry Party criticism. During the Hundred Flowers period there was a slight relaxation. But when in the summer of 1957 the Party dealt its blows to the critics of the preceding weeks, the storm broke once again, and this time publicly, over Ting Ling and her friends: they were 'unmasked' as enemies who had allegedly engineered a conspiracy against the Party. It was even hinted that Ting Ling had worked for Chiang Kai-shek's secret police in the thirties. The witch trial, to which numerous writers were summoned as spectators, continued for more than two dozen sessions, recalling Stalin's mock trials; it ended with the expulsion of all the accused from the Party.

The man whose job it was to keep the writers in line was Chou Yang. Ever since the thirties he had been active as a literary whip, and he finally rose to be Deputy Director of the Propaganda Department of the CPC Central Committee; he was also the vice president and driving force of the All-China Federation of Literary and Art Workers (modeled on the Soviet pattern). The utterances of this man are on a par with those of the literary functionaries and inquisitors in Russia during the Stalin era; he too regarded literature as a function of propaganda. Everything was to be shown in black or white; the Communists had to be noble and perfect (apart from rare and bravely countered temptations) and the enemies abysmally wicked—they were not permitted even the smallest deviation from the path of unrelieved devilry. Psychological subtleties were frowned upon; what was required were stereotype figures, *the* landowner, *the* cadre, *the* soldier.

*

As in the Soviet Union, the greatest call was for 'production novels'. To this end writers were sent (and are still being sent) to the factories and rural areas,[87] and are exhorted to create in their books true-to-life, 'positive' heroes. As in the Soviet Union during the period of Stalin's literary despotism, in China there is also the grave-yard hush of conformity. But at least in the USSR such stories as *The Wedding*, by Chou Li-po, are no longer fashionable: the point of this tale is that at her wedding the bride declares she is going to challenge the bridegroom to a 'socialist work contest', while the latter is not present at the ceremony because he has remembered some urgent work to be done at the factory—both of which actions are held up as specimens of exemplary behavior.[88] Since the end of 1960 there seems to have been a slight relaxation, although for a depressing reason: the food situation and general atmosphere became so bad that the Party obviously considers it advisable to open a few safety valves.[89]

This does not change the overall picture of Mao's cultural policy. While monuments were being put up to the dead Lu Hsün, his closest friends and kindred spirits were silenced. Of the others, Mao Tun became Minister of Culture and thus the extended arm of the Party as well as President of the Chinese Writers' Association; he administered more than he wrote. Ch'ien Chung-shu, author of the novel *The Besieged City* (1947), emerged in 1958 after a long silence—but with an anthology of poems from the Sung dynasty, prefaced by an introduction containing numerous Mao quotations. Nothing more was heard from Shi To (1908), who wrote the successful novel *The Marriage* (1947). Pa Chin fell silent; his last great novel, *Cold Nights*, had appeared back in 1946–47. Shang Tsung-wen (1902), known chiefly for his short stories, tried to commit suicide.

Among the authors of the early days there was only one who, if one is to believe appearances, found no difficulty in falling into step, and that was Lao She. He produced a quantity of shallow plays in the style of social realism which were much praised by the Party. Like Chou Yang, he was vice president of the Federation of Literary and Art Workers.[90] Even the industrious Kuo Mo-jo (1892) did not give the impression of being at ease. He had been an avowed Communist since 1924 and played a leading part in Communist literary affairs—without, however, producing literary works of his own of any lasting value; finally he became Director of the Academy of Science and President of the Federation of Literary and Art Workers. But in the days of the Hundred Flowers, even he had not been able to conceal his critical attitude, and he criticized the interference of the Party in the research activities of scholars.[91] The words of an intelligent Indian written after a visit to China at the beginning of the fifties still apply:

> For the first time I realised what for many years I had sensed vaguely but never grasped. To have your body imprisoned behind prison walls is degrading. But to have your mind captive with invisible chains is far more degrading. In the democratic beholder such a spectacle creates a pain and nausea difficult to describe or overcome.[92]

Writers of the second rank, men like Ai Wu, had less trouble finding their niche in the Communist State than those of the first order. Ai Wu cheerfully set about imitating the Soviet authors, and for one of his books he even adopted (with a slight variation) the title of Ostrovsky's novel, calling his own work *The Tempering of the Steel*.[93] Another of these was Tsao Ming, who for his novel borrowed Gladkov's title *Energy*.[94]

*

In addition to all this, literary functionaries did their best to encourage new pro-Communist authors such as Chao Su-li, who sang the praises of collectivization in his novel *San-li Wan* (1956). In this milieu the duty of literature, like the production of coal or iron, is judged entirely from the point of view of quantity and of benefit to the State. In the Soviet Union under Stalin, industrial terminology was applied to literature, writers were described as 'engineers of the human soul', and the call went out for a '*Magnitostroy* [the name of the new industrial area on the eastern slopes of the Urals] of literature'. The same thing happened in China: after the announcement of the Great Leap (1958), Shanghai writers undertook to produce three thousand literary works in two years. Soon they had far exceeded their plan: on one single evening three thousand Shanghai workers and soldiers 'produced' three thousand poems and 360 songs; among the authors singled out for special praise was a 'work hero', who in one single year fulfilled the norm for seventeen years. His prize-winning poem, 'Ode to the Red Sun', is as follows:

> When Chairman Mao comes forth,
> The East shines red.
> All living things prosper,
> The earth is 'red'.

> Six hundred million, peony bright:
> Each one is 'red'.
> For all our beautiful hills and streams,
> Eternal time is 'red'.[95]

Meanwhile Shanghai alone has turned out over five million poems.[96]

The Chinese intellectual class as a whole suffered just as much under Mao's methods as their brothers had in the Soviet Union. But the reason for the particular harassment to which they were exposed lay, paradoxically enough, in the fact that Mao had a deeper respect than Stalin for the intellect, as well as a greater optimism with regard to the 'learnability' of Marxism-Leninism; in both these characteristics one discerns a part of the Chinese heritage.

In other respects the Maoist era of Chinese literature is scarcely distinguishable from the Stalinist era in Russia. The question remains: when Maoism comes to an end in China, will there be signs of a thaw as there were in Russia after Stalin's death? No one can say yet. One can only hope that this will be the case for, during the period of the Hundred Flowers, non-Communist works quickly made their appearance, works which dealt with human problems, like the story (by an as yet unknown author), 'A New Young Man Arrives at the Organization Department'. This story describes the disillusionment of a devout young Party comrade over the bureaucratic reality of Communist China and prompted 1,300 letters from readers.[97] Optimists may take heart at this and hope that in the post-Maoist era, as in the Soviet Union today, many more 'new young men' will speak up.

*

We see that the Chinese Communists and the Russian Communists adopted a different attitude toward all four of the social strata of the country which we have examined—workers, peasants, bourgeoisie, and intellectuals. The reasons for this difference we found in Chinese tradition, in China's historical situation at the time of the Communist revolution, in the person of Mao himself, and in the relatively protracted course of the revolution. Lenin rose within a few months from an outsider, living abroad and practically unknown in Russia, to master of the whole Russian empire. On the other hand, twenty-five years before its victory the CPC had, as a partner of Sun Yat-sen's, already had a responsible share in governing the country. Furthermore, even after the loss of this position, it continued to control vast areas with millions of inhabitants; for some two decades it possessed its own effective army; and as a champion against the national enemy, the Japanese, it enjoyed widespread sympathy among the Chinese people, whose patriotism had been fanned into flame by the Japanese invasion. After these long years of preparation, the victory of the CPC in 1949 was so complete that the country was spared a civil war such as rocked and bled the Soviet Union for years after Lenin's assumption of power. As in the Communist states of Eastern Europe, the absence of civil war after the seizure of power in China undoubtedly facilitated the maintenance of the multi-party façade.

If one asks what Mao had learned from his twenty years of provincial rule, one would assume the answer to be: guerrilla warfare, and an understanding of the peasant mentality. That he knows something about conducting a war, Mao proved in Korea and on the Himalayan border, but his understanding of the peasant seems doubtful, considering the disastrous experiences with the people's communes (to be discussed in Chapter XIV). Of the three other strata of the population—with which he had far less to do before his victory than with the peasants—the one he handled with the greatest amount of skill and success was, surprisingly enough, the bourgeoisie, while it was the intellectuals who, comparatively speaking, gave him the most trouble. The one we know least about is the one of which Mao and the CPC constantly claim to be exponents: the working class. Here again we find a contrast to the Soviet Union, where—at any rate during the first fifteen years of Communist rule—there was no doubt that it was in the working class that the Party had its greatest supporters.

CHAPTER VIII

THE PARTY AND ITS STYLE

EVER SINCE MARX, THE COMMUNISTS have steadfastly maintained that the proletariat is the avant-garde and champion of revolutionary development. But the overwhelming majority of the men who ushered in the revolution in Russia and in China were not proletarians. Lenin made no secret of this. As early as 1902 in his *What Is To Be Done?* he called for an organization of conspirators formed by 'professional revolutionaries', instead of a workers' movement or party in the usual sense of the words—'it is immaterial whether a student or a worker is capable of becoming a professional revolutionary'.[1] One year later this view was accepted by the Second Party Congress of the Russian Social Democrats, at which he and his supporters formed the majority (= *Bolshinstvo*, hence Bolsheviks) over the more moderate minority (= Mensheviks).

Even before Lenin, the men who had been the driving force in the revolutionary groups had for the most part been intellectuals and included many students. But it was Lenin who provided the ideological basis for the paradox that the proletarian revolution predicted by Marx should be led by non-proletarians. He had found to his annoyance that, among the men who were politically active, those who could truly be said to be workers felt obliged first and foremost to improve the lot of their fellow workers by such measures as promotion of trade unions and wage battles. Lenin, whose goal was political revolution and the seizure of power, impatiently scorned this method of carrying on the struggle and dubbed it 'economism', 'trade-unionism' (using the English term) and even 'tailism' (*khvostizm*, from the Russian *khvost* = tail) because in his eyes the advocates of a prosaic step-by-step policy of this kind formed not, as he wanted, the head of the revolution but the tail. All the discontent existing in the Tsarist empire—not only among the workers but among all other social and national groups—was grist to the mill of Lenin's revolution; but the leadership of the revolution he claimed for himself and his kind.

In the top echelon which prepared and directed the October revolution of 1917 there was not a single one of working-class origin. Among those who rose to a position of Party leadership during the civil war and managed to maintain that position, Voroshilov was the only one with a proletarian background. Most of them were from the bourgeoisie, many from the minor aristocracy, and they had found their way to the Party via the melting pot of the intelligentsia described above. The only peasant to hold high office, although he did not belong to the innermost circle of power, was Kalinin; it was his job to convince the peasants by his very existence that they were not being forgotten. The actual positions of leadership were reserved for professional revolutionaries, men sworn to serve the Party, 'graduates' of the revolutionary 'universities' of Tsarist prisons and Siberian exile, virtually classless and certainly not proletarian, men who had never earned their daily bread as ordinary workers.

*

When we look at the main executive bodies in the USSR, particularly the Politburo, which was founded in 1917 (renamed 'Presidium' in 1952), we see that in this respect nothing has changed in the last fifty years. Even when Stalin killed off the first echelon of the revolutionary leaders and moved up new men, these latter were not workers. Nor were they any longer professional revolutionaries, the revolution being a thing of the past. The leaders of the Stalin era belonged to a type of functionary appropriately known as *apparatchik*—a man who pursued his career within the Party apparatus. Among the *apparatchiki* there were at first many who came from the proletariat, but the proportion of those belonging to the new intelligentsia increased rapidly. In 1930 at the Sixteenth Party Congress only 22·9 per cent of the delegates had had high school, advanced technical school, and/or university education, while in 1952 at the Nineteenth Party Congress there were already 85·2 per cent. In 1961 (Twenty-second Party Congress) the number of advanced technical school and university graduates alone amounted to 72·8 per cent.[2] One *apparatchik* who has retained some 'proletarian' characteristics is Nikita Khrushchev, who in his youth was a village shepherd and a laborer. Hence members of the new upper class speak of him—as I myself heard in Moscow in 1959—with irony and a certain amount of suspicion as 'the last of the proletarians' (*posledny proletary*).

In China there was a similar trend, but with some slight differences. In the revolutionary groups, which may be regarded as the fore-runners of the subsequent Communist Party of China, the most active men were professors and students, and here the respect due to one's teacher in Asia created particularly strong bonds of loyalty. After the founding of the Party in 1921, the proportion of non-academic members in the Party's leadership did, it is true, increase, but only a small minority came from the working class. This shrank even further when the center of gravity of the struggle shifted from the cities to the provinces. A study of the Communist leading class at the beginning of the forties shows the following: only 17 per cent might be called proletarian even if we use the term in its widest sense; 70 per cent were intellectuals from non-proletarian families.[3] In other words, the old Chinese tradition whereby the leaders of peasant revolts were often intellectuals was apparent in the Communist revolution also.

Symptomatic of this are the men who have led the CPC since its foundation: Ch'en Tu-hsiu (1921–27) was a professor at the National University of Peking and a journalist; Ch'ü Ch'iu-pai (1927–28) was a typical intellectual, from an impoverished upper-class family and the grandson of a high official; Li Li-san (1928–1930) who as a student in 1920 had founded a Communist cell in France with Chou En-lai, had from his earliest youth been an organizer and functionary, i.e., one of those professional revolution-aries spoken of by Lenin; Wang Ming (alias Ch'en Shao-yu, 1930–1932), the son of a well-to-do peasant,[4] was for a time a student in Moscow and a true *apparatchik* in the way he occupied his post; even Mao Tse-tung (the *de facto* leader of the CPC since Wang Ming's resignation) came, as we have seen, from a prosperous peasant family and was a student and political organizer.

A look at the men who went to make up the Central Committee which was elected at the Eighth Party Congress in September 1956 is also very revealing. Of the ninety-seven members of the CC who to-gether occupied the 585 principal official posts in China, we know something about eighty-one, and of this number only seven were workers. Of the remaining seventy-four, fifty-five came from the country: twenty-eight from well-to-do peasant families, and four from poor ones; the rest have merchant (ten), civil service (five), and teacher (four) family backgrounds. Thirty-nine have studied abroad, the greater part of them in the Soviet Union and the rest (in this order) in France, Japan, Germany, and the United States. At the time they joined the Party, a total of fifty members of the Eighth CC were students.[5] As recently as 1961 Foreign Minister Ch'en Yi, a veteran Communist, stated: 'Among the leading comrades of the Party Central Committee there are many who come from families of higher social standing and there are not many who come from worker and peasant families.'[6]

*

If we compare Mao—China's leading Communist since the end of the twenties—with the two men who ruled the CPSU during the same period, i.e., with Stalin and Khrushchev, we see that the Chinese leader is more of an intellectual than Stalin, the runaway seminarian, or the decidedly unintellectual Khrushchev. After all, for eight years (from 1911 to 1919) Mao had contacts with the intellectual world, first as a student in Changsha and then as an assistant in the library of Peking University. But even Mao is above all else a practical revolutionary, and most of his publications—essays and (usually heavily edited) lectures—remind one in their style, and particularly in their artlessness, of those of Stalin.

Beginning with the thirties, Mao's position as head of the Party was never seriously disputed; nor does it seem to have been impaired by the fact that in 1959 he resigned the highest government post of all, that of Chairman of the People's Republic, in favor of Liu Shao-ch'i. The outward maintenance of intra-Party democracy was of even less concern to Mao than to Stalin. Under Stalin, once he was in control, there were four more Party Congresses (1930, 1934, 1939, and 1952) while in China after 1928 there were only two and a half (two full Congresses, in 1945 and 1946, and one intermediate Congress in 1958) and this in spite of the fact that the Party Congress is supposed to meet every three years according to the Party Constitution (Article 29) of 1945, and annually according to the Party Constitution of 1956 (Article 31). For four years (from 1950 to 1954) Mao did not even call a meeting of the CC of the CPC.

It must be emphasized that the function of the Party in both countries is exactly the same. And yet the proportional strength of the Party is almost twice as great in the Soviet Union today as in China. In 1961 the CPSU had 9·7 million members (of which 0·8 million were candidates) and the CPC had 'more than seventeen million'.[7] Or—in round figures—in the Soviet Union there is one Party member per twenty-two of population, and in China one in forty. (As a comparison: in imperial China there was approximately one member of the gentry per four hundred inhabitants.)

One frequently hears it said that Party leadership in China has been spared the internal conflicts such as frequently rocked the CPSU. This is certainly not true of the first ten or twelve years of the CPC's existence. On the contrary, this period was marked by an unrelieved series of acrimonious clashes and quarrels; personal and ideological struggles—including the question of Moscow's influence—and accusations of betrayal and deviation from the true doctrine were quite customary.[8] There is even reason to suspect that in these clashes Party members were handed over to the tender mercies of the police.[9]

We do not know much about Mao's activities during those early Party days. He, too, seems to have been involved in these rivalries. But ever since he has been firmly in the saddle as Party leader, the internal quarrels have lost much of their intensity. Those of his one-time enemies who are still alive were graciously readmitted to favor, and Li Li-san was even a member of the Seventh as well as the Eighth CC. Under Mao the CPC experienced nothing comparable to the Stalinist murder-years of 1936 to 1938. A list compiled by Chinese anti-Communists in Hongkong of the twenty-two principal purges of the years 1949 to 1959 contains among the names of ninety-seven Party members affected only one whose death could be attributed to the purges—Kao Kang, who was said to have committed suicide. All the other 'deviationists' or 'enemies of the revolution' were merely expelled from the Party and at worst were sentenced to imprisonment.[10] Since the completion of this list two more prominent veteran Communists have fallen into disfavor: Marshal P'eng Teh-huai and Ch'en Yün. (We shall return to Kao Kang and P'eng Teh-huai later on.) In their case also there were no long-drawn-out vilification campaigns such as were customary in Moscow; they simply ceased to appear before the public. For this reason, continuity in the CPC is far greater than in the CPSU with its sharp fluctuations. The forty-four members who belonged to the CC elected in 1945 all became CC members again in 1956.[11] It remains to be seen, of course, what effect Mao's death will have.

The difference between the Russian and Chinese methods could be explained as follows. After nearly ten years of internal strife, Stalin became the ruler of a party which had been built up by someone else —by Lenin; a party whose leaders dating from Lenin's times were not sworn to Stalin's service and many of whom, for personal as well as objective reasons, rejected him and were rejected by him. (Among the exceptions were Molotov and Voroshilov.) Stalin was determined to assemble his own team which would unconditionally support his course of action. The fact that this was brought about in a particularly horrible bloodbath, which lasted many years and the psychological consequences of which will not be overcome for a long time, may be attributable to the pathological characteristics of the 'Red Tsar', who in many ways reminds us of Ivan the Terrible—a figure deliberately rehabilitated. In any event, it is noticeable that, with some exceptions (such as Voznesensky, d. 1949), Stalin put an end to the murders, if not the arrests, within the Party after the Party had become thoroughly 'Stalinist' and had evolved a uniform ideology.

Mao, on the other hand, developed his own branch of the CPC in the remote rural areas, and after the destruction of the urban Party headquarters (and many of its leaders) by Chiang Kai-shek, this branch formed the new central organization of the Party, with Mao and his friends at the helm. Ever since the early thirties, Mao was the real leader of a party of which the principal 'cadres'—to use the popular Communist term—were 'Maoist' from then on, since they consisted of his friends and supporters. Thus for Mao there was no reason to undertake a massive 'purge' of the Party machine: Chiang had already done it for him. The only one of the pre-Maoist Party leaders still active in the topmost echelon is Chou En-lai.

When Li Li-san—to take him once more as an example—after his long years as a refugee in the USSR, returned at the end of World War II in the train of the Soviet Army to a China in which Mao's complete victory was only a matter of time, he and his fellow exiles were such isolated outsiders that Mao, conscious of his historic triumphs, found it easy to be generous. (I shall not deal here with the numerous speculations concerning intra-Party disputes.)[12] When we consider, however, how Stalin behaved toward the Party after it had been fully 'Stalinized' (i.e., after 1938) and compare this with Mao's behavior after the complete 'Mao-ization' of the CPC (after 1935) we see that the difference, as far as the 'liquidation' of Party members is concerned, is not so great after all. Whether it is true that in Russia in 1953 a new wave of terror was about to begin and was only stopped by Stalin's death, is something no one can say with certainty.

However, we are struck by a difference of another kind between Mao and Stalin. Mao has devoted a great deal of energy—including his own personal energy—to the education of his cadres, to their 'rectification' (the Chinese Communists' own translation for their word for this process—*ch'eng feng*). Outwardly this process of his recalls the original bloodless purges in the Soviet Union in which Party members were examined on their ideological knowledge. (Elsewhere I have related how in Moscow early in the thirties I once for my own amusement took part in the preliminary test for one of these examinations.)[13] But the intensity with which these rectification campaigns—especially the best known one, from 1942 to 1944[14]—were carried on far exceeded anything to be found in similar manifestations in the USSR.

The first Communist cells in China, early in the twenties, were study groups, and even today one of the chief duties of the cell (*hsiao tsu* = small group) is still that of becoming a 'study group' (*hsüeh hsi hsiao tsu*). Not only the CPC, but the great majority of the population, with its hundreds of millions of people, is divided up into study groups averaging ten members which meet frequently, sometimes daily, to discuss prescribed topics under the direction of the group leader. There is nothing which cannot serve as a topic, from the most intimate details of private life to new Party resolutions. On my travels through China in 1957 I often came across study groups of this kind. Once in a small rural clinic I found the entire staff, from the doctor in charge to the cleaning woman, sitting around a table studying Mao's speech 'On Contradictions'. The method devised by the Bolsheviks called 'criticism and self-criticism' has been greatly intensified in China, and the main principle in its application seems to be to keep each cell member alternating between two states: bliss at being accepted or fear of being rejected.

Attempts have been made to explain the significance of rectification for the Chinese mentality by the fact that the CPC had been split up into many small battle units, often forced to rely on themselves for years at a time, during the civil war and the Sino-Japanese war, and there is certainly some truth in this. But there is a further reason, and that is the particular attitude of the Chinese toward the problem of 'knowledge and action' which we discussed in the chapter on the intellectuals.

*

During the first rectification period, Mao's speeches contained an element which then disappeared for a while—a note of patriotism.

He upbraided his audience for not knowing enough about China's history. Many of them, he said, preferrred what 'they have picked up bit by bit from the rubbish heap of obsolete foreign books' and parroted what had been imported from abroad, thus playing 'the role of a talking-machine'. He called upon them to 'take over the rich legacy and succeed to the fine tradition of Chinese and foreign art and literature of the past'.[15]

Russian historical awareness is also stronger today than anyone would have expected in the early iconoclastic days of Bolshevism. This is apparent to anyone who has visited the lavishly redecorated Kremlin or who has followed the development of historiography in the Soviet Union during the last twenty or thirty years—particularly under the influence of the Second World War.[16] But just as the awareness of history and tradition was incomparably stronger in imperial China than similar feelings were in Tsarist Russia, so today it is a far more powerful force in China than in the USSR. The fact that I found the temple at Ch'ü-fou, the town of Confucius, in considerably better condition in 1957 than when I had first visited it some thirty years earlier and that some of the larger buildings were being thoroughly renovated, or that the palaces in the Forbidden City at Peking were being restored by the Communists in all their former glory, is not too significant. The domes of the Kremlin and the Trinity Monastery near Moscow are also resplendent with fresh gilt. It is much more significant that, in the speeches and writings of Mao and his followers, historical overtones are to be heard to a much greater extent than in parallel utterances on the part of Russian Communists, and that a sense of history makes itself felt in countless phrases and turns of speech. This is not due merely to the idiosyncrasy of Chinese speech and writing, where historical images and associations live on in every word and character; it is the result of deliberate intention.

The most striking example of this is the speech made by Liu Shao-ch'i in Yenan in the summer of 1939. Although the event took place in the 'Marx-Lenin Academy', he quoted from the Chinese classics much more often than from Marxism-Leninism.[17] Many of those sayings which had formed part of popular wisdom for two thousand years suddenly reappeared—right at the beginning, twelve of them in five paragraphs, among them Confucius' saying which we have already mentioned: 'What you do not want done to yourself, do not do to others', and others such as 'as public as an eclipse [of the sun]', 'being right, he is strong', and the maxim we have already met: 'When you are alone, watch over yourself!'

Above all it was Mao himself who loved to adorn his utterances with classical quotations. The idea that the east wind would conquer the west wind, which he announced to Moscow in 1957 (and to which we shall return later), has its origin in a remark of beautiful Black Jade in *Dream of the Red Chamber*.[18] The 'hundred schools which are to contend with one another', according to his promise in his Hundred Flowers speech, were, as we know, an echo from the classical era of China's intellectual history. Mao's famous principle of guerrilla warfare, 'When the enemy advances, we retreat. / When he escapes, we harass. / When he retreats, we pursue./ When he is tired, we attack', was taken by Mao, with a slight alteration in form, from the works of a military writer of the pre-Confucian period.[19] And the phrase, 'It is upon bad fortune that good fortune leans, upon good fortune that bad fortune rests', which occurs in his Contradictions speech of 1957, is a quotation from Lao-tzu.[20]

There is one publication which more than any other falls outside the Marxist-Leninist framework and proves Mao's ties with the intellectual past of China. Neither in Marx nor Engels, neither in Lenin, Stalin, nor Khrushchev, would it be possible to imagine anything resembling Mao's classically constructed 'Nineteen Poems', published at the beginning of 1957,[21] in which he deferred to the ancient Chinese conception of a classically educated statesman.

If these poems were really written by Mao (which we may assume to be so) they betray a certain measure of classical education as well as literary talent, and a lack of self-consciousness which is absent among European Communists (because the latter are either much too concerned with being taken seriously or, like Khrushchev, lack the necessary education). The following short poem, which has nothing to do with politics, gives Mao's impressions of a mountain range seen from a peak:

> Mountains!
> Like surging, heaving seas with your billows rolling,
> Like a myriad horses
> Rearing and plunging away in the thick of the battle.

The twenty-three poems of another Communist leader in Asia, the Vietnamese Ho Chi Minh, are quite different; most of them are rather naive 'poems for special occasions' (there are nine commemorating the new year alone) and have an unmistakably political bias.[22]

Mao himself has said[23] that in his youth the great Chinese folk novels, especially *The Three Kingdoms* (fourteenth century) and *All Men Are Brothers* (sixteenth century), made a deep impression on him. Hence we may take him for a man educated in the classics, although probably not very thoroughly, a man who is influenced by the great traditions of his people. He shows almost no trace of foreign influence, other than Russian. He is the only leading statesman of our time who has never gone beyond the borders of his own country, except to the Soviet Union. Moreover, even while in China he spent twenty years entirely in the remote hinterland. Of his collaborators, there are only a few—like Chou En-lai—who are acquainted with the outside world, let alone that of the West.[24]

Mao is probably also responsible for the publication in Peking early in 1961 of a little book called *Stories About Not Being Afraid of Ghosts*.[25] With the aid of thirty-five tales from the world of Chinese legends and fairy stories, the reader is taught, by looking at the old familiar figures, to realize the harmlessness of all manner of enemies. The idea behind it is: If you are not afraid of ghosts, the ghosts will be afraid of you. Who these ghosts are it is not difficult to imagine— imperialists, reactionaries, revisionists, and other villains—a Chiang Kai-shek, a Kennedy, perhaps even a Nikita Khrushchev? One has only to follow the example of that scholar of old to whom, in the midst of his studies, a ghost appeared with a black face and goggling eyes, whereupon the fearless scholar immediately blackened his own face with ink, rolled his eyes, and thus put the confused apparition to flight.

*

Other authors are trying to follow in Mao's footsteps. In the struggle against the rightist opposition (after 1957) in order to show how tiny and yet how disagreeable this opposition was, the slogan 'A speck of mouse dirt ruins a whole pot of soup'[26] was borrowed from the novel *The Three Kingdoms*. The members of this opposition group were accused of wearing a 'painted skin' (like the demon in an old tale who pulled on a painted skin over his own in order to look like a beautiful woman) or they were challenged to 'reveal their original forms' (using the words employed toward the animals in fairy stories who temporarily change into human beings).[27] Those who were attacked replied likewise with classical allusions. They accused the Party of 'opening graves to whip the corpses' (as one man is said to have done in olden times with the corpse of his father's murderer).[28] Not long ago Foreign Minister Ch'en Yi said that in him were combined the influences of Communism with those of Confucius and Mencius.[29]

However, Mao was quite capable of making unclassical remarks. In his knowledge of proverbs he is almost a match for Khrushchev. He is fond of using them (for example, to 'cut the dress according to the figure', or 'insects don't make their home in the door hinge'),[30] and in vulgar comparisons he is his equal. Of Marxism-Leninism he said that China needed it like a constipated man needs a laxative. In order to make his audience understand that this doctrine was an introduction to action and not a dogma, he said that a dogma was of less value than excrements, for at least they could be used for fertilizing the fields.[31]

Communist writing has never made enjoyable reading. With the Chinese it is no different. Nevertheless, from time to time one comes across effective phrases such as occur but rarely in Bolshevik publications. (Among the few memorable puns of Lenin's is the title of his essay, 'Better Fewer, But Better'.) When Mao's old Party enemy Li Li-san confessed his sins at the Eighth Party Congress, he said of his mistaken political leanings that they were 'like weeds which not even the burning of the steppe can exterminate and which grow again with the spring wind'.[32] While in the Soviet Union those who were sympathetic to the West are called 'lickspittles' or lackeys of monopolistic capitalism, the head of the Propaganda Department of the CPC referred to them more imaginatively as people who thought that 'the moon in America is rounder than the moon in China'.[33] Mao made the expression 'paper tiger' popular ('the atom bomb is a paper tiger',[34] i.e. it looks dangerous but it is not really) and from Liu Shao-ch'i comes the terse phrase 'red and expert';[35] and how much coarser it sounds when the Russians explain their wage-system based on achievement by saying that the 'material self-interest' of the individual must be considered, while the Chinese said: 'Wages must correspond to work performed as a shadow corresponds to the length of a stick.'[36]

The tendency of the Chinese to use turns of speech consisting of two parallel halves has its roots in ancient literary tradition; the most common example is the sentence consisting of four characters, such as: 'Hundred smeltings produce iron', in other words: Good iron (= success) can only result from a hundredfold effort. Or: 'Heal disease save man' (i.e. treat the illness in order to save the man) which is one of the slogans proclaimed by Mao during the rectification campaign in Yenan.[37] 'Down [from] horse observe flowers!' cried Mao to the Party functionaries in his speech 'On Contradictions', an expression used to exhort a haughty official of imperial days to become better acquainted with the common people.[38] In 1955 the University of Peking compiled a book with more than two thousand such old and new four-character phrases; it is available everywhere, including Hongkong, for a moderate price.[39]

The Chinese love of numbers, attributable to the already noted significance of numerology in Chinese tradition, is also very much alive today. In the past there have been: three dependencies (of the woman: on father, husband, and son); four demon kings (in front of Buddhist temples); five poisonous creatures (snakes, toads, lizards, scorpions, and centipedes); eight immortals (in Taoism); ten archcrimes; and dozens of similar formulas.[40] Today this love of numbers has become a veritable mania. I am inclined to believe that in the few years the Communists have been in power they have produced more numerological slogans than have existed during the previous two thousand years. Among these are the familiar Three-Anti and Five-Anti; also, three strengths (strong in land, cattle, and laborers = rich peasant); three good things (for young people: work, study, health); three assessments (of class origin, of fulfilment of duty, of fighting spirit); four pests (rats, flies, mosquitoes, sparrows); five guarantees (for the peasants: food, clothing, heating, education of the young, burial); five poisonous creatures (as above, but now applied to class enemies); five excesses (of bureaucratic committees, meetings, documents, written reports, telephone calls); five daggers (i.e. Party directives aimed at writers); eight modes of behavior (for Party members); eight basic rules (for agriculture)—and so forth.[41]

I do not know of any study of this passion of the Chinese Communists for numbers, but I would assume that they find it convenient to work with slogans which link up with the age-old familiarity of the people with maxims based on numbers. The seriousness with which the Party regards its numerological didacticism is shown by the example of a school board which added a fourth 'good thing' (good order) to the 'three good things' (for young people) and was duly reprimanded for attempting to improve on the Party.[42]

Even where the Russians simply speak of the CC of the Party, the Chinese usually put a number in front: hence the CC that has existed since the Eighth Party Congress of the CPC (i.e. since the autumn of 1956) is known as the Eighth CC. And while for decades the Russians in somewhat looser and less systematic fashion have been defining the plenary sessions of their CC according to the month in which they take place and, for example, call the session of March 1962, in which Khrushchev demanded a thorough reform of agriculture, merely the 'March plenum' (without giving the year), the Chinese neatly label theirs: the 'Sixth Plenary Session of the Eighth CC'.

*

Does this intellectual and pseudo-intellectual activity on the part of the *kan pu* (from *kan* = to work, and *pu* = component part; i.e. working part, or 'activist') or cadres mean that this body of Party functionaries is to be regarded as a resurrected gentry? A fleeting glance might indeed detect some parallels. Both gentry and *kan pu* belong to a privileged group in society which is sharply distinguished from the rest of the population; its members, whether or not they occupy government posts, form the backbone of the administration, one might even say of the State as a whole. The road to this position is open to every citizen—in theory, at least, and to some extent also in fact. It is true that this road to the gentry was barred to persons of certain occupations which were considered dishonorable and the promotion to cadre status is obstructed by certain social backgrounds. It is also true that in both cases admission presupposed adherence to the dominant ideology—Confucian or Marxist—rather than occupational training, thus enabling the State to use these people in almost any required position. A comprehensive Western work on Chinese intellectual history comes after nearly a thousand pages to the following conclusion:

> Despite important ideological differences, the new Communist elite resembles the old one in its combination of ideological and political authority, in its identification with a specific intellectual orthodoxy, and in its claim to quality for leadership by conforming to a rigorous code of conduct.[43]

Continuing this line of thought one might be tempted to explain the differences between the Bolshevik Party functionary and his Chinese counterpart—for example, the greater independence and higher authority of the *kan pu*—by saying that the *kan pu* carries on the tradition of the gentry, which performed its duties without detailed

instructions from the capital and to which the population reverently
kowtowed. It may indeed be true that the *kan pu* is benefiting today
from such residue of the authority of the old élite as may still remain
after all these years of confusion and upheaval.

Yet similarities of this kind are superficial and fortuitous. The
differences and contrasts are far more significant. A member of the
gentry was the upholder and guardian of ancient tradition, the
personification of Chinese culture, the symbol of stability in the flux
of time. The *kan pu*, on the other hand, through the denial and
complete overthrow of the old order, rose to power as the champion
of a fresh young ideology, an ideology, moreover, which was born in
the westernmost corner of the Eurasian continent. A member of the
gentry was considered an ideal official when, as a true disciple of
Confucius, he governed as little as possible and left people to themselves and their non-government associations, particularly the clans.
In the name of the State and the Party, the *kan pu* must continually
interfere, exhort, threaten, punish, and drive the people to actions
and forms of behavior which, if left to themselves, they would not
contemplate. In his person a member of the gentry united the realms
of the intellect and the State—in normal periods of Chinese history,
an unbeatable combination. The *kan pu* (apart from a few specimens
for display purposes) is anything but an intellectual; he is much more
likely to be a coarse, shirt-sleeved type whose contrast to the intellectual élite is but thinly veiled and who is far more inclined to regard
it as consisting of weeds rather than flowers. A member of the gentry
was imbued with a highly humanistic ideology in which the art of
government meant the discreet adjustment of personal relationships,
the elimination of friction, the promotion of balance and harmony,
here and now. The *kan pu* is obliged to serve the attainment of a goal
which lies in the distant future and to this end continually has to
release new forces, but at the same time new friction, imbalance, and
discord. Hence the *kan pu* class is the antithesis of the gentry rather
than its spiritual descendant. The most one could say is that its
ancestors were the anti-Confucian 'legalists' whose brief appearance
on the Chinese scene we noted in Chapter III.

*

Actually it is the 'veteran fighters' of a very recent past who today
still determine the *kan pu* type. Some three and a half million of the
total of seventeen million Party members joined the Party in the

period before the founding of the Chinese People's Republic, i.e. before 1949.[44] From their ranks come not only the entire top Party leadership but the bulk of the intermediate ranks. They were molded in the twenty years of guerrilla fighting; in thousands of little partisan units—often existing for years on end with no personal contact with headquarters—they waged war on Chiang and the Japanese.

It is here that the natural explanation for the differences between the Chinese and Soviet functionary is to be found. The school through which this guerrilla Communist, as we may call him, passed was a completely different one from that of the Russian Communist. The latter's struggle against Tsarism had been of a conspiratorial nature—underground work in urban settlements, the organizing of strikes and demonstrations, years as *émigrés* in the editorial offices of illegal papers and in the coffee houses of Vienna and Zürich, when they suddenly found themselves (after the brief interlude of the civil war) faced with the task of ruling the largest country in the world. And even that happened over forty years ago, years in which a clearly discernible type has emerged: that of the manager who is part of a tightly organized hierarchy. At the same time, many of the most talented have switched from a purely Party career to that of industrial management, primarily because they found greater possibilities of development in this area due to the 'one-man leadership' in the economic field (*yedinonachalie*) introduced by Stalin in 1929. For years Khrushchev has been trying to lead the Party out of rigid Stalinist bureaucratism, to imbue it with fresh vigor, to bring it into closer contact with the masses. He has decentralized and again centralized the economy, increased the Party's supervisory functions in industrial concerns and agriculture, and handed over certain government tasks (such as dealing with juvenile delinquency and the black market) to mass organizations run by the Party. But he does not seem to have been particularly successful in these efforts.

The Chinese Party leadership, on the other hand, has so far managed to keep the Party more flexible and to preserve its position of power, in economic life as well. The 'one-man leadership' adopted in industrial concerns in the early days in imitation of the Soviet pattern has been done away with;[45] the role of the *kan pu* in the economy has been strengthened.[46] Elements of guerrilla Communism were revived, especially during the phase of the Great Leap; Party members were encouraged to indulge in independent thinking and to make their own decisions—within the framework, of course, of the 'small study groups', where problems which could be solved on the spot were discussed and dealt with.

Such differences in style are not to be dismissed lightly, although it will not be possible to assess their importance for another ten or twenty years. For what will happen when Mao, that embodiment of guerrilla Communism, is no longer alive, when the 'veteran fighters' no longer form a fifth of the Party, but only a tenth or a twentieth? When Chinese industry has reached the same stage of development and differentiation as Soviet industry had at the time when 'one-man leadership' was put into effect throughout Russia's economy? Only then we will be in a position to judge whether the CPC is fundamentally different from the CPSU, or whether here too the differences are merely temporal ones due to varying levels of development.

Side by side with the distinctions in style which we have observed, especially in linguistic style, there is, of course, no lack of common elements. Like the Russians, the Chinese Communists are fond of militarizing the language; and although ever since World War I this process is also to be found in other languages, in China this tendency is emphasized—no doubt in order to condition a people more inclined to adjustment and harmony than to division and struggle, and to render them more useful to the Party. In the Soviet Union the challenge of one factory to another to vie with it in production is simply called a competition (or a socialist competition) but the Chinese call it 'the lighting of the beacons of war'. The written challenge is called a 'declaration of war', and in cases where—to the satisfaction of the Party—a number of these are to be found on a factory notice board, the factory is commended for its 'warlike atmosphere' (*chan tou ch'i feng*).

The passion for making everything relating to Communism appear grandiose by means of adjectives is another feature the Chinese have in common with the Russian Communists. Mao, of course, is 'great' or 'brilliant', the Party functionaries are always 'of high caliber', the Party is 'the glorious Party which is always right', and the masses are not simply masses but 'broad, great masses'.

As far as I know, there is as yet no comprehensive monograph on the new speech usages of our time, but presumably it would reveal that in the early stages of a revolution, when people have to get used to an unfamiliar, constantly shifting situation, the power of linguistic creativity is stronger than at a later stage when the population has settled down. As far as the Soviet Union is concerned,[47] this has already been ascertained. The number of new words, particularly large during the revolution and the first Five-Year Plan, has diminished. Will we find one day that the same thing has happened in China?

*

For the foreign observer who is familiar with the Soviet Union and who has followed day-to-day events in Communist China (at least in the years immediately after 1949) the common elements far outweighed the differences. Almost all the distinguishing features which had been observed in the Soviet Union were to be found again in Red China. As in Russia, one was struck everywhere by the insistence on fulfilling the plan ahead of time: a Chinese truck driver, for instance, had reached his 1961 norm in April 1960,[48] for which feat praises have been heaped upon him. (By this time he must be approaching his quota for the 1970's.) As in the Soviet Union, the sports badge in China bears the inscription 'Prepared for work and defence'; in China, too, the foreigner finds himself dealing with a tourist bureau modeled to the last detail on the Soviet Intourist; just as Moscow paraded Lenin's widow as a symbol of the continuity of the Russian revolution, so Peking has its Soong Ching Ling (Sun Yat-sen's widow), whose job it is to appear before the Chinese public as well as foreign visitors as the 'grand old lady of the revolution'. When one reads the pamphlets about Liu Hu-lan, the young woman activist who was killed by Chinese anti-Communists,[49] one finds they hardly differ from the Soviet descriptions of the struggle and death of Zoya Kosmodemyanskaya, the girl-partisan who was hanged by the Germans; and a relationship was also established between the mothers of these two heroines. What Stakhanov was to the Russians, Wu Yun-to is to China.[50] In China as in Russia, Sino-Soviet friendship is guarded 'like the apple of the eye';[51] there is a 'general line';[52] on revolutionary anniversaries the masses march past the beloved leader; in both countries youth is organized along very similar lines[53] —and yet a surprising amount of effort still goes into dealing with juvenile delinquents, known in the USSR as khuligany (from 'hooligans'), in China as liu ming (= wandering tramp). In Red China, too, in speeches where it is desired to haul a Party comrade over the coals, sentences begin with: 'Some comrades believe . . .' A desperate (but apparently unsuccessful) battle is being waged against bureaucratism in which parallel slogans and even anecdotes are used. (Just like the tale is told in the Soviet Union of a senior official who paid so little attention to his outgoing mail that he unwittingly signed his own death warrant, so there was a report in the Chinese press of someone signing a delivery slip on which some pranksters had entered '500 sheets of paper, 40 pairs of gloves, and one woman.'[54])

It goes without saying that painters in China also turn out collective works of art ('collective paintings of the Central Academy of Fine Arts'),[55] a practice which, apart from a few exceptions, has meanwhile been stopped in Russia and one to which even in China objections are beginning to be made.[56] In China, too, those who have fallen into disfavor turn into Orwellian 'unpersons': just as Beria no longer appears in the Great Soviet Encyclopedia, whose subscribers were instructed to cut out the page containing his biography and to replace it with one about the Bering Sea, so Kao Kang's name was expunged from Mao's *Selected Works*.[57] Cadres riding the crest of the revolution get themselves new—younger—wives,[58] in spite of the fact that puritanical primness and decorum form part of the style demanded by Party leadership in both Red countries. (However, lapses are becoming more and more common in the USSR.)

*

The phase of widespread adoption of Soviet models coincided with the anti-national period of the Chinese revolution, when it was apparently believed—as the Russians had done before—that it was possible to start again with the Year One and throw everything which had gone before onto the rubbish heap of history. These trends probably did not originate with Mao himself, but for a time, while he was consolidating his power, he let them take their course.

As in Russia after 1917, the combination of revolutionary excess of zeal with hatred of the traditional resulted in the loss of irreplaceable treasures. In the struggle against the landlords, for example, their libraries were either destroyed as 'feudalistic' or handed over to the peasants, who used them for fuel or sold them as waste paper. During that time, a single paper mill in Anhwei province annually 'processed' more than sixty thousand pounds of classical books. When in the fall of 1956 the Hundred Flowers started to put out their first hesitant blossoms, protests were raised against this national self-mutilation. 'Classical books are no longer to be destroyed', said an editorial in a Peking newspaper containing the item about the paper mill in

Anhwei;[59] and the Szechwan province newspaper wrote: 'The classics are the most precious cultural heritage of our people.'[60] Soon afterwards, in January 1957, the musicians and dancers who still survived after the traditional Confucius celebrations had been abolished in 1937, were instructed by the Ministry of Culture to provide for the training of young artists.

The new note of patriotism among the Communists found a lively and responsive echo in China, more so even than in the Soviet Union, because to the Chinese his 'cultural heritage' is so very important. Moreover, the humiliations he had undergone at the hands of the West (and of the Japanese) left him with far deeper spiritual wounds than we realized. In the course of my numerous visits and many years spent in China, I never once experienced any unpleasantness aimed at me as a white man—from the Japanese, yes, but never from a Chinese. Only Mao's victory, and the anti-foreign feeling in China which contributed to it, revealed how much resentment, if not hatred, must have existed behind the sometimes friendly, sometimes reserved, but always courteous faces of the Chinese.

Among the young Chinese with whom I talked in Hongkong after their flight from China, one student, who had only recently gained his freedom, said to me: 'I myself couldn't stand it any longer; but as far as I am concerned, Mao can do what he likes, as long as he makes China strong.' We would have to search for quite a long time among the students of the Soviet Union before we found one who would apply this phrase to his own country. Of course, the Russians had and still have inferiority complexes toward the West, but even the older ones among them do not have the memory of a long period of humiliation by Western powers.

The stage during which Soviet citizens greedily drank in everything Stalin had to tell them about the many alleged 'first discoveries' by Russians is past, while the Chinese are still in the throes of it. Since the production of stamps has become more of a political than a geographical matter, even I, although I am not a collector, had to take a look at philately. What did I find? Portraits of Mao, naturally, and red flags, doves of peace, dams, happy working girls at the polling booths, high tension cables, threshing combines, record-breaking sportsmen, raised gun barrels, fighter pilots in the sky, Marx, Engels, Lenin, Stalin, scenes from the revolution and the Korean war, people's furnaces. But side by side with these (although not for the first few years after 1949) pictures of quite a different kind

—symbols of the 'cultural heritage': portraits of two astronomers of the second and eighth centuries (one a monk, as is evident from the picture), one of a mathematician and another of a pharmacologist of olden times; also one of a dramatist of the Mongol period with illustrations depicting his works; a beautifully designed series entitled 'Our Great Mother-Country', with eight reproductions of early wall-paintings, including some decidedly 'feudalistic' scenes; others called 'Ancient Inventions', including the compass and the seismograph, and 'Archeological Treasures', showing ceramics and bronzes from the second and first centuries B.C.; and five views of old Peking and four of ancient pagodas. In the Soviet Union stamps devoted to the cultural heritage did not appear till eighteen years after the triumph of the revolution: the first was in 1935 commemorating the twenty-fifth anniversary of Tolstoy's death, and even then they remained rare exceptions. During World War II the patriotic motifs became more frequent.

Whether these historical series were mainly intended to impress the West or the Russians it is impossible to say: in my opinion the Chinese certainly also had their Russian neighbors in mind. In some cases this is quite clear, as for example an illustrated book which proudly enumerates the early Chinese inventions;[61] or an article appearing in the *People's Daily* in 1957 which in dealing with rocket technology has this to say:

We Chinese have played a glorious role in this field. At the beginning of the eleventh century [A.D.] T'ang Fu and Shih Pu invented the rocket. . . . In the presence of the emperor they fired a rocket into the sky, using black powder as fuel. This was the first step on the road to a man-made satellite. The invention reached Europe. Nine hundred years later [!] a Russian schoolteacher studied the problems of interplanetary space flight.[62]

*

It is by no means impossible that the zeal with which the 'cultural heritage' has been emphasized in China, particularly during the last few years, represents the result of the internal clash with the powerful but, in the eyes of many Chinese, barbarically immature Russian neighbor. Mao has managed to give Marxism-Leninism a Chinese coloring—without, it must be emphasized, altering its substance. Even when in 1958 he took a different path from that of the Soviet Union, especially in regard to people's communes and wage policy, he remained within the boundaries of the common ideology and, like his opponent Khrushchev, he was always able to justify himself with a number of apt quotations from Marx and Lenin. Here, then, we see the very beginnings of a process which we came across earlier in discussing the Sinification of Buddhism (to some extent, of Christianity also). Nor is it surprising that this Sinification is taking place chiefly via the language, that most Chinese of instruments created by the genius of this people over the last few thousand years.

An expert in linguistic research at the University of California, who is of Chinese descent, has been following this process for some years, and she has published some detailed papers on the subject.[63] From the latter it is clear that this, like the acceptance of Buddhism in China long ago, is a case of mutual interpenetration: a Sinification of Communism on the one hand and, on the other, a Bolshevization of all that is Chinese. However, we have already shown in our discussion of Buddhism that a comparison of the respective effects of Buddhism and Marxism-Leninism on China certainly does not warrant any unqualified predictions.

Leninism, too, represents a Russianization of Marxism and an application of this non-Russian ideology to conditions which were not only economically primitive but also specifically Russian. This is too well known for me to have to substantiate it here. The path from Marx to Lenin and to Mao is, therefore, to some extent the path of Russianization and then Sinification of Marxism, and this fact cannot remain entirely without influence on the relationship between Moscow and Peking.

When we look back on the traditional, i.e. pre-Communist, world view of the Russians and the Chinese, as outlined in Part I, we recall that their Communist leaders found themselves in dissimilar situations. Lenin and his adherents profited from their country's Messianic spirit, and one may well ask whether the Bolshevik revolution would have successfully overcome its serious setbacks and trials if it had not gained supremacy over a people which was prepared in its idealism 'to take upon itself the sufferings of the world' and at the cost of its own travail to bequeath mankind with what it believed to be a better tomorrow. Not long ago I was talking to a Soviet engineer who is not only far from being a romantic enthusiast but regards the realities in the Soviet Union with some scepticism and reservations, and he said to me: 'What we Russians have gone through in the last forty-five years in the way of evil [he was referring here to Stalin, as the conversation showed] and good, will make it very much easier for the rest of the world to find the right path in the future.' The only thing was that Lenin could not lay claim to this metaphysical spirit of self-sacrifice as such, since the materialistic doctrine of salvation applies to the body, not the soul. The forces with which Lenin turned his mill wheels came from springs beyond his experience, and which he even despised; he mobilized the religious fervor of the people for worldly, anti-religious purposes.

Mao was in the opposite position. He was dealing with a people who by tradition had been striving since the days of Confucius to adapt themselves to the here and now as best they might, a people who sincerely believed in the possibility of establishing a social order on earth which would approximate the ideal of mankind living together in peace and harmony. To this extent, therefore, the Communist doctrine of the imminent establishment of an ideal, classless, fraternally-minded State which would give security to every Chinese, fell on receptive soil.

Had Mao stopped here, he would have remained within the framework of Chinese tradition and would have been assured of the support of the overwhelming majority of his people. But Mao went further, a great deal further. While marching toward the alleged harmony of tomorrow, the Communists forced the people to the actual disharmony of today, to behavior which was extremely repugnant to them: to public criticism of their fathers, to vilification of their neighbors, to class warfare, to the relentless search for the 'enemies of socialism', to uncompromising decisions for or against—in a word, to actions which run counter to their traditions. It is true that the Chinese has taken all this upon himself, but who can believe he has done so willingly?

The threat to Communism in Russia, then, is the possibility of the people's faith in their world mission declining. For Chinese Communism, however, it lies in the prospect that the people, although they have subjected themselves to an uncongenial way of life, advance no nearer toward the harmony they dream of, the minimum level of prosperity they hope for, but that—as has been happening since 1958 —they find these goals receding.

Part III

NEIGHBORS

INTRODUCTION

COMMUNISM HAS GAINED TOTAL SUPREMACY in two countries. In spite of all the ways in which they differ, we have established in Part II of this book that there were a preponderant number of parallel features in both states, especially in the end results. By the time Mao had been in power a few years, the Chinese People's Republic had already traveled a fair distance along the road marked by Lenin and to an even greater degree by Stalin: the peasantry had been collectivized (the 'advanced agricultural producers' co-operative' differed in name only from the Soviet kolkhoz), trade and commerce were completely in government hands, the intellectuals had been integrated (outwardly at least) and the Communist Party of China—which in matters of style often differed from the Bolshevik Party but which, like it, was a tightly centralized organization of functionaries—represented the sole authority in the country. The preceding four chapters have shown us that, in all material points, Mao was the pupil and imitator of the men in the Kremlin, and the conclusion seemed inevitable that Russia and China, moving in the same direction along very similar paths over the terrain of the same world outlook, must be close allies and friends. But, as we shall see in Part III, at a very early stage there also existed between the Communist movements of the two neighboring countries something more than the 'socialist brotherhood' which so many people have expected —namely, a coldly calculating self-interest, a tightening up of the frontier of language and script, a highly 'unbrotherly' creditor-debtor relationship, and a growing coolness due to what one might call an excess of 'friendship'—all this long before the Sino-Soviet conflict became one of the cardinal issues in world affairs.

CHAPTER IX

STALIN—CHIANG—MAO

FOR A LONG TIME the Russians, like all Europeans, were in the eyes of the Chinese 'foreign devils', the only difference being the not very important fact that they came by land. Anyone who wishes to study the early history of Russo-Chinese relations will find an extensive literature on the subject.[1] As far as we are concerned, this relationship did not begin to be of interest until 1917, for, as Mao has said, 'Before the October Revolution, the Chinese were not only ignorant of Lenin and Stalin, they did not even know of Marx and Engels.'[2]

Classical Marxism of the pre-Lenin stamp had been unable to gain a foothold in China since it was designed for an industrial society such as did not exist in China at that time. Modern intellectual circles in China had, of course, been interested in the Russian revolutionary movement before the autumn of 1917, but rather for its liberal aspects than for the Bolshevist group of conspirators. The significance of Lenin's seizure of power for world politics was at first recognized even less in China than in the West.

Among the first to welcome the Bolshevik victory was Li Ta-chao, who in July 1918 wrote an article entitled 'On the Revolution in France and Russia', praising it as 'the dawn of a new world culture'.[3] During the days of chaos in Europe at the close of World War I, he published another article under the revealing title of 'Victory of Bolshevism'; for, he argued, the real conquerors of the epoch were not the liberal democrats of the West but 'Lenin, Trotsky, Kollontay, Liebknecht, Scheidemann and Marx', and he called Bolshevism the standard-bearer of mankind and freedom.[4] For the time being, however, such voices were but rarely heard.

Communist influences were hardly at work in the May Fourth Movement. However, twenty years later Mao maintained: 'The May 4 Movement came into being at the call of the world revolution of that time, of the Russian Revolution and of Lenin.'[5] Since then history writers in the Soviet Union as well as in China have attributed the 4th of May to Communism. In actual fact, however, as we have seen, the movement which exploded into the consciousness of the Chinese public on May 4, 1919, had been born before the Bolshevik revolution and without the influence of Communism.

*

Wider circles among the revolutionary intelligentsia of China did not become aware of the upheaval in Russia until they heard of what is known as the Karakhan Declaration. In July 1919 Leo Karakhan, at that time Deputy People's Commissar for Foreign Affairs in Moscow, announced that the Soviet Government would annul all unequal treaties made by the Tsars with China and would give back to the Chinese people the acquisitions therein defined. Owing to the some-what chaotic conditions prevailing in China, eight months went by before this statement was made known there in March 1920, and then in a version which specifically promised the return of the railway which had been built by the Tsarist empire. However, the Soviets later maintained that this section of the Karakhan Declaration, which had had a particularly sensational effect in China, had been forged and inserted at a later date. In fact it had unquestionably formed part of the original version.[6]

The declaration gave rise to great enthusiasm in China. The sympathies it aroused for Soviet Russia were all the stronger for the fact that the Western powers were not inclined to relinquish any of their privileges in China, and even accepted the Japanese claims to Chinese soil which the Chinese had angrily rejected.[7] The represent-atives of the Chinese intelligentsia turned more and more to the study of Marxism. The countless intellectual groups, both large and small (such as Mao's New People's Studies Society in Changsha) and their publications which, especially in Peking, sprang up like mush-rooms,[8] concerned themselves increasingly with the radical doctrines of the West, and with every 'ism' then in existence.

At first only a few committed themselves to a definite direction. Generally speaking, they were interested in everything at once. From what Mao has himself said, we know that, in the few years between 1911 and 1920, he was a Buddhist and a K'ang Yu-wei-ist, a mon-archist, idealist, liberal, democratic reformer, utopian socialist, anti-militarist, autonomist (for his native province of Hunan), anar-chist, and a Marxist.[9] At that time thousands of young Chinese intellectuals could have said the same of themselves. Nevertheless Mao was among the few who openly acknowledged Marxism and the model of the Bolshevik revolution in the very early days, i.e. before the announcement of the Karakhan Declaration. He did this in his essay, 'The Great Community of the Masses of the People', which appeared in serial form in July and August 1919 in a newspaper published by him in Changsha, and in his letters which were later published in the 'Collection of Letters from Members of the New People's Studies Society'.[10] 'By the summer of 1920 I had become, in theory and to some extent in action, a Marxist,' Mao says of himself.[11]

Of all the encounters which the Marxists had with other revolutionary doctrines, the most interesting was the conflict with the anarchists in China, because here the ancient anti-government doctrines dating from Chinese antiquity, particularly those of Lao-tzu and Chuang-tzu, combined with the parallel ideas of Bakunin and Kropotkin.[12] These discussions showed, moreover, how quickly Lenin's Chinese followers appropriated his jargon. When, for instance, they wrote: 'Revisionists and reformists, like Kautsky and Bernstein & Co., who are infected with the poison of rationalism . . .',[13] they were obviously taking a leaf from his book.

In the summer of 1920 Grigor Voytinsky was sent to China by the Comintern. He was present at the founding of the Socialist Youth Corps, a forerunner of the CPC (August 1920), and then of the CPC itself. July 1, 1921, is considered the official founding day of the Party.

From the first moment of its creation to the shifting of its Central Committee to Mao's stronghold in the autumn of 1932, that is to say, for more than eleven years, the ties between the CPC and Moscow were of the closest. Many decisions which vitally affected the CPC were actually not made in China but in the 'capital of world revolution'. It is scarcely an exaggeration to say that at that time the fate of the CPC was dependent on the struggles for power in Moscow. Its leaders were appointed and dismissed by Moscow; its policies were determined by Moscow's agents. The historians' final word concerning this period of the CPC's utmost dependence on Moscow has not yet been written, as there are still too many gaps in our knowledge, but some detailed studies have been published covering the extent of this knowledge.[14]

During those eleven years, world Communism suffered one of its most serious defeats. A swift rise of the CPC to power and influence, a rise which seemed to render its victory throughout China imminent, was followed in 1927 by a sudden plunge to a position of almost total insignificance: the loss of any kind of influence among the workers, the miserable stagnation of a divided and powerless 'general staff without an army', and finally the flight to the remote guerrilla areas in which Mao together with his peasant bands barely managed to hold out against Chiang Kai-shek's troops. No wonder Moscow and Peking do not care to recall this period. Here again, the most momentous of the decisions which led to this disaster originated in Moscow: the alliance of the CPC with Sun Yat-sen's party, the Kuomintang (KMT). Against its better judgment and under pressure of a representative of the Comintern (the Dutchman Sneevliet, alias Maring), the CPC leadership resolved on this alliance with the KMT at its founding congress in July 1921, and a year later, likewise under his influence, on the entry of CPC members into the KMT.

As long as the KMT was a loose, undisciplined body, it represented no great threat. But the Russians had such high hopes of the alliance with Sun Yat-sen that in the autumn of 1923 they sent their agent Mikhail Borodin to China to reorganize the KMT into a strong, effective weapon. Together with the ablest of the KMT leaders, Chiang Kai-shek, who at that time enjoyed Moscow's favor, Borodin was so successful in these efforts that in April 1927 the KMT was able to extinguish the CPC almost completely. Even after that, improbable though it may sound, Moscow insisted for nearly six months on the continuation of the Communists' alliance with the KMT in the vain hope that its left wing would successfully oppose Chiang. The remnants of the Communist cadres in the cities were sacrificed in a number of ventures inspired chiefly by Moscow, such as the Canton rebellion of December 1927, which was put down by Chiang with much bloodshed but without great difficulty.

*

During the years 1934 to 1936, which I spent in Moscow, I frequently came in contact with a sad-faced man who worked in the editorial department of an English-language Communist newspaper and gave one the impression of a disused locomotive rusting away on a siding. It was Grusenberg, alias Borodin, eating Stalin's bread of charity in these uncharitable surroundings. He had no objection to telling me about his career: his membership as a young man in the Russian Social Democratic Party (in the right, i.e. Menshevik wing), his emigration to America (under the impact of the failure of the 1905 revolution), his return to politics after the 1917 revolution, his work as an agent in Mexico and then, as an adviser to Kemal (later Ataturk), in Turkey, his journey to China, and his efforts to re-organize the KMT.

But the closer he came to the year 1926, the more reticent Borodin became. For it was he who time and again had placed his bet on Chiang Kai-shek—even after Chiang's coup in March 1926 brought him control over Canton, even after the temporary arrest of the Soviet advisers (except for Borodin, who was absent at the time), even after Chiang ordered the exclusion of Communists from all important posts in May 1926; in fact, almost until the spring of 1927, when Chiang destroyed the Communist organization in Shanghai and paralyzed it throughout China. Not until his last hope, the left wing of the KMT, had turned against the Communists did Borodin realize that he had backed the wrong horse; he returned to Moscow a beaten man in the summer of 1927. Whether he had merely carried out Stalin's instructions to the bitter end, or whether his reports had played a part in Stalin's decisions, he would not say—it was just before the bloody purges in the Soviet Union. But one thing is certain: next to Chiang himself there was scarcely one individual who contributed as much to Chiang's unquestioned victory in 1927 as Borodin. No wonder Mao called him a 'blunderer'.[15]

Borodin's departure from China represented the end of a discreditable phase in relations between Russian and Chinese Communists, a phase which in retrospect is still embarrassing for all parties concerned. Stalin's influence on the CPC dwindled after the urban centers of gravity had been destroyed and was soon negligible; his interest in events in China declined, as did his interest in the Comintern after his decisive victory over Trotsky under the banner of 'Socialism in one country'. The word China, so frequently uttered during the quarrel with Trotsky, was scarcely mentioned during the years 1931 to 1935;[16] and, apart from the German military adviser who went by the name of Li Teh (and who has still not been identified with certainty) not a single representative of the Comintern appears to have entered Mao's domain.[17] Hitler's accession to power caused Stalin to turn his eyes more toward the West. As far as his foreign policy was concerned, for the time being his maxim was: safety first—i.e. the safety of the Soviet Union before the speedy establishment of the world revolution.

As a reaction to the rise of Hitler, the Seventh Comintern Congress, which took place in Moscow in July and August of 1935, instructed the Communist parties to form a united front with all anti-Fascist groups. In the case of the CPC this was easier said than done, for the only body which could be an ally in a united front of this kind was the KMT. During that summer of 1935, the Communists were fleeing from the KMT. Not until Mao had established himself in the far northwest, early in 1936, did the declarations appear in which cooperation with the KMT was pronounced feasible.

*

Whether willingly or not, the Chinese Communists now fell once again into step with Moscow's line. The most dramatic instance of this was in the Sian affair in December 1936, when to everyone's surprise the Kremlin and the Chinese Communists supported the liberation of Chiang Kai-shek after his capture by rebel troops. A further instance occurred some months later, when a treaty was concluded between Moscow and Nanking (nominally a non-aggression pact but actually a treaty of friendship aimed at Japan) in August 1937, and a few days later the united front between the KMT and the CPC was proclaimed in Yenan and Nanking.

Even today it is still not clear whether this parallel attitude on the part of Moscow and Yenan toward Nanking was of spontaneous origin, whether it was the result of consultation, or whether Yenan was acting on instructions from Moscow.[18] But since the events in the Sian affair followed so closely on each other (Chiang was captured on December 12; in the night of the 13th to the 14th, *Pravda* and *Izvestiya* published articles urging his liberation; immediately after that Chou En-lai, speaking on behalf of the CPC, expressed a similar view) one cannot regard an agreement between the Russian and Chinese Communists as a certainty, especially when we consider the technical difficulties involved in reaching remote and primitive Yenan from Moscow. However, I think we may assume the following to be true: after the Comintern resolution of the summer of 1935—perhaps not immediately but in the course of the next few months—Moscow and Yenan agreed in principle that a united front of the CPC and the KMT against Japan was desirable, and on this basis Moscow and Yenan followed parallel paths, although each did so on its own.

Fundamentally, the Kremlin took the same position it had occupied a dozen years earlier: at that time it had wanted the alliance with Sun Yat-sen, now it wanted one with Chiang Kai-shek. But there was a difference: Sun had been weak; thus there had been some sense in Moscow's instructions to undermine the KMT from within. But Chiang was strong, and the Kremlin wanted him to be strong. That is why this time there was no talk in Moscow of crippling the KMT. In the twenties Moscow had got its way against the Chinese Communists' better judgment. When from 1935 on it once again urged the CPC to co-operate with the KMT, it had no opposition to overcome. On the contrary, Mao worked hard at a rapprochement with the KMT.

Naturally Stalin and Mao were not pursuing identical ends at that time. Moscow needed a strong national government under Chiang with no time limitations, while Yenan promoted the alliance with the KMT with the intention of undermining and then destroying the KMT—not at once, but as quickly as possible.[19]

Almost without exception the Soviet press reported most favorably on Chiang and had far more to say about him than about Mao, whose first biography (based on Snow's report) did not appear in the Soviet Union until 1939.[20] The co-operation of the CPC with the National Government was frequently referred to as a long-term association. Conflicts between Mao and Chiang found no echo in Soviet publications; even a clash between their troops in Anhwei in January 1941 received only a brief—and delayed—mention in the Soviet press. The Communist plans, insofar as they concerned China, were passed over in discreet silence.

By contrast the CPC never lost sight of its ultimate goal, even during the period in which the alliance was functioning quite smoothly (till the end of 1938) and was often outspoken about it. When increasing tension with the National Government recurred, Mao immediately spoke again of an armed struggle against the enemies of the revolution (end of 1939).[21] His reaction to the Anhwei incident was sharply to attack the KMT, and Chiang himself.[22]

During the Sino-Japanese war the Soviet Union provided Chiang with extensive military and economic aid, to a total value of at least 300 million US dollars. In contrast to this, there are no indications that the Soviets supplied the Communists during the same period—nor, incidentally, that Mao resented this. He seems to have accepted the fact—although it must be assumed he did not like it—that Soviet aid was mainly or even entirely for the benefit of Chiang.

*

Direct contacts between Moscow and Yenan were at a minimum. At the end of 1937, Wang Ming, whom we have already met as one of the leaders of the CPC before Mao, moved from Moscow to Yenan, without, however, gaining much influence there, and early in 1940 Chou En-lai spent some months in Moscow.[23] That seems to have been about all.[24] The common interest which had grown up between Yenan and Chungking, Chiang's emergency capital in the far west, as a result of the war with Japan was expressed by the fact that both Yenan and Chungking welcomed the Hitler-Stalin pact of August 1939 as an indication of a possible estrangement on the part of Germany from its Japanese ally. And both regarded the pact concluded between Stalin and Tokyo in April 1941 with uneasiness: in spite of Moscow's assurances to the contrary, the Chinese were afraid it would result in a falling off of Soviet aid to China and encourage Japan's aggressive desires—a fear which Chungking expressed openly and which Yenan may be assumed to have shared, although it remained silent on the subject. The fact that Stalin guaranteed the Japanese the territorial inviolability of 'Manchukuo' (Japanese-occupied Manchuria) must have been a particularly bitter pill for Chungking and Yenan to swallow. But the riddle of how Stalin's policy toward China would be influenced by his pact with Japan dwindled in significance when two months later Hitler's tanks rumbled eastward.

Now the Kremlin's attention was concentrated on the war with Germany, and China disappeared almost entirely from its field of vision. The Soviet press barely mentioned China, least of all Yenan. It is true that anxiety in Moscow over the Soviet eastern frontiers diminished after Japan attacked Pearl Harbor and Singapore instead of Siberia; but in view of the overwhelming initial victories of the Japanese anything was possible. Stalin therefore still wanted a strong Chiang.

Moreover, Stalin was in a predicament: since 1935 he had regarded Chiang, not Mao, as the main brake to Japanese aggression and as China's legitimate head of state, and, considering the situation as it was at that time, he was justified in doing so. His plans for future acquisitions in the Far East, on which he had been working since the

Teheran conference (November 1943) had, therefore, to be based on this view of Chiang's position. Furthermore, these plans required America's consent, and this was only obtainable if Chiang were regarded as representing China. The Americans in turn, who in 1943 were still overestimating Japan's military strength and were afraid they would have to fight for every foot of Japanese soil for the rest of the war, were prepared to force Chungking to accept Stalin's demands in order to obtain his entry into the war with Japan. And so it came about that, after Teheran, decisions in the Far East were made within the triangle of Roosevelt (and later Truman), Stalin, and Chiang—with Chiang by far the weakest partner—while nobody bothered to mention Mao.

The outcome of Teheran was Yalta (February 1945). Stalin committed himself to enter the war with Japan not more than three months after the end of the war in Europe, and Churchill and the mortally ill Roosevelt promised him—at the expense of China—a half-share in the Manchurian railway network, the use of Port Arthur as a naval port, a privileged position in the commercial port of Dairen, and the preservation of the *status quo* for Outer Mongolia (as a satellite of Moscow).[25] By this time Stalin had gone so far that the only way he could protect his acquisitions in China was to treat Chiang as the sole Chinese partner. Otherwise he would have run the risk of having Chiang refuse to honor promises—which others had made for him at Yalta.

Yalta led in turn to the treaty between Moscow and Chungking of August 14, 1945, in which, under American pressure, Chiang fulfilled the promises made by the Anglo-Saxons to Stalin in Yalta and for which Stalin in return traded his promise that the Soviet Union's 'moral support and aid in military supplies and other material resources . . . [was] to be entirely [i.e. exclusively] given to the National Government [Chiang Kai-shek] as the central government of China',[26] and that it would recognize China's sovereignty over Manchuria and not interfere in the domestic affairs of China.

What Mao thought of this treaty, whether he regarded it with resentment or with a knowing smile, we do not know. In his report of April 1945 he did 'enthusiastically approve' of the resolutions made at the conferences of Teheran and Yalta (a phrase which was subsequently reduced to the one word 'approve').[27] And the official organ of the Communists in Yenan unhesitatingly praised the treaty.[28]

*

For the ten years, therefore, between the Seventh Comintern Congress in the summer of 1935 and the Stalin-Chiang treaty of the summer of 1945, the picture of Stalin's policy toward China is quite clear. In the first place, he needed a united China under a strong national government, i.e. a government led by Chiang, as a counterweight to Japan; secondly, in order to gather in his rich harvest in the Far East with the consent of the United States, he was obliged to recognize Chiang's government as the sole government of China. August 1945 brought him the fulfilment of both desires within a few days: first Japan capitulated, then Chiang's government underwrote all the Kremlin's demands. What effect would this have on Stalin's policy toward China?

We know very little about the relationship between Stalin and Mao during the four years from August 1945 to the founding of the Chinese People's Republic in the autumn of 1949, a critical period for the continued relations of the two neighbor states.[29] The few facts known to us allow two different interpretations: that Stalin planned everything just as it happened, in close co-operation with Mao, or the other way round—that the course of events, i.e. Mao's rapid victory, took Stalin completely by surprise. The fact that Stalin spoke contemptuously of Mao in his conversations with Western representatives, for example with Harry Hopkins on May 26, 1945 (when he said he did not believe the Communist leaders in China were as capable as Chiang or that they would be able to unite China),[30] or when he was talking to Wang Shih-chieh, Chiang's Foreign Minister, during negotiations in the summer of 1945,[31] does not necessarily mean very much. But even the Yugoslavs report that, shortly before the break with Tito in 1948, Stalin spoke as follows to a delegation from Belgrade:

It is true that we have also made mistakes. For example, after the war we invited the Chinese comrades to Moscow to discuss the situation in China with them. We told them frankly that we felt the prospects of a revolt in China were nil, and that the Chinese comrades should seek a modus vivendi with Chiang Kai-shek, take part in his government, and disband their army. The Chinese agreed with this Soviet view, but went back to China and did something quite different. They assembled their forces, organized their army, and are now, as we see, in the process of defeating Chiang Kai-shek's troops. In the case of China, therefore, we admit we were wrong. It turned out that the Chinese comrades were right and not the Soviets.[32]

It seems to me that these words which are attributed to Stalin come very close to what actually happened. For after August 1945 Stalin did not abruptly shift Soviet support from Chiang to Mao; on the contrary, he carried on in the same way, as if he were counting on China being ruled by Chiang for a long time to come. His manoeuvering in Manchuria, of which we shall hear more in the next chapter, was guided exclusively by Soviet interests: the fact that in the end Manchuria found itself in Mao's hands instead of Chiang's is to be regarded as a delayed result but not the goal of Stalin's policy.

Stalin was intelligent enough to realize that he would lose his booty on Chinese soil as soon as Mao took the helm; *vis-à-vis* Mao he could not afford an expansionist policy. One can perceive a distinct reserve on the part of Moscow toward Mao when one sees how for almost a year—until the summer of 1946—the Soviet press practically ignored the Chinese Communists.[33] Their victories over Chiang's troops which followed shortly and astonished the whole world were given no prominence in Moscow. In the commemorative speech of the thirty-first anniversary of the October revolution, for instance, which occurred in the period of tremendous Red Chinese successes, these victories were not even mentioned.[34]

On the other hand, the Red Chinese utterances of those days likewise contained very few references to the Soviet Union, possibly also out of consideration for the United States where there was at the time a strong inclination to regard the Chinese Communists as harmless 'social reformers' who had nothing in common with world revolution and would never harm anybody, if only that wicked Chiang Kai-shek would stop harassing them. Here one is reminded of the would-be witty remark made by the US Ambassador to China, Patrick J. Hurley, in November 1945 to the effect that 'the only difference between the Chinese Communists and the Oklahoma Republicans was that the Oklahoma Republicans aren't armed'.[35] Not until July 1, 1949, did Mao make one of his rare public acknowledgments of the Soviet Union; even then it was comparatively carefully worded in that he made use of the idea of 'leaning'. Mao replied to the accusation that the Chinese Communists were leaning on the Soviet Union as follows:

Exactly. The forty years' experience of Sun Yat-sen and the twenty-eight years' experience of the Communist Party have taught us to lean to one side, and we are firmly convinced that in order to win victory and consolidate it we must lean to one side. In the light of the experiences accumulated in these twenty-eight years, all Chinese without exception must lean either to the side of imperialism or to the side of socialism. Sitting on the fence will not do, nor is there a third road.[36]

*

We shall have more to say later about events in Manchuria, occupied by Malinovsky's troops in August 1945. We have no reliable information. One is struck by the overlapping of the departure, constantly postponed, of the Soviet Army from Manchuria and the moving up of Red Chinese units, to whom in the process the Russians handed over extensive supplies of Japanese arms (a fact which nullifies the significance of the Red Chinese protestations that they received no *Soviet* arms whatever for the war with Chiang). Nevertheless it is conceivable that the mobility and shrewd tactics of Mao's troops took Malinovsky by surprise.

When, after the capture of Mukden in November 1948, the Chinese Communists had gained firm control of the whole of Manchuria, it looked at first as if China would remain for the time being divided— with Mao as master of Manchuria and Chiang of the rest of China. Yet regardless of what Stalin may have expected, Mao's series of sweeping victories, which began with the occupation of Tientsin and Peking in January 1949 and within a few months embraced the whole country, created an entirely new set of circumstances.

Even then Stalin did not immediately alter course: when the National Government fled before the Communist armies to Canton, Stalin's representative was the only ambassador to follow it there.[37] Not until it became clear that Chiang's disaster was irrevocable did Stalin accept the consequences: the day after the Chinese People's Republic was proclaimed in Peking on October 1, 1949, the Kremlin announced its recognition of the new government. It was as well for Stalin that he did not delay. On December 16 the victorious Mao arrived in Moscow.

CHAPTER X

BOTH SIDES OF THE
LONGEST FRONTIER

Manchuria

EVER SINCE I BEGAN writing a Ph.D. thesis on the significance in
world politics of the Russo-Japanese war, which was fought in
Manchuria, this country has interested me more than almost any
other outside Europe. I visited Manchuria over and over again:
while it was still Chinese; when it was occupied by the Japanese;
when it was known as Manchukuo and had to worship the Sun
Goddess of Japan; and under the Communists who, so as not to
recall the memory of the Manchu Emperors, refer to it as the 'Three
Northeastern Provinces'. This magnificent country, with its sparkling
frosty winters and hot summers, its deep forests and endless fertile
fields, its vast industries, has cast its spell over me, and I have faith
in its economic future. The Tsars had faith in it too; so had the
Japanese when, more than half a century ago, they won a major war
against the empire of the Tsars and then sent their best adminis-
trators, officers, railway engineers, and industrialists to Manchuria;
and, finally, Stalin too. On one of the very rare occasions when he
expressed any emotion, he referred to Manchuria; a few days after
its conquest by the Soviet Union he said (on September 2, 1945):

> The defeat [in the Russo-Japanese war] weighed on our country like a
> dark blot. Our people believed in and waited for the day when Japan
> would be beaten and the blot wiped out. For forty years we of the older
> generation have waited for this day. And now this day has come.[1]

*

None of Manchuria's conquerors found it easy to leave the country
when the bell tolled. For the Russians it came with the peace treaty
of Portsmouth (1905), when they lost southern Manchuria to Japan

(they sold their rights in the north to Manchukuo in 1935); for the Japanese, a few days after Hiroshima when they were suddenly attacked by the Soviet Union in spite of their non-aggression pact with the Soviets which was valid until 1946; and for the Soviets, in February 1950 when they promised Mao to relinquish the rights in Manchuria which Chiang Kai-shek had granted them in 1945 after a short transitional period.

Stalin must have found it particularly hard to keep this promise on account of the Manchurian railways. In spite of the Karakhan Declaration, he had laid claim to Russia's colonial rights in the railways, and in 1929 he even went to war in Manchuria—against the local warlord Chang Hsueh-liang—to enforce his demands. As late as 1945, when negotiating with the National Government, he told Chiang that he definitely needed the Manchurian railway system as otherwise he would be unable to defend the Pacific coast provinces of the Soviet Union against enemy attack.[2] As early as 1952 in the treaty with Mao he lost the many privileges connected with the railways which Chiang had been forced to grant him till 1975.

According to this treaty, Stalin would actually have had to vacate Port Arthur by the same date. But here the Korean war came to his aid, for this allegedly necessitated the continued existence of a Soviet base at this naval port. It was only after Stalin's death that his successors promised Mao, in a new treaty concluded in the autumn of 1954, to relinquish Port Arthur by May 31, 1955,[3] and this they actually did. (Rumors that in exchange they obtained the port of Chefoo remained unconfirmed.[4]) In order to sweeten this bitter pill for the Russians, a seventy-foot 'Tower of Sino-Soviet Friendship' was built in Port Arthur.[5]

*

The departure of the Soviet army, first scheduled for the end of November 1945, was, as we have noted, constantly postponed. It was said that the first delay, announced by the Russians on November 30, was at the request of the Chinese National Government. The latter was not yet in a position to despatch its own troops to ensure order in Manchuria, as Malinovsky was putting every possible obstacle in the way of the transportation of its troops, and this gave the Communist units a head start of several weeks. Yet the question of whether Chungking really asked for a delay of this kind remains in dispute.[6] The Soviet Union was undoubtedly solely responsible for further delays. At the end of February 1946 there were violent protests in many Chinese cities against the continued presence of Soviet troops in Manchuria—'Ivan Go Home!' demonstrations, so to speak. It was early in May of 1946 before the last Soviet soldiers left Manchurian soil.

After the departure of the Soviets it was revealed that they had taken with them the greater part of the equipment of this, the most important heavy industrial area in Asia. The advancing Chinese found only empty factory buildings.[7] We do not know what Mao thought about this; he made no comment. What many other Chinese thought about it came to light in 1957 in the weeks of the Hundred Flowers. Lung Yün who, after nearly twenty years as governor of Yunnan province, had gone over to the Communists and was now a leader of one of the smaller parties, made the following public statement:

> The Soviet army dismantled and removed a portion of the machinery in our factories when it liberated Northeast China. How much did the Soviet Union pay for this? Will we be compensated for it?[8]

These critical remarks were soon exploited to the full in the campaign against Lung Yün. When he apologized for them to the National People's Congress, his heretical views were paraded once more throughout the Red Chinese press; and when the secretary-general of the Sino-Soviet Friendship Association defended the Soviet Union against its critics—also to the National People's Congress—the Chinese press did not pass up the opportunity of covering this in detail too, and reporting that he had said:

> When China with the aid of the Soviet Union liberated the Northeast [Manchuria] the Americans dropped KMT troops there by plane. If the machinery had not been removed [and taken to Siberia] from these areas, it would have fallen into Chiang Kai-shek's hands. The rightist-opposition elements among us know very well that the aid given China by the Soviet Union since the liberation outweighs many times over the value of the machinery removed from the Northeast, and that the Soviet Union is granting us credit at a low rate of interest.[9]

This was another way of saying—as every Chinese immediately understood: first, we, the Chinese, liberated Manchuria from the Japanese; second, the Soviets removed the machinery and equipment which were there; third, they have since supplied us with new machinery, but against payment. Every Chinese with whom I talked

about this public controversy had been following it, and almost all
of them let it be understood (when speaking without witnesses) that
Lung Yün's undiplomatic remarks had gratified them.

At the time of my visit to Mukden in 1943, it had been Japan's
great mainland arsenal. I had driven for miles through streets where
factories on both sides were working day and night. Among others
I saw a big machine factory employing several thousand workers.
Fourteen years later, my wish to see this very factory was granted;
it was now called 'Machine Tool Factory No. 1' and belonged to the
Red Chinese government. In the manager's office I was given the
Communist version of what had happened to the factory. At the end
of the war it had been in quite good condition, but Chiang Kai-shek's
people had wrought havoc in Mukden and had practically given
away the machines, so that, when the Red Chinese occupied Mukden,
I was told, there were only a few machines left.

'As far as I know,' I put in, 'after the conquest of Manchuria the
Soviets removed the machines from Mukden *before* Chiang's troops
got there.'

The Chinese looked at me without expression. 'No, the Soviets
did not remove any machinery from here.'

I would not let it go at that: 'But this was openly admitted at
a session of the National People's Congress—I read about it myself!'

Again the expressionless mask: 'That happened in other factories,
not here.' I did not argue any further.

*

In Manchuria I came upon another shadow which falls across the
relationship between Peking and Moscow. A strange interlude had
taken place there after Mao's victory. Kao Kang, the man around
whom this affair revolved, had been the local CP leader in Shensi
before Mao reached this province in 1935 at the end of the Long
March. A self-made man, vigorous and determined, he had worked
his way up to the position of, so to speak, a Mao Tse-tung of Shensi
and it was to his domain that Mao escaped when he fled from South
China. Although Kao Kang retained his independent attitude, for a
long while everything went smoothly. He rose step by step and became a member of both the CC and the Politburo. When the Communists began to take Manchuria, he was transferred there. In 1948
he was commander in chief of all Communist troops in Manchuria

and the head Party boss of that area; at that time there was even a 'Northeastern Bureau of the CC' in Manchuria. In July 1949 he went to Moscow with his own (Manchurian) trade delegation and concluded a trade agreement with the Soviet Union which applied solely to Manchuria.[10] The following month a 'People's Congress of the Northeastern Provinces' [i.e. of Manchuria] met in Mukden and formed a 'People's Government of the Northeastern Provinces'— all under Kao Kang.

After that Kao Kang ruled for five years as the all-powerful regional head of Manchuria—also during the Korean war when Manchuria gained special importance as the hinterland of the war theater. In February 1954, however, charges were made against him in a closed session of the CC in Peking. In June the far-reaching administrative independence of Manchuria was done away with. And in the following year it was announced that since 1949 Kao Kang had been trying to turn Manchuria into his own 'independent kingdom', had led a conspiracy to take over the control of the Party and the government, and, after the disclosure of this conspiracy in 1954, had committed suicide.[11]

Two years later, while the memory of this most sensational of all purges in the CPC was still fresh, I constantly asked people I talked to in Red China what they thought of the background to this case. No one seemed to know exactly, but nearly all of them expressed the belief that Kao Kang, in his struggle for independence, had co-operated more closely with Stalin than was permissible for a provincial governor. Owing to a lack of concrete evidence, I myself prefer to refrain from passing judgment. However, it would not be surprising if Stalin, when he saw his Manchurian venture collapsing after Mao's victory throughout China, had encouraged the formation of a government more or less independent of Peking in order to make it a satellite of Moscow—like Outer Mongolia, which had once belonged to the Manchu empire. Peking gave a significant hint of this in the spring of 1956 in a declaration on de-Stalinization, when it was said that Kao Kang's anti-Party group had represented 'reactionary forces at home *and abroad*'.[12] (Author's italics.) One cannot help being struck by the fact that the charges against Kao Kang were not made until after Stalin's death, and that Marshal P'eng Teh-huai, who fell into disfavor in 1959, was Kao Kang's neighbor during the years when Kao Kang was governor of Manchuria and P'eng Teh-huai was commander in chief of the Chinese army in North Korea; presumably they had a lot to do with one another.

*

During that summer of 1957 I found Manchuria more Chinese than ever. There were only a few Russian advisers left. In order to emphasize their complete departure from Manchuria, the Soviets had in the previous year dissolved the 'Association of Soviet Citizens', to which every technical expert from the Soviet Union who was in Manchuria had belonged, and shortly before my arrival they even closed their consulate-general in Mukden (renamed Shenyang in 1928 so as not to remind people of the deposed Manchu dynasty, whose old capital it had been).

The only place where I saw Russians in large numbers was Harbin. After the Bolsheviks' victory in Siberia in 1922, this city, once the metropolis of Russian influence in Manchuria, became the haven for more than a hundred thousand 'White Russian' refugees. Even in the thirties, when many of them had already moved on to other Chinese cities (mainly to Shanghai) and to America, Harbin reminded me of a pre-revolutionary provincial Russian town in which a few Chinese had also happened to settle. In 1957 Harbin gave a quite extraordinary impression: the whole plan of the city, the houses, streets, and churches, were Russian, but the population thronging these streets consisted almost entirely of Chinese, of whom more than a million are now living there. Harbin remained the only city in Manchuria in which Russian as well as Chinese street signs were to be seen. Yet in what had once been the largest Russian club, the Railway Club on the banks of the Sungari, I saw no Russians at all; there were hundreds of young Chinese dancing Western dances to Western music. One landmark of the old days was left: the principal department store was still called Churin, although now it was called the 'Chinese State Company Churin'. At one time the Churin branches scattered throughout Manchuria had been meeting-places for the Russians, for all Europeans in fact; today they are purely Chinese department stores.

But in about a dozen Russian churches services were still being held. It was Sunday, and I went to the main church. The service was conducted by a Chinese priest, and there were also some Chinese among the congregation. When the service was over I sat for a while with a very old Russian refugee on a bench outside the church. He had come to Manchuria during the last century as a railway official and mainly entertained me with tales of his heroic exploits during the Boxer rebellion. The intervening decades seemed to be of less interest to him. Finally he informed me that he intended to commit suicide soon: life had become so exceedingly boring.

In Harbin I came upon two stone witnesses to the fact that it had been Stalin's intention to establish himself in Manchuria on a long-term basis. In front of both the railway station and the Hotel Harbin, not five minutes' walk apart, stand two monuments to Soviet soldiers who fell in 1945 in the fighting against the Japanese. The inscriptions indicate that they were put up in honor of the men who gave their lives 'for the freedom and independence, for the honor and victory, of the Soviet Union'. Not a word about a 'liberation of Chinese soil', in fact, not a single word about China. But these monuments had been put up at a time when Mao was still in Yenan and Stalin could count on maintaining the Russian position until 1975 as provided for in his treaty with Chiang.

My wish to go to the Amur River (Chinese: Heilungkiang) was not granted. I would like to have seen the mighty frontier-river again, particularly to see for myself what was going on in the joint Sino-Russian Amur project. One year earlier (August 18, 1956) a Sino-Soviet agreement had been signed for the joint survey and development of the mineral wealth and natural resources of the Amur basin, the Chinese signatory being the vice president of the Academy of Sciences, Ch'u Ko-ch'en. I called on Professor Ch'u and found him to be a scholar of the old type (he is a meteorologist) with an excellent command of English, and he told me something about the work that had been done so far.

'I have read that it is a joint undertaking of the Soviet Union and China,' I said. 'Does that mean that each section consists of Soviet *and* Chinese scientists?'

'No, not at all,' replied Professor Ch'u. 'The Russians work on their side of the border, and we on ours.'

'Have you come up with any solution to the main problem of the Amur—its outlet into the Sea of Okhotsk, way up there in the north?'

'There are two different opinions about that. The Russians have proposed the building of a waterway from the Heilungkiang via the Ussuri River and Lake Khanka as far as the Bay of Vladivostok. We Chinese would benefit more from a waterway being built via the

Sungari and Liao Rivers straight across the Northeastern Provinces [Manchuria] to the south, ending in the Gulf of Liaotung.'

The atmosphere of cool matter-of-factness which made itself felt in these words of the professor does not appear to be an entirely new feature of this touchy border area on the Amur. I also noticed it in the Sino-Soviet agreement on the frontier-waterways of January 2, 1951, the full text of which has only recently become available in the West. This document could not have been more down-to-earth if the agreement had been concluded with Chiang instead of Mao. Nothing about brothers crossing back and forth, but plenty about passports, visas, and restrictions. Even then each side regarded the other with suspicion. Article 15, for example, dealing with the Joint Commission for the Survey of Frontier-Waterways, stipulated that workers and technical personnel were only permitted to cross the frontier when they were in possession of a list of names which had been signed by the members of one of the two high contracting parties to the Joint Commission and acknowledged by the signature of the other high contracting party. This personnel was only allowed to cross the frontier in daylight and had to be accompanied by a representative of the other side of the Joint Commission. Every time works of this nature were begun, the Joint Commission had to inform the defense organs of the two high contracting parties in advance.[13]

The Soviet Far East

WHEN KARAKHAN in his declaration of 1919 promised the Chinese the restitution of all territories and privileges they had lost to the Tsarist empire, he did not mention the Soviet Far East, although this area had also fallen to the Russian empire as a result of 'unequal treaties', just as Annam had become part of a foreign colonial empire—in that case the French. The only difference was that the French had used force to compel Peking to give up their sovereignty over Annam, while the Russians (without themselves going to war with China but exploiting the awkward position Peking was in as a result of her war with England and France) persuaded the violently protesting Chinese government in the treaties of 1858 and 1860 to hand over to them the area east of the Stanovoy Range as far south as the region of what is today Vladivostok, on the pretext of aiding China against England. This fact is one of which they do not care to be reminded today.

Furthermore, to judge by Soviet and Red Chinese maps the owner-ship of the large islands at the confluence of the Amur and the Ussuri is still in dispute.[14]

I asked young Chinese who had grown up in Red China but had then left it what they had learned in school about Vladivostok. Almost all of them replied that they had been taught that the place had been called Haishenwei 'before the Russians took it away' (and renamed it Vladivostok = 'Rule the East'). The two next most important cities of the Soviet Far East, Khabarovsk (after the Russian conqueror of the Far East, Khabarov), and Blagoveshchensk, are shown on Red Chinese maps by the Chinese names (side by side with the Russian ones) of Poli and Hailanpao.

That the Soviet Far East—outwardly at least—has been com-pletely 'Russianized' was apparent as early as 1929, when I first traveled through this area on a journey from Vladivostok to Chita. But even then I was wondering whether the Chinese, with their strong national pride, really had accepted the loss of an area which until a few decades ago they claimed as theirs, and whose principal city, with its truly imperialistic name, is ten times as far from Moscow as the crow flies than from China's most important industrial region.

In 1963 it became clear that the Chinese had not abandoned their claim to these areas. During the dispute between Moscow and Peking arising out of the withdrawal of Soviet missiles from Cuba, Khrush-chev had answered Chinese reproaches by hinting that after all the Chinese themselves had been pretty cautious—in such places as Hongkong and Macao. This infuriated the Chinese. It is true, they said, that Hongkong and Macao had been torn from China by imperialist aggression, but these were by no means the only territories of which China had been robbed. They then listed nine unequal treaties from the consequences of which they were still suffering; of these, three had been concluded with Russia! The first two were the ones already referred to which had ceded to the Russians their Far Eastern territories from the Stanovoy Range to Vladivostok; the third one, of 1881, related to the area around the Ili River in Central Asia. The following comments reveal Peking's violent indignation over Krushchev's dig about Hongkong and Macao.

These heroes [in the USSR, who had mentioned Hongkong and Macao] are apparently very pleased with themselves for having picked up a stone from a cesspool, with which they believe they can instantly fell the Chinese. But whom has this filthy stone really hit? . . . It may be asked: In raising questions of this kind, do you intend to raise all the questions of unequal treaties and have a general settlement? Has it ever entered your heads what the consequences would be? Can you seriously believe that this will do you any good?[15]

Mongolia

FOR MANY YEARS I had wanted to see Outer Mongolia.[16] What finally made me go ahead and obtain a visa for the Mongolian People's Republic was a map of China which I had bought in the bazaar at Peking during the summer of 1957. It was brand new (June 1957) and showed China with all its adjacent territories. The surprising thing about it was that it used two different markings to indicate the frontier of China. One marking looked like this: —.—.—. and was defined in the explanatory note as 'frontier'. The other looked like this: — — — — and indicated 'frontier not yet finally determined'. The entire frontier between China and the Mongolian People's Republic was shown with — — — —. To make sure, I compared this map with a number of other Chinese maps: it was the same thing everywhere. Even in a Russian-language magazine[17] published by the Red Chinese, the frontier was shown like this. There could be no doubt about it: the roughly 2,700-mile-long frontier with the Mongolian People's Republic was not recognized by the Red Chinese government as final, while on Soviet maps it has been shown as a normal, valid frontier. And even the frontier indicated provisionally on the Red Chinese maps differed up to sixty miles and more from the one shown as final on the Soviet maps.[18]

The officials at the Peking embassy of the Mongolian People's Republic were extremely friendly. I must admit I had to have a certain amount of patience, but in the end I got a visa. One morning I left Peking by train; the last landmark was the deep-blue tiled roof of the Temple of Heaven. My railway coach was a new, typically Russian, 'hard'-class one, built—to judge by the little plate on the coach-steps—in Görlitz on the River Neisse, i.e. in the Soviet Zone of Germany. There were two Russian conductors looking after the coach, but all the passengers traveling in it with me were Chinese workers on their way to the Mongolian People's Republic with long-term contracts. They proved to be thoroughly agreeable traveling companions, clean, well-behaved, and friendly. Only once did they have a good go at the bottle—they sang and then slept off the effects for several hours. Even when they were tipsy they were not objectionable.

The first big station was Kalgan. I had been there in the thirties, at that time via the old railroad which passes through the Great Wall at the Nankao Pass. Now, however, the Red Chinese had built a second line: from Peking it first goes westward, then northwest as far as Shacheng, where it meets the old line. The new route is scenically more impressive, but it has one drawback—one cannot see the Great Wall from it. The train passes underneath it through one of the many tunnels, of which there are almost seventy. Between the tunnels are magnificent views of wild, rugged country and of the valley of the Yungting River, whose waters rush down toward the plain through deep gorges between high mountains. Three hours after Peking and immediately to the north of the Great Wall, the valley widens out, and a dam is visible to the right—the Kwanting Dam, begun in the years 1951 to 1954, which has backed up the Yungting River into a great lake. It is an astonishing sight, this wide blue lake surrounded by bare mountains. Work at the reservoir was not yet complete; as the level of the water rose, so the dikes were built higher and higher. Thousands of Chinese laborers were carrying buckets of stones and earth; they looked like the proverbial ants crawling over the slopes.

By evening we were in Tatung, famous for its caves in which, during a catacomb period in Buddhist history, giant statues were hewn out of the rocks. Late at night we reached Tsining. At this point the Trans-Mongolian Railway branches off to the north. Although it runs for another 220 miles or so on Chinese soil as far as the frontier station of Erhlien, the track changes to the Russian gauge at Tsining. Coaches traveling between the Soviet Union and China are provided with an interchangeable undercarriage. The switch to the wide-gauge track took place so smoothly that I never noticed it and slept right through.

*

When I woke up we were already speeding across the Gobi Desert. At that time of year it was covered with a light carpet of green. The railway line was almost completely straight and flat. We were now some three thousand feet above sea level, and compared to Peking with its oppressive heat the air was cooler and pleasantly dry.

On many of the maps we are accustomed to using, Erhlien is

shown as being inside the borders of the Mongolian People's Republic. But when we reached Erhlien I was told it was another six miles to the border. Except for the new railway station and customs building, and a new housing settlement for railway employees and border officials, there was not much to see at Erhlien. Before the railway was built there was apparently no settlement here. After a three-hour stop we went on, the train now being pulled by a modern Soviet diesel locomotive. Or wasn't it so modern after all? It had a portrait of Stalin cast into its front end.

The station beyond the border was called Samyn Ude. Like all the new stations on this new line, this was an impressive building with large rooms and a tiled roof to give it an Asiatic appearance. In the station restaurant the menu was in Russian, and I ordered a typically Russian soup, borscht. From here on the train crossed a landscape entirely devoid of human beings. Far and wide there were neither yurts nor herds. Here, too, the only human habitations were those built for the railway. In contrast to the station buildings, they were all Russian in type.

The track is single-gauge, necessitating frequent sidings for oncoming trains. But there was not much traffic. The train I was on only went three times a week. We also saw a few freight trains, perhaps two or three a day. I test the quality of a railway line with my portable typewriter: if it rests securely on my knees and I do not miss the keys too often, the roadbed is good. This was the case on the section (built in the days of the wicked imperialists) as far as Tsining. But on the Trans-Mongolian Railway the same coach bounced so much that I was forever hitting the wrong keys and finally gave up typing. The tracks were laid on the bare ground. Once when I was watching a locomotive being shunted, I noticed how the rails sank into the ground every time the wheels passed over them.

We crossed the barren, desert-like portion of the Gobi during the night. When I got up early on the third morning of the journey, we were just approaching Choyir station. Another oversized railway station, out of proportion to the small settlement of railway employees' houses behind it. Some Mongolians joined the train. Those who had accompanied them were on horseback. Some of them rode right up to the coaches and chatted with their departing friends from the saddle. Now there was steppe-like grass again, but so little that each nomad required a wide grazing area for his herds. Further to the north the steppe became greener. Then hills appeared in the distance, and finally mountains. The last portion of the line before Ulan Bator contained a surprising number of curves, although it could have crossed the empty countryside in an almost straight line if only the ground had been leveled to cope with the differences in altitude. Obviously they had been at pains to save excavation work in this part of the world where labor was so scarce and had preferred to lay rails for an additional few dozen miles. Fifty-four hours after leaving Peking we were in Ulan Bator, capital of the republic.

*

Here the desires and demands of the Russians and the Chinese confronted each other on the soil of a third race, the Mongolians, who once, thanks to Genghis Khan, were the 'lords of the earth' and today, in spite of their small numbers (less than three million), inhabit vast areas spread out over three countries, from the Amur to the Volga.

Of the 360,000 Mongolians who, according to Soviet figures,[19] live within the borders of the Soviet Union, the greater part inhabit the Lake Baikal area, which in the treaties of 1689 and 1728 was handed over by the Manchu empire to the Tsarist government; in the Buryat (until 1958 Buryat-Mongolian) Autonomous Soviet Socialist Republic, where the Mongolian Buryats form only a minority as against the immigrant Russians; and in two National Districts forming part of Russian provinces. Then there is the Mongolian tribe of the Tuvinians living in the Tuva region, which in the autumn of 1961 was given the status of the Tuva Autonomous Region. However, the Kalmucks along the Lower Volga are also Mongols. In the case of both the Kalmucks and the Buryats, Moscow is trying to prevent the creation of any Pan-Mongolian awareness and for this reason blocked all efforts of scientists in the Mongolian People's Republic to bring Kalmuck delegates to the International Mongolian Congress which took place in Ulan Bator in September 1959.[20]

More than half of all Mongols (some one and a half million) live within the borders of Red China: two thirds of them in the Inner Mongolian Autonomous Region, which with its area of about 460,000 square miles is nearly as large as the Mongolian People's Republic, the rest in Manchuria, Kansu, and Sinkiang.

As far as the relationship between Moscow and Peking is concerned, however, the most important Mongol-inhabited area is, of course, Outer Mongolia ('outer' as seen from the direction of and as called by the Chinese) with a population of less than a million.

Until 1911 Outer Mongolia belonged to the Manchu empire, and then—not without Russian aid—made itself autonomous, the justification being that it had recognized the sovereignty of the Manchu dynasty (which fell in 1911) but not that of China. From 1919 to 1921 Outer Mongolia was once again occupied by Chinese troops. White Russians under Ungern-Sternberg drove out these detachments and were in turn defeated by Soviet troops and Mongolian nationalists. Since 1921 Outer Mongolia has been nominally an independent state; in actual fact it was the Soviet Union's first satellite. A series of agreements, the chief of which were the military alliance of 1934 and the mutual-aid treaty of 1936, bound the Mongolian People's Republic—as the country had meanwhile been named—more and more closely to the Soviet Union.

During the first quarter-century of its existence Outer Mongolia maintained relations virtually only with the Soviet Union and was basically a subsidiary of Moscow: its leaders were trained in the Soviet Union (among the early Mongolian revolutionaries, the Soviet Buryat intelligentsia played a prominent role);[21] and the Mongolian Revolutionary People's Party (i.e. Communist Party) was formed on Soviet territory. Its political structure corresponded largely to that of the Soviet Union; in it, the Party assumes the same role as the CPSU (as in the Soviet Union; when 'elections' are held a 'bloc of Communists and non-Party candidates' are the only nominees); and the 'purges' were carried out with slogans very similar to those used in the Soviet Union. The Party organ is called, as in the Soviet Union, 'Truth'—in Russian *Pravda*, in Mongolian *Unen*; and similarly the semi-official humorous magazine is called 'Crocodile'— in Mongolian *Matar*. Religion—Lamaism, that is—was handled in principle as in the USSR, although, in view of the different initial situation, not in all tactical details; and during World War II there was also a slackening of tension in the Mongolian People's Republic in the relationship between state and priests.

The collectivization of agriculture, which consisted principally of animal husbandry, differed somewhat from the Soviet process. The first wave came, as it did in the USSR, between 1929 and 1932, with similar disastrous results as in the case of the nomads of Soviet Kazakhstan. But while in the USSR collectivization was thereupon merely slowed down and then resumed without further interruption, it was decided in the Mongolian People's Republic to call the measures of those years premature, a leftist deviation, and the existing collectives were dissolved.

*

The Mongolian People's Republic was the first country in which the Soviets tried to put into practice Lenin's thesis of the Second Comintern Congress (1920) which was that, since the founding of the Soviet Union, a pre-capitalist people could advance from feudalism to socialism without going through the intermediate capitalist stage which Marx had considered essential.[22] The transition of Outer Mongolia to a form of society for which Marx had stipulated the existence of a proletariat is supposed to have been performed by replacing Outer Mongolia's non-existent proletariat with the support of the proletarian Soviet Union. (In actual fact there was no question of an organic process of transformation such as Marx had in mind: it was an abrupt and radical change imposed from without, which, of course, is possible at every stage of development.) Early in the fifties an interesting discussion took place in Moscow on this subject, during which remarks such as the following were made by Soviet participants:

> The constant selfless aid, the ideological and political support of the Soviet Union, assured the Mongolian People's Republic . . . of the necessary proletarian leadership. . . . The working class of a country in which socialism has been victorious assumes the leadership of a backward country with a peasant population.[23]

For the government and social forms of Outer Mongolia during their transition from feudalism to socialism, Moscow used the formula 'new type of bourgeois-democratic republic'.[24] The fact that this formula was first put into practice in backward Mongolia, which for centuries had belonged to the Chinese empire, may have contributed to Mao's decision not to apply it in China; it is more than likely that he did not care for the implication that the lack of an indigenous proletariat was to be compensated for by aid supplied by another socialist country, in this case the USSR.

The Mongolian People's Republic would have continued to exist as a faraway, underdeveloped, and inaccessible satellite country of Moscow if Mao's victory had not intervened. Outwardly it looked as if the trend set by Moscow would continue: in Ulan Bator's Central Square, corresponding to Moscow's Red Square, stands a

monument copied from the Moscow Mausoleum, the tomb of
Sukebatur, the Mongolian Lenin, and Choibalsang, the Mongolian
Stalin (who incidentally was promptly 'de-Stalinized' in the winter
of 1961–62 although not yet removed from the Mausoleum).[25] There
is clearly greater justification for drawing a parallel between Choibalsang and Stalin than for comparing Sukebatur with Lenin, as
Sukebatur was more of a Mongolian nationalist than a Marxist
Communist. In Sukebatur's widow Yangjima, Mongolia even had its
'Krupskaya' (as Lenin's widow was called).[26] Tsedenbal (married
to a Russian), who became the leader after Choibalsang's death in
1952, alternated, on the Moscow pattern, between the dual function
of prime minister and Party leader (1952–54 and since 1958) and
the single function of prime minister (1954–58). The Mongolian
People's Republic based its economic 'Plans' on the Soviet rhythm
pattern (First and Second Five-year Plan, 1948–52 and 1953–57;
Three-year Plan, 1958–60; Third Five-year Plan, 1961–65). And
the postponed collectivization was resumed: starting in 1955 a
method developed in Soviet Kazakhstan was imposed on the
Mongols. This consists of settling the cattle-owning population and
having its livestock driven out by herdsmen onto the grazing lands,
which are often some distance away.[27] A virgin land campaign was
even undertaken (starting in 1959) modeled on the Soviet pattern.[28]
But the realization of these plans required time: by July 1956 only
fifteen per cent of the nomad households had been collectivized; and
when it was reported at the end of 1959 that practically all private
nomad groups and roughly three quarters of the cattle had been
rounded up into collectives, the process of settling the nomad
population was still spoken of as being a 'gradual' one.[29]

At first sight, therefore, it may have looked as though the Sovieti-
zation of the Mongolian People's Republic continued on unchanged
after the end of World War II. Actually, though, the whole Mongolian
question was revived in 1945. At first it was the Russians who took
the offensive. They consolidated their position in Outer Mongolia:
in the treaty of August 1945 Chiang Kai-shek was obliged officially
to abandon all claims to the country. In addition, scarcely had
Stalin's armies overrun Manchuria together with its Mongol-
inhabited western regions than he immediately attempted to gain
control of Inner Mongolia also, by encouraging and manipulating
certain Mongolian groups, especially the anti-Chinese Inner Mongolian Revolutionary People's Party. Stalin's intention was presumably

to incorporate Inner Mongolia into the Mongolian People's Republic already in his hands. (A subsequent Soviet publication, the purpose of which was obviously to retouch the events of those days to conform to the thesis of undying Soviet-Chinese friendship, made out that there was a spontaneous desire in Inner Mongolia to join the Mongolian People's Republic.[30]) But the resistance Stalin encountered was not so much that of Chiang as of the CPC, which was rapidly extending its influence in North China. With the aid of the veteran Mongolian Communist Ulanfu, and by the founding of the Inner Mongolian Autonomous Region (May 1, 1947), the CPC succeeded in outmanoeuvering Stalin and in eliminating within a few years the influence of pro-Moscow Mongolians in its territories.[31]

*

I have no doubt that the leading Communists, including Mao, desire eventually to annex Outer Mongolia for the Chinese People's Republic. Mao's words, recounted by Edgar Snow after a conversation with him in the summer of 1936, are well known. To the question as to what plans the Chinese Communists had for the areas outside the Great Wall, Mao replied: 'It is China's immediate task to win back all the territories we have lost, not merely to defend our sovereignty on this side of the Great Wall.' (Both Inner and Outer Mongolia are situated beyond the Great Wall.) Snow reports that at a later interview Mao had the following to say about Outer Mongolia in particular:

> The relationship between Outer Mongolia and the Soviet Union, now and in the past, has always been based on the principle of complete equality. When the people's revolution has been victorious in China the Outer Mongolian republic will automatically become a part of the Chinese federation, at their own will.[32]

The Chinese leader expressed the same view eight years later.[33] Other Chinese Communists have made similar comments, as, for instance, when the Red Chinese General P'eng Teh-huai said in the thirties 'that the Soviet Union had no ambition to annex Outer Mongolia, and that it clearly recognized it as a part of China'.[34] However, in the treaty with Stalin of February 1950 Mao consented to the independence of the Mongolian People's Republic.

I have asked a number of Chinese who 'chose freedom' during the last few years what explanation was given in China for the fact that the whole of Manchuria but not the whole of Mongolia came within the Chinese borders. The answer was unanimous: in recent times the subject was never discussed, they said, but in the first few years after 1949 they had been told that it did not matter on which side of the border a people lived, the important thing was whether it belonged to a higher or lower social system, and as Outer Mongolia with the aid of the Soviet Union was already on the road to socialism, there was no further problem. My informants regarded this as the official version and not as the personal opinion of the speakers. Incidentally, this argument is no longer valid since Red China claims to be among the countries furthest advanced along the road to Communism.

Actually the words of a leading Bolshevik in 1922 should, in somewhat varied form, still apply for Communists today. Zinovyev said at that time: 'It would be unrealistic to ask for its [Outer Mongolia's] return to China until China had driven the imperialists from its own territory.'[35] This condition has now been fulfilled. According to that, from the 'realistic' point of view the annexation of Outer Mongolia by China is now due.

Whatever Mao may think today of the political future of Mongolia, he had scarcely established his supremacy over China proper and Inner Mongolia when he turned his eyes toward Outer Mongolia. But in order to exert influence in Ulan Bator he needed a railway connection, and this is the real reason behind the building of the line from Ulan Bator to Tsining. When Choibalsang died in Moscow in January 1952, Peking sent a delegation, which included Ulanfu, to his state funeral, and it was there that the first contacts were made. In the autumn Chou En-lai and Tsedenbal met in Moscow, and on September 15 a tripartite pact (the Soviet Union, China, and the Mongolian People's Republic) was concluded on the building of the railway. The existence of this agreement was not made known for two years; possibly Stalin was not particularly interested in the project (Ulan Bator had been linked by rail with the Soviet Union since 1949, and it may well be that he felt that was sufficient) and did not give his consent until negotiations between Chou and Tsedenbal were fairly far advanced. The 220-mile stretch across Inner Mongolia was built by the Chinese, the section from Ulan Bator to the Chinese border by the Soviet Union and the Mongolian People's Republic, for which Moscow bore the cost in the form of a loan. Direct communication between Ulan Bator and Peking was opened on January 1, 1956.

Meanwhile Peking had taken other steps to tighten up its relations with Outer Mongolia. In July 1950 ambassadors were exchanged (Peking sent a native Mongolian).[36] A year later Peking despatched a delegation to Ulan Bator on the occasion of the thirtieth anniversary of the Mongolian revolution; a further delegation six months later to the state funeral of Choibalsang; and yet another in the late autumn to the Twelfth Party Congress at Ulan Bator. (Ulanfu was present on both occasions.) In October 1952 the Chinese signed a ten-year treaty with Tsedenbal in Peking covering economic and cultural co-operation.

During all this time Mao was developing the Inner Mongolian Autonomous Region. With this he accomplished two things. In the first place he created a type of administration which would attract the Mongols living beyond the Chinese borders in the Mongolian People's Republic (rather as Moscow, by establishing the Soviet republics of Armenia, Azerbaidzhan, and Tadzhikistan, sought to attract the Armenians in Turkey and the Azerbaidzhanis and Tadzhiks in Persia). In 1954 Mao pointedly gave the new capital of the Autonomous Region, formerly known by its Chinese name Kweisui, the Mongolian name Kuku-khoto (= blue city); and in 1955 in a similar gesture he swallowed his pride as a Chinese and had a mausoleum to Genghis Khan erected in the Autonomous Region, although the house of the Mongol conqueror had once ruled over China. In the same year building began in connection with a metallurgical industry in Paotou, i.e. on the soil of the Autonomous Region, not the least reason being to catch the eye of those Outer Mongolians who thought of modernizing their country. In the second place, however, Mao's remarkable expansion of the Autonomous Region resulted in the fact that Mongols inhabiting the area (about one million) now constitute only a small minority among the nine million inhabitants of the territory which bears their name. Consequently they no longer represent a threat.

In 1955 the Chinese concluded a treaty with Ulan Bator covering the recruiting of Chinese workers for Mongolia (men who were traveling to Mongolia under the terms of this treaty had been my companions on the train between Peking and Ulan Bator) with the result that, as Tsedenbal told Harrison E. Salisbury, the American author, twenty thousand Chinese workers went to the Mongolian People's Republic.[37] In 1956 the Chinese put 160 million rubles at the disposal of the Mongolian People's Republic, with no conditions as to repayment, and two years later a further 100 million rubles as a fifteen-year credit.[38] In 1957 Ulan Bator opened a consulate-general in the capital of Inner Mongolia. Most important of all: on December 26, 1962, Chou En-lai signed a treaty with Tsedenbal defining the Sino-Outer Mongolian border, thus removing a source of uneasiness for the Mongolians.[39] However, I have not yet been able to obtain a detailed map of the agreed course of the border line.

What was the Kremlin's reaction to this offensive on the part of Peking? With Mao now in the saddle, Stalin had had to bury his aspirations for Inner Mongolia, but he was of no mind to give up Outer Mongolia. In 1947 he built the railway from the Soviet border to Ulan Bator, and he raised the Soviet legation there to the rank of embassy;[40] above all, he granted loans to the Mongolian People's Republic and his successors carried on this policy. The Soviets claim that between 1947 and 1957 they extended credits to the amount of 'more than 1·1 billion rubles',[41] an average of over 100 million rubles a year to a country with a population of less than a million—far and away the largest per capita economic aid that the Kremlin has ever granted. (As a comparison, Red China has, as we shall see, received only 1·72 billion rubles in economic loans.) And on May 15, 1957, a Soviet-Mongolian declaration was signed in Moscow which makes it clear that the Kremlin has no intention of being pushed out of its oldest and for a long time sole satellite country. At the same time Ulan Bator received a further loan of 200 million rubles.[42] The Mongolians continued to be able to call on Moscow for further loans (in unspecified amounts) every year.[43]

What the Mongolians thought when Molotov (who had been 'unmasked as a Party enemy') was sent to Ulan Bator as ambassador in the fall of 1957,[44] I was unable to find out for myself as he did not arrive in the Mongolian capital until a month after my visit. Nor do I know how they reacted when three years later Molotov was sent to Vienna in the unimportant capacity of Soviet representative to the International Atomic Energy Commission and was replaced in Ulan Bator by A. Khvorostukhin (previously Party secretary of Irkutsk and Tula), a man hitherto almost unknown to the public.[45] Presumably they told themselves that Molotov's coming and going had less to do with them than with Soviet domestic policy. It may have gratified the ancient race of horsemen that Moscow appointed Marshal Budenny, the legendary cavalry leader from civil war days, as president of the Soviet-Mongolian Friendship Association, founded in May 1958.[46]

*

In any event, after Mao's victory the Mongolians found themselves in the typical situation of developing countries after the end of World War II—that of being courted and presented with gifts by two sides, only that this time the rivals for their favors both belonged to the same side, the 'socialist camp'. Since the end of the war the Mongolians have received well over two billion rubles from their two neighbors; had no such aid-rivalry existed they would probably have received scarcely a tenth of this amount from Moscow. The admission of their government to United Nations in 1961 at the instigation of Moscow has led to a strengthening of their independent attitude toward both neighbors.

One of the leading experts on Mongolia today, Robert A. Rupen, believes there is evidence that since 1958 Peking has slowed down its offensive in Mongolia.[47] On the other hand, Moscow has of late stepped up efforts to tighten relations with Ulan Bator. To be sure, the significance of the new purges in the Mongolian People's Republic (1959) from the point of view of the balance of power between Soviet Russia and China in Mongolia is a matter of dispute. But events since 1961 should make the present state of affairs—Moscow's continuing, although no longer overwhelming, advantage—quite clear. On the occasion of the fortieth anniversary of the Mongolian People's Army (May 1961), Moscow sent its Minister of Defense, Peking its Deputy Minister of Defense; at the Fourteenth Party Congress and the attendant celebrations for the fortieth anniversary of the Mongolian revolution (both in July 1961), Moscow was represented in Ulan Bator by Suslov, Peking by Ulanfu, who ranks below Suslov in the Party but who is a Mongolian. In Tsedenbal's speeches at the ceremonies the Soviet Union was consistently ranked above China; at the Twenty-second Party Congress in Moscow (October 1961) Tsedenbal took Khrushchev's side in the dispute with China and has continued to remain on it ever since, to the point where he called Chinese criticism of the USSR 'irresponsible and arrogant'.[48] The entry of the Mongolian People's Republic into Comecon, the economic organization of the *European* Communist states, early in June 1962,[49] created an additional tie between Moscow and Ulan Bator.

If, then, we finally ask who benefits most from the building of the Ulan Bator–Peking railway, the answer as it appears today is: the Mongolian People's Republic, at any rate the forces within it which hope to derive advantages for independence and economic development from the rivalry of the two neighbors. They can only welcome the shower of gold from north and south. The railway could have been a threat to the Mongolians if unlimited numbers of Chinese had used it to pour into the country. This did not happen, for it was possible to cope with twenty thousand of them, the majority of whom have left Outer Mongolia by now.

However, the last word has not yet been spoken. In the long run Red China may be the one to profit most by the railway, as it has opened the door to Outer Mongolia. (It is not necessary to enlarge on the obvious advantage of the trans-Mongolian connection with Moscow—and hence Europe—which is shorter by 875 miles than the trans-Manchurian.)

The one to derive least benefit from the railway is the Soviet Union. The reduction in distance means less to it than to the Chinese, as for the Soviet Union imports from China are far less vital than the import of Soviet (and Eastern European) goods is to the Chinese. While the Soviet Union has previously enjoyed a monopoly in Outer Mongolia, it must now share this position with China, and in order not to sacrifice its supremacy (which undoubtedly still exists) it is forced to pump enormous sums of money into the empty land. Conceivably the Kremlin has missed its chance in Outer Mongolia—perhaps for ever. When China was weak the Soviet Union could have incorporated this territory, possibly as an additional republic of the Union. But what would have been possible with Chiang is out of the question with Mao. Today Moscow can no longer annex a country which as recently as fifty years ago belonged to the Chinese empire, now ruled by Communists. Nevertheless it can try to turn the Mongolian People's Republic into a showcase for the Soviet version of Communism by a favorable comparison with crisis-ridden China.

China's Far West

THE EFFORTS OF THE RUSSIANS to gain a foothold in Sinkiang go back even further than their advance into Manchuria. They had hardly subjugated Western Turkestan (today the Soviet republics in Central Asia) when they started looking toward Eastern Turkestan. In 1878, however, this area—for centuries a sphere of influence of the Manchu empire—had been incorporated into the Chinese Empire under the name of Sinkiang (=new border-area). Russian plans were interfered with not so much by the declining Manchu dynasty as by the British Empire, which was trying to safeguard India from the north by the creation of a Central Asian buffer zone. Finally an agreement was reached in 1907 between the two European empires to respect Sinkiang as part of China. Four years later the Manchu dynasty collapsed, and China was in chaos.

What explanation is there for the fact that things turned out differently in Sinkiang from Outer Mongolia, that it did not become a satellite of the Soviet Union? I myself have no first-hand knowledge of Sinkiang, but it seems to me that some reasons for the differing fates of the two border provinces are apparent from information emanating from that area. These reasons are to be found partly in the Soviet Union and partly in China.

The region around Lake Baikal, in Russian hands since the seventeenth century, offered a much stronger base for an advance into Mongolia than did Western Turkestan, conquered only a few decades previously, for an advance into Sinkiang. Immediately after the fall of the Tsars, Western Turkestan broke away from the Bolsheviks, was then reconquered, and as a result manifested strong anti-Russian *and* anti-Bolshevik feelings. Moreover, among the Buryat-Mongols the Bolsheviks already had numerous supporters who helped them carry the torch of the revolution into Outer Mongolia. On the other hand, the ties of the one hundred thousand Uighurs on Soviet soil (whose ancestors fled from Sinkiang to Russia toward the close of the nineteenth century and who now live mostly in the two Soviet republics of Kazakhstan and Uzbekistan) with the bulk of their people who remained in Sinkiang (in 1953: 3·64 million) are so tenuous that they are of scant political importance.

The Kazakhs of Sinkiang are another matter. If Sinkiang were inhabited principally by Kazakhs it would probably be a satellite of the USSR today; indeed, the Russians have not been entirely unsuccessful in their attempts to exert influence from Soviet Kazakhstan on the Sinkiang Kazakhs. But since there are only about 500,000 of these they represent less than a tenth of the total population of six million. (According to the census of 1953, the third-largest group consists of several hundred thousand Chinese, the rest of the population being mainly Mongols, Kirgizes, and Tadzhiks.)

The Uighurs lack the great national tradition of the Mongols and the sense of cohesion kept alive by the memory of Genghis Khan and his empire. Moreover, during a decade which was a critical one for them (1932–42), the province was ruled by the shrewd, vigorous Governor Sheng Shih-ts'ai, who tried to turn Sinkiang into his own personal satrapy. In these efforts he made extensive use of aid from the USSR, and this gave the Soviet Union a strong position in Sinkiang. In November 1940, in a treaty in which the USSR appeared as a colonial power pure and simple, he gave the Soviet Union the sole rights for fifty years to the exploitation of tin and other non-ferrous metal deposits in this province, arid but rich in ore.[50] But China was lucky: the heavy initial defeats suffered by the Soviet Union in the war with Hitler weakened its position and forced it to withdraw. Sheng, deprived of his Soviet support, let himself be recalled by Chiang Kai-shek (and later fled with him to Taiwan).

*

As soon as the Soviet Union's military situation in Europe improved, efforts to gain control of Sinkiang recommenced. A revolt of the Sinkiang Kazakhs against Chinese domination in the winter of 1943–44 won Soviet sympathy, perhaps also support, as did another and still more threatening uprising in November 1944. This latter led to the founding of an anti-Chinese 'Republic of East Turkestan' (with its own flag and currency) in northern Sinkiang, i.e. in the triangle between the borders of the Soviet Union and the Mongolian People's Republic, an area that contains the principal known mineral resources of the province and its rich oil deposits. In 1945 and 1946 one might have imagined that the 'Republic of East Turkestan', if not all of Sinkiang, was well on the way to becoming a Soviet satellite outside the borders of China, along the lines of Outer Mongolia. But Stalin, who was fully occupied in Europe, was in no great haste; he probably thought there was still plenty of time to make sure of his booty in Sinkiang.

In this he was wrong. Early in 1949 the Chinese Communists advanced on Sinkiang. A last-minute attempt on the part of the Russians to have the independence of the province proclaimed, and thus to halt the advance of the Red Chinese, failed.[51] By the autumn of 1949 Mao had complete control of the province. Stalin could hardly continue to oppose Mao in Sinkiang.

In the negotiations which took place between Mao and the Soviets in the winter of 1949–50, Sinkiang—like Manchuria—was still represented by its own delegation, but the only thing Stalin achieved in the ensuing treaty with Mao was the formation of two Sino-Soviet companies for the exploitation of Sinkiang's oil and non-ferrous mineral resources for a period of thirty years; and even these positions were abandoned by his successors in the treaties of October 1954.[52] One year later Sinkiang—like Inner Mongolia—became an Autonomous Region of the Chinese People's Republic, called, after its principal tribe, the Sinkiang Uighur Autonomous Region.

Nevertheless, in Sinkiang there were repeated anti-Chinese rebellions (which were always suppressed), especially during the summer of the Hundred Flowers in 1957 and in the two following years, presumably due to the formation of the people's communes and the revolt in Tibet; and it is quite possible that the real source of the rebellions lay in the USSR. Outwardly the policy of the Russians toward national minorities is a more generous one than that of the Chinese in that the USSR permits the existence of numerous national republics within its Union, while in China there are only Autonomous Regions.[53] In actual fact, however, there is practically no difference between them. In both cases the minorities are steadily being absorbed by the ruling race of the country in question, and their total subjection to the authority of the Party and central government in Moscow or Peking is already an accomplished fact. The Uighurs or the Sinkiang Kazakhs would therefore scarcely enjoy any greater freedom if they lived in a republic of the Soviet Union: but the grass on the other side of the fence always looks greener.

Regardless of where the sympathies of the non-Chinese tribes in Sinkiang may lie, there remains hardly any trace of the position held there by the Soviets from 1932 to 1949. The Chinese show the border between Sinkiang and the USSR on their maps as final—apart from the westernmost corner, which extends into the Pamir region. The nomads living on both sides of the border used to be able to cross back and forth quite casually, but it is becoming more and more difficult for them. A regular national frontier now exists, strictly guarded, like the one between Manchuria and the Soviet Far East. In the spring of 1961 it was announced that in Soviet Kazakhstan 'Volunteer People's Militia Units of the Border Areas' had been organized to guard the frontier.[54] The only frontier there is the one with China.

*

David Chipp, a Reuter correspondent who went to Sinkiang in 1956 and saw it through the eyes of a trained observer, told me in Peking: 'Sinkiang is completely in Chinese hands. I saw no evidence of any political or economic predominance on the part of the Russians. The only Russians who appear to be there are working as experts with no power of their own.' As far as I can judge, this observation is even more applicable today, since in the meantime many of the experts have left. However, a film I saw in Hongkong, made by the Red Chinese in the autumn of 1959, does not quite conform to this image. For a whole hour it depicted the life of bliss led by the inhabitants of Sinkiang under the Communists and showed a number of instances of aid given by the Soviet Union and individual Russians who came from across the near-by border.

During the last few years, especially since the Tibetan revolt, rumors have repeatedly sprung up concerning the joint Soviet-Chinese industrial development projects in western Sinkiang. There was even talk of a joint production of raw materials for atomic weapons. But it has never been possible to substantiate these rumors. Even refugees from Sinkiang who from time to time have managed to escape from the country had no information on this score. They had, it was true, seen phenomena in the sky which could have been taken for long-range missiles but, as far as could be judged, they were fired from Soviet soil and not from Sinkiang territory. We may assume that there are concentrators for fissionable minerals in Sinkiang, as the presence of non-ferrous metals there is well known, but we cannot by any means be certain; and there is even less certainty as to whether the Russians had a hand—or still have a hand—in their exploitation.

The Trans-Turkestan Railway, the construction of which was officially decided upon in October 1954, is being built from the west as well as from the east; like the Trans-Mongolian Railway it will probably benefit the Chinese more than the Soviets. It goes from Aktogai (a station on the Turksib Railway at the eastern end of Lake Balkhash) via Urumchi, Hami, and Yumen to Lanchow. There has not been much news lately as to its progress.

It would appear that for the time being Moscow has become reconciled to the loss of its position in East Turkestan. Today Sinkiang can scarcely be regarded as a seriously disturbing element in the relationship between Moscow and Peking.[55]

*

Finally, in Tibet the Tsars had also had political ambitions since the latter part of the nineteenth century, but these ambitions met with strong British resistance and were not pursued by the Bolsheviks. In the negotiations between the Russians and Chinese preceding the treaty of August 1945, Tibet was never mentioned, while Stalin frequently showed a lively personal interest in Sinkiang.[56] Since 1951, when Red China established its rule over the theocratic state, there have been plenty of rumors about Soviet airfields and other bases in Tibet, but there are no reliable reports of their existence. When a Sino-Soviet Friendship Association was formed in Tibet in the summer of 1956,[57] its aims were, as its name suggests, Sino-Soviet and not Tibeto-Soviet.

Apart from Tibet, to which the Soviets never publicly laid claim, the Bolsheviks lost to Mao—within five years of his victory—all the positions they had established or at least prepared in Chiang Kai-shek's time on Chinese soil, in Manchuria, in Inner Mongolia, and in Sinkiang. Even though the last of these losses did not occur until after Stalin's death, the veteran lord of the Kremlin was shrewd enough to foresee the consequences of Mao's victory, and for this reason he must have followed the Chinese Communists' rapid series of victories after 1945 with very mixed feelings. In the imperial interests of the Soviet Union, a long tug-of-war between Chiang and Mao, weakening to both sides, would have been preferable. This partly explains why Stalin was so grudging in extending aid to Mao.

China's Population Pressure—Northward?

IT IS NOT OFTEN that a political theory has found such response in the world as the one named after Professor Starlinger. When I left for a trip around the world in 1954 hardly anyone had heard of it; by the time I returned in the following summer, every politically interested person had studied it. Even in the United States I was constantly being asked about it. Adenauer, along with many others, was influenced by it, and he in turn passed it on to Dulles[58] and President de Gaulle.[59]

Dr. Wilhelm Starlinger, former Professor of Medicine at the University of Königsberg, spent several years in Soviet concentration camps, and after his release and arrival in West Germany (early in 1954) he propounded a theory, in lectures, essays, and books, based on conversations he had held with Russian fellow prisoners.[60] According to this theory, China would have to expand owing to its rapidly growing population and would only be able to do this in the direction of Russia, since the neighboring countries to the south were already overpopulated; hence Moscow would either have to yield all land east of Lake Baikal to Red China, or go to war with Red China.[61] There have been many arguments over this theory, and the discussion went on even after Starlinger's death.

*

We have already gone into China's population dynamics in Part I of this book. Reliable figures are not available, but no one doubts that this pressure is of gigantic proportions. According to the latest census of June 30, 1953 (although these figures are viewed with scepticism by many Western experts), Red China (i.e. not counting Taiwan or overseas Chinese) had a population of 582·6 million.[62]

The result of the census, announced the following year, had two conflicting effects on the Chinese Communists. On the one hand, proof that they ruled over by far the largest country in the world (in terms of population) filled them with pride; on the other, they now realized for the first time the full extent of the task confronting them. Their attitude was complicated by the thesis hitherto proclaimed by all Communists, and especially by the Russians, that a strong population increase posed a problem only for the decadent West, and none for the Communist countries, and that therefore any measures to promote birth control were to be severely condemned. It seems that in Peking opinions differed: side by side with enthusiastic comments on the high population figures were demands for the enlightenment of the population concerning contraceptive methods. These demands were so strong that in August 1956 the Ministry of Health gave instructions that it was necessary 'to satisfy the demands of the masses for birth control'. Abortion continued to be illegal, but the law was subject to wide interpretation. Young people were advised not to marry too early. (The minimum age for marriage is eighteen for women and twenty for men.[63])

The wave of propaganda started in full force on 'Woman's Day' (March 8), 1957. When I arrived in China shortly afterwards it was still at its peak. I visited an exhibition in one of the Imperial Palace buildings in Peking where young women guides equipped with long pointers explained to the astonished spectators the exhibits displayed on the walls. There were sixty birth control clinics in the capital alone. In a provincial city I spent an hour listening to the daily explanatory lecture given by a woman doctor to an audience consisting mainly of women, and even in villages I came across lectures of this kind. Contraceptives were produced in large quantities and put on the market. No Communist country has ever gone to this extreme; on the contrary, Stalin, like Hitler, had introduced a premium system for mothers of large families.

But the new trend was short-lived. During the period of sweeping changes between the summer of 1957 and the spring of 1958 (of which we shall have more to say when we come to the people's communes), this question was obviously also reviewed. Propaganda for birth control ceased, and an increasing number of voices gaily declared that there was no reason for anxiety over too swift a growth in population. In line with the Great Leap (see Chapter XIV) announced in May 1958, Liu Shao-ch'i proclaimed: 'The more people there are to put wood on the fire, the higher the flames leap.'[64] But care was taken not to call off the birth control campaign officially. The result was phrases such as: 'We want to retain birth control but, generally speaking, we believe that a large population is a good thing.'[65] And in September 1960 Chou En-lai declared in an interview that birth control methods were being taught in China 'to protect the health of mothers and provide favourable conditions for bringing up children, not because of so-called "population pressure"'.[66]

In the Soviet Union there has also been a change in the government's attitude to population, but it is not to be compared with the change that took place in China. After the revolution the attitude of the regime to the family, which was supposed to become a thing of the past, greatly facilitated abortion without any particular thought being given to the effect on population figures or the health of women. When Stalin became aware of the consequences in the thirties he did a complete turnabout and decreed new, conservatively formulated laws governing the family which were all designed to encourage population growth.[67] In this enormous country, with its small population in relation to its total area (at present, some 225 million inhabitants) the problem of overpopulation is not of pressing importance.

We cannot tell what effect a year of enlightenment on sexual matters (1957–58) has had on China's birth rate, but it can hardly be supposed that it will be a lasting one in a country of such over-whelmingly peasant traditions and such deep-rooted desire for children. It is more likely that the tremendous efforts exerted in the Great Leap, together with the general distress and poverty resulting from the crop failures of 1959, 1960, and 1961, will have reduced the number of births and increased the death rate considerably. A Chinese girl refugee who had been a medical student in Nanking until 1961 told me in Hongkong that during field work in the countryside her student team had found that the birth rate in the villages visited had dropped to one tenth of the 1957 level. However, this may have been a special case.

The Chinese reckon on an annual population increase of over two per cent,[68] i.e. more than twelve million. In the interview (1960) already referred to, Chou En-lai spoke of ten million. If we take his figure as the average (assuming that the increase in the years 1950–57 was very pronounced and then tapered off), the population must have increased since Mao's victory in 1949 by 140 million, and by 1963 it must have reached 680 to 690 million. Truly an enormous increase, and a justifiable reason for speaking of population pressure.

*

But even population pressure is relative; to us it is of interest only from the standpoint of its possible effect on Sino-Soviet relations. And here we come to Peking's remarkable statement to the effect that in the last few years, in spite of the mass mobilization of women in the labor force (especially in the rural areas) China was suffering from a serious labor shortage! At first sight one might think that the Chinese Communists had been carried away by their own propaganda. But some careful recent researches[69] have shown that this shortage actually did exist. It is true that the labor potential in Chinese villages (not counting children and old people unable to work) is around 225 to 240 million, but undue demands have been made on this seemingly inexhaustible supply. For a new method of deep ploughing, for example, 100 million peasants were recruited, and for a fertilization project of unprecedented extent (partly using silt, which first had to be collected), 90 million; for irrigation and flood control projects of all kinds, 77 million; for backyard furnaces (of which more later), 50 to 60 million; and many additional millions for the new light industries in the people's communes and for the reforestation of large areas.

Only part of this work, of course, required the full-time employment of the individual over long periods. But for months at a time normal agricultural activity was deprived of many millions without China being able to replace them by machines. An official Party announcement stated in 1960 that only fifty per cent of the village labor force was employed in actual agriculture.[70] Countless billions of working hours were also lost to agriculture through the inordinate number of meetings and indoctrination courses, and sometimes premilitary training. Excessive demands and inadequate nutrition lowered productivity. Peasants, including some of the healthiest, moved in hordes to the city; in the second half of 1958 alone, their numbers reached ten million, apart from their dependents. The result was a shortage of agricultural manpower, and this no doubt contributed acutely to the food crisis of the last few years. It is not possible at present to obtain anything like a clear picture of the number of people employed in agriculture; even the regime itself does not appear to have one. In any case it is noteworthy that in the report on Red China's first decade (1949–59) designed for foreign propaganda purposes, the population figures only go as far as the end of 1957.[71] But everything we do know confirms the existence of a gaping hole in the agricultural labor market.

There are certainly still large areas in China which could be cultivated. As to just how large they are, opinions differ, for their extent depends chiefly on how much the Red Chinese are willing to spend on their development: if sufficient funds were invested, the Gobi Desert itself could be turned into fertile fields. At the time Mao came to power, of the roughly 2,500 million acres of all Chinese territory, about 250 million were cultivated; since then a further 40 million acres or so have been added. According to Chou En-lai's figures of the autumn of 1960, about another 250 million acres can be brought under cultivation.[72] In 1950, more than half a billion peasants lived on the first 250 million acres. Of the 250 million to be brought under cultivation (if we accept this figure) it would not be possible to settle the same number of people, these areas being much less fertile, but they should nevertheless be capable of absorbing some 200 million settlers. A very rough calculation, certainly, but sufficient to correct the idea that China has no reserves of arable land or any alternative but to thrust forward into Siberia.

*

A distorted picture also emerges from the simple statement that an overpopulated China borders on an unpopulated Siberia. According to the latest census figures, those of 1953, in the northeastern, northern, and northwestern border areas of China, in Heilungkiang province, Inner Mongolia, Kansu, Tsinghai, and Sinkiang, 41,301,000 people live in a total area of 1,694,000 square miles, i.e. an average of 24·3 people per square mile. In the corresponding areas of the Soviet Union (the Maritime Territory, the provinces of Khabarovsk, Amur, Chita, Irkutsk, and Altai, in Tuva and in the Kazakh, Kirgiz, and Tadzhik Republics) according to the latest Soviet census (January 15, 1959) 22,463,000 people inhabited an area of 2,349,000 square miles, i.e. 9·6 people per square mile.

Opinions may vary as to whether a direct comparison is justified between the Chinese and the Soviet border areas. But at least these figures give us something to go on. The difference between 24·3 and 9·6 people per square mile is certainly not such as to warrant speaking of an irresistible pressure on the one hand and a vacuum on the other. Furthermore, we should not imagine that the Soviet Far East and Siberia offer unlimited or even favorable opportunities for settlement. Although it has been estimated that there are about 115 million acres[73] of arable land in the trans-Baikal region (including the Amur and Ussuri areas), of which until now less than 7·5 million have been cultivated, to extend the cultivated areas to these inhospitable regions with their short growing season would demand no less of an investment than a corresponding opening up of the land in China itself.

No exact figures are available on the opening up of virgin territory within China since 1949. It did not begin on a large scale until after Khrushchev's virgin land campaign of 1954. The Chinese made extensive use of the slogans heard in the Soviet Union, as, for example, this appeal 'To youth on its march to virgin land!':

You will transform deserts into a paradise. . . . Birds and animals live there, why not people too? Difficulties only overwhelm people who are unable to withstand hardship; difficulties are afraid of warriors who can withstand hardship. You are an army of steel making an attack on Nature.[74]

As we have seen, since 1949 a total of some 40 million additional acres are supposed to have been brought under cultivation. In Harbin the official in charge of the settlement of Heilungkiang province told me in 1957 that, in the first seven years of Communist rule, some four million acres had been added to the cultivated land in that area. It is to be remembered that this particular province received special support in the planning of new settlements owing to its fertile soil and its proximity to the border. If we take as our basis Chou En-lai's figure of roughly 250 million acres which in 1960 he maintained were still available for cultivation, and remember that, once the Great Leap had begun, the virgin land campaign lost much of its impetus, we are forced to conclude that this land reserve—regardless of how large it may actually be—has hardly diminished since the day Chou En-lai spoke of it, and that it will satisfy the settlement potential of China's economy and population for a long time to come.

However, even if Peking should one day decide that it absolutely must have additional arable land, this does not mean that it would necessarily look toward the Arctic Circle rather than the equator. There are the Philippines, Borneo, and Sumatra, Australia and New Zealand, where many millions of thrifty settlers could be placed, according to some estimates more than 300 million. This would mean war—but does not this also apply to an expansion to the north? Hence for Peking it would be a political decision, certainly not one determined by the laws of nature, whether, if war is inevitable, China should 'explode' into the near-by but hard and inhospitable north in a struggle against the Soviet Union, or whether it would not be more profitable to wage war against the Western powers and seize the distant but immensely fertile southern regions. In any case, China has plenty of time to make up its mind.

*

No doubt Moscow is concerned over the Chinese population trend. I do not know whether there is a causative connection, but it is certainly a remarkable coincidence that, while Peking was computing the results of the 1953 census, Khrushchev was preparing a population offensive toward Soviet Asia. In February 1954 he launched his virgin land program.[75] A giant campaign then began to sweep the country, a campaign of propaganda and mass organization such as had not been seen since the end of World War II. Khrushchev's was the loudest voice in the battle; with all his dynamic energy he plunged himself and the people into this enterprise. He offered material inducements such as a bounty corresponding to three months' wages to everyone who responded to his call, and increased wages and special premiums for kolkhozes, sovkhozes, and machine tractor stations in the virgin territories.[76] However, it was not merely a question of these territories alone, but of all Siberia and the Soviet Far East. People who moved to the Maritime Territory on the Pacific were transported free of charge, together with their families, cattle, and two tons of luggage. They received a bounty of 1,000 rubles per head of family, and 300 rubles for each member of the family; they were also granted a ten-year building loan of 15,000 rubles, a further loan of 2,000 rubles, free food supplies to start off with, and a five-year tax remission.[77]

An appeal was made above all to the patriotism and idealism of the younger generation, and eulogies of heroic young people who settle in Siberia as farm-hands or industrial workers occupy a good deal of space in the officially inspired products of Soviet literature.[78] In Khrushchev's speeches the theme of population policy is particularly audible, for example in phrases such as these: 'Comrades, I was recently in the Far East [of the Soviet Union]. . . . It is an immensely rich land, but there are too few people there; it must be opened up and appropriated. . . . In the East we must appropriate the empty spaces more quickly and settle in them permanently. . . . We must root the people there firmly . . . that's the main thing!'[79] Although generally speaking the virgin land campaign has come to an end, appeals have continued to be heard in the style of 'Go east, young man!'[80]

Since the start of Khrushchev's virgin land offensive, some 92 million acres have been opened up in Soviet Asia (not counting the Ural and Volga regions and the four Central Asian Soviet republics, but including Kazakhstan),[81] and millions of people—especially young people—have been resettled there from the European Soviet Union. Between 1939 and 1959 the population of Soviet Asia (in the areas mentioned above) increased from 21·8 to 30·8 million,[82] i.e. by almost half.

It goes without saying that, in the official appeals for the resettlement of Siberia, no mention was ever made of China. There was no visible indication that these measures were designed to ward off a population pressure on the part of the Chinese. Indeed, Khrushchev specifically told foreign journalists that he did not have the slightest anxiety concerning the rapid growth of the Chinese population.[83] On the other hand, in Moscow in 1955 he hinted to Chancellor Adenauer that he was a little uneasy about China's high birth rate. In any case, among the Russian people themselves the constant appeal for the settlement of the East is definitely regarded as being connected with neighboring China. On a train journey through Manchuria I was standing by the window next to a Russian. We both looked at the crowded streets of a little town through which the train was passing. The Russian, who was going home after some years spent as a technical adviser in China, said, half to himself and half to me (whom he probably took for a Soviet colleague): 'The Chinese are really multiplying like rabbits. It's not for nothing Nikita Sergeyevich [Khrushchev] has said we have to populate Siberia.'

In view of China's teeming masses and the sparse settlement of Siberia, one might be inclined to believe the reports one reads from time to time, according to which millions of Chinese workers are employed in Siberia. Whenever I heard a rumor of this kind I followed it up, but I never found even the slightest confirmation. When I was traveling through Siberia in 1957 I asked everyone I spoke to whether he had seen any Chinese workers. The answer was always a surprised and emphatic No. Only small groups of students or technicians and engineers on a training course were, I was told, occasionally to be seen. (Soviet statistics give the total number of Chinese in the USSR during 1959 as 25,800.[84])

There appears to me to be no doubt that since the end of World War II Siberia has been chiefly settled by Russians (and Ukrainians), and not by members of the non-Slavic peoples living in Soviet Central Asia; whereas during the war the latter—presumably for fear of fraternization in the event of an advance by the German army into Central Asia—were resettled in large numbers in Siberia and the Soviet Far East, as I deduced in Shanghai at that time from the sudden increase of broadcasts in Central Asian languages by the Soviet Far Eastern radio.

*

This leads us to a further consideration. When we speak of population pressures, figures tell us very little; we must also bear in mind the ethnological and even the psychological factors. In the border areas of China as well as of the Soviet Union, there are, besides Chinese and Slavs, members of numerous other tribes which are all Asiatic. According to Peking's statistics, some 35 million non-Chinese (i.e. six per cent of the total population) were living in all of China at the time of the 1953 census, of whom some 13 million inhabited the regions on the Soviet border—mainly Koreans, Manchurians, Mongolians, Hui (mostly Mohammedans of Turkic origin), Uighurs, and Kazakhs. In the Soviet Union, according to official figures for 1959, there were 48 million non-Slavs (23 per cent of the total population); of these some 6·5 million inhabited the areas along the border with China (mainly Buryat-Mongols, Kazakhs, Kirgizes, and Tadzhiks). In the event of open conflict, to whom would the loyalty of these roughly 20 million people, who are neither Russian nor Chinese, belong?

One may assume that Pan-Asian feelings exist among the non-Slavs of the USSR. A German visitor tells us that an Uzbek said to him in 1960:

Here in Tashkent we often have a different idea of Communism from the people in Moscow. Well, of course we are Asians. Other Asian countries often understand us better. We are very pleased . . . at the contact with the Chinese. . . . Yes, we Asians are having a difficult time just now, very difficult. That's because of domestic policy. But as far as foreign policy goes, we understand one another—we are all Asians![85]

Or will the higher standard of living in the Soviet Union turn out to be the stronger attraction? And will these peoples react in any sort of unified manner and, even if they do, will they be able to exert any appreciable influence on the course of events? Nobody can answer these questions.

The Battle of the Alphabets

A COMPARISON OF THE border-territory policy of the two neighbors would be incomplete without a look at the language policy, both spoken and written. After a number of fluctuations, this policy finally ended up in the Soviet Union with the Russian language occupying a privileged position in the regions inhabited by non-Russians, regions which are, of course, to a large extent border areas. The fact that related language families, especially the Turkic, were split up into numerous individual languages with their own grammar and vocabulary, forced the members of these tribes to make Russian their common means of communication. In addition, a Buryat or a Kazakh can only rise above a certain level if he speaks fluent Russian. If he is talented and ambitious he must in his own interest master the Russian language. From an ideological point of view, this privileged position of Russian is supported by theses which can scarcely be very welcome to Chinese ears, theses which were perhaps most clearly expressed in the statement made by the Soviet literary historian Zazlavsky:

> No one may call himself a scholar in the full and true sense of the word who cannot speak Russian and who cannot read the works of Russian genius in the original. . . . In the history of mankind we see how the languages of the world have all had their turn through the ages. Latin was the language of antiquity and the early Middle Ages. French was the language of feudalism. English became the language of imperialism. And when we look into the future, we see Russian becoming the universal language of socialism.[86]

And yet, who knows? Perhaps the Chinese are consoling themselves with the thought that, although Russian is the 'language of socialism', Chinese has a chance of becoming the universal language of Communism?

*

In the three decades during which I have been able to see for myself what was going on in the Soviet Union, Russian has spread among the Asiatic peoples of the Soviet Union in two ways: first, more and more non-Russians speak or at least understand Russian, and secondly, more and more Russian words or Russianized Western expressions (such as *mashina, bukhgalter* [= bookkeeper, from the German *Buchhalter*], *marksizm*) are finding their way into the languages of other nationalities. As long ago as 1935 when I spent several weeks in Bashkiria, I was struck by the fact that I could more or less follow the conversations of Bashkir *kolkhozniki* or railway workers, as among themselves they used many expressions taken from the Russian. Twenty years later, in Uzbekistan, I found this process even further advanced.

The Bolshevik script policy went through three stages. In the first stage, the nationalities which had their own scripts were permitted to retain them; in the second, in compliance with Lenin's wish, Romanization was introduced for most of these languages; in the third, the Kremlin—a sign of its increased self-assurance—ordered the transition to the Cyrillic alphabet. In the case of the Buryat-Mongols this occurred in 1937, and with the countries using Arabic script two years later.[87] In Ulan Bator the CC and the council of ministers decided in March 1941 to introduce a modified Cyrillic alphabet.

Today there are only two peoples, the Georgians and the Armenians, who are allowed to use their traditional scripts (also the Baltic Soviet republics, who use the Latin alphabet). The aim of the Kremlin is undoubtedly to force all inhabitants of the Soviet Union to learn first the Russian alphabet and then the Russian language.

At first it looked as though Peking would go along with the claim that Russian was to be the universal language of the age of socialism. In August 1955 it decided to introduce the Cyrillic script for 'its' Mongols over a four-year period, and a year later the same plan was announced for the peoples of Sinkiang, including the Uighurs and Kazakhs.[88] But apparently the Chinese soon began to doubt the wisdom of this decision. In 1957, when I changed money in Peking, I noticed that the Mongolian script still appeared on brand-new banknotes, and in Inner Mongolia I saw nothing but Chinese and Mongolian characters on all official buildings.

'I wonder whether the Chinese will ever have Russian letters printed on their currency', I wrote in my notebook at that time. My curiosity has since been satisfied in a negative sense: the following year Romanization was introduced for Mongolian and the languages of Sinkiang. The justification for this measure was that it would facilitate the access of the non-Chinese inhabitants of China to the Chinese language, which was gradually being Romanized. In the resolution of the Second Forum for the Study of Minority Languages which took place in Urumchi at the end of 1959, it was pointed out that, although the languages of the minorities had played an important role in their cultural development, these languages were no longer compatible with the requirements of the Great Leap in economic growth and the cultural revolution.[89]

*

The Romanization of Chinese writing which was decided on in Peking in November 1956,[90] had been preceded—long before the rise of Communism—by decades of discussion. Even the Communists were at first unable to come to a decision. Then they inclined toward Romanization but wanted to add to it five non-Latin letters which bore a certain resemblance to the Cyrillic script. But the alphabet as finally introduced for the transcription of Chinese[91] contained *only* Latin letters. But, as demonstrated in Part I, it is no easy task to replace Chinese writing by the Latin alphabet. Recently the trend has been to use Latin letters mainly to explain the pronunciation of

Chinese characters. A keen observer of the Chinese scene states: 'Once the children know the characters, all their work is in characters, and the [Latin] alphabet is rapidly forgotten.'[92]

The fact that of the three alternatives—Romanization, Cyrillization, or the invention of an entirely new alphabet—the Chinese Communists chose Romanization must have been bitterly resented by the Russians. It is true that, as far as I know, they have never admitted this publicly, for Peking's decision to introduce the Latin alphabet took place at a time when Moscow was at pains to present an image to the world of complete solidarity with Peking.[93] Perhaps the Soviets were also embarrassed by the fact that the first Communists to recommend the Latin alphabet for Chinese writing had been Russians who, soon after the Bolshevik revolution, devised a simplified script for the Chinese living in Russia. At that time a Chinese Communist had become acquainted with this alphabet, which the Russians called Latinxua, and had taken it back with him to China.[94] Mao had also been fascinated for a time—while he was in Yenan—by Latinxua and had published newspapers in this script.[95]

Speaking as a neutral who grew up with Latin and Cyrillic letters and lived for a long time in China, it seems to me, although I am not a linguist, that the Cyrillic script is no worse—in fact is somewhat better—suited for the transcription of Chinese than the Latin, for it contains some letters, especially those for sibilants, which are well suited to convey certain Chinese sounds.

I would imagine that Peking's decision in favor of Romanization at the expense of the Cyrillic alphabet was in the last analysis based on two considerations: to show its people that China is not a satellite of Moscow, and to keep contacts open with the rest of the world, particularly with the developing countries, most of which use the Latin alphabet. It is, after all, to these latter that Red China desires to show itself off as the truest and best model on the road to Communism, outshining the Soviet Union.

The results of our study of the border and language policies of the two Red neighbors can be reduced to a simple formula: the Sino-Soviet frontier is visibly hardening; today it is already much more sharply dividing than, say, the frontier between Germany and France or between the United States and Canada. Although on both sides of the border the people profess to follow Marx and Lenin and carry on policies which are in many respects parallel ones, there is no question of a free-and-easy neighborly crossing back and forth.

Slavic settlement and the promotion of the Russian language and the Cyrillic alphabet on one side are faced on the other by Chinese settlement and the promotion of the Chinese language and Romanization. It will not be long before the tribes inhabiting this enormous border strip—tribes who, in the way of nomads, had hardly been conscious of a frontier and had shared common languages and scripts—grow completely apart.

In one place only—in Outer Mongolia—has a clear distinction as between Soviet and Chinese influence not yet been made.

CHAPTER XI

BETWEEN STATE AND STATE

DURING THE SIX MONTHS that followed Mao's victory the foundations for international relations between Peking and Moscow were laid step by step; on October 1, 1949, the official founding of the Chinese People's Republic, and the next day the Soviet Government's decision to recognize the new regime; twenty-four hours later, diplomatic relations were established. Ten weeks later Mao arrived in Moscow and was received by Stalin the same day. On February 14, 1950, the treaty between the two states frequently mentioned in these pages was signed in Moscow and followed by Mao's return to Peking. Then came (on March 27, 1950) an agreement on the establishment of joint Soviet-Chinese airlines and on the exploitation of the oil and non-ferrous metal resources of Sinkiang, as well as on the supplying of Soviet experts to China; and finally (on April 19, 1950) a trade agreement.[1] This took care of matters for the time being.

In spite of the Korean war, nearly two years went by before the next Red summit meeting. First Chou En-lai went to Moscow in the autumn of 1952 (he succeeded in having the Manchurian railway system handed over to Red Chinese administration, but in return granted the Soviets an extension of their rights to use Port Arthur); he was followed by Liu Shao-ch'i, representing the CPC at the Nineteenth Party Congress of the CPSU (the last under Stalin). Liu remained for more than three months. No plausible reason was given for the length of his stay. Did he negotiate for Soviet economic aid? Or for the termination of the costly Korean war? Or, in these months prior to Stalin's death, was the battle for his succession already casting its shadow?

Stalin died on March 5, 1953. The Chinese funeral delegation was headed by Chou En-lai; Mao stayed behind in Peking. China was now carrying more weight in the Red system of alliance than ever before. But for the time being this did not seem to lead to tensions. The new Moscow team (Beria had meanwhile been 'liquidated'), which under the leadership of Khrushchev and Bulganin had visited China in the fall of 1954 for the fifth anniversary of the People's Republic, felt obliged to go a long way toward meeting the wishes of the Chinese: on December 31, 1954, it sold the Chinese the Soviet shares in the Sino-Soviet companies and guaranteed the withdrawal of Soviet troops from Port Arthur by May 31, 1955.

These are the dates of the outward course of official relations up to the end of 1955. The new phase, beginning with the Twentieth Party Congress of the CPSU and the de-Stalinization process which was started at that time, resulted in 1957 in the visits to Moscow first of Chou En-lai and then Mao (for clarification of the problems arising out of the events in Hungary and Poland). Judging by the promptness of their support, which was telegraphed within twenty-four hours of the publication of the Moscow CC's resolution,[2] the Chinese had no objections to Khrushchev's victory over the 'Party enemies', Malenkov, Molotov, and company, in the summer of 1957. There followed Khrushchev's visits to China (in the summer of 1958 during the Near East crisis and in the fall of 1959 on the occasion of the tenth founding day of Red China), Chou En-lai's participation in the Twenty-first Party Congress of the CPSU early in 1959, the conference of the eighty-one Communist Parties in Moscow in November and December 1960, and the open conflict (over Stalin and Albania) at Moscow's Twenty-second Party Congress in October 1961. A proposal for a new Sino-Soviet summit meeting was made by Moscow early in 1963.[3] It is worth noting that Khrushchev (born in 1894) was in Peking three times (in 1954, 1958, and 1959), while Mao (born in 1893) has paid only one visit to Khrushchev (in 1957); furthermore, in contrast to the frequent discussions between leading statesmen in the West, these two met only on rare occasions, and since the fall of 1959 have not met at all.

*

When Moscow took up relations with the young People's Republic in 1949, one might have thought that now one of the leading men in the Kremlin would hurry to Peking to represent the Kremlin in the capital of the country with the largest population in the world, a country which had just joined the Communist camp. But nothing of the sort occurred. As if it were a case of a perfectly normal change of government, N. V. Roshchin, who had been Stalin's ambassador to Chiang Kai-shek since February 1948, stayed on for another three years in China; this might be taken as further proof that Stalin was finding it difficult to adjust to the full significance of the Chinese revolution. China is China, and what was good enough for Chiang is good enough for Mao, Stalin's attitude seemed to say. And then when a change did at last take place in February 1952, Stalin sent, not a leading Party man, but A. S. Panyushkin, long rated as a top intelligence man; he had also been ambassador to Chiang's government from 1939 to 1944.

One of the first steps taken by Stalin's successors was the recall of Panyushkin. Perhaps it was realized that it would not do to go on treating China as if nothing had been drastically altered by Mao's entry into Peking, or possibly Chou En-lai had contributed to this view during the funeral ceremonies in Moscow. The man who went to Peking as the new ambassador was V. V. Kuznetsov, the top trade union boss of the USSR since 1944. But even this choice was apparently not very satisfactory, for he only stayed nine months. Pavel F. Yudin, the fourth ambassador from Moscow to Peking in less than two years, was the first to take root there, and it was almost six years before he was recalled. Prior to being sent to Peking, Yudin had made a name for himself as an outstanding Soviet ideologist (director of the Philosophical Institute of the Academy of Sciences, 1934–44; editor-in-chief of the Cominform magazine, 1946–53) and as the man in charge of the Russian edition of Mao's works.[4]

One wonders whether in a man like Yudin the Chinese saw a tiresome governess on ideological questions; in any case they put up with him. Naturally the tensions created between Moscow and Peking in the fall of 1958 as a result of the people's communes must have also affected Yudin's position; it now became his difficult task to represent the ideological and practical misgivings of his masters over the new trend. Early in 1959, when the Chinese had abandoned their extreme position in the matter of the communes, Yudin made a speech at the Twenty-first Party Congress in Moscow on the correct path to Communism in which he took the Chinese to task without mentioning them by name.[5] And again in the late summer of 1961 he rebuked them in the press for the policy they had carried out in 1958.[6]

As Yudin was recalled in 1959 immediately after Khrushchev's visit to Peking, we may assume that the Chinese had asked for a change. The fact that Khrushchev replaced him with S. V. Chervonenko, who did not belong to the top echelon of the Party, was one more sign that relations were cooling off.

Mao's first ambassador to Moscow was Wang Chia-hsiang, and he was not a top man either; in the Party he ranked merely as a CC candidate. Peking probably realized that his appointment had been a mistake; in any case, after a year and a half he was replaced by the CC member Chang Wen-t'ien, who ranked twenty-second in the Party and then rose to be a member of the Politburo also. He stayed until the beginning of 1955. In his place came once again a man of lower Party rank, the CC candidate Liu Hsiao. Did Peking feel, in the full flush of equality achieved after Khrushchev's visit in 1954, that it could now afford not to look quite so high in its choice of an ambassador for Moscow?[7] And was it a political gesture that Wang and Chang, the two first ambassadors, who had meanwhile both become Deputy Foreign Ministers in Peking, simultaneously lost their new posts in the fall of 1959 following Khrushchev's visit to the United States, when the difference of opinion between the two Red powers became increasingly apparent? In November 1962 Liu was replaced by the CC candidate Pan Tzu-li, who, as ambassador to India since 1956, had had to represent his government's views in New Delhi during the disputes over Tibet and the Tibeto-Indian frontier.

On the tenth anniversary of the Chinese People's Republic its Moscow embassy moved into a magnificent new building, designed by Soviet architects but reflecting some Chinese architectural features. It stood on the Lenin hills, not far from the skyscraper of the new university. As for the Soviet Government, it had inherited spacious property in Peking's legation quarter from the Tsars. Like the rest of this suburb it was a quiet tree-studded oasis in the noisy hubbub of the capital. Naturally the new masters of Peking eventually wanted to divest the legation quarter of its characteristic quality, as it was too reminiscent of the era of national humiliation and foreign privileges. One day it was the Soviets' turn to move. But they had no desire to move to the area outside the eastern gate of the city which the government had set aside for a new embassy quarter. They insisted on setting up their embassy inside the city walls—on the former property of the Russian Orthodox mission whose historic churches were torn down. While the other new embassies are visible to the public the new Soviet embassy is hidden away behind high walls. The Chinese showed their sense of humor by moving their public prosecutor's office into the premises vacated by the USSR!

In the case of the ambassadors and embassies of the two governments, certain parallel features are to be found, but the consulates followed quite different paths. In pre-Communist China the Soviet Union had had nine consular offices: in Manchouli (on the Soviet-Manchurian border), Harbin, Mukden, Dairen, Tientsin, Shanghai, Canton, Urumchi, and Kashgar. When it closed its consulates-general in Tientsin (1955-56)[8] and Mukden (1957), it still had seven. It was only in the fall of 1962 that most of these were shut down too. Red China, which took over from Chiang's regime four consular offices (in Leningrad, Tashkent, Semipalatinsk, and Vladivostok) closed them all in 1951 and 1952 so that all it had was a consular department in its Moscow embassy. As far as I know, no explanation has ever been given for these measures, nor have I any to suggest.

*

The predilection for protocol which the Russians and Chinese have always had in common once again became apparent after their 'proletarian' revolutions—even in their relations with each other. In Stalin's day, when virtually nothing of what was going on behind the walls of the Kremlin reached the outside world, every photograph of groups of Party leaders at the Lenin Mausoleum, every list of those taking part in ceremonial functions, was looked at abroad under a magnifying glass in the hope that at least by this method it would be possible to find out whether the central figures in the Kremlin were on their way up or down.

Since relations between Moscow and Peking were as secret as intra-Party manoeuvering, the attempt has also continually been made in this field to examine carefully all manifestations of protocol for indications as to the true state of affairs. In order to check the impressions I have obtained by other means, let us do the same thing here.

A great deal of guessing went on as to whom the Chinese would have liked to see in Stalin's place. Many people think[9] their candidate was Khrushchev, as he was at that time considered to be a champion of the promotion of heavy industry, while Malenkov was believed to be in favor of increasing the production of consumer goods.

That may well be. But judging by the 'protocol' of Peking's

congratulations on the anniversaries of the USSR on November 7, this does not appear to be so, as we see when we compare the names of those to whom these congratulatory telegrams were addressed. From 1950 to 1952 Mao's congratulations were first (1950) addressed to 'Generalissimo Comrade Stalin', then to 'Prime Minister Comrade Stalin'. After Stalin's death, the picture is as follows:*

1953: From Mao to 'Prime Minister Comrade Malenkov'.

1954: From Mao and Prime Minister Chou En-lai (as joint signatories) to President Voroshilov, Prime Minister Malenkov, and Foreign Minister Molotov (as joint addressees).

1955: From Mao, Party Secretary Liu Shao-ch'i, and Chou to President Voroshilov, Prime Minister Bulganin, and Foreign Minister Molotov jointly. By contrast, the congratulations of the Poles, Czechs, Hungarians, and Rumanians had been addressed to Khrushchev (since 1953 First Party Secretary).

1956: From Mao, Liu, and Chou to President Voroshilov, Prime Minister Bulganin, and Foreign Minister Shepilov jointly. Khrushchev was the recipient—or among the recipients—of telegrams from the Rumanians, Bulgarians, Albanians, and Outer Mongolians, but again not from the Chinese.

1957: The Chinese were the only ones not to send a telegram. (True, Mao was in Moscow himself on the occasion of the fortieth anniversary of the Bolshevik revolution; but this also applied to the leaders of the other CP's, who nevertheless still sent telegrams.)

1958: From Mao, Liu, and Chou to Prime Minister (since March 1958) and Party Leader Khrushchev (for the first time) and to President Voroshilov.

1959: From Mao, Liu, Marshal Chu Teh, and Chou to President Voroshilov and Khrushchev (in that order).

1960: As in 1959.

1961: From the same four to Party Leader and Prime Minister Khrushchev and President of State Brezhnev.

1962: As in 1961.

Next let us compare the degree of cordiality in relations between the two powers, first again on the basis of the telegrams in which the Chinese Communists congratulate their Russian colleagues on November 7, then on the basis of the traditional exchange of telegrams commemorating the treaty of February 1950, and lastly as evidenced by the so-called 'slogans' which Moscow publishes every year on November 7 and May 1.

Even the length of the telegram—that is, the number of lines it

* The following figures and quotations have all been taken from *Pravda*, hence no individual references will be given.

occupies as printed in *Pravda*—is not without significance from the point of view of protocol. So as not to weary the reader with figures, a graph has been composed to show the trend of three numerical series.

TEMPERATURE CHART OF DIPLOMATIC RELATIONS
(according to the number of lines in greetings telegrams)

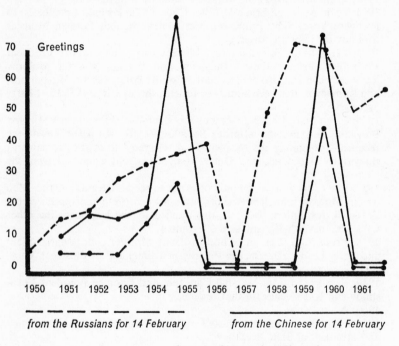

from the Russians for 14 February   *from the Chinese for 14 February*

- - - - - *from the Chinese for 7 November*

We see at once that the curves indicate a rhythm which corresponds strikingly to the relations that existed between the two powers: a low, flat curve under Stalin; a marked 'warming up' after his death, presumably in line with the desire—in the dangerous situation resulting from Stalin's elimination—to emphasize to all the world the close co-operation existing between the two Red powers; a sharp decline in the period of the first de-Stalinization and the people's communes; again an upward swing—probably to counteract the rumors of tension between Peking and Moscow; and finally another downward plunge, perhaps because it was realized that there was no longer any point in denying the already well-known tensions in the alliance.

Side by side with the length of the congratulations we must also examine the tone and frequency. Let us look at the exchange of telegrams sent for the anniversary of the treaty of February 1950:

1951: Stalin: 'Heartfelt congratulations'. Mao: 'Heartfelt gratitude and congratulations'.
1952: Stalin, as in 1951. Mao: 'Gratitude and warm congratulations . . . for selfless aid'.
1953: Stalin, as in 1951. Mao: 'Heartfelt gratitude and warm congratulations . . . for selfless aid'.
1954: Malenkov, same as Stalin in 1951. Mao, as in 1953.
1955: Voroshilov, Bulganin, and Molotov, same as Stalin in 1951. Mao, Liu, and Chou: 'Warm congratulations'.
1956: No exchange of telegrams published. (This might be because the first de-Stalinization was just beginning at the Twentieth Party Congress, which took place from February 14 to 25. Yet Chu Teh mentioned in his welcoming speech at the Party Congress that its opening coincided with the anniversary.)
1957: No exchange of telegrams published.
1958: No exchange of telegrams published.
1959: No exchange of telegrams published.
1960: (*Tenth* anniversary). Khrushchev and Voroshilov: 'Warm congratulations'. Mao, Liu, Chu Teh, and Chou: 'Warmest congratulations'.
1961, 1962, 1963: No exchange of telegrams published.

So we find: from Moscow, laconic, stereotyped congratulations until 1955, then no more, except for the tenth anniversary; from Peking, gratitude for 'selfless aid' up until 1954: after that, discontinuance of this phrase and, from 1956 on (but again with the exception of 1960) of the congratulations altogether. Possibly both sides had agreed henceforth to mark the anniversaries with an exchange of telegrams every ten years only, but even this would indicate a cooling off.

We now turn to the Moscow 'slogans' as they reflect the development of the Chinese revolution in Moscow's eyes: in 1950, 'Long live the CPC which has opened the path to socialism for the Chinese people'. Then for a few years nothing about socialism. In May 1954 the Chinese people were said to be 'fighting successfully for socialist industrialization'. From November 1954 China was already 'fighting successfully for the building of the foundations of socialism'; in May 1956 it was 'successfully realizing the socialist transformation'; from November 1956 it was 'building socialism'—at first 'successfully', from May 1957 without this adverb. Three times (May and

November 1957, and May 1958) the noun 'builders of socialism' was chosen for China; this was taken to indicate a promotion, i.e., the recognition of closer proximity to the socialist goal.[10] If that was the case, then from November 1958 these improved marks were withdrawn—following on the Chinese campaign for the people's communes; after that they were merely 'building' again, like the other countries in the bloc. Finally we note that Moscow called the Chinese People's Republic, at the peak of their friendship in November 1955 (and on this occasion only), 'a mighty world power'; and from May 1960 on—in a period of tensions—declared the friendship between the two peoples, which it had referred to in almost every slogan since May 1951 as 'unshakable', to be 'eternal and unshakable'.

Taken individually, the three curves and the other comparative series would not mean much. However, if we find very considerable agreement among them in rhythm, and if this rhythm in turn corresponds to the rest of our information, we are justified in believing that they are mutually corroborative.

Finally, if we take still further evidences of protocol in speech or action, such as the presence or absence of the leading men of one country at the official functions of the other, we find that certain parallels exist here too. For instance, some light is thrown on Peking's attitude to Moscow at the time of the Hungarian uprising of 1956 by the fact that Chinese protestations of friendship addressed to Moscow on the occasion of the state anniversary of that year—a few days after the Hungarian freedom fighters had been suppressed—were more cordial than usual. The evening before the celebrations Mao had made a point of attending the Soviet circus then in Peking, and after the performance he had greeted every member of the Russian troupe.[11] Peking and Moscow are standing side by side in this crisis—that was probably what these gestures were meant to convey. During the 'cool' year of 1960, on the other hand, not a single leading Russian or Eastern European (apart from, even then, an Albanian!) went to Peking for the Chinese state anniversary, and the jubilee article in the Moscow *Kommunist* praised the Chinese development with palpable reserve.[12] Yet five weeks later Mao together with the central figures in Party and government turned up at the Soviet ambassador's reception for the Soviet state anniversary, although neither he nor Liu had attended this function the year before, presumably because it took place shortly after Khrushchev's visit to Peking which had not gone particularly smoothly. From these facts the conclusion might be drawn that in 1959 the Chinese were not afraid of showing their annoyance, while in 1960—on the eve of the Communists' Conference in Moscow—they tried a more conciliatory tack.

*

When in 1949 the victory of the Chinese Communists fell—unexpectedly, we must assume—into the Soviets' lap, the latter found themselves in a quandary: either they could give the Chinese everything they did not absolutely need for themselves and thus through 'brotherly co-operation' get the Asian colossus on its feet in the shortest possible time; or they could leave things more or less as they were and go by the maxim 'business as usual'. Which did they decide to do?

The answer to this question can be dealt with briefly here; details can be found in a number of studies.[13] There is virtually nothing to indicate a powerful brotherly love, overriding national self-interest, in Moscow's dealings with China.

Since the USSR did not introduce its present rate of exchange for the ruble until January 1, 1961, here and elsewhere in this book we shall use only the old ruble valid until the end of 1960, and where necessary will convert the new ruble to the old. Officially the old ruble was worth about twenty-five cents, but its purchasing power was much less. The exchange rate between the Chinese yuan and the Soviet ruble is a science in itself and one into which we cannot go here.[14] For a long time no official rate was published; it was assumed that one yuan approximately equalled one old ruble. Now the official rate is one yuan = 0·45 new rubles.[15]

In the spring of 1961 trade negotiations between the two governments took place which lasted a very long time (from February 10 to April 7) and were evidently extremely difficult. Besides the joint communiqué which was published, the Soviets issued an additional, unilateral statement.[16] They bluntly informed the world, in a manner not exactly customary among friends, that, 'as a result of natural disasters', China was unable to meet its financial obligations and hence had not paid the Soviet Union trading debts due in 1960 amounting to 288 million new (= 1·28 billion old) rubles. The Soviets went on to say they had granted a moratorium and the debt was to be settled between 1962 and 1965. Hitherto neither Moscow nor Peking had given any information as to the state of the mutual payments; considering how extremely embarrassing these of all details must have been to the Chinese, it is remarkable that they were published.

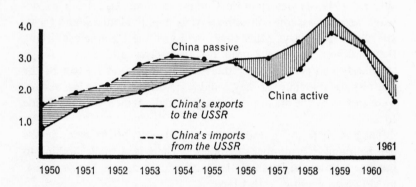

SINO-SOVIET BALANCE OF TRADE
– in Milliard Rubles

This statement contains no details as to the origin of this debt of 1·28 billion old rubles. However, we know from Soviet trade statistics that in the eleven years from 1950 to 1960 the Soviet Union supplied China with goods to the value of 29·2 billion rubles, and imported goods from China to the value of 27·8 billion rubles: in other words, that China's trade deficit on January 1, 1961, amounted to some 1·4 billion rubles (*see diagram*). The difference between this figure and the 1·28 billions mentioned by the Russians in April 1961 was 120 million rubles; it might represent a credit balance which was not due until the end of 1960 and thus did not need to be included in the moratorium. During these eleven years the Kremlin extended— as far as we can judge from the published figures—only two trade credits to its ally: the first in February 1950 amounting to 1·2 billion rubles, payable at the end of 1963; the second, the duration of which was not divulged, in October 1954 to the amount of 520 million rubles. Perhaps in the spring of 1961 Peking still had 120 million rubles at its disposal from these two credits.

But China's debts did not only originate in its trade deficit. In 1955 the USSR sold the Chinese its shares in the joint Soviet-Chinese companies together with part of its property in Dairen and Port Arthur. No figure was named, but a Chinese national economist working in the United States has put it at around 0·7 billion rubles (1·55 billion yuan at a rate taken by him of one ruble = 2·177 yuan).[17]

On top of all this, the Chinese had to pay the salaries of the 11,000 to 11,500 Soviet technical experts who were assisting them in their economic development. We shall have more to say about these people in the following chapter; we need only say here that from 1950 on, taking an average stay of two to three years, they had a total claim on Peking of some 30,000 annual salaries of about 20,000 rubles each, although, of course, the greater part of this was paid them in Chinese currency.

Then come the freight charges which Peking had to reimburse to the Soviets covering the transportation of goods in Soviet vessels. When we consider that marine transportation of one million tons from Europe to China costs, according to international freight rates, 60 to 100 million rubles, this also represents a sizeable figure. Added to this are the rail freight charges across the Soviet Union—by the longest railway in the world—for goods from Eastern European countries.

And finally the Soviets agreed to supply material for the building of a section of the Trans-Turkestan Railway (from the Soviet border to Urumchi, 320 miles)—against payment, of course.[18]

To these financial obligations arising from economic transactions must be added China's debts from the Korean war. These amounts can only be guessed at, but they must have been considerable, as the bulk of the up-to-date war material used by the Chinese was supplied by the USSR. One American expert has put this debt at two billion US dollars (= eight billion rubles).[19] It is possible to dispute this estimate, but it can scarcely be considered too high, since from the first involvement of the Chinese in October 1950 to the armistice in July 1953 the war lasted some one thousand days.

In view of these uncertain elements it is not worth while attempting to arrive at a total figure of China's indebtedness apart from straightforward trading debts. It is certain that this goes into billions of rubles, and it is highly probable that, as a result of their acute lack of foreign currency, the Chinese have so far repaid only a small portion of their indebtedness. In other words, their debts to the Soviets exceed by many times the sum named in the moratorium of April 1961, since this latter refers specifically to trade debts only.

*

By the beginning of 1961, therefore, things had reached a point where the Chinese, after the serious crop failures of 1959 and 1960, no longer knew which way to turn and were forced to ask Moscow for a deferment of repayment. They also asked their Big Brother for food. They obtained from him—also under the terms of the agreement of April 1961—500,000 tons of sugar (largely from Cuba) and promised to give back the same quantity of sugar during the years 1964–67. Apart from this, they obtained no food from the Soviet Union (had they done so, this would, like the sugar advance, have been announced) and therefore they were compelled to buy wheat on the world market—in 1961 alone over six million tons, almost all of it outside the Eastern bloc, the latter being unable (or unwilling) to supply any. This by itself means an indebtedness toward the non-Communist world of over a billion rubles. During 1962 further purchases were undertaken. To assist its languishing agriculture, Peking bought roughly one million tons of fertilizer from the West in 1961[20]—one more debt. Moreover, China's supply of foreign currency was already dwindling, since shortages within the country had led to a throttling of exports. Thus a reduced foreign currency reserve was being borrowed for food purchases on a totally unexpected scale, with the result that what was left over for the planned purchases of machinery was far less than had been provided for. This in turn set back the whole economic growth of the country, probably for years.

Owing to the secrecy affected by the two Red partners, the picture we have presented contains many unknown factors, but the main outlines are probably correct. In any event we can now answer the original question with some degree of certainty: it is quite clear that Moscow did not decide to throw all it had, in a spirit of brotherly self-sacrifice, into the aid of its Asian comrades. On the contrary, apart from the granting of a low rate of interest, it developed its economic relations with Red China along lines as 'capitalist' as those of a large Western industrial concern. It is true that an impressive amount of machinery and equipment has been delivered to China from the USSR since 1949, but it was not much in comparison to what China needed and expected (in value it was little more than what West Germany exported to Holland!) and, furthermore, it had—and still has—to be paid for.

From the United States, its enemy of yesterday, West Germany obtained some four billion dollars in the way of credits and gifts;

immense sums (in 1960 alone some $7\frac{1}{2}$ billion dollars)[21] were poured into the developing countries by the Western world, and from the Soviet Union they received billions of rubles—if not in gifts (which were very limited in extent), then in the form of credits on favorable terms. Even the countries of the Eastern European bloc, in comparison to which China has six times the population, received from the Russians up to 1957 more than 20 billion rubles in credits and gifts.[22] But the most populous country in the world, the Soviet Union's most important ally, obtained from Moscow over a period of thirteen years 1·72 billion rubles in credits and a few gifts which—in view of the projects to be tackled—are scarcely worth mentioning (the equipping of a state agricultural enterprise in Manchuria called 'Friendship'[23] and of a hospital in Peking,[24] twenty breeding sheep,[25] and a few other things). An American journalist reports that Chou En-lai, when asked whether the Soviet Union had rendered aid gratis to China, replied that, generally speaking, the answer was No.[26] And all this after China had not failed to mention, in its published statements regarding the friendship of the two nations, China's aid to the Soviet Union when the latter was suffering the ravages of famine in 1921.[27]

*

Not until the Chinese were at their last gasp in a situation which could almost be described as a national food disaster in 1961, did the Russians condescend (and even then only after two months of negotiations) to advance them sugar and grant a moratorium on their debts. I would like to be shown a developing country which was as shabbily treated by its benefactor as China was by the Soviet Union!

Why, one is bound to ask? There are many possible explanations: Stalin had, and Khrushchev has, his eyes turned more toward the West than the East; to both men it may have been more important to support the Eastern European countries, which figure more prominently in the world's field of vision, than a country of the magnitude of China, where aid even on a large scale can only be a drop in the bucket. Possibly the men in the Kremlin also reasoned that, seen from the standpoint of Communism's world victory, it was more sensible to establish economic positions in countries such as Cuba and Egypt, India, Burma, and Indonesia, than in China, which already belonged to the 'socialist camp'. But it is impossible to avoid the suspicion that behind the USSR's meager support of China stands the Kremlin's determination to keep the economic growth of the neighboring giant within certain bounds. The simplest way for Moscow to do this is to say to the Chinese: We will supply you with as much as you can pay for. In this way a clearly defined limit is drawn.

The Russians were probably assisted in this by the attitude of the Chinese themselves. As a result of their experiences with foreign credits during the last hundred years, the Chinese tend to see in every foreign credit a link in a chain which encroaches upon their independence. How many times had a Western government granted them credit and demanded privileges in return—for, say, the building of a railway? Hence it is quite possible that they themselves did not particularly press for Soviet credits. But, even assuming this to be correct, the Chinese could hardly have expected, after all they had heard from the Soviets about 'brotherly love between socialist states', to be treated by their Big Brother in quite so miserly a fashion as they have been by Khrushchev, even more so than by Stalin.

Probably the Russian Communists do not regard themselves as Shylocks at all. In their own country also they do not think much of brotherly love; there, too, the principle of strict accounting between individual enterprises reigns, and transactions are carried on according to the established rules of business; nothing is given away, and only short-terms credits are granted. Why should things be any different between 'socialist' states than between 'socialist' enterprises? Moreover, it is to be assumed that the Kremlin accuses the Chinese of two things: first, that, although short of funds, they give away billions in gifts and credits to other—principally Asian—countries; and secondly, that, with their Great Leap and above all their (in Soviet eyes) totally unnecessary people's communes, they have completely dislocated their whole economic system.

The Soviet planned economy resembles a gigantic machine which can only function when each cog fits neatly into the next. It lacks sufficient reserves or stockpiles to be drawn on in an emergency, as can be done in a system of private enterprise, and for this reason it must be extremely annoying when such an important economic partner as Red China goes completely off the rails (since 1958 especially) and suddenly announces an urgent need for huge supplies, which a few months previously had not been mentioned at all. This might explain why Red China was not—as had seemed likely in 1958 —included among the members of the 'Council for Mutual Economic Aid' of the countries of the Eastern bloc (Comecon).[28] No doubt the Kremlin wished to deal only with those countries which would obediently fall in line with its proposed economic plan.

Yet to a certain degree the role of mere observer at Comecon may have suited Peking, since the Chinese—at any rate until their economic crisis, which began in 1958, and presumably since then also—dream of establishing an economic world of their own. Chou En-lai was emphatic in letting this be known when in a speech at the Eighth Party Congress in Peking (September 1956) he demanded that a country as rich in raw materials and population as China must set up a 'complete industrial system'—i.e., as is to be seen from the context, an autarkic economy, and certainly not one merely geared to specialized production within the Communist bloc's division of labor. He rejected as false the view that China could dispense with 'its own independent and complete system of industry' and could 'rely exclusively on international support'.[29]

*

There is one field, however, in which the Soviets behaved generously to the Chinese: that of technical documentation. During the first visit of Stalin's successors to Peking (October 1954) an 'agreement on scientific-technical co-operation' was reached.[30] Both sides promised to make technical data available to the other and to exchange experts 'for technical aid and the exchange of information on the achievements of both countries'. At the same time it was decided to form a joint commission for scientific-technical co-operation.[31] Then in July 1956 came an agreement on cultural co-operation providing for the setting up of yearly plans for cultural exchange; similar agreements followed.[32] Reports by the Soviets that they put factory plans, machinery blueprints, etc., at the disposal of the Chinese in astonishing quantities are confirmed by Chinese reports. Only in this field, then, do we finally come upon some evidence of the much-vaunted 'brotherly love'.

The Chinese with their national pride are careful to see that these exchanges always take place on a reciprocal basis. When, for instance, they report that, in the first two years following the signing of the agreement on scientific-technical co-operation, the Russians put 600 plans for factory construction and the specifications for 1,700 types of machinery at their disposal, they do not omit to add that in exchange China likewise supplied the Soviet Union with plans for certain plants.[33] In the agreements, too, the reciprocal basis is emphasized. However, after an examination of Red Chinese sources, a survey carried out by a Chinese research institute in Hongkong comes to the following conclusion:

> No report has ever been seen about any Chinese scientist giving technical assistance or helping to solve a scientific problem in the Soviet Union.[34]

The crux of this scientific co-operation is in the field of atomic energy. This became apparent at a very early stage. The first meeting of the above-mentioned joint commission took place in Moscow on December 11, 1954, only a few weeks after the decision was made to form the commission. It sat until December 28.[35] And by the middle of January the Soviets already announced that they were prepared to put their knowledge in the atomic energy field at the disposal of other countries (those named were China, Poland, Czechoslovakia, Rumania, and the Soviet Zone of Germany) and to assist these countries in the construction of cyclotrons and atomic reactors up to 5,000 kilowatts, provided that they supplied the USSR with 'corresponding raw materials'.[36] The following year China was represented at a meeting in Moscow at which a 'United Institute for Nuclear Research' was founded.[37] The first Chinese atomic reactor was put into operation in September 1958. It was a reactor of 10,000 kilowatts:[38] in other words, the Chinese had succeeded in obtaining double the power originally provided for. At the same time a 20-million-volt cyclotron was dedicated.

The guessing game as to the date when Red China would explode its first nuclear bomb has been going on for years, and, like the 'Loch Ness Monster', new reports keep springing up in the press of Chinese nuclear tests which are said to be either imminent or to have already taken place. However, as distinct from the monster, which lives solely on printer's ink, one may be certain that the Chinese nuclear explosion will one day be a reality. The Chinese have never set a date; all they ever said (as, for example, Foreign Minister Ch'en Yi to two German newspaper correspondents in the spring of 1958)[39] was that they would have their own nuclear weapons 'in the future' or 'in the near future'.

Just as little is known in the West about Sino-Soviet military co-operation, and the little that is known is a strictly guarded secret there too. The fact that, according to the treaty of alliance of February 1950, the USSR is bound to extend military aid to China in the case of an attack by Japan or 'one of the countries allied to Japan' (the United States, in other words), can mean everything or nothing. It is to be presumed that the Kremlin will base its decision as to whether the alliance applies or not on circumstances rather than the text of the treaty.

*

By way of compensation the Chinese, like the Russians, see to it that we do not lack information about their 'cultural co-operation'. In China the instrument which is most broadly effective in promoting cultural rapprochement is the Sino-Soviet Friendship Association, founded in Peking on October 5, 1949, only a few days after Moscow's recognition of the People's Republic.[40] It has millions of members, branches all over the country, and magnificent 'palaces of Sino-Soviet friendship', and it organizes countless lectures, film showings, exhibitions, Russian-language courses, and artistic presentations. According to a report on its activities, during the first ten years of its existence the association published 46,566,000 copies of 1,829 books and pamphlets, and organized 204,500 lectures attended by 164,890,000 people.[41]

During the first five years its president was Liu Shao-ch'i, the second-most prominent man in the country; from 1954 it was the widow of Sun Yat-sen, sister of the most famous living Chinese woman, Madame Chiang Kai-shek. The fact that during the first phase Liu—known more for his harshness than for his kindness—was put at the head of the association but was then replaced by a woman surrounded by the nimbus of Sun Yat-sen's name may be taken as a sign that in the long run it was not so easy to make the friendship of the Soviet Union appear plausible to the Chinese people.

At first the association's principal organ was the daily newspaper *Druzhba* (Friendship), published from April 1955 in Russian; in October 1957 it was turned into a weekly paper of the same name; and in the summer of 1960 it ceased to appear. (Only the multilingual illustrated magazine, known in English as *China Pictorial*, continued to appear in Russian also under the name *Kitay*.) Since *Druzhba* was not only designed for the Soviet technicians working in China, whose number was sharply reduced at that time, but was also exported in one hundred thousand copies[12] to the Soviet Union, its decease can only be explained by the particularly unfriendly relations then existing between the two neighbors, especially as it was not long since the Sinological journal of the USSR, *Sovetskoye Kitayevedenie* (Soviet Sinology), ceased publication after only a few issues and was incorporated in a new journal, *Problemy Vostoko-vedeniya* (Problems of Oriental Studies). This has in turn also been renamed and is now devoted to the problems of Asia and Africa. The journal *Sovremyonny Vostok* (Contemporary East) was likewise adapted to include Asia and Africa.

Not until eight years after the founding of the Chinese association was its Soviet counterpart brought into existence in Moscow, in October 1957—the Soviet-Chinese Friendship Association, which in January 1958 began operations with the periodical *Su-chung Yu-hao* (Soviet-Chinese Friendship). Its first president was A. A. Andreyev, who had once belonged to Stalin's team but had now been demoted, and who ranked much lower than Liu and Sun's widow.

Mutual adulation was very marked—more so in the first few years after the founding of the People's Republic than today. Let us for instance look once more at the trend in Chinese postage stamps. Up until the time when the Great Leap began to have a detrimental effect on mutual relations, twenty-six stamps appeared in China extolling the friendship with Moscow, with portraits of Stalin, Stalin and Mao, Lenin, various scenes from the Bolshevik revolution, and pictures of sputniks and Soviet rockets. After that there were only six—on the tenth anniversary of the treaty of 1950, in commemoration of the moon rocket, and for the ninetieth anniversary of Lenin's birth. However, such Lenin stamps were a gesture against Khrushchev rather than for the Soviet Union; for Peking (as will become clear later) made use of this Lenin memorial day to present itself, rather than Moscow, as the true guardian of the master's teaching. On the other hand, as far as Soviet polito-philately (as it must indeed be called here) is concerned, in all these years I have run across only two stamps commemorating Soviet-Chinese friendship.

For many years the Chinese conscientiously commemorated every possible anniversary, including those of the birth and death of Pushkin, Gorky, and other Russian geniuses, and on one occasion even the 108th anniversary of the death of the Russian essayist Belinsky! During those years Peking never missed an opportunity to extol the Russians as teachers in all conceivable matters, even including the regulations of the railway system.[43] Those were the days when the Russians gave Chou En-lai an honorary doctor's degree, and returned to the Chinese the 'Manchurian archives' (1675 to 1900) which they had carried off during the Boxer rebellion.[44]

During that time most books were written—or at least planned—with mutual flattery and the greater glory of joint relationships in mind, even though many did not appear until later;[45] countless Soviet books were also published on China and vice versa.[46] Recent bibliographical material is more scarce; but if one day the number and tone of Soviet publications on China—and vice versa—from the years after 1949 are analyzed, it will probably be found that their curve, too, reached its most cordial point between Stalin's death and the Great Leap. After that, China disappeared to a large extent from Soviet publications. The Chinese reacted in similar fashion.

However, the fact that even relations between specialists did not remain untouched by political trends was clearly shown at the Congress of Orientalists in Moscow in August 1960. To the disappointment of the non-Russian guests and the embarrassed surprise of the Soviet hosts, the expected Chinese delegation stayed away from the Congress.[47] At the last moment the Russians tried—literally—to cover up the affront: from the July issues of *Sovremyonny Vostok* they cut out page six, which had presumably contained a welcome to the Chinese guests, and stuck in a new page which in their haste they did not even manage to fill entirely!

This, then, is the picture of relations between state and state. But how did the relations between people and people develop?

CHAPTER XII

BETWEEN PEOPLE AND PEOPLE

DURING THE LAST FOURTEEN YEARS the Russians and Chinese have become much better acquainted with one another, and they have flooded each other with goodwill visits, miles of film, and veritable mountains of books and pamphlets. Does this indicate a stronger affection between them than in 1949?

Let us then first inquire into the extent of this mutual 'getting acquainted'. It is in fact very considerable, judging by reports from Peking and Moscow. During the first ten years of the People's Republic, 295 million copies of Russian books were sold in Chinese, and 24 million copies of Chinese books in the languages of the USSR; 840 films were exchanged and seen by 2·4 billion people (by far more Chinese than Soviet citizens); 112 Soviet stage or concert ensembles (with 2,301 members) went to China, and 134 Chinese ensembles (with 2,334 members) went to the USSR.[1] The 'Exhibition of the Economic and Cultural Achievements of the Soviet Union', which was on display between the late fall of 1954 and the summer of 1956 in Peking, Shanghai, Canton, and Wuhan, is said to have been attended by 11·25 million visitors.[2] When during the winter of 1952–53 Soviet artists gave twenty-two performances over Chinese radio stations during a tour of the country, these broadcasts, according to Peking, had more than 25 million 'organized listeners'.[3]

Before the first decade of the People's Republic was over, 36,000 Chinese students, technicians, and specialists had gone to the USSR for training. In one way or another, even if it was by instruction over the radio, millions of Chinese took Russian lessons, and in some Soviet schools Chinese was introduced as a course.[4] Sinological research in the Soviet Union, and the study of Russian and Soviet problems in Chinese universities and institutes, increased,[5] as did the interest in each other's scientific journals, and the reviews of books appearing in the opposite country. Soviet Sinology paid special attention to the study of the modern Chinese language and developed some useful Russian textbooks and dictionaries on Chinese.[6]

From the point of view of quantity and quality, therefore, a great achievement. But in the relationship between nations—as between individuals—it is not so much a matter of the effort itself as of its effect. What effect, then, have these efforts had on the attitude of the Chinese to the Russians and vice versa?

*

There is no doubt that at first the campaign in China fell on fertile soil. After decades of civil war the Chinese were glad, not only to have order in their country again, but also to possess a powerful ally who had recently achieved such signal victories. Communism was, especially for the intellectuals, something new and exciting that they were anxious to explore—what better way to do so than by studying the Soviet Union, its ideological, literary, and artistic manifestations? Any uneasiness the Chinese may have felt at being once again exposed to a wave of European influence—even if it was in the guise of Soviet Russia—was allayed.

A certain parallel can be found when we reflect on conditions in Germany after World War II. According to the different zones of occupation, the inhabitants devoured British, American, French, or Russian books, swarmed over 'America Houses' and their counterparts, begged for foreign films, produced foreign plays, dreamed of obtaining a visa for France or even the United States. The craving to find out more about the other countries from which they had so long been isolated outweighed any inhibitions they may have had at first, and it was fully accepted that much of what was offered was part of a re-education campaign on the part of the victors.

A few more years of this, and difficulties would certainly have arisen (as they did in the Soviet Zone of Germany). But West Germany was spared this, for by the time people had satisfied their desire to catch up on what had been going on in the West, propaganda pressure began to relax; intellectual contacts with the outside world—owing to a change on the political level—lost their re-educational character and became more relaxed. The Germans were no longer obliged to absorb these influences: they were free to take them or leave them. The feeling of excess was never reached.

Not so in China. When I went there in 1957, pro-Soviet propaganda was still in full swing, in fact it was still approaching its zenith (which was to be reached in the autumn of 1957 with the celebrations of the fortieth anniversary of the Bolshevik revolution), but a feeling of surfeit was already apparent. The machine had been wound up as tight as it would go; now it was running, and producing, producing. It produced propaganda, and at the same time a surfeit of propaganda.

On the whole the Russians are friendly, helpful people, and there is no reason to doubt that the following incidents (hardly uncommon in other countries) actually did occur: that a Russian family in China took food to the sick elevator-boy in their hotel; that a Soviet soldier rescued a little Chinese girl; that Russian women doctors strove to save the lives of Chinese mothers and babies in difficult births, or that they snatched from certain death children who had swallowed rat poison during the campaign against the 'four pests'.[7] But when the Chinese people are served up these praiseworthy deeds over and over again (and in especially large helpings on Sino-Soviet anniversaries) and, moreover, not simply as facts but with all manner of fatuous embellishments (such as that the rescued child was named —inevitably—Su Hua, an abbreviation of Soviet Union—China), and when this is often used to find fault with the Chinese (a Soviet workman repairs a tractor on a Chinese state agricultural enterprise 'in less than one minute', after the Chinese had been unable to get it to work),[8] the whole business tends to produce a surfeit.

This is not mitigated by the fact that in his own newspapers the Chinese likewise reads of cases where his compatriots have been responsible for helpful deeds toward the Russians—for example, took a Russian boy home who had lost his way; rushed a sick Soviet woman specialist to hospital in difficult circumstances; or even, at the cost of half a day's efforts on the part of an expert 'with twenty years' experience', restored to a condition of pristine newness the hat of visiting Soviet President Voroshilov which had got wet in the rain.[9] Besides these everyday acts of heroism we have reports on the splendid co-operation of Soviet and Chinese frontier guards in the capture of 'imperialist spies', or the tender care lavished on the upkeep of monuments to Soviet soldiers who lost their lives in China.[10]

And all this not only in newspapers, magazines, and books, but also in children's picture books (along the lines of American comics), in which every page contains a drawing and a short text, and which are published by the million on cheap paper. I bought one of these little books in a children's bookshop. The cover showed two boys, one Chinese, the other an auburn-haired Russian. The story, illustrated with numerous pictures, was called 'Ling and Vitya'. This touching tale begins with Vitya's father, a Soviet admiral, arriving with his wife and son Vitya at the Chinese port of Dairen, occupied at that time by the Soviets. Vitya soon makes friends with Ling, the son of the Chinese neighbors. The next few pages show that Vitya has a definitely salutary influence on Ling, who at first cannot by any means be called 'kulturno'. Vitya shows him how to help his mother sweep the yard and his father to chop wood, teaches him Russian games, sees that he does his homework and helps him with it too. One day young Ling rescues a Russian girl from drowning. For this he is awarded a Soviet medal. But in his heart little Ling knows that without Vitya's beneficial influence he would not have been capable of this heroic deed. When the Soviet Union gives back Dairen (Talien, as it is called by the Chinese) to China and Vitya's father returns to the Soviet Union with his family, the two friends are very sad at being separated. As parting gifts they present each other with satchels for their schoolbooks. Since then they have been busily corresponding . . . and are no doubt living happily ever after.

One can have too much of a good thing. One can guess what the young Lings think of the Vityas when they have read two or three books in this mawkish moralizing style. The Chinese, who are by nature matter-of-fact and sceptical in outlook, are in any case not very receptive to obvious propaganda; when a thing has to be praised overmuch it can't be as good as all that, they say to themselves, and, vice versa, not as bad as all that when everything possible is done to belittle it. During a visit to a refugee camp in Hongkong I was eagerly questioned about America by a Chinese. I asked him why he was so particularly interested in America, and he replied: 'It must be a strange country. We are always being told how poor and weak it is, a pitiful paper tiger, and yet that it will take many years for the mighty Soviet Union to catch up with it.' The author of these remarks was twelve years old. This is the kind of person to make a political indoctrinator despair!

*

No wonder, then, that the anti-Communist feelings expressed during the days of the Hundred Flowers in China contained unmistakable anti-Russian undertones. When one glances through the critical remarks made at that time in the Chinese press, one comes across numerous indications of resentment over the fact that for years every-thing Soviet Russian had been praised to the skies and set up as a model. Professors complained that Chinese universities were being reorganized along Soviet lines; engineers that they had to make use of methods just because the Russians used them even though they were unsuitable for China; writers that they were required to imitate 'socialist realism'; experts in every field that Soviet technicians were preferred to them sight unseen.[11] In Peking I was told about a student who got into trouble during the wave of purges in July 1957 for having contemptuously said after attending a Soviet industrial exhibition: 'You can hear Soviet watches ticking on the other side of the street'; and about another who remarked that: 'Soviet machines are big and bad.' It was reported of the University of Peking that at that time half the the students held 'erroneous views on the Soviet Union'.[12] It was clear that Soviet propaganda had overreached itself and achieved the opposite objective: the feeling we all know after having too much of one particular dish.

The pride of the Chinese began to assert itself. This was to be seen in the fact that in all the agreements with the Soviet Union emphasis was laid on 'reciprocity'. Closer inspection of the 'exchange' defined in these agreements revealed, as we have seen, that China was mainly on the receiving end—but 'face' had been saved. Moreover, when I was in China I constantly had to listen to examples cited by Chinese of cases in which they did not lag behind the Russians or in which they even outdid them. On a visit to a factory, which had been built according to Russian specifications and equipped with Soviet machinery, I was told that a certain part which the Soviets produce in sixty-five minutes could be produced by the Chinese with the same machinery in sixty minutes. In another factory, also equipped with Soviet machinery, I was told: 'Our annual production is six per cent higher than the maximum figure set by the Soviet experts.'

An engineer engaged in the building of the new bridge over the Yangtze near Hankow said to me: 'The biggest problem in building the bridge was the erection of piers in the deep water of the river. The Soviet engineers proposed one method; our engineers had another idea. The Soviet engineers did not want to consent on their own to such a radical departure from Moscow's original specifi-cations, so the Chinese proposal was sent to Moscow for study. This took a long time. Meanwhile the Chinese managed to have their new method tested in the construction of one of the piers. It proved to be excellent, and it was decided to apply it with the other piers. While construction was still underway, word finally came from Moscow: the Chinese method was rejected as unsuitable! Of course no one paid any attention to this finding, and we went right on building according to the Chinese method.' It was not possible to prove the authenticity of this story, but, whether it is true or not, it went the rounds in China.

Interest in the Russian language had also diminished noticeably: it began to forfeit some of the priority it had been enjoying in education since 1949—English was reintroduced, not only in the universities but also in the high schools.[13] A questionnaire in one school revealed that out of 210 students 197 wanted to learn English.[14]

One hot summer evening in Peking I went out onto the roof garden of my hotel. I chose a spot with a bit of a breeze to watch the dancing. Most of the guests were students, and I soon got into conversation with some of them. I wanted to try out their Russian, but I did not get very far. Their English was better. They frankly admitted that they were not very interested in Russian. When I asked why, I got a variety of answers: 'There are enough Russian books being translated into Chinese anyway.' 'We hear about the Russians all the time and want to read something else once in a while.' 'Russian books are propaganda; we don't learn anything from them that we don't already know.' 'Russian is useful in the Soviet Union, but English is the key to the world.' And one student made his friends laugh by adding: 'Russian is only the key to the next room in the same house, and we know that inside out!'

What has suffered least from this surfeit is the popularity of Russian music. While I found Soviet films poorly attended—almost pointedly so—I often heard young Chinese humming Russian songs and hit tunes. One Sunday I was being rowed across the lake of the Summer Palace and kept hearing the sound of Russian songs coming from the pleasure boats; when I looked closely I saw it was always Chinese sitting in them. One song, however, I have never heard sung —except on the record I bought in Peking. The tune was written by the Soviet composer Muradeli; the first two verses are supposed to be sung in Chinese and the third in Russian. Here is the English version:

Moscow—Peking

The peoples of the Soviet Union and China are brothers for ever,/their friendship and unity are unbreakable./The peoples have arisen shoulder to shoulder,/gaily singing they march forward./Stalin and Mao are in our hearts,/in our hearts,/ in our hearts./Moscow-Peking, Moscow-Peking!/ The peoples stride forward to happy work,/to lasting peace, under the flag of freedom,/to happy work, to lasting peace, under the flag of freedom!

One can hear the Yangtze River on the banks of the Volga,/and the Chinese people see the red Kremlin star./Of threats we have no fear,/strong is the will of our peoples./The whole world extols our victory, our victory, our victory./Moscow-Peking, Moscow-Peking! (Refrain)

Never has the world seen stronger ties,/over our columns May rejoices./ Here the Soviet Union is marching,/the mighty Soviet Union,/and side by side new China, new China, new China!/Moscow-Peking, Moscow-Peking! (Refrain)

Since 1958 the pro-Soviet trumpeting in China has subsided noticeably; too late—the damage was already done. Moreover, the slowing down of propaganda was not the result of psychological insight. The overall climate of relations had deteriorated.

*

Strangely enough, the defensive attitude of the Chinese toward Soviet propaganda was extended as early as 1957 to Russian technicians who, after all, were assisting the Chinese in their economic development by the sweat of their brows and often (at least that was my impression) with great enthusiasm. According to Peking, in the first ten years of the People's Republic 10,800 Soviet experts went to China,[15] most of them for about three years. Since many of them took along their families, this must have brought between 25,000 and 30,000 Soviet citizens to China. What the courteous Chinese thought about this influx I discovered less from what they told me than from items in the Chinese press concerning the criticisms made during the Hundred Flowers period, and from the Russians themselves, with whom I spent a good deal of time during my stay in China as—apart from the nationals of a few Eastern European countries—they were almost the only Europeans with whom I came in contact.

For many of these Russians the *kommandirovka* to China was simply an adventure that they enjoyed; for many others it was a patriotic duty to which they dedicated themselves without giving much thought to what was going on around them. One Russian woman who was on her way home again with her husband complained to me that her husband, a mechanic, had ruined his health in the two and half years they had been in China. He could not stand the heat, she said, and suffered a great deal from intestinal troubles, but he had nevertheless done more than his share of duty. He did in fact look very ill and spent most of the time lying down. She gestured toward him and said bitterly: 'That's the price *we* have had to pay for China's development!' The more reflective among the Russian experts seemed to be rather saddened by the fact that their efforts were received with more politeness than cordiality.

As a Russian-speaking European I was often taken automatically for a Russian by the Chinese, but only once did I ever see a Chinese look spontaneously and convincingly pleased to meet me. It was during a night journey by train. I had the compartment to myself for a while and was asleep. At a station the door opened and the light was switched on. I woke up with a start. Two Chinese officers entered the compartment. When the first one saw me he beamed and said: 'Tovarishch!' (Comrade). There was no doubt that he was really pleased to meet what he thought was a Soviet comrade. I should add that this was the extent of his command of Russian; besides, it was two o'clock in the morning, so we were soon all three asleep. A few hours later the two officers got out.

A Russian engineer whose friendly, expansive nature was probably suffering from the polite reserve with which he was treated, said resignedly: 'Well, after all, who loves a schoolmaster? One can respect and admire a schoolmaster—but can one love him?'

*

However, it was not always the Chinese who maintained their distance. All the Soviet nationals had been instructed to keep to themselves as much as possible. In Peking alone, at the time I was there, there were many thousands of Russians (including families), but one hardly ever saw them. Some stayed at the old Hotel Wagons-Lits, which had been almost entirely set aside for them, but most of them lived in a new district in the west (outside the city) which was put exclusively at their disposal.

It struck me one day in Peking that Chinese sometimes took me for a Russian and at other times for a non-Russian. At first I could not understand why this was so. Finally I solved the mystery: when I arrived by car or on foot, I was taken for a Russian; I was assumed to be a non-Russian when I took a pedicab (the three-wheeled, man-powered substitute for the vanishing ricksha). Soviet nationals in China are instructed never to use pedicabs. This is to prevent arguments with the drivers, who are often quite cheeky, and presumably also to show that a Soviet citizen is above such primitive methods

of locomotion and considers this kind of personal service 'unsocia-
listic' (which, however, does not prevent the same citizen from
entrusting duties of a far less pleasant nature to his domestic
servants). Result: pedicab drivers, who are among the most agreeable
dwellers in the Heavenly Kingdom, are all anti-Russian.

Soviet nationals in China use their own cars or buses, and even
this they do as discreetly as possible. Their bus stops, for example,
are hardly noticeable: in Peking they were marked by little signs on
which there was nothing but one Russian letter indicating which line
stopped there, and most of these bus stops were situated some
distance away from those of the Chinese bus lines.

Even the children did not have much contact with Chinese of their
own age. They went to Soviet schools; if their fathers were stationed
in places without such schools, school-age children were left behind
in the Soviet Union. One day I was chatting with a six-year-old
Russian girl. This well-brought-up young person was on her way
with her parents to the Soviet Union, and I asked her if she were not
sad to leave her Chinese playmates behind. But it turned out that she
did not know any Chinese children. 'Didn't you play with them
then?' I asked. 'No', she said, 'Mama wouldn't let me.' On another
occasion a fourteen-year-old told me Chinese children were impudent
and always played in the dirt, so she never played with them. 'But
they always came into our garden, although they weren't allowed to,
and broke off the flowers.' The Russian conductors in a Soviet-
Chinese train also told me how glad they were when most of their
passengers were Russians, as they always had to clean up after every
Chinese passenger.

It is unnecessary to say more about reactions of this kind. They are
to be found wherever people of different nationalities and cultures
meet. I only mention them because they demonstrate that the human
relationships between Russians and Chinese are not as wonderful
and harmonious as their official propaganda would have one believe.

*

Side by side with the Chinese dislike of the patronizing attitude and
technical superiority of the Russians, and with the problems that are
the natural result of the clash of two self-contained cultures, the
difference in the standard of living of the two countries has also had a
detrimental effect on their mutual relationship. The Russians earned
considerably higher salaries than Chinese in corresponding positions.

As it was difficult for them to transfer to the Soviet Union the portion of their salaries which they received in Chinese currency, they were obliged to spend the money in China. They could convert it either into a standard of living far above the Chinese one or into articles which they eventually took back to Russia with them.

On one occasion I was traveling in the Peking-Moscow train through Manchuria toward the Soviet border with a Russian family consisting of husband, wife, and eleven-year-old daughter. The whole compartment was piled so high with trunks and cases that there was hardly room to sit. In addition these people had, so they told me, sent on some cases by freight. Why not the whole lot, I asked? Nine days in such a crowded compartment must be pretty uncomfortable for them. The reply was: 'Well, you see, right at the end we had to get rid of the last of our Chinese money. That's how we got all this, and there was no time to send it by freight.' A young woman technician, also traveling with a great many cases, told me she had bought her whole trousseau in China, including a complete dinner service for twelve people and a beautiful fur.

In the luxury departments of Chinese shops, it was mostly Russians I saw buying—woollen goods, silks, brocades, and silver. If the Chinese standard of living were higher than it actually is, all this would be less obvious and have no psychological consequences. But the Chinese standard of living is so low that it would be extremely strange if, in spite of their recognition of the achievements of the Soviet specialists, they did not sometimes say to themselves bitterly: 'These people live pretty well in China on our money! They shouldn't pretend they come only from motives of brotherly love.' Travelers from Western countries to the Soviet Union may find the Russian population poorly dressed; but in China it is the Russians, the representatives of an industrial country, who stand out against the drab background of this developing nation. The noisy, uninhibited Soviet tourists also irritated many Chinese; the stream from the USSR (which later subsided) was much stronger than the one in the other direction. When at the end of 1956 the first group of Chinese tourists set off on a forty-day trip to the USSR (cost: 1,522·44 yuan), the forty-first Soviet tourist group was already in China.[16]

The Russians have their own way of showing off, as, for instance, in the building of the ostentatious 'palaces of Sino-Soviet friendship'. Those in Peking and Shanghai were built, like their counterpart in Warsaw, at a time when the 'wedding cake style' was at its peak in the Soviet Union, which accounts for their multitudes of columns and turrets; they are a mixture of the Kremlin and Pennsylvania Railroad Station in New York. Many Chinese find them beautiful and admire them very much; others shrug their shoulders and consider them disturbing foreign elements, all too reminiscent of the Soviet Union. In Harbin I saw a precision-tool factory built according to Soviet designs; its administration building was surmounted by a tower in imitation of the Kremlin. Not far away was an agricultural college, likewise built from Soviet designs; its principal building was a copy (albeit a modest one) of the new Moscow University.

The most flamboyant example of interior decoration is the 'Moskva' restaurant in Peking, built by the Russians. It is a kind of Moscow subway station in the form of a restaurant: four columns of dark green stone carved with typical Russian symbols (bears, elks, squirrels, and fir cones) support the ceiling; their curvaceous glass capitals are illuminated from within. The walls are also of green stone, a little lighter in color than the columns. Here the decorative motif is oversized ice crystals. The windows are festooned with muslin curtains in a style popular in Paris at the turn of the century. The central wall is dominated by a giant painting of the Kremlin, also illuminated. This is all presented to the Chinese as representing victorious socialism, and indeed it has already started its own trend: in the new annex to the Peking Hotel there is an enormous banquet room for receptions, and the layout and decoration show the unmistakable influence of Moscow. It is only natural that many Chinese, with their powerful, age-old traditions of culture, should look with mixed feelings toward this stylistic invasion from the northwest.

An intelligent Russian woman, the wife of a Soviet engineer working in China, told me: 'It would be a good thing if the Chinese could soon manage without us. We are beginning to be a nuisance to them. When my husband and I came to China two and a half years ago, all was sweetness and light. But things have changed since then—not much, because the Chinese are polite and appreciate our assistance. But one thing I know for sure: they are fed up with us here.' (In Russian: *Nadoyeli my im.*)

                                        *

The reverse is also true; the Chinese get on the nerves of the Russians. On my last visits to the Soviet Union I asked Russians about their

Far Eastern allies whenever I could, and the answers I received were far more often neutral or unfavorable than favorable. The critically inclined man in the street was likely to say something like this: We have enough to do building up our own country; why should we now work for 600 million Chinese as well? Or: We are sending them our best machinery, and what do we get for it? Soybeans!

If Soviet citizens knew a little more about the Great Leap and the people's communes, they would probably have added that they had some misgivings about an ally who boasts about a twenty-hour working day as if it were a great victory. At Soviet universities Chinese students are as unpopular with their mania for work as a Stakhanov is among his co-workers for forcing the work-norms upward.

Moscow students feel more uneasy than amused when they hear about a Chinese classmate who went without the necessities of life and saved enough from his grant to buy a camera, but who then succumbed to the pressure of his fanatical countrymen, sold the camera, and handed in the money because, in order to satisfy a personal desire, he had not had enough to eat, had impaired his intellectual powers, and had thus harmed the Chinese state.[17] A young German from the Soviet Zone of Germany who had spent many years in Moscow as a student and had fled to West Germany in 1961, told me: 'After 1958 the Chinese formed a community of their own in the institute; they completely isolated themselves. The Soviet students smiled when, for instance, the Chinese sat in the reading rooms even on New Year's Eve, cramming Marx. The iron discipline of the Chinese went so far that they made a kind of 'Party resolution' for one and all to stop studying at midnight and go to bed. They kept to this too, and at three in the morning they all got up again to go on working. They went in for athletics in a body, they attended cultural events in a body, they didn't smoke and didn't drink, and they had half the money from their grants sent to Peking via the embassy. It always seemed to me that the different way of life of the Russians and the Chinese reflected a different interpretation of Marxism. The Russians were freer, more relaxed, and often regarded the Chinese as backwoodsmen who couldn't grasp what was new in Moscow's policy.'

To Westerners the Russian often seems tense, but compared to the Chinese Communist he is indeed 'freer, more relaxed'. Whenever I saw Russian and Chinese diplomats standing side by side at receptions abroad, the Chinese always seemed to me, with their buttoned-

up jackets and stern expressions, like people who had just been
brainwashed, as if they were in the grip of some inward command,
not simply 'to be', but 'to behave'—and to behave in one particular
manner (Chou En-lai is the great exception), while the Russians
have long since passed the stage of having apparently just emerged
from training-camp (here the exception is Gromyko, who usually
looks morose and grim).

*

It was remarkable how often I came across the phrase 'Chinese
cruelty' when talking to Russians, said with a note of revulsion.
After I had heard it a good many times I began to wonder what was
behind it. The explanation I was given was that, during the Russian
civil war (1918–22), the Chinese had behaved with 'bestial cruelty'.
Since to my surprise I was told this by young people who did not see
the light of day until ten or twenty years after the civil war, I
continued my inquiries and was told the following strange story.

When the fortieth anniversary of the Bolshevik revolution (1957)
was approaching, a supersmart Soviet (or it might have been
Chinese) propaganda expert hit on the brilliant idea of giving the
journalists of both countries certain directives by means of which
two birds could be killed with one stone. They were to write about
the part played by Chinese Communists in the Russian civil war—
to the greater glory of Lenin and Soviet-Chinese friendship combined.
In any case, on the occasion of the anniversary, and also subsequently in China and the Soviet Union, a number of articles appeared
celebrating the heroic deeds of the Chinese Red guards;[18] these were
also described in books on Soviet-Chinese friendship.[19] These reports
showed that at the time of the October revolution some 200,000
Chinese were living in Russia, most of whom had been brought into
the country as cheap labor during the First World War; some 30,000
to 40,000 were said to have joined the ranks of the Red Army. In
recent publications as well as in the contemporary reports mentioned,
the extraordinary toughness of the Chinese Bolsheviks is praised
over and over again. ('Even when his own brother falls in battle, he
does not turn a hair; he goes over to him, closes his eyes, and that's
that.'[20]) There were more than seventy of them in the unit detailed to
guard the Kremlin and, most important of all, Lenin's life. In
Rostov-on-Don a monument was put up to the Chinese Red guard.[21]

It goes without saying that the flood of articles which appeared in

1957 spoke only of toughness, never of cruelty. However, the to-do about the role played by the Chinese Red guards in the civil war seems to have backfired; it has reawakened in the Russian people the memory of the forgotten cruelties of the Chinese units, and this in turn is linked with the tradition, still extant, of the centuries of harsh Tatar rule over Russia.

If through this and similar propaganda China has been brought more prominently into the Russians' field of vision, it has not altered their outlook on the world. Since the day some years ago when a student in Moscow told me she was studying history 'from the beginning' and on being questioned explained that what she meant was history from the Egyptians up to Khrushchev, I have asked a number of Russians of varying ages what they considered to be the chief stages in world history. Their answers showed unfailingly that they still possess a Mediterranean-European-centered perspective. China was never mentioned.

Part IV

PARTNERS AND RIVALS

INTRODUCTION

WE DO NOT KNOW what the aging Stalin thought of the junior partner in the Red camp who had so suddenly entered the world arena. Stalin could not have failed to grasp that the Chinese masses represented an economic, political, and military potential that, once it was systematically developed by firm leadership, not only equalled but surpassed that of the USSR, and that, with Mao's triumph, this firm leadership had for the first time in centuries become a political reality. Neither do we know to what extent the young—or rather, the old—giant of the Orient, waking from his long sleep, was aware of his strength. One thing, however, Mao understood better than Moscow's organizer of terror and technician of power: the Chinese people's enormous potential of spiritual strength could enable them to catch up with the evolutionary head start of the West and Soviet Russia. Had not Japan, enriched long ago by China's genius, managed to accomplish that very thing? Had not Mao and his comrades in arms been victorious solely by virtue of their own efforts, with no significant aid from Moscow, and had they not in Chiang Kai-shek conquered an enemy who had just won a war—though not without the assistance of powerful allies? Thirty years earlier Lenin had only to complete the downfall of a regime already tottering as a result of military collapse.

It could only be a question of time before China would lay claim to equal status. That hour came with Stalin's 'second death' in February 1956, when his successor wiped out the Stalin myth and thus removed the moral and psychological basis for Moscow's hitherto undisputed claim to leadership in the Communist world.

Chou En-lai's trip to Eastern Europe at the beginning of 1957 demonstrated that Peking had no intention of being satisfied with the negative success of a recognition of its 'special national position': it wanted something much more than that. Its attempted short cut to

325

Communism, entered upon two years later with the Great Leap and the people's communes, meant nothing less than that Peking was beginning to dispute the older brother's ideological leadership. The failure of this experiment, justifying Khrushchev's warnings, was not conducive to strengthening Peking's affection for its mentor.

Similarly, in world politics the Chinese claimed with increasing insistence the right to an equal voice in decisions and leadership. They observed Khrushchev's road to the summits of Camp David (1959) and Paris (1960) with scepticism, and soon with unmistakable disapproval; in the Asian sphere—in the Straits of Formosa and on the Himalayan border—as well as in their relations with the developing countries, they pursued their own line.

The methods by which this conflict was fought were at first strange indeed, and can only be understood when seen from the point of view of the political and ideological structure of the Communist world. After subsiding temporarily at the end of 1960, the quarrel flared up in the fall of 1961 more fiercely than ever: 'Albania' and 'second de-Stalinization' have become familiar catchwords. The Cuban crisis, the Sino-Indian war, the struggle for supremacy within the Communist world, added to the sharpness of the conflict. Partners had turned into rivals.

CHAPTER XIII

AFTER STALIN'S SECOND DEATH

WHILE STALIN WAS STILL ALIVE the superiority of the Soviet Union—which gained most in the Second World War—over the Chinese People's Republic, which was just getting onto its feet, was so overwhelming that the emergence of serious differences of opinion was unthinkable. Nor did the early edition of Mao's *Selected Works* which first appeared in Peking in 1951 postulate any special ideological positions for Chinese Communism.

With Stalin's death China's importance within the alliance was enhanced overnight, but even then there was at first no sign of tension. I remember that at the Geneva conference on Korea and Indo-China in the early summer of 1954, to which both Red powers sent delegations, I discussed the question every day with the political observers who were there at that time. The signs of tension were so small, and at that so disputed,[1] that they are not worth going into again here.

Let us therefore begin our examination with the Twentieth Congress of the CPSU in Moscow early in 1956. As this resulted in de-Stalinization and led to the Polish crisis as well as the Hungarian uprising, it represents a decisive turning-point in the history of the Eastern bloc.

I spent the first few months of 1956 in the Soviet Union and have described elsewhere[2] the consequences of the Twentieth Party Congress which suddenly robbed Josef Stalin of his infallibility. Of course, Moscow tried to keep de-Stalinization within bounds by referring to the dangers of an objectionable 'personality cult', thus depriving the situation of its dangerous quality. The directive for this new approach was contained in a *Pravda* article at the end of March 1956.[3] In the Soviet Union in particular, as with Communism in general, so the article stated, everything was in excellent shape; the blemishes which appeared for a while had nothing to do with the system but were attributable solely to the aging Stalin as a result of this personality cult.

Khrushchev may have thought that this settled the matter once and for all, but for Peking de-Stalinization had a whole series of additional aspects. First of all a very personal one. Mao's position in the spring of 1956 was similar in many ways to that held by Stalin during the last ten years of his life: it corresponded to the style of leadership dominant throughout the Soviet bloc during Stalin's lifetime. The hymns of praise to Mao were not quite as ecstatic as those to Stalin had been, but they differed only in degree, not in kind; in the Party indoctrination campaign of 1942–44 Mao—like Stalin—had already claimed to be the final authority in all matters, from the conduct of war to literature.[4] The destruction of the idol brought certain advantages to Khrushchev: he deflected the tide of hatred against the dead tyrant away from himself, and, in contrast to him, appeared a more humane leader; yet in doing so he sacrificed nothing, as at that time there was—as yet—no personality cult in honor of Khrushchev. The reputation of Mao, on the other hand, the Chinese counterpart to Stalin, was bound to be affected if the CPC should decide to condemn the personality cult too.

However, the loss of prestige of the dead Stalin (and thus also of the CPSU) automatically meant a gain in prestige for Mao within the Communist sphere. It was to be many years before Khrushchev would acquire an authority of his own; thus with Stalin's death in 1953 Mao became the 'Number One Communist'. This position was still further enhanced by Stalin's 'second death'—all the more so since, among the errors attributed to Stalin by Khrushchev in his 'secret speech' at the Twentieth Party Congress, Stalin's policy toward China was specifically referred to:

In our relations with China, it has been the lack of faith on Stalin's part in our Chinese comrades which led to an unnecessary retarding in their positive program relating to the establishment of a government of Popular Democracy and the elimination of the disastrous regime of Chiang Kai-shek and his bourgeois imperialist collaborators.[5]

Here, then, was a clear statement of Stalin's share of the blame for the Chinese Communists' embarrassing defeats of the early years, and it must have been gratifying to them.

Had Peking been notified in advance of the imminent de-Stalinization? We do not know. Although there were inklings of the change in course on the opening day of the Congress, Mao's message of greeting, read by Chu Teh (the leader of the Chinese delegation), praised 'the invincibility of the CPSU, created by Lenin and fostered by Stalin and his closest comrades in arms'.[6] If, therefore, the Chinese either knew of or suspected the coming massive attack on Stalin, which was to erupt in full force in the 'secret speech' of February 25, the wording of this message seems to indicate that they did not approve. But if—as is also possible—Khrushchev had kept the Chinese in the dark, they may very well have resented being passed over in the planning of a step of such vital importance to world Communism.

*

Whatever may have actually happened, for the time being Peking was silent, nor was it obliged to react to a speech of the Moscow Party leader made at a secret meeting. When the *Pravda* article appeared at the end of March, the Peking ideologists deliberated for a week: then they published a voluminous document entitled 'The Historical Experience of the Dictatorship of the Proletariat'.[7] The next step was the appearance in Peking of a 'Collection of Critical Views on the Problem of Stalin', an imposing pamphlet containing statements of leading Communists all over the world made during the months following the Moscow Party Congress.[8] Six weeks later a further pamphlet was published with supplementary documents.[9] If we add the second exposition of Peking's views published at the end of the year, and which by its title, 'Again on the Historical Experience of the Dictatorship of the Proletariat',[10] showed that it was a continuation of the April publication, we may consider that Peking's attitude toward de-Stalinization had in the main been defined.

Mao's reaction differed from both attempts made thus far to account for the sins of Stalinism. Khrushchev had placed all the blame on Stalin personally, as if a villain had appeared, so to speak, out of the blue, whose wicked deeds could otherwise only be explained as symptoms of old age. Critics outside the 'camp', on the other hand—including the Yugoslavs—believed the causes of Stalinism to lie in an excessive concentration of power. Peking did not want to accept the first explanation and could not accept the second. Mao accordingly reverted to his favorite old theory, which he had already defined nineteen years earlier (in 'On Contradiction', August 1937):[11] namely, that the dialectic principle, the principle of contradictions, far from being limited to the period of class warfare, continued to be effective even after the Communist victory.

A thorough study of Mao's intellectual evolution would be necessary to determine whether his interpretation of dialectics is based on Marxism or rather on Chinese tradition (here we are reminded of the ancient conception of Yang and Yin). In any event it is quite clear that the leading Chinese Marxists argue this question differently from the men in the Kremlin.

'Contradiction is universal, *absolute*, existing in all processes of the development of things and running through *all* processes *from beginning to end*,'[12] wrote Mao in 1937. (Author's italics.) This is a clear statement from which Mao has never since deviated. And in 1958 Liu Shao-ch'i said at the Party Congress, 'even ten thousand years from now' there would be 'poisonous weeds',[13] as he called the enemies of Communism.

The early Marxists were mainly interested in the problem of contradictions as it related to the period leading up to the victory of the revolution they were preaching; they were not particularly concerned whether there would still be contradictions afterwards, under socialism or even Communism. But Stalin felt differently. He was a *post*-revolutionary ruler, and the older he became the less he cared for contradictions—which, after all, could only be contradictions aimed at himself. Thus under his rule the distinction between contradictions of an antagonistic nature (i.e. irreconcilable, to be solved only by a struggle) and a non-antagonistic nature (capable of being solved without a struggle) acquired a special significance. In the Soviet Union, so his court philosophers proclaimed, the remaining contradictions were non-antagonistic; it was only in the capitalist society that antagonistic contradictions were inevitable.[14] On this point Khrushchev agreed with him in May 1957 (in an interview for an American television network; in the *Pravda* report of this interview the sentence in question was suppressed!)[15] As late as 1960 a leading Soviet philosopher declared that 'under socialism contradictions have lost their antagonistic character', and argued with the 'dogmatists' who see in contradiction 'always and everywhere' the cause of progress.[16] Mao, on the other hand (as early as 1937) stated, with no limitations as to time:

Based on the concrete development of things, some contradictions, originally non-antagonistic, develop and become antagonistic, while some contradictions, originally antagonistic, develop and become non-antagonistic.[17]

Twenty years later Mao again took up this theme in his speech

'On the Correct Handling of Contradictions Among the People',[18] to which we have already referred; even after the victory of the Communists, antagonistic contradictions 'among the people' (by which he meant, as the context shows, between Party and people) could arise, as witness the example in Hungary.

When someone denies, as Khrushchev did, the possibility of antagonistic contradictions once socialism has become a reality, he does indeed have no alternative but to represent Stalin as being an exceptional case. In doing so he really does not explain Stalinism. The Chinese, however, were able to include Stalinism within the framework of their doctrine of contradictions without tying themselves in knots. It would be naive, they said in their first statement on de-Stalinization, to believe that contradictions no longer existed in a socialist society; these would appear 'at all times', and, moreover, not only under socialism but 'even when a Communist society is established'.[19] Thus there was, they maintained, no reason whatever for alarm.

From the Olympian heights of this theory Mao looked down on his colleagues in the Kremlin with thoughts that presumably were not exactly flattering, since their primitive mode of attack on Stalin had placed them—and Communism throughout the world—in an awkward position. Furthermore, as Mao let it be known (in the second statement on the dictatorship of the proletariat), Stalin's errors were secondary as compared to his achievements. Criticism of Stalin within certain limits—that was all right; but it was 'extremely wrong' to deny the importance of leaders. In spite of its errors, Stalinism was first and foremost Marxist-Leninism. Khrushchev concurred with this view at a reception given by the Chinese Embassy in Moscow early in 1957; the name of Stalin, he said, 'is for us indissolubly linked with Marxist-Leninism'![20] The united front seemed to have been restored.[21]

Naturally the question of de-Stalinization as applying to Mao was never raised in the Chinese press. But insofar as infringements of the 'collective leadership' principle propagated by Khrushchev were publicly censured in China, these rebukes were directed solely at minor functionaries, such as the Party secretary of a Mukden transformer plant who forced his employees to agree with every notion that came into his head.[22]

There was one particular embarrassment which the Chinese were spared: in the Soviet Union thousands of enterprises, kolkhozes, streets, districts, mountain peaks, schools, libraries, and even a number of cities had to change their name in the wake of de-Stalinization. In China no places or institutions have—so far—been named after Mao.

*

Nevertheless the cult of Mao abated somewhat at that time. If, for instance, we compare the Party statutes of 1945 and 1956, we find that Marx's name occurs twice in the second paragraph of the introduction ('General Program') to the 1945 draft and that of Lenin and Mao once each; in the corresponding place of the draft of September 1956, Mao's name was not mentioned, while Marx and Lenin were each invoked seven times.[23] But that did not last long; from 1957 on, the cult of Mao began to put forth new blossoms. Countless portraits of Mao, both large and small, immediately reminded the visitor to China of Stalinism. In the spoken and written word, too, this adulation assumed 'Stalinist' forms. Mao, like Stalin before him, was frequently compared to the sun;[24] the era of Mao, it was said, was 'heaven on earth';[25] and in the fall of 1959 a song about Mao contained these rhapsodic lines:

> Chairman Mao is infinitely kind.
> Ten thousand songs are not enough to praise him.
> With trees as pens, the sky as paper
> And an ocean of ink,
> Much would still be left unwritten.[26]

It was above all 'Mao's thoughts' that were so continually quoted and eulogized. In 1960 the expression 'Mao's thoughts' (sometimes also 'Mao's writings') occurred sixty-one times in a single article in the leading Communist youth journal![27] Truly reminiscent of Stalin's best days.

In China portraits of Stalin never quite disappeared; while in Moscow after 1956 pictures of the dead dictator were no longer prominently displayed on state anniversaries, in Peking giant portraits of Marx, Engels, Lenin, and Stalin continued to adorn the parade ground in front of the Gate of Heavenly Peace as late as 1962. Stalin began to be quoted again relatively quickly.[28] The article in *Pravda* on the eightieth anniversary of Stalin's birthday (1959) consisted almost entirely of criticisms and was not illustrated, while the one in the Peking *People's Daily* contained very few derogatory remarks and was accompanied by a photograph of Stalin.[29] During the summer of 1961 the Red Chinese delegate to the Moscow film festival refused to support the anti-Stalinist Soviet film proposed for the highest award and voted instead for a non-Communist film from Italy.[30]

The Chinese edition of Stalin's works is still advertised in Peking in exactly the same way as editions of Marx, Lenin, or Mao, while in the Soviet Union the publication of the *Collected Works* ceased after Stalin's death with Volume XIII, which goes only as far as 1934. In China, therefore, Stalin—but not Khrushchev!—was numbered among the 'classical writers of Marxism' and Party members were advised to study his works.[31]

However, in talking to young Chinese—some who remained and some who had fled—I received the impression that de-Stalinization had had a similar although perhaps not quite so strong a disorganizing effect on them as on their Russian contemporaries. One young Chinese, who had been a student in Peking before he fled, told me later that after the Twentieth Party Congress he had read everything about Stalin he could lay hands on in an effort to understand the phenomenon he found so disturbing—the damnation of the former idol, and that de-Stalinization had contributed in no small measure to the loss of his illusions about Communism.

It was not until the Twenty-second Party Congress in Moscow, however, that the extent of the split between the two Red allies in their assessment of Stalin became fully apparent. Starting with his first speech on October 17, 1961, the opening day, Khrushchev ushered in a new de-Stalinization campaign which was carried on during the days that followed with increasing volume. But on October 21—at ten minutes past two in the afternoon, according to the Peking *People's Daily* report from Moscow under a big headline[32]—Chou En-lai conspicuously laid wreaths on the coffins of Lenin *and* Stalin, Stalin's wreath being provided with a ribbon bearing the inscription (also printed in the newspaper in bold type): 'To J. V. Stalin, the great Marxist-Leninist'—and this only a few days before Stalin's body was taken away from the mausoleum at dawn, on Khrushchev's orders, and Stalin's name was removed from above the entrance. By this time Chou, who had prematurely turned his back on the Congress, had already returned to China. (The Soviet press resorted to a rather farfetched explanation for his hurried departure by speaking of the 'imminent' session of the National People's Congress in Peking,[33] although this did not take place until April of the following year!) On the forty-fourth anniversary of the Russian revolution in November 1961, the Peking Party journal extolled Stalin for his achievements in building up the Soviet Union into a 'mighty socialist state';[34] and Albania, China's protégé, took every opportunity to acknowledge the greatness of the dead dictator even more emphatically. The first sign of coolness on the part of the Chinese toward the memory of the Soviet dictator came in March 1963, when no articles were published in China's leading newspapers on the tenth anniversary of his death.

*

We all remember the dramatic effects of de-Stalinization, and of the Twentieth Party Congress in general, on the Eastern European satellites. A great deal has been written about Peking's attitude to the events in Poland and Hungary—much of it incorrect. Let us look at the facts.

The headlines over the Chinese news reports from Warsaw are enough to indicate Peking's reaction to the uprising of June 28, 1956: ORDER RESTORED AFTER UPRISING IN POZNAN. WARSAW WORKERS CONDEMN PROVOCATEURS. POZNAN'S SABOTEURS CONDEMNED. LIFE IN POZNAN RETURNS TO NORMAL. POLES INDIGNANT AT POZNAN PROVOCATION.[35]

These, then, were the spontaneous reactions. Two weeks later the Peking *People's Daily* wrote in a final commentary that it had been 'definitely' established that the revolt had been staged by 'imperialist secret agents'. But the same article struck a note which continued to reverberate during the following months: namely, that the revolt had been possible because 'certain difficulties' had existed in supplying the population and local organs had made 'certain mistakes'.[36] Here, too, the Chinese commentators took refuge in Mao's doctrine of contradictions.

On the one hand, therefore, Peking had apparently unhesitatingly condemned the uprising as did the government (then still Stalinist) in Warsaw and the Moscow leaders; there was no trace of any sympathy for the men who had taken part in the revolt and thereby lost their lives. But on the other hand it became clear that, after due consideration, doubts began to arise in Peking (as well as in Warsaw) as to whether other factors should not be sought apart from the oversimplified theory of foreign agents. We have the same picture in

Moscow: FOREIGN PROVOCATION OF AN IMPERIALIST AGENCY IN POZNAN was the headline over the *Pravda* report of the incident;[37] but in Moscow too it was admitted that the incident was associated with 'economic difficulties and deficiencies in some Poznan enterprises'. Thus Moscow and Peking were in agreement.

We must remember that in 1956 the Hundred Flowers had begun to bloom in China, and that Mao presumably believed he had virtually the entire population behind him and could thus afford to loosen the reins a little. In the summer of 1956, therefore, Peking probably thought: if those people in Warsaw behaved a bit more sensibly, as we do in Peking, they surely ought to be able to create an atmosphere in Poland which makes uprisings impossible. Perhaps this view was also expressed to Ochab, at that time head of the CP in Poland, who in September 1956 was staying in Peking for the Eighth Party Congress of the CPC, and this may have led to the rumors circulating that autumn and long afterwards in Poland—and in the West—to the effect that Peking had stiffened the Poles' attitude toward Moscow. But even if Peking did encourage the Poles, as they in turn reported to an American journalist, to develop their own socialism as the Yugoslavs had done,[38] it certainly did not mean, as many Poles (and a great many Yugoslavs and Hungarians) would have liked to believe, that Mao wished Poland to dissociate itself from Moscow after the pattern of Tito.

The Chinese public heard little of the events which took place during Poland's 'spring in October' and nothing at all of the drama surrounding them. In its press, particularly in a long report of the *People's Daily* from Warsaw,[39] it was offered a cautiously sympathetic portrait of Gomulka, which no doubt corresponded to the view of the Peking Party leaders at that time. Mao did not commit himself, but we may assume that he preferred to see a popular Communist (like Gomulka) at the head of Poland rather than an unpopular one—provided, of course, that he remained loyal to the 'socialist camp'; and it was felt that this could be expected of Gomulka—rightly so, as things turned out. Accordingly, when the crisis had been finally overcome and the Soviet-Polish negotiations concluded, Peking heaved a sigh of relief.[40]

Meanwhile the Hungarian tragedy had run its course. The version recurring in the West (and in Eastern Europe) according to which Peking viewed the Hungarian uprising differently from—i.e. more favorably than—Moscow, is not borne out by the facts. A comparison of the day-by-day Soviet (TASS) and Chinese (NCNA) agency reports and newspapers (bearing in mind the six-hour time-differential between the two capitals) gives us the following picture.

*

Events in Hungary entered upon their acute stage with the mass demonstrations of October 23. The first reports from Budapest—both Russian and Chinese—were vague and short. TASS reported in somewhat more detail on October 25, followed by NCNA on October 26: taking advantage of an orderly and peaceful demonstration, an uprising of counter-revolutionaries had occurred; however, under the leadership of the newly appointed Prime Minister Nagy, Hungary was already returning to normal. Doubts about Nagy appeared for the first time in a TASS report of October 28, when he was no longer called 'Comrade'. But Moscow remained cautious and gave the reports from Budapest non-committal headlines such as 'The Situation in Hungary'. On the 31st, TASS still referred to the Nagy government as a 'coalition of democratic forces'. The Chinese showed similar reserve.

On November 1 Nagy announced Hungary's neutrality and withdrawal from the Warsaw Pact. NCNA reported this on November 2 and spoke for the first time of the 'betrayal of Hungary's national interests by the Nagy government'. On November 4 Nagy was compared by the Peking *People's Daily* to Chiang Kai-shek—the worst thing Chinese Communists can say about a politician. On the other hand, the *Pravda* editorial published the same day did not yet condemn Nagy and only indirectly reported Hungary's withdrawal from the Warsaw Pact. More or less unanimous reports from the press agencies of both countries announced on November 4 (for the papers of the following day) the intervention of the Soviet army, the dissolution of the Nagy government, and its replacement by the Kadar regime. On November 5 the Peking *People's Daily* came out with the headline: LET US CELEBRATE THE GREAT VICTORY OF THE HUNGARIAN PEOPLE, and the editorial in *Pravda* ran: THE TOILING HUNGARIAN PEOPLE DEFEND THEIR SOCIALIST ACHIEVEMENTS.

This unanimity was still further underlined in Moscow by the fact that on November 5 and 6 *Pravda* reprinted the editorials of the *People's Daily* from the preceding day.

Thus we see that views did not differ appreciably. One certainly cannot say that the Red Chinese were more favorably disposed toward the freedom fighters: on the contrary, they were the first—days before the Russians—to accuse the Nagy government of betrayal. In fact, one had the feeling that Peking, being further away and less directly involved, managed to collect its thoughts and recover more quickly than Moscow from the shock of the bad tidings from Budapest. By November 6 Peking had already offered aid to the Kadar government to the extent of 30 million rubles; and while *Pravda* did not bestir itself until November 23 to give a detailed analysis of the events in Hungary, the *People's Daily* published a long, comprehensive article two weeks earlier, on November 10, with the following reasoning:

Under Rakosi's rule (which preceded Nagy's) there had, according to this article, been serious infringements of 'socialist legality' in Hungary: numerous innocent, decent workers and Party members had been persecuted, imprisoned, and even executed; furthermore, the government at that time had committed the error of over-industrialization at the expense of agriculture [a mistake to be made later by Peking itself in a much more extreme form]; Party and government had not paid sufficient attention to the people's living conditions. Differences of opinion with the Soviet Union had arisen. The article continued:

After the Twentieth Party Congress the Hungarian people demanded an increase in democracy, the further improvement of living conditions, and the regulating of relations between Hungary and other socialist countries based on equality. . . . The Party and government authorities at that time behaved bureaucratically and showed themselves to be undecided and slow in the correction of their errors. This aroused even greater discontent among the masses. After the rapid development of the democratic movement in Poland, the Hungarian people finally launched a large-scale mass movement on October 23. The peaceful mass demonstration was quickly exploited by the counterrevolutionaries.

After the departure of the Soviet troops, the *People's Daily* went on to say, the Nagy government revealed itself as incapable of putting down the rebellion; it initiated negotiations with the rebels and on November 1 announced the withdrawal from the Warsaw Pact. On November 4 the people realized the true nature of the uprising; an opposition government under Kadar had been formed which, together with the righteous support of the Soviet army, put an end to the rebellion.

This made it clear that Peking wanted nothing more to do with Nagy once he had announced Hungary's withdrawal from the Warsaw Pact. Ever since the existence of the Red Chinese state, Mao had always supported the idea of the unity of the bloc, even though the leadership of this bloc was in Moscow. Doubts as to whether this unity really meant more to him than anything else were not to arise until four years later.

*

In January 1957 Chou En-lai ('at the invitation of the Soviet government', as Peking took care to point out)[41] undertook a memorable journey to Moscow and on to Poland and Hungary—memorable because here for the first time in history a Chinese politician mediated between European states and thus, for the first time since the days of the Mongol invasions, East Asia appeared on European soil. For the freedom-loving forces in Poland and Hungary, the visit of the Chinese proved a bitter disappointment. To the very last they had hoped that China, the great neighbor of their great Soviet neighbor, would support them in their defiance. But instead of encouraging them, Chou told the Poles and the Hungarians politely and coldly that they would just have to get along with Moscow and, that the unity 'of the socialist camp under the leadership of the Soviet Union' was to be preserved at all costs.[42]

Chou seems to have greatly enjoyed his role of mediator and teacher. He handed out report cards all round: the 'imperialists and counter-revolutionaries' got the worst marks; then came the Rakosi regime; and even Moscow was forced to listen to some critical comments. ('There were errors in the relations between the socialist countries. . . .')[43]

In spite of Chou En-lai's disappointing visit, the Poles clung obstinately to their illusions about China. In the summer of 1957 their ambassador in Peking told me his country was definitely counting on Mao's imminent visit, and he was not to be swayed from this hope even when I told him that there had not been a single official Chinese statement agreeing to such a journey. After the settling of the Polish crisis Moscow would certainly not have welcomed a visit of Mao's to the Poles, as this might have suggested Chinese support of Poland's desire for greater independence from Moscow. Anyway, what possible reason could Mao have for annoying the Russians without deriving any benefit to himself? Not even after his visit to Moscow in November 1957 did he make a detour to Warsaw.

When some months later the Hungarian government executed Nagy, after promising him safe conduct in November 1956 if he left his refuge in the Yugoslav embassy, indignation and sorrow were expressed in many different parts of the world—even among many people behind the Iron Curtain. Moscow refrained from comment and merely reprinted the Hungarian statement.[44] Only one country had the infamous cynicism to call the announcement of this legalized murder 'welcome news'[45]—Communist China. Of Eastern Europe's hopes of a 'liberal' China, nothing now remained.[46] A similar switch was to be found in Mao's relations with Tito.

*

For years the Chinese Communists had openly acknowledged Josip Tito and his partisans to be their valiant comrades in arms. But on June 27, 1948, the Cominform had excommunicated Tito; although the Chinese Communists were then in the throes of the civil war and, one would have imagined, had enough worries of their own, they found time to approve the Cominform resolution on July 15.[47] Nevertheless, the following year Yugoslavia was one of the first countries to recognize the Chinese People's Republic, on the fourth day of its existence. Peking completely ignored this and consistently refused to assume diplomatic relations with the outlaw country. Not until Moscow began to soften its attitude toward Tito after Stalin's death did Peking also begin to revise its position. In June 1955, a few weeks after Khrushchev's reconciliation with Tito, ambassadors were exchanged. China despatched a deputy foreign minister to Belgrade, and Yugoslavia sent one of its best diplomats to Peking in the person of Vladimir Popovic. In a message to Moscow's Party Congress at the beginning of 1956, Mao acclaimed as second among the foreign-political successes of the CPSU the normalization of its relations with Yugoslavia;[48] and in the first 'Historical Experience of the Dictatorship of the Proletariat' Stalin's 'wrong decision in the Yugoslavian question' of 1948 was censured.[49] Tito's visit to the Soviet Union in the summer of 1956 was commented on very favorably by Peking,[50] and approval expressed of the 'socialist nature of its [Yugoslavia's] government and social system'.[51] During the events in Poland and Hungary, Peking voiced no complaints against the Yugoslavs.

On November 16 Belgrade published a speech made by Tito in Pula five days earlier.[52] As the Hungarian fight for freedom progressed, Tito had begun to get cold feet, so that in Pula he leveled accusations at Nagy, praised Kadar, and defended the military intervention of the Soviets in Hungary. Nevertheless, he maintained the fundamental positions of what is known as Titoism, including the workers' councils, and his attacks on Stalinism. The Pula speech at once became the target of fierce criticism in Soviet[53] and many other Communist papers throughout the world.

A whole month went by before the Peking *People's Daily* reacted to the Pula speech,[54] but then it did so conspicuously, on the first page—although without comment, in the form of a report of the speech accompanied by its repercussions among leading Communists abroad. The next day the whole Pula speech was published, again without comment. The greater part of a speech made on December 7 by Kardelj, Tito's ideologist, following the line of the Pula speech, was printed without comment in Peking.[55] The Yugoslavs were delighted at this attention and believed it indicated Peking's agreement with them. In actual fact the scepticism of the Chinese toward Tito's and Kardelj's speeches was at first only indirectly discernible in their selection of foreign CP comments on the speeches, these comments—with the exception of those of the Italian and Polish Communists—being in the main critical of the Yugoslavs' attitude.

The fact that Peking gave great prominence to the Yugoslav speeches, but did not take a stand, was a sign of its uncertainty. It was six weeks before its reaction to the Pula speech was announced, in Part II of the second declaration on the dictatorship of the proletariat. Generally speaking it was unfavorable but not hostile; Tito and Kardelj were called 'Comrades' to whom brotherly advice was handed out, the chief accusation being that they had overshot the mark—which after all need not mean they had been shooting in the wrong direction; furthermore, it was admitted that the Yugoslavs had 'in difficult circumstances made valuable efforts to preserve socialism'.[56]

The Yugoslavs were justified in regarding Mao's speech of February 1957, 'On the Correct Handling of Contradictions Among the People', as being in line with their own thinking (although there for the first time it was stated that revisionism—later to be identified with Titoism—was more dangerous than dogmatism). At the end of July the Yugoslav ambassador Popovic told me when I called on him in Peking that he was optimistic about his country's relations with China, though he was unable to hide his misgivings over the terrible battle being waged against the Hundred Flowers, now declared poisonous weeds. Relations remained normal until well into the autumn. Thanks to the visits to China of Yugoslavia's Vice President Vukmanovic-Tempo and a group of Yugoslav deputies, September was virtually a month of friendship between the two states; when the West German government broke off relations with Tito, Peking stood firmly on his side,[57] and on November 1, 1957, a few hours before he flew to Moscow, Mao Tse-tung ratified a cultural agreement with Belgrade.[58] Meanwhile Khrushchev's relations with Tito had also improved again under the auspices of a new truce which the two had concluded at a meeting in Rumania early in August.[59]

The big change did not come until November 1957. Presumably Khrushchev and Mao had had the same idea in mind—that of finally bringing the troublesome outsider to heel. At the forthcoming assembly of the heads of the Communist Parties in Moscow to celebrate the fortieth anniversary of the Bolshevik revolution, they wished Tito, in common with all the others, to sign a declaration which would bind him to the Eastern bloc in the eyes of the whole world. However, Tito found out about this plan in time. He did not go to Moscow; according to his polite message, he had lumbago. His absence was noted with anger and no doubt contributed to the fact that in the Communist leaders' declaration revisionism was placed ahead of dogmatism as being the chief danger within the Communist world movement.[60] Tito's representative refused to sign the declaration, which was thus limited to the twelve full members of the Eastern bloc.

*

Outwardly, however, nothing dramatic had occurred as yet. A few days after his return from Moscow, Mao put his name to a telegram to Tito congratulating him and the Yugoslav people on their national holiday, wishing them 'new successes in the building of socialism', and extolling the growing friendship between the two peoples.[61]

Tito now decided on a step which revealed the extent of his self-confidence: in March 1958 he sent the voluminous draft of his new Party program to the leaders of all the Communist Parties, requesting his colleagues to study the document, let him have their reactions, and meet in the Slovenian city of Ljubljana on April 22, 1958, at the

Party Congress of the Yugoslav Communists, when the document would be discussed.

This Party program was a kind of new Communist manifesto embracing all that is commonly known as Titoism and setting out the ways in which it differs not only from Stalinism (and Maoism) but also from Khrushchev's brand of Bolshevism.[62] Needless to say, Khrushchev and Mao were no more inclined to accept the invitation to Ljubljana than Pope Leo X had once been to go to Wittenberg for a discussion with Martin Luther. The Communist Parties refrained—presumably on instructions from Moscow—from sending delegates to the Ljubljana Congress, and even the Eastern bloc diplomatic representatives who were present at the beginning staged a dramatic withdrawal from the Congress hall on the second day.

However, the sharpest public attack was that undertaken by the Chinese on May 5, 1958, in an editorial commemorating the one hundred and fortieth anniversary of Marx's birth. Completely abandoning the views expressed by the Chinese during the preceding two years, this editorial culminated in the statement that the (Stalinist) Cominform resolution against Tito of June 1948 had been correct.[63] The same thought was expressed in the final resolution of the (Intermediate) Congress of the CPC of May 23 dealing almost exclusively with Yugoslavia. Further attacks followed, especially in the bi-weekly journal *Hung-ch'i* (Red Flag)[64] which had begun to appear on June 1 and became the chief mouthpiece of the CPC in ideological questions (a counterpart to the Moscow journal *Kommunist*, previously *Bolshevik*) serving principally as a political forum against 'revisionism'. An editorial in the *People's Daily* expressing Peking's satisfaction over the execution of Nagy contained a sentence which had obviously been coined for Tito's benefit: 'That's what happens to people who collaborate with the imperialists.'[65] Peking's battle against the 'Judas Tito' was in full swing.

The situation in Moscow was a different one. Now it was the Russians who hesitated to make radical decisions. While the Chinese, from the sending of the Yugoslav program draft until the start of their offensive on May 5 (except for one brief comment)[66], remained wrapped in a silence which boded no good, Moscow admitted as late as mid-April that the Yugoslavs were 'building socialism'[67] and termed Soviet criticism of the draft program 'friendly'.[68] The new conflict between Moscow and Belgrade did not become obvious in the Soviet press until *Pravda* reprinted[69] the acrimonious article from the *People's Daily* of May 5 and three days later published its own sharp criticism of Tito.[70] On May 27 Khrushchev stopped the credits which had been solemnly promised to Yugoslavia; Ulbricht cried, 'Me too!' and did likewise. And on June 3 in a speech in Sofia Khrushchev himself engaged in the battle with Tito.[71]

Comparing the anti-Tito utterances of the two Red powers we find that the Russian ones were usually a shade or two more moderate and often sounded like echoes of the Chinese outbursts. Since the reconcilation of 1955 Moscow had, it is true, frequently quarreled with Belgrade, but, warned by the experiences of the years after 1948, had left the door to Belgrade ajar, while in the weeks following the Ljubljana Congress Peking had slammed it shut.[72]

No wonder I found the Yugoslavs full of disappointment and bitterness at Peking when I visited Belgrade a few weeks later. I was told the joke which some years earlier they had applied to the Soviet Union: there are three kinds of unnatural love—between men, between women, and for the Chinese People's Republic. What a long way from those rapturous dreams of Yugoslav-Chinese friendship of the spring and summer of 1956!

*

Peking has continued to maintain this position of strict anti-revisionism ever since, not only in its relationship to Tito. It was equally apparent in the powerful reaction to every hint of Soviet revisionism, and finally in the almost grotesque friendship with Albania, the most backward member of the bloc, a friendship which, during the Twenty-second Party Congress and after, reached a zenith of mutual adulation. To the Chinese reader it must have seemed that, apart from China, there was only one truly Marxist-Leninist country, only one country of world-political stature—known as Albania. For weeks Peking found new grounds almost every day for praising the Albanian comrades; and while events in the Soviet Union, including the Party Congress, were summarily dealt with in a few lines, the *Peking Review*, for example, glorified Albania in three articles in one single edition: GLORIOUS ALBANIAN PARTY OF WORKERS [i.e. CP]. MESSAGE OF GREETING [to the CC of the Albanian Party of Workers]. IN A LAND OF HEROES [i.e. Albania].[73] In every case Albania was extolled as a stronghold of Marxism-Leninism, and China's 'militant friendship' with Albania described as unbreakable.

Over the years the Peking leadership had already developed a strong preference for Albania based on the common 'uncompromising fight against modern revisionism, particularly that of Yugoslavia, and against all anti-Marxist phenomena',[74] and had allotted that country a disproportionate amount of space in its press;[75] it had also, in spite of its own very serious food shortage, given Albania economic assistance on several occasions, the biggest loan corresponding to half a billion (old) rubles at the beginning of 1961. But these indications of sympathy did not become openly anti-Soviet until the moment when Enver Hoxha and his comrades in Tirana began to inveigh against Khrushchev with such expressions as revisionist, anti-Marxist, divider, conspirator, calumniator, usurper, and dirty liar, and closed the Soviet submarine base, while Moscow returned the compliment with such endearments as murderer, hypocrite, and dogmatist, ordered the departure of the Russian and other Eastern European specialists from Albania, recalled its ambassador from Tirana, and requested the departure of the Albanian ambassador from the Soviet Union.[76]

Peking missed no opportunity to list the *twelve* member states of the socialist camp, with Albania, in alphabetical order, at the head of the list and the Soviet Union down toward the bottom,[77] while Khrushchev, who was having his ears boxed every day in the Albanian press, would only list *eleven*. All this was indeed very interesting, and at times extremely amusing, but actually it was nothing new, being merely the logical outcome of a development the causes of which we will now examine.

Since Stalin's second death Peking's policy toward Yugoslavia offers the best yardstick for the extraordinary changes which took place in the Red Chinese capital. Mao, who in the spring of 1956 had proclaimed the blossoming of the Hundred Flowers, who then became the hope of the liberals and revisionists in Poland, Hungary, and Yugoslavia, who—as we shall soon see—at the end of the year warned that dogmatism was the greatest danger and soon afterwards (in the speech on contradictions) called upon his people to express their criticisms freely—this was the same Mao who in November 1957 turned out to be the most orthodox of all those assembled in Moscow, where he succeeded in having revisionism—that is, the relatively free interpretation of dogma—labeled the principal danger, and who in the early summer of 1958 dubbed Tito a traitor and a Judas. Within a short period of time, Red China had gone through the same evolution as that covered by the Soviet Union between Stalin and Khrushchev, only in the opposite direction and with no change in leadership.

But were the changes in Peking really so great? The problem of the internal structure of the Communist camp had, and still has, for China two aspects: one has to do with its own relation to the 'camp' the other with that of the remaining member states to it. As far as the first aspect is concerned, there has been no change in China's insistence on greater independence (slogan: 'China's own road to Communism', which is actually a 'revisionist' slogan); in fact, over the years this insistence has become even more marked. And the second aspect (slogan: 'unity of the socialist camp', i.e. insistence on dogmatic co-ordination), which stands in opposition to the first, has also always been present. The logical contradiction between the two aspects is resolved for China by the fact that in the case of 'China's own road to Communism' it is thinking chiefly of itself, and in the case of the 'unity of the camp' it is mainly concerned with the co-ordination of the other Eastern bloc states.

In 1957 the Chinese recognized the instability of the Communist bloc structure and at the same time began attaching more and more importance to camp discipline (for the others, of course!). Not until after 1959 did their quarrel with Moscow become acute, and occupy their attention to the exclusion of all else and even push their concern over camp unity into the background, as is shown, for example, by the case of Albania. Let us now look a little more closely at the two aspects of Peking's relations with the Soviet bloc.

*

After the bitter experiences of the twenties, Mao and his friends were constantly concerned about the relationship of their own Communism to Moscow. As early as October 1938 Mao declared in a report to the CC: 'It is a matter of learning to apply the theory of Marxism-Leninism in the specific circumstances of China.'[78] Since then he has expressed this thought over and over again.[79] The uniting of 'the universal truth of Marxism with the specific practice of the Chinese revolution'—thus ran the standard formula to which Mao and all the other Chinese Communists reduced their relationship to dogma and thus also to Moscow. It was repeated a thousand times, and Chen Po-ta, one of the leading Party ideologists, has called the practical application of this formula Mao's real achievement.[80]

Mao's indoctrination campaign during the years 1942–44 in Yenan was devoted mainly to this very aim. Mao demanded that the classical writings of Marxism be adapted to China's needs. In order to overcome the excessive tendency—especially of the intellectuals—to think along the lines of the Communist ideologists of Russia and Europe, the Marx-Lenin Institute in Yenan was symbolically renamed the Lu Hsün Academy,[81] after the revolutionary Chinese poet.

At the Twentieth Party Congress Khrushchev had gone out of his way to praise the Chinese People's Republic for its originality in building socialism and had agreed that all the Party leaderships of the Eastern bloc were building socialism 'taking into account the special character and circumstances' of their countries.[82] Peking used this to back up its claim for consideration of its own road to Communism. Already in the first of the two declarations on 'The Historical Experience of the Dictatorship of the Proletariat' it had accused Stalin of failing to consider the independence and equal status of other Communist Parties, a criticism which had never been publicly made before his fall from grace. The Chinese noted with satisfaction that Mikoyan, as head of the Moscow delegation to the Eighth Party Congress of the CPC in September 1956 in Peking, conceded the right of the Chinese to a certain degree of independence, and specifically praised some of their measures which deviated from Soviet practice (such as their method of transforming private economy), as well as their 'great contribution to the theory of Marxism-Leninism' particularly by that 'outstanding Marxist-Leninist, Comrade Mao Tse-tung'.[83] At about the same time a *Pravda* editorial acknowledged that the Chinese had 'a creative attitude toward the theory of revolution as applicable to China's concrete circumstances'.[84] A little later Khrushchev praised

the wisdom of the Chinese comrades, who, taking into account the special circumstances of their country, creatively and with great originality are solving the problem of the methods of building socialism and thus overcoming many difficulties.[85]

*

Presumably matters would have gone no further than these mutually satisfying set phrases had not the events in Poland and Hungary intervened and once again focused attention on the discussion of the national road to Communism. China did not fail to make use of the opportunity to pin Moscow down to an increased consideration of its independence. One document in particular was highly suitable for this purpose: published by Moscow in its first alarm over Poland and Hungary, it was to become more important for Moscow's relations with China than for those with the other Eastern European 'people's democracies'—the document was known as the 'Declaration of October 30, 1956'.[86]

In its search for a formula for its relationship to the Eastern European members of the 'camp', one which would satisfy these states and at the same time keep its own dominant position more or less intact, the Kremlin came up with the expression *sodruzhestvo* (literally: co-friendship, like *sosushchestvovanie* = co-existence), which might be translated as 'friendship association' (in the sense of 'commonwealth'.) The expression 'sodruzhestvo of the socialist countries' had already made its appearance the year before,[87] but it was not defined until the Declaration of October 30: complete equality of status, respect for territorial immunity, national independence and sovereignty, mutual non-interference in domestic affairs, and co-operation in the fields of economy, politics, and culture.[88]

It is to be assumed that Moscow gave the Chinese access to this document before it was published, for only two days later Peking published a detailed commentary acclaiming the Soviets' declaration, although not without hinting that their 'big power chauvinism' had more than once impaired the unity of the Soviet bloc. *Pravda* printed the Chinese declaration the next day.[89]

Since then Peking has often referred to the document of October 30 and demanded adherence to the principles therein set out, usually in the manner of the *People's Daily*, November 21, 1956:

Even after the principles [of October 30] have been laid down, they do not prevent errors which infringe upon these principles and which have occurred in the past, which occur in the present, and may even occur in the future. . . . If in future relations between socialist countries the larger nations could make a greater effort to avoid 'big power chauvinism' (that is the main thing) and the smaller nations could make a greater effort to avoid nationalism (that is also important), then there is no doubt that friendship and solidarity based on equality would be strengthened and continue to grow. . . . The Hungarian people can now see that the Soviet policy toward the People's Democracies is truly a policy of equality, friendship, and mutual assistance, and not of conquest, aggression, and looting.[90]

What impertinence to suggest that anyone might have regarded

Soviet actions in Eastern Europe since World War II as 'conquest, aggression, and looting'!

By using the transparent excuse of also warning themselves against 'big power chauvinism', the Chinese took the Soviets to task—and presumably enjoyed doing so. They criticized countries which, 'even when they happen to be Communist', see good only in their own power, but not in other countries:

They develop a superiority complex and would always like to put their own interests above those of other nations. They always think that other countries have to look up to them; it never occurs to them on their part to treat other countries as equals.[91]

*

The second declaration on the dictatorship of the proletariat, published on the eve of Chou's journey to Moscow, Warsaw, and Budapest, was able in its Part III to extend the limits within which Chinese Communism was free to move. This occurred in the form of a discussion of dogmatism and revisionism, two concepts which had long been significant in the history of Communism and which were to play an important part in the ideological dispute between Peking and Moscow, although they gradually acquired a different meaning.

In the eyes of the Chinese, dogmatism (also doctrinairism and sectarianism), represented the unreasonable demand that Marxist-Leninist dogma be interpreted in strict adherence to the Soviet pattern, without due regard for 'special national circumstances'. They regarded revisionism as an over-emphasis of the 'special national circumstances' such as was to be found in the case of some Communists of Eastern Europe and which must inevitably threaten the unity and strength of the Soviet bloc. During their early years the Chinese Communists felt that dogmatism represented the greater danger, for it was the dogmatism of a Stalin which had hampered them for so many years, and the dogmatism of a Rakosi which had led to the uprising in Hungary.

Where the borderline lay between (good) 'special national circumstances' and (bad) revisionism was something Peking took upon itself to decide. Perhaps one might formulate Mao's attitude, particularly toward Yugoslavia, by varying the classical *Quod licet Jovi non licet bovi* to read: The 'special national circumstances' we Chinese lay claim to are by no means permitted to others. What the Chinese actually wanted was plenty of elbow room for themselves while outwardly acknowledging Moscow's priority: in other words, they wanted the Soviet bloc to be a structure which appeared monocentric—as if its sole center were Moscow—but which in actual fact was bicentric, with Peking as the second center. But Peking did not want, then or now, a polycentric system such as had been propagated from time to time since 1956, particularly by the Italian Communist leader Palmiro Togliatti.[92]

Until the turn of the year 1956–57 the Chinese continued to describe dogmatism as the greater danger. We can see the raised finger and feel how the authors of that second declaration on 'The Historical Experience of the Dictatorship of the Proletariat' must have enjoyed being able to let off steam, when we read passages such as the following which, if they issued from Tito's lips, would today be branded by Peking as rank revisionism:

The total, the fundamental experience of the Soviet Union is bound up with certain special national circumstances; other countries must not mechanically copy this experience. . . . It also includes the experience of errors and failures. The total experience—that of successes as well as failures—is a priceless treasure for those who study it intelligently, as it can help us avoid detours and suffer less harm. But when this experience is copied indiscriminately, even the experience of the Soviet successes, not to mention the experience of the Soviet failures, can lead other countries to failures.

From 1931 to 1934 the Chinese dogmatists [Mao is referring here to his previous opponents] denied the existence of China's special circumstances and copied the experience of the Russian revolution; the result was that the revolutionary forces in our country suffered a severe defeat. This defeat served as a great lesson to our Party. In the period from the enlarged Politburo session in Tsunyi in 1935 [where Mao was elected Party leader] to the Seventh Party Congress in 1945, our Party has had nothing more to do with dogmatism, which was responsible for so much damage; it [the Party] united all Party members, even those who had committed errors, it awakened the forces of the people and in this way won through to revolutionary victory. Had we behaved otherwise, victory would have been impossible. Now, since we have conquered dogmatism [i.e. since the Chinese Communists make all decisions themselves] our Party, thanks to the study of the experience of the Soviet Union and other brother-nations, makes comparatively few mistakes.[93]

*

But Peking did not stop at this negative goal of progressive emancipation. As a result of the events of 1956, Mao had acquired a special position in the Soviet bloc, a formidable junior partnership; he now shared responsibility for the policy of the 'socialist camp' and no longer wanted it left entirely in Moscow's hands. Even in getting rid of the weeds, he could not keep to his own garden.

Outwardly, of course, the old standard formula of the 'socialist camp headed by the Soviet Union' persisted for a long time; the formula had already been used in China before the founding of the ·People's Republic, for example in the CC resolution of March 1949,[94] and afterwards became obligatory. To everyone's surprise, in February 1955 it was extended by Molotov as follows: 'The world camp of socialism and democracy headed by the Soviet Union—or, more correctly: by the Soviet Union and the Chinese People's Republic.'[95] Was this how the wily old Stalinist sought to enlist Mao as the future savior and restorer of Stalinism in the Communist bloc? No doubt even then—not long before he expressed severe disapproval of Khrushchev's journey to see Tito—Molotov found a good many objectionable traits in his new boss. But Mao did not catch the ball tossed to him.

Nor did he in the crucial year of 1957; for meanwhile the Chinese Communists—like Stalin in the late twenties—had decided to exert almost superhuman efforts to bring about extraordinary achievements in their own country. The resultant changes envisaged for the social structure—indeed, for the entire mental and spiritual outlook of the people—were so immense that they could only be effected, if at all, under extreme pressure. At such a time Mao was no more inclined for a discussion in his own country of 'different roads to socialism' than Stalin had once been. Under the banner of 'One People, One State, One Leader, One Ideology!' and looking neither right nor left, the Chinese were to be rushed through the narrow channel of blitz-industrialization and super-collectivization. There had to be absolute unity not only in China but in the whole camp while China risked the 'Great Leap'. Anyone who, like Tito, deviated from the straight and narrow path, was bound to be regarded by Peking as an enemy.

So for the time being Peking continued to make its traditional obeisance to the Soviet Union as the 'camp's' leader. In both declarations of 1956 on the dictatorship of the proletariat, the role of the Soviet Union as the center of the international Communist movement was acknowledged. At the Communists' Conference in Moscow of November 1957 the Soviet Union's special position within the camp was confirmed in the document signed by the representatives of the twelve ruling Communist Parties.[96] In Moscow, Mao reduced the reasons for this to a simple formula; in a speech to Chinese students at Moscow University he said:

The socialist camp must have a leader, and this leader is the Soviet Union. In the same way there must be a leader among the Communist and workers' parties of all countries, and this leader is the CPSU.[97]

We may well doubt whether this acknowledgment of Moscow's priority, derived as it was from a purely practical line of reasoning, made very pleasant listening to Kremlin ears: the Kremlin wanted a better justification than that for its claim to leadership. A. A. Andreyev, for example, president of the Soviet-Chinese Friendship Association, wrote in an article commemorating the tenth anniversary of the Chinese People's Republic:

The incredible sufferings, trials, and difficulties borne by the Soviet people for decades in the building and defense of the world's first socialist state, and the vast quantities of blood shed by the Soviet people in the civil war and the war for the Fatherland, have yielded a rich harvest, and continue to do so in the victories achieved by all the brother-nations, and in the march of all socialist countries in the common front toward Communism.[98]

However, Moscow had no desire to bear the consequences of this claim to leadership. At a press conference on October 6, 1959, Christian Herter, then US Secretary of State, stated that, if the Soviet Union called itself leader of the Communist bloc, then it was responsible for whatever happened within the bloc—including the aggressive attitude of Peking. It took two and half weeks for the otherwise quickwitted Khrushchev to think of a reply, and when it came it was not very convincing. The People's Republic of China, he said indignantly, was a world power which did not require a guardian.[99]

*

Khrushchev was not to have to carry this 'Red man's burden' for very much longer. When a year later at the Moscow conference of the eighty-one Communist Parties a declaration was finally arrived at after weeks of effort, it did not contain the formula of the 'socialist camp headed by the Soviet Union'.[100] And just as three years earlier Mao had explained that formula to the Chinese students in Moscow, so twenty-four hours after the declaration was published Liu Shao-ch'i, then heading the Chinese delegation, announced a new formula to twelve thousand Russians in the Lenin Stadium in Moscow. This formula made the shift in power in the Eastern bloc abundantly clear: 'The Chinese Communist Party and the Communist Party of the Soviet Union [in this order!] are the two biggest Parties in the international communist movement. China and the Soviet Union are the two biggest countries in the socialist camp.[101]

What went on behind the scenes before the previously indispensable formula 'headed by the Soviet Union' disappeared from sight, we do not know. We only know Khrushchev's version: some weeks later he announced in a speech that it had been the Soviet delegation which had asked for the elimination of the phrase; first of all, he said, it did not coincide with the facts, since the Soviet Union issued no directives to the other members of the camp, and secondly it led to nothing but difficulties.[102]

The Lord of the Kremlin did not disclose the nature of these difficulties. Perhaps he was thinking of Mr. Herter's uncomfortable thesis, or perhaps the Chinese comrades had objected to the continued use of the formula since it contrasted so blatantly with the violent criticism (of which we shall hear more in the final chapter) which Peking had been directing that year at Moscow's ideological positions?

One is bound to wonder, however, whether in eliminating this formula Moscow really sacrificed anything, whether on the contrary Khrushchev had not shrewdly succeeded on the one hand in discarding ballast (i.e. the responsibility implied in the old formula for the actions of the camp) and on the other in obtaining a confirmation by all Communist Parties of Moscow's dominant position. For in the declaration of 1960 we find the statement that the CPSU is the 'generally acknowledged avant-garde of the international Communist movement'. The word 'avant-garde' as used by Communists has always meant not only marching ahead but also leadership ('the Party as avant-garde of the proletariat').

But does this new formula still have any effective significance? Peking did not make much use of it. True enough, it is still to be found in the resolution on the Moscow declaration drawn up by the Chinese CC a few weeks later,[103] but after that it hardly ever appeared again.

That one must learn from the experience of the great Soviet Union had also always been one of China's set phrases; it was used by Mao,[104] by Liu Shao-ch'i,[105] by Chou En-lai,[106] all the way down to the last Party speaker in the rural areas. Recently, however, these obeisances of pupil to teacher have become very rare indeed.

The solidarity of the camp had thus become endangered. But Peking's anger with Moscow had meanwhile assumed such proportions that, in the fight to assert its own line, it was even prepared to jeopardize the unity of the Communist bloc—and this at a time when the chances of sustaining its rebellious spirit had been diminished by crop failures and serious economic crises.

CHAPTER XIV

SHORT CUT TO COMMUNISM?

The Chinese Sputnik

WHICH SPUTNIK EXERTED MORE INFLUENCE on world politics—the Russian or the Chinese?

How a historian will answer this question twenty or thirty years from now, we cannot tell. Looked at from the vantage point of today, it seems to me that the Chinese 'Sputnik'—as the first people's commune, formed in April 1958, was called—was no less significant than the Russian, the first space rocket of October 1957. One thing is certain: the mass organization of the people's communes was one of the most fateful events affecting the relationship between the two Red powers. How was such a drastic change in Chinese agrarian policy possible?

The causes are to be found on various levels. They extend from deliberate economic, political, and even military calculation to deep-seated psychological motives of which those concerned were probably only dimly aware. But it is here that the most powerful motivations are often to be sought. Hence, bearing in mind the picture derived from the preceding chapter, let us turn first to these.

While in the Soviet Union the heroic past of revolution and civil war had retreated to an almost legendary distance and was barely kept alive in the imagination of the younger generation, the China of Mao Tse-tung had managed to preserve the militant spirit of the fighting days, of guerrilla Communism, the Spartan spirit of that time of ordeal, of share-and-share-alike, the great sense of comradeship in campaigns and battles. Those fighting days played a vital part in forming the outlook of the leading men, and at the same time gave new impetus to the egalitarian Utopian visions existing in the Chinese (as in every other comparable) peasant movement. It was no accident that the first editorial of the Peking *People's Daily* on the

354

communes recalled the teachings 'of many outstanding Utopian [i.e. pre-Marxist] socialists'.[1]

Even the fanatics among the Chinese Communists knew quite well that for the first post-revolutionary phase Marx and Lenin had recommended that wages be paid 'according to work performance' (higher wages for more work) and that the principle of remuneration 'according to need' was reserved for a later, surplus-producing period. They were also aware that a wage scale based on work performance had been in effect in the Soviet Union since 1931 and that it had had favorable effects on production. But they saw that this appeal to the individual's 'material self-interest' (as the Soviets called it) had led to an ever-increasing cleavage between high and low incomes (involving countless additional privileges for the higher incomes, among them even summer residences on the Black Sea), to an outlook which always related work performed to wages paid. If in the course of time it were possible—perhaps—to arrive at a surplus of commodities by following in Soviet footsteps, would one not eventually be faced, the 'veteran fighters' must have wondered, by people who no longer had any desire to live 'under Communism'?

For more than twenty years the men around Mao had fought with their bare hands and an iron will against the well-equipped, well-trained troops of Chiang Kai-shek, and later against the then best soldiers in the Orient, the Japanese—and won. Mao's words from the civil war days had become part of their flesh and blood: 'Gruel [literally: millet, the guerrillas' staple diet] and guns [of the Red Chinese army] are stronger than Chiang Kai-shek's planes and tanks.'[2] Did not this maxim still hold good, now that the new struggle for economic development was beginning? Yes, it was wrong to base everything on technology and the technocrats as the Soviet Union had done. 'Marxist-Leninists have always maintained that in world history it is not technique but man, the masses of people, that determine the fate of mankind', to quote from an article written in Peking on the occasion of the Lenin jubilee of 1960.[3] This view has persisted until now, especially in the sharp controversies with Moscow during the winter of 1962–63.

*

It is certainly open to dispute whether this could be called an accurate interpretation of Marxism-Leninism. In any case, from theses such as this it is but a step to Peking's new doctrine, that of 'subjective dynamism'. This 'subjective dynamism', was to provide the impetus for the development in the desired direction, even when the 'objective possibilities' for such development required by the fathers of Marxism did not yet exist.[4] But in the final analysis 'subjective dynamism' was the will of the leaders imposing this dynamism on the people. This reasoning recalls Stalin's doctrine of 'revolution from above', which in a similar situation reserved the right to the Soviet leader to determine the laws by which this development was to be implemented.[5] In no other matter is Mao's kinship with Stalin more apparent than here, for did not Stalin say as long ago as 1934:

> There can be no justification for references to so-called objective conditions. Now that the correctness of the Party's political line has been confirmed by the experience of a number of years, and that there is no longer any doubt as to the readiness of the workers and peasants to support this line, the part played by so-called objective conditions has been reduced to a minimum; whereas the part played by our organisations and their leaders has become decisive, exceptional. What does this mean? It means that from now on nine-tenths of the responsibility for the failures and defects in our work rest, not on 'objective' conditions, but on ourselves, and on ourselves alone.[6]

When the Chinese fanatics looked at the Soviet Union of the mid-fifties, they saw a country which had developed of late along comparatively calm, orderly, and highly bureaucratic lines; they certainly did not see a people in a process of revolution. That was not what they wanted for their country. They preferred to keep to the old Marxist concept of 'permanent revolution', a concept which they now filled with new meaning. Actually, of course, it referred to the speedy and complete transition of political power from the 'bourgeoisie' to the 'proletariat'; but if, according to Mao (as we saw in the preceding chapter), contradictions persist even after the triumph of the revolution, there also persists the necessity to continue the revolution.[7]

Liu Shao-ch'i stressed this in his important speech of May 1958 on the permanent revolution (*pu tuan ko ming*) in China,[8] and a year later Lu Ting-yi, chief of propaganda, said:

> Revolution is the locomotive of history, the motive force of the progress of human society. This is so in class society and *it will remain so in the future communist society*, only the revolution of that time will be different in nature and method.[9] (Author's italics.)

If the transition from the rule of the bourgeoisie to the dictatorship of the proletariat could be accelerated with the aid of the permanent revolution, then surely the road from that dictatorship to Communism could also be shortened with similar aid. Although as far as I know this was never expressed, the Chinese deliberations amounted to asking whether it was not possible to skip the stage of socialism (with wages based on performance)—just as Lenin had advised the peoples living under feudalism to skip the capitalist stage on the road to socialism—and to find the direct route to Communism by means of the permanent revolution in a gigantic effort of will. For such an underdeveloped country as China, this prospect must have been particularly attractive. What a triumph, if the backward latecomer were to outdistance all others and place itself at the head of human evolution, faithful to its ancient tradition as the leader of mankind!

We know from authoritative sources that by no means all Communists in China thought this way. Liu Shao-ch'i, self-appointed spokesman of this policy, said more than once that 'some people' did not agree on speeding up the pace.[10] It appears that the conflict over the future line to be taken, and above all the future pace, was fought out in the summer and fall of 1957. Perhaps we can reconstruct what happened, although we do not know the details, somewhat as follows: There must have always been two 'wings in the Chinese leadership, we might call them the radicals and the moderates. The Hundred Flowers policy, which began in 1956, followed the line of the moderates. After the fiasco of the weeks of free speech in the early summer of 1957, the radicals got their way—and got it, moreover, all along the line: in the economic policy, in relations with the other bloc countries, and in international affairs.

However, the public did not become aware of this victory of the radicals until May 1958: in his speech at the second session of the Eighth Party Congress, Liu Shao-ch'i informed the Chinese people of the new line, using the catch phrase which has since been repeated so many millions of times: the 'Great Leap Forward'.

This was more than just a vivid, inspiring image for the masses; for every trained Communist there was a familiar ring to it. According to dialectic materialism, historical evolution takes place not at a continuous, steady pace but in such a way that during extended periods of apparent inactivity the tensions continue to mount until they are dramatically released, so that with one 'leap' a new level is reached in the historical process. This new hour in the world's history had now come. Mao and his closest associates had been the first to hear it strike and had proclaimed it to their comrades.

*

During the preliminary years of their rule over China the leaders had been content to imitate the Soviet model. This attitude was expressed in the first Five-Year Plan (1953–57), which in its design corresponded essentially to the first Soviet Five-Year Plans. Gradually, however, Peking seems to have realized that China's conditions for economic development differed considerably from those in the Soviet Union of the thirties.

However much the Soviet people may have achieved under the most rigorous conditions, we must remember that, instead of having to start from scratch, the Soviets were able to carry on a development already begun under the Tsars; and, moreover, that the disruptions of World War I and the civil war were briefer and hence easier to overcome than the standstill at which China had arrived after decades of utter confusion.

Comparison of per Capita Production
On the Eve of the Respective First Five Year Plans[11]

			Russia 1928	China 1952
Gross national product (in 1952 dollars)			240·0	50—60
Cereal crops (incl. rice) (in kilograms)			491·0	270·0
Coal	,,	,,	273·0	110·5
Pig iron	,,	,,	22·0	3·27
Steel	,,	,,	29·0	2·35
Cement	,,	,,	13·0	4·97
Electric power capacity (in kilowatts)			·01	·005
Cotton spindles			·05	·01

This comparison of the principal areas of production just before the Five-Year Plans of each country, taking figures which in some cases are only estimated but which suffice for our purposes, shows that the USSR had a considerable advantage over China. In addition, the inadequate basis for the start of China's Five-Year Plan coincided with an immense population increase.

From the founding of the Chinese People's Republic in 1949 up to the end of 1960, the population is said to have increased from 542 to 682 million, i.e. by some 140 million (nearly 26 per cent).[12] For the same eleven years Moscow reported an increase from 179 to 216 million, i.e. of 21 per cent.[13]

Moreover, while in other developing countries the gaps in supply were at least partially closed by Western economic aid, Peking was disappointed by Moscow's considerably smaller contributions; also, it had to reckon with these dwindling still further. Hence it was not a question of the Chinese merely *wanting* to rely on their own efforts—they had no alternative. They were compelled to utilize the only surplus raw material they had—human beings—to an extent never experienced by the Soviet Union, and to compensate for the lack of 'horsepower' by the ruthless all-out exploitation of manpower, down to the last housewife.[14]

*

With the 'Great Leap' Peking was at last to make up for the bitter experiences of the recent past, during which it had had to be content to play second fiddle in the Communist bloc and to be a grateful pupil of the complacent Russians. For the proud Chinese, with their ambition to be the Middle Kingdom and a model for the world, this had been hard to take; and this wounded pride, together with their disappointment over the—as they felt—meagre and all too commercial aid of the Soviet Union, made them resolve to accomplish something that had never been done before, something that would astonish the whole world and even impress the Soviet Union. They were sick of always being told by Moscow that decades of patient toil still lay ahead; they wanted with one supreme effort to break through the bottleneck in which they found themselves and actually to overtake the Soviet Union on the road to a better future.

It was presumably a coincidence that the day after the resolution of the Chinese CC on the creation of the people's communes the Russian CC (together with the Council of Ministers) issued a proclamation on the expansion of the gas industry;[15] but it was certainly not a coincidence that the Russians announced the liberation of the Soviet housewife from some of her kitchen chores thanks to the forthcoming introduction of gas into millions of homes, while during those same days the Peking press gave the Chinese housewife the prospect of imminent liberation from the same chores through mass feeding in communal kitchens—and appallingly primitive ones at that.

No 'dolce vita', then, for the Chinese, at any rate not for the next few years—this soon became a recurrent theme in their propaganda. Young Chinese frequently asked such questions as: What's the terrible hurry? Who says we have to catch up with Great Britain in production (one of Peking's declared goals)? Would it really be so bad if we went ahead a little more slowly and got more out of life? What's the point of living like this—scarcely is one job finished before the next one starts? In reply to such questions they were informed that speed is inherent in mass revolution, and after all no one would think of killing a pig slowly; and because of their objections they were denounced as sluggards and as 'putrid stagnant water'.[16]

*

Making a virtue of necessity is not a maxim of private life only; nations do it too. The knowledge that they are poor but not for that reason inferior is uppermost among many Chinese, especially when compared to the—in their eyes—prosperous Russians. This feeling of being 'poor but proud' became particularly acute when they saw how the Soviet Union extended gigantic loans to the Nehrus and the Nassers on favorable terms, while to China it sold only in exchange for goods or cash, yet behaved as if it were a benefactor. It must have infuriated them when in an article reprinted by a number of Soviet newspapers Moscow threatened, in a scarcely veiled allusion, to cancel deliveries:

> Could one imagine the successful construction of socialism going on in present day conditions even in so great a country as, let us say, China, if that country were in a state of isolation and could not rely on the collaboration and aid of all other socialist countries?[17]

Chinese pride was to find its most significant expression in a speech by Li Fu-ch'un, head of the State Planning Commission. Imperialists and revisionists, he said (and we know that many Chinese regard Russian Communists as revisionists), had been trying to isolate China since 1958. The date is interesting too, and again points to the Soviet Union, with which the Chinese had been having serious disputes since 1958. And he added:

> For us, their anti-Chinese activity is a good thing, not a bad thing. It ... has not harmed a single hair of China. On the contrary, it has roused the whole Party and the people to unite still more closely, to set bold targets, rely on our own efforts, to press ahead bravely.[18]

It was also an unmistakable dig at Moscow when shortly afterwards

Lin Piao, then Minister of Defense, wrote in a review of the civil war that in 1946 Chiang Kai-shek had 'received immense support . . . and large quantities of arms and equipment and economic aid "from U.S. imperialism",' while 'its [the Chinese Red army's] weapons and equipment were poor, and it had no foreign aid'.[19]

One can almost hear what the Chinese must have been saying to the Russians in their imagination: You boast that in the next few years you intend to reduce the working day to seven, six, even five hours. That doesn't impress us. Our peasants work twelve, fourteen, sixteen, even twenty hours a day in order to reach Communism quickly via the Great Leap. You Russians don't want to supply us with enough blast furnaces—all right then! We will mobilize millions of Chinese peasants who will supply the steel we need from backyard furnaces. We will do it all by ourselves!

In the light of this frame of mind we may assume that the name for the first people's commune revealed a definite trend: Let the Russians be the first to reach the moon with their sputnik, we Chinese will be the first to reach Communism with ours! In other words: the Chinese had waited long enough, especially as practical considerations were making new decisions imperative. Thus the dramatic experiment of the people's communes came about. The immediate reasons behind this decision are not only economic, but also political and even military and sociological. In assembling these reasons we will compare the measures taken by the Soviet and Chinese governments to deal with similar situations.

*

Economic Aims. Only a small part of the capital required for the speedy modernization (and that means industrialization) of their country was available to the Chinese from abroad (i.e. from the 'camp'); hence they had to provide most of it themselves, namely by means of reduced consumption on the part of the population, especially in the rural areas. It would be possible to feed new armies of workers at relatively minor additional cost if they were recruited from the peasant labor potential and remained within their natural areas of food supply. Put to work on a mass basis they could then, by the construction of dams, irrigation systems, and roads, contribute to an increase in national wealth, and by developing rural light industry (such as agricultural tools or clothing) they would be able to free the corresponding work force in urban industry for other tasks. Moreover, the State would also lighten its budget by assigning some of the tasks which would normally devolve upon it, such as rural education and the lower levels of administration, to the people's communes.[20]

So far the Soviet State has been satisfied with the kolkhoz form of exploiting the peasants, and indeed by this method it has not only extracted countless billions of rubles from the peasantry by paying the latter only a fraction of the market value for their products, but has also been able to rely largely on the resultant enormous profits to finance its industrialization. Mao, however, was obviously not content with this; from the people's communes he anticipated a much more effective exploitation. But when we consider the disastrous crop failures of 1959, 1960, and 1961, admitted by Peking,[21] and attributable not only to unfavorable weather conditions but also to the confusion and discontent caused among the peasants by the people's communes, we are bound to wonder whether Mao has not miscalculated.

*

Political Aspects. Evidently the Chinese government regarded the political control over the peasants such as was offered by the comparatively loose association of kolkhozes as inadequate. The year before, at the peak of the Hundred Flowers, it had recognized the extent of peasant opposition to collectivization; it was also aware that at every opportunity the peasants tried to loosen the bonds of collectivization.[22]

Nor had the Russian Communists found it easy to keep the peasants in line by means of the kolkhoz, but they evidently believed that under the circumstances it sufficed as an instrument of control. There is, after all, a difference between dealing with a population of which (as in the Soviet Union of 1958) only 52 per cent live in the rural areas, or a rural population (as in China) of more than half a billion peasants (in 1957 there were only 25 million workers and employees—plus families).[23]

*

Military Aspects. As master of the world's most populous country Mao must have felt that China has the best chance of surviving a nuclear war if it consists of a vast number of more or less autarchic economic units which can continue to exist even if the industrial centers should crumble into atomic dust.

For similar reasons the Soviet Union has for a long time been spreading its industry all across the country; but, except within certain very modest limitations, it has not gone to the extreme of industrializing the village.

*

Socio-political Plans. That the Chinese Communists (like all Communists) should oppose clan solidarity, because they regard the clan as a state within a state, is not surprising. However, as we have seen in Part I, before the arrival of Communism the clan had already lost much of its solidarity and strength, and as modernization progressed it would have automatically lost its former significance. The struggle against what has been called the 'biological family' (parents and children only, perhaps grandparents), such as encouraging the denunciation of the father by the 'progressive' son, had at first been carried on by Peking purely as a temporary measure arising out of the revolution and the ensuing turmoil—i.e. only against those families, or members of families, which were regarded as 'strongholds of reaction', but not against the biological family as such.[24] Now this was to change too, and this change is clearly apparent from the policy of the leading youth journal. During the Hundred Flowers period it had exhorted young people to honor their parents and to regard supporting them as a 'sacred duty'. But under the banner of the Great Leap it wrote:

The framework of the individual family, which has existed for thousands of years, has been shattered for all time . . . We must regard the people's commune as our family and not pay too much attention to the formation of a separate family of our own. . . . For years mother love has been glorified. . . . but it is wrong to degrade a person from a social to a biological creature. . . . The dearest people in the world are our parents, yet they cannot be compared with Chairman Mao and the Communist Party. . . . for it is not the family which has given us everything but the Communist Party and the great revolution. . . . Personal love is not so important; therefore women should not claim too much of their husbands' energy.[25]

Parents' influence on their children declined sharply as a result of living and working conditions in the commune; but grandparents' influence was also to be eliminated by moving them to old people's homes—called 'Homes of Happiness'. Wages and distribution of supplies no longer went to the head of the family but to each separate wage earner. Thus in its effect on the people, the entire rhythm of life in the communes was anti-family; it was as if one were dealing only with sexless work-animals.

I have described elsewhere[26] what happened to the Russian family under Bolshevism; since the mid-thirties the policy of the Soviet State has had a reinforcing rather than a weakening effect on the family. The principle of family solidarity is no longer disputed; the sending of children to boarding school is entirely voluntary, and so far only a very small percentage of the younger generation attend these schools. The millions of new apartments built during the last ten years are definitely family dwellings, designed as units suitable for family living. An elimination of the family by separating parents from their children at an early age is only envisaged for a far-off future 'under Communism'.

*

For the Chinese Communist, however, all these ideas, no matter how important they may be, are merely partial aspects of organizational and technical significance. The heart of the matter is still the over-riding ideological goal, and in this case is expressed in the question: How can China—a country of peasants and likely to remain so for a long time to come—be brought closer to the Communist way of life? In the eyes of the radicals in the CPC, the Russian-style kolkhoz was no longer sufficient. In the close circle of his neighbors the kolkhoz still allowed the individual a certain amount of personal leeway and might actually become an obstacle in the way of his complete integration in the larger community of all toilers; it is not surprising that the Communists regard collective ownership of the means of production, as in the kolkhoz, merely as a preparatory stage toward the ultimately desirable one of people's ownership (for which read: state ownership).

With this ideal in mind, every concentration of small collectives into new, larger ones which could be controlled and manipulated only from the highest level seemed to represent definite progress. Thus the Peitaiho resolution, which in the late summer of 1958 officially gave birth to the people's communes, emphasized the fact that the communes already contained 'elements of people's ownership' (i.e. the 'highest form of ownership').[27] In any case, so the official Party organ declared during those weeks, the transition from former collec-tive ownership to people's ownership would generally speaking take only three or four years, and in some cases would be effected even sooner[28]—while in the USSR this process had always been represented as a lengthy and complicated one.[29]

But quantity alone was not enough. If the new system was to make full use of China's greatest wealth—its labor potential—it had to meet every need and be able to put the same human columns to work today in the fields, tomorrow at the dam, the day after at the blast furnace or the factory bench—or in military exercises: as a working and producing community it had to be universal and total, so that all economic life could exist solely in it and through it.

Added to this was one last, supreme consideration: if the tiresome remnants of the bourgeois mentality, such as had come to light during the Hundred Flowers period, were finally to disappear, and the transition from private individual to collective existence were to become reality, it was essential that the individual depend on the commune for food, clothing, housing, even a minimum of enjoyment. If the communes were successful—and the modest standard of living and moderate requirements of the Chinese people gave the experiment some chance of success—then Mao's China, as far as the Communist nature of its way of life was concerned, would have reached the head of the 'camp' in one fell swoop.

Requirements, considerations, and—dreams of this nature led to the great decision, and also determined the manner of carrying it out. There is no need to go into the process in detail; besides, within a few months its early history became—no doubt deliberately—shrouded in a well-nigh impenetrable veil of confused and contradictory reports.[30] The public speeches and resolutions made at the Party Congress held in May 1958 proclaiming the Great Leap had given no hint of any imminent drastic change in the agricultural structure. And yet according to the later version, the people's commune 'Sputnik' had already been formed on April 20, 1958, from twenty-seven kolkhozes consisting of 9,300 farms and 43,000 people.[31] But once the decision was made to lift the veil, the people's communes were immediately given the utmost publicity.

This became apparent when on September 10, 1958, the resolution of the Chinese CC, which shortly before had been in session at the seaside resort of Peitaiho, was published in Peking[32] and cabled all over the world; it was unmistakable when the Chinese press dramatized the events in the rural areas far beyond the comparatively matter-of-fact text of the resolution and stamped it as being of world-wide significance. Much of what happened during the ensuing weeks is known to us from numerous Chinese publications[33] and even some reports by Western eye-witnesses,[34] allowing us to draw certain conclusions.[35]

*

The period up to the end of November 1958 seems to me to contain seven features of special significance. In the case of each one I shall indicate the corresponding situation in the USSR.

1. New order of magnitude

In China, according to official information, only a few weeks after the Peitaiho resolution about 120 million peasant families were combined in some 26,000 people's communes; accordingly an average of 4,600 families was assigned to each people's commune, while there had previously been 740,000 kolkhozes with about 160 families each.[36] In the Soviet Union at the corresponding time there were some 76,500 kolkhozes containing an average of 245 peasant families each.[37] These figures show that, in the period before the establishment of the people's communes, the Chinese kolkhozes were comparable in membership—although not in area—to the Russian, while later we find completely divergent trends.

2. Integration with public administration

Efforts were made[38] to combine the duties of local administration with the control of the people's communes and thus to demonstrate that the communes represent a step on the road toward the 'withering away' of the state as proclaimed by Engels. In the Soviet Union, kolkhoz administration and state administration were separate at that time.

3. Regimentation

It is apparent from the very first reports that the people's communes were militarized in more senses than one: first, by establishing militias within them ('Every Chinese a soldier!'), and second, by requiring the peasants (both men and women) to march to work every day in companies and regiments, and by 'throwing' them—as if they were military units—often for weeks at a time into other areas where labor forces happened to be needed in large numbers, for irrigation projects, for example, or for road construction. In the Soviet Union there was no such thing as military units in the kolkhoz; the training of young people in semi-military organizations (originally Osoavia-khim, later DOSAAF) was quite separate from the work of the kolkhoz. Pictures of peasants working in the fields beside pyramids of rifles, such as were published in China in the autumn of 1958, never existed in the Soviet Union. Also, as far as I know, people in the USSR have never set off for work (except in penal colonies) in military formations.

4. Industrialization of the village

Typical of the people's communes was the creation of large numbers of non-agricultural production sites. They were not so much 'factories', however—as they were called in the enthusiasm of those months—as workshops, and usually very primitive ones. This is obvious, unless we want to believe in fairy stories, from the report that, for example in a district in Honan 'within ten days 4,530 factories for the production of steel, iron, machines, chemical fertilizer, cement, etc', were established.[39] The best known are the backyard furnaces, many of them barely eight or ten feet high, of which two million were constructed during 1958 and into which everything made of iron was thrown, as well as ore from available local deposits. In the Soviet Union there was never anything like this. Of course, many Soviet kolkhozes have their own repair work-shops as well as equipment for the further processing of their products, and also building enterprises; but the Russian Communists have always left industrialization to large-scale undertakings consisting of huge plants.

5. Remuneration 'according to need'

Until the summer of 1958 wages were paid in the Chinese kolkhoz according to performance, and in the Russian kolkhoz this is still the case. Wages were calculated on more or less accurate records of the work performed by each individual. (Sometimes it was the perform-ance of a work group, which in turn distributed the group wages among its members according to work performed.) However, in the people's commune the members received part of their wages in kind, the free distribution on a per capita basis of the barest essentials of life (a bowl of soup in the communal kitchen; a pair of cloth shoes when the old ones were in rags), independent of the amount of work performed. The rest of their wages were still paid them according to work performance (the piecework system being retained), and partly according to wage categories based on each individual's qualifications.[40]

The Peitaiho resolution contained a warning against premature experimentation with new wage systems, but distribution in kind caught on very quickly, perhaps mainly because in the general confusion it was no longer possible to keep records of the performance of every individual. Many communes introduced the so-called 'seven guarantees', or 'ten guarantees', according to which every commune member was entitled to certain goods or services free of charge: food, clothing—often a haircut too—and housing; assistance in birth, marriage, and burial; medical treatment; schooling for children; visits to the cinema or other entertainment.[41] (Whether these 'guaranteed' claims could be met was another matter!) Cash was often only paid out in the form of a small amount of pocket money, and even part of this was kept back for government bonds.[42] During the fall of 1958, there was every indication that the cash portion which depended on performance would soon disappear entirely and wages would be paid exclusively by distribution in kind. The Party acclaimed the new form of wage payment as being the germ cell of Communism,[43] and voices were already to be heard calling for the transition to a system whereby all wages should be paid in kind.[44]

The basic difference between payment in cash and in kind is obvious: when the individual receives his wages in kind he can no longer exercise any personal choice, while when he is paid in cash based on performance, be this amount ever so small, he still retains this choice. When someone is dependent on rations he must accept whatever 'they' hand out—'they' being the bosses, on whom he now depends almost to the point of slavery. In the Soviet Union payment according to performance has been strictly and without exception the rule, in both town and country, ever since the early thirties, even if it was sometimes at an inconceivably low level. Within his wage category each person was, and still is, paid according to work performed. As late as April 1962 the Soviet Union minister responsible for matters pertaining to wages strongly opposed any attempt to alter this procedure.[45]

6. Drastic curtailment of private ownership

In order to render absorption in the collective still more effective, the members of the commune were continually urged to transfer their modest private possessions, which they had retained in the kolkhoz, to the commune: vegetable plots, fruit trees, livestock, and household belongings. In cases where this sacrifice was not yet demanded, it was announced as a prospect for the future. In the Soviet Union—except during the twenties—a sharp distinction has always been made between private ownership, permitted to every Soviet citizen, of *consumer goods* (including even house and car) and ownership of *means of production*, to which he was not entitled and which may belong only to the state (or a collective such as the kolkhoz). Since the early thirties the principle of private ownership of consumer goods has remained in theory (if not always in practice) inviolate. In Article 10 of the Soviet constitution of 1936 it is specifically guaranteed.

7. Collectivization of private life

But even with these restrictions the limit had still not been reached: in the people's communes during those months, the Communists launched an attack on all fronts of private life. Meals were eaten in communal dining halls (there were people's communes in which pressure was brought to bear on the peasants until they handed over their kitchen utensils and crockery to the commune) and punishment was meted out when smoke rising from a cottage betrayed the cooking of a private meal;[46] children too young to work in the fields were rounded up in hastily constructed crèches and kindergartens; the elderly who until then had lived with their children's families had to move to old people's homes and take over light duties in kindergartens or repair workshops; married couples were assigned to different work units and did not see each other for weeks at a time; in many places the tearing down of farmhouses was begun and the material obtained was used to build dormitory barracks[47] in which married couples were housed in separate quarters;[48] in new buildings there was no provision for private kitchens, and individual privies were replaced by large latrines;[49] and finally, a particularly harsh measure for Chinese: the removal of the ancestors' graves from the fields and the gathering of them into mass graves was not only planned[50] but in many cases actually put into effect. In the Soviet Union, apart from the few communes existing in the twenties, nothing of this kind was ever undertaken. It is true that some Bolsheviks, including Khrushchev, were in favor of building so-called 'agro-cities' with large apartment houses into which the peasants were to be moved; but, knowing what the peasants' reaction to such plans would be, they have not carried them out so far.

We may ask whether it was possible for the Chinese Communists to believe that they could really accomplish a program of such Utopian extent. In the summer and fall of 1958 functionaries and leaders apparently egged each other on in a steadily mounting ecstasy of victory. Some of the local Party propaganda functionaries believed in the imminent arrival of Communism and the willingness of the masses to work day and night without pay; others probably sensed a new general line and were hoping for increased prestige and personal advantages if they adjusted to it quickly enough. They began to persuade themselves that there were signs of the new line in their own field of operation and did what they could to promote it. As a result, reports piled up on the leaders' desks of new mass enthusiasm, of voluntary waiving of wages, of expressions of delight from the peasants whose ancestors' graves were being filled in and whose pigs were taken away. Consequently the leaders saw their propaganda confirmed and themselves began to believe that one could do without material prerequisites and by a mere act of will on the part of millions of people bring about the 'Great Leap Forward', straight into Communism.[51]

The First Serious Dispute

WHAT HAD BEEN HAPPENING in the villages of China during the latter part of 1958 was not the taking of emergency measures to overcome a temporary impasse, but something entirely new. For the first time a way of life was forced upon a whole nation as an example and model for all, a way of life which had formerly existed only in limited communities dedicated to a strict purpose, such as monastic orders: the total collectivization and absolute subjection of the human being. Peking itself announced this to the world in loud triumph, and the world buzzed with horrified excitement.

In the capital of the Soviet bloc, however, there was no sign of emotion. Moscow was silent—for weeks and months on end. *Pravda*, as was customary in the case of important events in the Communist world, reprinted the Peitaiho resolution the day after it was published, but without comment.[52] Nor in the days that followed was there a word of either praise or criticism for the new venture, although China occupied a good deal of space in the Soviet press due to the tension over Taiwan. Even in the special articles commemorating the Chinese state anniversary there was not a single word about the new development—with one exception: the Moscow literary journal published a somewhat rapturous story describing the people's communes.[53] Who can tell whether this article had been inspired at a higher level, or whether it merely 'slipped through'?

With this single exception—utter silence, month after month. While the Chinese press was outdoing itself in enthusiasm over the communes, while every Western newspaper and journal was registering the creation of the people's communes as one of the most significant events of postwar history, Moscow said not a word. It is impossible to imagine a stronger token of disapproval than this stony silence.

*

For the Soviet Union, the people's commune was the most serious political challenge since Tito had dared to defy Stalin and claim for Yugoslavia its own separate road ten years earlier. And the challenge of 1958 was far more serious than that of 1948, if only because China was infinitely more important than Yugoslavia.

What must have angered the Russians most was the Chinese insistence that the people's commune was far more progressive than the kolkhoz. As compared to the kolkhoz, it had, according to Peking, 'considerable advantages in the deployment of productive mass activity'; 'the relatively narrow organizational form' of the kolkhoz, which was concerned 'with a relatively simple economy', no longer corresponded to the demands of the times.[54] Compared to the people's commune, the kolkhoz was 'backward' and 'obsolete'.[55] Hence the people's commune was far superior to the kolkhoz, so it was claimed, and surpassed it in productivity by twenty per cent.[56]

This was bad enough, but worse was to come. Peking publicly proclaimed the people's commune to be the decisive step on the road to Communism. The relatively cautiously formulated Peitaiho resolution had already stated: 'The people's commune represents the best organizational form for the gradual transition from socialism to Communism; it will become the basic unit of future Communist society.'

In a bloc of states given over to a certain ideological goal, the country which can convince the member states that it knows the road to this goal better, and will reach this goal faster, than any other country, will be the most successful in its claim to leadership. Up until the summer of 1958 the Russian Communists were justified in believing that they were the undisputed leaders in the 'socialist camp'. Now their Red brothers in Peking appeared with a claim which was tantamount to saying: We Chinese, in spite of bad initial conditions, have come closer to Communism in the eighth year of our state than you Russians have in more than forty years since the founding of yours.

Since then Peking has tried indefatigably to fan the flames in its own country and in the Soviet bloc; its chief political utterances, especially the statements made on the Lenin anniversary (April 1960), are full of a revolutionary fervor nowadays rare in the 'socialist camp'.

We do not know whether Peking gave the Kremlin advance information on the people's communes. If during his visit to Peking in July and August 1958 Khrushchev was told by Mao what was going on, certainly nothing was said publicly about it. If Mao concealed from his guest the mass movement which was then already under way, or even its scope (and there are many indications that this is what happened),[57] this must have been an additional reason for Moscow's anger.

Moreover, the Kremlin leaders must have recognized that the hymns of praise to the people's communes contained an exhortation to the other countries in the Red camp, as well as to the developing countries, to follow not the Russian but the Chinese example. And finally it must have seriously alarmed Khrushchev that the Chinese with much fanfare had turned off onto a road which the Soviet leaders had also once explored but long since abandoned as being impassable. I have reported elsewhere my own observations on how the Soviet Union experimented with communes, in which everything belonged to everybody, and how these communes then vanished from sight.[58] At the Party Congress of 1930, the type of kolkhoz known as the 'agricultural artel' was designated (together with the state farms) the sole agricultural organizational form.[59] In Stalin's Russia, which reckoned, not with the population's selfless devotion to duty but, to use the catch phrase, with the individual's 'material self-interest' and striving for promotion, there was no room for the Utopian-egalitarian communes; nor have they ever existed since then. And now, almost thirty years after the Soviet Union had called off the experiment as unsuccessful, the Chinese were suddenly insisting that in the communes they had hit on the perfect solution.

The Russians discussed their later disputes with Peking openly, but in the autumn of 1958 they remained silent. Why? First of all, they did not want to offer the West the spectacle of a quarrel with their biggest ally (the lessons they had learned from the open conflict with Tito ten years before had left a sore spot), and secondly they probably wanted to avoid alarming their own peasant population. Nothing could upset the Russian peasants more and thus endanger their steady productivity than a description of the people's communes and the implication that this 'higher form' of rural life was also in store for them. Although in the Soviet kolkhoz, land, labor, machinery, and all other equipment have been collectivized for the past thirty years, the Russian kolkhoznik lives in his own house, has his own garden, even though it is small, with his own fruit trees and berry bushes, has his own chickens or goats, usually his own cow and a few pigs; and when he comes home from the kolkhoz fields in the evening, he stretches his legs under his own table, on which his wife sets their own meal in front of him and his children. He can work in his own garden until it gets dark. He earns his own money; and whether it is a lot or a little, it is his, and he can do what he likes with it.

*

So Moscow said nothing. If they expressed any criticism at all, they did so very indirectly, as, for example, when they stated through Stepanyan, one of their leading ideologists, that the Soviet Union and the Eastern European people's democracies would reach Communism before China and the Asian people's democracies. This disposed of the Chinese claim to have discovered a short cut to Communism.[60] A delightful variation of this theme appeared in *Izvestiya*: one well-to-do, efficient, and economically advanced kolkhoz is addressed by others who are greatly inferior to it: 'We will all reach Communism at the same time!'[61]

Or here is an example of a more subtle criticism: the Soviet government organ published an article by Po I-po on the occasion of the Chinese state anniversary. In quoting the Peitaiho resolution the author had spoken of the 'realization *of Communism*' in China; the Russian version spoke only of a 'realization *of the communes*'.[62]

(Author's italics.) (In the translation of the Peitaiho resolution in *Pravda* a few weeks earlier the phrase 'realization of Communism' had been accepted verbatim.[63] Evidently the editor had not yet grasped how dangerous it was.)

Similar concealment and obliqueness marked the speech of the Soviet ambassador Yudin at the Soviet Union's anniversary celebrations in November 1958. On that occasion whenever Yudin mentioned China he referred only to that country's achievements in building socialism (i.e. not Communism) and emphasized that China was utilizing the Soviet Union's experience.[64] The term 'people's communes', used so many millions of times in China during those weeks, never once occurred in his speech.

When mention was made of the people's communes in Soviet technical journals, in order to provide information to the specialists, they were referred to in a deliberately aloof manner: mention was made, for instance, of the people's communes 'which *the Chinese comrades* regard as the best method of building *socialism*. . . .'[65] (Author's italics.)

*

Although the Russians at that time avoided any public expression of opinion, or restricted themselves to veiled allusions, their actual views on the matter are now known to us. In a long discussion with US Senator Hubert Humphrey on December 1, 1958, Khrushchev expressed strong disapproval of the people's communes, which he termed old-fashioned and reactionary; the Soviet Union was aware, he said, that for the time being there would be no high productivity without material inducements. I was told by someone who was at that time attached to the US Embassy in Moscow that this part of the conversation was to remain confidential; but Marguerite Higgins quoted Khrushchev's words in the *New York Herald Tribune*,[66] and not long afterwards Humphrey himself made them public.[67]

For Khrushchev this indiscretion was embarrassing. In his speech at the Twenty-first Party Congress he compared Humphrey—without mentioning the people's communes!—to that arch-liar Baron Münchhausen; in his picturesque way he likened the senator to a newsboy who in order to get rid of his wares shouts: 'Read all about it! Woman gives birth to girl with moustache!' although the newspaper contains nothing of the sort.[68]

The Russians did not speak more openly until, as we shall soon

see, the Chinese began to dissociate themselves from their enthusiastic utterances concerning the people's communes. At the Twenty-
first Party Congress early in 1959 Khrushchev spoke as follows,
unmistakably addressing himself to Peking, since there was no one
in the Soviet Union at that time who might be considered the target
of his remarks:

> The socialist principle of distribution [of goods] according to work
> performed is based on the recognition of the impossibility of equalizing
> distribution during the socialist era. . . . For existing circumstances it is the
> only sensible and fair principle of distribution. . . . Equalization would not
> mean the transition to Communism but the discrediting of Communism. . . .
> The kolkhoz system corresponds completely to the level and needs of the
> development of present productive forces in the rural areas.[69]

That was the same speech in which Khrushchev said it was impossible
to *leap* into Communism without first going through the stage of
socialism. Nor had Moscow ever conceded to the Chinese that they
had already achieved socialism, the formula being always that they
were engaged in 'building' it. Furthermore when a few weeks earlier
the boss of the Kremlin had used the expression 'Great Leap', it was
clear that he was referring not to the trend in China but to the
progress made in cattle-breeding in the USSR![70] There were to be
plenty more of these verbal thrusts, as, for instance, in the article by
a Moscow ideologist who wrote in *Pravda*:

> The attempt to skip whole historical stages merely plays into the hands
> of the enemies of the working class. . . . Friedrich Engels long ago criticized
> the Blanquists of his day, who wanted to leap over all intermediate stages
> right into Communism, without taking into account the process of
> historical development . . . It is like wanting to teach a four-year-old child
> higher mathematics.[71]

Khrushchev was still more explicit during his visit to Poland in July
1959. There had been people in the Soviet Union during the twenties,
he said in a speech, who thought that, in order to have Communism,
it was necessary to create communes. But 'obviously there were
many people at that time who did not properly understand what
Communism is and how it is built'. The communes, he went on, had
not corresponded to either material or political conditions and had
been replaced by kolkhozes.[72] In this he agreed with Stalin, who in
1934 had listed the objections to the communes.[73]

  The strongest argument against the people's communes has never
yet been officially used by the Russians (it was not, of course,

available to them in all its acuteness till later): the argument that the commune must inevitably disrupt work in the rural areas and jeopardize the food situation, indeed the whole economy, of China.

*

Peking backed down. To what extent the Soviet Union's admonitions (and perhaps also its powerful economic pressure) contributed to this, and how far Peking's own disappointment because of the chaotic conditions caused by this most drastic of all experiments in modern times was responsible, we cannot tell. All we know is the CC conference held from November until December 10, 1958, in Wuhan (more correctly: in Wuchang, part of the city of Wuhan), which on its final day drew up the 'Resolution on Some Questions Concerning the People's Communes'.[74] This resolution, which was almost five times as long as the Peitaiho resolution, started off with a resounding chord ('In 1958 a new social organization appeared, fresh as the morning sun, above the broad horizon of east Asia. This was the large-scale people's commune'), but in the rest of the text there was little of this lyrical rapture to be seen. (This time Moscow published only a short summary[75]—again without comment. In other words, the Russians were handling Peitaiho and Wuhan at arm's length and with averted eyes.)

A comparison of the Wuhan resolution with what was said and published during the preceding months about the people's communes shows that it is a document of retreat. Needless to say it did not abandon the communes; indeed, it praised them assiduously. But it was governed by a word which contrasted with the hectic atmosphere of the fall, the word 'gradually'. Not at one blow, therefore, not in one all-conquering revolutionary sweep, was the transition to Communism to be brought about, but—gradually. The difficult nature of this transition was emphasized constantly—it would be accomplished 'not very soon', on the contrary a 'fairly long time' would be required; the whole process would take 'fifteen, twenty or more years'. Phrases indicating its long-drawn-out nature appeared in the Wuhan resolution altogether twenty-nine times

The resolution had hard things to say about the—apparently quite numerous—comrades who had grievously overestimated the speed of the process; they had been 'over-eager' and had mistakenly believed the transition to Communism to be 'a very easy thing'. Twice they are called 'Utopians' (now, in contrast to Peitaiho, a term of disfavor), and people who follow 'an incorrect line of thought' concerning wages, prices, and money. They were told 'not to be in a hurry'.

Both Moscow's central countertheses were accepted in Wuhan. The building of a powerful heavy industry was an essential requirement for the transition to Communism; in other words, China's low level of productivity must first be raised. The text ran:

We should not groundlessly make declarations that the people's communes . . . 'enter communism immediately', and so on. To do such things is not only an expression of rashness, it will greatly lower the standards of communism in the minds of the people, distort the great ideal of communism and vulgarize it, strengthen the petty-bourgeois trend towards equalitarianism and adversely affect the development of socialist construction.

In the second place, the resolution stated that wages must be paid predominantly according to work performed. This principle was to be retained until a state of surplus had been reached, and that was a long way off. To want to give up this principle prematurely was a 'Utopian concept', and to believe one could skip the socialist stage (with its piecework wage system) and arrive directly at Communism, was nothing but pure fantasy.

The biggest retreat took place in the realm of communal life: house, clothing, furniture, fruit trees, tools, livestock, poultry, and savings, were for the time being to remain private property; new buildings were to provide for each family to live together in one apartment; the sending of children to crèches and kindergartens was to be voluntary. Numerous study commissions, to which as many as ten thousand functionaries from each province were to be delegated, would eliminate all abuses in the people's communes by April 1959 and create order. Although the peasant militia was to remain, in saying that the peasants were to be organized 'along military lines' for their work all that was meant was a general, closely knit organization 'on the pattern of the factories'.

We must not overlook the fact, however, that the retreat in Wuhan, although a long-range one, was nevertheless meant to be only temporary. Even the Wuhan resolution clung to some of Peitaiho's principal positions, for it stated that the people's communes represented the best method for the transition of the village from collective to people's ownership and for the transition of the country from the socialist to the Communist society, and that the 'introduction of a distribution system which combines the wage system and the free supply system . . . includes the first shoots of Communism'. Thus the claim remained that the people's commune is closer to Communism than the kolkhoz.

That opinions in the Party differed considerably on this point and that it was not easy to reduce them all to one common denominator, is shown by the very fact that the conference in Wuhan had been preceded by two others—under the chairmanship of Mao—which had occupied a good deal of November.[76]

However, I would prefer to remain within the scope of known facts rather than embark on speculation as to who in Wuhan might have belonged to the moderates (who engineered the retreat), and who to the radicals (who during the preceding months had held the reins). Mao himself had in the autumn been called the founder of the people's communes, but his name was never associated with the abuses that ensued. Consequently the question remains unanswered as to how we are to interpret his refusal, announced in Wuhan at the same time, to be nominated again for the post of president. It was at first taken by many to indicate an admission of errors, yet there was no sign of any lessening of his personal reputation.

*

At the Twenty-first Party Congress in Moscow a truce was concluded with Moscow. Chou En-lai listened quietly to Khrushchev's lectures on the correct road to Communism, and then in his own speech stated: 'Under China's present conditions the people's commune is the best way of developing socialism.'[77] It was understood in the compromise proclaimed between Moscow and Peking in the Wuhan formula that: in the first place, the people's commune is a *specialty of China* (hence not automatically applicable to other countries); secondly, it is for the time being only an intermediate station on the road to *socialism*. Although Chou En-lai could not refrain from adding that the commune was also essential to the subsequent transition from socialism to Communism, he clarified the Wuhan resolution in one important point by making it clear that the period mentioned in it of 'fifteen or twenty years or more' was necessary to make China a *socialist* country. Since the Russians for their part claim to have been living in a socialist country for a long time, China is not a competitor if it admits that it will not become socialist until 1974–79 or even later.

A few days after this Chou and Khrushchev signed an agreement whereby the USSR would supply the Chinese between 1959 and 1967 with machinery and equipment to the value of about five billion rubles.[78] Whether this satisfied the insatiable desires of the Chinese is open to question; presumably they were disappointed that the deliveries were not to be made on a credit basis but against prompt payment. But anyway it was—after a long interval—at least something.

Furthermore, Khrushchev did make one ideological concession. If, as we have seen, Peking's high hopes of an imminent transition to Communism had been brushed aside in the autumn with the observation that China and the other Asian people's democracies would reach Communism later than the Soviet Union and the Eastern European states — to which the Chinese doubtless objected indignantly—now Khrushchev stated at the Twenty-first Party Congress that the economically backward states of the 'socialist camp' would develop so fast with the aid of the more advanced countries that one day all countries in the camp would be able to reach Communism 'more or less simultaneously'.[79]

For the Chinese this was a concession of the highest significance; for if they were to reach the goal at this speed they could, with the backward condition of their productivity, demand economic aid from Moscow far in excess of anything they had hitherto received. However, it cannot possibly be maintained that the Soviet Union granted them this, as we saw when we looked at Soviet-Chinese economic relations. Chinese hopes had already received one damper in a (second) article by Stepanyan. In this the author, following Khrushchev's example, reviewed his thesis, already familiar to us, of the non-simultaneous transition to Communism; he stated in a cool and matter-of-fact manner that the Soviet Union needed another 'ten to twelve years' to reach the desired economic level and would only then (i.e. in the seventies) provide the remaining member states of the camp with the assistance which would enable them to reach Communism 'more or less simultaneously' with the Soviet Union.[80]

That the Russians in their continued disputes with the Chinese found even this watered-down 'more or less simultaneously' concession distinctly embarrassing, is to be seen from the fact that Khrushchev felt obliged at the Twenty-second Party Congress to review once again the formula reached at the Twenty-first: the states of the Soviet bloc are admittedly to reach Communism 'more or less simultaneously', but this formula is understood to mean 'within the framework of a [i.e. the same] historical era'.[81] The Middle Ages also represent a historical era; they lasted about a thousand years.

*

Even after the truce of the Twenty-first Party Congress, Moscow remained cool toward the people's communes. In books reaching the expert but not the general reading public, the people's communes were briefly mentioned here and there, although not very often, but they were never emphasized, much less acclaimed; and the very thing that had given them their particular dramatic quality—the complete transformation of daily life—was never made clear to the Soviet reader.[82] The only exception was *New Times*, the multilingual journal designed for foreign propaganda. In the spring of 1959, no doubt out of consideration for readers in foreign countries who were closely following Moscow's reaction, it finally published an article on the people's communes.[83] However, this was not so much an evaluation of the communes as an attack on their Western critics.

In late August of 1959, the Chinese press devoted columns and often pages to the first anniversary of the Peitaiho resolution; the Soviet press remained silent. A few weeks later the Chinese People's Republic celebrated its tenth anniversary; the Soviet press published numerous congratulatory articles but not a single word about the communes. In the commemorative issue of the official Party journal *Kommunist*, A. A. Andreyev refrained from mentioning the people's communes in his article on the first ten years of the Chinese People's Republic by the simple device of describing China's agricultural progress during the first eight years only! The anniversary article in *Kommunist* merely referred to 'the co-operativized peasantry' of China.[84] In its own special article *Pravda* made no mention whatever of the people's communes.[85] The only place where the Soviet reader could find the Chinese version—and pretty scantily at that—was in an article by the First Secretary of the CPC published in *Pravda*.[86]

Suslov, who made the anniversary speech in Peking as Khrushchev arrived too late from Camp David, took pains to avoid mentioning the words 'people's commune', the formation of which had, after all, been by far the most striking event during Red China's first decade. He contented himself with the dry observation that the Chinese peasants had 'entered' upon the 'socialist path of development'.[87]

And when Khrushchev reached Peking on September 30 his address did not contain a single reference to the communes.[88]

Not even in their Chinese-language journal designed specifically for China could the Russians bring themselves to utter a word of praise for the people's communes. In a report of a visit of some Soviet representatives to two Chinese communes, the most they managed to do was acknowledge the 'industriousness of the Chinese in the building of socialism';[89] and when the new Soviet ambassador Chervonenko, at the celebrations marking the tenth anniversary of the first treaty between Moscow and Peking, made a half-way friendly remark about the people's communes (all he did was quote from Chinese statements, without expressing any opinion of his own),[90] even that was ignored by the Soviet press.[91] Two and a half years after the formation of the people's communes, Moscow's official Party journal, in a review of the 'international socialist system', observed that at the beginning of 1961 the 'co-operativization of agricultural production in China, Bulgaria, Korea, the German Democratic Republic [Soviet Zone of Germany], Mongolia, Albania, Rumania, and Czechoslovakia' had been completed or almost completed.[92] China was thus mentioned in the same breath with Bulgaria and Mongolia; no special place was reserved for it in the sphere of agricultural organization.

*

The Chinese defended themselves against Moscow's attitude without mentioning Moscow. The *People's Daily* wrote on the occasion of the first anniversary of Peitaiho: 'Why don't those who have doubts about the people's commune movement make a serious study of the facts of history and this fundamental Marxist view of historical development?'[93] In a long article marking the tenth anniversary, Liu Shao-ch'i attacked all opponents of the communes, and many of his remarks applied more to critics in the USSR than to those in China. He reproached them bitterly for their 'capitalistic lordly airs', for their claim that the people's communes had been created 'much too early' and were in advance of social developments as well as of the level of the people's political awareness. He said menacingly that a mass movement of this kind would not collapse merely 'because someone opposes it'.[94]

This acrimonious although oblique mutual needling continued, although the importance of the people's communes has declined considerably since 1959. (In spite of its penchant for celebrating anniversaries, China ignored the second anniversary of the Peitaiho resolution.) In order not to lose face, and also no doubt so as to be able at a later date to resume the campaign for the wholesale institution of the people's communes, they were allowed to remain, but the kolkhozes, from which the communes had been created, became once more the mainstay of agricultural production. This was explicitly set out in the resolution of the CC meeting which took place in August 1959 in Lushan.[95] Accordingly since 1959 Chinese agriculture has consisted of people's communes composed of kolkhozes, which again represented the center of gravity of production; the kolkhozes were in turn divided into brigades, as had been the case before 1958 and still is in the Soviet Union. Since 1961 emphasis has even shifted from the kolkhoz down to the brigade.[96] (English-language reports from China often refer to the kolkhoz as a production brigade, and to the brigade as a production team; for purposes of easier comparison with the USSR we shall keep to the terms people's commune, kolkhoz, and brigade to signify the three levels).

Of the two guiding principles of the commune venture—the transformation of private individuals into a Communist collective mass, and the mobilization of every possible ounce of the labor potential, especially of women—the first was temporarily postponed following upon Wuhan. It had become obvious that it is not so easy to turn the population into mere members of a collective with no private life, and that furthermore the attempt to bring about such a transformation by force endangered production. Consequently, measures which the people resented and which at the same time did not increase their productivity, such as the tearing down of private dwellings, were dropped; those which promoted the total mobilization of the population, such as crèches and kindergartens, were preserved. Now it was possible to tell the women: Your children are being looked after, you don't need to worry about them any more; instead you can go out into the fields while your husbands build dams.

The enforced 'industrialization' of the village by backyard furnaces, etc., had already been slowed down considerably in 1959, because it deprived agriculture of inordinate quantities of the labor potential and also produced results which, as far as quality was concerned, left a great deal to be desired.[97] In the first half of 1960 the development of people's communes in the towns was again pursued with some vigor; after that there was less heard about them too.[98] In any case it continued to be part of the ritual of public speeches to praise the 'successes of the Great Leap and of the people's communes', and this was still the case in the communiqué of the CC plenary session of September 28, 1962,[99] although by that time there was not much left of either of them.

*

Nevertheless the people's communes have also exerted a continuing influence on the Soviet Union. Relations between Moscow and Peking are no longer a one-way street between master and pupil; instead, they are now in a 'dialectic' stage in which it is possible to discern reciprocal effects. After the summer of 1958 Moscow was no longer able to avoid the discussion of the 'transition to Communism'. As long as Stalin was alive, this expression was not much more than a stereotyped formula, which, although it was constantly used, remained vague and without concrete meaning. In the main section of his last work, *Economic Problems of Socialism in the USSR*,[100] Stalin did not touch on this subject at all, and in the second of his three letters referring to this book he dealt with it summarily and with the implication: that is all a long way off yet. Hence no actual discussion on this point ever took place in his time, while as a rule every trivial remark of the dictator was publicly quoted and interpreted over and over again in the Soviet Union. Six months later Stalin was dead.

For five years nothing was said in Moscow about the 'transition to Communism'; only in commemorative speeches was it sometimes referred to, as, for instance, in those marking the fortieth anniversary of the revolution.[101] Any discussions known to have taken place on this subject had been carried on in a matter-of-fact, academic atmosphere. For example at the session of the social science departments of the Academy of Sciences of the USSR (which dealt with the theme 'On Economic Problems in the Building of Communism'),[102] neither the organizers nor the participants in this session (which was not much publicized) seemed to have any inkling of the storm brewing in China. The dry deliberations in the Moscow Academy, and the clarion calls issuing from Peking when the Peitaiho resolution was made known were pitched on utterly different levels.

The first important statement on the subject of the 'transition to Communism' to come from Soviet lips since the Stalin work of 1952 was to be found in the already quoted speech of Khrushchev at the Twenty-first Party Congress. This marked the start of busy activity on the part of the Soviet ideologists. The number of relevant articles rose by leaps and bounds.[103] Up to the fall of 1958 there had been hardly any monographs at all on this subject and by the summer of 1959 only a few: starting with the autumn of 1959 the country was swept by a flood of pamphlets and books—more than a hundred in twelve months[104]—describing life under fully developed Communism, for example life in housing communes.[105] At some time during the winter of 1958–59, then, the directive must have gone out to the Moscow ideologists to start thinking about the transition to Communism as quickly as possible and to write about it.

Presumably the Western analyses of Soviet society also prompted Moscow to deal with the subject. In any case, reference is constantly made in the relevant Soviet works to Western publications, including my own book *Soviet Man*,[106] which appeared in Moscow in 1960 in a limited Russian edition for a restricted circle of readers, i.e. not for general sale. The ideological authorities of the Soviet Union saw themselves attacked on two fronts—from the East by the claim: China is on the threshold of Communism; and from the West under the slogan: Communism and Communist man are Utopian ideas.

Other Soviet measures which could be regarded as answers to the people's communes are the creation of comrades' courts, neighborhood courts, and workers' militias. The purpose of these is to take over a portion of the functions hitherto carried out by the law courts and the police and thus to prove that the State is beginning to 'wither away' on the road to Communism.[107] Khrushchev had already hinted at this in April 1958,[108] and it may well be that he would have introduced extrajudicial processes anyway; yet one cannot help noticing that the campaign for them did not start until the people's communes had been formed, and only really got under way with Khrushchev's speech at the Twenty-first Party Congress.

We must also mention the new regulation (announced at the end of 1960) prohibiting the transfer of land to private individuals for the construction of private country homes.[109] a practice which had been quite common and very popular among the upper class. It was felt that the all-too bourgeois character of these country homes conflicted somewhat with Moscow's claim to be the leader on the road to Communism. The 'brigades of Communist labor' must also be mentioned here, created at the end of 1958 and likewise assiduously promoted after the Twenty-first Party Congress.[110] But the system of wages based on performance was not touched.

The peak of Moscow's reaction to the challenge of the people's communes has been represented by the new 'program of the CPSU', which takes that very subject of 'transition to Communism' as its general theme and ends with the triumphant words (in bold type): 'The Party solemnly announces: The present generation of Soviet people will live in Communism!'[111] Truly an echo of Peitaiho.

*

If we summarize the course of events in China since Wuhan and the Russian reaction thereto, we see that the ideological rift caused in the late summer of 1958 by the Chinese and their people's communes has to a certain extent been narrowed. In China emphasis moved away from the commune to the kolkhoz and even to the brigade, and payment based on performance again became the standard wage form. The Russians for their part have become absorbed in the discussion of the 'transition to Communism'. In the wage question, however, that basic problem, they have stood firm. For the next twenty years, said Khrushchev at the Twenty-second Party Congress, wages based on performance will remain, although that portion of the national product which the individual receives without regard for performance (medical care, school, and housing) is to increase steadily.[112] Following the plans for agriculture of the new Party program of 1961[113] and the resolutions of the CC plenary sessions of March and November 1962[114] a new administrative unit, the Territorial Production Administration, was introduced in rural areas. It combines the political and economic functions of State and Party, thus taking many decisions out of the hands of Kolkhoz leadership, and to this extent resembles the people's commune.[115]

It can scarcely be said that Khrushchev has become more popular among Soviet citizens as a result of his participation in the race to Communism, into which he let himself be coaxed by China and the people's communes. While the trend in the Russian population toward private life, toward a personal sphere of interests, has become increasingly marked since Stalin's death, Khrushchev has become the driving force on the road to collectivism—to a far greater extent than if there had not been this ideological rivalry with Mao. Tension between the Kremlin and the majority of the population has not yet become acute simply because so far the 'transition to Communism' has not figured in the ordinary life of the Soviet citizen of today.

CHAPTER XV

WORLD POLICY OF THE 'CAMP'

PRIOR TO THE ESTABLISHMENT of the People's Republic, the Chinese Communists had been too busy with their own problems to concern themselves with international politics that did not immediately affect them. On those occasions when they did express their views on the subject they merely reiterated the stock phrases of world Communism.

However, one very serious involvement of the new state in world affairs arose in the first year of its existence—in Korea. We have practically no direct information on the scope and content of the Sino-Soviet consultations on Korea before and after the outbreak of the war. However, Moscow's and Peking's behavior in 1950 indicate that the planning of the war took place initially in Moscow—involving, of course, the Korean Communist leaders who, almost without exception, had been trained by Moscow.

On the other hand there is no indication that Peking opposed the war. When US troops had pulled out of Korea, and Secretary of State Dean Acheson had specifically designated South Korea as being outside the US defense zone in January 1950, a swift victory of the North Koreans over the South Koreans seemed inevitable. This, of course, was just what Peking wanted.

When things turned out differently, and the Americans returned to Korea with UN support and General MacArthur marched on the Yalu River, Peking decided to intervene. Whether this was done on its own initiative or under pressure from Stalin, we do not know, nor has it much bearing on the subsequent relationship between the two Red neighbors, since the joint efforts—Chinese 'volunteers' plus Soviet arms—led to a satisfactory outcome for the Chinese: they had entered the arena of world politics.[1] The only serious reverse—the decision of thousands of Chinese soldiers who had been taken prisoner to go to Taiwan after their release instead of returning to Red China—represented no threat to Sino-Soviet relations.

The Indo-China war also enhanced Peking's international prestige, as did the Geneva conference of 1954 on Korea and Indo-China, at which China was directly represented by Chou En-lai. Only a few months later, early in 1955, the Chinese tested their new position of power in their first attack on Chiang Kai-shek, as a result of which the Tachen Islands (about two hundred miles south of Shanghai) fell into their hands. In the spring of 1955—in Bandung—they played a dominant role at a large international conference. This was followed, however, by a period of withdrawal from world affairs; during 1956 and 1957, as we have seen, Peking was principally occupied with the internal problems of the Soviet bloc. Not until that period was over did it re-enter the arena of world politics, and now it remained to be seen whether or not this was done in agreement with Moscow.

*

In the foregoing chapter we dealt with the assumption that, after the fiasco of the Hundred Flowers, the radicals and the moderates among the top Chinese leaders wrestled for supremacy in the shaping of China's economy, and that the radicals won. It would seem that a similar battle was being fought out at the same time over foreign policy. In both instances it was a question of speed—on the one hand, of China's transition to Communism, and in this case of carrying the revolution to the rest of the world.

An American expert, in an excellent and detailed study of Sino-Soviet relations from 1956 to 1961, has come to the conclusion that the Chinese radicals used the two great space achievements of the Soviet Union between the end of August and the beginning of October, 1957 to bolster their aggressive line: the launching of the first intercontinental rocket and of the first man-made earth satellite.[2] This theory may be correct, although it would contradict the Chinese Communists' contempt for technology—particularly the technology of another country. 'The outcome of a war is decided by the people, not by one or two new types of weapons,' Mao had said in 1946 with reference to the atom bomb,[3] and this has been reiterated many times since. Yet beginning with Mao's statement in his speech to the students in Moscow that the east wind was now stronger than the west wind (November 1957), the Chinese continually spoke of a 'decisive turning-point' in world politics, the superiority of the 'socialist camp' over the West, and the grave mistake of over-estimating the 'imperialistic forces' in the future. Moreover Mao called the United States a 'paper tiger' in 1958 in a pamphlet also containing the notorious phrase: 'The atom bomb is a paper tiger'.[4]

The Russians, on the other hand, who after all were in a better position to judge, restricted themselves to the more modest formula: the power relationship of the Soviet bloc to the Western world had developed in favor of the former, although the Soviets did not lay claim to absolute superiority.

Whatever significance Soviet penetration of outer space may have had, the real reason for China's growing aggressiveness seems to lie in the fact that the radicals wanted to extend their policy of the Great Leap from internal to external politics. They were convinced that only a strong state of tension in every field, including relations with other countries, could yield the pressure necessary to force the people into producing all that was demanded of them. Hence they rejected all moderation whether it related to domestic economy or foreign policy.

It is of special relevance to our subject that the victory of those Chinese who advocated an aggressive world policy began to take effect at a time when Khrushchev, in spite of his obvious final goal, was preparing for a relaxation of tension and a summit meeting with Eisenhower. He thought this would offer him better prospects for an economic upsurge of the Soviet Union and an extension of his influence in the uncommitted world. However, since this diverging trend did not become apparent—even to the leaders of the two Red powers—all at once, it would be a distortion to try and dramatize its initial phases.

Episode in the Near East—Summer 1958

THE VERY FIRST EPISODE shows that we are dealing with an area in which great care must be exercised in forming judgments, and even then only after taking all available documents into account. We shall therefore study this test case in some detail. Some Western descriptions contained a good deal of wishful thinking, in particular the widespread attempt to find symptoms of Sino-Soviet conflict everywhere. From the first reports in the summer of 1958, I also derived a distorted picture, based most of all on the oft-repeated statement that it had been two full days before the Chinese could bring themselves to approve of Khrushchev's decision to hold a summit conference within the framework of the UN Security Council. What actually did happen?

Since the winter of 1957–58 Moscow had been working toward a new summit conference; this was the theme of the innumerable letters which—then still being signed by Bulganin—went out to every Foreign Office in the world. The Chinese press had backed up the Kremlin loyally in these efforts, among other things with editorials supporting Moscow's demand.[5]

After the overthrow of the government in Iraq on July 14, 1958, which cost the king his life and led to the arrival of American and British troops in Lebanon and Jordan, Khrushchev saw a chance of having his desire for a summit meeting fulfilled. On July 19—perhaps also because he was seriously afraid that the Americans and the British would march into Iraq—he called for a meeting, to take place on July 22, of the heads of government of the Soviet Union, the United States, Great Britain, France, and India.

What made him pick this particular combination? He wanted to avoid the 1 : 3 ratio between the USSR and the Western powers that had existed at the first summit meeting in Geneva in 1955. He could not suggest that Red China take part, as then the Western powers would have stayed away from the meeting, and it was their participation he so much desired. The only possible fifth candidate of world status was India.

Or did Khrushchev propose India in order deliberately to pass over China? Hardly. Presumably he was thinking only of Moscow's interests and not at all of China. Furthermore, in an editorial some months earlier the *People's Daily* had described the Middle East problems as being a suitable topic for a summit conference, without demanding that Peking participate,[6] and the Chinese press showed no signs of resentment when Khrushchev's proposal became known.

On July 22 Macmillan agreed to Khrushchev's proposed conference of the five heads of government; but he insisted it be held within the framework of the UN Security Council in New York. Washington sent a similar reply. For Khrushchev this counterproposal had the disadvantage that the five, instead of meeting in strict privacy, would presumably negotiate in the presence of the other members of the Security Council, which included Nationalist China. No one was surprised, therefore, when the Moscow press reacted unfavorably. Did America seriously believe the Soviet Union would discuss important international matters in front of Chiang

Kai-shek? asked *Izvestiya* indignantly; *Pravda* expressed similar disapproval.[7] Peking's comments were obviously also unfavorable: the majority of the Security Council members, they declared, were under the thumb of the United States, including the men who represented the half-dead Chiang and the quite dead King of Iraq.[8]

*

Great was the surprise, therefore, when on the evening of the 23rd—the same day on which the Moscow morning papers had sharply rejected Macmillan's proposal—Radio Moscow announced Khrushchev's decision to accept that same proposal. It was, of course, to be expected that on the following day the Soviet press would express no criticism of this about-face of the Lord of the Kremlin.[9] But how would Peking react?

To begin with there was no word from Peking, and this was construed as registering Chinese disapproval of Khrushchev. But this silence had a perfectly natural explanation: as a result of the six-hour time differential, day was already breaking in Peking when the news of the Moscow change-of-heart arrived—that is to say, the papers bearing the date of July 24 were already off the press. But that same evening, while it was still noon in Moscow, the Chinese news agency cabled out into the world the editorial to appear in the *People's Daily* of the following day; it described Khrushchev's new decision as an 'important step toward peace'. The nations of the world, it went on, 'hope that on the basis of the Soviet proposal a special session of the Security Council with the participation of the five heads of government may take place as soon as possible'.[10] In other words, far from registering their disapproval of Khrushchev, the Chinese approved his actions as quickly as was technically possible—including, moreover, the formula of the 'five heads of government', i.e. with India and without China. During the days that followed, the Chinese press continued to support Khrushchev's decision unreservedly.[11]

The first sign of a divergency of opinion was to be found in the question of the use of 'volunteers' in the Near East. Peking threatened this (on July 21 and 25),[12] the Russians did not; indeed, Khrushchev declared (on July 29) that he was opposed to the sending of volunteers of third (i.e. uninvolved) countries, as this gave rise to 'the danger of a real war'.[13] One should not take small differences too lightly; but this statement of Khrushchev's came a few days after the Chinese threat, at a time when the political situation in the Near East had already calmed down, and the sending of Chinese volunteers—if, indeed, this had ever been seriously contemplated—was no longer very likely.

Khrushchev's motive in accepting Macmillan's proposal was obviously understood in Peking, or at least acknowledged: a summit conference was important enough to justify accepting the presence of a representative of Nationalist China (even Chiang himself). Moreover, according to the British note, Khrushchev could assume that, although he would be negotiating in New York within the Security Council, he would not be bound by its rules of procedure and would be dealing quite informally with the other heads of government, particularly Eisenhower.[14] When these hopes were shattered by the next communications from Washington and London (July 25 and 26), his attitude stiffened. On July 28 he declared that an ordinary session of the Security Council, instead of an early meeting of the five heads of government, was useless, as such a session, on account of the 'mechanical majority' of the West, could lead no-where. It was necessary, therefore, to revert to his original plan of July 19—a summit meeting of the five outside the Security Council.[15]

The lapse of time between the two proposals of the Western heads of government (on July 25 and 26) and Khrushchev's reply (of 28th) might indicate that Khrushchev had also to cope with a protest on the part of Peking. For even if, for the sake of the solidarity of the Red bloc, the Chinese publicly applauded Khrushchev's decision of July 23, they must have been very displeased by the fact that their ally was going to negotiate in New York on an Asian problem in a group in which India and Taiwan, but not Peking, were represented. In any event, Khrushchev decided at short notice to negotiate personally with the Chinese in Peking.

The Red summit conference lasted from July 31 to August 3. Again we do not know exactly what happened there. On August 5, shortly after his return from China, Khrushchev stated definitely that he was not interested in a special session of the Security Council,[16] and it might be thought that this decision was the result of the Peking talks. However, it must not be forgotten that his proposal of July 28 had meanwhile also been rejected, and that, with the recognition of the new Iraqi government by London and Washington on August 1 and 2, the danger of British-American intervention in Iraq had been averted.

From the study of this Near East episode two factors emerge. Outwardly Peking behaved like a thoroughly loyal partner, and in every instance it promptly approved whatever Moscow did, even when this must have gone against the grain;[17] one is therefore not justified in maintaining that those three weeks produced documentary evidence of Sino-Soviet differences of opinion. However, this episode made Moscow aware, probably for the first time, of the full extent of its Chinese partner's weight and insistence on being heard. Henceforward international problems could no longer be solved without consulting Peking, as had formerly been taken for granted. In other words, Moscow had reached the boundary of its freedom to make its own decisions, and this boundary was Peking.

The Bombardment of Quemoy—Autumn 1958

WHETHER THE PROBLEM of Taiwan was dealt with, let alone decided upon, at the Peking conference, is still not known; the final communiqué says nothing about it. It can be assumed the talks included military matters as the two Defense Ministers, Malinovsky and P'eng Teh-huai, were present. This much is certain: on August 23, twenty days after the conclusion of Khrushchev's discussions with Mao, firing was resumed on the offshore islands held by Chiang's troops. On some days the bombardment was so intense that communications between the threatened islands and Taiwan could only be maintained with the utmost difficulty.

But Taiwan and Washington stood firm, and the Red Chinese air force with its Russian MIG fighter planes suffered a severe defeat in the air battle against the American-armed Nationalist Chinese. The expected invasion of the islands never came. On October 12 a new chief of general staff was appointed to the Red Chinese army. On October 25 Peking announced its decision—equally senseless from a military or a psychological point of view—from then on to bombard the islands on odd days only. The Taiwan crisis was over.

Certainly there is much to be said for the theory that all the publicity given to the demand for the 'liberation of Taiwan' was intended to impress not so much the enemies—Chiang and Dulles— as the five hundred million Chinese peasants and, with the assistance of a newly awakened anti-American patriotism, to facilitate the unpalatable transition to the people's communes.

Again, the only thing that interests us in this crisis is the Sino-Soviet aspect. Until August 1958 Moscow had shown a noticeable reserve in matters pertaining to Taiwan. In the joint declaration of October 1954, all that had been said was that 'the continued occupation . . . of Taiwan Island by the United States was not compatible with the tasks of maintaining peace in the Far East and lessening international tension'.[18] This was not an especially vigorous phraseology, containing as it does the term 'Far East', an expression which, with its Europe-centered connotation, is not very popular in China. A few months later, in his first big speech after Malenkov's downfall, Bulganin went somewhat further. He stated that the Soviet Union gave 'full approval and support' to Chinese claims on Taiwan, and that the Chinese people could count on the assistance of the Soviet Union in this respect.[19] Matters went no further than statements of this kind, and it is possible that Peking regarded this attitude as lukewarm and non-committal.

In the Taiwan crisis of the late summer of 1958 Moscow's editorial support did not begin immediately. Its first contribution was an article in *Pravda*—a week after the start of the bombardment[20]—followed after yet another week had elapsed by full-scale support in the form of a message from Khrushchev to Eisenhower, in which he said: 'An attack on the People's Republic, the great friend, ally, and neighbor of our country, is tantamount to an attack on the Soviet Union.'[12] (Statements of this kind have since been repeated from time to time, for example in Khrushchev's electoral speech of February 1963.[22]) However, Khrushchev had not made his position known until Chou En-lai (on September 6) had offered to resume the interrupted talks between the Red Chinese and American ambassadors, thus bringing about a lessening of tension. Another twelve days went by before Khrushchev, in a new letter to the President of the United States, warned the Americans of reprisals with atomic weapons should these be used by the Americans against China.[23]

This message ostensibly went further than Moscow's previous commitments in the Far East. While in the treaty of 1950 the alliance was limited to an attack by Japan or one of the countries allied with Japan, it was now extended to cover every type of conflict. But the Taiwan crisis of 1958 proved one thing: the Russians no more want to have their actions dictated to them by Mao than the Americans want theirs dictated to them by Chiang.

*

China is not a member of the military alliance within the Soviet bloc
—the Warsaw Pact[24] concluded in May 1955; the military obligations
laid down in this pact (Article 4) relate only to Europe (not even to
the Asiatic part of the Soviet Union). Nevertheless, through its
representative who was an observer at the concluding of the pact,
Peking stated that it was 'in complete unanimity' with it and
'supports it'. Whether this entails an obligation to extend military
aid in a European conflict is an open question.[25] It is true that Chou
En-lai has often stated in conversation that China would regard an
attack against any country of the Soviet bloc 'as an attack against
China and the whole socialist camp and in such a case would not
calmly look on'.[26] The fact that Moscow regards the Warsaw Pact
as one of the Kremlin's instruments of leadership vis-à-vis the
European 'people's democracies', is shown by the most recent of the
Soviet monographs on the pact, for it makes no reference to the
Asian member states of the Soviet bloc.[27] Peking has not yet brought
into existence any formal system of alliance between itself and the
Asian members of the 'camp'.

Since the decision 'to bombard on odd days', no new factors
worth speaking of have emerged in the Taiwan question. The Red
Chinese have from time to time stepped up their bombardment, they
have varied their propaganda methods toward the population of
Taiwan, they have continually declared Taiwan to be a Chinese
province temporarily occupied by the American imperialists and its
liberation to be imminent—in other words, there were not and never
would be two Chinas;[28] and their propaganda against the United
States has fluctuated in intensity. Echoes of approval have usually
been forthcoming from the Kremlin, and Moscow has supported the
thesis that Taiwan is the exclusive concern of the Chinese People's
Republic, which, of course, also indicates its aloofness and the fact
that it had no intention of interfering in a domestic Chinese quarrel.[29]

The Chinese Communists knew that no invasion of Taiwan—or
even, presumably, of the offshore islands—was possible without
provoking the Americans into using atomic weapons. Although they
had induced the Kremlin to state officially that in such case it would
assist them with atomic weapons, they had not been able to persuade
it to provide Red China with atomic weapons. In spite of the volume of
their propaganda (and their artillery), the bombardment of Quemoy
ended in failure. Mao could blame Dulles and Khrushchev for this.

From Camp David to Peking—Autumn 1959

THAT MOSCOW AND PEKING differed widely in their tactical attitude toward the United States became still more obvious in the following year. There had been talk for some time of Khrushchev going to the United States. The visit was officially announced on August 3, 1959, as a first step, to be followed by the next step—a return visit of the American President to the Soviet Union. Moscow was jubilant: the long-sought summit of all summits, the dual meeting of Khrushchev and Eisenhower, was in sight. In the exuberance of this success, Khrushchev described the Soviet Union and the United States in his statement to the press as 'the two greatest states in the world' on whose relationship depended war or peace on earth, and he quoted the Russian proverb: 'When the masters quarrel, the servants tremble.'[30]

As seen from Moscow, the picture was perfectly clear: the meeting of the two masters of the world was imminent, the first event of this kind since 1807 when Napoleon and the Tsar, at a meeting on a raft anchored on the River Memel, divided Europe between them. The other nations—servants all—were to rejoice. . . .

The Chinese press duly 'rejoiced', although with a note of warning: one must be suspicious of the sincerity of the Americans. To under-line this, the Party journal quoted the counterpart to our: 'The leopard cannot change his spots.'[31]

While during the ensuing months Moscow almost completely suspended its attacks on the United States and the American President, Peking continued its accusations. Nevertheless Peking treated Khrushchev's American visit as a success of the 'Soviet peace policy' and a 'strengthening of the forces for peace in the world'.

The visit to the United States ended, we recall, with the talks at Camp David; the joint declaration of September 27—on the whole optimistically phrased—also announced Eisenhower's return visit for the following spring. A new summit meeting, to include other heads of government (although not of China) was envisaged. In the report which Khrushchev delivered the very next day to a mass meeting in Moscow, he was full of praise for President Eisenhower, whose 'statesmanlike wisdom in judging the present international situation' and whose 'courage and determination' he extolled.[32]

The Chinese press held to the old line: it congratulated Khrushchev on his success in the United States but continued to attack the

latter as malicious and insincere.[33] This attitude contained the
implied question to Khrushchev: What is the point of discussing
peace with the enemies of peace?

The day after his arrival in Moscow, the tireless Khrushchev flew
on to Peking for the celebrations marking the tenth anniversary of
the Chinese People's Republic. That the Soviets attached far more
importance to his stay in the USA than to his subsequent visit to
China was also shown by the fact that the two issues of the most
widely read illustrated magazine, *Ogonyók*, dealing with Red China's
anniversary,[34] were filled almost entirely with photographs of the
American visit. This third visit of Khrushchev's to China (the first
had taken place five years earlier, during the fifth anniversary, the
second during the Near East crisis of the summer of 1958), was not
marked by a particularly cordial atmosphere. The man who arrived
in Peking on September 30 was still under the spell of his weeks in
the United States. The overwhelming friendliness of the Americans,
the tremendous wealth and enormous power of the country, the
human warmth of the President—all this had its effect even on
Khrushchev. At the same time he was justified in regarding his
journey as a great personal triumph and thus as a triumph for
Communism.

*

Arriving in this almost festive mood, Khrushchev now had to face for
the next three days the cold, sceptical gaze of Mao and the other
Chinese leaders. But he would not have been Khrushchev if he had
let himself be daunted by this. Immediately after landing he stated—
not without pride—that, after a short change of planes in Moscow,
he had come straight from America.[35] Mao said nothing; he did not
even come to the microphone. Khrushchev declared at the banquet
'that the President of the United States has recognized the necessity
of a relaxation of international tension' and that 'he is supported in
this by not a few men'; he added that so great a cause as socialism
must not be imposed upon the peoples by force of arms. He warned
against 'testing the stability of the capitalist system by force'. That
would be wrong, for: 'The peoples would not understand this
and would never support those who acted in this manner.'[36] Mao
remained silent, and not a single Chinese paper commented on these
remarks of the guest from Moscow.

It was not only by his silence that Mao expressed his disapproval;

in various other ways he avoided conferring any special honor on his guest in the New York suit. Not even the customary 'spontaneous reception' was accorded him; he had been driven from and to the airport through empty streets. The man who for several weeks had been regarding himself and Eisenhower as the two masters of the world once again found himself one among many in the circle of Communist leaders and, moreover, exposed to the overwhelming display of might of his Red brother.

Before his departure it was again only the Soviet leader who spoke at the airport ('We Communists of the Soviet Union', he said pointedly, 'want to liquidate the Cold War.').[37] Contrary to usual practice, no communiqué on the Sino-Soviet talks was issued. On his return journey through the Soviet Far East and Siberia, Khrushchev in several speeches acclaimed the results of his trip to the United States and the improved prospects for peace. Mao still said nothing.

We do not have to look far to find the reasons for Mao's hostile reaction to Khrushchev's Washington bias. If the two 'greats'—the leaders of the Eastern and the Western camps—were to divide up the world between them as Napoleon and Alexander or Mark Antony and Augustus had once done, Chinese interests would soon be reduced to bargaining points between Moscow and Washington. Furthermore, in a situation of relaxed world tension, the already inadequate aid offered by a Soviet Union no longer so dependent on its fellow bloc members would be still further reduced. It already looked as if this new Khrushchev could think of nothing else but catching up with the American standard of living, reducing working hours, and supplying domestic kitchens with gas outlets, instead of doing his utmost to help China build up its economy. If, finally, the Russians considered the meaning of co-existence to be a prosperity race with the Americans, thus justifying, for instance, the spending of billions on housing,[38] while the Chinese were suffering extreme privation at all levels, this did not make the Russian pursuit of prosperity or co-existence à la russe any more palatable to the Chinese.

Some years later, when the quarrel between the two neighbors had become public property, the Chinese could express their disapproval not merely by silence but in so many words. An editorial in the *People's Daily* openly voiced disapproval of Khrushchev's policy of 1959:

Particularly around the time of the Camp David talks in September 1959, certain comrades of a fraternity Party [the CPSU] put forward a series of erroneous views on many important issues relating to the international situation. . . . They pinned their hopes for defending world peace on the 'wisdom' of the heads of the major powers, holding that the historical fate of the present epoch is actually decided by individual 'great men' and their 'wisdom', and that summit meetings of the major powers can determine and change the course of history. . . . They portrayed the Camp David talks as a 'new stage', a 'new era' in international relations'. . . . They were especially ardent in lauding Dwight Eisenhower, the chieftain of US imperialism, as one who had 'a sincere desire for peace', who 'sincerely hopes to eliminate the state of "cold war",' and who 'also worries about ensuring peace just as we do'.[39]

Thus we learned in 1963 that what many of us had assumed to be true in 1959 was correct. However, there was one more field in world politics, and a very wide one, in which opinions in Moscow and Peking were growing further and further apart.

The Two Red Powers and the Developing Countries

TODAY PEKING AND MOSCOW are in touch with dozens of countries in Asia, Africa, and Latin America. It is not necessary to examine the relations with each individual state; in order to judge their effects on the relationship between the two Red capitals it is enough to know the general line.[40]

Lenin had been fully aware of Asia's importance in the world revolution to which he was aspiring. Although it is not possible to trace the phrase so often ascribed to him—that the road to Paris leads via Shanghai and Calcutta (or other cities of Asia)—he did write, in his last essay: 'In the last analysis, the upshot of the struggle will be determined by the fact that Russia, India, China, etc., account for the overwhelming majority of the population of the globe.'[41] Stalin also expressed himself in a similar vein.[42]

The prospects for a revolution in large parts of Asia seemed particularly favorable after World War II had stirred up the people and disrupted their way of life. With the gradual disintegration of the war-time alliance between the victorious powers, Moscow discarded its scruples about instigating unrest in the spheres of influence of its recent allies. At first, Western observers assumed that the call to a general revolt went out at the Communist Youth Congress in Calcutta in February 1948, but it is now doubtful whether any clear directive of this kind was ever given. The fact remains that, ever since the summer of 1947, the Moscow leaders had set the storm signals, although not uniformly or all at the same time.[43] In the Soviet press Nehru's image was distorted to that of an imperialist lackey, and for the Indian Communists he became the object of a bitter—and to them highly damaging—attack. The Communist revolts in the Philippines, in Indo-China and Indonesia, in Malaya and Burma, also failed to lead to lasting successes, although it must not be forgotten that Stalin supported these revolts somewhat half-heartedly since his interests lay principally in Europe.

After the dictator's death, events in this field also took a new turn. This became apparent in 1954 when both the Korean and Indo-China wars ended in a draw. Moreover, when the Bandung conference took place in the spring of 1955 without the Russians, and when at that conference Chou En-lai, overshadowing even Nehru and showing his best side, made a deep impression on the admiring Asians and Africans, Khrushchev with his customary vigor executed a political change of front. In the summer of 1955 Nehru was invited to the USSR as an honored guest, he and Gandhi having meanwhile been transformed by the Soviet press into freedom-fighters against imperialism; and that winter Khrushchev—then still arm in arm with Bulganin—went on a propaganda trip to India, Burma, and Afghanistan.

From then on the Kremlin's policy was one of the closest possible co-operation with the official leaders of the young states, regardless of their form of government—even with Nasser, who locked up his Communists; with U Nu, who for years had been engaged in fierce skirmishes against the Communist guerrillas of Burma; with Sukarno, whose nationalistic policy had brought great hardship to the Chinese living in Indonesia; with Nehru, who fought the CP with every means permitted under the constitution; and with Kassem, of whom no one really knew which way he wanted Iraq to go. Moscow did not demand a public show of sympathy from these men either for itself or for Communism; the main thing was that they should not openly align themselves with the Western camp. (Tito, being a renegade, is an entirely different case; had he achieved power not as a Communist guerrilla chieftain but as a nationalist-revolutionary colonel à la Nasser, he could have done and said as he pleased in his country without being the target of constant censure from the Kremlin.)

*

The Soviet Union followed its tradition of maintaining diplomatic relations as far as possible with all recognized governments. My own observations during Adenauer's negotiations in Moscow in the fall of 1955 convinced me that, if only for reasons of protocol, the Soviets definitely wanted to create outwardly normal relations with Bonn, even the Bonn of Konrad Adenauer. On the other hand, the Kremlin was unwilling to maintain official relations with non-legitimate governments even when their aspirations fitted neatly into its plans. For example, it did not recognize the exile government of Algiers, formed in 1958, until 1962—i.e. not until after the armistice with de Gaulle. And just as Stalin closed both eyes when his treaty partner Hitler continued to keep the German Communists in concentration camps, so Khrushchev merely sent protests when the developing countries took action against Communists, but he did not withdraw his economic assistance, not even from Iraq when, early in 1963, Kassem's successors killed off and imprisoned their country's Communists by the hundreds. Nor did Moscow ever raise such a storm over the death of a foreign Communist as it did over that of the non-Communist Lumumba.

In his ideas on world politics, Khrushchev, like Stalin, is basically an 'infantryman'—although an infantryman equipped with nuclear rockets; he does not automatically think in terms of overseas bases, a way of thinking natural to the old maritime powers of Europe, to Japan, and to the United States of today. The thought that the fate of his empire and of world Communism is linked with the decisions of men who are playing with gunpowder in the jungles of Africa or on the distant island of Cuba might well cause him many a sleepless night. Without hesitation he had the Soviet flag pulled down in Leopoldville in September 1960 when this was demanded by the new government after Lumumba's downfall; without demur he recalled his ambassador from Guinea in December 1961 after Sekou Touré— whom he had called his friend—accused him of interfering in Guinea's internal affairs;[44] and in April 1962 Khrushchev dropped the Cuban Communist leader Anibal Escalante, then in opposition to Fidel Castro, in favor of Castro himself.[45] The reason for this was not far to seek: whatever Fidel Castro may one day do in Cuba, Khrushchev does not need to feel responsibility for a non-Communist; if necessary he could even look on at Castro's downfall without too great a loss of prestige. But should a real Communist like Escalante take over power in Cuba and then get into trouble, it would be much more difficult for Khrushchev to leave him in the lurch. It was symptomatic of Khrushchev's 'infantryman's' attitude that in the autumn of 1962 he quickly removed his missiles from Cuba when this was demanded by President Kennedy. In the eyes of the Chinese this was, of course, a terrible thing to do. They promptly published the Khrushchev-Kennedy exchange[46] and criticized the Soviet attitude,[47] comparing it with the appeasement policy toward Hitler, and even labeled it 'doing a Munich'.[48] Moscow in turn used another historical simile, hinting that Peking wanted to 'do a Sarajevo' in Cuba,[49] i.e. utilize it to touch off a new world war.

Obviously Khrushchev does not believe mankind to be on the verge of world revolution, and so for the time being he is still counting on the 'bourgeois nationalists' in all the developing countries and not on the Communists (even in a country like Afghanistan, although it borders on the Soviet Union). Through his ideological expert for Asia he describes as 'sectarians of the most dangerous type', doomed to self-imposed isolation, those who refuse to understand that in the national struggle for liberation 'under certain circumstances non-proletarian elements move to the fore', and recalls Lenin's words to the effect that in the early stages of every nationalist movement the bourgeoisie occupies the dominant position.[50] For Khrushchev, the neutrality of the developing countries has a certain value of its own: he knows that the fear of a Communist seizure of power among the bourgeois-nationalist leaders would drive these countries into the arms of the West.

*

Thus Khrushchev has no qualms about giving extensive economic aid to countries under non-Communist rule, even to countries where many Communists are in prison. According to Soviet statistics (whose accuracy it is not our task to examine here), the credits extended by the USSR to the developing countries from 1954 (prior to that hardly any credits were given) to 1960 exceeded ten billion old rubles.[51] Up to 1960 the lion's share went to: India (3·2 billion rubles), the United Arab Republic (2·35 billion), Indonesia (1·47 billion), Iraq (730 million), Afghanistan (400 million), and Ethiopia (400 million). In other words the non-Communists Nehru, Nasser, Sukarno, Kassem, Daud, and Haile Selassie, who together rule over fewer people than there are Chinese, have received during this period exactly five times as much in credits as Mao, the Communist ally, in all the years since he came to power in 1949.

For the Chinese, looking at the low level of their own under-developed economy, the thought of Moscow's generosity toward the non-aligned countries must have been particularly galling. Presumably they spoke their minds to the Russians. For at the peak of the dispute with Tirana, one of the top Soviet ideologists described the Albanian leaders 'and their like-minded comrades' as 'narrow-minded nationalists' and egoists because they reproached the Soviet government on account of its economic aid to the developing countries; they merely showed by this, he said, that they did not understand the role of the neutral countries in world politics.[52]

The want of understanding for the non-Communist governments of the developing countries—where else could Tirana's 'like-minded comrades' be but in Peking?—is psychologically quite easily explained by the fact that the Chinese Communists were still suffering from the shock of their experience in 1927 when, in obedience to Moscow's orders, they had supported Chiang Kai-shek, only to be routed by him. Since then Mao has had a poor opinion of bourgeois-nationalist-led revolutions; that is also why he developed his theory of the 'new democracy', according to which even a so-called bourgeois-democratic revolution must definitely be led by the proletariat (i.e. by the Communists). It is true that, when he needed Chiang in his desperate struggle against the Japanese, Mao let this theory slip temporarily into the background, but he never abandoned it and, particularly in recent years and in connection with the non-aligned countries, he has frequently put it forward again.[53]

*

Under the influence of the radical wing which, as we must assume, gained ascendancy in China during the second half of 1957, Peking attacked the co-operative attitude of the Kremlin toward the anti-Communist governments of the developing countries. Accusations such as the following were leveled at Khrushchev: 'The modern revisionists . . . try to make people believe that it is possible to achieve socialism without a revolutionary party of the proletariat. . . . This is sheer nonsense and pure deception.'[54] Whoever spreads this belief 'will deprive the oppressed peoples of their fighting spirit and . . . prevent them from arming themselves to actively fight the enemy . . .

and to liberate themselves. This will, in effect, keep the oppressed peoples for ever in the state of enslavement.'[55]

Lately the Chinese have gone still further. They claim that Moscow does not even want liberation struggles on the part of the dependent countries.

What these persons want is that . . . the oppressed nations should not fight imperialism and colonialism . . . for otherwise, they say, a world war would be touched off, causing the death of millions upon millions of people.[56]

The Chinese Communists have long believed that their revolution represents a far more appropriate model for the developing countries than the Russian. Here is a selection of quotations (all italics are the author's):

This kind of revolution [a new type of bourgeois-democratic revolution] is developing *in China as well as in all colonial and semi-colonial countries*. . . . Therefore the form of state to be adopted by the revolutions *in colonial and semi-colonial countries* during a given historical period can only be a third one, namely, the new-democratic republic.[57]

Mao Tse-tung's great accomplishment has been *to change Marxism from a European to an Asiatic form.* Marx and Lenin were Europeans; they wrote in European languages about European histories and problems, seldom discussing Asia or China. . . . Mao Tse-tung is Chinese. . . . He has created *a Chinese or Asiatic form of Marxism.* . . . There are similar conditions [similar to China] in other lands of Southeast Asia. The courses chosen by China will influence them all.[58]

The classic type of revolution in the imperialist countries is the [Russian] October revolution. *The classic type of revolution in the colonial and semi-colonial countries is the Chinese revolution.*[59]

Thanks to the success of our revolution, the thoughts of Lenin, supplemented by the thoughts of Mao Tse-tung and the experiences of the CPC, have inspired further *hundreds of millions of people in Asia, Africa, and Latin America.*[60]

Naturally revolution and construction in China have their specific characteristics for this country. But it is possible that some of these important characteristics will appear in other countries. In this sense Chinese experiences are to a certain degree *of international significance.*[61]

Here is a variation of particular interest to Europeans:

First of all *the absurd theory*, current in modern bourgeois historical science, *of 'Europe as the center of the world', must be destroyed.* . . . The revolutions of the East, especially the great victory of the Chinese revolution, had a strong and *widespread influence on Asia, Africa, and Latin America.*[62]

*

Two quotations which go beyond this idea of the exemplary significance of the Chinese revolution seem to me especially revealing. At the
end of his speech 'On the Correct Handling of Contradictions Among
the People' (1957) Mao spoke of the solidarity of the Chinese, first
'with all socialist countries' and secondly with 'the *Asian and
African countries*, and all the peace-loving countries and peoples',
and added: 'United with these *two* forces, we will not stand alone.'[63]
(Author's italics.) With this statement, coming with such emphasis
at the close of one of his most important utterances, Mao voices the
view that for China the Soviet bloc is not the only ally. And the
Sino-Nepalese communiqué of March 1960 is—as far as I know—the
first official Chinese document[64] to speak merely of the 'solidarity of
the Asian countries' (not counting, of course, the 'Afro-Asian
Solidarity Conferences' in Cairo (1958), Conacry (1960) and Moshi
(1963), as well as similar 'Afro-Asian' functions). It is to be presumed
that in signing the treaty with Nepal Chou had his mental reservations.
He must have been aware that in 1939 Mao had described Nepal (also
Korea, Burma, and Annam) as a territory of which the Chinese state
had been robbed by the imperialists.[65]

There were some years in which the Chinese did not allow their
aggressive imperialism to come forward—at the time of the Geneva
conference on Korea and Indo-China (1954) and immediately
following. At that time Chou En-lai undertook numerous trips to
Asian countries, concluded the agreement with India on the Five
Principles of Co-Existence (April 1954), shone in Bandung (1955),
and generally conducted himself peaceably. That was the period in
which in China itself a somewhat less drastic course was being
pursued. But all that changed when in 1958 the tone and tempo
toward the developing countries, as in all areas of Chinese policy,
were sharply stepped up. The prompt recognition of the Algerian
government in exile the same year (from which Moscow had
refrained), was a symptom of this change; the virulent speech against
Nasser which the Syrian Communist leader Khaled Bagdash was
permitted to make at the celebrations for the tenth anniversary of the
founding of the Chinese People's Republic (1959), was another. At
this point we must also mention the flood of pamphlets and radio
broadcasts with which Peking has ever since been exhorting the
developing countries to battle and revolution; also the rapid increase
in newspaper reporting on these areas at the same time that the
amount of news concerning the Soviet bloc was diminishing.

The climax to this Chinese policy toward the new states, whose friendship Peking had courted in Bandung, was reached with the conflict with India.

*

In the spring of 1959 I was traveling by train from Moscow to Berlin. I bought a Soviet newspaper en route and saw an item about a revolt in Tibet—not previously reported—having been put down by Chinese troops. The Russians in my compartment had also seen it and made no attempt to hide their misgivings. When I let fall the word 'Hungary', it was received in subdued silence. One man said gloomily: 'This means trouble with India.'

No doubt the men in the Kremlin were also uneasy over the news of the great Tibetan revolt which had broken out on March 10. In principle, of course, they agreed with their Chinese colleagues: whether they are Tibetans or Hungarians, Turkmen or Ukrainians— they all have to be 'socialistically' integrated, and anyone opposing this process is a 'reactionary' and a 'running dog of the imperialists' who needs to be rapped over the knuckles. But the Soviet leaders could foresee that what was going on in Tibet was bound to have unfavorable repercussions not only on Peking's relations with Asia but also Moscow's relations with Asia, just as the Hungarian incident two and a half years earlier had had on the reputation of the Soviet Union in Europe. Hence on the whole Moscow's reports on events in Tibet were somewhat guarded although they faithfully reiterated Peking's theses (which of course corresponded to Moscow's views).[66] However, the attacks on India[67] found in the Peking press at that time were totally absent.

Shortly before the Tibetan revolt, Moscow had been able to look with satisfaction on the considerable improvement of its relations with the peoples and governments of Asia. It had gained a lot of ground and earned a name for itself in Asian eyes as an industrial power of the first order, capable of supplying its friends and customers with ready-made steel plants on favorable credit terms.

India's indignant cries and the Dalai Lama's successful flight to India infuriated the Chinese leaders; the Indians were dubbed imperialists, interventionists, expansionists, even 'lurking tigers'. And when, in the wake of the suppression of the Tibetan revolt, feelings in Peking began to subside, a new conflict arose between Peking and New Delhi: the dispute over the Sino- (actually Tibeto-)

Indian border which has dragged on for years and in October 1962 was to flare up into a full-fledged war. Until the revolt in Tibet, this frontier had been one of the most peaceful—because one of the most remote—in the world. One has only to look at this mightiest of the earth's barriers from the foothills of the Himalayas to feel any frontier must lose its normal function in this virtually uninhabited mass of rock and ice—especially when peace-loving people live on either side of it.

This practically lifeless frontier, however, suddenly came very much to life (according to Nehru)[68] when Peking set up a regime of terror in Tibet from which tens of thousands fled and hundreds of thousands wanted to flee. Now that the frontier was sealed off, the question of its exact position became vital. It suddenly became apparent that the frontier claimed by Peking cut deep into Indian territory; further, for long stretches (on the western part of the border) the claim had become a fact, complete with watchtowers and soldiers. In other words, undetected by the Indian public, the Chinese had already acquired a firm grasp on an enormous area covering tens of thousands of square miles—an area which the Indians considered their property but had not guarded as such.

Nehru was a deeply shaken man, he had to fight for his reputation and his confidence in the new China, and to defend himself against parliament's charge that he had made mistakes in dealing with China which 'in geography and magnitude' were 'Himalayan'.[69] The details are to be found in the highly dramatic White Books of the Indian government and in the reports of the Indian parliament sessions in the fall of 1959.

*

A few months after the Chinese invasion of Indian territory became known, I spent eight weeks in India. The change in the political climate brought about by China's actions was extraordinary. The peaceloving Indians were now calling for a militarily strong India, for an armed nation, and they turned Eisenhower's visit to India in December 1959 into a triumphal procession. Even Nehru declared before an applauding parliament that, when it was a matter of honor, self-respect, and freedom, no price was too high, and that it was better to perish than to yield and capitulate.[70]

We have no means of knowing whether the Chinese wanted this conflict with India, or whether they landed in it unintentionally. To judge by what we do know of the feelings of the radicals among the CPC, it is quite possible that they wanted to impress on the two world powers, the USSR and the USA—which during the months before and after Khrushchev's visit to the United States had been talking so much about co-existence—that there could be no lessening of tension without Peking. And indeed the shadow of the Himalayas lay over Camp David when Eisenhower welcomed Khrushchev there.

The extent of Khrushchev's annoyance was to be seen in his remarkable reaction: while in the past he had automatically and unequivocally taken sides with a Communist partner who became involved in a dispute with a third country, he did not do so in the case of the Sino-Indian border dispute. In fact, in a TASS statement of September 9, 1959—which the Chinese press then ignored—he called upon *both sides* to put an end to the quarrel, as if their positions were more or less equal. The significant passage was as follows:

> One cannot help regretting that an incident has occurred on the Sino-Indian frontier. The Soviet Union has friendly relations with the Chinese People's Republic as well as with the Republic of India. The Chinese and Soviet peoples are bound to one another by indissoluble friendship, founded on the great principles of socialist internationalism. Co-operation between the Soviet Union and India is developing amicably corresponding to the ideas of peaceful co-existence. . . . In leading Soviet circles . . . the belief is expressed that both governments [China and India] will eliminate the misunderstanding in consideration of their mutual interests in the spirit of traditional friendship between the peoples of China and India.[71]

*

It was only three and a half years later that the Chinese told the world how outraged they had been by this cool attitude on the part of Moscow. In fact, they claimed that the TASS statement had been the beginning of the rift between Peking and Moscow. (The reader knows that this is not the author's view, but it is interesting to note that this is what the Chinese now claim.) In an article directed against the French Communist leader, the *People's Daily* said:

> The internal differences among the fraternal Parties were first brought into the open . . . on the eve of the Camp David talks in September 1959—on September 9, 1959, to be exact. On that day a socialist country [the USSR], turning a deaf ear to China's repeated explanations of the true situation and to China's advice, hastily issued a statement on a Sino-Indian border incident through its official news agency [TASS]. Making no distinction between right and wrong, the statement expressed 'regret'

over the border clash and in reality condemned China's correct stand. They even said that it was 'tragic' and 'deplorable'. Here is the first instance in history in which a socialist country, instead of condemning the armed provocations of the reactionaries of a capitalist country [India], condemned another fraternal socialist country [China] when it was confronted with such armed provocation.[72]

It so happened that I was in India when Khrushchev arrived there in January 1960. Within an hour of landing in India, Khrushchev must have realized the consequences of Peking's actions: not only was his reception by the populace far less cordial than it had been four years earlier—it paled in comparison with Eisenhower's tremendous success two months before. The mood of the Indians was aggravated when it became known that Khrushchev had not brought a Chinese compromise proposal with him and actually had nothing more to offer than the oft-repeated admonition: now be sensible and make up! He totally ignored the fact that the aggressor China was showing no inclination whatever to yield.

At a reception for the press in New Delhi's modern Ashoka Hotel, Nehru was surrounded—as he was whenever he appeared—by a flock of correspondents, when two Russians who had arrived with Khrushchev tried to break through the crowd in order to get closer to Nehru. The Indian who was standing in front of me refused to give way, but did not look to see who was pushing him. At that moment one of the Russians pushed him aside, pointed to the other Russian, and said by way of explanation: 'That's Khrushchev's son-in-law!' [Adzhubei, editor-in-chief of Izvestiya], whereupon the Indian turned round and indignantly replied: 'And I'm not a Czech but an Indian!' Khruschhev himself was also regarded more critically by the Indians than during his first visit; half-amused, half-indignant, they shook their heads when they heard that, after a performance by an interpreter of religious dances who was revered throughout India, Khrushchev had asked her how much she was paid.

*

I was also in Burma at the same time as Khrushchev. His reception there was cool, at times unfriendly. The Burmese saw themselves also exposed to Chinese frontier demands, and this had influenced their attitude toward the Communist world as a whole. Khrushchev went to Burma—as to India—uninvited. The Burmese extended the minimum hospitality required by courtesy. It must have been the most unenthusiastic reception Khrushchev has ever encountered on all his travels: a few hundred Communists and Communist-sympathizers at the airport, a scattering of people along the road to the city, hardly any flags, no one—apart from a few government officials—to see him off at the airport, no farewell speeches, and an icy atmosphere in the press. The Rangoon *Guardian* wrote that four wicked capitalists were not as bad as one Communist; and its competitor, the *Nation*, headed its editorial with the words: AN UNWELCOME VISITOR, and called Khrushchev a heavy-drinking politician at whose appearance one felt like calling out, as at the approach of invading soldiers, Hide the silver and the girls!

In Indonesia, where I arrived shortly after Khrushchev, the visit had also not gone off well. There, too, it had been overshadowed by tension with Peking, which affected the overseas Chinese living in Indonesia, whom the Indonesians wished to get rid of. Each new shipload of repatriated Chinese from Indonesia brought Chinese blood to boiling point, for Peking felt obliged to go to the defense of the overseas Chinese even when the latter possessed foreign or dual nationality. Article 98 of the new Chinese constitution expressly states: 'The People's Republic of China protects the well-earned rights and interests of the overseas Chinese'; and Article 23 reserves places for them in the National People's Congress.

The dispute between Djakarta and Peking, which lasted for many months, showed that the more than ten million Chinese living out-side of China (and Taiwan) in some ways represent a liability for Peking. Its relations with the Philippines, Cambodia, Malaya, Thailand, and Indonesia would be better if these countries were not continually faced with the problem of dealing with overseas Chinese, who are in many cases very unpopular on account of their business acumen. On the other hand, these overseas Chinese are an asset (as well as the nucleus for a 'fifth column') in that, despite a good deal of anti-Communist feeling—especially among the older ones—they have no desire to be on bad terms with whatever government happens to be in control in China.[73]

The Soviets have no such problem; the Pan-Slavism of Tsarist times is no longer acute.[74] Apart from the period of World War II, Red Moscow has seldom played its Slavic card; the journal *Slavyáne* (The Slavs), which first appeared in 1942 and was embellished with Old Slavic motifs, lost its significance after the war and soon ceased publication.

The implied support against Peking which Djakarta read into Khrushchev's friendly visit naturally did nothing toward making the Indonesians more amenable to Chinese demands. No wonder Peking also reported this part of Khrushchev's trip scantily and without a word of approval.

Thanks to his visits and the gifts he brought with him, Khrushchev was apparently able, in the spring of 1960, to improve Moscow's relations with the three countries in South and Southeast Asia to which he had traveled, and demonstrate that the Soviet Union was really much more generous and easy to get along with than the new China. To this extent Moscow derived some benefit from Peking's unruly behavior since the revolt in Tibet. On the whole, however, more harm than good was done to the Soviet bloc, reason enough for Moscow to view its ally in Peking—the cause of it all—with some resentment.

*

The repercussions on Sino-Soviet relations in 1959–60 due to the events on the Tibeto-Indian frontier were repeated three years later when Chinese armies marched in full force across the border into India, but this time the exchanges were more heated. The very thing the Russians had done their best to prevent, now came to pass within a few hours: India had no choice but to turn to the West for aid. It must have been a nightmare to Khrushchev to learn that US planes had established an air bridge from Frankfurt, Germany, to Calcutta, transporting war material to the hard-pressed Indians. Again it so happened that I was in India during the crucial first days of the Chinese attack, so I had a chance to see for myself the long faces of the Russians in New Delhi at that time. Although the Soviets refrained, as they had three years earlier, from censuring Peking, and sought refuge in their stock phrase about a deplorable conflict between their Chinese 'brothers' and their Indian 'friends',[75] they were furious, and so were the Chinese. Some time later Peking gave vent to its feelings in the *People's Daily*:

The surprising thing is that when a fraternal socialist country [China] was facing the Nehru government's provocations and attacks, certain self-styled Marxist-Leninists [the Kremlin leaders] should abandon the principle of proletarian internationalism and assume a 'neutral' stand. In practice, they have not only been giving political support to the anti-China policy of the Nehru government, but have been supplying that government with war material.[76]

The last sentence, of course, referred to the Soviet delivery of MIG fighters to India. Whether the Chinese withdrawal behind a line corresponding more or less to that from which they had started in October 1962 was the result of Soviet pressure or Chinese strategy, we cannot tell.

On the ideological level—particularly with regard to relations between the Communist bloc and the developing countries—a slight, temporary relaxation was brought about at the conference of eighty-one Communist Parties late in 1960. For a long time the Soviets had been resisting the claim of the Chinese to be the model for the developing countries. ('It would be dangerous to regard the Chinese revolution as a kind of yardstick for people's democratic revolutions in other Asian countries.')[77] But finally they acknowledged it—to a limited degree. The declaration of 1960 contains the following passage:

> The people's revolution in China dealt a crushing blow at the positions of imperialism in Asia. . . . By giving a further powerful impetus to the national-liberation movement, it exerted tremendous influence on the peoples, especially those of Asia, Africa, and Latin America.[78]

At the same time, however, the Soviets managed to include the term 'national democracy'—which, although they had not invented it, had recently been introduced into Communist speech—in the declaration, thus pushing Mao's 'new democracy' into the background. For while 'new democracy' is understood to mean leadership by 'the proletariat' (the Communists), 'national democracy' is so defined as to make it applicable to countries like Cuba (before Castro's avowal of Marxism); as extensive as this definition is, it does not contain the words 'proletariat' or 'socialism'—not to mention 'Communism'.[79] Everything was eliminated which might have offended the 'bourgeois nationalists'—but which at the same time might have sweetened the pill for the Chinese.

*

There is one other damaging consequence that must not be overlooked: the events in the Himalayas brought confusion to the ranks of the Asian Communists, and the Indian Communist Party was now split right down the middle.

Moscow's ties with the Indian CP were older and closer than that with any other CP in Asia. M. N. Roy, for decades the leading Indian Communist, had been introduced to Marxist doctrine as a young man when he met Borodin (later the China agent for the Comintern) on a visit to Mexico. He had already made a name for himself in the world Communist movement when Chinese Communism was still in its infancy. Recent studies of Moscow's relations with India's CP[80] show without a doubt how intensively Moscow had devoted itself to directing the Indian CP, and how it managed to steer it more or less intact through some difficult decades in spite of numerous abrupt changes in course.

The aggression in the Himalayas forced the Communist Party of India into a desperate quandary: should it defend the behavior of the Chinese Communists and thus fly in the face of the prevailing national mood in India? Or should it take a nationalistic stand against Red China? Since 1959 the life of the Indian CP has been haunted by this dilemma. Today one might almost speak of two Communist Parties in India: one pro-Chinese, the other nationalist and prepared to co-operate with Nehru. This latter group is led by the Party's chairman, S. A. Dange, a favorite object of Chinese attack as a 'traitor', 'revisionist', and 'fanatical national chauvinist'.[81]

When the Chinese realized toward the close of 1959 that their behavior had stiffened India's attitude rather than weakened it, they decided to isolate India in Asia and so began to adjust their relations with their other neighbors. With Nepal and Burma they concluded comparatively reasonable agreements in 1960 which settled the long-drawn-out dispute over the frontiers;[82] and the visit of the Chinese Foreign Minister Ch'en Yi to Djakarta and Sukarno's return visit to Peking in 1961 helped restore relations with Indonesia to normal.[83] The borders with the Mongolian People's Republic were determined in December 1962,[84] those with the Pakistan-occupied part of Kashmir in March 1963;[85] boundary negotiations with Afghanistan were agreed upon. The purpose of all this activity was no doubt to show the world: we Chinese can get along with everybody except the wicked Indians.

*

Of the three Communist states in Asia (apart from China) we have already dealt with Outer Mongolia (in Chapter X). We know much more about its position between Moscow and Peking than about that of the two other 'camp' states, North Korea and North Vietnam. The results of my researches on two visits to South Korea and four to South Vietnam were meager. The view, still widespread, that the North Korean Communists are Moscow puppets, no doubt applied to the first few years after 1945, but today it is no longer valid. During the Korean war the Chinese have greatly strengthened their positions in Korea, and the Koreans, like the Mongolians, realize that it can be an advantage to have two powerful neighbors who in many respects disagree. No one particularly enjoys the role of satellite, so the Number One Korean Communist Kim Il-sung is trying to maintain good terms with both neighbors—and to play off one against the other. To please the Russians he praised their new Party program,[86] and he gratified the Chinese by attacking 'revisionism'.[87] In ticklish controversial questions he has a way of not becoming involved: de-Stalinization, according to him, was an internal affair of the CPSU in which he would not interfere, and he was 'deeply concerned' over the Albanian issue—a formula with which he avoided making any clear commitment.[88] After the Cuban and Himalayan affairs, the tendency to lean a good deal closer toward Peking was to be observed in Pyongyang, but there is probably no Korean who wishes his country to become an outright satellite of China.

As for Soviet credits, the Koreans, as far as we know, have obtained nearly as much as the Mongolians—but only as to the total, not per capita, amount, for their population is twelve times as great as that of Outer Mongolia. The exact sum is not known.[89] Apart from credits, the Koreans have received goods to the tune of 1·3 billion rubles as out-and-out gifts from the USSR. Aid from China—nonrepayable amounts as well as credits—is well below that from the Soviet Union.

Like North Korea, North Vietnam borders on China and, again like North Korea, has with China's assistance waged a successful war (against France). But the Soviet Union is far away, so the chances of playing one big brother off against the other are limited. It has been calculated that 64·5 per cent of economic aid received by North Vietnam came from China; only 27·8 per cent came from the Soviet Union, and the rest from the other Soviet bloc countries.[90] This ratio should also correspond roughly to the degree of the pressures to which North Vietnam is exposed on the part of both its 'camp' comrades.

Ho Chi Minh, one of the most outstanding leaders of the Communist world, has done everything to prevent his country from coming entirely under the influence of its overbearing Chinese neighbor. Rumor has it that, during the Moscow conference of 1960, he worked more than anyone else toward a settlement between Peking and Moscow for this very reason. But he is a sick old man, and the question of his successor is closely related to his country's foreign-political orientation. There are already indications of two distinct groups: the nationalists, who look toward Moscow because only Moscow can save them from becoming a province of Red China; and the realists, as we might call them, who, although they presumably have little love for the Chinese, believe that they have no alternative but to lean heavily on their powerful neighbor.[91] Over the last few years Hanoi's political course has not run in a straight line. During the war with France and for the first few years after, it was closely linked with Peking; from 1956 on the position of the pro-Chinese wing became weaker; since 1960 it has won back much of its lost ground.[92] In the Albanian controversy Hanoi tended to support Peking's position; on the occasion of the twentieth anniversary of its Albanian brother-Party it sent congratulations and published an article which was quite flattering to Albania. North Vietnam simply cannot afford to tread on China's toes.

*

The reaction to the conflict over Albania has also shed some light on the attitude of the Communist Parties in the other developing countries toward the two rival Red powers.[93] The Indonesian CP supported China's stand.[94] The Communists in Malaya, Burma, and Thailand generally followed the Chinese line, for they are illegal and openly opposed to their governments. Moscow's attack on Albania was supported by the Parties in Ceylon, the Near East, Algeria and Morocco, and in Latin America.

One would have thought Khrushchev might have been satisfied with this result. But was he really? The stand taken by the Communist Parties in the developing countries toward his dispute with Mao merely reveals the mood and the tactical considerations prevailing among the leading Communists in those countries, men who have been closely associated with Moscow in years—in some cases decades—of co-operation. But how does the bulk of the Party members feel—and the rest of the population, to whom the Party must appeal in the case of elections?

For these nations there exist in the world today not just two models of development—the Western and the Communist—but three: the Western, the Soviet, and the Red Chinese. For the effectiveness of Communist propaganda this is, of course, a handicap. In countries with a pronounced population increase, a low standard of living, and a preponderantly peasant population, the Chinese model might exert a stronger appeal than the highly industrialized and comparatively well-to-do Soviet Union—particularly on the radicals pressing for an early revolution and rapid transition to 'socialism'. 'The Chinese are the only people in the world who really understand us', said a young Nigerian to a German journalist;[95] and the Secretary General of the Nationalist Party of Zanzibar, after returning from a trip to the Communist states, told a German visitor: 'In Peking I found the true revolutionary spirit; Moscow seemed far too complacent to me, a bourgeois society under the hammer and sickle.'[96] Perhaps it was in an attempt to eradicate this impression that in the fall of 1960 Khrushchev took off his shoe at the UN session.

*

In the treaty of Tordesillas in 1494, the great powers of the day— Spain and Portugal—divided the world between them, so as not to interfere with each other's expansion—and mission! I have asked myself whether Moscow and Peking have secretly come to a similar arrangement, but on none of my journeys did I find anything to confirm this theory. I consulted Alexander Kaznacheyev, who until the summer of 1959 worked at the Soviet embassy in Rangoon and then sought freedom, because I had been told of a remark of his to the effect that Indonesia, Burma, and Cambodia belonged to the Chinese sphere of influence, while India, Ceylon, and Afghanistan belonged to the Russian.[97] However, even in a long conversation he was unable to furnish any concrete support for his conjecture. Today I am inclined to the view that no agreement exists on a dividing line between the spheres of influence of the two Red centers.

Instead there are signs of an unnegotiated 'Tordesillas line'; instead of following longitudes it runs between the poor, underdeveloped peoples on the one side, and the industrialized, already fairly prosperous nations on the other. Among the first group, Chinese propaganda seems to be more successful than Moscow's, and in the second group vice versa. Within the Communist Parties of the developing peoples it is possible to discern a further dividing line:

that between the older cadres, who still maintain strong personal contacts with Moscow, and the younger ones, who have no such ties.

We have now seen that by early 1960 numerous differences of opinion between Peking and Moscow had accumulated. It may well be that Khrushchev's journey through South Asia was the last straw as far as China was concerned, ushering in a new phase in the relations between the two Red powers.

CHAPTER XVI

TARGET PRACTICE—WITH
LIVING TARGETS

IN THE EARLY THIRTIES I once watched, not far from Moscow, a rather unusual kind of shooting contest. The idea was to make it as realistic as possible by having one team win, not just by scoring more points, but by 'shooting down' its opponents—symbolically, at least. The two teams A and B, each consisting of six marksmen, lay side by side on the ground; opposite them, a hundred yards away, were two sets of six targets representing prone marksmen. If a member of team A, for example, hit target No. 4, marksman No. 4 of team B was considered to have been hit and had to withdraw. Only those who were not hit were allowed to continue firing, and the winning team was the one which first shot down all members of the opposing team. In other words, although they were firing at targets made of inanimate wood which were distinguished by anonymous numbers, they actually scored their 'hits' on an 'enemy' who was very much alive and not in the least anonymous. I have often been reminded of this when observing the strange game in which the ideologists of Moscow and Peking have been engaged since early 1960.

However, Peking's and Moscow's targets have been identified not merely by numbers but by terms drawn from the treasure house of Communist catchwords, such as revisionism, reformism, opportunism, dogmatism, sectarianism, and so on; but here too the shots were actually aimed, not at inanimate targets, but at rivals—rivals who were exchanging heavy fire while lying side by side in neighboring foxholes.

One of the favorite targets of the Red Chinese team was not even anonymous: it went by the name of Tito, that arch-revisionist. What was sauce for the goose was sauce for the gander: Moscow also found a non-anonymous scapegoat—he lived in the Balkans and his name was Enver Hoxha.

Another device used to convey Chinese criticism was to sing the praises of the Russian comrades but never to go beyond Lenin, or at most Stalin, just as one might pointedly praise a man's father and grandfather by saying, 'Ah, what fine fellows those were!' and pass over the man himself in pitying silence, until there is no doubt in anyone's mind as to the sad decline of the once respected family. . . .

No Synchronization of Watches

MY INTRODUCTION TO THIS SHOOTING GAME came about through rather a strange incident. While I was in New Delhi at the time of Khrushchev's visit to India—early in February 1960—I heard that K'ang Sheng had just given a remarkable speech at the recently concluded session of the Warsaw Pact conference in Moscow. In *Pravda*, however, I found the final declaration of the session[1] but no mention of this speech, let alone its text. I went to the Red Chinese embassy, where they were well prepared for my question (thus I had not been first on the scene) and promptly handed me the text.[2] When I compared it with *Pravda* I found that it varied considerably from the declaration published in the Soviet paper. What had been going on?

Judging by previous experience with Soviet bloc official functions and conferences, the story behind this incident provided sufficient indication that something was amiss. Initially there had been talk in Moscow merely of an agricultural conference, limited to the European Soviet bloc states, which was to meet on February 1. Two days later it was reported that 'invited' delegates from the Mongolian and Korean People's Republics had arrived, but two days after this the report was corrected again: the two Asian delegations were said to have come 'at their own wish'. Next it was reported that on February 2 a group of Chinese, headed by K'ang Sheng, had arrived as 'observers' to the conference of the Warsaw Pact states, which actually began on February 4. Traveling in the same plane as the Chinese, there also arrived a delegation from North Vietnam 'by invitation'. The final communiqué of the Warsaw Pact conference named three observer delegations (the Chinese, Mongolian, and Korean) without mentioning the Vietnamese.[3]

Quite a mix-up all round—especially for the protocol-minded Soviet capital. Possibly it had originally been intended for the conference to take place without the Chinese and Vietnamese, so that, when the Chinese began to show an interest, the invitation to Mongolia and North Korea was denied, and then finally the Chinese (together with the Vietnamese) were allowed to participate. However, the chief observer of the Chinese delegation, far from being of the second echelon, was one of the leading Party theoreticians, a Party member since 1924, and for a long time Party boss of his important native province of Shantung.

While the declaration of the Warsaw Pact countries faithfully reiterated the Party line which Moscow had been following since Camp David (particularly Moscow's optimism concerning the possibilities of co-existence with America where, it maintained, there were sensible people amenable to discussion), K'ang held fast to the Peking line of the unalterable wickedness of the United States and all its leaders. For those who had read Peking's and Moscow's utterances over the preceding months, these two documents contained nothing new. Their significance lies in the fact that, at the conclusion of a conference which included all the Communist bloc states, two declarations on the same subject were issued which virtually contradicted each other: on the one hand the Chinese attitude as read by K'ang, and on the other the final declaration of the eight Pact countries, which K'ang, as a mere 'observer', had not signed and from which he dissociated himself. Moreover, not one of the Pact countries published his speech.

For the first time in the recent history of the Communist movement (apart from Tito, who was no longer a member of the 'camp'), it had been found impossible to arrive at a single common denominator for one declaration. Needless to say, in accordance with the rules of this type of target practice, neither document mentioned its object of attack by name.[4]

*

The next 'exchange of shots' was begun by the Chinese in April 1960; they were warning shots, for it was just at the time when Khrushchev was getting ready for the summit conference in Paris. Peking took as its excuse the ninetieth anniversary of Lenin's birthday (April 22). Resounding salvos were delivered: an unusually long editorial in both the Peking *Red Flag*[5] and the *People's Daily*[6] (the special significance of each being stressed by the comment that they emanated from the editorial office itself), and the anniversary speech of the Party Chief of Propaganda, Lu Ting-yi.

Soon after that all the Communist bookstores in Hongkong (where I happened to be at the time) were resplendent in red; they had decked out their windows from top to bottom with copies of a book, bound in red and displaying a picture of Lenin, which had just arrived in large quantities and a number of languages, bearing the gilt-lettered title: *Long Live Leninism.*[7]

This book contained those Chinese statements made in connection with the Lenin anniversary which Peking considered especially important.

They all abounded in an impatient, aggressive revolutionary spirit; studded with numerous quotations from Lenin, they called for the struggle against all opportunists and revisionists in the camp who chattered with the enemy about compromises, cherished the disgraceful illusion that the enemy could change, and naively underestimated the danger of war.

The full significance of these Chinese documents was emphasized by their counterpart, the anniversary speech made a few hours later at the Lenin celebrations in Moscow. Even the speaker had been unmistakably chosen with Peking in mind: it was Otto Kuusinen, at that time seventy-nine years old, who had been active in the Communist movement in Lenin's days and for that reason alone could be considered better able to understand the master's teachings than the Chinese, to whom Lenin was only an embalmed figure in Red Square. In contrast to the gloomy warnings of the Chinese, Kuusinen's words were full of optimism; he aimed his shots at the dogmatists who refused to see that the prospects for building socialism would be considerably better if world war were avoided. One feature of this speech must have been particularly galling to the impatient Chinese: while looking ahead at the remainder of the century (another forty years, after all!) Kuusinen did not mention any further extension of the 'socialist camp' by the addition of new member states.[8]

So, repeating their performance at the Warsaw Pact conference, the Chinese and the Russians appeared on the scene at Lenin's birthday anniversary celebrations with diametrically opposed theses. This was the position in the days when Khrushchev was preparing for the four-man summit meeting in Paris.

*

The next shot was fired by the Russians: the Soviet shot which on May 1, 1960, brought down the United States U-2 plane over the

Urals. This hit was also a boomerang for Khrushchev in that now the whole world was aware of the embarrassing fact that US observer planes had been photographing the Soviet Union for a long while, and, what was more, from such an altitude that until then the Soviets had been unable to do anything about it.

Nothing could have suited the Chinese better. Implicit in their indignation over the American action was the sarcastic query to the Russians: now do you understand what scoundrels the Americans are?[9] But Peking's big moment really came when, contrary to Khrushchev's expectations, the President of the United States decided to assume personal responsibility for the U-2 flights.[10] From that instant on, everything Khrushchev had been saying to his colleagues in Peking in defense of his American policy must have sounded even more ridiculous to their ears. 'Some people', said Mao sarcastically to a group of foreign guests, had regarded Eisenhower as a friend of peace—he hoped they now realized the truth.[11] Thirty million Chinese were mobilized for anti-American demonstrations.[12]

Peking must have particularly resented the fact that, after Eisenhower's refusal to apologize, Khrushchev did not alter his line. On the contrary he let it be understood in Paris that, although he would never again negotiate with Eisenhower, he would do so with his successor.[13] And so the target practice went merrily on.

At a meeting of the (Communist) World Federation of Trade Unions in Peking, a few weeks after the big row in Paris, the Chinese found themselves once again talking about the inevitability of war[14] as opposed to the Russians who were defending their version of co-existence. From the published reports of the speeches we know that sharp exchanges took place, during which some of those present—a minority—sided with the Chinese, including the delegates from Japan, North Vietnam, Indonesia, Burma, Ceylon, Somalia, the Sudan, and Argentina.[15] The final resolution, however, followed the Russian line in its essentials.

Moscow's view was to be found in a detailed article in *Pravda* published—Moscow also knew its calendar of Lenin anniversaries!—in commemoration of the fortieth anniversary of the appearance of Lenin's '*Left-Wing*' *Communism, an Infantile Disorder*, and aimed at the target of 'leftist deviation' (i.e. over-hasty transition to Communism).[16] On the other hand, the existence of a letter attacking China which, according to rumor, Khrushchev was supposed to have sent during those weeks to the Communist Parties,[17] was disputed by Chou En-lai.[18]

The next verbal duel took place at the congress of the Rumanian CP held in Bucharest in June, 1960; it was the largest meeting of Communist representatives since 1957. It had obviously been Moscow's intention to take this opportunity of at last—as Khrushchev put it[19] —'synchronizing watches'. But although he gave an interesting speech in Bucharest, emphasizing his line,[20] he did not manage to bring round the Chinese, led this time by Peking's aggressive mayor and Politburo member P'eng Chen.[21] The significance of P'eng Chen's speech was withheld from the Soviet reader[22] and that of Khrushchev's speech (as of the conference as a whole) from the Chinese.[23]

It was several years before the Chinese were told Peking's version of what had happened at Bucharest. Early in 1963 the *People's Daily* stated:

It was a fact of particular gravity that late in June 1960 someone [the reader is aware by now that this 'someone' and Khrushchev are one and the same] went so far as to wave his baton and launch an all-out and converging surprise attack on the Chinese Communist Party at the meeting of the fraternal Parties in Bucharest. This action was a crude violation of the principle that questions of common interest should be solved through consultation among fraternal Parties. It set an extremely bad precedent for the international Communist movement.[24]

Thus the watches were still at variance. Intermittent skirmishing went on during the months following Bucharest. Rumors increased as to the withdrawal of Soviet experts from China. This event was probably one of the grievances the Chinese had in mind when at a much later date they wrote in their Party organ:

After the Bucharest meeting, some comrades who had attacked the Chinese Communist Party lost no time in taking a series of grave steps to apply economic and political pressure, even to the extent of perfidiously and unilaterally tearing up agreements and contracts they had concluded with a fraternal country, in disregard of international practice.[25]

The Chinese made use of the publication of the fourth volume of Mao's works (in September 1960, covering the years 1945 to 1949) to renew their sniping by quoting everything from Mao which fitted into their aggressive line,[26] and the Russians were not silent either.[27] Thus the idea of a new world conference to clarify matters under dispute acquired urgency.

*

Who initiated the choice of date (the forty-third anniversary of the Russian revolution) and of the participants (representatives of all eighty-one Communist Parties in the world) has never been revealed. No invitation to the meeting was ever published. Week after week went by with many rumors circulating. The mystery was not solved until early in December 1960: Communist newspapers all over the world published a statement, the result of weeks of deliberations.[28]

Three main features strike the observer: first, the length of the session. (There had been nothing like it since the Comintern conferences, the last of which, the seventh, met in the summer of 1935 and went on for a month.) Second, the air of mystery surrounding the session: while it was taking place it was never confirmed. (This was also in contrast to the usual practice of the Comintern, whose meetings were never kept secret and most of whose stenographically recorded speeches were published.) And third, the composition of the delegations, of which only the Soviet and the Chinese need concern us here.

The exact membership of the Soviet delegation was never announced as all the prominent Soviet leaders were in Moscow anyway. The photographs of the conference which were published in *Pravda* showed, among others, Khrushchev, Kozlov, Mikoyan, Brezhnev, Suslov, Pospelov, and Mme. Furtseva.

The Chinese delegation consisted of eleven persons.[29] Liu Shaoch'i, the Number One Chinese Communist after Mao, is as familiar to the reader as are P'eng Chen, the disputatious mayor of Peking, K'ang Sheng, who held forth at the Warsaw Pact conference in February, and Lu Ting-yi, the speaker at Lenin's anniversary celebrations. Among the remaining seven were Teng Hsiao-p'ing, Secretary-General of the CPC, and two foreign-propaganda experts (whose specialty was the developing countries). Five of the eleven had at some time or another spent fairly long periods in the Soviet Union. Missing among the top-ranking men were Mao—as Peking evidently did not want to bring up its heaviest artillery, but perhaps also because it wanted to reserve the final decision for itself—and Chou En-lai; also absent, for reasons unknown, was the ideologist and editor-in-chief of *Red Flag*, Ch'en Po-ta. Politically and ideologically, the Chinese team was just about as strong as any Mao could have sent that did not include himself.

From this composition of the Moscow and Peking delegations we may assume that both sides attached great importance to the meeting.

From the length of the discussions and the secrecy with which they were shrouded we may infer that the clash was a violent one and that its outcome was undecided up to the very last minute.

However, agreement was eventually reached, and two joint documents were published, a declaration and an 'appeal to the peoples of the world',[30] which, together with a number of commentaries in Peking and Moscow[31]—particularly a long speech of Khrushchev's early in January 1961[32]—represented a serious attempt to arrive at a compromise on the basis of discussion.

The result was a victory for the Russians. There were no doubt considerably more passages in the declaration reminiscent of earlier Soviet formulas than there were corresponding to Chinese views. Neither the people's communes—until yesterday Red China's pride and joy—nor other aspects of the Great Leap, were mentioned by so much as a word. There was nothing in the declaration to indicate that, since the late summer of 1958, Peking had been making gigantic sacrifices to pioneer a short cut to Communism for the developing countries. The Moscow thesis, according to which the 'transition to Communism' could only be achieved under conditions of abundance (still very remote even in the Soviet Union) was firmly embedded in Section II of the declaration. Such conditions were in turn only to be achieved—also one of Moscow's central theses—by the encouragement of material incentives.

In the brief paragraph devoted to China (also in Section II of the declaration) it was merely stated that China dealt a crushing blow to imperialism in Asia and gave a powerful impetus to the movement for national liberation. China appears, in alphabetical order, as one state among eleven in the paragraph listing the 'people's democratic republics'; the Soviet Union, on the other hand, is in a class by itself. It is claimed that the Soviet people are 'rapidly building up a material and technical basis for Communism', thus putting the Soviet Union far ahead of all other countries in the 'camp', including China.

China's main achievement was the sharp attack on 'revisionism', especially on Yugoslavia (Section VI of the declaration), which was to cause the Russians many a headache yet. The old formula of the 1957 Moscow declaration regarding revisionism as the principal danger was taken up once more, but, as in 1957, with the corollary that in some Communist Parties dogmatism might also become the principal danger.

*

However heated feelings may have been during the Moscow conference, as soon as it was over they subsided for the time being. The theme of the 'unshakable unity of the socialist camp' dominated the Communist press throughout the world. The weeks of argument seemed to have exhausted and sobered those taking part. Even Peking was apparently willing to learn from the resistance its aggressiveness had encountered on the part of the majority of its comrades: in an editorial in the *People's Daily* commenting on the Moscow conference, the words 'peace' and 'peaceful' appeared sixty-six times.[33]

That differences of opinion persisted, however, was revealed from time to time. Moscow, for example, welcomed the taking over of the reins of government by Kennedy, expressing its optimism in the conciliatory telegram despatched by Khrushchev on the occasion of the inauguration of the new President of the United States.[34] Peking, on the other hand, had not a single word to say in Kennedy's favor. First Mao, then Liu Shao-ch'i, announced that Kennedy was even more dangerous than Eisenhower,[35] and one Peking newspaper called him a 'hundred per cent imperialist gangster'.[36]

As a further example, the duel which had been fought a year earlier on the occasion of the ninetieth anniversary of Lenin's birth was resumed (although in a considerably milder form) in the utterances of both sides in honor of another event which had taken place ninety years previously: the founding of the 'Paris commune' in the revolution of 1871. In their commemorative articles the Chinese clearly divided the development of the modern revolution into three stages: the first was the Paris commune and revolved around Marx and Engels; the second consisted of the Russian revolutions of 1905 and 1917 led by Lenin; and the third was the Chinese revolution under Mao. Events in the Soviet Union since Lenin were not discussed, and as for Khrushchev, he was not even mentioned. In other words, the impression was encouraged—at least among Chinese readers—that the Chinese revolution represented the most modern form of revolution.[37] By contrast the Soviet commentators laid all their emphasis on the further development of the ideas of the Paris commune by the Soviet Union. In their articles no reference whatever was made to Mao.[38]

The ensuing months brought no new sensation. In such matters as Laos, Cuba, Berlin, the Congo, and the Belgrade conference, the official pronouncements of the two governments were basically in agreement, even though those of the Chinese were couched in sharper terms throughout. Moscow's decision to resume nuclear tests was applauded the very same day by the Chinese,[39] who in any event were not stinting in their praise whenever Moscow showed an aggressive front.

Meanwhile the Communist world was preparing for the Twenty-second Congress of the CPSU. At the end of July 1961 Moscow had published the draft of the new Party program[40] and thus laid it open to discussion. In Peking it was printed without comment.[41] Mao was doubtless far from pleased that in this copious document China was summarily dealt with in eleven words ('The victory of the revolution in China was of special significance'), and that he himself was not mentioned at all. Dissociation, but no open hostility—that was the position on the eve of the Party congress.

But during the very first days of the congress (it began on October 17, 1961), Peking's and Moscow's differences of opinion became fully apparent—more acutely and more publicly than ever before. We recall that, after Khrushchev, together with the entire Soviet elite, had just denounced Stalin as an evil tyrant and a murderer, Chou En-lai laid that now famous wreath, with the ribbon reading 'To the great Marxist-Leninist', at Stalin's glass coffin. And after Khrushchev, again with the entire Soviet elite, had just directed acrimonious attacks on the—absent—leaders of Albania, Peking promptly began an overwhelming campaign of praise and friendship for Albania. Chou stated from the congress platform, before his sudden departure, that the public and one-sided censure of a fraternal party did not correspond to the Marxist-Leninist view and gladdened the hearts of the enemies.[42] In an attempt to cope with this grave crisis in the Communist bloc, Peking called for a new Communist conference. It pointed out that in the previous year the declaration of the eighty-one Parties had provided for the calling of meetings for the express purpose of clearing up differences of opinion.[43]

*

The whole of 1962 went by without any such conference taking place. Instead, the open quarrel continued: first, Moscow continued to make ceaseless bitter attacks on the Albanians,[44] keeping them away from the Comecon sessions in December 1961 and June 1962, while the Chinese did everything in their power to proclaim their sympathy and solidarity with Tirana and published Albanian attacks on

Moscow in their press; and second, numerous articles were published in Moscow and Peking[45] showing a divergent evaluation of fundamental issues, in particular of the problem of co-existence.

When Moscow called a meeting of the CC of the CPSU for March 5, 1962, and at about the same time Peking announced that the National People's Congress would meet on the same day, it was expected in many quarters that a verbal battle of Homeric proportions would take place between the two Red capitals. But then the Peking meeting was postponed.

Thus Khrushchev had the stage to himself when he mounted the platform in the Kremlin on March 5. With the utmost emphasis, many quotations from 'classical works', and frequently interrupted by applause, the Soviet leader stated his view, dealing mainly with those points in which he differed from Mao.[46]

What was the Chinese answer going to be? Apparently a fight was going on at that time in Peking between the radical and the moderate wings. In February the Chinese Party cadres had conducted a verbal campaign up and down the country against Khrushchev, the 'rightist opportunist and modern revisionist', adding in each case that they were merely expressing their personal opinions. (A refugee from Red China told me this in April 1962.)[47] On the other hand, the disastrous economic situation had weakened the radical forces in the Party.

The session of the People's Congress in Peking which began on March 27, 1962, was a secret one; not even the representatives of the Soviet bloc were admitted. But when it was over (April 16), a long communiqué and the text of a resolution—which needless to say was unanimous—were issued.[48] These two documents contained the admission of a serious economic crisis. The surest sign of this was the order of economic priority established for the immediate future: first, agriculture; second, consumer goods industry; third, heavy industry.

There were other signs of Peking's low ebb: claims which the Chinese normally took every opportunity of making were absent from these documents. There was no mention of the 'unlikelihood of avoiding wars', of the urgency of 'encouraging revolutions in the developing countries', or of American 'paper tigers'.

On one point the Chinese admitted their defeat more openly in that spring of 1962. As we have seen, the Soviet leaders, who thought in terms of long-range planning, were not happy about the chaos wrought in China by its belief in the 'initiative of the masses', the continued existence of guerrilla-Communism, the neglect of 'objective possibilities' in favor of 'subjective dynamics',[49] and especially by the headlong speed. The retreat in this field was carried out by Peking in a manner which offers an amusing example of Sino-Soviet discussions during the early sixties in all their enigmatic and Aesopian nature. The *People's Daily* editorial in question seems at first sight to deal with nothing more than the regulation of the Urumchi River in Sinkiang. Perhaps it would not have occurred to anyone to connect this editorial with Peking-Moscow relations had not *Pravda* reprinted it a few days later.[50]

Since 1959 the Moscow Party organ had published very few articles from the Chinese press, and since 1960 scarcely any at all. Consequently it was bound to attract attention when it chose this particular article, which occupied almost an eighth of that day's *Pravda*, to present to the Russian public. What was so important about regulating the Urumchi? Nothing. The Urumchi was not the point: the river was only a pretext for some basic comments on the dispute between Peking and Moscow concerning the vital question of tempo. Within two paragraphs we come across the expressions 'step by step' and 'one step at a time' nine times; while 'leap', hitherto the favorite word in the Communist Chinese vocabulary, does not occur at all. Now, a step and a leap are two different forms of progression. The virtue of patience also came in for praise; great achievements, so the article said, were not accomplished from one day to the next. 'Children and grandchildren, generation after generation', must toil, and then the goal would finally be achieved. All appeals to 'subjective dynamics' were suppressed, and the importance of 'objective laws' was all the more frequently emphasized.

*

However, this period of relative Chinese meekness did not last long. For reasons unknown to us (perhaps due to a slightly improved economic situation) the Chinese pendulum was swinging back toward a tough line. The communiqué of the Chinese CC at the end of September 1962 showed that the radicals were firmly in the saddle.[51] A good deal was said there about the 'rightist opportunism' and 'revisionism' within the Party, and, while it was claimed that these wicked forces had been 'victoriously smashed' in August 1959 (when P'eng Teh-huai was dismissed from the leading group of the Party), the repeated call for vigilance indicated that this had not been quite the case. Among those promoted to membership in the CC's secretariat were two men well known as representatives of an aggressive policy, Lu Ting-yi and K'ang Sheng. It was even decided that 'the collective economy of the people's communes' was to be 'further consolidated', in spite of their failure. We must assume that the CC session also approved the plan of attacking India in the Himalayas, for on October 20, 1962, less than a month after its conclusion, war broke out on the Tibeto-Indian border. And again a few days later the Cuban crisis reached its climax.

From then on the Sino-Soviet quarrel became rapidly more heated. Now it was not just a question of what the other had said or thought, but of what he had done. And what the Chinese had done in the Himalayas was just as distasteful to Moscow as Soviet actions in Cuba had been to Peking. The congresses of some Communist Parties (normally routine affairs, but since the congress of Rumania's CP in 1960, a forum, as we have seen, for Sino-Soviet disputes) added fuel to the fury: notably those held between November 1962 and January 1963 in Sofia, Budapest, Prague, Rome and East Berlin. From one congress to the next tempers rose.[52]

It was almost always the same picture: after Moscow's representatives or ideological allies had attacked the Albanian—and by implication the Chinese—position, a Chinese speaker would climb the rostrum and blast those 'fraternal parties' which had committed the disgraceful act of abusing other 'fraternal parties' in public, in turn to be reprimanded by speakers representing the Moscow point of view. The Party congress in East Berlin finally witnessed a scene totally without precedent: the Chinese speaker's attacks on Yugoslavia and its defenders at the congress caused—to quote the *People's Daily*—'an uproar of booing, whistling and foot-stamping in the congress hall'.[53]

Yet it was during this same congress that Khrushchev finally answered in public the Chinese request for a new world conference of all Communist Parties, a request which, according to the Chinese,[54] had first been made by them on April 7, 1962. He agreed in principle on the desirability of a new big meeting of Parties, but advised against holding it 'when political passions are at the boiling point' as this might lead to a split in the world Communist movement.[55]

However, the Chinese gave no indication of being willing to let passions simmer down, and they pressed their attacks, evidently in order to force Khrushchev to agree to a world conference at which they hoped to present their case and to win the following, if not of a majority, at least of a sizeable minority of the Communist Parties, particularly of those in the developing countries. This, of course, was the very reason why Khrushchev did not cherish the idea of such a giant assembly. Instead he expressed—through *Pravda* on February 10, 1963—the Russians' willingness to meet the Chinese on a bilateral basis 'on any level and at any time'. They embodied this idea some days later in a letter from their CC to the Chinese CC which their ambassador handed to Mao on February 23, 1963. Mao agreed on March 9, 1963, and invited Khrushchev to Peking. But being well aware how difficult it would be for Khrushchev to make a fourth visit to Peking while Mao had visited the USSR only once since Stalin's death, he added:

If this is not convenient for you the CC of the CPSU can send to Peking a delegation headed by another responsible comrade, or we can send a delegation to Moscow.[56]

On March 30, 1963, Moscow in turn suggested that Mao either come to Moscow himself or send a delegation.[57] By the time it had been settled that the Sino-Soviet conference on a high (but not a summit level) was to start on July 5 in Moscow's guesthouse on Friendship Street, the observer might have thought that both sides had defined their position to their satisfaction: the Soviets principally by Khrushchev's speech of December 12, 1962,[58] and three long articles in *Pravda*;[59] the Chinese in a number of articles in the *People's Daily* and *Red Flag*.[60] But the two most violent blasts were still to come. The Chinese one, a letter summarizing in twenty-five points all the grievances which Peking felt against Khrushchev, was handed over in Moscow on June 15 and immediately published by the Chinese press.

The outraged Russians refused to print it, whereupon the Chinese proceeded to distribute it—in Russian. After expelling three members of the Chinese Embassy from the USSR (they received a heroes' welcome in Peking!), the Soviets published a lengthy counterstatement (along with the Chinese letter) in *Pravda* of July 14, accusing the CPCh of trying to split the world Communist movement and of raising the racial issue (against the Soviet Russians as 'whites'). Made public after days of futile negotiations between the Chinese delegation (in which there were, among others, Teng Hsiao-p'ing, P'eng Chen and K'ang Sheng) and the Soviet ideologists (headed by M. A.

Suslov), this Russian statement showed that the conflict had become irreconcilable, at least for the forseeable future. On the day the Chinese delegation left Moscow, Communism entered a new and unprecedented phase.

What Was It All About?

After considering the arguments of both sides I am inclined to say that the Chinese have taken the battle more seriously than their ideological opponents; their statements were more forceful and in many cases also more convincing and more logical, at least if one accepts the fact that this is a conflict between two parties both basing their positions on the tenets of Marx and Lenin. Although the economic situation of China remained precarious, the men in Peking had succeeded, by sheer drive and aggressiveness and by exploiting every weakness of their impulsive and sometimes erratic opponent, in forcing Khrushchev to argue with them from a clearly defensive position.

When we try to understand the background, the political substance, of this target practice that has been going on since 1960, the first thing to remember is that the dispute was carried on by both sides on the same ideological plane. The main issue was the interpretation of texts, of the jointly issued documents (such as the Moscow declarations of 1957 and 1960), or the 'classical works' of Marx, Engels, and Lenin. In these arguments Stalin was rarely quoted by the Chinese and never by the Russians, Khrushchev never by the Chinese—at least not by name, only in the guise of 'someone' or 'some comrades'—and Mao never by the Russians. In other words, each side ignored the existence of the head of the other side. Never for a moment, however, was the question argued of whether or not Communism was to remain the goal: it was always a matter of the correct interpretation of doctrine, of who was following it more faithfully and working hardest to make it a reality.

Actually there is nothing remarkable about this dispute. Whenever any sort of revolution reaches the stage of interpretation of doctrine, it is found that the same texts admit of widely divergent conclusions. In the same way, since the principles remain basically the same, no dramatic, mutually exclusive opposites of the oil-and-water type can be expected, but merely variations in nuance. The job is to explore these nuances and define them. The point of deviation frequently forms a minute angle; it is later that the lines may diverge so widely that often they never run parallel again.

The differences of opinion between Peking and Moscow which have been noticeable since early 1960 will be dealt with in the following pages, with the exception of those we have already examined in other contexts, such as the people's communes or the policy toward the developing countries. Stress will be laid on the earlier documents, i.e. those of 1960, because it is important to trace the earliest known beginnings of the ideological dispute. Later quotations will be given only if they add something new. But with few exceptions, cited at the end of the chapter, the arguments of 1962 and 1963 are not new: they are merely more outspoken and more vehement.

*

The quarrel among the interpreters had mainly to do with Lenin. Had the Russian and Chinese Communists sat down under normal circumstances to a quiet talk, undisturbed by heated arguments, they would no doubt soon have agreed that many of Lenin's theses from the first two decades of this century no longer apply to conditions as they exist in the seventh decade. But the circumstances were not normal; suspicion reigned on either side, and old Lenin quotations were used as arguments in basic and highly controversial questions of present-day policy.

Since 1956 the Russian stand has been an uncompromising one. At the Twentieth Party Congress Khrushchev said: 'In that period [in which Marx and Lenin lived] the afore-mentioned thesis [on the inevitability of war] was absolutely correct. Now, however, the situation has radically altered . . . war is no longer fatally unavoidable.'[61] In Bucharest Khrushchev was even more explicit. He declared:

It should not be forgotten that Lenin's propositions on imperialism were advanced and developed tens of years ago, when the world did not know many things that are now decisive for historical development, for the entire international situation. . . . One cannot mechanically repeat now on this question what Vladimir Ilyich Lenin said many decades ago on imperialism. . . . One cannot ignore the specific situation, the changes in the correlation of forces in the world and repeat what the great Lenin said in quite different historical conditions. . . . We live in a time when we have neither Marx, nor Engels, nor Lenin with us. If we act like children who, studying the alphabet, compile words from letters, we shall not go very far.[62]

The corresponding Chinese position is equally clear, especially as set out in the Lenin anniversary article in *Red Flag*:

> The present world situation has obviously undergone tremendous changes since Lenin's lifetime; but all these changes [are] far from proving that Leninism is obsolete; on the contrary . . . The modern revisionists claim that in what they call the 'new epoch', because of the progress of science and technology, the 'old conceptions' advanced by Marx and Lenin no longer apply . . . As pupils of Lenin and as Leninists, we must utterly smash the attempts of the modern revisionists to distort and carve up the teachings of Lenin.[63]

It was to the advantage of the Chinese that from the outset they were able to refer to a text to which the Russians had also put their names only a few years earlier, the Moscow declaration of 1957, in which the sentence occurs: 'Modern revisionism seeks to smear the great teachings of Marxism-Leninism, declares that it is "outmoded".'[64] Presumably it was Khrushchev himself who at that time desired the inclusion in the declaration of this sentence aimed at Tito, Nagy, and the anti-Soviet Poles, because, owing to the events which had taken place since the summer of 1956, he had lost the confidence, still shown at the Twentieth Party Congress, in his own ability to modernize the dogma. He had not foreseen that one day the Chinese would turn this very phrase against him. For the Chinese were now assuming the right, based on the 1957 declaration, to call everything 'modern revisionism' which, in their view, did not correspond to an orthodox interpretation of the dogma. Throughout the quarrel they insisted: revisionism is the main danger, while one of Khrushchev's allies, the CP of France, in a resolution of its CC in December 1962, maintained that 'latterly the danger of dogmatism and sectarianism has become the main danger'.[65] In almost all of the many instances in which the Chinese made use of the term revisionism since 1960 it was directed against Khrushchev and his ideological confederates.

*

The reader will recall the stony silence with which the Chinese reacted in the autumn of 1959 when Khrushchev reported to them on Eisenhower—who in his opinion was a very sensible man—and his negotiations with him. This silence continued until Lu Ting-yi stated in his Lenin anniversary speech:

The modern revisionists have completely betrayed the revolutionary spirit of Marxism-Leninism, betrayed the interests of the people of the world, and submitted and surrendered to the bourgeoisie and imperialism. They maintain that the nature of imperialism has changed and that imperialism has abandoned the war policy of its own accord, and that therefore there is no need for anti-imperialist struggles or revolutions. They are doing their utmost to camouflage the U.S. imperialist policies of aggression and war, to prettify imperialism and Eisenhower, the chieftain of U.S. imperialism . . . In a word, according to the modern revisionists . . . whoever persists in fighting against imperialism and in revolution is hindering peace and peaceful co-existence and is a 'rigid dogmatist'.[66]

The two sides also quarreled over the Western leaders as a whole. After Camp David, Moscow divided them into good and bad—as Khrushchev did, for example, in his statement in Peking[67] and Kuusinen in the Lenin anniversary speech.[68] Even after the summit clash in Paris, Khrushchev stated (in Bucharest):

People of sound mind—and they are in the majority even among the most deadly enemies of Communism— . . . cannot but be aware of the fatal consequences of another war.

At the same time he described Macmillan and de Gaulle as being relatively sensible people and added that even the 'thick-skulled ones' among the Americans would become sensible.[69] Mao, however, was convinced that imperialism would never alter its 'aggressive and predatory nature'.[70]

*

Feeling as they did about the US leaders, the Chinese could not understand Moscow's enthusiasm for negotiations with the enemy. The Soviet directive in this connection was contained in Kuusinen's speech. Since the founding of the Soviet State, Lenin's whole policy, according to Kuusinen, had been based on a businesslike co-operation with the capitalist states. Kuusinen went on to say:

Businesslike relations, including cultural contacts, are being established [on Moscow's initiative] between states with different social systems. The most burning questions of the international situation have, at long last, become the object of serious East-West negotiations.

The Soviet government is to be congratulated, he said, for 'cultivating personal contacts with both statesmen and public leaders of bourgeois countries'.[71]

The Chinese attacked such opinions as 'naive' and demanded (in bold type) that priority be given to the struggle of the peoples and that diplomatic negotiations should be relegated to second place.[72] They ridiculed 'persons' who are 'infatuated with the idea of summit meetings'.[73] The Russians in their turn called the aversion to negotiations with the enemy 'leftist sectarian' and attacked people who 'mistakenly regard the trend toward the creation of a peaceful co-existence between countries with different political systems . . . and negotiations between the leading politicians of the socialist and capitalist countries as a kind of deviation from the Marxist-Leninist positions', for Lenin had taught that, in the struggle with the international bourgeoisie, one must not abandon in advance the idea of agreement and compromise.[74]

*

A similar quarrel arose over the question of whether a capitalist state can make the transition to socialism peacefully, without revolutionary war. Since the Twentieth Party Congress Khrushchev had, with certain reservations, claimed that this was possible. The Chinese, on the other hand, wrote on the anniversary of Lenin's birth that only opportunists and revisionists could maintain that political power was to be achieved without revolution. With the aid of suitable quotations from Lenin they described the theory that it was possible to make a peaceful transition from capitalism to socialism as 'nonsense', 'empty talk', 'most utter stupidity', 'swindling the workers', and the chances of such a process being successful as 'extraordinarily rare'.[75]

The Russians replied with further quotations from Lenin and wrote that, since his time, in a number of states the attainment of power without civil war or armed revolt had become, thanks mainly to the existence of the Soviet Union and the Soviet bloc, 'even more likely'.[76] Here the Russians had a tactical advantage in that the Moscow declaration of 1957, to which Mao had been one of the signatories, had described the acquisition of power without civil war in 'a number of capitalist countries' as possible, and this formula had at their insistence also been included in the Bucharest communiqué. The 1960 Moscow declaration (Section III) provides for both possibilities, the peaceful and the nonpeaceful.

So Khrushchev adhered to his course of adapting ideology to the altered circumstances of the present day and was not afraid to break even more taboos: the CPSU program of 1961 declared that the dictatorship of the proletariat would lose its *raison d'être* even before the withering away of the state (second part, III), and that the CPSU had developed from the avant-garde of the proletariat to a 'Party of the entire people' (second part, VII).[77] By ignoring this newest idea of Moscow's, the Chinese let it be understood that they did not think much of Khrushchev as an ideologist. 'File it for the record', they may have said; 'it might come in handy some day as material for ideological target practice'.

In view of the frequently displayed impatience of the Chinese one could not help noticing that, among the many controversial topics, one was absent: the atom bomb. Presumably this subject was, in every sense, too explosive. But it was not necessary to mention it: it was in any event clear (at least since the interview with two German journalists in the spring of 1958)[78] that the Chinese wanted atom bombs, and it was equally clear that the Russians, who love to boast of their enormous supply of atom bombs in all shapes and sizes, had not given the Chinese a single one, a fact which doubtless did little to enhance Peking's affection for Moscow.[79]

As far as disarmament is concerned, the Chinese have in their official pronouncements supported up to a point the Soviet nuclear and disarmament policy.[80] But they did not conceal their scepticism, preferably by quoting Lenin's doctrine that 'only after the proletariat has disarmed [by force, naturally], the bourgeoisie will it be able . . . to throw all armaments on the scrap heap'.[81] The fact that they have explicitly stated they were not bound by any international disarmament agreements which might be arrived at without China[82] will not surprise anyone, nor will their scornful remark that 'the proposition of aiding so-called underdeveloped countries with money supposedly to be saved from disarmament is an illusion and deceitful nonsense', designed only 'to weaken the fighting spirit . . . against imperialism'.[83]

*

But while nothing was said about the matter of Soviet atom bombs for Red China, the dispute became that much more outspoken over another, closely related, question: whether or not a new war was inevitable. This argument also started at the Twentieth Party Congress early in 1956. In the same section of his speech in which Khrushchev described Lenin as partially obsolete, he used for the first time the phrase about war being 'no longer fatally unavoidable'.

This thesis was later included in the 1957 Moscow declaration: 'So long as imperialism exists there will always be soil for aggressive wars ... [But] at present the forces of peace have so grown that there is a real possibility of averting wars'.[84]

At the Twenty-first Party Congress Khrushchev went one step further. One has more reason now, he said, than three years ago to speak of the avoidability of war. 'Before the complete victory of socialism on earth, while capitalism continues to exist in part of the world, the real possibility emerges of banishing world war from the life of society.'[85] And a few months later: 'Only a stupid person can fail to fear war today.'[86]

Hence while the Russians referred to the second sentence in the above quotation from 1957, the Chinese took the first as their text. Their pronouncements on the anniversary of Lenin's birth contained the statement: 'Until the imperialist system and the exploiting classes come to an end, wars of one kind or another will still occur.'[87] Indeed, in the same way that Stalin, during the days of his most murderous purges, had justified his actions by saying that class warfare would increase in violence the nearer the victory of socialism approached, so the Chinese stated: 'With increasing decadence imperialism is becoming more and more wicked.'[88] Mao had always had a predilection for warlike phrases; from the year 1938 came his famous dictum that 'political power grows out of the barrel of a gun' and 'that the whole world can be remoulded only with the gun'.[89] Peking's ideologists were also fond of quoting von Clausewitz's dictum that 'war is the continuation of politics by other means' which Lenin had taken over from the German general of the Napoleonic era.[90] Again following Stalin's example, but in contradiction of Khrushchev, the Chinese refused to admit that the basic principles of war had been altered by the emergence of nuclear arms.[91] The Russians in turn quoted, not Lenin because no such quotation could be found among his sayings, but at least his widow: Lenin had, so she claimed, spoken of the day when, on account of its destructive power, war would render itself impossible.[92]

Thus two viewpoints stood in direct opposition: the Russian (since the Twenty-first Party Congress)—that war was avoidable before imperialism came to an end; and the Chinese—that it was unavoidable until imperialism came to an end. In order to cut the ground from under the Chinese objections, supported as they were by Lenin quotations, Khrushchev stated that of course it was true that imperialism would not change its wicked nature but that, in comparison to the 'socialist camp', it was getting weaker and weaker and thus less dangerous. In Bucharest he used this comparison:

It is common knowledge that a wolf is just as bloodthirsty a beast of prey as a lion or a tiger, although he is much weaker. That is why man fears less to meet a wolf than a tiger or a lion. Of course, small beasts of prey can also bite, essentially they are the same but they have different possibilities, they are not so strong and it is easier to render them harmless.[93]

*

As the year progressed, however, Peking embarked on a distinction in the use of the word 'war'. At the conference of the World Federation of Trade Unions, which took place in June 1960 in Peking, the Chinese delegate stated that it was necessary to distinguish between different kinds of wars. As for world war (which he did not define in detail), there was a possibility of preventing it, although the danger that the imperialists might cause one must always be borne in mind. But as for other wars, particularly between the oppressed peoples and the imperialists, it was mistaken, he said, to speak of them as being avoidable.[94]

The reasons for this difference of opinion are not far to seek. An article in *Pravda* clearly stated Moscow's view: in the first place, militant speeches made by Communists would assist the imperialists in spreading lies about the alleged aggressiveness of Communism and hence would damage its cause. Second, 'leftist sectarian views' of that kind 'would have a demoralizing effect on the builders of the new society'; for these builders would then ask: 'To what purpose are we building, working, creating, if it is already a foregone conclusion that all the fruits of our labors will be destroyed in the whirlwind of a war?'[95] In other words: the 'builders of the new society' —i.e. the inhabitants of the Soviet Union—would be unfavourably influenced in their willingness to work and their loyalty to the State if there were a serious threat of war; hence the people should not be unnecessarily alarmed.

The Chinese took the opposite point of view. Their speaker at the Trade Unions Congress said it was dangerous to keep talking so optimistically about the avoidability of war, because this gave rise to a feeling of false security and the risk was then run of falling victim to confusion at the moment of danger. 'The spreading of such illusions about imperialism . . . will lead to evil consequences of a serious nature and, in fact, we can already see such consequences at present.'[96]

A Chinese youth journal became even more explicit in connection with a letter from a reader who had said: if the socialist camp was getting stronger and stronger, and the imperialist camp weaker and weaker, there would be no war; why, then, this constant tension and excessive work tempo? The journal called the writer of this letter a revisionist and asked him indignantly how he could dare maintain there would never be another war since he was after all not the American chief of staff? The article said among other things: 'What you call "tension" is nothing but the normal law of evolution of a mass revolution.'[97] Here again we have the idea of the 'permanent revolution'.

For Peking a lessening of anxiety and tension was tantamount to falling asleep at the wheel, indeed to a betrayal of the Chinese revolution. Hence the Chinese leaders wanted to fan the flames of a militant atmosphere—both at home and abroad—as high as they would go.

Early in 1961, in an address to prominent Party ideologists, Khrushchev defined his views on war somewhat more closely, distinguishing among three kinds. First, world wars: of those he said, 'We can avoid them.' Second, local wars: although these might break out in the future it was possible, he said, for the 'socialist camp' to extinguish fires of this kind immediately, as witness the Suez war. (Khrushchev's claim for the significance of Moscow's warning to the swift termination of the Suez incident is highly exaggerated; what is important for us here is the fact that he used it as an argument.) Third, national wars of liberation: wars of this kind are unavoidable, he said, as long as there are imperialists, since the latter refuse to hand over their colonies voluntarily; national wars of liberation are justified as, for instance, the war of the Algerians, which Khrushchev called a 'holy war'. The Soviet Union had supported wars of this kind and would continue to do so.[98]

What Khrushchev had to say on this third category came close to the Chinese view; but the emphasis remained different. To the Chinese the avoidability of a world war seemed by no means as certain as it did to the Russians, and above all they felt that in practice the Soviet Union was a long way from according the 'national wars of liberation' the support desired by Peking. They were prepared all along the line to run far greater risks in world politics. In the age of the nuclear balance of power, states which possess no nuclear arms can afford a greater display of bravado than those who do have them and who, when it comes to a showdown, would have to use them.

*

The destructive force of a new war was also something which Moscow and Peking saw in different lights. The Russians painted it in darker colors. Malenkov had already said that a new war meant 'the destruction of world civilization',[99] and on this point Khrushchev's ideas were not very different when, for instance, he said: 'Millions of people might burn in the conflagration of hydrogen explosions.'[100] In the fall of 1960 the Moscow journal *Kommunist* contained the following passage:

> A world war with nuclear weapons would know practically no distinction between the front and the area behind the lines; it would lead to complete annihilation of the principal centers of civilization and to the destruction of entire nations and would bring immeasurable disaster upon all mankind.[101]

And in January 1961 Khrushchev said: 'We know that the first to suffer in the event of war would be the working people and their vanguard—the working class.' Referring to the estimates of an American scientist he stated that, of the thousand million people living in the area most likely to be affected, half to three quarters would be likely to perish within sixty days.[102] In other words, there can be no question of only the inhabitants of the Western world perishing while those of the Communist bloc gaily assume their inheritance.

Here again the Chinese were of a different opinion: as early as the summer of 1958 Tito referred in a speech to a remark (never admitted in China) by an (unnamed) Chinese statesman to the effect that, even if a nuclear war should destroy three hundred million people, the Chinese People's Republic would still be left with three hundred million people.[103] Officially, when they referred to a nuclear war, the Chinese Party ideologists always spoke only of the destruction of the enemy, as for instance:

> If the U.S. or other imperialists . . . should dare to . . . launch a war using atomic and nuclear weapons, the result will only be the very speedy destruction of these monsters themselves . . . and certainly not the so-called annihilation of mankind.[104]

The cynical expression 'so-called annihilation of mankind'—clearly aimed at Moscow's declarations—is significant and reveals a moral callousness which, although it also exists among Russian Communists, is usually less blatant.

Obviously hinting at Moscow's warnings about a new war, Lu Ting-yi said in his Lenin anniversary address:

> The modern revisionists are panic-stricken by the imperialist policy of nuclear-war blackmail. They develop from fear of war to fear of revolution, and proceed from not wanting revolution themselves to opposing other people's carrying out revolution.[105]

And after Bucharest a Chinese general attacked the modern revisionists who exaggerate the destructive consequences of nuclear war and beg the imperialists for peace at any price.[106] There was no reason to be afraid of war: that was the lesson which was emphasized over and over again in the articles marking the publication of the fourth volume of Mao's works.[107] The Kremlin, however, according to the slant of this whole polemic, had betrayed the cause of the revolution because it was afraid of a war.

After Cuba particularly, the Chinese enjoyed showing up their Soviet comrades to be fundamentally cowards who stressed the horrors of nuclear war in order to cloak the fact that they were panic-stricken. When Khrushchev reminded the Chinese that it was all very well to call America a paper tiger, but one should not forget that, after all, it was a paper tiger with nuclear teeth,[108] the Chinese scornfully retorted:

> No matter what kind of teeth imperialism may have . . . its rotten, decadent and paper-tiger nature cannot change. . . . Those who attack the proposition that 'imperialism and all reactionaries are paper tigers' have obviously lost every quality a revolutionary ought to have and instead have become as short-sighted and timid as mice.[109]

They even called the 'logic of survival' in an atomic age, which the Russians had invoked, the 'logic of slaves'.[110] The highest, or rather lowest, point in the Chinese discussion of war and peace was this vision of the glorious consequences of a nuclear war:

> On the debris of imperialism, the victorious people would create very swiftly a civilization thousands of times higher than the capitalist system and a truly beautiful future for themselves.[111]

The horrified echo called forth in the world by these perverted words by an unnamed writer in *Red Flag* provoked counterstatements on the part of the Russians: 'Only madmen and maniacs can now call for another world war,' said Khruschhev in Bucharest.[112] *Pravda* and *Kommunist* wrote:

> Mankind would face tremendous difficulties should it try to erect the new social system on the ruins of a military disaster.[113]
>
> The working class has no thought of building the Communist civilization on the ruins of the world's cultural centers, on an earth laid waste and contaminated by thermonuclear fall-out.[114]

But the Chinese blandly maintained that they were speaking only of the ruins of imperialism, not the ruins of mankind—still clinging to the illusion that nuclear war would destroy only the enemy.[115]

These contrasting views might well be used to demonstrate the Marxist thesis of the dependence of thinking on the social circumstances of the thinker. The inhabitants of the Soviet Union, who have begun more and more to enjoy the pleasures of prosperity and have moved by the million into their long-awaited new flats, look at the prospect of a destructive war in quite a different light from the Chinese, the majority of whom have little more to lose than their harassed and unhappy lives.

*

There was only one new point which the angry exchange of pot-shots in the winter of 1962–3 added to the three-year-old dispute, and it was new in degree rather than in kind: the attempt to discredit the Soviet Union's and particularly Khrushchev's claim to leadership in the 'camp'.

In this book we have refrained throughout from guesswork. When questions have arisen to which we do not know the answer, instead of replying by speculation we have preferred to leave them open. Among these open questions is that of the personal relationship between the two dictators—between Mao and Khrushchev. It may well have been true that after Stalin's death Mao preferred the hard-hitting Khrushchev to the more ambiguous Malenkov, and that, vice versa, in 1957 he had less confidence in Khrushchev, who was experimenting (not very convincingly) with a new course, than in the old Stalinist Molotov, but we cannot be certain.

However, there is a great deal to indicate that, especially since Khrushchev's visit to Peking in the fall of 1959, the two men are far more inclined to mutual feelings of suspicion and dislike than to those of affection and respect. Apart from the stock phrases used on special occasions, neither Khrushchev nor Mao has had a good word for the other, and what Peking had to say lately about the revisionists, and Khrushchev about the dogmatists, was highly uncomplimentary. Moreover, the practically undisguised Chinese attacks on the Soviet leader were directed not only at his ideological stand: they also lashed out at him personally, pointing to his erratic behavior and speaking of 'the irresponsible self-contradictory statements made by the leader of a Party who talks this way one day and that way the next', calling the behavior at the Party congress of East Berlin, where Khrushchov was the dominant figure, 'extremely vulgar',[116] and claiming that a fellow who overestimates the significance of atomic weapons is 'scared out of his wits'.[117]

Khrushchev's public pronouncements were not aimed at Mao personally, but there was a good deal of personal venom in his attacks on the Chinese, as is shown by a story he told in one of his speeches in December 1962.[118] He recalled an experience from his youth when he lived in a miners' settlement. There had been some perverse types there who took a delight in teaching obscene expressions—in which the Russian language abounds!—to little boys who had barely learned to talk. They told the children to go home and say these words to their mothers, and for this they were promised a few kopeks. 'Well', Khrushchev went on, 'the Albanian leaders are behaving just like those silly kids. Someone has taught them these foul expressions and now they are going around shouting rude words at the CP of the Soviet Union which, after all, is their mother! For this they are paid the promised three kopeks, and if they think up still dirtier words they are given a bonus and praised.'

The full text of Khrushchev's address was printed in millions of copies, and every reader knew who the 'someone' was who was praising the Albanians and reprinting their vituperations against Moscow. It is hard to see how Khrushchev could have shown his violent aversion to Chinese leadership more clearly than by comparing it to these perverted louts.

*

In trying to discredit Khrushchev, the Chinese of course tried to discredit the Soviet claim to leadership. For this purpose they took up the familiar accusation of 'great nation chauvinism', exemplified in Moscow's attitude toward Albania and thus aimed unmistakably at Khrushchev.[119] They insisted that all 'fraternal Parties are equal', from which they argued that the Albanians had the 'full and equal right' of publicly answering the accusations publicly made against them by the Soviets. They also denied Moscow the right to expect that other Parties follow its lead:

> No one has the right to demand that all fraternal Parties should accept the theses of any one Party. No resolution of any congress of any one Party can be taken as the common line of the international Communist movement or be binding on other fraternal Parties.[120]

This was obviously directed against Moscow's claim that Tirana was wrong because it did not follow the course of de-Stalinization adopted by the CPSU at its Party congresses of 1956 and 1961. The Chinese claimed

> that the only common principles of action which can have binding force on us and on all other fraternal Parties are Marxism-Leninism and the common documents agreed upon by the fraternal Parties [i.e. the declarations of the Communist Parties assembled at Moscow in 1957 and 1960], and not the resolutions of the congress of any one fraternal Party, or anything else.[121]

At the same time Peking lashed out against those 'fraternal Parties' which had accepted Moscow's lead, notably those of Italy, France, and the United States.[122] Here they introduced a new term: the baton. Some 'fraternal Parties', Peking said, 'suddenly changed their stand' and made 'complete turns of 180 degrees' whenever 'a foreign comrade' (easily identified as Khrushchev) raised 'the baton'. Following the baton of Moscow 'unconditionally' is, so the Chinese say, indicative 'of abnormal, feudal, patriarchal relationship. . . . Here there is all too much ability to parrot and all too little of Marxist-Leninist principle.'[123] The same article in *Jen-min Jih-pao* reminds the French Communists of their 'glorious revolutionary tradition', urging them to return 'to the revolutionary principles' of the declarations of 1957 and 1960, and thus in fact telling them to rebel against their Moscow-oriented leadership.

What all this means is quite clear: Peking is trying to win over as many Parties as possible to its way of thinking, and where it cannot win over the leadership it is trying to isolate this leadership from the bulk of the members. There are now two factions in the world Communist movement, and the conflict is being felt in many, if not most, Communist Parties. Whether Khrushchev's Russian opponents are conspiring with Peking, we do not know, but the downfall of Marshal P'eng Teh-huai in the summer of 1959 has been interpreted as a result of too close relations with Moscow,[124] and it may well be that the carriers of 'revisionist ideas in the Party' who were condemned in the CC communiqué in Peking in September 1962[125] were the 'Khrushchevists' of China.

But the Chinese know that for the time being they are still a long way away from the day when they will command a majority at a Communist world conference, if they ever reach that point at all. So they belittle the majority which Khrushchev now has:

Anyone with some common sense knows that such questions as who is right and who is wrong, and who has truth on his side, cannot be determined by who is in the majority or minority at a given moment. . . . Being in the majority at a given moment after all cannot turn falsehood into truth; being in the minority at a given moment cannot after all make truth turn into a falsehood.

They then go on to explain that at a certain period in history 'Lenin and the Bolsheviks were in the minority in the international workers' movement, but truth proved to be on the side of Lenin and the Bolsheviks'.[126] From this it was only a step virtually to identify Lenin with Mao, and Lenin's arch-enemy, the revisionist Karl Kautsky with Khrushchev.[127] This amounted to the indication of a possible split within the 'international workers' movement', like that which occurred when Lenin broke with the socialists of his time, leading to the establishment of his own party and international organization.

Mao's World and Khrushchev's

NO DOUBT KHRUSHCHEV assessed the actual power relationship more soberly and accurately than Mao. Although the Chinese have been credited more than any other people with the faculty of patience, Mao was far less patient than Khrushchev, indeed even than Stalin. It is true that the Bolsheviks had already turned Marxist doctrine upside down by anticipating the dictatorship of the proletariat in Russia, one of the least industrialized countries in Europe, a country which had barely reached the capitalist stage. Subsequently, with the aid of forced manual labor and large-scale imports of machinery (financed by the brutal exploitation of the people) they built up an adequate industrial foundation (which gave rise to the creation of the super compulsory state instead of a democratic socialism). But Mao outdid even this tour de force by trying, in one of the least industrialized countries in the world to create the economic basis for Communism even more swiftly than in Russia and by means of an even more flagrant exploitation of the peasantry. The much-vaunted Maoism can, I believe, best be explained as an intensified Stalinism: a people even poorer than the Russian is to be even more rapidly industrialized by even greater efforts.

Hence in our résumé of the conflict of the years since February 1960 we arrive at a conclusion similar to that reached in our study of the Great Leap and the people's communes: Stalin had tried to ennoble his deviation from the Marxist doctrine with his theory of the 'revolution from above', by claiming for himself, as interpreter and executor of the laws of evolution, the right to order from above the forced completion of developments which had not yet matured from below. Mao's deviation went even further: it culminated in the trend to give subjective will priority over objective possibilities.

The Russians were obviously finding it more and more difficult to recall their own situation during the twenties and to put themselves in the position of the Chinese. Moreover, as a result of their successes they now really believed that their increasing economic power (plus nuclear weapons in the background) would enable them to bring about the transition to socialism in the rest of the world 'without the use of force'; at the very least, they were convinced they could help their cause and that of Communism by appearing before the rest of the world in the garb of 'peaceful co-existence'. They had no objection, either, to banging the table now and again with their fist—or their shoe, but they wished to be the ones to decide when to smile and when to bang. It annoyed them when all of a sudden someone else turned up and started banging on his own—in the Straits of Formosa, for example, or in the Himalayas; and they said so.

*

There was a time—until the autumn of 1961—when some Western observers tried to explain these public disputes as a put-up job, with allotted roles, the aim being the utter confusion of the true opponent, the West. But this theory has by now lost all credibility and need no longer concern us. The confusion created by the quarrel must be far greater in their own, the Communist, ranks. In the spring of 1963 the Chinese themselves openly stated that for a long time they had 'made Yugoslav revisionism the target of the struggle' [rather than

Moscow itself] because they 'set store by unity'.[128] This disposes of the question: did the Chinese really mean the Russians when they attacked the Yugoslavs?

The question still remains, however, of why the two centers of Communism decided to fight it out in the open. One can assume that the Chinese gradually lost patience, when all their efforts to persuade Khrushchev to change his policy—for instance, during his visit to Peking on his return from Camp David—had been in vain. What alternative did they, the temporarily weaker partners of the alliance, have but to raise their voice so that all could hear? In February 1960 (at the conference of the Warsaw Pact states) they undertook this with a certain measure of discretion, but when this still had no effect and Khrushchev unconcernedly continued on his course toward the new—Paris—summit, they decided to use the ninetieth anniversary of Lenin's birth to unleash a public bombardment of their partner's ideological positions.

An American expert on Eastern affairs has suggested a plausible explanation for this behavior: the unity of the 'camp' is its greatest asset; hence a rupture represents a serious danger to all its members. Thus when the weaker partner makes it clear to all and sundry that there are some things which to him are more important than unity, and that if necessary he is prepared to sacrifice this unity, he exerts the greatest possible pressure on the stronger partner, like a black-mailer when he threatens the life of a hostage particularly dear to his victim.[129]

For the public record, of course, the Chinese claim, as we have seen, that it was the Russians who first 'exposed the differences before the enemy', by their behavior in China's conflict with India in 1959.[130]

Since the demonstration at the Lenin anniversary celebrations, Peking has openly disputed the monopoly of its Moscow comrades to interpret the doctrine, until it finally came to maintain that they were completely wrong in their interpretations. As time went on the Chinese became increasingly eager to bring the debate into the open; they even published a number of speeches and articles by foreign Communists who were hostile to Peking's point of view, including even Khrushchev's speech about the perverted young miners,[131] and ridiculed the Soviets for not daring to publish the Chinese attacks against them by saying:

As cowardly as mice, they are scared to death. They dare not let the people of their own countries read our articles, and they have tried to impose a watertight embargo. They are even using powerful stations to jam our broadcasts and prevent their people from listening to them.[132]

Thus a somewhat dangerous situation has developed for Moscow. Since Lenin's rise to power, disputes on matters of ideology in the Communist sphere have at the same time been disputes over the leadership and hence over power. In a chiliastic world movement, ideological leadership is bound to fall to whoever can convince the others that he holds the key to paradise; within the Communist bloc, this alone endows its holder with a legitimacy comparable to that of inherited succession in a ruling house.

Moscow's position of leadership, until recently unchallenged, was thus exposed to extreme danger. It was faced with the possibility that other members of the bloc would desert it and turn to the younger, more radical rival, and that its supporters in the Communist Parties —both in and outside the 'camp'— would be replaced by 'Maoists'. For this reason Khrushchev had to accept the challenge and to proceed from the still fairly restrained disapproval of the people's communes to increasingly open criticism. His language had to be so unmistakably clear that everyone knew: a flirtation with Mao and his ideas would be regarded by the Kremlin as a serious affront.[133] This accounts for the fury with which Khrushchev fell on the Albanians; this accounts for the cold determination with which he let the Chinese starve for years without supplying them with a single ton of grain.

PROSPECTS AND CONCLUSIONS

WE HAVE NOW REACHED THE THRESHOLD beyond which lies the unknown future. The trends which emerged from our study of the past and present do not stop at this threshold but, as far as the future is concerned, we can only trace them as possibilities, at best as tendencies. What curves the graph of relations between Peking and Moscow will follow, by what as yet undisclosed factors it will be influenced, we cannot foresee. The whole world has now become a web of interlocking causes and effects.

The reader will not expect an analysis based on reflection and sober appraisal to end in speculations which nurture the widespread euphoria of the affluent mentality, or alternatively confirm the gloomy prognoses of a fashionable pessimism. The storming of the British Crown Colony of Hongkong in 1962 by masses of starving Chinese was greeted by some as a harbinger of the disintegration of the Red Chinese imperium, but, although we cannot overlook the possibility of something of this nature happening, it must not be forgotten that, as the history of the last few decades has shown, the Soviet State has overcome similar crises without the regime collapsing or the infinitely long-suffering population being forced by desperation to revolt. The Chinese are second to none in the passive virtue of suffering, of bending before the storm, and there is no reason to believe that Mao is any more soft-hearted than Stalin was, or that he would allow himself to be swayed by the plight of starving millions.

The Great Leap of 1958, instead of leading directly to Communism, did, it is true, result in a still unresolved crisis and compelled Peking to slow down its headlong pace. But here again the Soviet example should be a warning to us not to interpret the tactical adjustment of a Communist regime to temporary realities as a change of strategy, let alone an abandonment of the goal, as Western observers once did when Lenin proclaimed his New Economic Policy

449

after the civil war. This was followed in a very few years by total collectivization. It remains to be seen whether, as a result of disappointments, the same view will triumph in Peking which dominated Stalin's economic policy after the thirties and which, notwithstanding all Peking's censure, is still upheld by Khrushchev: namely, that the building up of even a total state economy is impossible without the personal incentive provided by a wage system based on performance, without a certain measure of private life for the people, and that the prospect of an ant society is the last thing to encourage joyful co-operation among the masses. If Chinese are today compared to ants, this is merely a reflection of the consequences of Mao's Communism, and not of their true nature and aspirations.

Since Stalin's death Moscow, being well aware of these problems, has embarked on a trend which, all of us hope, is irreversible. First of all, the new, highly stratified and diversified upper class has no desire to gamble with its privileges, and even the dynamic Khrushchev recommends himself to the Soviet masses by holding out the prospect of more cars, more homes, more freedom, and more vacations—one might even say he offers the Western slogan: Prosperity for All! In the USSR this has entailed far-reaching changes in the political style; an intensely industrialized and hence highly complicated State can no longer be governed by primitive methods of terror.

But China? No one will believe that the militant spirit of guerrilla-Communism is dead; nor has the patriotic fervor abated, the enthusiasm which won Mao, the liberator, the devotion of large sections of the population, regardless of the disappointment felt by the bulk of the Chinese at the effect of Communism and regardless of how they may hate it today in many of its manifestations. And the economic difficulties, which contributed largely to the decision to make the Great Leap, have only increased during the last few years. Although it is impossible to obtain a reliable picture of the country's present economic situation, Peking in recent years having published almost no production figures, one has only to look on the one hand at the widespread famine, the throttling of machinery imports, the forced resettlement of peasants who had migrated to the towns, and on the other at the avalanche of population increase (amounting annually to an average of something like ten million), to see that China's per capita production today lags far behind its minimum requirements.

The problem of tempo, therefore, has become still more acute for the Chinese leaders, and the temptation to solve it by a relentless forward thrust through the bottleneck of the early stages of industrialization has become even stronger.

Timing has become the crucial issue of the Sino-Soviet controversy. In an obvious allusion to an earlier wish expressed by Khrushchev that Moscow and Peking should synchronize their watches, the Chinese coldly stated: 'There are *two* watches' (author's italics), adding ominously: 'Which is to be the master watch?'[1] Which indeed? That is the question.

And even the champions of a more moderate policy in Peking will have doubts—since they are Communists—about recommending the only sure way to extricate the country from dire straits: the liberation of the peasants. No matter which of the Communist wings triumphs, China has still a long way to go before it reaches the level attained by the Soviet Union at Stalin's death, a point, that is to say, at which the Soviet State made the transition from the era of total absolutism to that of an 'enlightened absolutism', to the era of Khrushchev. Thus we must assume that the further development of the *Chinese revolution*, regardless of whether it be fast or slow, will continue to affect relations between Peking and Moscow.

The problem of the advance or retrogression of *world revolution* also gives rise to differences of opinion between the two Red capitals. It is conceivable that they will agree on an acceptable line for both sides; but it is inconceivable that the Chinese will abandon their efforts to create, within the world Communist movement, their own position of power and a majority at future international Communist conferences. It is not the first time that proclaimers of the same faith have disagreed in their attempts to demarcate their 'mission fields'. In view of the relative stability and great strength of the industrial West, it is in the developing countries that the two Red rivals' efforts at proselytization and expansion meet and clash. The Chinese exploit to the utmost the tactical advantage of being able to present themselves as brothers and comrades to the peoples of Asia and Africa—and perhaps even the non-white sections of the Latin American countries—more easily than the delegates from the Soviet Union, who cannot quite rid themselves of the taint of their European origin or, propaganda notwithstanding, the odium of an imperialist past—and present!

We are reminded of the tale of the two shoemakers: one, the more influential of the two, displayed a sign boasting: 'Best Shoeshop in the Whole World!' But his neighbor stole his thunder with his more modest sign, which read: 'Best Shoeshop in this Street!' Today Peking is also trying to gain an advance on Moscow in its 'street', although the latter is more powerful in the 'whole world', by appealing specifically to the peoples of non-European origin.

The effects of this global rivalry cannot be predicted with certainty. But one thing we do know: the relationship between the two great powers in the Red camp has passed beyond the stage in which the master can guide the pupil, in which the stronger element can keep the weaker one in a state of permanent dependence through economic, political, and military superiority. It has entered upon its dialectic phase, resembling the relationship of the two political and spiritual centers of Rome and Byzantium in the late classical period and Middle Ages, or that of England and its former colony North America, although, needless to say, Peking and Moscow will persist in their efforts to find a common line in order not to jeopardize the ultimate goal by a breach.

In our family we have been telling the story for years of a little boy who, after being urged over and over again to love the cousin he was constantly quarreling with, finally promised to do so, but added: 'I only love him because I must.' I know of no more apt way of expressing the present, and probably future, relationship of Mao to Khrushchev—and vice versa. Never again will relations between the Red neighbors be undialectic and uncomplicated. Most of the causes of tension set out in this book will continue to have effect (even— and, as far as the border problem is concerned, especially—if Mao's regime should be swallowed up in chaos). The Russians have to reckon with this fact just as much as the Western leaders. It will continue to remain a cardinal theme of world politics, the more so as the number and variability of the factors determining the relations between the Red partners make it unlikely that a firm, mutually agreed line of any duration will ever be established.

*

How, then, can and should the West behave? Ought it to offer Khrushchev—or Mao?—a price sufficiently high to induce him to split up with his partner? The fixing of such a bounty would be enough to cause serious tension among the governments of the West, and the payment of it would strengthen the hand of the recipient to an extraordinary degree. Nor would the reward alone be enough to induce one of the two allies to break with the other; at best it might act as an additional incentive if a breach had already been decided upon. But such a decision would presuppose that one of the two had written off the common goal of world Communism and was prepared to share the world with the 'monopoly capitalists' of the West rather than with the Communist rival.

Among the conflicts known to have taken place within the Red alliance, not one has been caused by the actions of a third power. They all arose from contradictions and conflicting interests *within* the alliance. There will certainly be no lack of conflicts of this kind in the future. Once they have arisen, they can be intensified or mitigated by a calculated policy on the part of the West, by deliberate action—or refraining from action—above all in the area of the developing countries, where the interests of the West, Moscow, and Peking overlap. The closer China comes to possessing its own nuclear weapons, the more frequent might be the instances of joint interests between the Soviet Union and the West, especially the United States.

Of more lasting effect, however, on the relations between the two Red powers than even the most active policy on the part of the West would be the continuous manifestation of the West's own strength. Should it show itself to be weak, undecided, and disunited, it would confirm Mao's image of it as a 'paper tiger'. This would remove one of the most serious differences of opinion between Peking and Moscow, and one could then await the day when the two Red powers would combine to overthrow the 'decadent West' and divide up the globe between them. It is up to us to keep the Moscow rulers on the path of a realistic assessment of Western strength and thus of *true* co-existence, and gradually to force them away from their pernicious idea that 'co-existence' is nothing but a new and highly advantageous method of conducting a cold war.

*

I have spent many happy years in Russia and China and have felt at home among the Russians and the Chinese. But as a European I felt closer to the old Russia than to the old China, and even the establishment of a similar regime over both countries could not alter these natural ties. That the overwhelming majority of the Soviet population feels a greater sense of kinship with the non-Communist Europeans and Americans than with the Communist Chinese, I am quite certain. Perhaps one day even the men in the Kremlin will realize that they are more closely linked to the West by their European origin than to China by Communism.

In the long run, however, in the 'one world' of today, the significance of racial and national divisions is bound to decrease. All the more reason, then, for us to offer the Russian and Chinese people an alternative way of life so that, once able to envisage a different prospect, they will realize that they are not totally and forever at the mercy of their Red rulers.

Yet it is not enough to preach an alternative way of life: it must be lived. That is why in China's case it is so important whether Taiwan flourishes or stagnates, whether its neighbor Japan carries on its upsurge of recent years (truly a 'great leap') or sinks into unemployment and poverty; whether in the Philippines, India, and Pakistan the graphs of contentment and order go up or down.

In the final analysis it all depends on whether the West succeeds in developing its own way of life to the point where its spiritual freedom and richness, its social justice, its assured prosperity, its willingness to assist other nations, its moral standards and its tolerance, will one day exert an irresistible attraction on all the peoples of the earth, including those of China and the Soviet Union.

NOTES

Part 1: PEOPLES

INTRODUCTION

1 Felix M. Keesing, *Cultural Anthropology* (New York 1958), pp. 34 f.
2 Riencourt, *Soul*, pp. xviii, 216, 250
3 Moraes, *Report*, p. 21
4 Chiang Kai-shek, *Soviet Russia in China; a Summing-Up at Seventy* (New York 1957), p. 349

Chapter I: THE MAN

1 Hsu, *Americans*, p. 10
2 Yang Lien-sheng, 'The Concept of Pao as a Basis for Social Relations in China', in Fairbank, *Thought*, pp. 303 f.
3 M. Mead, quoted by Gerhard Piers and Milton B. Singer, in *Shame and Guilt* (Springfield, Ill. 1953), p. 50
4 Ruth Benedict, *The Chrysanthemum and the Sword* (Boston 1956), pp. 222 f.
5 Francis Hsu, 'Suppression versus Repression', in *Psychiatry*, XII, No. 3 (August 1949), p. 223
6 A detailed discussion is contained in Piers and Singer, see note 3
7 Weakland, 'Organization', pp. 361–70
8 Lucian W. Pye, 'Communist Strategies and Asian Societies', in *World Politics* (October 1958), pp. 118–27
9 Hsu, *Americans*, p. 118
10 Lin Yutang, *The Little Critic*, Vol. I (Shanghai 1936), p. 88
11 Hsu, *Americans*, p. 358
12 Mencius, III/2, Ch. IX/9
13 Creel, *Chinese Thought*, p. 82
14 *All Men Are Brothers*, translated by Pearl S. Buck (New York 1933)
15 Moraes, *Report*, p. 19
16 Hsu, *Americans*, p. 379
17 Abegg, *Ostasien*, p. 255
18 Arthur H. Smith, *Chinese Characteristics*, 15th ed. (Edinburgh, London), p. 29

455

19 Hsu, *Americans*, p. 100
20 *Ibid.*, pp. 10, 52–65
21 *Ibid.*, pp. 25, 37
22 Lin Yutang, *Country*, p. 159
23 *Dream of the Red Chamber*, translated by Chi-chen Wang (New York 1958)
24 Hsu, *Americans*, pp. 349 f.
25 R. H. van Gulik, *Sexual Life in Ancient China. A Preliminary Survey of Chinese Sex and Society from ca. 1500 B.C. till 1664 A.D.* (Leiden 1961), 392 pp.
26 Arthur Koestler, *Von Heiligen und Automaten* [Of Saints and Automata] (Berne-Stuttgart-Vienna 1961), pp. 116 f., 169 f.
27 Wolfgang Franke, 'Die Rolle der Tradition im heutigen China' [The Role of Tradition in Modern China], in *Moderne Welt*, III (1961–2), No. 2, p. 150
28 Chin, *A Study*, pp. 11 f.
29 Eberhard, *Geschichte* [History], p. 31
30 *Das Geheimnis der Goldenen Blüte* [The Secret of the Golden Blossom. Translated into German with commentary by Richard Wilhelm, with European commentary by C. J. Jung.] 5th ed. (Zürich, Stuttgart 1957), p. xvii
31 Abegg, *Ostasien*, pp. 85, 88 f.
32 Benjamin L. Whorf, quoted by Harry Hoijer (ed.), *Language in Culture* (Chicago 1954), p. 92
33 Mao Tse-tung, *Selected Works* (London and New York), IV, p. 54 (speech of 8 February 1942)
34 Abegg, *Ostasien*, p. 48
35 Weakland, 'Organization', p. 366
36 de Groot, *Universismus*, pp. 119 f.
37 Granet, *Pensée*, p. 387
38 Hellmut Wilhelm, *Chinas Geschichte* [History of China] (Peking 1942), pp. 35 f.
39 Abegg, *Ostasien*, p. 101
40 de Groot, *Universismus*
41 Quoted by Granet, *Pensée*, p. 15
42 Leo Trotzki: *Tagebuch im Exil* [Diary in Exile] (Cologne-Berlin 1958), p. 115

Chapter II: THE HERITAGE

1 *Istoriya yestestvoznaniya v Rossii*, ed. N. A. Figurovsky, Vol. 1, Part 1 (Moscow 1957), 495 pp.
2 Alexander Vuchinich, 'Mathematics in Russian Culture', in *Journal of the History of Ideas*, XXI, No. 2 (April–June 1960), pp. 161–79
3 *Der Feuervogel* [The Firebird. Old Russian fairy tales.] (Stuttgart 1960), p. 346
4 Joseph Needham, 'The Dialogue of Europe and Asia', in *Eastern Horizon*, I, No. 1 (July 1960), p. 18

5   Joseph Needham, *Science and Civilization in China*. To date Vols.
    I–IV (Cambridge, Mass. 1954, 1956, 1959, 1962)
6   Fung Yu-lan, *History*, Vol. I, p. 249
7   Quoted by Hu Shih, *Religion*, p. 15
8   Fung Yu-lan, *History*, Vol. I, pp. 150 f.
9   Mencius, VII/I, Ch. 26, 4
10 *Li Gi, Das Buch der Sitte* [Li Chi, The Book of Rites]. German rendi-
    tion with commentary by Richard Wilhelm (Düsseldorf-Cologne),
    p. 205
11 Arthur F. Wright, 'Struggle vs. Harmony. Symbols of Competing
    Values in Modern China', in *World Politics* (October 1953), p. 34
12 James Legge, *The Chinese Classics* (London 1861–72), Vol. I, pp. 384 f.
13 Fung Yu-lan, *History*, Vol. II, p. 571
14 *Ibid.*, Vol. I, p. 429
15 Confucius, *Analects*, XIII, 5
16 Graf Hermann Keyserling, *Das Reisetagebuch eines Philosophen*
    [Journal of a Traveling Philosopher], 3rd ed., Vol. II (Darmstadt
    1920), p. 544
17 Wilhelm, *Li Gi* (see note 10), p. 206
18 Confucius, *Analects*, IV, 16
19 *Ibid.*, XV, 23
20 Mencius, II, 1, Chap. 6, 3
21 Mencius, III/2, Chap. 6, 1
22 Hu Shih, *Renaissance*, p. 87
23 Confucius, *Analects*, XVIII, 8
24 *Ibid.*, II, 17
25 *Ibid.*, VI, 20
26 Wilhelm, *Li Gi* (see note 10), p. 203
27 Fung Yu-lan, *History*, Vol. I, p. 91
28 Wilhelm, *Li Gi* (see note 10), pp. 96–103
29 Confucius, *Analects*, I, 9
30 Hu Shih, *Religion*, p. 11
31 Wing-tsit Chan (Chan Wing-tsit), *Religious Trends in Modern China*
    (New York 1953), pp. 240, 138
32 *Ibid.*, p. 256
33 Frederick W. Mote, 'Confucian Eremitism in the Yüan Period', in
    Wright, *Persuasion*, pp. 202–40
34 Lin Yutang, *The Importance of Living*, 26th ed. (New York 1942), p. 17
35 H. Wilhelm, *Gesellschaft und Staat in China* [Society and the State in
    China] (Hamburg 1960) (reprint of 1944 ed.), p. 53
36 Hu Shih, *Religion*, p. 31
37 Wing-tsit Chan, *Religious Trends*, p. 174
38 *Ibid.*, p. 144
39 The relevant works are James Legge, *The Religions of China* (London
    1880), 310 pp.; and Jan J. M. de Groot, *Sectarianism* and *Uni-
    versismus*, also by the same author *The Religious System of China*,
    Vols. I–VI (Leiden 1892–1910), and *Religion in China* (New York
    and London 1912)

40 Arthur F. Wright, *Buddhism in Chinese History* (Stanford 1959), p. 105

41 Hervell Glessner Creel, *Sinism. A Study of the Evolution of the Chinese World View* (Chicago 1929), p. 115

42 Eberhard, *Geschichte*, p. 75

43 Wright (see note 40), pp. 36, 77, 110

44 Cf. *Der Heilige als Eulenspiegel* [The Saint as Trickster] (Basel, Stuttgart 1958), 167 pp.

45 F. C. M. Wei, *The Spirit of Chinese Culture* (New York 1947), pp. 161–77

46 de Groot, *Sectarianism*

47 Confucius, *Analects*, II, 16

48 From Chap. 17 of *Hsi Ming* by Cheng Tsai, quoted by Fung Yu-lan, *History*, Vol. II, p. 496

49 Cf. Chiang Yee, *Chinese Calligraphy*, 2nd ed. (London 1951), 230 pp.

50 Tschizewskij, *Geistesgeschichte*, Vol. I, pp. 111 f.

51 Iwan Kologriwow, *Das andere Russland* [The Other Russia] (Munich 1958), pp. 25–31; Tschizewskij (see note 50), pp. 31–32

52 Tschizewskij (see note 50), p. 149

53 *Ibid.*, p. 131

54 See *inter alia* Alexander Steininger, 'Die Wundertätige—Zum Problem der Religiosität in der Sowjetunion' [The Miracle Worker—On the Problem of Religious Feeling in the Soviet Union], in *Osteuropa*, IX, No. 5/6 (May/June 1959), pp. 339–54; 'Chronik: Religion und Kirchen' [Chronicle—Religion and Churches], in *Osteuropa*, X, No. 5 (May 1960), pp. 354–6; also the series of reports on Soviet literature by Barbara Bode in *Osteuropa*, IX (1959) f.; Gerd Ruge, '"Aber die Frau geht in die Kirche"—Bericht über die Religionsausübung in der USSR' ['But the woman goes to church'—Report on the Practice of Religion in the USSR], in *Aus Politik und Zeitgeschehen. Beilage zur Wochenzeitung Das Parlament* [Political and Contemporary Events. Supplement to the weekly journal *Parliament*], 1961, No. 16; Walter Kolarz, *Religion in the Soviet Union* (London 1961), 518 pp.

55 Kologriwow (see note 51), p. 13

Chapter III: THE SOCIETY

1 Hsu, *Americans*, p. 74

2 *Ibid.*, p. 131

3 Yang, *Family*, pp. 7 f., and Chang, *Gentry*, pp. 112 f.

4 The most concise survey of the present state of clan research is to be found in Hsiao, *Rural*, pp. 323–70 (Chap. 8); in more detail: Liu Hui-chen Wang, *The Traditional Chinese Clan Rule* (Locust Valley, N.Y. 1959), 264 pp.; Hu Hsien-chin, *The Common Descent Group in China and its Functions* (New York 1948), 204 pp.

5 Yang, *Village*, p. 12

6 Snow, *Red Star*, p. 292

7 T. S. Chen and J. R. Shryock, 'Chinese Relationship Terms', in *The American Anthropologist*, XXXIV (1932), pp. 623–69; Yang, *Family*, pp. 231–3

8 *The Book of Songs*, trans. by Arthur Waley (London 1937), 358 pp.

9 Lin Yutang, *The Little Critic*, Vol. I (Shanghai 1936), p. 174

10 Yang Lien-sheng, 'The Concept of Pao as a Basis for Social Relations in China', in Fairbank, *Thought*, pp. 303 f.

11 *The Works of Hsüntze*, trans. by Homer H. Dubs (London 1928), pp. 124, 135, 152

12 These and other sayings compiled by Ch'ü T'ung-tsu, in Fairbank, *Thought*, pp. 235 ff.

13 *Lao Dse: Führung und Kraft aus der Ewigkeit (Dan-Dö-Ging)* [Lao-tzu: Leadership and Strength from Eternity]. Trans. by Erwin Rousselle (Wiesbaden 1952), p. 32

14 H. Wilhelm, *Gesellschaft*, p. 52

15 John Lossing Buck, *Chinese Farm Economy. A study of 2866 farms in 17 localities and 7 provinces in China* (Chicago 1930), also *Land Utilization in China. A study of 16,786 farms in 168 localities and 38,256 farm families in 22 provinces in China, 1929–1933* (Nanking 1937)

16 Yang, *Village*, p. 123

17 George B. Cressey, *China's Geographical Foundation. A Survey of the Land and its People* (New York, London 1934), p. 90

18 Yang, *Village*, p. 68

19 Chang, *Gentry*, pp. xviii f.

20 *Ibid.*, pp. 165 ff.; Max Weber, *The Religion of China—Confucianism and Taoism*, Vol. 1 of Weber's *Collected Essays in the Sociology of Religion*, trans. and edited by H. N. Gerth (Glencoe, Ill. 1951), p. 128

21 E. A. Kracke Jr., *Civil Service in Early Sung China (960–1067)* (Cambridge, Mass. 1953), p. 140

22 *Ibid.*, p. 69

23 Chang, *Gentry*, pp. 165 f.

24 *Ibid.*, p. 116

25 *Ibid.*, pp. 216 f., and Chang, *Income*, p. 197; also see Franz H. Michael and George E. Taylor, *The Far East in the Modern World* (New York 1956), p. 27

26 Joseph R. Levenson, 'The Amateur Ideal in Ming and Early Ch'ing Society', in Fairbank, *Thought*, pp. 320–41; and C. K. Yang, 'Some Characteristics of Chinese Bureaucratic Behaviour', in Nivison-Wright, *Confucianism*, pp. 137 f.

27 Confucius, *Analects*, XII, 5

28 A. Tschepe, *Histoire des Trois Royaumes Han, Wei et Tschao* [History of the Three Kingdoms of Han, Wei and Ch'ao] (Shanghai 1910), p. 128

29 Hsiao, *Rural*, pp. 25–205

30 Confucius, *Analects*, IV. 19

31 Chang, *Gentry*, p. 6
32 Ralph C. Powell, *The Rise of Chinese Military Power (1895–1912)* (Princeton 1955), p. 16
33 A recent reference to this is T'ung-Tsu Ch'ü, *Law and Society in Traditional China* (Paris, The Hague 1961), 304 pp.
34 Confucius, *Analects*, II, 3 and VIII, 18
35 Joseph Needham, 'Human Laws and Laws of Nature in China and in the West', in *Journal of the History of Ideas*, XII (1951), p. 10
36 C. K. Yang, 'Some Characteristics of Chinese Bureaucratic Behaviour', in Nivison-Wright, *Confucianism*, pp. 153 f.
37 Creel, *Chinese Thought*, pp. 120 and 129
38 Confucius, *Analects*, II, 1; XII, 17–18
39 Mencius, VII/2, Chap. XIV, 1
40 Charles O. Hucker, 'Confucianism and the Chinese Censorial System', in Nivison-Wright, *Confucianism*, pp. 182 f.
41 Confucius, *Analects*, VIII, 9; XIV, 27
42 Cf. here D. S. Nivison and W. Th. de Bary in Nivison-Wright, *Confucianism*; also Hsiao, *Rural*, p. 721, n. 6
43 Quoted from H. Wilhelm, *Gesellschaft*, pp. 79 f.
44 Quoted in Hsiao, *Rural*, p. 629, n. 191
45 Erich Hauer, *Chinas Werden im Spiegel der Geschichte* [China's Development in the Mirror of History] (Leipzig 1928), p. 36
46 Joseph Needham, 'Human Laws and Laws of Nature in China and in the West', in *Journal of the History of Ideas*, XII (1951), pp. 14 f.
47 Max Weber, *The Religion of China—Confucianism and Taoism* (see note 20), p. 131
48 Creel, *Chinese Thought*, pp. 11 f.
49 Quoted from H. Wilhelm, *Gesellschaft*, p. 59
50 Confucius, *Analects*, XI, 23; XIV, 23; XIII, 15
51 Quoted by Charles O. Hucker, 'Confucianism and the Chinese Censorial System', in Nivison-Wright, *Confucianism*, pp. 194 f.
52 *Ibid.*, p. 201, and E. A. Kracke Jr., *Civil Service in Early Sung China (960–1067)* (Cambridge, Mass. 1953), p. 37
53 Yang, *Village*, p. 108
54 Hsu, *Americans*, p. 172
55 Hsiao, *Rural*, p. 371
56 Frederick W. Mote, 'Confucian Eremitism in the Yüan Period', in Wright, *Persuasion*, pp. 229, 238 f.
57 Hsu, *Americans*, p. 153
58 From a letter written at the end of 1869 by Griffith John, a missionary, as quoted by M. Wright in *Last Stand*, p. 64
59 On this subject see Harold J. Wiens, *China's March Toward the Tropics* (Hamden, Conn. 1954), 441 pp.
60 Baron Egon von Eickstedt, *Rassendynamik von Ostasien* [Race Dynamics of East Asia] (Berlin 1944), p. 70
61 Creel, *Chinese Thought*, pp. 122 f.
62 Eberhard, *Geschichte*, p. 307; Ho Ping-ti, *Studies on the Population of China, 1368–1953* (Cambridge, Mass. 1959), pp. 281 f.

63 Pososhkov to Peter the Great, as quoted by Karl Stählin, in *Geschichte Russlands* [History of Russia] (new edition, Graz 1961), Vol. II, p. 143

64 Tschizewskij, *Geistesgeschichte*, Vol. I, pp. 105, 107

65 Hildegard Schaeder, *Moskau das Dritte Rom* [Moscow the Third Rome], 2nd ed. (Darmstadt 1957), pp. 207, 209

66 A. de Riencourt, *The Soul of China* (New York 1958), p. 186

Chapter IV: THE PENETRATION OF THE WEST

1 On the Taiping Rebellion see George E. Taylor, 'The Taiping Rebellion. Its Economic Background and Social Theory', in *Chinese Social and Political Science Review*, XVI, No. 4 (January 1933), pp. 545–614; *Taipinskoye vosstanie 1850–1864 gg. Sbornik dokumentov.* [The Taiping Rebellion of 1850 to 1864. A collection of documents]. Compiled by V. P. Ilyushechkin and O. G. Solovyov (Moscow 1960), 324 pp. For new Chinese literature see Franz Michael, 'T'ai-p'ing T'sien-kuo' [The Heavenly Kingdom of Peace], in *The Journal of Asian Studies*, XVII, No. 1 (November 1957), pp. 67–76

2 Levenson, *Confucian*, p. 105

3 Teng-Fairbank, *Response*, p. 76, and Levenson, *Confucian*, pp. 70 f.

4 Teng-Fairbank, *Response*, p. 164

5 Feng Kuei-fen (1809–1874), 'Protests from the Study of Chiao-pin' (1861) as quoted by De Bary (*et al.*), *Sources*, pp. 708 f.

6 E.g. by Fan Wön-lan, *Neue Geschichte Chinas* [New History of China], Vol. I (1840–1901) ([East] Berlin 1959), p. 124; a somewhat different opinion is given by the Soviet Sinologist S. L. Tikhvinsky, *Dvizhenie za reformy v Kitaye i Kan Yu-wei* [The Reform Movement in China and K'ang Yu-wei] (Moscow 1959), 418 pp., where Tseng is assessed as neutral, and *inter alia* (p. 352) described as a 'respected court dignitary'.

7 Levenson, *Confucian*, p. 64

8 Wang T'ao (1828–1897), quoted by De Bary (*et al.*) in *Sources*, p. 720

9 Chang, *Gentry*, p. 205

10 *Li Gi* (see Chap. II, note 10), p. 56

11 *Ta T'ung Shu: The One-World Philosophy of K'ang Yu-wei.* Trans. from the Chinese with introduction and notes by L. G. Thompson (London 1958)

12 Quoted from De Bary (*et al.*), *Sources*, pp. 734 f.

13 M. Wright, *Last Stand*, p. 279

14 See Wolfgang Franke, *The Reform and Abolition of the Traditional Chinese Examination System* (mimeographed) (Cambridge, Mass. 1960)

15 Levenson, *Confucian*, pp. 98–104

16 E.g. the philosopher and language reformer Hu Shih (according to Chow, *May Fourth*, p. 300)

17 E.g. the author Lu Hsün in May 1918 (according to Tse-Tung Chow, 'The Anti-Confucian Movement in Early Republican China', in Wright, *Persuasion*, p. 294)

18 W. Franke, *Jahrhundert* [Century], pp. 137 f.

19 Concerning the path of the Kuomintang from anti-Confucianism to Confucianism, see M. Wright, *Last Stand*, pp. 300 f.

20 Hsu, *Americans*, p. 394

21 Lifton, *Thought Reform*, p. 373

22 *Dostizheniya sovietskoy vlasti za 40 let v tsifrakh* [The Achievements of Soviet Power in Forty Years in Figures] (Moscow 1957), p. 49

23 P. I. Lyashchenko, *Istoriya narodnogo khozyaystva SSSR* [Economic History of the USSR], Vol. II, 2nd ed. (Moscow 1950), p. 367

24 Hoetzsch, *Russland*, p. 193

25 Alexander Gerschenkron, 'Problems and Patterns of Russian Economic Development', in Black, *Transformation*, p. 58

26 Concerning China's most recent economic history see Albert Feuerwerker, 'Materials for the Study of Economic History of Modern China', in *Journal of Economic History* (March 1961), pp. 41–60

27 Cf. Karl A. Wittfogel, *Oriental Despotism. A comparative study of total power* (New Haven 1957), 556 pp.

28 John K. Fairbank, Alexander Eckstein, L. S. Yang, *Economic Change in Early Modern China* (Cambridge, Mass. 1960), p. 16

29 Albert Feuerwerker, *China's Early Industrialization, Sheng Hsuan-huai (1844–1916) and Mandarin Enterprise* (Cambridge, Mass. 1958), p. 12

30 Paul M. A. Linebarger, *The Political Doctrines of Sun Yat-sen* (Baltimore 1937), pp. 145 f., 252 f.

31 Wing-tsit Chan, *Religious Trends in Modern China*, pp. 3, 19, 91, 145–6, 152–3

32 See Chap. I, note 23

33 A more recent edition of the English translation: Pa Chin, *The Family* (Peking 1958)

34 M. H. van der Valk, *Conservatism in Modern Chinese Family Law* (Leiden 1956), 90 pp.

35 Hsiao, *Rural*, p. 407

36 Franz Michael, 'The Military Organization and Power Structure of China During the Taiping Rebellion', in *Pacific Historical Review*, XVIII, No. 4 (November 1949), pp. 478 f.

37 Powell, *Rise*, p. 114

38 *Ibid.*, p. 79

39 Cf. for example Marshal Malinovsky's speech during the Twenty-second Congress of the Communist Party of the Soviet Union in *Pravda*, 25 October 1961

40 See chapter 'Family and Home' in Mehnert, *Soviet Man*

41 The best comprehensive survey of the whole subject is still Geroid Tanquary Robinson, *Rural Russia under the Old Régime* (London, New York 1932), 342 pp. (2nd ed. New York 1949)

Part 2: REVOLUTIONARIES

INTRODUCTION

1 Books dealing with these questions in the Soviet Union can fill whole libraries, whereas literature on China is still very limited.

Among the few comparative studies which have been published to date are: Hans Georg Glaser, 'Einige Unterschiede im Partei- und Staatsaufbau zwischen der Sowjetunion und der Volksrepublik China' [Some Differences in Party and State Organization Between the Soviet Union and the People's Republic of China], in *Europa-Archiv*, XV (1960), No. 1/2, pp. 1–12; and H. F. Schurmann, 'Organizational Contrasts . . .', in London, *Unity*.

The reader is therefore directed to general works on Communist China. The only specialized publications on education are: K. E. Priestley, *Education in China* (Hongkong 1961), 70 pp.; Leo A. Orleans, *Professional Manpower and Education;* Robert D. Barendsen, *The 1960 Educational Reforms*; Robert D. Barendsen, *The Agricultural Middle School*; John M. H. Lindbeck, 'The Organization and Development of Science', in *The China Quarterly*, No. 6 (April–June 1961), pp. 98–132. On religion: Holmes Welch, 'Buddhism under the Communists', and C. K. Yang, *Religion in Chinese Society*, Ch. XIV. (Complete titles in the bibliography, pp. 501–12.)

There are already numerous books and articles on the CPC and the CPSU. We cite here (if listed in the Bibliography, pp. 501–12, in abbreviated form only): F. W. Houn, 'The Eighth Central Committee', and the excellent study by R. C. North, *Moscow and Chinese Communists*; also H. L. Boorman, *Men and Politics*; B. I. Schwartz, *Chinese Communism*; H. A. Steiner, 'Trade Unions in Mao's China'; Chao Ku-chün, 'Leadership in the Chinese Communist Party', in *The Annals of the American Academy of Political and Social Science*, CCCXXI (January 1959), pp. 40–50; H. C. Hinton and R. MacFarquhar (see note 12 of Chap. VIII); from the Red Chinese point of view there is the extensive work by Ho Kan-chih, *A History*. Standard works on the CPSU: J. S. Reshetar, *A Concise History*; Leonard Schapiro, *The Communist Party of the Soviet Union*.

Chapter V: PROLETARIANS OR PEASANTS?

1 *Pravda*, 22 October 1961; see Boris Meissner, 'Die soziale Struktur der Partei' [The Social Structure of the Party] in *Osteuropa*, XII, No. 1/2 (January–February 1962), pp. 21 f.

2 Ch'en Tu-hsiu, quoted in Schwartz, *Communism*, p. 48

3 Schwartz, *Communism*, p. 129

4 Cf. Arthur Steiner, 'Trade Unions in Mao's China', in *Problems of Communism*, V, No. 2 (March–April 1956), pp. 27–33; Suzanne

Labin, *The Anthill*, trans. from the French by Edward Fitzgerald (London 1960), pp. 244–79 (Chap. 12: 'The Workman Tsong and the Trade-Union Official Liang')

5 Hughes-Luard, *Development*, p. 116
6 Cf. 'How can the Party exert a still stronger leadership over the trade unions?' Chinese in *Kung-jen Jih-pao*, 19 September 1961
7 Ho Kan-chih, *A History*
8 Krymov-Shafir, pp. 586–9
9 Hughes-Luard, *Development*, p. 115; see also *Labour Laws and Regulations of the People's Republic of China* (Peking 1956), 87 pp.
10 *NCNA*, 13 September 1956
11 Calculated according to the speech of the Party Secretary Teng Hsiao-p'ing of 23 September 1957, in *NCNA*, 19 October 1957
12 A concise, lucid account of Communist peasant policy is given by Karl A. Wittfogel in *Handbuch des Weltkommunismus* [Handbook of World Communism], ed. by Joseph M. Bochenski and Gerhart Niemeyer (Freiburg/Munich 1958), pp. 421–72
13 Lenin, *Sochineniya* [Works] XIII, 'The Agrarian Program of the [Russian] Social Democracy in the First Russian Revolution', p. 322
14 *Pravda*, 20 November 1924, quoted by Arthur A. Cohen, 'How Original is Maoism?' in *Problems of Communism*, X, No. 6 (November–December 1961), p. 37
15 Lenin, *Selected Works*, II (Moscow 1947), ' "Left-Wing Communism", An Infantile Disorder', p. 573
16 A comprehensive work on this subject is Otto Schiller, *Das Agrarsystem der Sowjetunion. Entwicklung seiner Struktur und Produktionsleistung* [The Agrarian System of the Soviet Union. Development of its Structure and Production Achievements] (Tübingen 1960), 171 pp. (Contains a detailed bibliography on pp. 147–71)
17 Apart from Mao, the most outstanding was P'eng Pai in Kwangtung, see Chinkichi Eto, 'Hai-lu-fen: The First Chinese Soviet Government', in *The China Quarterly*, No. 8 (October–December 1961), pp. 166 f.
18 Snow, *Red Star*, pp. 123, 130
19 Mao Tse-tung, *Selected Works* (London and New York), Vol. I, p. 19
20 *Ibid.*, pp. 21, 22
21 *Ibid.*, pp. 26 f.
22 *Inter alia*, Karl A. Wittfogel, 'The Legend of Maoism', in *The China Quarterly*, No. 1 (January–March 1960), pp. 72–86, and No. 2 (April–June 1960), pp. 16–34; Benjamin Schwartz, 'The Legend of the "Legend of 'Maoism'"', *ibid.*, pp. 35–46; Karl A. Wittfogel: '"Maoism"—"Legend" or "Legend of a Legend"?' *ibid.*, No. 4 (October–December), pp. 88 f.
23 Brand-Schwartz-Fairbank, p. 83; in Mao Tse-tung, *Selected Works* (London and New York, Vol. I, pp. 24–26), this embarrassing sentence no longer occurs
24 See Snow, *Red Star*, esp. p. 169

25 See the differing views of Schwartz, *Communism*, and Karl A. Wittfogel (see note 12), also the controversy between Schwartz and Wittfogel in *The China Quarterly* (see note 22)

26 'Revolyutsionny Vostok' [Revolutionary East] (1927), No. 2 (Brandt-Schwartz-Fairbank, p. 487)

27 Lenin, *Selected Works*, Vol. II (Moscow 1947), 'Draft of Theses on the National and Colonial Question', p. 657

28 *Ibid.*, 'Preliminary Draft of Theses on the Agrarian Question', for the Second Congress of the Communist International, 4 August 1920, p. 654

29 Cf. Mao Tse-tung's report to the Central Committee of 25 November 1927, in Mao Tse-tung, *Selected Works* (London and New York), Vol. II, pp. 79 f., as well as numerous later utterances

30 Schwartz, *Communism*, pp. 198 f.

31 See *The Agrarian Reform Law of the People's Republic of China and Other Relevant Documents* [of 1950], 4th ed. (Peking 1953); *Co-operative Farming in China* [Text of CC's resolution of 16 December 1953] (Peking 1954); Tung Ta-lin, *Agricultural Cooperation in China* (Peking 1960) (incl. model regulations for 'higher' and 'lower' types of agricultural producers' co-operatives). Chao Kuo-chun gives a summary of the statistical trend in *Agrarian Policy*, p. 293

32 *Decisions on Agricultural Co-operation* [CC resolution of 11 October 1956] (Peking 1956), 54 pp.; Mao Tse-tung, 'The Question of Agricultural Co-operation' [Speech of 31 July 1955] (Peking 1956) and *Model Regulations for Advanced Agricultural Producers' Co-operatives* (Peking 1956). For Red Chinese agrarian policy as a whole, see Chao Kuo-chun, *Agrarian Policy*, a comprehensive work published in the West but with a certain pro-Communist slant; also the Soviet Russian surveys: I. Korkunov (*et al.*), *Sotsialisticheskoye preobrazovanie selskogo khozyaystva v Kitayskoy Narodnoy Respublike (1949–1957)* [The Socialist Transformation of Agriculture in the Chinese People's Republic (1949–1957)] (Moscow 1960); A. Ye. Kaminsky, *Kooperirovanie selskogo khozyaystva Kitaya* [The Co-operativization of Agriculture in China] (Moscow 1959); W. A. Zhamin, *Selskoye khozyaystvo Kitaya* [China's Agriculture] (Moscow 1959)

Chapter VI: WITH OR WITHOUT THE BOURGEOISIE?

1 Lenin, *Sochineniya* [Works], Vol. XVIII, 'Democracy and Populism in China', pp. 146–8

2 Lenin, *Collected Works*, Vol. 9 (Moscow 1962), 'Two Tactics of Social-Democracy in the Democratic Revolution', p. 50

3 *Ibid.*, 'Petty-Bourgeois and Proletarian Socialism', p. 443

4 *Ibid.*, 'Social-Democracy's Attitude Toward the Peasant Movement', pp. 236–7

5 *Ibid.*, 'Two Tactics . . .', p. 112

6 *Ibid.*, p. 100

7 *Ibid.*, p. 57
8 'Declaration of the Rights of the Working and Exploited People', 16 January 1918, as quoted by William Henry Chamberlin in *The Russian Revolution 1917–1921*, Vol. 1 (New York 1935), p. 492
9 Decree of 28 June 1918
10 Lenin, *Sochineniya*, Vol. XXX, 'Report to the Second All Russian Congress of the Communist Organizations of the Far Eastern Peoples', 22 November 1919, pp. 130–41
11 Lenin, *Selected Works*, Vol. II (Moscow 1947), 'Draft of Theses on the National and Colonial Questions', p. 658
12 Brandt, *Stalin's Failure*, p. 15
13 Degras, *Communist International*, Vol. I, pp. 389 f.
14 Mao Tse-tung, *Selected Works* (London and New York), Vol. I, pp. 13–20
15 *Ibid.*, Vol. I, p. 99
16 *Inprecor* [International Press Correspondence], 21 December 1935, pp. 172 f. (quoted by McLane, *Soviet Policy*, pp. 66 f.)
17 Mao Tse-tung, *Selected Works* (London and New York), Vol. I, pp. 171–3
18 *Ibid.*, p. 265
19 *Ibid.*, Vol. III, pp. 106–56
20 Anna Louise Strong, *The Chinese Conquer China* (New York 1949), p. 53 (quoted by McLane, *Soviet Policy*, p. 156)
21 Miao Chu-huan, *Kratkaya istoriya Kommunistischeskoy Partii Kitaya* [A Short History of the Communist Party of China] (Moscow 1958), p. 175; Ho Kan-chih, *A History*, p. 351
22 Stalin, *Sochineniya*, Vol. VIII (Moscow 1948), pp. 357 f.
23 Mao Tse-tung, *Ausgewählte Schriften* [Selected Works], Vol. IV ([East] Berlin 1956), pp. 356 f., 359
24 Lenin, *Collected Works*, Vol. 8 (Moscow 1962), 'Social-Democracy and the Provisional Revolutionary Government', p. 279; also *ibid.*, pp. 293–303, the basic discussion of this question by Lenin, 'The Revolutionary-Democratic Dictatorship of the Proletariat and the Peasantry'
25 Cf. Snow, *Random Notes*, p. 82, and Liu Shao-ch'i in his pronouncement at the 10th Founding Day of the People's Republic of China on 1 October 1959, in *Peking Review* (1959), No. 40, p. 8
26 Mao Tse-tung, *Ausgewählte Schriften*, Vol. IV, p. 362
27 Lenin, *Collected Works*, Vol. 8 (Moscow 1962), 'Social-Democracy and the Provisional Revolutionary Government', p. 291
28 Mao Tse-tung, *Ausgewählte Schriften*, Vol. IV, p. 362
29 The standard source for this period is the White Book published by the US Government on the subject: *United States Relations with China*.
30 Text of this resolution in Brandt-Schwartz-Fairbank, pp. 443–5
31 Mao Tse-tung, *Selected Works* (Peking), Vol. IV, pp. 411–24
32 Lenin, *Collected Works*, Vol. 8 (Moscow 1962), 'Social-Democracy and the Provisional Revolutionary Government', p. 284
33 Stalin, *Socheninya*, Vol. VIII (Moscow 1948), pp. 357 f.

34 Brandt-Schwartz-Fairbank, p. 133
35 Victor A. Yakhontoff, *The Chinese Soviets* (New York 1934), p. 217
36 *Handbook on People's China* (Peking 1957), pp. 84–94
37 *Peking Review*, No. 35 (1 Sept. 1961), p. 12. The earlier plan, which
   provided for the continued existence of the parties even in the
   classless society, is to be found *inter alia* in an article on the question
   of parties in the magazine *Chung-kuo Ching-nien-pao*, 17 October 1956
38 Mao Tse-tung, *Selected Works* (Peking), Vol. IV, p. 418
39 E.g. in May 1942, see Mao Tse-tung, *Selected Works* (London and
   New York), Vol. IV, p. 71
40 E.g. in the Organic Statute for the People's Government of Sept. 1949
   (according to Brand-Schwartz-Fairbank, p. 463), or in *Peking
   Review*, No. 46 (15 November 1960), p. 12
41 E.g. Mao Tse-tung, *Selected Works* (Peking), Vol. IV, p. 417
42 Stalin, *Problems of Leninism*, 11th ed. (Moscow 1947), p. 557
43 MacFarquhar, *Flowers*, pp. 226–30
44 Klaus Mehnert, 'Pekings Kampf gegen die Rechtsopposition im
   Sommer 1957' [Peking's Struggle against the Rightist Opposition
   in the Summer of 1957] in *Osteuropa*, VII, No. 11 (November 1957),
   pp. 804 f.
45 *Peking Review*, No. 9 (3 March 1961), p. 15
46 According to the resolution of the National People's Congress of
   16 April 1962, see *Peking Review*, No. 16 (20 April 1962), p. 6
47 Peter S. H. Tang, *Communist China Today* (New York 1957–8),
   Vol. II, p. 93
48 Kuan Ta-tung, *The Socialist Transformation of Capitalist Industry
   and Commerce in China* (Peking 1960), p. 45
49 *Ibid.*, p. 64
50 *Ibid.*, p. 87
51 *Pravda*, 18 September 1956
52 Part I, Para. 5, in *Pravda*, 2 November 1961
53 Lenin, *Selected Works*, Vol. II (Moscow 1947), 'The Tax in Kind',
   pp. 707 f.

Chapter VII: THE TROUBLESOME INTELLECTUALS

1 Lenin, *Collected Works*, Vol. 5 (Moscow 1961), 'What is to be Done?',
   p. 375
2 Richard Pipes (ed.), *The Russian Intelligentsia* (New York 1961);
   Stuart R. Tompkins, *The Russian Mind from Peter the Great through
   Enlightenment* (Norman, Okla. 1953), 291 pp.
3 Lenin, *Selected Works*, Vol. II (Moscow 1947), 'How to Organize
   Competition', p. 260
4 *Ibid.*, 'The Immediate Tasks of the Soviet Government', Section
   headed 'The New Phase of the Struggle Against the Bourgeoisie',
   p. 319
5 David Joravsky, 'Soviet Scientists and the Great Break', in R. Pipes
   (ed.), *The Russian Intelligentsia*, pp. 122–40; A. Vucinich, *The Soviet
   Academy of Sciences* (Stanford, Calif. 1956), pp. 9 f.

6 Stalin, *Works*, Vol. XIII (Moscow 1955), 'New Conditions—New Tasks in Economic Construction', pp. 71–75

7 Cf. Edward Hallett Carr, *Socialism in One Country*, Vol. I (= *A History of Soviet Russia*, Vol. V) (London 1958), pp. 111–36; Boris Meissner, 'Der Wandel im sozialen Gefüge der Sowjetunion' [Changes in the Social Structure of the Soviet Union] in *Europa-Archiv*, V (1950), No. 9, pp. 2989–3004

8 Klaus Mehnert, *Stalin Versus Marx* (New York-London 1954), 92 pp.

9 Stalin, *Problems of Leninism*, 11th ed. (Moscow 1947), p. 638

10 Mehnert, *Soviet Man*

11 Brandt-Schwartz-Fairbank, p. 350

12 Mao Tse-tung, *Selected Works* (London and New York), Vol. III, pp. 69–71

13 *Ibid.*, p. 90

14 E.g. in December 1940, *ibid.*, p. 215

15 *Ibid.*, Vol. IV, pp. 67–68 (Speech of 2 May 1942)

16 Lenin, *Selected Works*, Vol. II, 'The Tasks of the Youth League', pp. 661–74

17 Ch'en Yün, *How to Become a Good Party Member* (quoted by Brandt-Schwartz-Fairbank, p. 335)

18 Chen, *Thought Reform*, p. 12

19 Chalmers A. Johnson, 'An Intellectual Weed in the Socialist Garden: The Case of Ch'ien Tuan-sheng', in *The China Quarterly*, No. 6 (April–June 1961), p. 37

20 *Ta Kung Pao*, Shanghai, 6 February 1952

21 Li Chi, *Studies*, Vol. II, p. 22

22 E.g. the full text of the 'Confessions' of Prof. Chin Yüeh-lin (in Lifton, *Thought Reform*, pp. 473–84)

23 Chen, *Thought Reform*, pp. 62–69, 209–11

24 Lifton, *Thought Reform*, p. 13. Others on this subject: Edward Hunter, *Brain Washing in Red China* (New York 1951), 311 pp.; Dries van Coillie, *De enthousiaste Zelfmoord* [The Enthusiastic Suicide] (Antwerp 1958)

25 Lifton, *Thought Reform*, pp. 253–300

26 Lifton, in *Thought Reform*, gives similarly detailed reports of many other cases. Also of interest are the careers of two intellectuals who became well known in the Hundred Flowers period, reported in detail in Chalmers A. Johnson (see note 19), pp. 29–52, and Ronald Hsia, 'The Intellectual and Public Life of Ma Yin-ch'u', in *The China Quarterly*, No. 6 (April–June 1961), pp. 53–63

27 Mao Tse-tung, *Selected Works* (London and New York), Vol. IV, p. 49

28 Lifton, *Thought Reform*, p. 393

29 Confucius, *Analects*, XIII, 18

30 David S. Nivison, *Communist Ethics and Chinese Tradition* (mimeographed), (Cambridge, Mass. 1954), pp. 47–54

31 Entry in his diary of 14 November 1900 (according to the Russian jubilee edition of Tolstoi's works, begun in 1928, Vol. LIV, p. 63)

32   Wolfgang Leonhard, *Child of the Revolution*, trans. by C. M. Wood-
      house (London 1957)
33   Arthur Koestler, *Darkness at Noon*, trans. by Daphne Hardy (London
      1940)
34   Robert E. MacMaster, 'In the Russian Manner. Thought as In-
      cipient Action', in *Harvard Slavic Studies*, IV (The Hague), pp.
      281–300
35   Alfred Forke, *Geschichte der alten chinesischen Philosophie* [History
      of Ancient Chinese Philosophy] (Hamburg 1927), pp. 160 f.
36   Hu Shih, *The Development of the Logical Method in Ancient China*
      (Shanghai 1922)
37   Abegg, *Ostasien*, p. 341
38   *Selected Short Stories of Franz Kafka* (New York 1952), p. 104
39   From an unpublished account of his travels by Dr. Max Biehl, Kiel.
40   Reuter's News Agency, Peking, 19 April 1958
41   Chou En-lai, *Report on the Question of Intellectuals* (Peking 1956)
42   *Jen-min Jih-pao*, 21 March 1956
43   Chen, *Thought Reform*, pp. 112, 114
44   Lu Ting-yi, *Let Flowers of Many Kinds Blossom, Diverse Schools of
      Thought Contend!* (Peking 1957), p. 3
45   Li Chi, *Studies*, Vol. V, p. 32
46   Lu Ting-yi (see note 44), pp. 8, 14, 25
47   Chen, *Thought Reform*, p. 123
48   *NCNA*, 25 August 1956
49   *Kung-min Jih-pao*, 7 August 1956
50   *Jen-min Jih-pao*, 4 October 1956
51   *NCNA*, 18 June 1957. Later also published by Peking in brochure
      form in numerous languages, the following quotation being taken
      from one of them (with no date given); in Russian in *Pravda*,
      19 June 1957
52   *NCNA*, 30 April 1957
53   *Jen-min Jih-pao*, 19, 23, and 24 March 1957 (according to Chen,
      Thought Reform, pp. 146–8)
54   Li Wei-han, in *Jen-min Jih-pao*, 15 May 1957, according to *The China
      Quarterly*, No. 8 (October–December 1961), p. 35
55   Yeh Tu-yi in *Kung-min Jih-pao*, 8 May 1957
56   Chang Nai Ch'i in *Kung-min Jih-pao*, 14 May 1957
57   *Jen-min Jih-pao*, 31 May 1957 (according to Chen in *Thought Reform*,
      pp. 164 f.)
58   MacFarquhar, *Flowers*
59   *Jen-min Jih-pao*, 1 July 1957. Liu Shao-ch'i expressed similar ideas on
      5 May 1958, see *Die Dokumente der zweiten Plenartagung des VIII.
      Parteitages der Kommunistischen Partei Chinas* [The Documents of
      the Second Plenary Session of the Eighth Congress of the CPC],
      (Peking 1958), pp. 60 f.
60   *Jen-min Jih-pao*, 4 August 1957
61   Chen, *Thought Reform*, pp. 185–93
62   Dennis Doolin: 'The Revival of the "Hundred Flowers" Campaign

'1961', in *The China Quarterly*, No. 8 (October–December 1961), pp. 34–41

63 See e.g. the frequently published comprehensive report of Thomas R. Henry, which also appeared in *Hong Kong Tiger Standard*, 27 and 28 April 1960

64 Riencourt, *Soul*, p. 263

65 Lifton, *Thought Reform*, p. 401

66 *Ibid.*, p. 412

67 Wing-tsit Chan, *Religious Trends in Modern China*, pp. 4–20

68 *Index to Survey of China Mainland Press, Extracts from China Mainland Magazines, and Current Background* (Hongkong 1957), No. 6, pp. 25–28

69 *Dokumente der 2. Plenartagung* (see note 59), p. 57

70 *Hung-ch'i*, 16 January 1960

71 *Peking Review*, No. 46 (15 November 1960), p. 3

72 Mencius, III/I, IV, 3–6

73 A reliable survey of Soviet Russian literature and literature policy is given by Gleb Struve, *Soviet Russian Literature 1917–1950* (Norman, Okla.), 414 pp. For the post-Stalinist period, see also George Gibian, *The Interval of Freedom; Soviet Literature during the Thaw* (Minneapolis, Minn. 1960), 180 pp.; Harold Swayze, *Political Control of Literature in the USSR, 1946–1959* (Cambridge, Mass. 1962). Modern Chinese literature is discussed by C. T. Hsia, *Chinese Fiction*, and in a special issue of *The Chinese Quarterly*, No. 13 (January–March 1963), 262 pp.

74 Cf. Edward J. Brown, *The Proletarian Episode in Russian Literature 1928–1933* (New York 1953), 311 pp.

75 Lenin, *Sochineniya* [Works], Vol. X, p. 27 ('Party Organization and Party Literature')

76 A Shdanov, *Über Kunst und Wissenschaft* [On Art and Science] (Stuttgart 1952), p. 9 (Speech made at the First Congress of Soviet Authors 1934)

77 Cf. chapter entitled 'Not By Bread Alone' in Mehnert, *Soviet Man*. Recent developments are discussed in a special issue of *Survey, A Journal of Soviet and East European Studies* (London, January 1963), No. 46

78 Lu Hsün [pseudonym *inter alia* for Chou Shu-jen], *Ah Q and Others, Selected Stories of Lusin* [pseud.]. Translated by Chi-Chen Wang (New York 1941)

79 C. T. Hsia, *Chinese Fiction*, p. 30

80 Howard L. Boorman, 'Literature and Politics in Contemporary China', in *Thought Patterns* (ed. Arpad F. Kovacs, Institute of Asian Studies, St. John's University, New York), VII (1960), p. 106

81 C. T. Hsia, *Chinese Fiction*, p. 122. Among the numerous works on Lu Hsün the following may be noted: Huang Sung-k'ang, *Lu Hsün and the New Culture Movement of Modern China* (Amsterdam 1957); Jef Last, *Lu Hsün—Dichter und Idol* [Poet and Idol] (Frankfurt, Berlin 1959)

82 Eileen Chang, *Naked Earth* (Hongkong 1956), 365 pp.

83 Boyd Compton (ed.), *Mao's China*, pp. 16 f.

84 Mao Tse-tung, *Selected Works* (London and New York), Vol. IV, p. 83 (Speech of 23 May 1942)

85 C. T. Hsia, *Chinese Fiction*, pp. 277 f.

86 Detailed account in Yang I-fan, *The Case of Hu Feng* (Hongkong 1956) (The Union Research Institute); Chen, *Thought Reform*, pp. 85–90

87 Lao Sheh [pseudonym for Shu Ch'ing-ch'un], 'Theme and Life' (in Chinese) in *Tsü-i* (1961), No. 5/6 (in English in *Union Research Service*, XXV (1961), No. 2, p. 28)

88 Chou Li-po, *The Wedding* (translated into Russian in *Neva* (1959), No. 10)

89 Cf. 'Changing Tone of the Press', in *China News Analysis*, No. 393 (20 Oct. 1961), pp. 1–5. On the trend since 1958 see also Cyril Birch, 'The Literature of the Great Leap Forward', in *Current Scene* (Hongkong), I, No. 31 (5 May 1962), pp. 1–9

90 Cyril Birch, 'Lao She. The Humourist in his Humour', in *The China Quarterly*, No. 8 (October–December 1961), pp. 45–62

91 *Jen-min Jih-pao*, 18 December 1956

92 Moraes, *Report*, p. 34

93 Russian edition: *Ai U, V ogne roshdayetsya stal* (Moscow 1959)

94 Tsao Ming, *Yüan-tung-li* [Energy] (Peking 1949)

95 *Peking Review*, No. 15 (12 April 1960), p. 30

96 *Wen-i Pao* (1958), No. 6 (according to C. T. Hsia, *Chinese Fiction*, p. 495); *Peking Review*, No. 15 (12 April 1960), p. 30; S. H. Chen, 'Multiplicity and Uniformity—Poetry and the Great Leap Forward', in *The China Quarterly*, No. 3 (July–Sept. 1960), pp. 1–15

97 Wang Mong in *Jen-min Wen-hsüeh* [People's Literature] (Sept. 1956) (English trans.: 'A New Young Man Arrives at the Organization Department', in *Current Background*, Hongkong, No. 459 (June 1957); see also *NCNA*, 21 March 1957, and *China News Analysis*, No. 176 (12 April 1957), pp. 1–7

Chapter VIII: THE PARTY AND ITS STYLE

1 Lenin, *Collected Works*, Vol. 5 (Moscow 1961), 'What is To Be Done?', p. 462

2 Boris Meissner, *Das Ende des Stalin-Mythos* [The End of the Stalin Myth] (Frankfurt 1956), p. 20; Boris Meissner, 'Die soziale Struktur der Partei' [The Social Structure of the Party], in *Osteuropa*, XII, No. 1/2 (Jan.–Feb. 1962), pp. 22 f.

3 Nym Wales, *Inside Red China* (New York 1939), p. 335

4 Snow, *Random Notes*, p. 139

5 Franklin W. Houn, *The Eighth Central Committee*, p. 398

6 *Kung-min Jih-pao*, 3 September 1961; cf. *China News Analysis*, No. 393 (20 October 1961), p. 7

7 *Pravda*, 22 October 1961 (Titov's report) and *Peking Review* (1961), No. 26/7 (July 7), p. 10 (Liu Shao-ch'i).

8   See especially Schwartz, *Communism*; or a Red China source, Ho Kan-chih, *A History*

9   Schwartz, *Communism*, p. 166

10   *Communist China 1949–1959* (Communist China Problem Research Series, No. 25) (Hongkong 1961), Vol. I, pp. 40 f.

11   Franklin W. Houn, *The Eighth Central Committee*, p. 393

12   See Harold C. Hinton, 'Intra-Party Politics and Economic Policy in China', in *World Politics*, XII, No. 4 (July 1960), pp. 509–24; and Roderick MacFarquhar, 'Communist China's Intra-Party Dispute', in *Pacific Affairs*, XXXI, No. 3 (December 1958), pp. 323–35

13   Mehnert, *Soviet Man*, p. 68

14   See especially Compton, *Mao's China*

15   Mao Tse-tung, *Selected Works* (London and New York), Vol. IV, pp. 15, 71

16   See Cyril E. Black, *Rewriting Russian History* (New York 1956), 413 pp.; Klaus Mehnert, *Stalin Versus Marx* (London and New York 1952), 128 pp.

17   Compton, *Mao's China*, pp. 108–55. Re-edited by Liu Shao-ch'i and republished in *Hung-ch'i* (1962), No. 15–16 (1 August)

18   Li Chi, *Studies*, Vol. V, pp. 58 f.

19   Robert Payne, *Mao Tse-tung* (New York 1950), p. 103

20   Mao Tse-tung, *On the Correct Handling of Contradictions Among the People* (Peking 1957), p. 63

21   Mao Tse-tung, *Nineteen Poems*. With notes by Chou Chen-fu and an appreciation by Tsang Keh-chia (Peking 1958)

22   Kho Shi Min [Ho Chi Minh], *Izbrannye statyi i rechi* [Selected Essays and Speeches] (Moscow 1959), 814 pp.; cf. 'Statyi Kho Shi Mina' [The Essays of Ho Chi Minh] in *Inostrannaya literatura* [Foreign Literature] (1960), No. 5, p. 37

23   Snow, *Red Star*, p. 127

24   Donald W. Klein, 'Peking's Leaders. A Study in Isolation', in *The China Quarterly*, No. 7 (July–September 1961), pp. 35–43

25   *Stories About Not Being Afraid of Ghosts* (Peking 1961); cf. *New York Times*, 3 March 1961

26   *Hung-ch'i*, 1 November 1959

27   Li Chi, *Studies*, Vol. V, p. 62

28   *Kung-min Jih-pao*, 13 October 1957

29   *Ibid.*, 3 September 1961 (Speech to an audience of artists); cf. *China News Analysis*, No. 393 (20 October 1961)

30   Mao Tse-tung, *Selected Works* (London and New York), Vol. IV, p. 50; and Mao Tse-tung, *Ausgewählte Schriften* ([East] Berlin 1956), Vol. IV, p. 410

31   Mao Tse-tung in his speech of 1 February 1942; in the expurgated *Selected Works* (London and New York, Vol. IV, p. 28) this remark has been omitted, but it is to be found in the collection, Compton, *Mao's China*, pp. 21 f., based on earlier publications

32   *Der VIII. Parteitag der Kommunistischen Partei Chinas* [Eighth Party Congress of the CPC] (Peking 1956), Vol. II, p. 282

33   Lu Ting-yi, *Let Flowers of Many Kinds Blossom* (Peking 1957), p. 5

34 Mao Tse-tung, *Selected Works* (Peking), Vol. IV, p. 100 (to Anna Louise Strong in August 1946)
35 Speech of 5 May 1958 in *Die Dokumente* (see note 59, ch. VII), p. 60
36 Editorial in *Jen-min Jih-pao*, 6 July 1956
37 Mao Tse-tung, *Selected Works* (London and New York), Vol. IV, p. 44
38 According to Kuo Mo-jo in *Jen-min Jih-pao*, 17 July 1957, although not contained in the edited text of the speech itself
39 *Chengyu Xiaocidian* (Hongkong 1958)
40 See relevant sections in R. H. Mathews, *Chinese-English Dictionary* (Cambridge, Mass. 1960)
41 These number-slogans occur so frequently that it would be superfluous to name sources
42 *Jen-min Jih-pao*, 13 November 1955
43 de Bary (*et al.*), *Sources*, p. 945
44 Calculation based on the speech of Liu Shao-ch'i of 30 June 1961 in *Peking Review* (1961), No. 26/27 (July 7), p. 10
45 Li Hsueh-feng, director of the Industrial Work Department, in *Der VIII. Parteitag* (see note 32), Vol. II, pp. 336 f.
46 See, also regarding this whole section, the stimulating study made by the American expert, H. F. Schurmann, 'Organizational Contrasts Between Communist China and the Soviet Union', in London, *Unity*, pp. 65–99
47 Egon von Bahder, 'Die russischen Neuwörter' [New Russian Words], in *Osteuropa*, II, No. 3 (June 1952), pp. 181–87
48 *Peking Review*, No. 46 (15 November 1960), p. 4
49 E.g. Liang Hsing, *Liu Hu-lan. Story of a Girl Revolutionary* (Peking 1953), 87 pp.
50 Wun Yun-to, *Son of the Working Class. Autobiography* (Peking 1961), 226 pp.
51 See speeches in connection with the anniversary of the Bolshevik revolution in China on 6 and 7 November 1956
52 *Jen-min Jih-pao*, 1 October 1953
53 Klaus H. Pringsheim, 'The Functions of the Chinese Communist Youth Leagues (1920–1949)', in *The China Quarterly*, No. 12 (October–December 1962), pp. 75–91
54 *Jen-min Jih-pao*, 29 November 1956
55 E.g. jacket of *China Reconstructs*, IX, No. 5 (May 1960)
56 *China News Analysis*, No. 393 (20 October 1961), pp. 4 f.
57 Cf. Mao Tse-tung's speech of 1 February 1942, in the original version in Compton, *Mao's China*, p. 25, with the revised version in Mao Tse-tung, *Selected Works* (London and New York), Vol. IV, pp. 28 f.
58 *Ta Kung Pao*, 22 December 1956
59 Editorial in *Jen-min Jih-pao*, 25 October 1956
60 *Szechwan Jih-pao*, 26 November 1956
61 Mao Tso-pen, *Eto izobreteno v Kitaye* [That Was Invented in China] (Moscow 1959) (A Russian translation of the Chinese edition which appeared in 1957)
62 *Jen-min Jih-pao*, 19 February 1957
63 Li Chi, *Studies*

Chapter IX: STALIN—CHIANG—MAO

1 See Notes on the Bibliography
2 Mao Tse-tung, *Selected Works* (Peking), IV, p. 413; *re* Sun Yat-sen's acquaintance with Marxism, see Paul M. A. Linebarger, *The Political Doctrines of Sun Yat-sen* (Baltimore 1937), 278 pp. (espec. pp. 137 f.)
3 Din (*et al.*), p. 55
4 Quoted from de Bary (*et al.*), *Sources*, pp. 862–65
5 Mao Tse-tung, *Selected Works* (London and New York), III, p. 146
6 Whiting, *Policies*, pp. 28–33; text of the declaration, *ibid.*, pp. 269–71
7 Chow, *May Fourth*, pp. 209–14
8 Listed in Din Schou-che (*et al.*), pp. 72–75
9 Snow, *Red Star*, pp. 128–55
10 Din (*et al.*), pp. 87–90
11 Snow, *Red Star*, p. 155
12 Din (*et al.*), pp. 113–25; Robert A. Scalapino and George T. Yu, *The Chinese Anarchist Movement* (Berkeley, Calif. 1961), 81 pp.
13 *Ibid.*, p. 110
14 See Notes on the Bibliography
15 Snow, *Red Star*, pp. 164 f.; see also Robert C. North, 'M. N. Roy and the Fifth Congress of the Chinese Communist Party', in *The China Quarterly*, No. 8 (October–December 1961), pp. 184–95
16 McLane, *Policy*, p. 47
17 Snow, *Red Star*, p. 417
18 A detailed discussion of the pros and cons is to be found in McLane, *Policy*, pp. 78–100; Snow, *Random Notes*, pp. 1–14, supports the theory that the Chinese Communists obeyed Stalin's instructions without enthusiasm
19 McLane, *Policy*, pp. 101–55
20 *Mao Tse-dun, Biografichesky ocherk* [Mao Tse-tung, Biographical Sketch] (Moscow 1939)
21 Mao Tse-tung, *Selected Works* (London and New York), III, p. 85
22 *Ibid.*, III, p. 237; IV, p. 21
23 *New York Times*, 26 March 1940
24 Chin Szu-k'ai, *Communist China's Relations*, pp. 56 f. The author, a non-Communist, believes that there were additional contacts but has no definite proof
25 For text of Yalta agreement see *United States Relations*, pp. 113 f.
26 Text of the agreement, *ibid.*, pp. 585–96
27 Brandt-Schwartz-Fairbank, p. 313; Mao Tse-tung, *Selected Works* (London and New York), IV, p. 302
28 McLane, *Policy*, p. 191
29 The standard source for this period is *United States Relations*; see also Beloff, *Policy*
30 Based on a publication of the US State Department, according to *Neue Zürcher Zeitung*, 9 May 1961
31 Verbal information given to the author by Wang Shih-chieh in the summer of 1960

32 Vladimir Dedijer, *Tito* (Berlin 1953), p. 314. Corroborated by Milovan Djilas, *Conversations with Stalin* (London and New York 1962), pp. 164 f.
33 McLane, *Policy*, p. 254
34 *Pravda*, 7 November 1948
35 McLane, *Policy*, p. 3
36 Mao Tse-tung, *Selected Works* (Peking), IV, p. 415
37 Beloff, *Policy*, p. 64

Chapter X: ALONG BOTH SIDES OF THE LONGEST FRONTIER

1   J. Stalin, *Über den Grossen Vaterländischen Krieg der Sowjetunion* [On the Great Patriotic War of the Soviet Union] (Moscow 1946), pp. 229 f. On the subject of the border territories, in so far as it concerns the Soviet Union, see Walter Kolarz, *The Peoples of the Soviet Far East*; E. Thiel, *Sowjet-Fernost* [The Soviet Far East]; and the Soviet author Udovenko, *Dalny Vostok* [Far East]; on China, see Boorman (*et al.*), *Axis*, and O. Lattimore, *Pivot of Asia*. (For complete titles, see Bibliography)
2   According to verbal information given to the author by Fu Ping-ch'ang, Chiang Kai-shek's last ambassador to Moscow
3   German text in supplement to *Neue Zeit* (Moscow 1954), No. 42 (16 October)
4   Tang, *Communist*, I, p. 389
5   *Jen-min Jih-pao*, 15 October 1956
6   McLane, *Policy*, p. 208; Beloff, *Policy*, pp. 42 f.
7   Detailed eyewitness account in Edwin W. Pauley, 'Report on Japanese Assets in Manchuria', in *United States Relations*, pp. 598–604
8   *NCNA*, 18 June 1957
9   *Ibid.*, 15 July 1957
10 *Pravda*, 3 July 1949 (acc. to Beloff, *Policy*, p. 70)
11 *Jen-min Jih-pao*, 5 April 1955; *Pravda*, 6 April 1955
12 *Jen-min Jih-pao*, 5 April 1956; in English: *The Historical Experience of the Dictatorship of the Proletariat* (Peking 1959), p. 18
13 *US Joint Publications Research Service* (Hongkong, 15 July 1961) (No. 8585/SS 1267)
14 For a Soviet version glossing over Russia's action, see Ye. M. Zhukov (ed.), *Mezhdunarodniye Otnosheniya na Dalnem Vostoke (1870–1945 gg.)* [International Relations in the Far East, 1870–1945] (Moscow 1951), pp. 24–29. Concerning the Amur islands see Th. Shabad, in *New York Times*, 26 February 1961, p. 16
15 *Peking Review*, 1963, No. 10/11 (15 March), p. 61
16 In addition to the articles by Rupen and Ballis cited in notes 20, 21, 24, 26 and 46, see also *re* Mongolia: E. Thiel, *Die Mongolei* [Mongolia]; J. N. Knutson, *Outer Mongolia*; G. M. Friters, *Outer Mongolia*; also H. E. Salisbury, *To Moscow—and Beyond*, and *Mongolskaya Narodnaya Respublika* [Mongolian People's Republic],

published by the Academy of Sciences in Moscow, and the Statistical Handbook of the Central Statistical Office of the Mongolian People's Republic with English and Russian texts, *National Economy of the Mongolian People's Republic*. (For complete titles, see Bibliography)

17 *Narodny Kitay* [People's China], 1957, No. 9

18 Th. Shabad, see note 15

19 P. G. Podyachikh, *Naselenie SSSR* [The Population of the USSR] (Moscow 1960), p. 103

20 Robert A. Rupen, 'Outer Mongolia 1957–1960', in *Pacific Affairs*, XXXIII, No. 2 (June 1961), p. 133

21 Robert A. Rupen, 'The Buriat Intelligentsia', in *Far Eastern Quarterly*, XV (3 May 1956), pp. 383–98

22 Lenin, *Sochineniya* [Works], XXXI, p. 219 (Report of the Commission on the National and Colonial Questions)

23 *Izvestiya Akademii Nauk SSSR, seriya istorii i filosofii* [Bulletin of the Academy of Sciences of the USSR, Historical and Philosophical Series], Vol. IX (January–February 1952), p. 86

24 S. Viktorov, N. Khalkhin, *Mongolskaya Respublika* [The Mongolian Republic] (Moscow 1936), p. 28, as quoted by William B. Ballis, 'The Political Evolution of a Soviet Satellite. The Mongolian People's Republic', in *The Western Political Quarterly*, IX, No. 2 (June 1956), p. 310

25 *Pravda*, 3 February 1962 (Report of Tsedenbal at the Plenary Session of the CC of the Mongolian Revolutionary People's Party)

26 Robert A. Rupen, 'Notes on Outer Mongolia since 1945', in *Pacific Affairs*, XXVIII, No. 1 (March 1955), p. 78

27 George G. S. Murphy, 'Planning in the Mongolian People's Republic', in *Journal of Asian Studies*, XVIII, No. 2 (February 1959)

28 *Pravda*, 25 November 1960; see also report on a visit to a Mongolian state farm by Harrison E. Salisbury, *To Moscow—and Beyond* (New York 1959), pp. 213 f.

29 Cf. Resolution of the 4th Plenary Session of the CC of the Mongolian Revolutionary People's Party, *Jen-min Jih-pao*, 20 December 1959; see also Tsedenbal in *Pravda*, 19 February 1960

30 S. D. Dylykov, *Demokraticheskoye dvizhenie mongolskogo naroda v Kitaye* [The Democratic Movement of the Mongolian People in China] (Moscow 1953), pp. 54 f.

31 Chin Szu-k'ai, *Communist China's Relations*, pp. 57–62

32 Snow, *Red Star*, p. 96

33 Gunther Stein, *The Challenge of Red China* (London 1954), pp. 195 f., 356; see also McLane, *Policy*, p. 179, note 84

34 Snow, *Random Notes*, p. 106

35 Degras, *International*, I, p. 286

36 Howard L. Boorman, 'The Borderlands and the Sino-Soviet Alliance', in Boorman (*et al.*), *Axis*, p. 167

37 Harrison E. Salisbury, *To Moscow—and Beyond* (New York 1959), p. 228

38 [Kurt Müller], *Entwicklungschilfe innerhalb des Ostblocks* [Development Aid within the Eastern Bloc] (Frankfurt/Main–Berlin 1960), pp. 38 f.
39 *Peking Review*, 28 December 1962 (No. 52), pp. 5 f.
40 *New York Times*, 4 April 1950
41 [Kurt Müller] (see note 38), pp. 36 f.
42 *Pravda*, 17 May 1957
43 [Kurt Müller] (see note 38), p. 40
44 *New York Times*, 8 September 1957
45 *Ibid.*, 28 September 1960
46 Robert A. Rupen, 'Outer Mongolia 1957–1960', in *Pacific Affairs*, XXXIII, No. 2 (June 1961), p. 131; Rupen also mentions a Sino-Mongolian Friendship Association several times
47 Robert A. Rupen, 'Russian-Mongol-Chinese Conference', in *The Journal of Asian Studies*, XVII, No. 3 (May 1958), pp. 537–41; and his *The Mongolian People's Republic* (multigraphed—no place given) (1961), p. 13; see also his 'Sino-Soviet Rivalry in Outer Mongolia', in *Current Scene* (Hongkong), I, No. 11 (31 August 1961), pp. 4 f.; I. Ya. Slatkin, S. W. Kiselyov, 'Soveshchanie istorikov Mongolskoy Narodnoy Respubliki, Kitayskoy Narodnoy Respubliki i Sovetskogo Soyuza v Ulan Batore' [Conference of Historians from the Mongolian People's Republic, the Chinese People's Republic, and the Soviet Union in Ulan Bator], in *Voprosy istorii* [Questions of History] (1957), No. 2, pp. 211–13
48 Yu. Tsedenbal, in *Pravda*, 3 February 1962 and 10 January 1963
49 *Pravda*, 9 June 1962
50 Whiting, *Sinkiang*, pp. 280 f.
51 *Ibid.*, pp. 117 f.
52 On the treaties of 1954, see Klaus Mehnert, 'Peking und Moskau', in *Osteuropa*, V, No. 1 (February 1955), pp. 17–20
53 A survey of the treatment of the nationality problem in China is given by S. Chandra Sarker (Chandrasekhar), 'China's Policy Toward Minorities', in *The World Today*, XV, No. 10 (October 1959), pp. 408–16
54 Theodor Arnold, 'Die Zukunft der Sowjetarmee' [The Future of the Soviet Army], in *Osteuropa*, XI, No. 7/8 (July–August 1961), p. 496
55 Of the sparse literature of recent date on Sinkiang may be mentioned O. Lattimore, *Pivot of Asia*; A. S. Whiting, *Sinkiang*; B. Davidson, *Turkestan Alive* (complete titles in the Bibliography)
56 Verbal information given to the author by Fu Ping-ch'ang, Chiang Kai-shek's last ambassador to Moscow
57 *NCNA*, 30 June 1956
58 For the spread of the Starlinger theory, see John E. Tashjean, *Where Russia Meets China. An Analysis of Dr. Starlinger's Theory* (multigraphed) (Washington, D.C. 1959), pp. 1–3
59 Cf. de Gaulle's statement at the press conference of 10 November 1959
60 Wilhelm Starlinger, *Grenzen der Sowjetmacht im Spiegel einer West-Ost-Begegnung hinter Palisaden von 1945 bis 1954* [The Frontiers of

Soviet Power as Reflected in an East-West Encounter Behind
Barbed Wire between 1945 and 1954] (Kitzingen a. Main 1954),
131 pp. By the same author, *Hinter Russland, China* [Beyond Russia
—China] (Würzburg 1957), 141 pp.

61 *Ibid.*, pp. 116 f.
62 John S. Aird, 'Population Growth. Evidence and Interpretation', in
The China Quarterly, No. 7 (July–September 1961), pp. 44–56
63 For a comprehensive study of the Chinese population policy see
Leo A. Orleans, 'Birth Control. Research or Postponement', in
The China Quarterly, No. 3 (July–September 1960), pp. 59–73; see
also *Kung-min Jih-pao*, 3 August 1956, *Chung-kuo Ching-nien-pao*,
19 August 1956, *Jen-min Jih-pao*, 28 August 1956, and 5, 29 and 31
March 1957
64 Speech of 5 May 1958, in *Dokumente der 2. Plenartagung*, p. 51
65 *Jen-min Jih-pao*, 15 April 1959
66 BBC radio interview, text in *Peking Review*, 1960, No. 45 (8 November 1960), pp. 24 f.; the recent trend is discussed by Leo A. Orleans,
'A New Birth Control Campaign?', in *The China Quarterly*, No. 12
(October–December 1962), pp. 207–10
67 Rudolf Schlesinger (ed.), *The Family in the USSR. Documents and
Readings* (London 1949), 408 pp.
68 S. Chandrasekhar, *China's Population* (Hongkong 1959)
69 Leo A. Orleans, 'Problems of Manpower Absorption in Rural China',
in *The China Quarterly*, No. 7 (July–September 1961), pp. 57–68;
and John Philip Emerson, 'Manpower Absorption in the Non-
Agricultural Branches of the Economy of Communist China 1953–
1958', *ibid.*, pp. 69–84
70 *Hung-ch'i*, 16 March 1960 (as quoted by Orleans, see note 69, p. 66)
71 *Ten Great Years. Statistics of the Economic and Cultural Achievements
of the People's Republic of China* (Peking 1960), p. 8
72 *Peking Review*, 1960, No. 45 (8 November 1960), pp. 24 f.; cf. *NCNA*,
3 February 1957, and *Nash drug Kitay* [Our Friend China] (Moscow
1959), pp. 298 f.
73 Erich Thiel, *Sowjet-Fernost* [Soviet Far East] (Munich 1958), p. 127
74 *Chung-kuo Ching-nien-pao*, 1 December 1955
75 Speeches of 22 and 23 February 1954, in *Pravda*, 23 February and
21 March 1954
76 Resolution of CC and Cabinet Council, in *Pravda*, 28 March 1954
77 Reuter's News Agency, Moscow, 19 February 1957
78 Cf. e.g. the novel by Ivan Koshevnikov, *Utro moyey zhizni* [The
Morning of My Life] (Moscow 1959) or the story by Anatoly
Kuznetsov, 'Devochki' [Girls] in *Yunost* [Youth], 1960, No. 8
79 *Pravda*, 8 January 1955
80 E.g. *Pravda*, 10 July 1960, 22 and 29 March and 26 May 1961
81 A recent survey, Frank A. Durgin, 'The Virgin Lands Programme,
1954–1960', in *Soviet Studies*, XIII, No. 3 (January 1962), pp. 255–
80; see also 'Neulandgewinnung' [The Development of Virgin
Lands], in *Osteuropa*, IV, No. 4 (August 1954), pp. 304–13; Soviet

statistics on the development of virgin land in *Narodnoye khozy-aystvo SSSR v 1961 godu* [The Agricultural Economy of the USSR in 1961] (Moscow 1962), pp. 373 f.

82 P. G. Podyachikh, *Naselenie SSSR* [The Population of the USSR] (Moscow 1961), pp. 63, 170–73

83 *Pravda*, 27 March 1959

84 Podyachikh (see note 82), p. 104

85 Rolf Italiaander, *Schwarze Haut im roten Griff* [Black Skin in the Red Grip] (Düsseldorf 1962), p. 312

86 D. I. Zaslavsky, 'Veliky yazyk nashey epokhi' [The Great Language of our Era], in *Literaturnaya gazeta* [Literary Gazette], 1 January 1949; see also Elliot R. Goodman, *The Soviet Design for a World State* (New York 1960), pp. 246–84; Paul Urban, 'Moskaus heutige Kulturpolitik gegenüber den nichtrussischen Völkerschaften' [Moscow's Cultural Policy Toward the Non-Russian Peoples], in *Osteuropa*, XI, No. 3 (March 1961), p. 221

87 Hans Niedermeier, 'Schriftreform und Nationalität' [Script Reform and Nationality] in *Osteuropa*, III, No. 6 (December 1953), pp. 413–16

88 *NCNA*, 27 August 1956

89 According to *The Times of India*, 30 January 1960

90 *NCNA*, 21 November 1956

91 Published *inter alia* in *Jen-min Jih-pao*, 11 December 1957

92 *China News Analysis*, No. 443, 26 October 1962, p. 6

93 Cf. G. P. Serdyuchenko, *Kitayskaya pismennost i yeyo reforma* [Chinese Writing and Its Reform] (Moscow 1959), p. 41

94 C. T. Hsia, *Fiction*, p. 130

95 Robert Payne, *Mao Tse-tung. A Biography* (New York 1950), p. 160

Chapter XI: BETWEEN STATE AND STATE

1 Sladkovsky, *Ocherki*, pp. 301 f., 439 f.; Kurdyukov (*et al.*), pp. 227–29

2 Telegram of the CC of the CPC of 5 July 1957, in *Pravda*, 6 July 1957

3 *Pravda*, 10 February 1963

4 *Re* his career, P.A., 'Berater in Karlshorst—Pawel F. Judin' [Adviser in Karlshorst—Pavel F. Yudin], in *Osteuropa*, III, No. 3 (June 1953), pp. 206 f.

5 *Pravda*, 6 February 1959

6 P. F. Yudin, 'Zakonomerniy kharakter perekhoda ot sotsializma k kommunizmu' [The Predetermined Nature of the Transition from Socialism to Communism], in *Kommunist*, 1961, No. 12 (August 1961), pp. 44–56

7 Chin Szu-k'ai, p. 18

8 *Ibid.*, p. 19

9 Cf. Myron Rush, *The Rise of Khrushchev* (Washington, D.C. 1958), pp. 6 f.; Zagoria, *Conflict*, p. 21

10 Zagoria, *Conflict*, p. 112

11 *NCNA*, 5 November 1956

12 S. Tikhvinsky, 'Odinnadsataya godovshchina Kitayskoy Narodnoy Respubliki' [The Eleventh Anniversary of the Chinese People's Republic], in *Kommunist*, 1960, No. 14 (September), pp. 76–83

13 See *inter alia* [Gross, Müller], *Verflechtung*; Handke, *Wirtschaft Chinas*; Grossmann, *Wirtsch. Entwicklung*; Sladkovsky, *Ocherki*; A. Eckstein, 'Moscow-Peking Axis. The Economic Pattern', in Boorman (*et al.*), *Axis* (complete titles in Bibliography); Oleg Hoeffding (see note 28)

14 Cf. [Gross, Müller], *Verflechtung*, pp. 29–36

15 *Izvestiya*, 3 January 1962, p. 4

16 Both in *Vneshnyaya torgovlya* [Foreign Trade], 1961, No. 5 (May), pp. 11–18

17 Li Choh-ming, *Economic Development of Communist China* (Berkeley, Los Angeles 1959), p. 173; cf. Chin Szu-k'ai, p. 29

18 Sladkovsky, *Ocherki*, p. 332

19 Allen S. Whiting, 'Contradictions in the Moscow-Peking Axis', in *The Journal of Politics*, XX, No. 1 (February 1958), p. 130

20 Deutsche Presse Agentur from Hongkong, 16 January 1962

21 OECD Report of 21 March 1962 (as quoted in *New York Times*, 22 March 1962)

22 [Gross, Müller], *Verflechtung*, p. 43

23 Sladkovsky, *Ocherki*, pp. 449 f.

24 *NCNA*, 12 March 1957

25 *Ibid.*, 23 July 1956

26 Edgar Snow, in *Look*, 31 January 1961

27 E.g. Pyn Min, *Istoriya*, p. 100

28 More details in Oleg Hoeffding, 'Sino-Soviet Economic Relations in Recent Years', in London (ed.), *Unity*, pp. 295–312

29 *Der VIII. Parteitag*, I, p. 268

30 Text of the communiqué given by Sladkovsky, *Ocherki*, p. 448, and in *Pravda*, 12 October 1954

31 Text of the communiqué in Kurdyukov (*et al.*), p. 304

32 A list of the principal agreements is contained in the handbook *Nash drug Kitay* [Our Friend China] (Moscow 1959), pp. 237–42

33 *Jen-min Jih-pao*, 5 November 1956

34 Chin Szu-k'ai, p. 35

35 *Ibid.*, p. 28

36 *Pravda*, 15 and 18 January 1955

37 *NCNA*, 29 March 1956

38 *New York Times*, 28 September 1958

39 *Stuttgarter Zeitung* and *Die Welt*, 10 May 1958

40 *Re* the early stages, see Klaus H. Pringsheim, *The Sino-Soviet Friendship Association* (*October 1949—October 1951*). Master of Arts Thesis, Columbia University (New York, no year given), 224 pp.

41 *Druzhba* [Friendship], 1949, No. 41, pp. 21 f.

42 Kapitsa, p. 387

43 *Jen-min Shu-tzu* [People's Handbook] (Tientsin 1956), p. 509

44 *NCNA*, 9 January 1957

45 *Pravda*, 24 August 1956; *NCNA*, 19 September 1956
46 Skachkov, *Bibliografiya*, pp. 276–82, lists 236 titles of Russian books and magazine articles concerning Soviet-Chinese relations between 1949 and 1957; in the same bibliography there are over 2,400 books and articles listed on the Chinese People's Republic itself between 1949 and 1957
47 From the large number of reports on the Congress we cite here: William B. Ballis (*Michigan Alumnus*, 20 May 1961), Heinz Friese (*Mitteilungen des Instituts für Asienkunde* [Reports of the Institute for Oriental Affairs], Hamburg, No. 5), Joachim Glaubitz (*Osteuropa*, XI, No. 10), Walter Z. Laqueur (*Forum Service*, London, Nos. 273 and 274), Roderick MacFarquhar (*The China Quarterly*, No. 4, 1960), Franz Michael (*The American Slavic and East European Review*, XX, No. 1), Alvin Z. Rubinstein (*Orbis*, IV, No. 4)

Chapter XII: BETWEEN PEOPLE AND PEOPLE

1 Liu Hsiao (Chinese ambassador in Moscow) in *Inostrannaya Literatura* [Foreign Literature], 1959 No. 10, pp. 181–84
2 *NCNA*, 29 July 1956
3 Pyn Min, *Istoriya*, p. 333
4 E.g. *Pravda*, 29 September 1959 (with photo.)
5 Rodger Swearingen, 'Asian Studies in the Soviet Union', in *The Journal of Asian Studies*, VII, No. 3 (May 1958), pp. 515–37; Peter Berton (ed.), *Soviet Works on China. A Bibliography of Non-Periodical Literature* (Los Angeles 1959), 158 pp.
6 The standard modern dictionary is I. M. Oshanin (ed.), *Kitaysko-russkiy slovar* [Chinese-Russian Dictionary], 2nd enlarged and improved edition (Moscow 1955), 898 pp.; an excellently constructed textbook is B. Isayenko, N. Korotkov, I. Sovetov-Chen, *Uchebnik kitayskogo yazyka* [Textbook of the Chinese Language] (Moscow 1954)
7 *Wen Hui Pao* (Shanghai), 20 November 1957; *Changchow Kung-jen Jih-pao*, 6 November 1957; *Heilungkiang Jih-pao*, 17 November 1957; *Peking Kung-jen Jih-pao*, 14 February 1958; *Neimengku Jih-pao*, 8 November 1958; *Jen-min Jih-pao*, 22 October 1957
8 *Druzhba*, 27 July 1957
9 *Jen-min Jih-pao*, 24 October 1957; *Shenyang Jih-pao*, 30 April 1957
10 *Changchow Kung-jen Jih-pao*, 5 November 1957
11 See in MacFarquhar, *Flowers*, the numerous references to the Soviet Union in the index (p. 322)
12 Chen, *Thought Reform*, p. 15
13 *Chung-kuo Ch'ing-nien-pao*, 25 December 1960
14 *Kung-min Jih-pao*, 13 August 1961
15 *NCNA*, 7 November 1957 (article by Mme. Soong Ching-ling, widow of Sun Yat-sen)
16 *NCNA*, 23 December 1956; *Jen-min Jih-pao*, 24 December 1956
17 Harrison E. Salisbury in *New York Times*, 11 September 1959

18 The most complete Soviet report that I know of is G. Novogrudsky, A. Dunayevsky: 'Pau Ti-san i yego tovarishchi' [Pao Ti-san and His Comrades] in *Noviy mir*, 1959, No. 4 (April), pp. 115–35, and No. 5 (May), pp. 100–29; Chinese articles in *Sinkiang Jih-pao*, 23 October 1957; *Chiefang Jih-pao*, 31 October 1957

19 Kapitsa, pp. 27–32; Pyn Min, *Istoriya*, pp. 96–99

20 I. Ye. Yakir, *Vospominaniya o grazhdanskoy voyne* [Memories of the Civil War] (Moscow 1957), p. 12 (as quoted by Kapitsa, pp. 28 f.)

21 *Kung-min Jih-pao*, 4 November 1958

Chapter XIII: AFTER STALIN'S SECOND DEATH

1 Cf. Klaus Mehnert, 'Die Indochina-Konferenz in Genf' [The Conference in Geneva on Indo-China], in *Osteuropa*, IV, No. 5 (October 1954), pp. 378 f.

2 Mehnert, *Anatomy of Soviet Man* ('Crises—and Repercussions')

3 *Pravda*, 28 March 1956 ('Why is the Personality Cult Foreign to the Spirit of Marxism-Leninism?')

4 Cf. Compton, *Mao's China*

5 Bertram D. Wolfe, *Khrushchev and Stalin's Ghost* (New York 1957), p. 82

6 *Pravda*, 16 February 1956

7 *Jen-min Jih-pao*, 5 April 1956; in English: *The Historical Experience of the Dictatorship of the Proletariat* (Peking 1959), pp. 1–20

8 *NCNA*, 16 July 1956

9 *Jen-min Jih-pao*, 1 September 1956

10 *Ibid.*, 29 December 1956; in English: *The Historical Experience of the Dictatorship of the Proletariat* (Peking 1959), pp. 21–64

11 Mao Tse-tung, *Selected Works* (London and New York), II, pp. 13–52

12 *Ibid.*, p. 21

13 *Second Session of the Eighth National Congress*, p. 57

14 B. Kedrov, 'O formakh skachkov v razvitii prirody i obshchestva' [On the Forms of the Leaps Made in the Evolution of Nature and Society], in *Kommunist*, 1951, No. 15 (August), espec. p. 15. Not long before his death, Stalin issued a warning—perhaps for fear some impetuous successor might endanger his work—that a mistaken policy in socialism, too, might lead to the creation of dangerous contradictions (J. Stalin, *Ökonomische Probleme des Sozialismus in der USSR* [Economic Problems of Socialism in the USSR] (German edition, Stuttgart 1952), pp. 67 f.)

15 Text of the interview of 28 May 1957, contained in the *New York Times*, 6 and 9 June 1957; Soviet version in *Pravda*, 4 June 1957

16 B. Ukraintsev, 'Voprosy dialektiki pererastaniya sotsializma v kommunizm' [Questions of the Dialectic of the 'Growing Over' of Socialism into Communism], in *Kommunist*, 1960, No. 13 (September), pp. 62 f., 71

17 Mao Tse-tung, *Selected Works* (London and New York), II, p. 50

18 Mao Tse-tung, *On the Correct Handling of Contradictions Among the People* (Peking 1957), pp. 7–27

19 *The Historical Experience of the Dictatorship of the Proletariat* (Peking 1959), pp. 10 f.

20 *Pravda*, 19 January 1957

21 A useful compilation of material on de-Stalinization: *The Anti-Stalin Campaign and International Communism. A Selection of Documents.* Edited by the Russian Institute, Columbia University (New York 1956), 342 pp.

22 *Jen-min Jih-pao*, 7 April 1956

23 Text of both statutes in Tang, *Communist*, II, pp. 70 f. and 112 f.

24 E.g. *Jen-min Jih-pao*, 4 November 1958

25 *Ibid.*, 1 October 1958

26 Quoted by Richard L. Walker, 'Chairman Mao and the Cult of Personality', in *Encounter* (June 1960), p. 36

27 Hu K'o-shih in *Chung-kuo Ching-nien-pao* (1960), No. 3

28 E.g. in an article on legal problems in *Chung-kuo Ching-nien-pao*, 20 October 1956

29 *Pravda* and *Jen-min Jih-pao*, 21 December 1959

30 *New York Times*, 3 August 1961

31 *Jen-min Jih-pao*, 24 October 1961 (in an article on Party Schools)

32 *Ibid.*, 22 October 1961

33 *Pravda*, 24 October 1961

34 *Peking Review*, 1961, No. 45 (10 November), p. 5

35 *NCNA*, 29 and 30 June, 1 July 1956

36 *Jen-min Jih-pao*, 12 July 1956

37 *Pravda*, 30 June 1956

38 Sydney Gruson in *New York Times*, 16 October 1956

39 *Jen-min Jih-pao*, 26 October 1956

40 *Ibid.*, 21 November 1956

41 *NCNA*, 23 December 1956

42 Thus in Moscow (*NCNA*, 8 January 1957) and in Warsaw (*NCNA*, 11 January 1957)

43 In Budapest (*NCNA*, 16 January 1957) and prior to that similarly in Warsaw (*NCNA*, 13 January 1957)

44 *Pravda*, 17 and 18 June 1958

45 *Jen-min Jih-pao*, 18 June 1958

46 On the situation in the Eastern bloc regarding Hungary and Poland, see *National Communism and Popular Revolt in Eastern Europe. A Selection of Documents on Events in Poland and Hungary, February–November 1956.* Editor: Paul E. Zinner (New York 1956)

47 Brandt-Schwartz-Fairbank, p. 44

48 *Pravda*, 16 February 1956

49 *Jen-min Jih-pao*, 5 April 1956

50 *Ibid.*, 22 June 1956

51 *Ibid.*, 13 July 1956

52 *Borba*, 16 November 1956

53 *Pravda*, 19 and 23 November 1956
54 *Jen-min Jih-pao*, 11 December 1956
55 *Ibid.*, 23 December 1956
56 *Ibid.*, 29 December 1956
57 *NCNA*, 22 October 1957
58 *Ibid.*, 2 November 1957
59 *Borba*, 4 August 1957
60 *Pravda*, 22 November 1957
61 *NCNA*, 28 November 1957
62 *The Programme of the League of Yugoslav Communists* (English edition) (Belgrade 1958)
63 *Jen-min Jih-pao*, 5 May 1958
64 One article in No. 1 (1 June 1958) and two in No. 2 (16 June 1958); also attacks on 'revisionism' in *Jen-min Jih-pao*, 4, 14 and 18 June 1958
65 *Jen-min Jih-pao*, 20 June 1958
66 *Ibid.*, 26 April 1958
67 *Pravda*, 13 April 1958 ('Slogans' for May 1)
68 P. Fedoseyev, I. Pomelov, V. Cheprakov, 'O proyekte programmy Soyuza kommunistov Yugoslavii' [On the Draft of the Programme of the League of Yugoslav Communists], in *Kommunist*, 1958, No. 6 (April), p. 39
69 *Pravda*, 6 May 1958
70 *Ibid.*, 9 May 1958
71 *Ibid.*, 4 June 1958
72 The relevant documentary texts are assembled in *The Second Soviet-Yugoslav Dispute*. Edited by V. L. Benes, R. F. Byrnes, U. Spulber (Indiana University Publications 1959)
73 *Peking Review*, 1961, No. 46 (17 November)
74 *Jen-min Jih-pao*, 20 October 1960
75 Cf. Joachim Glaubitz, 'China im Ostblock' [China in the Eastern Bloc] in *Osteuropa*, XI, No. 4/5 (April–May 1961), pp. 364 f.
76 Literature on Albania is rapidly increasing. A comprehensive study is presented by William E. Griffith, *Albania and the Sino-Soviet Rift*
77 See e.g. the speech of Wu Yü-chang in *Jen-min Jih-pao*, 7 November 1961
78 Mao Tse-tung, *Selected Works* (London and New York), II, p. 260
79 E.g. *Ibid.*, III, p. 154, and IV, pp. 19, 20
80 Chen Po-ta, *Mao Tse-tung's Theory of the Chinese Revolution is the Combination of Marxism-Leninism with the Chinese Revolution* (Peking 1951), p. 1
81 Brandt-Schwartz-Fairbank, p. 374
82 *Pravda*, 15 February 1956
83 *Ibid.*, 18 September 1956
84 *Ibid.*, 15 September 1956
85 *Ibid.*, 19 November 1956
86 *Ibid.*, 31 October 1956

87 'Svyaz teorii s praktikoy i partiynaya propaganda' [The Connection between Theory and Practice and Party Propaganda], editorial in *Kommunist*, 1955, No. 14 (September), p. 5

88 See also Kurt L. London, 'The "Socialist Commonwealth of Nations"', in *Orbis*, III, No. 4 (Winter 1960), pp. 424 f.

89 *Pravda*, 2 November 1956

90 *Jen-min Jih-pao*, 21 November 1956

91 *Chung-kuo Ch'ing-nien-pao*, 28 November 1956

92 Togliatti's article: '9 Domande sullo Stalinismo', in *Nuovi Argomenti* [New Arguments], 1956, No. 20 (16 June); English translation in *The Anti-Stalin Campaign and International Communism. A Selection of Documents* (New York 1956), p. 139

93 *Jen-min Jih-pao*, 29 December 1956

94 Brandt-Schwartz-Fairbank, p. 445

95 *Pravda*, 9 February 1955

96 *Ibid.*, 22 November 1957

97 *Ibid.*

98 A. A. Andreyev, '10 let Kitayskoy Narodnoy Respubliki' [Ten Years of the Chinese People's Republic], in *Kommunist*, 1959, No. 14 (September), p. 31

99 *Pravda*, 1 November 1959 (Speech to the Supreme Soviet on 31 October 1959)

100 *Ibid.*, 6 December 1960

101 *Peking Review*, 1960, No. 49/50 (13 December), p. 32

102 N. S. Khrushchev, 'Za noviye pobedy mirovogo kommunisticheskogo dvizheniya' [For New Victories of the International Communist Movement], in *Kommunist*, 1961, No. 1 (January), pp. 33 f.

103 *Peking Review*, 1961, No. 4 (26 January), p. 9

104 E.g. in his speech of 15 September 1956, at the Eighth Party Congress of the CPC (*Pravda*, 16 September 1956)

105 E.g. at the founding ceremonies of the Sino-Soviet Friendship Association on 5 October 1949

106 E.g. in his speech of 5 March 1957

Chapter XIV: SHORT CUT TO COMMUNISM?

1 *Jen-min Jih-pao*, 3 September 1958 (editorial)

2 *Hung-ch'i*, 1960, No. 19 (1 October), p. 8; cf. Zagoria, *Conflict*, pp. 189–94, on the Chinese military conference of May–July 1958

3 *Long Live Leninism*, p. 20

4 Klaus Mehnert, 'Einige politische Theorien aus Peking' [Some Political Theories from Peking], in *Osteuropa*, X, No. 7/8 (July–August 1960), pp. 514, 517

5 Klaus Mehnert, *Stalin Versus Marx*, pp. 67 f.

6 Stalin, *Works* (Moscow 1955), XIII, 'Report to the Seventeenth Party Congress', p. 374

7 See Zagoria, *Conflict*, pp. 79–83

8 *Second Session of the Eighth Congress*, p. 39

9 *Long Live Leninism*, p. 102

10 See for example *Second Session*, p. 36

11 Figures quoted from Alexander Eckstein, 'Moscow-Peking Axis. The Economic Pattern', in Boorman (*et al.*), *Axis*, p. 63, except for those on cereal crops; for the Soviet Union these have been calculated for a five-year average from *Narodnoye khozyaystvo SSSR v 1958 godu* [The Economy of the USSR in 1958] (Moscow 1959), pp. 7, 31 and 352; for China, they have been calculated from official Chinese statistics in *Ten Great Years* (Peking 1960), pp. 8 and 119

12 Bernhard Grossman, *Die wirtschaftliche Entwicklung der Volksrepublik China*' [The Economic Development of the Chinese People's Republic] (Stuttgart 1960), p. 310 (as far as the end of 1957; for 1958–60, based on figures for the preceding years)

13 Based on *Narodnoye khozyaystvo SSSR v 1958 g.* (Moscow 1959), pp. 7 and 31

14 Cf. Mah Feng-hwa, 'The Financing of Public Investment in Communist China', in *The Journal of Asian Studies*, XXI, No. 1 (November 1961), pp. 33–48. Red China's economic development is dealt with in a general way by Bernhard Grossmann, Werner Handke, Li Choh-ming, and Hughes-Luard, *Development* (see Bibliography)

15 *Pravda*, 30 August 1958

16 See the highly revealing article by Wei Wei in *Chung-kuo Ch'ing-nien-pao*, 16 July 1960

17 See Titarenko in *Sovetskaya Latviya* (and other newspapers), 16 August 1960, quoted in the documentation of R. MacFarquhar in Hudson-Lowenthal-MacFarquhar, p. 150

18 *Peking Review*, 1960, No. 34 (23 August), p. 11; similarly Chou En-lai in Moscow on 19 October 1961, see *Peking Review*, 1961, No. 43 (27 October), p. 8

19 *Hung-chi'i*, 1960, No. 19 (1 October), according to the English version in *Peking Review*, 1960, No. 41 (11 October), p. 9

20 Cf. Art. 7–11 of the Model Constitution of the People's Commune 'Sputnik', in *People's Communes in China*, pp. 64–68

21 E.g. *Peking Review*, 1961, No. 44 (3 November), p. 3

22 *Chinese Communes*, pp. 16–18; *Hung-ch'i*, 16 September 1958

23 P. G. Podyachikh, *Naselenie SSSR* [Population of the USSR], (Moscow 1961), p. 71; *Ten Great Years* (Peking 1960) (Official Bureau of Statistics), p. 180

24 See Vermier G. Chin, 'The New Marriage Law of Communist China', in E. Stuart Kirby (ed.), *Contemporary China. Economic and Social Studies*, II (Hongkong 1958), pp. 64–72; M. H. van der Valk, *Conservatism in Modern Chinese Family Law* (Leiden 1956)

25 This selection of particularly striking passages is from *Chung-kuo Ch'ing-nien-pao*, 30 November and 16 March 1956; 27 September 1958; 1 May, 16 July and 1 March 1960

26 Mehnert, *The Anatomy of Soviet Man* ('Family and Home')

27 Peitaiho resolution, Para. 5, in *Jen-min Jih-pao*, 10 September 1958; official English text in *Peking Review*, 1958, No. 29 (16 September); also *Pravda*, 11 September 1958

28 *Jen-min Jih-pao*, 3 September 1958 (editorial)

29 E.g. again by Khrushchev at the Twenty-first Party Congress of the CPSU, *Pravda*, 28 January 1959, p. 9

30 Cf. the attempts made to penetrate this darkness in Zagoria, *Conflict*, pp. 70 f., 87 f., 93 f.

31 *Jen-min Jih-pao*, 4 September 1958

32 See note 27

33 Some of them conveniently collected in *People's Communes in China* (Peking 1958)

34 E.g. Fritz Steck, 'Besuch einer Volkskommune im Norden Chinas' [Visit to a People's Commune in North China], in *Neue Zürcher Zeitung*, 16 November 1958; Rolf Gillhausen and Joachim Heldt, *Unheimliches China. Eine Reise durch den roten Kontinent* [Mysterious China. A Journey Across the Red Continent] (Hamburg 1959), 152 pp.

35 See pamphlet published by 'Soviet Survey', *The Chinese Communes* (London [1959]) (with contributions by Geoffrey Hudson, A. V. Sherman, and A. Zauberman), and Cheng Chu-yuan, *The People's Communes* (Hongkong 1959)

36 *Peking Review*, 1958, No. 43 (23 December), pp. 10 f. (=Wuhan resolution of 10 December 1958, Part I; official English text)

37 These figures for the end of 1957 in *Narodnoye khozyaystvo SSSR v 1959 godu* (Moscow 1960), p. 307

38 Art. 2 of the 'Sputnik' Model Constitution (as in note 20), p. 68

39 *Jen-min Jih-pao*, 3 September 1958 (editorial)

40 Wuhan resolution (see above), Part IV

41 Wu Chih-p'u, in *Hung-ch'i*, 16 September 1958

42 Fritz Steck in *Neue Zürcher Zeitung*, 16 November 1958

43 *Hung-ch'i*, 1 September 1958 (editorial)

44 Zagoria, *Conflict*, p. 101

45 A. Volkov in *Pravda*, 4 April 1962

46 Lily Abegg in *Frankfurter Allgemeine Zeitung*, 27 December 1958

47 Art. 20 of the 'Sputnik' Model Constitution (as in note 20), pp. 74 f.

48 Rolf Gillhausen and Joachim Heldt, *Unheimliches China* (Hamburg 1959), p. 59

49 *Chinese Communes*, p. 27

50 Art. 19 of the 'Sputnik' Model Constitution (as in note 20), p. 74

51 *Chinese Communes*, p. 41

52 *Pravda*, 11 September 1958

53 *Literaturnaya gazeta*, 30 September 1958

54 *Hung-ch'i*, 1 September 1958 (editorial)

55 *Ibid.*

56 Wu Chih-p'u in *Hung-ch'i*, 16 September 1958

57 Cf. Zagoria, *Conflict*, pp. 90 f., 94 f.

58 Klaus Mehnert, *Youth in Soviet Russia* (London and New York 1933), pp. 159–86; also Mehnert, *The Anatomy of Soviet Man* ('Family and Home' and 'Prosperity')

59 *KPSS v rezolyutsiyakh i resheniyakh* [The CPSU in its Resolutions and Decisions], Vol. II (Moscow 1953), p. 595; see also Robert G. Wesson, 'The Soviet Communes', in *Soviet Studies*, XIII, No. 4 (April 1962), pp. 341–61

60 A. D. Stepanyan, 'Oktyabrskaya revolyutsiya i stanovlenie kommunisticheskoy formatsii' [The October Revolution and the Creation of the Communist Formation] in *Voprosy filosofii*, 1958, No. 10 (October), pp. 39 f.

61 *Izvestiya*, 13 April 1960

62 *Ibid.*, 1 October 1958

63 *Pravda*, 11 September 1958

64 *Jen-min Jih-pao*, 7 November 1958

65 *Promyshlenno-ekonomicheskaya gazeta* [Gazette for Industry and Economy] (Moscow, 21 November 1958)

66 Marguerite Higgins in *New York Herald Tribune* (European edition), 27–28 December 1958

67 In *Life*, XLVI, No. 2 (12 January 1959), p. 86

68 *Pravda*, 6 February 1959

69 *Ibid.*, 28 January 1959

70 *Ibid.*, 16 December 1958, p. 4

71 N. Matkovsky, *Pravda*, 12 June 1960

72 *Pravda*, 21 July 1959

73 Stalin, *Works* (Moscow 1955), XIII, p. 358 f.

74 English text of the 'Wuhan Resolution' in *Peking Review*, 1958, No. 43 (23 December), pp. 10–19

75 *Pravda*, 18 December 1958

76 See communiqué from Wuhan, note 74

77 *Pravda*, 29 January 1959

78 *Peking Review*, 1959, No. 7 (17 February), p. 12

79 *Pravda*, 28 January 1959

80 Ts. Stepanyan, 'Étapy i Sroki' [Stages and Periods] in *Oktyabr*, 1960, No. 7 (July), p. 152

81 *Pravda*, 2 November 1961

82 E.g. A. Ye. Kaminsky, *Kooperirovanie selskogo khozyaystva Kitaya* [The Co-operativization of Agriculture in China] (Moscow 1959), pp. 150 f.; Shkarenkova (ed.), *Nash drug Kitay* [Our Friend China] (Moscow 1959), p. 206

83 V. Bereshkov, 'People's Communes and Paper Tigers', in *New Times* (Moscow), 1959, No. 12 (March); shortly beforehand *New Times* had published a short contribution on the subject of the people's communes by a Chinese author, but then in the article by L. Delusin, 'The Great Leap' (No. 39/1959) it expressed criticism

84 A. A. Andreyev, '10 let Kitayskoy Narodnoy Respubliki' [Ten Years of the Chinese People's Republic], in *Kommunist*, 1959,

No. 14 (September), pp. 23 f.; 'Veliky podvig kitayskogo naroda' [Editorial: The Heroic Feat of the Chinese People], *ibid.*, p. 12

85 *Pravda*, 2 October 1959

86 *Ibid.*, 1 October 1959

87 *Ibid.*, 29 September 1959

88 *Ibid.*, 1 October 1959; see also Joachim Glaubitz, 'Das Echo der chinesischen Volkskommunen im Ostblock' [The Echo of the Chinese People's Communes in the Eastern Bloc], in *Osteuropa*, XI, No. 11/12 (November–December 1961), pp. 823–28

89 *Sovietsko-kitayskaya druzhba* [Soviet-Chinese Friendship], 1959, No. 38

90 *NCNA*, 13 February 1960

91 *Pravda*, 14 February 1960

92 'Neuklonnyy rost sil sotsialisma' [The Steady Growth of the Forces of Socialism], in *Kommunist*, 1961, No. 6 (April), p. 95

93 *Jen-min Jih-pao*, 29 August 1959; English version in *Peking Review*, 1959, No. 36 (8 September), p. 9

94 Liu Schao-tschi [Liu Shao-ch'i], *Der Sieg des Marxismum-Leninismus in China* [The Victory of Marxism-Leninism in China] (Peking 1959), pp. 33, 35, 37

95 *Peking Review*, 1959, No. 35 (1 September), pp. 7 f.

96 See the issue of *Union Research Service*, Vol. 29, No. 21 (11 December 1962) devoted to: The Present Stage in the Operation and Management of Production Teams

97 See the Lushan resolution of the CC of the CPC, in *Peking Review*, 1959, No. 35 (1 September), pp. 5 f.

98 See Joachim Glaubitz, 'Die Kommunisierung der chinesischen Stadt—eine Episode im "Grossen Sprung"' [The Communization of the Chinese Town—a Stage in the 'Great Leap'], in *Osteuropa*, XII, No. 4/5 (April–May 1962), pp. 311–15

99 *Peking Review*, 1962, No. 39 (28 September), pp. 5 f.

100 Stalin, *Economic Problems of Socialism in the USSR* (English edition) (Moscow 1952), 103 pp.

101 E.g. in Khrushchev's anniversary speech, Part II, in *Pravda*, 7 November 1957

102 See *Voprosy ekonomiki*, 1958, No. 9, pp. 84–118

103 See especially the Moscow journals *Kommunist* and *Oktyabr*

104 See the bibliographical survey by A. Loginov, 'Chitaya knigu o kommunizme' [Reading a Book about Communism], in *Kommunist*, 1960, No. 12 (August), pp. 111 f.

105 S. Strumilin, 'Rabochiy byt i kommunizm' [Workers' Life and Communism], in *Novyy mir*, 1960, No. 7 (July), pp. 203 f.

106 E.g. A. Kharchev, 'Semya i kommunizm' [Family and Communism], in *Kommunist*, 1960, No. 7 (May), p. 53; O. Yurovitskiy, 'Materialnye i moralnye stimuly sotsialisticheskogo proizvodstva' [Material and Moral Stimuli of Socialist Production] in *Kommunist*, 1960, No. 12 (August), p. 31; Ts. Stepanyan, 'Obshchaya zakonomernost kommunisticheskogo stroitelstva' [The General

Course of the Building of Communism], in *Politicheskoye samo-obrazovanie* [Political Self-Education], 1961, No. 2

107 Reinhart Maurach, 'Das Sowjetrecht auf dem Wege zur Restalini-sierung?' [Soviet Law on the Road to Re-Stalinization?], in *Osteuropa*, XII, No. 4/5 (April–May 1962), pp. 280 f.

108 *Pravda*, 19 April 1958

109 Directive of 30 December 1960, published in *Sotsialisticheskaya zakonnost* [Socialist Legality], 1961, No. 3, p. 83

110 Cf. the announcement of the CC of the Komsomol, in *Pravda*, 22 November 1958, and the editorial in *Pravda*, 25 November 1958

111 *Pravda*, 2 November 1961

112 *Ibid.*, 19 October 1961, p. 6

113 See Part 2, Paragraphs I/2/A and III/1 (*Pravda*, 2 November 1961, p. 7)

114 *Pravda*, 24 March 1962

115 Cf. Boris Meissner, 'Die grosse Verwaltungsreform Chruschtschows', in *Osteuropa*, XIII, No. 2/3 (February/March 1963), pp. 81–107; Roy D. Laird, 'Die Reformen von 1962 in der sowjetischen Agrarverwaltung', *ibid.*, No. 6, pp. 394–8

Chapter XV: WORLD POLICY OF THE 'CAMP'

1 See Allen S. Whiting, *China Crosses the Yalu*

2 Zagoria, *Conflict*, pp. 154 f., 160–65, 187 f.

3 Mao Tse-tung, *Selected Works* (Peking), IV, p. 100

4 *Genosse Mao Tse-tung über 'Der Imperialismus und alle Reaktionäre sind Papiertiger'* [Comrade Mao Tse-tung on 'Imperialism and all Reactionaries are Paper Tigers'] (German edit., Peking 1958)

5 *Jen-min Jih-pao* and *Ta Kung Pao*, 11 and 12 January 1958

6 *Jen-min Jih-pao*, 11 January 1958

7 *Izvestiya* and *Pravda*, 23 July 1958

8 *NCNA*, 22 July 1958

9 *Pravda*, 24 July 1958

10 *NCNA*, 24 July 1958

11 *Jen-min Jih-pao*, 25, 26 and 27 July 1958

12 *NCNA*, 21 and 25 July 1958

13 *Izvestiya*, 5 August 1958

14 This latter view expressed by the *New York Times*, 10 August 1958

15 *Pravda*, 29 July 1958

16 *Izvestiya*, 6 August 1958

17 A similar conclusion is reached by Herbert Ritvo, 'Sino-Soviet Relations and the Summit', in *Problems of Communism*, VII, No. 5 (September–October 1958), pp. 47–49

18 *Pravda*, 12 October 1954

19 *Ibid.*, 10 February 1955

20 *Ibid.*, 31 August 1958

21 *Izvestiya*, 8 September 1958

22 *Pravda*, 28 February 1963

23 *Izvestiya*, 20 September 1958
24 Treaty text first published in *Pravda*, 15 May 1955
25 Cf. Boris Meissner (ed.), *Der Warschauer Pakt. Dokumentensamm-lung* [The Warsaw Pact. Collected Documents] (Cologne 1962), pp. 32 f.
26 First to Field Marshal Montgomery, then to Edgar Snow, according to *Look*, 31 January 1961, pp. 85 f.
27 G. P. Zhukov, *Varshavsky dogovor i voprosy mezhdunarodnoy bezopasnosti* [The Warsaw Pact and Problems of International Security] (Moscow 1961)
28 E.g. *Jen-min Jih-pao*, 8 July 1956, and 19 June 1960
29 E.g. Khrushchev's reply to TASS, *Pravda*, 6 October 1958
30 *Pravda*, 6 August 1959
31 *Hung-ch'i*, 16 August 1959
32 *Pravda*, 29 September 1959
33 E.g. *Jen-min Jih-pao*, 15 September 1959, and *Peking Review*, 1959, No. 40 (6 October), p. 35
34 *Ogonyok*, 1960, Nos. 40 and 41
35 *Pravda*, 1 October 1959
36 *Ibid.*
37 *Ibid.*, 5 October 1959
38 Boris N. Ponomarev, in *Pravda*, 12 August 1960
39 *Peking Review*, 1963, No. 9 (1 March), p. 9, and No. 10/11 (15 March), pp. 60 f.
40 For Communism in Asia, see among others Ball, *Nationalism and Communism in East Asia*; Brimmel, *Communism in South East Asia*; Kennedy, *A History of Communism in East Asia*. For Communist policy in the Near East: Laqueur, *The Soviet Union and the Middle East*; Rodger Swearingen, *A Decade of Soviet Policy in Asia*; Paul F. Langer, *Independence or Subordination? The Japanese Communist Party Between Moscow and Peking* (Los Angeles 1962) [mimeographed], 54 pp.; in Africa: Italiaander, *Schwarze Haut im roten Griff* [Black Skin in the Red Grip]; Fritz Schatten, *Afrika—schwarz oder rot?* [Africa—Black or Red?]; in Latin America: Allen, *Soviet Influence in Latin America*; Daniel Tretian, 'Sino-Soviet Rivalry in Latin America', in *Problems of Communism*, 1963, Vol. XII (January–February), pp. 26–40 (complete titles in Bibliography)
41 Lenin, *Selected Works*, II (Moscow 1947), 'Better Fewer, But Better', p. 854
42 Stalin, *Works*, V, pp. 57 and 242 f.
43 John H. Kautsky, *Moscow and the Communist Party of India* (New York and London 1956), pp. 24–43; Gene D. Overstreet and Marshall Windmiller, *Communism in India* (Berkeley and Los Angeles 1959), pp. 253–275
44 See *Osteuropa*, XII, No. 6 (June 1962), p. 438; also *Neue Zürcher Zeitung*, Foreign Edition, 4 January 1962
45 *Pravda*, 11 April 1962

46 *Jen-min Jih-pao*, 29 and 30 October 1962
47 *Ibid.*, 31 October 1962
48 *Peking Review*, 1962, No. 45 (9 November), p. 13
49 *Pravda*, 18 November 1962. For a summary of events, see 'Communist China in the Cuba Crisis', in *Current Scene*, 1963, Vol. II, No. 8 (28 January), 9 pp.
50 Ye. Zhukov, 'Znamenatelniy faktor nashego vremeni' [A Significant Factor of Our Time], in *Pravda*, 26 August 1960
51 V. Rymalov, V. Tyagunenko, *Slaborazvitye strany v mirovom kapitalisticheskom khozyaystve* [The Less Developed Countries in the Capitalist World Economy] (Moscow 1961), p. 441; the standard Western work for the period from the early days until the spring of 1958 is Berliner, *Soviet Economic Aid*; see also *Sino-Soviet Economic Offensive in the Less Developed Countries*, edited by the US State Department. On development aid for the members of the Asian Soviet bloc, see [Kurt Müller], *Entwicklungshilfe innerhalb des Ostblocks* [Development Aid Within the Soviet Bloc]
52 F. Konstantinov, 'Raskolnicheskaya, antimarksistskaya deyatelnost albanskikh rukovoditeley' [The Divisive Anti-Marxist Activity of the Albanian Leaders], in *Kommunist*, 1961, No. 17 (November), p. 48
53 E.g. through Teng Li-chun and Wu Chiang, 'Dialectic is the Algebra of Revolution', in *Peking Review*, 1960, No. 46 (15 November), p. 12
54 *Long Live Leninism*, pp. 49 f.
55 Thus the Chinese representative before the (Communist) World Federation of Trade Unions, see *Peking Review*, 1960, No. 24 (14 June), p. 14
56 Mao Tse-tung, *Selected Works* (London and New York), III, pp. 96 and 119
57 Liu Shao-ch'i to Anna Louise Strong ('The Thought of Mao Tse-tung', in *Amerasia*, June 1947, p. 161), quoted by Zagoria, *Conflict*, pp. 14 f.; Liu Shao-ch'i made similar statements at the Trade Unions Conference in Peking on 25 November 1949, see *Pravda*, 4 January 1950
58 Statement at the 30th anniversary of the founding of the CPC, July 1951, according to Howard L. Boorman, 'The Sino-Soviet Alliance. The Political Aspect', in Boorman (*et al.*), *Axis*, p. 43
59 Soong Ching-ling (widow of Sun Yat-sen), in *Jen-min Jih-pao*, 8 November 1956
60 Closing words of Liu Shao-ch'i's article marking the tenth anniversary of the founding of the Chinese People's Republic, in *Jen-min Jih-pao*, 1 October 1959
61 Teng To, 'Mao Tse-tung's Ideology Opens Up the Way for Chinese Historical Science', in *Peking Jih Pao*, 24 February 1961, quoted in *Ost-Probleme*, XIII, No. 22 (27 October 1961), p. 712
62 *Peking Review*, 1963, No. 9 (1 March), p. 12
63 Mao Tse-tung, *On the Correct Handling of Contradictions Among the People* (English edition, Peking 1957), p. 70

64 *Peking Review*, 1960, No. 13 (29 March)
65 Robert C. North, 'The New Expansionism', in *Problems of Communism*, IX, No. 1 (January–February 1960), p. 25; in the later edition of Mao Tse-tung's works (*Selected Works* (London and New York), III, p. 78), reference to these areas has been omitted
66 *Pravda*, 29, 30 and 31 March 1959
67 Cf. *Pravda*, 5 April 1959
68 Speech of 23 December 1959, before the Indian Lower House
69 Thus Member of Parliament Masani, in the Indian Lower House on 25 November 1959
70 Speech of 23 December 1959, before the Indian Lower House
71 *Pravda*, 10 September 1959
72 *Jen-min Jih-pao*, 27 February 1963; English version: *Peking Review*, 1963, No. 9 (1 March), p. 10
73 The standard work on this question is Victor Purcell, *The Chinese in Southeast Asia*
74 Cf. Hans Kohn, *Pan-Slavism: its History and Ideology* (Notre Dame, Indiana 1953)
75 *Pravda*, 5 November 1962
76 *Peking Review*, 1963, No. 9 (1 March), p. 13
77 *Izvestiya Akademii Nauk SSSR* [Bulletin of the Academy of Sciences of the USSR], Seriya istorii i filologii [Historical and Philological Series], January–February 1952, p. 87
78 *Peking Review*, 1960, No. 49/50 (13 December), p. 9
79 *Ibid.*, p. 16
80 John H. Kautsky, *Moscow and the Communist Party of India*; Gene D. Overstreet and Marshall Windmiller, *Communism in India*
81 *Peking Review*, 1963, No. 10/11 (15 March), pp. 63 f.
82 *Re* the treaty with Nepal, see *Peking Review*, 1960, No. 1 (29 March), pp. 6–10, and 1963, No. 4 (25 January), pp. 9 f.; *re* relations with Burma, see Dai Shen-yu, 'Peking and Rangoon', in *The China Quarterly*, No. 5 (January–March 1961), pp. 131–44
83 David Mozingo, 'New Developments in China's Relations with Indonesia', in *Current Scene* (Hongkong), I, No. 24 (5 February 1962)
84 *Peking Review*, 1962, No. 52 (28 December), pp. 5 f.
85 Full text of agreement in *Peking Review*, 1963, No. 10/11 (15 March), pp. 67–70
86 *Pravda*, 4 December 1961
87 E.g. in the Sino-Korean communiqué of 15 July 1961, see *Peking Review*, 1961, No. 29 (21 July), p. 21; cf. John Bradbury, 'Sino-Soviet Competition in North Korea', in *The China Quarterly*, No. 6 (April–June 1961), pp. 15–28
88 *Pravda*, 4 December 1961
89 [Kurt Müller], *Entwicklungshilfe innerhalb des Ostblocks* (Frankfurt and Berlin 1960), p. 70; *Pravda*, 11 July 1961
90 *Ibid.*, p. 101

91 J. P. Honey, 'The Position of the DRP Leadership and the Succession of Ho Chi Minh', in *The China Quarterly*, No. 9 (January–March 1962), pp. 24–36

92 Bernard B. Fall, 'Power and Pressure Groups in North Vietnam', in *The China Quarterly*, No. 9 (January–March 1962), p. 39

93 A useful summary is given by Robert A. Scalapino, 'Moscow, Peking and the Communist Parties of Asia', in *Foreign Affairs*, Vol. 41, No. 2 (January 1963), pp. 323–34

94 Speech of the Indonesian CP leader Aidit, in *Jen-min Jih-pao*, 1 December 1961

95 Fritz Schatten, *Afrika—schwarz oder rot?* (Munich 1961), p. 241

96 W. Weise, in *Die Welt*, 28 December 1961

97 Alexander Y. Kaznacheyev, 'Soviet "Operation Burma"', in *New Leader*, 18 January 1960, p. 15

Chapter XVI: TARGET PRACTICE—WITH LIVING TARGETS

1 *Pravda*, 5 February 1960

2 It has been taken from the magazine *China Today*, of 12 February 1960; see also *Peking Review*, 1960, No. 6; originally it had been published in *Jen-min Jih-pao*, 6 February 1960

3 *Pravda*, 29 January, 1, 3, 4, and 5 February 1960

4 The texts of most of the 1960 documents mentioned here are contained in Hudson (*et al.*), *The Sino-Soviet Dispute*

5 *Hung-ch'i*, 16 April 1960; cf. in the preceding issue of *Hung-ch'i* the preparatory article, 'Imperialism, the Cause of War Today, and the Road of the Peoples' Struggle for Peace'

6 *Jen-min Jih-pao*, 22 April 1960

7 *Long Live Leninism* (Peking 1960), 106 pp.

8 *Pravda*, 23 April 1960

9 E.g. *Jen-min Jih-pao*, 12 and 13 May 1960; also *Ta Kung Pao*, 12 and 13 May 1960

10 Peking's reaction was reflected in the editorials in *Jen-min Jih-pao*, 13 and 20 May 1960, and *Ta Kung Pao*, 13 May 1960

11 *Wichtige Gespräche des Vorsitzenden Mao Tse-tung mit Persönlichkeiten aus Asien, Afrika und Lateinamerika* [Important Conversations between Chairman Mao Tse-tung and Personalities from Asia, Africa and Latin America] (Peking 1960), p. 8

12 *NCNA*, 22 May 1960

13 *Pravda*, 19 May 1960

14 See the issue of *Peking Review*, 1960, No. 24 (14 June) devoted to this conference

15 Zagoria, *Conflict*, pp. 320–23

16 *Pravda*, 12 June 1960

17 Edward Crankshaw, 'The Moscow-Peking Clash Exposed', in *The Observer*, 12 and 19 February 1961

18 In his interview with Edgar Snow, in *Look*, 31 January 1961

19 Cf. editorial in *Pravda*, 20 June 1960, and report on Khrushchev's speech at the session of the Hungarian CP in December 1959, in *Pravda*, 2 December 1959

20 *Pravda*, 22 June 1960

21 P'eng Chen's speech in *NCNA*, 22 June 1960, and *Peking Review*, 1960, No. 26 (28 June), pp. 4 f.

22 *Pravda*, 23 June 1960

23 *Jen-min Jih-pao*, 24 June 1960

24 *Peking Review*, 1963, No. 9 (1 March), p. 10

25 *Ibid.*, p. 11

26 The principal articles are in *Peking Review*, 1960, Nos. 40, 41, 45 and 46 (4 and 11 October, 8 and 15 November)

27 E.g. A. Belyakov and F. Burlatsky, in *Kommunist*, 1960, No. 13 (September); Ye. Zhukov, in *Pravda*, 26 August 1960

28 *Pravda*, 6 December 1960. For an excellent reconstruction of the course of the conference, see William E. Griffith, 'The November 1960 Moscow Meeting. A Preliminary Reconstruction', in *The China Quarterly*, 1962, No. 11 (July–September), pp. 38–57. In March 1963 the Chinese indicated that they intended one day to publish their own version of what really happened at the 1960 Moscow conference, see *Peking Review*, 1963, No. 9 (1 March), p. 11

29 *NCNA*, 4 November 1960

30 Declaration published in *Pravda*, 6 December 1960, appeal in *Pravda*, 11 December 1960

31 Editorial in *Pravda*, 7 December 1960, and Suslov's report to the CC of the CPSU in *Pravda*, 23 January 1961; resolution of the CC of the CPC in *NCNA*, 20 January 1961, also editorials in *Jen-min Jih-pao*, 7, 10 and 12, December 1960, all published in English in *Peking Review*, 1960, Nos. 49/50 and 51 (13 and 20 December)

32 Text in *Kommunist*, 1961, No. 1 (January), pp. 3–37

33 *Jen-min Jih-pao*, 12 December 1960; *Peking Review*, 1960, No. 51 (20 December), p. 10

34 *Pravda*, 21 January 1961

35 Mao to a group of Africans, see *NCNA*, 28 April 1961, and Liu Shao-ch'i in his speech of 30 June 1961, see *Peking Review*, 1961, No. 26/27 (7 July), p. 12

36 *Ta Kung Pao*, 20 April 1961

37 See editorial as well as articles by Ai Su-ch'i and Ch'ang Ch'ung-hsi, in *Jen-min Jih-pao*, 18 March 1961

38 Yu. Frantsev, in *Pravda*, 18 March 1961 and A. Molok: Istoricheskoye znachenie Parizhskoy Kommuny [The Historical Significance of the Paris Commune] in *Kommunist*, 1961, No. 4 (March), pp. 80–88

39 Official government statement of 31 August 1961, in *Peking Review*, 1961, No. 36 (8 September), p. 6

40 *Pravda*, 30 July 1961

41 *Jen-min Jih-pao*, 5 August 1961

42 *Peking Review*, 1961, No. 43 (27 October), p. 9

43 *Jen-min Jih-pao*, 1 December 1961 (editorial); *Peking Review*, 1961, No. 49 (8 December), p. 8

44 See especially F. Konstantinov, 'Raskolnicheskaya, anti-marksist-skaya deyatelnost albanskikh rukovoditeley' [The Divisive Anti-Marxist Activity of the Albanian Leaders], in *Kommunist*, 1961, No. 17 (November), pp. 38–53

45 E.g. N. Inozemtsev, in *Pravda*, 17 January 1962, and P. Pospelov, in *Pravda*, 18 January 1962; *Jen-min Jih-pao*, 1, 10 and 11 December 1961

46 *Pravda*, 6 March 1962

47 See also 'The Anti-Khrushchev Movement in Communist China', in *Union Research Service*, Vol. 29, No. 5 (16 October 1962), pp. 66–75

48 *NCNA*, 16 April 1962; *Pravda*, 18 April 1962

49 E.g. L. Ilyichev, in *Pravda*, 21 April 1961

50 *Jen-min Jih-pao*, 29 March 1962; *Pravda*, 3 April 1962

51 *Peking Review*, 1962, No. 39 (28 September), pp. 5–8

52 For a detailed study of the five congresses see Robert F. Lamberg, 'Kommunistische Parteikongresse im Winter 1962–63' [Communist Party Congresses during the Winter of 1962–63], in *Osteuropa*, 1963, No. 2/3 (February/March 1963), pp. 158–71

53 *Peking Review*, XIII, No. 5 (1 February), p. 5

54 *Ibid.*, 1963, No. 4 (25 January), pp. 7 f.; and No. 12 (22 March), p. 7

55 *Pravda*, 17 January 1963

56 Both letters were published by *Pravda* on 14 March and by *Peking Review* on 22 March 1963

57 *Pravda*, 3 April 1963

58 *Ibid.*, 13 December 1962

59 *Ibid.*, 18 November 1962, 7 January and 10 February 1963

60 In: *Peking Review*, 1962, No. 47/48 (30 November), pp. 26–30 and 30–34; 1962, No. 51 (21 December), pp. 5–10; 1963, No. 1 (4 January), pp. 9–21; 1963, No. 2 (11 January), pp. 5–10 and 10–15; 1963, No. 5 (1 February), pp. 5–10; 1963, No. 9 (1 March), pp. 7–16; 1963, No. 10/11 (15 March), pp. 8–58 and 58–62; 1963, No. 25 (21 June), pp. 6–22

61 *Pravda*, 15 February 1956

62 *Ibid.*, 22 June 1960, as quoted by Hudson (*et al.*) in *The Sino-Soviet Dispute*, pp. 136–37

63 *Long Live Leninism*, pp. 16 f.

64 *Pravda*, 22 November 1957, see note 62, p. 53

65 *Peking Review*, 1963, No. 10/11 (15 March), p. 50

66 *Long Live Leninism*, pp. 100 f.

67 *Pravda*, 1 October 1959

68 *Ibid.*, 23 April 1960

69 *Ibid.*, 22 June 1960

70 *Long Live Leninism*, p. 102

71 *Pravda*, 22 April 1960, see note 62, p. 119

72 Speech of the Chinese delegate at the Congress of the (Communist) World Federation of Trade Unions, in *Peking Review*, 1960, No. 24 (14 June), p. 14

73 *Peking Review*, 1963, No. 10/11 (15 March), p. 60

74 N. Matkovsky, *Pravda*, 12 June 1960

75 *Long Live Leninism*, pp. 2, 37, 39, 43, 60

76 A. Belyakov, F. Burlatsky, 'Leninskaya teoriya sotsialisticheskoy revolyutsii i sovremyonnost' [The Leninist Theory of Social Revolution and the Present Day], in *Kommunist*, 1960, No. 13 (September), pp. 23, 25, 27

77 See Boris Meissner, *Das Partei-Programm der KPdSU* [The Party Program of the CPSU], p. 104

78 *Stuttgarter Zeitung*, 10 May 1958

79 Cf. the detailed study of this question in Alice Langley Hsieh, *Communist China's Strategy in the Nuclear Age* (Englewood Cliffs, N.J. 1962)

80 E.g. *Jen-min Jih-pao*, 21 Sept. 1959; *Peking Review*, 1959, No. 40 (6 October), p. 23, and No. 42 (20 October), pp. 10 f.; *Jen-min Jih-pao*, 22 January 1960

81 *Peking Review*, 1963, No. 10/11 (15 March), p. 25

82 K'ang Sheng at the Warsaw Pact conference on 4 February 1960, in *Peking Review*, 1960, No. 6 (9 February), pp. 6–9; Chou En-lai to Edgar Snow, in *Look*, 31 January 1961

83 *Peking Review*, 1963, No. 10/11 (15 March), p. 8

84 *Pravda*, 22 November 1957, see note 62, pp. 48, 49

85 *Ibid.*, 28 January 1959

86 *Ibid.*, 8 October 1959

87 *Long Live Leninism*, p. 30

88 *Chungkuo Ch'ing-nien-pao*, 16 February 1960

89 Mao Tse-tung, *Selected Works* (London and New York), II, pp. 272, 273

90 *Peking Review*, 1963, No. 10/11 (15 March), p. 30

91 Sung Tu, in *Chungkuo Ch'ing-nien-pao*, see note 88

92 As quoted by Kuusinen in his speech at the ninetieth anniversary of Lenin's birth, in *Pravda*, 23 April 1960

93 *Pravda*, 22 June 1960, see note 62, p. 137

94 *Peking Review*, 1960, No. 24 (14 June) p. 13

95 Yu. Frantsev, in *Pravda*, 7 August 1960

96 *Peking Review*, 1960, No. 24 (14 June), p. 13

97 *Chungkuo Ch'ing-nien-pao*, 16 July 1960

98 *Kommunist*, 1961, No. 1 (January), pp. 16–22

99 *Pravda*, 13 March 1954

100 *Ibid.*, 22 June 1960, see note 62, pp. 132–33

101 A. Belyakov, F. Burlatsky (see note 76), p. 16

102 *Kommunist*, 1961, No. 1 (January), p. 20

103 *Borba*, 16 June 1958

104 *Long Live Leninism*, pp. 21 f.

105 *Ibid.*, p. 104

106 General Li Chi-min, in *Jen-min Jih-pao*, 25 June 1960
107 Especially the editorial in *Jen-min Jih-pao*, 30 September 1960— English version in *Peking Review*, 1960, No. 40 (4 October), p. 14
108 *Pravda*, 13 December 1962
109 *Peking Review*, 1963, No. 1 (4 January), p. 14
110 *Ibid.*, 1963, No. 2 (11 January), p. 8
111 *Long Live Leninism*, p. 22
112 See note 62, p. 133
113 Yu. Frantsev, in *Pravda*, 7 August 1960
114 A. Belyakov, F. Burlatsky (see note 76), p. 16
115 *Peking Review*, 1963, No. 10/11 (15 March), p. 27
116 *Ibid.*, 1963, No. 5 (1 February), pp. 9 and 5
117 *Ibid.*, 1962, No. 51 (21 December), p. 6
118 *Pravda*, 13 December 1962
119 *Peking Review*, 1962, No. 51 (21 December), p. 8
120 *Ibid.*, 1963, No. 9 (1 March), pp. 7 f.
121 *Ibid.*
122 *Ibid.*, 1963, No. 1 (4 January), pp. 9–21; No. 9 (1 March), pp. 7–16; No. 10/11 (15 March), pp. 8–62
123 *Ibid.*, 1963, No. 9 (1 March), pp. 13, 15
124 David A. Charles, 'The Dismissal of Marshal P'eng Teh-huai', in *The China Quarterly*, No. 8 (October–December 1961), pp. 63–76
125 *Peking Review*, 1962, No. 39 (28 September), p. 7
126 *Ibid.*, 1962, No. 51 (21 December), p. 9
127 *Ibid.*, 1963, No. 10/11 (15 March), pp. 9 f.
128 *Ibid.*, 1963, No. 9 (1 March), p. 10
129 Zbigniew K. Brzezinski, 'The Problematics of Sino-Soviet Bargaining', in Kurt London, *Unity*, pp. 392–405
130 *Peking Review*, 1963, No. 9 (1 March), p. 10
131 *Jen-min Jih-pao*, 20 February 1963
132 *Peking Review*, 1963, No. 10/11 (15 March), p. 56
133 See the report on the conference on Sino-Soviet problems at Kawaguchi, Japan, in September 1960, in *Osteuropa*, X, No. 11/12 (November–December 1960), pp. 729–770, and part of the papers of Kawaguchi in Kurt London, *Unity*

PROSPECTS AND CONCLUSIONS

1 *Peking Review*, 1963, No. 10/11 (15 March), p. 50

NOTES ON THE BIBLIOGRAPHY

A COMPLETE BIBLIOGRAPHY covering the subject of this book would run into some two hundred pages. Since the author has drawn on more than 1,200 books and other publications, in addition to thousands of articles in newspapers and magazines, the following bibliography can contain only a selection, and in the case of some authors only the principal work is listed. Many of the books mentioned include comprehensive bibliographies of their own. The American *Bibliography of Asian Studies* lists several thousand titles every year (most of which, although not all, are in English); the Soviet bibliography on China by P. E. Skachkov comprises nearly 20,000 titles.

Among the Communist periodicals the sources most frequently used were the Moscow *Pravda* and its Peking counterpart, *Jen-min Jih-pao* (People's Daily); others are the Moscow Party organ *Kommunist* and its equivalent *Hung-ch'i* (Red Flag), published in Peking since June 1958, and the news services of the two official news agencies, TASS of Moscow and NCNA (New China News Agency) of Peking. In the case of Chinese publications, the author has made use of the invaluable translation services of the United States Consulate-General and the Union Research Institute, both of Hongkong, as well as of the Joint Publications Research Service of Washington, D.C. Most of the quotations and documentary material supplied by these services have been checked by his assistants wherever access to the original was possible. Since 1958 an English-language periodical, *Peking Review*, representing the official viewpoint, has been published in Peking. (It had previously appeared, starting in 1950, as *People's China*.) A number of other foreign-language periodicals are also published regularly in Peking.

The following Western periodicals are relevant: *China News Analysis* (Hongkong, weekly since 1953), publishing excellent interpretations based on thorough and expert knowledge of the subject, and *Current Scene* (Hongkong, biweekly since May 1961—originally in multigraph form). The foremost British journal dealing with present-day China is *The China Quarterly* (London, quarterly since the beginning of 1960); while the leading American equivalent is *Asian Survey* (Berkeley and Los Angeles, monthly since 1961). Articles on China frequently appear in *Problems of Communism* (Washington, D.C., bimonthly since 1952), and in *Osteuropa* (Stuttgart, German Federal Republic, since 1951—originally six times a year, from 1957 monthly), the latter also regularly publishing reports on Sino-Soviet relations.

As regards the author's quotations from the Communist 'classics', wherever possible the translator of the present book has substituted the corresponding passages and references from standard English-language editions of the works of Lenin, Stalin, and Mao Tse-tung. Occasionally the author, in his original version of his book, drew on material of which a German but not an English translation was available, and in these isolated instances the translator has either translated directly from the available German version or, if some other source was used (in one case, the original Russian), clarified this in the relevant footnote.

Material covering Russian-Chinese, and Soviet-Chinese, relations is increasing by leaps and bounds. For the pre-Communist era, see Yakhontoff (for the years from 1240 to 1930) and Dallin (from the nineteenth century to 1930); also three non-Communist Chinese: Ch'eng T'ien-fang (Middle Ages to 1956), Wu Aitchen (from 1618 to 1950), and Weih Ken Shen (seventeenth century to 1924); in Russian, the Communist writers P. E. Skachkov (from 1689 to 1916), Sladkovsky (Middle Ages to 1956, mainly economic relations), and Pyn Min (Middle Ages to 1955; translated from the Chinese). The somewhat obscure twenties and thirties of this century are dealt with in the United States by Whiting (1917 to 1924), Schwartz (1918 to 1933), North (1919 to 1951), Eudin and North (1920 to 1927), Brandt (1924 to 1927), and Dallin (Soviet Russia and the Far East, 1930 to 1948), as well as by the non-Communist Chinese Wei (1917 to 1954) and Hsiao Tso-liang (1930 to 1934), and the Soviet authors Kapitsa (1917 to 1958), Perevertaylo (1923 to 1927), and the Red Chinese work by Din, In, *et al.* (1917 to 1923).

Analyses of the years following the end of World War II, and in particular since the founding of the Chinese People's Republic, are to be found in the works of the following writers published in England or the United States: Beloff (1944 to 1951), Boorman *et al.* (principally the first half of the 1950's), Zagoria (1956 to 1961), Hudson *et al.* (1957 to 1960: some English quotations from Russian and Chinese sources have been taken by the translator from this book), and Chin Szu-k'ai (1949 to 1957), who lives in Hongkong. A comprehensive collection of documents on Soviet-Chinese relations covering the period from 1917 to 1957 was published in Moscow, edited by Kurdyukov *et al.* One of the best surveys of the internal problems of the Soviet bloc is that by Brzezinski, while Konstantinov and Sanakoyev dealt with the subject from the Soviet point of view.

BIBLIOGRAPHY

Abegg, Lily, *The Mind of East Asia* (London, New York 1952), 344 pp.

Allen, Robert Loring, *Soviet Influence in Latin America. The Role of Economic Relations* (Washington, D.C. 1959), 108 pp.

Anand, Shanta, *Communist China in the Bandung Conference*. Master of Arts Thesis. (Berkeley, Calif. 1957), 130 pp.

Ball, William MacMahon, *Nationalism and Communism in East Asia* (Melbourne 1953), 210 pp.

Ballis, William B., 'The Political Evolution of a Soviet Satellite: The Mongolian People's Republic', in *Western Political Quarterly*, IX, No. 2 (June 1956), pp. 293–328

Ballis, William B., 'Soviet Russia's Asiatic Frontier Technique: Tannu Tuwa', in *Pacific Affairs*, XIV, No. 1 (March 1941), pp. 91–96

Barendsen, Robert D., 'The 1960 Educational Reforms', in *The China Quarterly*, No. 4 (October–December 1960), pp. 55–65

Barendsen, Robert D., 'The Agricultural Middle School in Communist China', in *The China Quarterly*, No. 8 (October–December 1961), pp. 106–33

Barnett, A. Doak, *Communist China and Asia* (New York 1960), 575 pp.

Bary, Wm. Theodore de, Wing-tsit Chan, Burton Watson, *Sources of Chinese Tradition* (New York 1960), 976 pp.

Beloff, Max, *Soviet Policy in the Far East. 1944–1951* (London 1953), 278 pp.

Benz, Ernst, *Geist und Leben der Ostkirche* (Hamburg 1957), 203 pp.

Berliner, Joseph S., *Soviet Economic Aid* (New York 1958), 232 pp.

Berton, Peter (ed.), *Soviet Works on China. A Bibliography of Non-Periodical Literature 1946–1955* (Los Angeles 1959), 158 pp.

Bibliography of Asian Studies. Annual Supplement (since 1956) to *Journal of Asian Studies* (Ann Arbor, Mich.)

Black, Cyril E. (ed.), *The Transformation of Russian Society. Aspects of Social Change Since 1861* (Cambridge, Mass. 1960), 695 pp.

Black, Cyril E., 'Political Modernization in Russia and China', in Kurt London (ed.), *Unity and Contradiction* (New York 1962), pp. 3–18

Bodde, Derk, 'Harmony and Conflict in Chinese Philosophy', in Arthur F. Wright (ed.), *Studies in Chinese Thought* (Chicago 1953), pp. 19–80

Bodde, Derk, 'Feudalism in China', in Rushton Coulborn (ed.), *Feudalism in History* (Princeton, N.J. 1954), pp. 49–92

Boorman, Howard L. (ed.), *Contemporary China and the Chinese* (The Annals of the American Academy of Political and Social Science, CCCXXI) (Philadelphia, Jan. 1959), 220 pp.

Boorman, Howard L., 'Literature and Politics in Contemporary China', in *Thought Patterns*, No. 7 (New York 1960), pp. 101–23

Boorman, Howard L., *Men and Politics in Modern China* (New York 1960) (multigraphed), 173 pp.

Boorman, Howard L. *et al.*, *Moscow-Peking Axis* (New York 1957), 227 pp.

Boyd, R. G., *Communist China's Foreign Policy* (New York 1962), 147 pp.

Brandt, Conrad, *Stalin's Failure in China. 1924–1927* (Cambridge, Mass. 1958), 226 pp.

Brandt, Conrad, Benjamin Schwartz, John K. Fairbank, *A Documentary History of Chinese Communism* (London 1952), 552 pp.

Brière, O. (S.J.), *Fifty Years of Chinese Philosophy, 1898–1950* (New York 1956), 159 pp.

Brimmell, J. H., *Communism in South East Asia* (London, New York 1959), 415 pp.

Brzezinski, Z. K., *The Soviet Bloc. Unity and Conflict* (Cambridge, Mass. 1960), 470 pp.

Byrnes, Robert F., 'Soviet and Chinese Communist Relations with Yugoslavia', in Kurt London (ed.), *Unity and Contradiction* (New York 1962), pp. 159–84

Chan Wing-tsit, *Religious Trends in Modern China* (New York, 1953), 327 pp.

Chandrasekhar, S., *China's Population. Census and Vital Statistics* (Hongkong 1959), 69 pp.

Chang Chung-li, *The Chinese Gentry* (Seattle, Wash. 1955), 250 pp.

Chang Chung-li, *The Income of the Chinese Gentry* (Seattle, Wash. 1962), 369 pp.

Chang, Eileen, *Naked Earth* (Hongkong 1956), 365 pp.

Chao Kao-chün, *Agrarian Policy of the Chinese Communist Party. 1921–1959* (Bombay, Calcutta, New Delhi, Madras, London, New York 1960), 399 pp.

Ch'en Po-ta, *Stalin and the Chinese Revolution* (Peking 1953), 55 pp.

Chen, Theodore H. E., *Thought Reform of the Chinese Intellectuals* (Hongkong 1960), 247 pp.

Ch'eng T'ien-fang, *A History of Sino-Russian Relations* (Washington, D.C. 1957), 389 pp.

Chiang Kai-shek (Chiang Chung-chen), *Soviet Russia in China; A Summing-Up at Seventy* (New York 1957), 392 pp.

Chin, Calvin Suey Keu, *A Study of Chinese Dependence upon the Soviet Union for Economic Development as a Factor in Communist China's Foreign Policy* (Hongkong 1959), 181 pp.

Chin Szu-k'ai, *Communist China's Relations with the Soviet Union, 1949–1957* (Hongkong 1961) (multigraphed), 143, ix, iv pp.

Chou En-lai, *Report on the Question of Intellectuals* (Peking 1956), 44 pp.

Chou Ts'e-tsung, *The May Fourth Movement. Intellectual Revolution in Modern China* (Cambridge, Mass. 1960), 486 pp.

Ch'ü T'ung-tsu, *Law and Society in Traditional China* (Paris, The Hague 1961), 304 pp.

Ch'ü T'ung-tsu, *Local Government in China under the Ch'ing* (Cambridge, Mass. 1962), xiv, 360 pp.

Chyzhevskyi, Dmytro, *History of Russian Literature from the Eleventh Century to the End of the Baroque* (The Hague 1960), 451 pp.

Coillie, Dries van, *De enthousiaste Zelfmord* (Antwerp 1958), 370 pp.; German translation: *Der begeisterte Selbstmord* (Donauwörth 1961), 472 pp.

Communist China 1955–1959, Policy Documents with Analysis (With a Foreword by Robert R. Bowie and John K. Fairbank) (Cambridge, Mass. 1962), 611 pp.

Compton, Boyd, *Mao's China: Party Reform Documents 1942–1944* (Seattle, Wash. 1952), 278 pp.

Confucian Analects—see *Four Books*

Creel, Herrlee Glessner, *Chinese Thought from Confucius to Mao* (Chicago 1953), 363 pp.

Dallin, David J., *The Rise of Russia in Asia* (New Haven, Conn. 1949), 293 pp.

Dallin, David J., *Soviet Russia and the Far East* (New Haven, Conn. 1948), 398 pp.

Davidson, Basil, *Turkestan Alive. New Travels in Chinese Central Asia* (London 1957), 255 pp.

Degras, Jane (ed.), *The Communist International, 1919–1943. Documents* (London, New York, Toronto). Vol. I: 1919–1922 (1956), 463 pp.; Vol. II: 1923–1928 (1960), 584 pp.

Der VIII. Parteitag der Kommunistischen Partei Chinas. 3 vols. (Peking 1956), 318, 428, 289 pp.

Der Heilige als Eulenspiegel. Zwölf Abenteuer eines Zenmeisters. Translated from Chinese into German by Liu Guan Ying (Basel, Stuttgart 1958), 167 pp.

Din Shou-khe, In Sui-i, Chan Bo-chao, *Vliyanie Oktyabrskoy revolyutsii na Kitay* [The Influence of the October Revolution on China] (Moscow 1959), 202 pp.

Druhe, David N., *Soviet Russia and Indian Communism, 1917–1947* (New York 1959), 429 pp.

Dutt, Vidya Prakash, 'India, China, and the Soviet Union', in Kurt London (ed.), *Unity and Contradiction* (New York 1962), pp. 248–62

Eberhard, Wolfram, *A History of China* (London 1950), 368 pp.

Elegant, Robert S., *The Dragon's Seed* (New York 1959), 312 pp.

Erkes, Eduard, *Geschichte Chinas von den Anfängen bis zum Eindringen des ausländischen Kapitals* ([East] Berlin 1956), 155 pp.

Eudin, Xenia J., Robert C. North, *Soviet Russia and the East 1920–1927. A Documentary Survey* (Stanford, Calif. 1957), 478 pp.

Fairbank, John K. (ed.), *Chinese Thought and Institutions* (Chicago 1957), 438 pp.

Fairbank, John K., Alexander Eckstein, L. S. Yang, *Economic Change in Early Modern China: An Analytic Framework* (Cambridge, Mass. 1960), 26 pp.

Fall, Bernard, *Le Viet-Minh. La République Démocratique du Viet-Nam. 1945–1960* (Paris 1960), 376 pp.

Fan Wön-lan, *Neue Geschichte Chinas*. Vol. I: 1840–1901. ([East] Berlin 1959), 575 pp.

Feuerwerker, Albert, *China's Early Industrialization. Sheng Hsuan-huai (1844–1916) and Mandarin Enterprise* (Cambridge, Mass. 1958), 311, xxxii pp.

Feuerwerker, Albert, 'Materials for the Study of the Economic History of Modern China', in *Journal of Economic History*, March 1961, pp. 41–60

Four Books: The Great Learning; The Doctrine of the Mean; Confucian Analects; The Works of Mencius. Based on the translation of James Legge. Chinese and English version. Reprinted in Hongkong (no year given), by the Hop Kuen Book Co. 351 pp.

Franke, Herbert, *Geld und Wirtschaft in China unter der Mongolen-Herrschaft. Beiträge zur Wirtschaftsgeschichte der Yüan-Zeit* (Leipzig 1949), 171 pp.

Franke, Wolfgang, *Das Jahrhundert der chinesischen Revolution 1851–1949* (Munich 1958), 297 pp.

Franke, Wolfgang, *The Reform and Abolition of the Traditional Examination System* (Cambridge, Mass. 1961), 100 pp.

Friters, Gerard M., *Outer Mongolia and its International Position* (London 1951), 358 pp.

Fung Yu-lan, *A History of Chinese Philosophy*. Vols. I–II (Princeton, N.J. 1952–53)

Giles, Herbert A., *A History of Chinese Literature* (New York 1923), 448 pp.

Gillhausen, Rolf, Joachim Heldt, *Unheimliches China. Eine Reise durch den roten Kontinent* (Hamburg, 1959), 191 pp.

Glasser, Hans Georg, 'Einige Unterschiede im Partei- und Staatsaufbau zwischen der Sowjetunion und der Volksrepublik Chinas', in *Europa-Archiv*, XIV (1960), No. 1/2, pp. 1–12

Granet, Marcel, *La Pensée Chinoise* (Paris 1950), 614 pp.

Griffith, William E., *Albania and the Sino-Soviet Rift* (Cambridge, Mass. 1963), 423 pp.

Groot, Jan Jakob M. de, *Sectarianism and Religious Persecution in China*. Vols. I–II (Amsterdam 1903–4)

Groot, Jan Jakob M. de, *The Religious System of China, its Ancient Forms, Evolution, History and Present Aspect, Manners, Customs and Social Institutions Connected Therewith* (Leyden, 1892–1910), 6 vols.

Groot, Jan Jakob M. de, *The Religion of the Chinese* (New York 1912), 230 pp.

[Gross, D. E., K. Müller], *Die wirtschaftliche Verflechtung der Volksrepublik China mit der Sowjetunion* (Frankfurt, Berlin 1959), 105 pp.

Grossmann, Bernhard, *Die wirtschaftliche Entwicklung der Volksrepublik China* (Stuttgart 1960), 413 pp.

Guillermaz, Jacques, *La Chine Populaire* (Paris 1959), 126 pp.

Guillermaz, Jacques, Basile H. Kerblay, 'The Question of Sino-Soviet Competition over North Vietnam', in Kurt London (ed.), *Unity and Contradiction* (New York 1962), pp. 233–47

Hackmann, Heinrich, *Chinesische Philosophie* (Munich 1927), 406 pp.

Hamm, Harry, *Rebellen gegen Moskau. Albanien—Pekings Brückenkopf in Europa* (Cologne 1962), 189 pp.

Hayit, Baymirya, *Sowjetrussische Orientpolitik am Beispiel Turkestans* (Cologne-Berlin 1962), 289 pp.

Herbert, Jean, *Asien. Denken und Lebensformen der östlichen Welt* (Munich 1959), 297 pp.

Ho Kan-chih, *A History of the Modern Chinese Revolution* (Peking 1959), 627 pp.

Ho Ping-ti, *Studies on the Population of China, 1368–1953* (Cambridge, Mass. 1960)

Hoetzsch, Otto, *Russland. Eine Einführung auf Grund seiner Geschichte vom Japanischen bis zum Weltkrieg.* 2nd ed., completely revised (Berlin 1917), 439 pp.

Houn, Franklin W., 'The Eighth Central Committee of the Chinese Communist Party. A Study of an Elite', in *The American Political Science Review* (June 1957), Vol. 51, pp. 392–404

Hsia, C. T., *A History of Modern Chinese Fiction 1917–1957* (New Haven, Conn. 1961), 662 pp.

Hsia, T. A., *Metaphor, Myth, Ritual and the People's Commune* (Studies in Chinese Communist Terminology. VII) (Berkeley, Calif. 1961) (multigraphed), 60 pp.

Hsia, T. A., *Enigma of the Five Martyrs, A Study of the Leftist Literary Movement in Modern China* (Berkeley, Calif. 1962), 150 pp.

Hsiao Tso-liang, *Power Relations Within the Chinese Communist Movement 1930–1934. A Study of Documents* (Seattle, Wash. 1961), 404 pp.

Hsiao Kung-ch'üan, *Rural China. Imperial Control in the Nineteenth Century* (Seattle, Wash. 1960), 783 pp.

Hsieh, Alice Langley, *Communist China's Strategy in the Nuclear Era* (Englewood Cliffs, N.J. 1962), 204 pp.

Hsu, Francis L. K., *Americans and Chinese. Two Ways of Life* (New York 1953), 457 pp.

Hsüeh Chün-tu, *The Chinese Communist Movement 1937–1949.* An Annotated Bibliography of Selected Materials in the Chinese Collection of the Hoover Institution on War, Revolution, and Peace (Stanford, Calif. 1962), 312 pp.

Hu Hsien-chin, *The Common Descent Group in China and Its Functions* (New York 1948), 204 pp.

Hu Shih, 'Religion and Philosophy in the Chinese History', in Sophia H. Chen Zen (ed.), *Symposium on Chinese Culture* (Shanghai 1931), pp. 31–58

Hu Shih, *The Chinese Renaissance* (Chicago 1934), 110 pp.

Hudson, G. F., Richard Lowenthal, Roderick MacFarquhar, *The Sino-Soviet Dispute.* Documented and Analyzed (London, New York 1961), 227 pp.

Hughes, Richard, *The Chinese Communes* (London 1960), 90 pp.

Hughes, T. J., D. E. T. Luard, *The Economic Development of Communist China 1949–1958* (London, New York, Toronto 1959), 223 pp.

Ilyushechkin, V. P., O. G. Solovyov, *Taypinskoye vozstanie 1850–1946* [The Taiping Rebellion 1850–1946] (Moscow 1960), 324 pp.

Italiaander, Rolf, *Schwarze Haut im roten Griff* (Düsseldorf, Vienna 1962), 421 pp.

Johnson, Chalmers A., *Freedom of Thought and Expression in China. Communist Policies Toward the Intellectual Class* (Hongkong 1959), 130 pp.

Kalb, Marvin, *Dragon in the Kremlin. An Illuminating Report on the Menacing Russian-Chinese Alliance* (New York 1961), 258 pp.

Kapitsa, M. S., *Sovetsko-kitayskiye otnosheniya* [Soviet-Chinese Relations] (Moscow 1958), 423 pp.

Kara-Murtsa, G. S., *Taypiny-Velikaya krestyanskaya voyna i taipinskoye gosudarstvo v Kitaye. 1850–1864* [The Taipings. The Great Peasant War and the Taiping State in China 1850–1864]. 2nd edition (Moscow 1950), 141 pp.

Kardelj, Edvard, *Socialism and War; a Survey of Chinese Criticism of the Policy of Coexistence* (London 1961), 238 pp.

Kardelj, Edvard, *Vermeidbarkeit oder Unvermeidbarkeit des Krieges. Die jugoslawische und die chinesische These* (Hamburg 1961), 173 pp.

Kautsky, John H., *Moscow and the Communist Party of India* (New York, London 1956), 220 pp.

Kaznacheev, Aleksandr, *Inside a Soviet Embassy. Experiences of a Russian Diplomat in Burma* (New York 1962), 250 pp.

Kennan, George F., 'Stalin und China', in *Aus Politik und Zeitgeschehen.* Supplement to the weekly *Das Parlament* (9 August 1961), pp. 455–71

Kennedy, Malcolm, *A History of Communism in East Asia* (New York 1957), 556 pp.

Klemann, Friedrich, *Europäer und Ostasiaten. Die Verschiedenheit ihres Intellekts* (Munich-Basel 1957), 258 pp.

Knutson, Jeann Nickell, *Outer Mongolia: A Study in Soviet Colonialism* (Hongkong 1959), 174 pp.

Kolarz, Walter, *Russia and Her Colonies* (New York 1952), 324 pp.

Kolarz, Walter, *The Peoples of the Soviet Far East* (New York 1954), 193 pp.

Konstantinov, F. I., A. I. Arnoldov (ed.), *Sodruzhestvo stran sotsializma* [The Friendship Alliance of the Socialist Countries] (Moscow 1958), 337 pp.

Kracke, E. A. Jr., *Civil Service in Early Sung China, 960–1067* (Cambridge, Mass. 1953), 262 pp.

Krymov, A. G., M. A. Shafir (ed.), *Konstitutsiya i osnovniye zakonodatelniye akty Kitayskoy Narodnoy Respubliki (1954–1958)* [Constitution and Legislative Documents of the Chinese People's Republic, 1954–1958] (Moscow 1959), 727 pp.

Kurdyukov, I. F., V. N. Nikiforov, A. S. Perevertaylo (ed.), *Sovyetsko-kitayskiye otnosheniya 1917–1957. Sbornik dokumentov* [Soviet-Chinese Relations 1917–1957. Collected Documents] (Moscow 1959), 465 pp.

Lang, Olga, *Chinese Family and Society* (New Haven, Conn. 1946), 395 pp.

Langer, Paul F., 'Moscow, Peking and Tokyo: Views and Approaches', in Kurt London (ed.), *Unity and Contradiction* (New York 1962), pp. 207–32

Laqueur, Walter Z., *The Soviet Union and the Middle East* (London 1959), 366 pp.

Lattimore, Owen, *Pivot of Asia. Sinkiang and the Inner Asian Frontiers of China and Russia* (Boston 1950), 288 pp.

Leng, Shao Chuan, Norman D. Palmer, *Sun Yat-sen and Communism* (New York 1960), 234 pp.

Lenin, V. I., *Collected Works* (London 1960–)

Lenin, V. I., *Selected Works* (London 1947), 2 vols.

Lenin, V. I., *Sochineniya* [Works] (Russian), 4th edition. Vols. I–XXXIX (Moscow 1941–60)

Lenin o druzhbe s narodami vostoka [Lenin on Friendship with the Peoples of the East] (Moscow 1961), 399 pp.

Levenson, Joseph R., *Confucian China and its Modern Fate. The Problem of Intellectual Continuity* (Berkeley, Calif. 1958), 223 pp.

Levy, Marion J. Jr., Shih Kuo-heng, *The Rise of the Modern Chinese Business Class* (New York 1959), 64 pp.

Li Chi, *Studies in Chinese Communist Terminology*. Vols. I–V (Berkeley, Calif. 1956–58) (multigraphed)

Li Gi, Das Buch der Sitte. Translated from the Chinese into German, with explanatory notes and introduction, by Richard Wilhelm (Düsseldorf-Cologne, no year), 355 pp.

Li Choh-ming, *Economic Development of Communist China. An Appraisal of the First Five Years of Industrialization* (Berkeley, Los Angeles 1959), 284 pp.

Lifton, Robert Jay, *Thought Reform and the Psychology of Totalism. A Study of 'Brainwashing' in China* (New York 1961), 510 pp.

Lin Yutang, *My Country and My People* (London, Toronto 1956) (new edition), 419 pp.

Liu Hui-chen (Wang), *The Traditional Chinese Clan Rules* (Locust Valley, N.Y. 1959), 264 pp.

London, Kurt, 'Sino-Soviet Relations in the Context of the "World Socialist System"', in Kurt London (ed.), *Unity and Contradiction* (New York 1962), pp. 409–21

London, Kurt (ed.), *Unity and Contradiction. Major Aspects of Sino-Soviet Relations* (New York 1962), 464 pp.

Long Live Leninism (Peking 1960) (Contains editorials from *Hung-ch'i* of 16 April 1960, and *Jen-min Jih-pao*, 22 April 1960; also Lu Ting-yi's speech of 22 April 1960.) 106 pp.

Lu Hsün, *Selected Works*. Vols. I–IV (Peking 1956–60)

MacFarquhar, Roderick, *The Hundred Flowers* (London 1960), 324 pp.

McLane, Charles B., *Soviet Policy and the Chinese Communists 1931–1946* (New York 1958), 310 pp.

Mao Tse-tung, *Selected Works* (London, New York 1954–62), 5 vols.

Mao Tse-tung, *Selected Works*. Vol. IV (Peking 1961), 459 pp.

Mao Tse-tung, *Ausgewählte Schriften*. Vols. I–IV (East Berlin 1956)

Mao Tse-tung, *On the Correct Handling of Contradictions Among the People* (Peking 1957), 69 pp.

Marx, Karl, *Marx on China, 1853–1860; articles from the New York Daily*

Tribune, with an introduction and notes by Dona Torr (London 1951), 98 pp.

Mayer, Peter, *Sino-Soviet Relations Since the Death of Stalin.* (Union Research Institute, Hongkong 1962), 172 + 32 + 89 pp.

Mehnert, Klaus, *Asien, Moskau und wir* (Stuttgart, 1956 and following editions), 433 pp.

Mehnert, Klaus, *Soviet Man and His World* (New York 1961); published in Great Britain under the title, *The Anatomy of Soviet Man* (London 1961), 310 pp.

Mencius—see *Four Books*

Michael, Franz, T'ai-p'ing T'ien-kuo, in *The Journal of Asian Studies*, XVII, No. 1 (November 1957), pp. 67–76

Mongolskaya Narodnaya Respublika 1921–1961 [The Mongolian People's Republic 1921–1961] (Moscow 1961), 247 pp.

Moraes, Frank, *Report on Mao's China* (New York 1953), 212 pp.

[Müller, Kurt], *Entwicklungshilfe innerhalb des Ostblocks* (Frankfurt, Berlin 1960), 122 pp.

Mu Fu-sheng, *The Wilting of the Hundred Flowers* (London, Melbourne, Toronto 1962), 324 pp.

National Economy of the Mongolian People's Republic for 40 Years. Collection of Statistics (Ulan Bator 1961). (State Central Statistical Board of the Council of Ministers of the MRP.) 195 pp. (English and Russian text)

Needham, Joseph, *Science and Civilization in China*, Vols. I–IV (Cambridge, Mass. 1954–)

Nivison, David S., 'The Problems of "Knowledge" and "Action" in Chinese Thought since Wang Yang-ming', in Arthur F. Wright (ed.), *Studies in Chinese Thought*, pp. 112–45

Nivison, David S., Arthur F. Wright (ed.), *Confucianism in Action* (Stanford, Calif. 1959), 390 pp.

North, Robert C., *Moscow and Chinese Communists* (Stanford, Calif. 1953), 306 pp.

North, Robert C., *Kuomintang and Chinese Communist Elites* (Stanford, Calif. 1952), 130 pp.

North, Robert C., and Xenia J. Eudin, *M. N. Roy's Mission to China. The Communist-Kuomintang Split of 1927* (Berkeley, Los Angeles 1963), 399 pp. (Arrived too late to be used)

Onoe, Masao, 'Factors Binding the U.S.S.R. and Communist China', in Kurt London (ed.), *Unity and Contradiction* (New York 1962), pp. 142–55

Orleans, Leo A., *Professional Manpower and Education in Communist China* (Washington D.C.; no year—1960?), 260 pp.

Overstreet, Gene D., Marshall Windmiller, *Communism in India* (Berkeley, Los Angeles 1959), 603 pp.

Pa Chin, *The Family* (Peking 1958), 320 pp.

Paloczi-Horvath, György, *Mao Tse-tung, Emperor of the Blue Ants* (London 1962), 424 pp.

Payne, Robert, *Mao Tse-tung, Ruler of Red China* (New York 1950), 303 pp.

Perevertaylo, A. S. (ed.), *Sovetskiye dobrovoltsy o pervoy grazhdanskoy revolyutsionnoy voyne v Kitaye. 1923–1927. Vospominaniya* [Soviet Volunteers in the First Civil and Revolutionary War in China. 1923–1927. Reminiscences] (Moscow 1961), 161 pp.

Pipes, Richard (ed.), *The Russian Intelligentsia* (New York 1961), 234 pp.

Porshnev, Boris F., *Ocherk politicheskoy ekonomii feodalizma* [Outline of the Political Economy of Feudalism] (Moscow 1956),205 pp.

Powell, Ralph L., *The Rise of Chinese Military Power 1895–1912* (Princeton, N.J. 1955), 383 pp.

Pringsheim, Klaus H., *The Sino-Soviet Friendship Association (October 1949–October 1951)*. Master of Arts Thesis, Columbia University, New York (no year, hectographed), 224 pp.

Purcell, Victor, *The Chinese in South East Asia* (London, New York, Toronto 1951), 801 pp.

Pyn Min [Peng Ming], *Istoriya kitaysko-sovetskoy druzhby* [History of Sino-Soviet Friendship] (Moscow 1959), 359 pp.

Reform of the Chinese Written Language (Peking 1958), 69 pp.

Reshetar, John S., Jr., *A Concise History of the Communist Party of the Soviet Union* (New York 1960), 331 pp.

Rigby, T. H., 'The Embourgeoisement of the Soviet Union and the Proletarianization of Communist China', in Kurt London (ed.), *Unity and Contradiction* (New York 1962), pp. 19–36

Riencourt, Amaury de, *The Soul of China* (New York 1958), 298 pp.

Rostow, W. W., *The States of Economic Growth. A Non-Communist Manifesto* (Cambridge, Mass. 1960), 178 pp.

Rostow, W. W., *The Prospects for Communist China* (New York 1954), 379 pp.

Rupen, Robert A., 'Outer Mongolia, 1957–1960', in *Pacific Affairs*, XXXIII, No. 2 (June 1960), pp. 126–43

Rupen, Robert A., 'Mongolian Nationalism', in *Royal Central Asian Journal*, XLV, April and July–October 1958 (special printing edition), 46 pp.

Rupen, Robert A., 'The Buriat Intelligentsia', in *Far Eastern Quarterly*, XV, No. 3 (May 1956), pp. 383–98

Rupen, Robert A., 'Sino-Soviet Rivalry in Outer Mongolia', in *Current Scene* (Hongkong), I, No. 11 (31 August 1961), pp. 1–6

Rush, Myron, *The Rise of Khrushchev* (Washington, D.C. 1958), 116 pp.

Salisbury, Harrison E., *To Moscow—and Beyond* (New York 1959), 301 pp.

Sanakoyev, S., 'The Basis of the Relations between the Socialist Countries', in *International Affairs* (Moscow), July 1958, pp. 23–33

Sarkisyanz, Emanuel, *Russland und der Messianismus des Orients* (Tübingen 1955), 419 pp.

Scalapino, Robert A. and George T. Yu, *The Chinese Anarchist Movement* (Berkeley 1961), 81 pp.

Schapiro, Leonhard, *The Communist Party of the Soviet Union* (New York 1960), 631 pp.

Schatten, Fritz, *Afrika—schwarz oder rot? Revolution eines Kontinents* (Munich 1961), 425 pp.

Schiller, Otto, *Das Agrarsystem der Sowjetunion. Entwicklung seiner Struktur und Produktionsleistung* (Tübingen 1960), 171 pp.

Schiller, Otto, 'The Agrarian Systems in the Soviet Union and Communist China: A Comparison', in Kurt London (ed.), *Unity and Contradiction* (New York 1962), pp. 331–50

Schurmann, H. F., 'Organizational Contrasts Between Communist China and the Soviet Union', in Kurt London (ed.), *Unity and Contradiction* (New York 1962), pp. 65–99

Schwartz, Benjamin I., *Chinese Communism and the Rise of Mao* (Cambridge, Mass. 1951), 258 pp.

Second Session of the Eighth National Congress of the Communist Party of China (Peking 1958), 95 pp.

Seton-Watson, Hugh, 'The Communist Powers and Afro-Asian Nationalism', in Kurt London (ed.), *Unity and Contradiction* (New York 1962), pp. 187–206

Sherwani, Latif Ahmed, 'Sino-Soviet Aid Programs in Asia', in Kurt London (ed.), *Unity and Contradiction* (New York 1962), pp. 313–27

Shih Ch'eng-chih, *The Status of Science and Education in Communist China and a Comparison with that in USSR* (Hongkong 1962) (mimeographed), 76 pp.

Shkarenkova, G. (ed.), *Nash drug Kitay. Slovar-spravochnik* [Our Friend China. Reference Dictionary] (Moscow 1959), 630 pp.

Skachkov, K. A., *Pekin v dni taypinskogo vozstaniya* [Peking in the Days of the Taiping Rebellion] (Moscow 1958), 358 pp.

Skachkov, P. E., *Bibliografiya Kitaya* [Bibliography of China] (Moscow 1960), 690 pp.

Skachkov, P. E., V. S. Myasnikov (ed.), *Russko-kitayskiye otnosheniya 1689–1916* [Russo-Chinese Relations 1689–1916] (Moscow 1958), 136 pp.

Sladkovsky, M. I., *Ocherki ekonomicheskikh otnosheniy SSSR s Kitayem* [Sketches Concerning the Economic Relations Between the USSR and China] (Moscow 1957), 454 pp.

Smedley, Agnes, *The Great Road. The Life and Times of Chu Teh* (New York 1956), 461 pp.

Smith, Arthur H., *Chinese Characteristics* (Edinburgh and London; no year), 342 pp.

Snow, Edgar, *Red Star Over China* (New York, 1937), 474 pp.

Snow, Edgar, *Random Notes on Red China (1936–1945)* (Cambridge, Mass. 1957), 148 pp.

Solich, Eduard J., *Die Überseechinesen in Südostasien* (Frankfurt a.M., Berlin 1960), 112 pp.

Sorok let Narodnoy Mongolii [40 Years of People's Mongolia] (Moscow 1961), 165 pp.

Spector, Ivar, *The First Russian Revolution. Its Impact on Asia* (Englewood Cliffs, N.J. 1962), 180 pp.

Stählin, Karl, *Geschichte Russlands von den Anfängen bis zur Gegenwart*. Vols. I–IV/2 (Graz 1961) (Unchanged reprinting of edition published in Berlin in 1930)

Stalin, J. V., *Sochineniya* [Works] (Russian), Vols. I–XIII (Moscow 1946–51)

Stalin, J. V., *Works*, Vols. I–XIII (Moscow 1953–55)

Starlinger, Wilhelm, *Grenzen der Sowjetmacht* (Kitzingen/M. 1954), 131 pp.

Starlinger, Wilhelm, *Hinter Russland, China* (Würzburg, 1957), 141 pp.

Steiner, H. Arthur, 'Trade Unions in Mao's China', in *Problems of Communism*, V, No. 2 (March–April 1956), pp. 27–33

Swearingen, Rodger, 'A Decade of Soviet Policy in Asia 1945–1956', in *Current History*, No. 32 (186) (February 1957), pp. 89–96

Tang, Peter S. H., *Communist China Today*, Vols. I–II (New York 1957–58)

Tang, Peter S. H., *Russian and Soviet Policy in Manchuria and Outer Mongolia 1911–1931* (Durham, N.C. 1957), 494 pp.

Taylor, George E., 'The Taiping Rebellion. Its Economic Background and Social Theory', in *Chinese Social and Political Science Review*, XVI, No. 4 (January 1933), pp. 545–614

Teng, Ssu-yü, *New Light on the History of the Taiping Rebellion* (Cambridge, Mass. 1950), 122 pp. (multigraphed)

Teng, Ssu-yü, John K. Fairbank, *China's Response to the West. A Documentary Survey 1839–1923* (Cambridge, Mass. 1954), 296 pp.

The Anti-Stalin Campaign and International Communism. A Selection of Documents (New York 1956; Russian Institute, Columbia University), 342 pp.

The Chinese Communes. A Documentary Review and Analysis of the 'Great Leap Forward' (with articles by Geoffrey Hudson, A. V. Sherman, A. Zauberman) (London [1959]; edit. of *Soviet Survey*), 79 pp.

The Sino-Soviet Economic Offensive in the Less Developed Countries (Washington, D.C. 1958 (State Dept.)), 111 pp.

Thiel, Erich, *Die Mongolei. Land, Volk und Wirtschaft der Mongolischen Volksrepublik* (Munich 1958), 495 pp.

Thiel, Erich, *The Soviet Far East; a Survey of its Physical and Economic Geography* (London 1957), 388 pp.

Tikhvinsky, S. L., *Dvizhenie za reformy v Kitaye XIX veka i Kan Yu-vei* [The Reform Movement in China at the End of the XIXth Century and K'ang Yu-wei] (Moscow 1959), 418 pp.

Tongas, Gérard, *J'ai vécu dans l'Enfer communiste au Nord Viet-Nam* (Paris 1960), 463 pp.

Trager, Frank N., *Marxism in Southeast Asia. A Study of Four Countries* (Stanford, Calif. 1959), 381 pp.

Tutayev, M., *U istokov russko-kitayskikh revolyutsionnykh svyazey* [On the Origins of Russo-Chinese Revolutionary Associations] (Kazan 1961), 177 pp.

Udovenko, V. G., *Dalny Vostok. Ekonomichesko-geograficheskaya kharakteristika* [The Far East. Economic-geographical Characteristics] (Moscow 1957), 246 pp.

United States Relations with China, with Special Reference to the Period 1944–1949 (Washington, D.C. 1949 (State Dept.)), 1054 pp.

Ushakov, Alexander, *Der Rat für gegenseitige Wirtschaftshilfe* (Comecon) (Cologne 1962), 199 pp.

Valk, M. H. van der, *Conservatism in Modern Chinese Family Law* (Leiden 1956), 90 pp.

Verträge der Volksrepublik China mit anderen Staaten. Teil 1: Süd- und Ostasien. (Prepared at the Institute for Asian Study, Hamburg, espec. by Wolfgang Mohr.) (Frankfurt a.M., Berlin 1962), 243 pp.

Wang, Y. C., *Intellectuals and Society in China 1860–1949.* Comparative Studies in Society and History, in *An International Quarterly*, III, No. 4 (July 1961), pp. 395–426

Weakland, John H., 'The Organization of Action in Chinese Culture', in *Psychiatry*, III, No. 3 (August 1950), pp. 361–70

Weber, Max, *The Religion of China: Confucianism and Taoism* (Glencoe, Ill. 1951), 308 pp.

Wei, Henry, *China and Soviet Russia* (Princeton, N.J. 1956), 379 pp.

Weih, Ken Shen, *Russo-Chinese Diplomacy* (Shanghai 1928), 382 pp.

Welch, Holmes, 'Buddhism under the Communists', in *The China Quarterly*, No. 6 (April–June 1961), pp. 1–14

Whiting, Allen S., *Soviet Policies in China, 1917–1924* (New York 1954), 350 pp.

Whiting, Allen S., *Sinkiang: Pawn or Pivot?* (East Lansing, Mich. 1958), 314 pp.

Whiting, Allen S., *China Crosses the Yalu. The Decision to Enter the Korean War* (New York 1960), 219 pp.

Whiting, Allen S., 'Contradictions in the Moscow-Peking Axis', in *The Journal of Politics*, XX, No. 1 (February 1958), pp. 127–61

Wilhelm, Hellmut, *Gesellschaft und Staat in China* (Hamburg 1960) (new printing of edition of 1944), 149 pp.

Wittfogel, Karl A., *Oriental Despotism. A Comparative Study of Total Power* (New Haven, Conn. 1957), 556 pp.

Wright, Arthur F. (ed.), *Studies in Chinese Thought* (Chicago 1953), 317 pp.

Wright, Arthur F. (ed.), *The Confucian Persuasion* (Stanford, Calif. 1960), 390 pp.

Wright, Mary C., *The Last Stand of Chinese Conservatism. The T'ung-Chih Restoration, 1862–1956* (Stanford, Calif. 1957), 426 pp.

Wu, Aitchen K., *China and the Soviet Union. A Study of Sino-Soviet Relations* (London 1950), 434 pp.

Yakhontoff, Victor A., *The Chinese Soviets* (New York 1934), 296 pp.

Yakhontoff, Victor A., *Russia and the Soviet Union in the Far East* (London 1932), 454 pp.

Yang, C. K., *A Chinese Family in the Communist Revolution* (Cambridge, Mass. 1959), 246 pp.

Yang, C. K., *A Chinese Village in Early Communist Transition* (Cambridge, Mass. 1959), 284 pp.

Yang, C. K., *Religion in Chinese Society* (Berkeley, Los Angeles 1961), 473 pp.

Yang I-fan, *The Case of Hu Feng* (Hongkong 1956), 169 pp.

Zagoria, Donald S., *The Sino-Soviet Conflict 1956–1961* (Princeton, N.J. 1962), 484 pp.

Zhukov, Ye. M. (ed.), *Mezhdunarodniye otnosheniya na Dalnem Vostoke 1840–1949 gg.* [International Relations in the Far East in the Years 1870–1945] (Moscow 1956), 783 pp.

INDEX

DATE DUE